PRINCIPLES OF CORPORATE
FINANCE LAW

N

Principles of Corporate Finance Law

EILÍS FERRAN

OXFORD
UNIVERSITY PRESS

OXFORD
UNIVERSITY PRESS

Great Clarendon Street, Oxford OX2 6DP

Oxford University Press is a department of the University of Oxford.
It furthers the University's objective of excellence in research, scholarship,
and education by publishing worldwide in

Oxford New York

Auckland Cape Town Dar es Salaam Hong Kong Karachi
Kuala Lumpur Madrid Melbourne Mexico City Nairobi
New Delhi Shanghai Taipei Toronto

With offices in

Argentina Austria Brazil Chile Czech Republic France Greece
Guatemala Hungary Italy Japan Poland Portugal Singapore
South Korea Switzerland Thailand Turkey Ukraine Vietnam

Oxford is a registered trade mark of Oxford University Press
in the UK and in certain other countries

Published in the United States
by Oxford University Press Inc., New York

British Library Cataloguing in Publication Data

Data available

Library of Congress Cataloging in Publication Data

Data available

Typeset by Newgen Imaging Systems (P) Ltd., Chennai, India
Printed in Great Britain
on acid-free paper by
CPI Antony Rowe, Chippenham, Wiltshire

ISBN 978–0–19–923050–1 (Hbk.)
ISBN 978–0–19–923051-8 (Pbk.)

3 5 7 9 10 8 6 4 2

This book is dedicated to my mother, Kay Ferran, and
to the memory of my father, Gerry Ferran

Preface

This book is derived from *Company Law and Corporate Finance*, which was published in 1999. The book has been reoriented to concentrate on the parts of company law that are most directly relevant to the financing of the corporate sector and to include more securities regulation relating to corporate issuers' access to the public markets. The law in these areas has developed significantly since 1999 and I have sought to explain the changes, explore their underlying aims, and assess their overall significance.

Although the book is about British law, the regulatory agenda relating to corporate finance is increasingly set at the EU level. This trend, which was certainly evident in 1999 but which has increased dramatically since then, is reflected in the text. I have benefited greatly from a rich and growing body of literature on EC corporate and securities law by European scholars, and from comparative scholarship by researchers from other parts of the world. Luca Enriques, Howell Jackson, and Niamh Moloney merit special mention for their willingness to read working papers in which some of the ideas that made their way into this book were first expressed and to give invariably incisive, yet constructive, criticism.

The challenges involved in following the many twists and turns that arose in the reform process leading up to the UK Companies Act 2006 and in coming to terms with that colossal instrument were made easier by having friends and colleagues with whom to discuss its more mystifying aspects. This group includes John Armour, Martina Asmar, Philip Bovey, Kathryn Cearns, Brian Cheffins, Paul Davies, James Palmer, Caroline Quinnell, Jonathan Rickford, Pippa Rogerson, Carol Shut Kerer and, especially, Richard Nolan, whose trenchant views never fail to stimulate. I am grateful also to the partners of Herbert Smith for enabling me to keep in touch with changes in practice.

I was privileged to be able to share ideas and draft chapters with groups of LLM students at Cambridge University, particularly the 2006–07 and 2007–08 year groups. Their feedback helped to clarify my thinking on numerous points. I also learnt a lot from my two former research students, Dr Thomas Bachner and Dr John Vella. I would also like to thank the OUP commissioning and production team, in particular John Louth, Gwen Booth, Bethan Cousins, and Alison Floyd.

My father and a close friend both died a few weeks before I completed the manuscript. Those sad events and the gatherings of family and friends that followed them affected me deeply and reminded that even though I am lucky enough to have an enriching and fulfilling job, it is only one part of life and not the most fundamentally important aspect. My husband, Rod, and my two children, Aoife and Oliver, are at the centre of my life and I am profoundly grateful to them for all that they do.

Eilís Ferran

St Catharine's College, Cambridge
17 December 2007

Contents

III. DEBT CORPORATE FINANCE

List of Abbreviations

General

ABI	Association of British Insurers
AIM	Alternative Investment Market (London Stock Exchange)
ASB	Accounting Standards Board
ASBJ	Accounting Standards Board of Japan
BERR	Department for Business, Enterprise and Regulatory Reform
BIS	Bank for International Settlements
BVA	base value of assets
BVL	base value of liabilities
CAPM	Capital Asset Pricing Model
CARD	Consolidated Admission and Reporting Directive
CESR	Committee of European Securities Regulators
DTI	Department of Trade and Industry (now the BERR, see above)
DTR	FSA *Disclosure Rules and Transparency Rules*
EC	European Community
ECB	European Central Bank
ECJ	European Court of Justice
EEA	European Economic Area
ESME	European Securities Market Expert Group
FASB	Financial Accounting Standards Board (US)
FEE	Federation of European Accountants
FMLC	Financial Markets Law Committee
FRS	Financial Reporting Standards
FSA	Financial Services Authority
FSAP	Financial Services Action Plan (European Commission)
FSMA 2000	Financial Services and Markets Act 2000
GAAP	Generally Accepted Accounting Principles
HMT	Her Majesty's Treasury
IAS	International Accounting Standards (now IFRS, see below)
IASB	International Accounting Standards Board
ICAEW	Institute of Chartered Accountants in England and Wales
ICAS	Institute of Chartered Accountants of Scotland
IDS	International Disclosure Standards
IFRS	International Financial Reporting Standards
IMA	Investment Management Association
IOSCO	International Organization of Securities Commissions
IPO	initial public offer
LIBOR	London Inter-Bank Offered Rate
LR	FSA *Listing Rules*
MiFID	Markets in Financial Instruments Directive
MJDS	Multi-jurisdictional Disclosure System (between the US and Canada)

MM theorem	Modogliani-Miller theorem
NAPF	National Association of Pension Funds
NASDAQ	National Association of Securities Dealers Automated Quotations
Nomad	nominated adviser (under AIM *Rules for Companies*)
NYSE	New York Stock Exchange
PAL	provisional allotment letter
PR	FSA *Prospectus Rules*
PSM	Professional Securities Market
QIB	qualified institutional buyers
RIE	recognized investment exchange
RIS	Regulatory Information Service
SEC	Securities and Exchange Commission (US)
SIMEX	Singapore International Monetary Exchange
SLIM project	Simpler Legislation for the Internal Market project (European Commission)
SMEs	small and medium-sized enterprises
SPEs	special purpose entities
SPVs	special purpose vehicles
SUSMI	substantial US market interest
TIFFE	Tokyo International Financial Futures Exchange
TRACE	Trade Reporting and Compliance Engine
UKLA	United Kingdom Listing Authority
WACC	weighted average cost of capital

Publications

ALJ	Australian Law Journal
CFILR	Company Financial and Insolvency Law Review
CLJ	Cambridge Law Journal
Conv	The Conveyancer and Property Lawyer
JBL	Journal of Business Law
LMCLQ	Lloyd's Maritime and Commercial Law Quarterly
LQR	Law Quarterly Review
MLR	Modern Law Review
NLJ	New Law Journal
NZLJ	New Zealand Law Journal
OJLS	Oxford Journal of Legal Studies

Table of Cases

Table of Legislation

UK STATUTORY INSTRUMENTS

OTHER JURISDICTIONS

Note on the Implementation of the Companies Act 2006

The Companies Act 2006 received Royal Assent in November 2006 and is being brought into force in stages. The final implementation timetable published in December 2007 is indicated below. Except where otherwise indicated, the book is written as if the Companies Act 2006 is fully in force. Some of the delegated legislation to be made under the Act is only available in draft form at the time of writing.

Commencement dates

Parts of the Act	Contents of Part	Date of entry into force
1	General introductory provisions (1–6) Section 2: 6 April 2007	1 October 2009
2	Company formation (7–16)	1 October 2009
3	A company's constitution (17–38) Sections 29 and 30: 1 October 2007	1 October 2009
4	A company's capacity and related matters (39–52) Section 44: 6 April 2008	1 October 2009
5	A company's name (53–85) Sections 69 to 74: 1 October 2008 Sections 82 to 85: 1 October 2008	1 October 2009
6	A company's registered office (86–88)	1 October 2009
7	Re-registration as a means of altering a company's status (89–111)	1 October 2009
8	A company's members (112–144) Sections 116 to 119: 1 October 2009 Sections 121 and 128: 6 April 2008	1 October 2007
9	Exercise of members' rights (145–153)	1 October 2007
10	A company's directors (154–259) Sections 155 to 159: 1 October 2008 Sections 162 to 167: 1 October 2009 Sections 175 to 177: 1 October 2008 Sections 180(1), (2)(in part), and (4)(b), and 181(2) and (3): 1 October 2008 Sections 182 to 187: 1 October 2008 Sections 240 to 247: 1 October 2009	1 October 2007
11	Derivative claims and proceedings by members (260–269)	1 October 2007
12	Company secretaries (270–280) Section 270(3)(b)(ii): 1 October 2009 Sections 275 to 279: 1 October 2009	6 April 2008

Continued

Parts of the Act	Contents of Part	Date of entry into force
13	Resolutions and meetings (281–361) Sections 308 and 309: 20 January 2007 Section 333: 20 January 2007 Sections 327(2)(c) and 330(6)(c) are not being commenced for the time being.	1 October 2007
14	Control of political donations and expenditure (362–379) Provisions relating to independent election candidates: 1 October 2008 Part 14 comes into force in Northern Ireland on 1 November 2007, except for provisions relating to independent election candidates.	1 October 2007
15	Accounts and reports (380–474) Section 417: 1 October 2007 Section 463: 20 January 2007 for reports and statements first sent to members and others after that date	6 April 2008
16	Audit (475–539) Sections 485 to 488: 1 October 2007	6 April 2008
17	A company's share capital (540–657) Section 544: 6 April 2008 Sections 641(1)(a) and (2)–(6), 642, 643 and 652: 1 October 2008 Section 654: 1 October 2008	1 October 2009
18	Acquisition by limited company of its own shares (658–737) Repeal of the restrictions under the Companies Act 1985 on financial assistance for acquisition of shares in private companies, including the 'whitewash' procedure: 1 October 2008	1 October 2009
19	Debentures (738–754)	6 April 2008
20	Private and public companies (755–767)	6 April 2008
21	Certification and transfer of securities (768–790)	6 April 2008
22	Information about interests in a company's shares (791–828) Sections 811(4), 812, 814: 6 April 2008	20 January 2007
23	Distributions (829–853)	6 April 2008
24	A company's annual return (854–859)	1 October 2009
25	Company charges (860–894)	1 October 2009
26	Arrangements and reconstructions (895–901)	6 April 2008
27	Mergers and divisions of public companies (902–941)	6 April 2008
28	Takeovers, etc (942–992)	6 April 2007
29	Fraudulent trading (993)	1 October 2007
30	Protection of members against unfair prejudice (994–999)	1 October 2007
31	Dissolution and restoration to the register (1000–1034)	1 October 2009
32	Company investigations: amendments (1035–1039)	1 October 2007
33	UK companies not formed under the Companies Acts (1040–1043) Section 1043: 6 April 2007	1 October 2009
34	Overseas companies (1044–1059)	1 October 2009

PART I
OVERVIEW

1

The Regulatory Framework

Scope of the book

The limited company is the most popular organizational form for modern businesses of economic significance in the UK.[1] The company occupies this preeminent position because it has advantages over other types of business vehicle, such as unincorporated associations and partnerships, as an organizational form through which to limit financial risks and to raise large amounts of finance from investors whilst keeping the day-to-day running of the business concentrated in the hands of a relatively small group of managers.[2] These advantages are supplied by the state through its system of company law.[3] These special features of company law act as incentives to trade and commerce and can play a critical role in promoting enterprise and investment.[4]

---

[1] At the start of 2004 there were 4,282,845 enterprises in the UK, of which the majority in number (2,719,410) were unincorporated; incorporated companies (1,024,125) formed only the second largest group numerically. On other measures, however, the incorporated company comes out very clearly ahead. For example, of the 2,719,410 unincorporated businesses, all but a relatively small number (329,230) had no employees and were sole proprietorships and partnerships comprising only self-employed owner managers. These figures are drawn from DTI, 'SME Statistics UK 2004' (2004).

[2] The limited liability partnership, which in theory also has certain advantages as an organizational structure suited to raising finance, was introduced by the Limited Liability Partnerships Act 2000. This structure has been embraced by some large professional firms, such as accountants and lawyers, but, contrary to some expectations, it has not become very popular with small commercial businesses, possibly because of a rather unwieldy legal framework: M Lower, 'What's on Offer? A Consideration of the Legal Forms Available for Use by Small- and Medium-sized Enterprises in the United Kingdom' (2003) 24 *Company Lawyer* 166; J Freedman and V Finch, 'The Limited Liability Partnership: Pick and Mix or Mix-up?' [2002] JBL 475. Government statistics indicate that at the end of 2003–04 there had been 7,396 Great British LLPs formed under the 2000 Act as compared to 1,639,700 companies on the Great British register of companies, with new incorporations in 2003–04 alone numbering 371,400: DTI, 'Companies in 2003–2004' (Report for the year ended 31 March 2004).

[3] These features, in particular the shielding of the firm's assets from claims by personal creditors of its shareholders (which is important to those dealing with companies because it gives them confidence that they alone have a claim on the firm's assets) could not be fully replicated by contracts: H Hansmann and RR Kraakman, 'The Essential Role of Organizational Law' (2000) 110 *Yale Law Journal* 387.

[4] DTI, *Company Law Reform* (Cm 6456, March 2005) 3 (foreword by Secretary of State for Trade and Industry).

Since it is company law that provides the basic features that make the company an especially attractive organizational form for the channelling of finance to business, this book begins with company law and then branches out into other areas of law that are relevant to corporate finance. Part I, which includes this chapter, provides an introduction to the regulatory and business framework governing corporate finance in the UK and examines ways in which the corporate form can be used to limit financial risks. Part II is about company law, with an emphasis on the parts of company law that are particularly concerned with the ways in which limited companies are financed through share issues. Part III reviews some major legal issues arising in relation to the debt financing of companies. Corporate finance theory establishes that companies fund their operations through a combination of capital raised through share issues, retained earnings, and debt. A book on the law relating to corporate finance would therefore be incomplete if it did not include a section on the law relating to corporate borrowing, even though this is a very large subject in its own right. The final section of the book, Part IV, considers aspects of securities law. The capital markets constitute a rich source of corporate finance but, in order to gain access to them, companies must submit to an extensive array of obligations, particularly disclosure requirements, that are intended to support the operation of the markets as a mechanism for the efficient allocation of resources and to bolster investor confidence.

Throughout the book, the discussion relates to companies formed and registered under the Companies Act 2006, the Companies Act 1985, or former Companies Acts.[5] Although it is possible under the companies legislation to form an unlimited company[6] or a company limited by guarantee,[7] the book concentrates mainly on companies limited by shares.

Types of company limited by shares

Companies limited by shares are either public companies or private companies. Only about 1 per cent of the total number of registered companies are public companies, although in terms of size of operations, market capitalization, number of employees and the like, public companies tend to be much larger than private companies. The distinction between public and private companies is enshrined in the companies legislation. It is a requirement of the legislation that, subject to certain limited exceptions, every company must make plain its status by its suffix: 'public limited company' ('plc' for short) or 'private limited

---

[5] Companies can also be formed by Royal Charter or by specific Acts of Parliament but incorporation by these methods is now uncommon.

[6] An unlimited company is not subject to the maintenance of capital rules and is therefore free to return capital to its members.

[7] This form of corporate structure tends to be adopted by non-profit making organizations.

company' ('Ltd' for short).[8] The fundamental point of distinction between public and private companies is that only public companies are allowed to raise capital by offering their shares and other securities to the investing public at large.[9] The companies legislation also distinguishes between public and private companies with regard to the rules relating to the raising and maintenance of share capital where, broadly speaking, private companies operate under a more relaxed regime than public companies.[10] The more stringent rules applying to public companies are commonly derived from European Community (EC) law, which Member States are obliged to incorporate into their domestic legislation. Private companies are also relieved of some of the administrative obligations imposed by the companies legislation, such as the requirements to hold an annual general meeting (AGM) and to have a company secretary.[11]

For the purposes of exposition, it is often convenient to contrast a public company with a large number of shareholders, each of whom holds only a tiny fraction of its shares and virtually all of whom perform no managerial functions, with a private company which has a few shareholders, all or most of whom are also involved in the management of the company. This practice should not be allowed to obscure the fact that there are many different types and sizes of company that can be accommodated under the 'public' and 'private' banners. There is no upper limit on the number of shareholders in a private company. It is possible to have private companies which have managerial structures similar to those of the paradigm public company, ie where most shareholders are investors who do not participate directly in the management of the company. On the other hand, the shareholder base of a public company can be very small; the minimum number of shareholders in a public company has been progressively relaxed over the years and now stands at one, which is the same as for a private company.[12] However, the burden of complying with more onerous requirements would usually deter the operators of a small business from seeking public company status at least until such time as it has established a sufficient reputation to make raising capital from external investors a viable financing option. In the context of public companies, it is important to recognize that there can be some companies where the shareholding is so widely dispersed that no one shareholder or group of shareholders holds more than a tiny fraction of its shares and others where one shareholder, or a group of shareholders, holds a significant portion of the share capital.[13] A widely-dispersed shareholder base is a common ownership structure for the largest public companies in the US and the UK but elsewhere in the world

---

[8] Companies Act 2006, ss 58–65.

[9] ibid s 755.

[10] ibid Pts 17–18, considered in detail in Part II of this book.

[11] ibid s 336 (requirement for public companies to hold AGMs) and s 270 (private company not required to have a secretary).

[12] ibid s 7.

[13] ES Herman, *Corporate Control, Corporate Power* (CUP, 1981) ch 3.

public companies are often controlled by a single shareholder or by a concentrated group of shareholders.[14] As dispersal of share ownership increases, the percentage shareholding that any one shareholder needs in order to exercise some form of practical control decreases.[15]

Companies where all, or most, of the shareholders participate in management are sometimes described as 'quasi-partnership' companies, reflecting the fact that the management structure is akin to that of a partnership. Quasi-partnership companies tend to be private companies with just a few shareholders. The companies legislation does not specifically recognize the category of quasi-partnership companies but, in relieving private companies from certain administrative requirements, it acknowledges that there may be companies for which the demarcations between one group of corporate actors (the directors) and another group (the shareholders) are unnecessary and inappropriate. Quasi-partnership companies have achieved recognition in case law concerned with the protection of minority shareholders. A petitioner may be entitled to relief where the conduct complained of is contrary to what the parties have actually agreed.[16] The House of Lords has said that the promises that the parties have actually exchanged in the case of a quasi-partnership company will usually be found in the understandings between the members at the time they entered into association.[17]

In its accounting and audit requirements, the companies legislation contains a lighter regime for 'small' private companies and groups of companies, with the relevant criteria for this purpose being turnover, balance sheet totals, and number of employees.[18] Many quasi-partnership companies will satisfy the criteria to be small companies for the purposes of the statutory accounting rules and for exemption from audit requirements. The accounting rules also distinguish between 'quoted'[19] and 'unquoted' companies, with more extensive financial disclosure obligations attaching to those companies that are quoted.[20] Other parts of the legislation, particularly those concerned with transparency and shareholder rights, also single out quoted companies for a heavier burden of regulation.[21] The obligations with regard to filing of financial statements and reports

[14] RJ Gilson, 'Controlling Shareholders and Corporate Governance: Complicating the Comparative Taxonomy' (2006) 119 *Harvard Law Review* 1641.

[15] JE Parkinson, *Corporate Power and Responsibility* (OUP, 1993) 59–63.

[16] *O'Neill and anor v Phillips and ors, Re a company (No 00709 of 1992)* [1999] 2 BCLC 1, [1999] 1 WLR 1092, HL.

[17] ibid.

[18] Companies Act 2006, ss 381–384 (accounting requirements) and ss 477–479 (conditions for exemption from audit).

[19] Defined in Companies Act 2006, s 385 as a company that is officially listed in the UK or another EEA State or admitted to dealing on either the New York Stock Exchange or NASDAQ.

[20] See Companies Act 2006, Pt 15, ch 6 (directors' remuneration report required of quoted companies), ch 7 (publication requirements in respect of financial statements), and ch 9 (members' approval of directors' remuneration reports).

[21] See eg Companies Act 2006, Pt 13, ch 5 (provisions relating to company meetings) and Pt 16, ch 5 (members' rights to raise audit concerns).

employ an additional categorization, as they distinguish between 'small', 'medium-sized' (determined by reference to turnover, balance sheet total, and number of employees),[22] unquoted, and quoted companies.[23]

Another type of company that is recognized by the companies legislation is the company that is part of a larger group of companies. Corporate groups are subject to specific regulation in the context of accounting requirements. Certain other legislative rules also have a particular application to companies within a group. However, the British companies legislation does not contain a specialized part that is dedicated to the regulation of corporate groups.

Despite the recognition of different types of company for various specific purposes, in broad terms the underlying approach to company law in the UK is that the same legal framework applies to all companies regardless of the number of shareholders or employees, managerial structure or size of financial operations. From time to time there have surfaced proposals for a separate form of incorporation for small businesses[24] but that option was specifically rejected in the major review of company law that preceded the Companies Act 2006.[25] In that debate, a powerful argument against adopting a special and distinct corporate regulatory framework for small businesses was that thresholds established for the scope of the special regime could operate as barriers to growth.[26] Instead, the government sought to address the needs of small business by using the Companies Act 2006 as an opportunity to refashion company law so as to make it more accessible to small businesses.[27] This Act did not go as far as to structure the entirety of the companies legislation so as to give priority to the needs of small businesses ('think small first'). Radical restructuring had been considered as part of the review but some of the more ambitious plans were scaled back during the legislative process, with the result that the basic design remains the same but provisions that are of particular importance to small companies have been significantly revised and, throughout the legislation as a whole, efforts have been made to express the law in more accessible language.

The regulatory framework for corporate finance

A range of actors, including the domestic and regional (ie EC) legislatures, national and international standard-setting bodies, and private and voluntary sector organizations, supply the legal and non-legal norms, principles, standards,

---

[22] Companies Act 2006, s 445 and ss 465–467.
[23] ibid ss 444–448.
[24] eg *A New Form of Incorporation for Small Firms* (Cmnd 8171, 1981). See WJ Sandars, 'Small Businesses—Suggestions for Simplified Forms of Incorporation' [1979] JBL 14.
[25] DTI, *Modernising Company Law* (Cm 5553, 2002) paras 1.5–1.6.
[26] ibid.
[27] DTI, 'Company Law Reform Small Business Summary', URN 05/927.

guidelines, and rules that go to make up the regulatory framework governing corporate finance activity in the UK. The common purpose underlying this vast body of regulatory activity is to establish an optimal package of commands and incentives to stimulate desirable behaviour and to curb undesirable behaviour by affected parties. Some of the main elements of the regulatory framework are as follows.

Legislation

The Companies Act 2006 is the principal piece of primary legislation relating to the formation, operation, and control of companies. This Act applies to companies incorporated in Great Britain (England, Wales, and Scotland) and also to companies incorporated in the remaining region of the UK, Northern Ireland.[28]

The Companies Act 2006 is intended to bring company law more into line with the realities of modern business. Extensive changes made by this legislation were largely based on an independent review of company law which was conducted between 1998 and 2001 by an independent group of experts appointed by the government department now known as the Department of Business, Enterprise and Regulatory Reform (BERR, previously the Department of Trade and Industry or DTI). This group of experts, known as the Company Law Steering Group, produced a series of consultation documents and helped to build a broad consensus in favour of reform.[29] Not all of the Companies Act 2006 is entirely new, however. Some sections are simply re-stated versions of provisions that were in the Companies Act 1985. At the start of the legislative stage of the reform process, the government's intention had been to keep some important company law provisions in the Companies Act 1985 but as the discussion in Parliament progressed it became clear that it would be preferable, as a government spokesperson put it, 'to make the new legislation much closer to a complete code of company law for the majority of users'.[30] The aim of making the Companies Act 2006 a near complete code has been achieved. The Companies Act 1985 remains in force only for certain specialized purposes that are outside the scope of this work.

The Financial Services and Markets Act 2000 provides the regulatory framework for issuing securities to the public and for the admission of securities to trading on a regulated market. As a framework Act, it contains fundamental elements of the regulatory regime but much of the detail is to be found in delegated legislation. Delegated legislation under the Financial Services and Markets Act 2000 comes in the form of both statutory instruments (made by HM Treasury

---

[28] Companies Act 2006, Pt 45 extends the mainland legislation to Northern Ireland (this was not previously the case).

[29] The work of the Steering Group and the company law reform process generally are reviewed in E Ferran, 'Company Law Reform in the UK' (2001) 5 *Singapore Journal of International and Comparative Law* 516.

[30] Lord Sainsbury, *Hansard*, HL vol 682, col 795 (23 May 2006).

or (HMT)) and rules made by the Financial Services Authority (FSA) in the FSA *Handbook*. The FSA *Handbook* includes the *Prospectus Rules*, the *Listing Rules*, and the *Disclosure Rules and Transparency Rules*. When acting as the competent authority for listing, the FSA may refer to itself as the UK Listing Authority (UKLA).

Corporate insolvency is regulated by the Insolvency Act 1986 and detailed rules made thereunder. Provisions relating to the winding up of solvent companies are also contained in this Act.

As a Member State of the EU, the UK is obliged to give effect within its domestic laws to legislation that is adopted at the European level. A considerable amount of the domestic company law that is relevant to corporate finance has its roots in EC law. The influence of Europe is stronger still in the regulation of public offers of securities and the admission of securities to trading. Establishing a regulatory framework to facilitate the development of a genuinely integrated pan-European capital market has been a priority for EC policymakers in recent years and a large body of centralized legislation has been adopted in pursuit of that goal. Member States retain some discretion to impose their own additional requirements but the major decisions on the shape of regulatory policy relating to the capital markets are now taken at the European, rather than the domestic, level.

Internal constitutional instruments

Companies are permitted considerable flexibility in the internal constitutional regulation of their own affairs. Historically, companies were required to have a constitution set out in two documents: the memorandum of association and the articles of association. The Companies Act 2006 retains the concept of a memorandum of association but it no longer has constitutional significance as all that is required (and permitted) as its contents is a statement that the subscribers wish to form a company, agree to become members of the company, and, in the case of a company that is to have a share capital, to take at least one share each. For companies incorporated before the Companies Act 2006 that had detailed constititutional provisions in their memoranda, those provisions are now to be treated as provisions of the company's articles.[31] A company's objects are unrestricted unless a company's articles specifically provide otherwise.[32] A company, once registered, is capable of exercising all the functions of an incorporated company.[33]

It is the articles of association that now constitute the main constitutional document, although it can be supplemented by certain shareholder resolutions or agreements.[34] Separate model form articles for public companies, private

---

[31] Companies Act 2006, s 28.
[32] ibid s 31.
[33] ibid s 16(3).
[34] ibid s 17.

companies limited by shares, and private companies limited by guarantee are provided in delegated legislation made under the Companies Act 2006.[35] The relevant model form will apply by default if articles are not registered as part of a company's constitution or, if articles are so registered, in so far as they do not exclude or modify the relevant model articles.[36] However, subject to certain constraints under the general law, companies can depart from the model forms.

The companies legislation gives legal effect to the articles as a contract between the company and its shareholders and between the shareholders among themselves.[37]

Case law

The judiciary has made an immense contribution to the development of British company law. One of the main functions of company law is to regulate conflicts of interest between directors and shareholders and, historically, it was the courts that played the major role in discharging that function by applying to directors a range of duties analogous to those they had developed in relation to trustees. Over the years, additional statutory rules were added as well but case law remained the primary source for the law on the general duties of directors. The Companies Act 2006 makes a significant break with the past in this respect because it has introduced a statutory statement of directors' duties.[38] This statutory statement of general duties replaces the common law and equitable rules made by the judiciary[39] but the general duties are to be interpreted and applied in the same way as the common law rules or equitable principles, and regard is to be had to the corresponding common law rules and equitable principles in interpreting and applying the general duties.[40] It was indicated by a government spokesperson in Parliamentary scrutiny of the Bill that became the Companies Act 2006 that it was intended that the courts should continue to have regard to developments in the common law rules and equitable principles applying to other types of fiduciary relationships so that the statutory duties could develop in line with relevant developments in the law as it applies elsewhere.[41] The extent to which authorities on the common law and equitable principles will remain relevant and the scope left for the judiciary to play a 'developmental' role in relation to directors' duties can only be a matter for conjecture at present. The likelihood is that codification will reduce the judiciary's role as a maker, as opposed to an interpreter, of company law. The justification put forward by the government for this shift is

---

[35] The Companies (Model Articles) Regulations 2007, SI 2007/(draft).
[36] Companies Act 2006, s 20.
[37] ibid s 33.
[38] ibid Pt 10, ch 2.
[39] ibid s 170(3).
[40] ibid s 170(4).
[41] Lord Goldsmith, *Hansard*, vol 678, GC col 243 (6 February 2006).

that a statutory statement should make directors' duties more consistent, certain, accessible, and comprehensible.[42]

Codes and guidelines

For a full view of the regulatory environment in which companies with a dispersed shareholder base operate within the UK, it is necessary also to look beyond the traditional legal sources, as a few well-known examples can quickly demonstrate. The Combined Code on Corporate Governance sets out standards of good practice in relation to issues such as board composition and structure, remuneration, accountability and audit, and relations with shareholders. The Combined Code, which began life as a private sector initiative and which is now maintained by the Financial Reporting Council, the body responsible for the oversight of financial reporting and corporate governance in the UK, is not legally enforceable in any direct way, although it is underpinned by a requirement in the FSA *Listing Rules* whereby listed companies that are incorporated in the UK must report on how they have applied the Combined Code in their annual report and accounts.[43] Despite the lack of direct enforceability, the Combined Code is an important element of the UK's regulatory framework. It has been said that 'for the director of a listed company the precepts of the Combined Code may well dominate his thinking, to the virtual exclusion of any question of law'.[44] For directors of companies involved in mergers and acquisitions activity, historically much the same has been true of the City Code on Takeovers and Mergers, which governs the takeover of public companies in the UK. This too began life as a private sector initiative that was not supported by direct legal sanctions. Over time, however, the City Code has acquired increasingly significant legal underpinning. The first step was endorsement by the official securities regulator (which in the UK is now the FSA), a formal step that has the effect of allowing the FSA to take enforcement action against regulated firms and some of their senior officers in the event of contravention.[45] The second, and more radical, change of finally putting the Takeover Panel and the City Code onto a statutory footing (which was necessitated by the obligation to implement the EC Takeover Directive)[46] was effected first by interim regulations (passed to meet EC implementation deadlines)[47] and then by the Companies Act 2006.[48]

---

[42] DTI, *Company Law Reform* (Cm 6456, 2005) para 3.3.
[43] *LR* 9.8.6.
[44] LS Sealy, 'Directors' Duties Revisited' (2001) 22 *Company Lawyer* 79, 83.
[45] Financial Services and Markets Act 2006, s 143 and FSA *Handbook*, Market Conduct, MAR 4.
[46] Directive (EC) 2004/25 of the European Parliament and of the Council of 21 April 2004 on takeover bids [2004] OJ L142/12.
[47] The Takeovers Directive (Interim Implementation) Regulations 2006, SI 2006/1183.
[48] Companies Act 2006, Pt 28.

2

Use and Abuse of the Corporate Form as a Vehicle for Raising Finance and Managing Financial Risk

Issues considered in this chapter

It is easy to incorporate a company under British law. There is an administrative process involving form-filling and the disclosure of information but the requirements are not burdensome. Indeed, as a result of the Companies Act 2006, a process that by international standards was already quite straightforward should be further simplified.[1] Making the corporate form so readily available is a deliberate policy choice, which is intended to encourage entrepreneurship and enterprise.[2] Old-fashioned notions of incorporation as a privilege or concession granted by the state are thus very far removed from the modern legal reality.[3] Not only can people who operate businesses set themselves up within a company with a minimum of fuss, they can sub-divide the business into a number of different

---

[1] See the World Bank 'Doing Business Map' (an interactive map powered by Google), which complements the Bank's annual 'Doing Business' report by displaying key information on ease of doing business, at <http://www.doingbusiness.org/map/>. The UK was ranked 6th in 2006, one place down from its 2005 ranking.

An example of simplification is that with effect from 1 January 2007, the registrar of companies has been able to offer a web incorporation facility. This change gives effect to an amendment to the First Council Directive (EEC) 68/151 of 9 March 1968 on co-ordination of safeguards which, for the protection of the interests of members and others, are required by Member States of companies within the meaning of the Treaty, Art 58, second paragraph, with a view to making such safeguards equivalent throughout the Community [1968] OJ L65/8 (amended by Directive (EC) 2003/58 [2003] OJ L 221/13).

[2] E Ferran, 'Company Law Reform in the UK' (2001) 5 *Singapore Journal of International and Comparative Law* 516.

[3] On the historical development of English law, see PL Davies, *Gower's Principles of Modern Company Law* (Sweet & Maxwell, 6th edn, 1997) chs 2–3. On the decline of the theory that incorporation should be regarded as a concession or privilege awarded by the State, see WW Bratton, 'The New Economic Theory of the Firm: Critical Perspectives from History' (1989) 1 *Stanford Law Review* 1471; M Stokes, 'Company Law and Legal Theory' in S Wheeler (ed), *The Law of the Business Enterprise* (OUP, 1994) 80, 89 (reprinted from W Twining (ed), *Legal Theory and Common Law* (Blackwell, 1986) 155). Wheeler's own comments on the concession theory are at 6–8. See also JE Parkinson, *Corporate Power and Responsibility* (OUP, 1993) 25–32.

companies within a group so as to enjoy many times over the advantages of the corporate form.

This chapter considers the standard features of the company that help to explain why, either in single entity form or as multiple entities linked within a corporate group, it is the organizational form chosen by most businesses that want to raise large amounts of capital. The advantages of the corporate form as a mechanism for shielding those who run or own a business from personal financial exposure are outlined. The shielding effect of the corporate form supports business innovation because it provides room for the kind of risk-taking that is often needed to get new ventures off the ground. At the same time, however, the fact that the operators of a business in corporate form do not shoulder all of the financial exposure is potentially problematic because it means that they may be tempted into excessive risk-taking, which if it is unsuccessful and the business fails, will result in creditors of the company being left with worthless claims. The policy challenge is to strike a sensible balance between these competing considerations. How lawmakers in the UK have responded to this challenge and how the choices they have made compare with those made in certain other developed economies, are also issues considered in this chapter. These issues go to the heart of what company law is really about, as recent debate in Europe has recognized:[4] if company law's primary goal is to be facilitative and helpful to those who establish and operate businesses, the policy choices on striking the balance between competing concerns may be quite different from those that would be made from the starting point that company law's essential role is to protect people who deal with businesses whose operators are protected by the shielding effect of the corporate form.

Distinctive features of the company limited by shares

An incorporated company limited by shares has two distinctive features that are of particular significance in relation to corporate finance: separate legal personality and limited liability.

Separate legal personality

An incorporated company is a legal person separate and distinct from the people who hold shares in it and the people who manage it. This has been a foundation stone of company law in the UK ever since the decision of the House of Lords in *Salomon v Salomon & Co Ltd*.[5] Mr Salomon was a boot and shoe manufacturer

---

[4] European Commission, 'Report of the High Level Group of Company Law Experts on a Regulatory Framework for Company Law in Europe' (Brussels, November 2002) 29–31.
[5] [1897] AC 22, HL.

who had been in business for over thirty years as a sole trader. He then converted his business into the newly fashionable company limited by shares incorporated under the companies legislation of the time. Mr Salomon financed the company partly by investing in its shares and partly by lending to it and taking security. The incorporated business failed and the company became insolvent. An action brought by the company's liquidator gave the House of Lords the opportunity to consider fully for the first time the consequences of incorporation. It held that an incorporated company was a legally different person from the persons who had formed the company. Accordingly, even though Mr Salomon controlled all the shares in the company, it was legally distinct from him and he could not be made personally liable to make good the shortfall in the company's assets.

Various consequences follow from the fact that a company is a separate legal personality. A company continues in existence even though managers and share-holders may come and go.[6] It is the company, not its managers or shareholders, that acquires the contractual rights and undertakes the contractual liabilities that are involved in the running of the business. A contract between a company and a substantial shareholder, even one who controls all of the shares in the company, is a valid bilateral contract.[7] A company can have as one of its employees the controller of all its shares.[8] As a legal person, a company can incur tortious liability and can be prosecuted for committing crimes. The property of the business is owned by the company, and its shareholders do not have an insurable interest in it.[9] If shareholders misappropriate the company's property they may be guilty of theft.[10]

The designation of a pool of assets that belongs to the business rather than to its operators personally, which is achieved through incorporation, has been described as 'affirmative asset partitioning'.[11] Affirmative asset partitioning shields the assets of the business from the people behind it and, importantly, from the personal creditors of those people. Affirmative asset partitioning is one of the features that makes the corporate form attractive as a vehicle for raising finance: financiers can concentrate their risk-assessment processes and investigative and monitoring efforts on the particular entity to which they are supplying capital, thereby avoiding costs that would otherwise be passed through to the business that is seeking external finance.

---

[6] *Standard Chartered Bank v Pakistan National Shipping Corp and ors (Nos 2 and 4)* [2003] 1 AC 959, HL, para 36 *per* Lord Rodger.

[7] *Salomon v Salomon & Co Ltd* [1897] AC 22, HL.

[8] *Lee v Lee Air Farming Ltd* [1961] AC 12, HL. But whether a controlling shareholder can be viewed as an employee will depend on the context: *Buchan v Secretary of State for Employment* [1997] BCC 145 (director and controlling shareholder was not an employee for the purpose of receiving redundancy and other payments from the Secretary of State under Employment Protection (Consolidation) Act 1978, ss 106 and 122). Cf *Secretary of State for Trade and Industry v Bottrill* [1999] BCC 177.

[9] *Macaura v Northern Assurance Co* [1925] AC 619, HL.

[10] *Re AG's Reference (No 2 of 1982)* [1984] QB 624, CA.

[11] H Hansmann and RR Kraakman, 'The Essential Role of Organizational Law' (2000) 110 *Yale Law Journal* 387.

Lifting the veil of incorporation

When the veil of incorporation is lifted, the shareholders rather than the company itself are regarded as the relevant actors and, therefore, the shareholders are personally responsible for any liabilities incurred. The vital commercial significance of incorporation is respected by the law and it is therefore exceptional in British law for the veil to be lifted.[12] British law's stance in this respect is broadly consistent with international practice in which veil-piercing is regarded generally as being available only in extreme circumstances.[13] Veil-piercing has been described as 'rare, unprincipled, and arbitrary' by one US commentator, who has suggested that it should be abolished altogether.[14]

Specific statutory provisions may require or permit lifting the veil in particular circumstances: a historical example, which is no longer current because the minimum number of shareholders has been reduced to one for all types of company, was that the companies legislation used to provide for remaining shareholders in a public company to be made personally liable for company debts incurred after the number of shareholders had fallen below the prescribed minimum. These days, where there is statutory intervention to impose personal liability for company debts, this tends to be targeted at those involved in the management of the company rather than at its shareholders as such.[15] The courts do not have a discretionary power to lift the veil in the interests of justice[16] and, aside from those situations where veil-lifting can be justified by reference to the construction of a particular statute, the only clearly established basis for judicial intervention is where the corporate form is a façade that is being used in order to evade an existing legal obligation or to practise some other deception.[17] The precise scope of the courts' power in this respect has not been fully articulated.[18] The Court of Appeal has

---

[12] *Standard Chartered Bank v Pakistan National Shipping Corp and ors (Nos 2 and 4)* [2003] 1 AC 959, HL, para 37 *per* Lord Rodger.

[13] RR Kraakman, P Davies, H Hansmann, G Hertig, KJ Hopt, H Kanda, and EB Rock, *The Anatomy of Corporate Law* (OUP, 2004) 92–4.

[14] SM Bainbridge, 'Abolishing LLC Veil Piercing' [2005] University of Illinois Law Review 77; SM Bainbridge, 'Abolishing Veil Piercing' (2001) 26 *Journal of Corporation Law* 479.

[15] eg Companies Act 2006, s 767(3)–(4) (plc doing business without trading certificate); Company Directors Disqualification Act 1986, s 15 (involvement in management while disqualified); Insolvency Act 1986, s 17 (contravention of restrictions on re-use of company names).

[16] *Woolfson v Strathclyde Regional Council* 1978 SLT 159, HL; *Adams v Cape Industries plc* [1990] Ch 433, CA; *Yukong Lines Ltd of Korea v Rendsburg Investments Corp of Liberia* [1998] 1 WLR 294; *Ord v Belhaven Pubs Ltd* [1998] BCC 607, CA; *Trustor AB v Smallbone and ors (No 2)* [2001] 3 All ER 987.

[17] *Woolfson v Strathclyde Regional Council* 1978 SLT 159, HL, 161 *per* Lord Keith; *Adams v Cape Industries plc* [1990] Ch 433, CA, 544 *per* Slade LJ; *Re Polly Peck plc* [1996] 2 All ER 433, 447; *Trustor AB v Smallbone (No 2)* [2001] 2 BCLC 436; *Kensington International Ltd v Republic of the Congo* [2006] 2 BCLC 296.

[18] S Ottolenghi, 'From Peeping Behind the Corporate Veil to Ignoring it Completely' (1990) 53 MLR 338 reviews the authorities and the earlier literature in an attempt to provide a structure based on four categories. The article acknowledges that there can be no closed list of the circumstances in which the court will lift the veil.

identified the motives of the persons responsible for the use of the corporate structure as a relevant consideration in determining whether an arrangement involving a company is a façade, but has declined to give a comprehensive definition of the principles which should guide a court in determining whether an arrangement involving a company amounts to a façade.[19] It is understandable that the higher courts should resist any temptation to prescribe comprehensively the elements of a façade, since that would be an invitation to the unscrupulous to devise new and previously unenvisaged misuses of the corporate form, but the absence of fuller guidance at a senior judicial level, say in the form of a non-exhaustive list of relevant considerations, makes the law on this point vulnerable to the charge that it is unpredictable and arbitrary.[20]

An example of an attempt to use the corporate form to evade an existing obligation is provided by *Gilford Motor Co v Horne*[21] where an individual attempted to side-step a restrictive covenant that had been imposed on him by his former employer by carrying on business through a limited company. The Court of Appeal held that the company was a façade and lifted the veil of incorporation so as to ensure that the restrictive covenant continued to bite. A more recent illustration of the veil-lifting process at work in this type of situation is provided by *Trustor AB v Smallbone and ors (No 2)*[22] where the veil was lifted in circumstances where a company acted as a device or façade in that it was used as the vehicle for the receipt of money misappropriated from another company by its managing director.

Whilst the courts will lift the veil in circumstances where a company is a sham to evade an existing obligation, they are not receptive to lifting the veil where the corporate form is adopted in order to limit the future obligations of its shareholders. The freedom to use incorporation as a means of reducing future legal liability is an inherent part of company law.[23]

---

[19] *Adams v Cape Industries plc* [1990] Ch 433, CA, 540 *per* Slade LJ.

[20] DD Prentice, 'Groups of Companies: the English Experience' in KJ Hopt (ed), *Groups of Companies in European Laws* (W de Gruyter, 1982) 99, 101. The plea 'is it not time to know just when a company is a "sham" and when the veil of incorporation *can* be "torn aside"?' (Lord Wedderburn, 'Multinationals and The Antiquities of Company Law' (1984) 47 MLR 87) has gone largely unanswered, save that it can be gleaned from recent decisions that the fraud category will be strictly confined: *Ord v Belhaven Pubs Ltd* [1998] BCC 607, CA (where *Creasey v Breachwood Motors Ltd* [1993] BCLC 480 was said to be no longer authoritative); *Yukong Lines Ltd of Korea v Rendsburg Investment Corp of Liberia (No 2)* [1998] 1 WLR 294 (noted J Payne, 'Reaching the Man Behind the Company' [1998] *Company, Financial and Insolvency Law Review* 147); *HR v JAPT* [1997] Pensions Law Review 99 (noted C Mitchell, 'Beneficiaries' Rights Against Trustee Company Directors' [1998] *Company, Financial and Insolvency Law Review* 133).

[21] [1933] Ch 935, CA. See also *Jones v Lipman* [1962] 1 All ER 442; *Re a Company* (1985) 1 BCC 99, 421, CA. cf *Coles, Hunter and Parker v Samuel Smith Old Brewery Tadcaster* (27 November 2007, CA).

[22] [2001] 3 All ER 987.

[23] *Adams v Cape Industries plc* [1990] Ch 433, CA, 544 *per* Slade LJ. See also *Multinational Gas and Petrochemical Co v Multinational Gas and Petrochemical Services Ltd* [1983] Ch 258, CA, noted Lord Wedderburn, 'Multinationals and The Antiquities of Company Law' (1984) 47 MLR 87.

Lifting the veil of incorporation between companies that are in the same corporate group is considered later in this chapter.

Limited liability

Shareholders in a company limited by shares are liable to contribute only a limited amount to its assets. The minimum amount of the contribution in respect of each share is its par value—ie its fixed nominal value[24]—because that constitutes the minimum allotment price.[25] Where a share is allotted at a price higher than its par value (described as an issue at a premium), then the required contribution is par value plus the premium.[26] Company law does not impose mandatory par values for shares, nor does it require companies to issue their shares at specific premiums. These are matters for companies to decide on an individual basis.[27] Many private companies start life with a nominal share capital of £100 divided into 100 £1 shares. The par value of shares in public companies is often much less than £1 because this can enhance liquidity, the argument being that, for example, ten shares of 10p each will be easier to sell than one share of £1. The mandatory rule that shares cannot be allotted by the company at less than par provides another explanation for low par values. When a company is planning to raise capital by offering its shares for investment it will have in mind the price at which it intends to offer the shares but must take into account that the offer price may have to be adjusted downwards in response to market conditions at the time when the offer is made. To enable this fine-tuning to take place, the par value of shares must be virtually irrelevant, which means that there must be a large margin between the intended premium at which the shares are to be offered and their par value.

Limited liability does not follow automatically from the principle of separate legal personality.[28] Corporate personality means that the company, not its shareholders, is the person responsible for the debts of the business. The extent to which the company can require its shareholders to provide the finance to meet the liabilities of the business is a logically distinct issue. The legislation of 1844[29] that first established the procedure for incorporating a company by an administrative registration process did not provide for limited liability of the shareholders. Limited liability did not become part of the law relating to companies incorporated

---

[24] Companies Act 2006, s 542.

[25] ibid s 580.

[26] ibid s 582.

[27] It may be a breach of duty by directors if they fail to offer new shares at the best price obtainable (*Shearer v Bercain* [1980] 3 All ER 295) but the company would not be in breach of any general requirement of company law in that event.

[28] PI Blumberg, *The Multinational Challenge to Corporation Law: The Search for a New Corporate Personality* (OUP, 1993) 7.

[29] Joint Stock Companies Act 1844.

by registration[30] until over ten years later, when the Limited Liability Act 1855 was passed.[31]

People who lend to companies also have limited exposure: they, too, are liable to contribute no more than the principal amount that they agree to lend. The basic distinction between the shareholder and the lender is that, whilst both contribute a fixed amount, only the shareholder hopes for open-ended capital gain in respect of the investment. This distinction can easily become blurred— preference shares can resemble debt finance by offering the investor only a limited capital return, lenders may make their profit on a loan by advancing less than the agreed principal on the basis that the full amount of the principal is to be repaid— but it suffices as a point of departure for the present discussion.[32] Provided the company remains solvent, lenders get back what they lent, but no more; it is the shareholders of a solvent company who are entitled to claim the residue remaining after all liabilities and claims have been met (hence shareholders can be described as the 'residual claimants'). The flip side of the contrast between a lender and a shareholder is the position in an insolvent company: there, in simple terms,[33] the order of repayment is: first, creditors who have taken security on the company's property, secondly, unsecured creditors and, finally, shareholders. Shareholders, at the bottom of the pile, have the least chance of recovering their investment but, because they benefit from limited liability, they do not have to make good any shortfall in the company's assets. The risk of corporate insolvency is thus borne in part by a company's creditors.[34]

For shareholders, therefore, limited liability operates as a shield against having to contribute over and above the fixed amount of the investment they agree to

---

[30] The principle of limited liability already applied to companies incorporated by Charter or by specific Act of Parliament.

[31] On the struggle for limited liability in the UK: PL Davies, *Gower's Principles of Modern Company Law* (Sweet & Maxwell, 6th edn, 1997) 40–6; A Muscat, *The Liability of the Holding Company for the Debts of its Insolvent Subsidiaries* (Dartmouth, 1996) 103–6. The Limited Liability Act 1855 contained various safeguards, including regulated minimum par values (£10), but most of these disappeared almost immediately when that Act was repealed and replaced by the Joint Stock Companies Act 1856. The historical background to limited liability in the US is explored in SB Presser, 'Thwarting the Killing of the Corporation: Limited Liability, Democracy and Economics' (1992) 87 *Northwestern University Law Review* 148, 155–6 and PI Blumberg, *The Multinational Challenge to Corporation Law: The Search for a New Corporate Personality* (OUP, 1993) 10–14.

[32] It has been argued that capital markets would nullify the practical impact of any widescale attempt to withdraw shareholders' limited liability by devising synthetic securities which replicated all of the advantages of shares but which did not adopt that legal form: JA Grundfest, 'The Limited Future of Unlimited Liability: a Capital Markets Perspective' (1992) 102 *Yale Law Journal* 387.

[33] This rank order ignores such matters as the costs of the insolvency process, priorities between secured creditors (see ch 12 below), subordinated creditors (ch 11 below), and different classes of shareholders (ch 6 below).

[34] Some writers regard limited liability as a device for shifting risk from shareholders to creditors. See DW Leebron, 'Limited Liability, Tort Victims, and Creditors' (1991) 91 *Columbia Law Review* 1565, 1584; but contrast BR Cheffins, *Company Law Theory, Structure and Operation* (OUP, 1997) 497.

make in return for their shares. This aspect of the shielding effect of limited liability leads to a number of positive consequences, which, for convenience, can be considered under the following headings, although they are in fact inter-related: promotion of entrepreneurial activity; passive investment; portfolio diversification; cost of capital; transferability of shares; and insulation from tort liabilities.

Promotion of entrepreneurial activity

Limited liability encourages entrepreneurial activity because it allows people to limit the risks involved in conducting business. This is the main function of limited liability in quasi-partnership type companies where raising share capital from persons other than the controllers of the business, or their families, is usually not a realistic option.[35] The importance of this aspect of limited liability should not be overstated because in a real-life situation it is likely to be whittled away by unlimited personal guarantees which some providers of debt finance to the business may demand from its controllers. To the extent that personal guarantees are given, contractual stipulation overrides the limited-liability position established by company law.[36] Yet not all creditors of the business will be in a position to demand personal guarantees. Some will lack the necessary bargaining strength whilst others may have no opportunity to bargain because they are the victims of a tort committed by the company. The controllers can thus still derive some benefit from limited liability.[37]

Passive investment

Limited liability facilitates passive investment, ie investment on the basis that the investor will not play a part in management. The fact that there is a cap on the amount at risk is an encouragement to investors to allow other people to run a business using their money. Without such a cap, a prudent[38] investor might be disinclined to invest in shares at all or, at least, would undoubtedly expect a very high return to compensate for the risks involved. The investor might also want to monitor more closely the way in which the managers of the business conduct its affairs, and that would lead to additional costs.[39]

---

[35] SB Presser, 'Thwarting the Killing of the Corporation: Limited Liability, Democracy and Economics' (1992) 87 *Northwestern University Law Review* 148, 163 argues that limited liability was developed in the 19th century to facilitate investment in smaller firms and that it 'reflects a traditional American policy to favour the small-scale entrepreneur'.

[36] FH Easterbrook and DR Fischel, *The Economic Structure of Corporate Law* (Harvard University Press, 1991) 55–6.

[37] Cheffins (n 34 above) 500–1.

[38] A reckless investor, especially if he or she is virtually insolvent anyway, might not mind taking on such a degree of risk because there is always the option of bankruptcy.

[39] Easterbrook and Fischel (n 36 above) 41–2. But the extent to which shareholders would intensify their monitoring of management could depend on the potential return. If high enough they might still adopt a fairly passive role: Presser (n 35 above) 159.

There is a risk that, because they enjoy limited liability, shareholders may allow the managers of their company to take greater risks in the running of the business than they would have permitted if they had to face the prospect of being personally liable without limit for the failure of that business. In the event of such failure, it is the creditors who will have to absorb the loss over and above the amount of share capital that has been invested. Here we begin to see a problem with limited liability (sometimes described as a 'moral hazard'): it is the shareholders who reap the benefit from success because they get capital gains but they do not bear all the risk of failure.[40] The moral hazard aspects of limited liability are considered further in this chapter in the context of groups of companies because they can arise especially strongly in that context. Here the emphasis is on the upside. Successful risk-taking, which may be funded by passive investment, is a positive outcome facilitated by limited liability. As well as benefiting shareholders and ensuring that debts to creditors can be paid when due, successful risk-taking, funded by passive investment, may also produce new jobs for employees and contribute to general economic prosperity. Thus there is a public interest in the facilitation of passive investment through the provision of limited liability.[41]

Passive investment means that companies can expand their capital base whilst retaining a cohesive managerial structure involving relatively few individuals who, between them, own only a small portion of the company's issued share capital: in other words, ownership (through shareholding) and control (through managing the business) are able to separate. It was exactly because large businesses, such as railway companies, needed to expand their capital base in this way that there was such pressure for the enactment of limited liability for the shareholders of registered companies in the middle of the nineteenth century.[42] When it became available, it immediately prompted a spate of new incorporations.[43] The limited liability company rapidly became the means whereby businesses could raise large amounts of finance from a large spread of investors.[44]

Portfolio diversification

Limited liability also facilitates portfolio diversification. This is the process whereby an investor can reduce the risks involved in investing in volatile securities

[40] Cheffins (n 34 above) 497–8; P Halpern, M Trebilcock, and S Turnbull, 'An Economic Analysis of Limited Liability in Corporation Law' (1980) 30 *University of Toronto Law Journal* 117, 144–5.

[41] PL Davies, *Introduction to Company Law* (Clarendon Press, 2002) 63–5.

[42] JB Baskin and PJ Miranti, *A History of Corporate Finance* (CUP, 1997) 138–45 traces the 19th-century development of limited liability in the UK and the US.

[43] PL Davies, *Gower's Principles of Modern Company Law* (Sweet & Maxwell, 6th edn, 1997) 46, n 64; PI Blumberg, *The Multinational Challenge to Corporation Law: The Search for a New Corporate Personality* (OUP, 1993) 17–19.

[44] P Halpern, M Trebilcock, and Turnbull (n 40 above) 118–19; M Radin, 'The Endless Problem of Corporate Personality' (1983) 32 *Columbia Law Review* 643, 654; HG Manne, 'Our Two Corporation Systems: Law and Economics' (1967) 53 *Virginia Law Review* 259, 260.

by constructing a portfolio of investments in which those securities are balanced by others that are lower risk and which offer a lower return. Portfolio diversification does not eliminate systematic risk—ie the risk of variability in returns on investments because of the way that capital markets in general respond to macroeconomic developments, such as changes in the tax regime, or exchange-rate and interest-rate swings. It is all about reducing the specific risks arising from factors which are unique to the individual companies whose shares are included in the portfolio.[45]

Without limited liability, portfolio diversification could not eliminate or reduce the risks associated with investing in specific companies.[46] It would have the opposite effect of increasing risk because every time an investor added a new share to his portfolio that would create exposure to the risk of being personally liable for all of that company's debts.[47] Without portfolio diversification, and in the absence of some alternative way of dealing with risk such as the purchase of insurance,[48] companies seeking to raise share capital from investors would have to offer them a return that compensated them for taking on specific risk as well as systematic risk, with the result that share capital would become a more expensive form of finance. Some investors might be prompted to withdraw altogether from holding shares, which could cause the costs associated with raising capital by issuing shares to increase still further because of the diminution in the size of the pool of finance available in that form.[49] Other investors might concentrate their investment on one or two companies and engage in closer monitoring and control of the management of those companies, which could generate inefficiencies.

Cost of capital

The return required by the providers of a company's share capital and debt constitutes its cost of capital. Minimizing the cost of capital is a crucial part of running a business, and corporate finance decisions such as how much debt or share capital to have in the balance sheet, or how much profit to pay out by way of dividend, are all fundamentally about cost of capital.[50] It might be argued that limited liability should not affect cost of capital because all it does is to cause part of the risk of

---

[45] Manne, (n 44 above) 262.

[46] FH Easterbrook and DR Fischel, *The Economic Structure of Corporate Law* (Harvard University Press, 1991) 43.

[47] This assumes a rule of joint and several personal liability. For an analysis of portfolio diversification under a pro rata personal liability rule, see DW Leebron, 'Limited Liability, Tort Victims, and Creditors' (1991) 91 *Columbia Law Review* 1565, 1597–1600.

[48] On insurance as an alternative to limited liability, see Easterbrook and Fischel (n 36 above) 47–9.

[49] Though if investors simply switched to synthetic securities devised by companies to replicate the features of share capital, query whether the overall cost of capital would increase significantly. On the response of the capital markets to the withdrawal of limited liability, see JA Grundfest, 'The Limited Future of Unlimited Liability: a Capital Markets Perspective' (1992) 102 *Yale Law Journal* 387.

[50] See ch 3 below.

insolvency to fall on creditors rather than shareholders. Thus, to the extent that shareholders can limit their risk, the creditors' risk is increased and that will be reflected in the interest rates charged in respect of debt finance.[51] This argument is superficially appealing but it begins to break down on closer examination.

First, if shareholders did not have limited liability and were personally liable for all of the company's debts, that would still not eliminate the risk to creditors because their chances of being repaid would depend on the creditworthiness of all of the shareholders. Checking the creditworthiness of a large number of persons would be time-consuming and costly, as would enforcing claims against a large number of shareholders in the event of default. Limited liability reduces the costs that creditors have to incur in transacting with companies because they need check only the creditworthiness of the company itself and, in the event of default, need only sue the company. In theory, the reduction in transaction costs that follows from limited liability should impact positively on the rates at which the company can borrow.[52]

Secondly, a bank or other professional lender that is considering lending a large amount of money to a company can be expected to investigate the company closely. Specific investigation, in combination with the lender's accumulated general knowledge and experience of lending to companies, should put it in a strong position to assess the risks involved, with the consequence that a professional lender may price more accurately the risk for which it requires compensation than potential equity investors would have done had the company sought additional finance in that form.[53]

Another possible reason why the savings in cost of capital that flow from limited liability may not necessarily be cancelled out by higher interest rates charged by creditors to compensate them for bearing part of the risk of insolvency is that interest rates are not the only risk-management tool available to creditors. Depending on respective bargaining positions, creditors may be able to reduce their risk by taking security or imposing contractual restrictions on the operation of the business. However, some caution is appropriate here because if one creditor accepts a lower rate of interest in return for security, another unsecured creditor may charge a higher rate to compensate it for the risk that, in insolvency, it will rank behind the secured creditor and will have to absorb loss remaining after the shareholders' funds (the equity cushion) have been wiped out. Whether alternative risk-management mechanisms that are available to creditors reduce the total amount of interest charged to a borrowing company is thus a debatable point, which is considered further in chapter 3 below.

---

[51] Halpern, Trebilcock, and Turnbull (n 40 above) 126–9.
[52] RC Clark, *Corporate Law* (Little, Brown, 1986) 8–9; Halpern, Trebilcock, and Turnbull (n 40 above) 134–5.
[53] Clark (n 52 above) 8.

Transferability of shares

Unless the articles of association of a particular company restrict dealings, shares in limited companies are freely transferable. Shares which are admitted to CREST, the UK's mechanism for the electronic trading of securities, are bought and sold without a document of transfer. Otherwise shares are transferred by means of an instrument of transfer in accordance with the formalities prescribed in the Stock Transfer Act 1963 (where the shares have been paid for in full) or the company's articles (where they are not fully paid).[54]

If shareholders had joint and several personal liability for all of their company's debts,[55] a relevant consideration for a person investing in shares would be the ability of other shareholders to pay the company's debts. Prudent shareholders would engage in costly monitoring of each other's wealth[56] and they would want to restrict the transfer of shares so as to ensure that any new shareholders were at least as wealthy as the persons whose shares they acquired. Moreover, share prices would not be uniform: the wealth of the person acquiring the shares would affect the price because a wealthy investor could expect to pay less for the same shares than an impecunious one on the basis that he or she would be taking on more of the risk in the event of corporate default.[57] With limited liability, shares are fungible securities and trading can take place on an anonymous basis.

Tort liabilities

Another function of limited liability is that it insulates shareholders from tort liabilities that may be incurred by their company. If, say, a company pollutes a river or one of its factories blows up, then the persons who are injured or who suffer physical damage to their property can seek compensation from the company. Depending on the seriousness of the accident and the number of victims involved, the compensation costs may be very large. Limited liability means that the shareholders do not have to meet the claims from their personal resources. The victims of the tort will be unsecured creditors in the company's insolvency. They may also have a claim against the company's directors or senior managers

---

[54] Companies Act 2006, Pt 21.

[55] This is only one of the ways in which an unlimited-liability regime might operate. Another is that shareholders might incur liability pro rata to their investment: see DW Leebron, 'Limited Liability, Tort Victims, and Creditors' (1991) 91 *Columbia Law Review* 1565, 1578–84; H Hansmann and RR Kraakman, 'Towards Unlimited Shareholder Liability for Corporate Torts' (1991) 100 *Yale Law Journal* 1879, 1892–4. Pro rata liability would remove the incentive to monitor other shareholders' wealth: DW Leebron, ibid 1607–8; H Hansmann and RR Kraakman, ibid 1903–6; SB Presser, 'Thwarting the Killing of the Corporation: Limited Liability, Democracy and Economics' (1992) 87 *Northwestern University Law Review* 148, 160–1.

[56] FH Easterbrook and DR Fischel, *The Economic Structure of Corporate Law* (Harvard University Press, 1991) 42.

[57] P Halpern, M Trebilcock and S Turnbull, 'An Economic Analysis of Limited Liability in Corporation Law' (1980) 30 *University of Toronto Law Journal* 117, 130–1. Again, the position would be different under a rule of pro rata personal liability: Leebron (n 55 above) 1608–10.

as joint tortfeasors but, for this to succeed, they will need to establish a distinct personal liability in tort attaching to those individuals.[58]

The present practice of the courts in the UK is not to view tort claimants more favourably than contractual creditors in relation to lifting the veil.[59] However, whether the courts should be more willing to favour tort claimants is a issue that is much debated in the literature.[60] Some commentators consider that the veil of incorporation should not be allowed to shield those involved in a company from the consequences of its hazardous activities. It is argued that preserving the veil of incorporation in this situation may encourage excessive risk-taking by companies and operate unfairly in relation to the victims of the tort who, unlike contractual creditors of the company, do not have an opportunity to protect their position through a bargaining process. The debate on this topic is particularly concerned with the situation where the tortfeasor is a subsidiary within a corporate group, and this is therefore an appropriate point to start looking more closely at corporate groups as an organizational form for the conduct of business activity.

The corporate group

It is commonplace for business to be conducted through a network of connected companies rather than by a single corporate entity.[61] There are a variety of reasons why a structure involving a goup of companies may be adopted, including tax planning, regulatory requirements, and administrative convenience.[62] Group

---

[58] *Williams v Natural Life Health Foods Ltd* [1998] 1 WLR 830, HL. See further R Grantham and C Rickett, 'Directors' ' "Tortious" Liability: Contract, Tort or Company Law?' (1999) 62 MLR 133. For the liability of company officers for fraud see *Standard Chartered Bank v Pakistan National Shipping Corp and ors* [2003] 1 AC 959.

[59] *Adams v Cape Industries* [1990] Ch 433, CA.

[60] The literature includes the following: DW Leebron, 'Limited Liability, Tort Victims, and Creditors' (1991) 91 *Columbia Law Review* 1565; H Hansmann, and RR Kraakman, 'Towards Unlimited Shareholder Liability for Corporate Torts' (1991) 100 *Yale Law Journal* 1879; SB Presser, 'Thwarting the Killing of the Corporation: Limited Liability, Democracy and Economics' (1992) 87 *Northwestern University Law Review* 148, 166–72; D Goddard, 'Corporate Personality— Limited Recourse and its Limits' in R Grantham and C Rickett (eds), *Corporate Personality in the 20th Century* (Hart, 1998) 11, 39–40.

[61] T Hadden, *The Control of Corporate Groups* (Institute of Advanced Legal Studies, 1983) ch 2, analyses in detail the group structure of four multinational enterprises. Three of the four groups studied in detail comprised at least 170 active companies. The largest British groups at the time of the study (Unilever and BP) were not included in the survey but the author notes that, between them, they had some 2,100 subsidiaries. On the emergence of corporate groups in the US: PI Blumberg, *The Multinational Challenge to Corporation Law: The Search for a New Corporate Personality* (OUP, 1993) ch 3 and PI Blumberg, 'The American Law of Corporate Groups' in J McCahery, S Piccoitto, and C Scott (eds) *Corporate Control and Accountability* (Clarendon Press, 1993) 305. For comparative studies see JE Antunes, *Liability of Corporate Groups* (Kluwer, 1994) ch 1 and T Hadden, 'Regulating Corporate Groups: International Perspective' in McCahery, Piccoitto, and Scott (eds) (above) 343.

[62] V Finch, *Corporate Insolvency Law Perspectives and Principles* (CUP, 2002), 407–8.

structures may reflect geographical considerations, as was the factual position in an important decision of the European Court of Justice on the tax treatment under English law of losses incurred by Belgian, German, and French subsidiaries of Marks & Spencer plc.[63] Where business is diversified into a number of different and distinct activities, it may be judged to be convenient to establish separate subsidiaries to conduct those separate businesses. Companies may be brought into a corporate group by acquisition and then allowed by their new owner to retain their existing form as part of the network.[64] Analysis of business structures suggests that enterprises which are divided into separate divisions operating as separate profit centres with responsibility for their own administration may be preferable to enterprises that have one central management because the divisional structure reduces the length of chains of command and facilitates the setting of goals and consequential monitoring.[65] However, although the legal rules concerning groups of companies would seem to fit well with the achievement of a multi divisional management structure, evidence suggests that the divisionalization that occurs in practice within large organizations may be unrelated to the formal corporate structure of the group.[66]

The cornerstone principle of company law that each company in the network is a separate legal person and its shareholders have limited liability is a powerful consideration in favour of a group structure. It means that the corporate group is a structure that can be used to minimize liability and to shield assets of one part of the business from claims arising from the activities of another part. For a multi national business, a group structure may provide protection against the risks involved in operating in politically unstable countries.[67] Furthermore, it limits the jurisdiction of the courts of a particular state only to those parts of the business that have a connection with that state. Profits can be taken out of successful companies within a group by means of intra-group dividends[68] but unsuccessful companies can be left to fail with only the loss of the original investment in their share capital and without any further liability to the creditors of those concerns.

---

[63] Case C-446/03 *Marks & Spencer plc v David Halsey (Her Majesty's Inspector of Taxes)* [2005] ECR I-10837, ECJ.

[64] RP Austin, 'Corporate Groups' in CEF Rickett and RB Grantham (eds), *Corporate Personality in the Twentieth Century* (Hart, 1998) 741; A Wyatt and R Mason, 'Legal and Accounting Regulatory Framework for Corporate Groups: Implications for Insolvency in Group Operations' (1998) 16 *Corporate and Securities Law Journal* 424; A Muscat, *The Liability of the Holding Company for the Debts of its Insolvent Subsidiaries* (Dartmouth, 1996) 14.

[65] OE Williamson, 'The Modern Corporation: Origin, Evolution, Attributes' (1981) 19 *Journal of Economic Literature* 1537; N Kay, 'Corporate Governance and Transaction Costs' in McCahery, Piccoitto, and Scott (eds), (n 61 above) 133.

[66] T Hadden, *The Control of Corporate Groups* (Institute of Advanced Legal Studies, 1983) 10, 12–13; Muscat (n 64 above) 8–10.

[67] G Jones, 'Structuring the Relationship—the Group's Viewpoint' in RM Goode (ed), *Group Trading and the Lending Banker* (Chartered Institute of Bankers, 1988) 1.

[68] Tax considerations may mean that different structures (eg administration payments) are used in order to move profits around the group: T Hadden, 'Insolvency and the Group—Problems with Integrated Financing' in RM Goode (ed) (n 67 above) 71.

There is no separate branch of British company law that deals with corporate groups generally,[69] but for particular purposes the Companies Act 2006 does recognize and attach legal significance to two main[70] types of corporate group: namely, the holding or parent company and its subsidiary companies, and the parent undertaking and its subsidiary undertakings. The latter type of group is relevant for the purposes of consolidated group accounts; the former is employed in other specific statutory contexts.

The definition of the corporate group for accounting purposes

The purpose of group accounts is to give shareholders and creditors of the holding company a clearer picture of the use of their investment than could be gleaned from its individual accounts.[71] The process of drawing up group accounts involves treating the assets and liabilities of all of the companies in the group as if they were part of the assets and liabilities of the company that heads the group. This results in the financial statements of a group being presented as those of a single economic entity.[72] The production of annual consolidated group accounts is mandatory for parent companies that are incorporated in the UK, save for those that are subject to the lighter disclosure regime for small companies, and certain other limited exceptions.[73]

The informational value of consolidated accounts depends crucially on the rules defining the entities to be included in a consolidation (scope rules). The narrower the scope, the more room there is for reporting entities to establish off-balance sheet special purpose vehicles (SPVs) in which they have significant economic stakes and whose activities could have significant adverse ramifications for them. The notorious story of the Enron Corporation, which grew spectacularly during the 1900s and collapsed, equally spectacularly, in 2001 after announcing a US$1 billion plus adjustment to its published accounts, shows what can happen

[69] T Hadden, *The Control of Corporate Groups* (Institute of Advanced Legal Studies,1983) 2–3; A Tunc, 'The Fiduciary Duties of a Dominant Shareholder' in CM Schmitthoff and F Wooldridge (eds), *Groups of Companies* (Sweet & Maxwell, 1991) 1–3. DD Prentice, 'Some Comments on the Law Relating to Corporate Groups' in McCahery, Piccoitto, and Scott (eds) (n 61 above) 371, 372 argues in favour of the status quo and the absence of an area of law on group enterprises generally. His argument is that there is already an abundance of law relating to corporate groups, but for specific purposes and in specific contexts.

[70] Although not developed in the text, it may be noted that other groupings are also recognized in certain contexts (such as associated companies where one has the right to control at least one-third of the voting rights in the other; eg Companies Act 2006, s 823 (attribution of corporate interests for the purpose of disclosure obligations)).

[71] C Napier and C Noke, 'Premiums and Pre-Acquisition Profits: the Legal and Accountancy Professions and Business Combinations' (1991) 54 MLR 810, 811; KJ Hopt, 'Legal Issues and Questions of Policy in the Comparative Regulation of Groups' [1996] *I Gruppi di Società* 45, 54–5.

[72] International Accounting Standard 27, *Consolidated and Separate Financial Statements* (IAS 27).

[73] Companies Act 2006, ss 399–402.

when scope rules are restrictive. Key problems in the Enron situation involved its use of special purpose entities (SPEs) to engage in 'off-balance sheet' activities.[74] Enron used SPEs, which were not part of its corporate group for accounting purposes, to conceal debt and to manipulate financial results.[75] In a submission by The Institute of Chartered Accountants in England and Wales (ICAEW) to a Treasury Select Committee that examined, in the light of the Enron collapse, the arrangements for financial regulation of public limited companies in the UK, the Institute commented on the apparent centrality in relation to Enron of off-balance sheet accounting treatment of SPEs. The Institute noted that difficulties lay in deciding to whom the assets and liabilities of SPEs 'belonged' and therefore whether they should be included in the consolidated accounts. It contrasted the British and US approaches on scope in the following terms: 'In the United Kingdom, the consolidation model is based on the principle of control of economic benefits, not just control of a company. The IAS approach is broadly comparable. However, under United States GAAP (generally accepted accounting principles), consolidation is more often based on legal ownership, with specific rules regarding non-consolidation of certain SPEs.'[76]

On the other hand, an overly broad definition could also be problematic in that it could inhibit the entrepreneurial development of new ventures. Those who make the rules in this area thus face the familiar challenge of achieving a balance between competing concerns. They also have to contend with the fact that the off-balance sheet industry will immediately respond to new requirements by trying to find loopholes that will avoid consolidation obligations. To address this problem, financial disclosure regimes need to include 'catch all' or anti-avoidance provisions whereby particular entities that are not otherwise caught by the general scope rules must be consolidated or at least mentioned in notes to the accounts where they represent a source of material risks and/or benefits for the reporting group.[77]

The British domestic position on the scope of consolidation requirements is now found in the Companies Act 2006, which gives domestic effect to the Seventh Company Law Directive on consolidated accounts,[78] and in accounting

[74] *Arthur Andersen LLP v US* 125 SCt 2129, US, 2005, 2132.

[75] *Re Enron Corp Securities, Derivative & ERISA Litigation* 235 F Supp 2d 549 (SD Tex 2002), 618. SL Schwarcz, 'Enron and the Use and Abuse of Special Purpose Entities in Corporate Structures (2002) 70 *University of Cincinnati Law Review* 1309.

[76] ICAEW, 'Submission to the Treasury Committee' s Inquiry into the Financial Regulation of Public Limited Companies' (March 2002), accessible at <http://www.icaew.co.uk/index.cfm?AUB=TB2I_31988%7CMNXI_31988#the%20background> (accessed December 2007).

[77] See eg Directive (EEC) 83/349 on consolidated accounts [1983] OJ L193/1 (as amended (most recently) by Directive (EEC) 2006/46 [2006] OJ L 224/1) Art 43.7(a), which was added in response to concern about off-balance sheet activities. In the IFRS disclosure regime, see SIC-12, which deals with the accounting treatment of special purpose entities that are not within the scope of the group, as determined under the general requirements of that regime.

[78] Seventh Company Law Directive, Directive (EEC) 83/349 [1983] OJ L193/1.

standards.[79] Section 404 of the Companies Act 2006 provides that where a parent company prepares Companies Act group accounts, all the subsidiary undertakings of the company must be included in the consolidation, subject to limited exceptions. In this context, 'undertaking' means a body corporate, partnership, or unincorporated association carrying on a trade or business, with or without a view to profit.[80] An entity is a subsidiary undertaking (SU) of another entity (the parent or 'P') where: (1) P holds a majority of the voting rights in SU; (2) P is a member of SU and has the right to appoint or remove the majority of its board of directors; or (3) P is a member of SU and controls alone, pursuant to an agreement with other shareholders, a majority of the voting rights in SU.[81] References to voting rights in a company are to rights conferred on shareholders in respect of their shares or, in the case of a company not having a share capital, on members, to vote at general meetings of the company on all, or substantially all, matters.[82] The reference to the right to appoint or remove a majority of the board of directors is to the right to appoint or remove directors holding a majority of the voting rights at meetings of the board on all, or substantially all, matters.[83]

In addition, there exists a parent and subsidiary undertaking relationship giving rise to an accounting consolidation obligation where: (1) P has the right to exercise a dominant influence over the SU by virtue of provisions contained in the SU's articles or by virtue of a control contract (legal control);[84] or (2) P has the power to exercise or actually exercises dominant influence over SU, or P and SU are managed on a unified basis (factual control).[85] Both of these tests recognize that a company can effectively control other entities even without majority voting control: for example, if the majority of the shareholders are diversified passive investors, each holding a small proportion of its shares, one shareholder with a substantial shareholding may in practice (as a consequence of the voting apathy of other shareholders) be in a position to control the outcome of shareholder meetings notwithstanding that it does not formally control the majority of the votes.

The test based on factual control is more significant in practice because the criteria for legal control are quite formal and rigid.[86] Where the operators of a business want to avoid a consolidation obligation, they are unlikely to regard the legal control limb of the statutory scope rules as being a major impediment to the achievement of this goal. The factual control test is less easy to circumvent. According to the relevant accounting standard,[87] actual exercise of a

---

[79] Financial Reporting Standard 2, *Accounting for Subsidiary Undertakings* (FRS 2).
[80] Companies Act 2006, s 1161.
[81] ibid s 1162 (a), (b) and (d) and Sch 7.
[82] ibid Sch 7, para 2.
[83] ibid Sch 7, para 3.
[84] ibid s 1162(20(c) and Sch 7, para 4.
[85] ibid s 1162(4).
[86] These requirements are specified in Companies Act 2006, Sch 7, para 4.
[87] FRS 2.

dominant influence means the exercise of an influence that achieves the result that the operating and financial policies of the undertaking influenced are set in accordance with the wishes of the holder of the influence and for its benefit. The power to exercise dominant influence is a power that, if exercised, would give rise to the actual exercise of dominant influence. The actual exercise of a dominant influence is to be identified by looking at the effect in practice. Power of veto may amount to exercise of a dominant influence in an appropriate case, although it is more likely that this would be so where the veto power is held in conjunction with other powers and no similar veto is held by anyone else. The actual exercise of dominant influence may be interventionist or non-interventionist—the latter meaning that the parent's interference occurs only rarely on critical matters. The accounting standard also defines 'managed on a unified basis'. This exists where the whole of the operations of the undertakings are integrated and they are managed as a single unit.

Where a company has its securities admitted to trading on a regulated market in the European Economic Area (EEA), it is obliged under EC law to produce its consolidated accounts in accordance with International Financial Reporting Standards (IFRS)/International Accounting Standards (IAS) rather than under its national accounting system.[88] The consolidation requirements in this system are set out in IAS 27, *Consolidated Financial Statements and Accounting for Investments in Subsidiaries*. Under IAS 27, a corporate group means a parent and all of its subsidiaries. A subsidiary is an entity that is controlled by its parent. Control is presumed when the parent acquires more than half of the voting rights of the enterprise. Where this threshold is not met, control may be evidenced by power: (a) over more than one half of the voting rights by virtue of an agreement with other investors; (b) to govern the financial and operating policies of the other enterprise under a statute or an agreement; (c) to appoint or remove the majority of the members of the board of directors; or (d) to cast the majority of votes at a meeting of the board of directors.[89]

The definition of the corporate group for other purposes

Other sections of the companies legislation also employ the concept of the corporate group: for example a subsidiary is prohibited from holding shares in its parent (or holding) company[90] and financial assistance by a subsidiary for the acquisition of shares in a parent is prohibited where the subsidiary or the parent is a public company.[91] The definition of the corporate group that applies for the

---

[88] Regulation (EC) 1606/2002 of the European Parliament and of the Council of 19 July 2002 on the application of international accounting standards [2002] OJ L243/1 (hereinafter the 'IAS Regulation').

[89] IAS 27.13.

[90] Companies Act 2006, s 136.

[91] ibid ss 677–680.

non-accounting provisions overlaps with, but is narrower than, the accounting definition. A company is a parent (or holding) company and another company is a subsidiary if (1) P holds a majority of the voting rights in S; (2) P is a member of S and has the right to appoint or remove the majority of its board of directors; or (3) P is a member of S and controls alone, pursuant to an agreement with other shareholders, a majority of the voting rights in S.[92] If S in turn has a subsidiary (SS), SS is also a subsidiary of P.[93] A wholly owned subsidiary is one in which S has no members apart from P or P and other wholly owned subsidiaries of P.[94] These tests are identical to the first set of tests that are used for the accounting definition of the corporate group and, as there, it is the control of the majority of the voting rights, not the majority in number of the shares or of the directors, that matters.[95] The Companies Act 2006 tests for the existence of a corporate group that are based on legal control and factual control do not apply outside the accounting context.

Where a company enters into a contract containing provisions that relate to it and other members of its group, or has such provisions in its articles, it is necessary to establish contextually how the group is defined. This is a matter of drafting and there is no presumption that any of the statutory definitions is imported into contracts or other arrangements to which a company is a party.

Company law and the corporate group: a general overview

The fundamentals are clear: each company within a corporate group is a separate and distinct legal entity; assets and liabilities belong to the individual companies, not to the group as a whole; and directors of subsidiaries owe the duties that attach to their office to the particular companies on whose boards they serve, not to the parent company or to the group as a whole. However, the fact the companies are related to each other can affect the way in which general principles of company law, such as those relating to directors' duties, actually operate. For example, whilst it is technically correct to say that a director of a subsidiary company owes his duties to the subsidiary rather than the parent company,[96] the core obligation is that, outside insolvency situations, directors must promote the success of their company for the benefit of its *members*.[97] This means, therefore, that directors of a solvent subsidiary can discharge their duties to the subsidiary by acting for the benefit of the parent company, at least so long as the subsidiary is wholly owned or the interests of the parent company and any minority shareholders in the subsidiary coincide. Where a subsidiary is in, or near, insolvency the position

---

[92] ibid ss 1159 and Sch 6.
[93] ibid.
[94] ibid s 1159 (2).
[95] ibid Sch 6.
[96] *Lindgren v L & P Estates Ltd* [1968] Ch 572, CA.
[97] Companies Act 2006, s 172.

is different, however, because the directors of the subsidiary must consider creditors' interests rather than members' interests and, moreover, this means creditors of their own particular company rather than of the group as a whole.[98] Insolvency concerns also affect the position of directors of subsidiary companies in another important respect: directors can usually protect themselves from breach of duty claims by having their actions ratified by the company's shareholders but shareholder ratification is ineffective when a company's solvency is in doubt.[99]

In the context of petitions for relief from unfairly prejudicial conduct under (now) section 994 of the Companies Act 2006, the courts have sometimes been willing to move away from a rigid, legalistic approach to the entities within a corporate group. To succeed under this section, a petitioner must show that the affairs of the company of which he is a member have been conducted in an unfairly prejudicial manner. It has been held that, in an appropriate case, the conduct of a parent company—or of such of its directors who happen to be directors of the relevant subsidiary—towards a subsidiary may constitute conduct in the affairs of that subsidiary[100] and that the conduct of a subsidiary—or of some or all of its directors who happen as well to be directors of the parent company—may be regarded as part of the conduct of the affairs of the parent company.[101]

Despite the fact that, as these examples illustrate, company law does not completely ignore intra-group relationships between companies and there is some 'legal adaptation to reality',[102] the overriding general legal principle that all companies are separate and distinct entities and are not, in law, a single enterprise even where they are part of a group, continues to exert a powerful force. The emphasis on the separate entity principle is especially noticeable in situations where a group is affected by insolvencies at the subsidiary level: the directors of the failed subsidiaries may be personally liable for breach of their duties but, generally speaking, the parent company and other companies in the group can walk away from the failed subsidiaries with no financial consequences beyond writing off their equity investment and any intra-group debts that will not be repaid.

---

[98] *West Mercia Safetywear Ltd v Dodd* [1988] BCLC 250, 252; *Facia Footwear v Hinchliffe* [1998] 1 BCLC 218, 228; *MDA Investment Management Ltd* [2004] 1 BCLC 217.

[99] *Re New World Alliance Pty Ltd; Sycotex Pty Ltd v Baseler* (1994) 122 ALR 531, 550; T Ciro, 'The Twilight Zone Revisited: Assessing the Enforceability of Pre Liquidation Transactions in Corporate Group Insolvency' 2005, 20(11) *Journal of International Banking Law and Regulation* 590; A Keay, 'Directors Taking Into Account Creditors' Interests' (2003) 24 *Company Lawyer* 300; A Keay, 'Directors' Duties to Creditors: Contractarian Concerns Relating to Efficiency and Over-Protection of Creditors' (2003) 66 MLR 665; A Keay, *Company Directors' Responsibilities to Creditors* (Routledge-Cavendish, 2007). See also P Davies, 'Directors' Creditor-Regarding Duties in Respect of Trading Decisions Taken in the Vicinity of Insolvency' (2006) 7 *European Business Organization Law Review* 301.

[100] *Scottish Co-operative Wholesale Society Ltd v Meyer* [1959] AC 324, HL; *Nicholas v Soundcraft Electronics Ltd* [1993] BCLC 3, CA.

[101] *Re Citybranch Group Ltd, Gross v Rackind* [2004] 4 All ER 735, CA. R Goddard and HC Hirt, 'Section 459 and Corporate Groups' [2005] JBL 247.

[102] J Dine, *The Governance of Corporate Groups* (CUP, 2000) 43.

The corporate group and liability for the debts of insolvent subsidiaries[103]

The starting point here is that companies that hold shares in other companies enjoy limited liability in respect of their investment. There is no legal distinction between the liability position of a parent company with respect to the debts of its subsidiaries and that of an individual investor who acquires shares: each is liable only up to the nominal amount of the shares which comprise the investment plus any premium charged in respect of the shares when they were first issued. This means that a network of companies can be formed in order to limit a group's contractual liability to outsiders and to create contractual liability between members of the group. It also means that it is possible to limit the group's potential exposure to tort victims by conducting hazardous activities through subsidiaries. Should the risky venture end in disaster, the parent will lose the value of its investment in the subsidiary but the creditors of the subsidiary cannot look to it to make good the shortfall in the subsidiary's assets.

An illustration of the use of the corporate form to create contractual liabilities within a group is provided by *Re Polly Peck plc*.[104] In this case a subsidiary, incorporated in the Cayman Islands, made a public issue of debt securities and lent the proceeds to its parent company. The parent company guaranteed the issue. It was held that the subsidiary was entitled to prove in the insolvency of its parent in respect of the on-loan. The court rejected the argument that the subsidiary was simply acting as the agent of its parent in issuing the debt securities, which would have meant that the on-loan had no legal significance, and also held that the arrangement was not a sham.

Whether a parent company should be liable for the debts of its insolvent subsidiaries is an issue that is much discussed by academics.[105] An argument for preserving the veil of incorporation between companies within a group is that this facilitates managerial risk-taking, which is important if companies are to expand for the benefit of all of the constituencies who have an interest in them and for general economic prosperity.[106] According to this argument, investors

---

[103] See generally, V Finch, *Corporate Insolvency Law Perspectives and Principles* (CUP, 2002) 406–18.

[104] [1996] 2 All ER 433.

[105] See in particular, JM Landers, 'A Unified Approach to Parent, Subsidiary, and Affiliate Questions in Bankruptcy' (1975) 42 *University of Chicago Law Review* 589; RA Posner, 'The Rights of Creditors of Affiliated Corporations' (1976) 43 *University of Chicago Law Review* 499; JM Landers, ' Another Word on Parents, Subsidiaries and Affiliates in Bankruptcy' (1976) 43 *University of Chicago Law Review* 527. For an English law perspective, see CM Schmitthoff, 'The Wholly Owned and the Controlled Subsidiary' [1978] JBL 218; Lord Wedderburn, 'Multinationals and the Antiquities of Company Law' (1984) 47 MLR 87; DD Prentice, 'Some Comments on the Law Relating to Corporate Groups' in J McCahery, S Piccoitto and C Scott (eds), *Corporate Control and Accountability* (Clarendon Press, 1993) 371; H Collins, 'Ascription of Legal Responsibility to Groups in Complex Patterns of Economic Integration' (1990) 53 MLR 731.

[106] DW Leebron, 'Limited Liability, Tort Victims and Creditors' (1991) 91 *Columbia Law Review* 1565, 1617–18.

will be encouraged to invest in the shares of a holding company which caps its potential losses in respect of particularly risky activities to the amount of share capital that it invests in the subsidiaries through which those activities are conducted.[107] Another argument for preserving the veil is that contractual creditors assume that each company will be liable for its own debts but no more, and bargain accordingly. If lifting the veil within a corporate group were to become commonplace, with the result that the principle that a company's assets are only available to pay the debts owing to its own creditors is not maintained, that would be likely to add to companies' costs of borrowing because creditors would need to extend their investigations into the creditworthiness of the group as a whole.[108]

The primary argument for lifting the veil within a corporate group relates to control: a corporate group is, ultimately, an integrated economic enterprise and the parent controls, or has the power to control, its subsidiaries' activities for the benefit of the group as a whole; therefore, the parent should be liable for the activities of its subsidiaries.[109] Whilst the individuals who hold shares in a small private company may also be its controllers, it can be argued that their position is not analogous to that of a parent company because they could be personally ruined in the event of lifting the veil to make them liable for the company's debts; lifting the veil between parent and subsidiary companies might make the parent insolvent but the shareholders in the parent would still be shielded from personal liability by the limited liability that they would continue to enjoy in respect of their investment.[110] The point can also be made that the economic arguments about limited liability being necessary to enable companies to attract passive investment, to allow investors to engage in portfolio diversification, and to permit the functioning of capital markets do not apply in relation to a parent company's investment in a subsidiary.[111] Strict adherence to the preservation of the veil of incorporation may encourage excessive risk-taking by managers:[112] should an independent company which is not part of a group (or which is the holding company of a group) fail, the management will lose their jobs but that constraint against risk-taking is less powerful in relation to a subsidiary because there is always the possibility of its management being redeployed in other parts

---

[107] SB Presser, 'Thwarting the Killing of the Corporation: Limited Liability, Democracy and Economics' (1992) 87 *Northwestern University Law Review* 148, 174–5; PI Blumberg, *The Multinational Challenge to Corporation Law: The Search for a New Corporate Personality* (OUP, 1993) 130–3.

[108] In other words, asset partitioning benefits, discussed earlier in this chapter, would no longer apply.

[109] Blumberg (n 107 above) 123–4; JE Antunes, *Liability of Corporate Groups* (Kluwer, 1994) 131–2.

[110] RA Posner, 'The Rights of Creditors of Affiliated Corporations' (1976) 43 *University of Chicago Law Review* 499, 511–12.

[111] Blumberg (n 107 above) 133–40.

[112] ibid 134.

of the group in the event of its failure.[113] Moreover, although directors are legally obliged to act in the interests of their own company and not in the interests of the group of companies to which it may belong,[114] the distinction between group interests and those of the individual companies can easily become blurred in practice; and, except where there are insolvency concerns, irregularities, or breaches of duty by the directors of a group company can, in any event, be cured by the passing of a ratifying resolution by any other companies in the group which are the owners of its shares. The net result of these considerations is that companies within a group may deal with each other otherwise than on an arm's length basis to the detriment of creditors who cannot object unless they have imposed contractual restrictions on such activities and can monitor compliance effectively,[115] and of minority shareholders in the subsidiaries whose only effective means of redress may be to allege that such dealing constitutes unfairly prejudicial relief from which they should be granted relief under section 994 of the Companies Act 2006.[116] A particular argument for lifting the veil within a corporate group is that limited liability operates unfairly in relation to the victims of torts by subsidiaries since they cannot negotiate around it.[117]

Whatever the theoretical attraction of these competing arguments, it is not the practice of the courts in the UK to adopt an enterprise approach[118] in relation to liability, even where tort liability of companies within a corporate group is involved. The courts emphasize the importance of maintaining the principle that the assets of a company are available to pay its creditors and no others.[119] The leading case is the decision of the English Court of Appeal in *Adams v Cape Industries*

---

[113] FH Easterbrook and DR Fischel, *The Economic Structure of Corporate Law* (Harvard University Press, 1991) 56–7.

[114] *Lindgren v L & P Estates Ltd* [1968] Ch 572, CA.

[115] The complexity of group activities may in fact make it hard for creditors to follow the movement of assets around the group: V Finch, *Corporate Insolvency Law Perspectives and Principles* (CUP, 2002), 409.

[116] *Stein v Blake* [1998] 1 All ER 724, CA, illustrates the type of problems that can occur within a corporate group (transfers of assets by the controlling shareholder). The Court of Appeal held that the other shareholder had no personal common law claim arising from the facts.

[117] H Hansmann and RR Kraakman, 'Towards Unlimited Shareholder Liability for Corporate Torts' (1991) 100 *Yale Law Journal* 1879; DW Leebron, 'Limited Liability, Tort Victims, and Creditors' (1991) 91 *Columbia Law Review* 1565, 1612–26; Blumberg (n 107 above) 135–6. But, as Blumberg notes (136–8), it may be overly simplistic to regard all contract creditors in the same way. Many contractual creditors have no real opportunity to engage in bargaining, junior employees being an example that springs readily to mind. DD Prentice, 'Groups of Companies: The English Experience' in KJ Hopt (ed), *Groups of Companies in European Laws* (W de Gruyter, 1982) 99, 105 describes employees (and the revenue authorities) as 'quasi-involuntary creditors' who normally do not contract around limited liability. Prentice would also include unsecured trading creditors in the category of those who do not normally engage in such bargaining.

[118] See AA Berle, 'The Theory of Enterprise Entity' (1947) 47 *Columbia Law Review* 343 and Blumberg (n 107 above) ch 5, both of whom discuss the acceptance of enterprise principles in the US courts and legislation.

[119] See *Charterbridge Corp v Lloyd's Bank Ltd* [1970] Ch 62; *Ford & Carter Ltd v Midland Bank Ltd* (1979) 129 NLJ 543, HL, 544 *per* Lord Wilberforce.

plc[120] which was an attempt by victims of a tort (ie personal injuries suffered as a consequence of exposure to asbestos dust) to enforce a judgment that had been obtained in the US. The company law point in issue was whether the US courts could assert jurisdiction over an English company on the basis of the presence within the US of certain subsidiaries. The Court rejected the argument that the various companies should be treated as one group enterprise. It reaffirmed the fundamental legal principle that each company in a group of companies is a separate legal entity possessed of separate rights and liabilities.[121] It distinguished earlier cases[122] appearing to support a group enterprise approach as being concerned with specific statutes or contracts which justified the treatment of parent and subsidiary as one unit. Rather surprisingly, in view of the outright rejection of it in the *Adams* decision, a group enterprise argument resurfaced in *Re Polly Peck plc*.[123] The Court there regarded as 'persuasive' the argument that, in reality, the issue of debt securities was by the group rather than by the Cayman Islands subsidiary through which it had been channelled but ruled that it was precluded by *Adams*, a decision of a higher court, from accepting the group enterprise approach.[124]

The Court of Appeal in the *Adams* case confirmed that the court does not have a general discretion to disregard the veil of incorporation on grounds of justice. With regard to the argument that the corporate structure in that case was a façade, because it had been adopted to remove group assets from the USA to avoid liability for asbestos claims whilst at the same time continuing to trade in asbestos there, the Court concluded:

> ...We do not accept as a matter of law that the court is entitled to lift the corporate veil as against a defendant company which is the member of a corporate group merely because the corporate structure has been used so as to ensure that the legal liability (if any) in respect of particular future activities of the group (and correspondingly the risk of enforcement of that liability) will fall on another member of the group rather than the defendant company. Whether or not this is desirable, the right to use a corporate structure in this manner is inherent in our corporate law. [Counsel] urged on us that the purpose of the operation was in substance that Cape would have the practical benefit of the group's asbestos trade in the United States of America without the risk of tortious liability. This may be so. However, in our judgment, Cape was in law entitled to organise the group's affairs in that manner.[125]

---

[120] [1990] Ch 433, CA.

[121] *The Albazero* [1977] AC 774, CA and HL, 807 *per* Roskill LJ.

[122] Including the notorious decision of the Court of Appeal in *DHN Food Distributors Ltd v Tower Hamlets LBC* [1976] 1 WLR 852, CA. The judgment of Lord Denning MR in this case is probably the most positive endorsement of the group enterprise approach in British law. The authority of the case is now slim: as well as being distinguished in *Adams*, its correctness was doubted by the Scottish House of Lords in *Woolfson v Strathclyde Regional Council* 1978 SLT 159, HL.

[123] [1996] 2 All ER 433.

[124] ibid 447. Counsel's argument was based on the acceptance in *Adams v Cape Industries plc* [1990] Ch 433, CA that there were special cases where contract or statute permitted or required a group enterprise approach, but the court refused to put the insolvency rule against double proof into this special category.

[125] [1990] Ch 433, CA, 544.

Looked at from the present British law perspective,[126] therefore, it is difficult to avoid the conclusion that lifting the veil as a means of achieving group liability is a non-starter even in relation to arguably the most deserving case, namely that of the tort victims of a subsidiary company.[127]

Alternatives to lifting the veil: agency[128]

If it can be shown that a subsidiary acted as the agent of its parent, then, on ordinary agency principles, the liability will attach to the parent as principal.[129] However, there is no presumption that a subsidiary acts as the agent of its parent and this will depend on the facts pertaining to the relationship between parent and subsidiary.[130] Insufficient capital to engage in business independently can be an indicator that the subsidiary is an agent,[131] but capitalization needs to be considered in conjunction with the purpose for which the subsidiary exists: for example, if a subsidiary is established purely as a vehicle for the raising of debt, it may have a small amount of equity (with alternative forms of credit enhancement being built into the terms of the issue) but still be an independent operator rather than an agent.[132] Evidence that the subsidiary has a board of directors, all or most of whom are also directors or senior executives of the holding company, does not necessarily indicate an agency relationship between it and the parent company.[133]

Alternatives to lifting the veil: contractual guarantees

It is a trite observation that creditors of a failing company who are in the fortunate position of holding guarantees from other companies in its group may be able to

---

[126] Judicial conservatism with regard to lifting the veil is not confined to the British courts. Discussing the position in Australia and New Zealand, see R Baxt and T Lane, 'Developments in Relation to Corporate Groups and the Responsibilities of Directors—Some Insights and New Directions' (1998) 16 *Corporate and Securities Law Journal* 628; JH Farrar, 'Legal Issues Involving Corporate Groups' (1998) 16 *Corporate and Securities Law Journal* 184.

For a view that the test for piercing the corporate veil propounded by Slade LJ in *Adams* is doctrinally unsustainable see: M Moore, 'A Temple Built on Faulty Foundations: Piercing the Corporate Veil and the Legacy of Salomon v Salomon' [2006] JBL 180.

[127] DD Prentice, 'Group Indebtedness' in CM Schmitthoff and F Wooldridge F (eds), *Groups of Companies* (Sweet & Maxwell, 1991) 77: 'piercing the corporate veil is very much the exception to the rule and probably in the majority of cases the courts will refuse to do so'. J Dine, *The Governance of Corporate Groups* (CUP, 2000) 48: 'The lower courts seem to be adopting a policy that would eliminate the agency route to lifting the veil and restrict any general doctrine to statute and cases of fraudulent misuse of the veil. Any concept of an "enterprise doctrine" is losing ground.'

[128] Some form of trust-beneficiary or nominator-nominee relationship between companies in a group could also suffice to shift liability.

[129] *Canada Rice Mills Ltd v R* [1939] 3 All ER 991, PC; *Firestone Tyre and Rubber Co Ltd v Lewellin (Inspector of Taxes)* [1957] 1 All ER 561, HL; *Rainham Chemical Works v Belvedere Fish Guano Co* [1921] 2 All ER 465, HL.

[130] *Adams v Cape Industries plc* [1990] Ch 433, CA.

[131] *Re FG Films* [1953] 1 All ER 615. JM Landers, 'A Unified Approach to Parent, Subsidiary, and Affiliate Questions in Bankruptcy' (1975) 42 *University of Chicago Law Review* 589, 621.

[132] *Re Polly Peck plc* [1996] 2 All ER 433, 445–6.

[133] ibid.

shift the liability around the group by enforcing their contractual claims. There are some potential pitfalls that persons considering lending to a group company on the security of personal guarantees from other companies in its group need to look out for. One is that the other group companies may seek to resist giving guarantees and instead offer comfort letters in which they state that it is their policy to ensure that other companies in the group are, and will be, in a position to meet their liabilities. In *Kleinwort Benson Ltd v Malaysia Mining Corporation Bhd*[134] the Court of Appeal held that a comfort letter in these terms was merely a statement of present fact regarding intentions and that it was not a contractual promise as to future conduct.[135] Another potential difficulty stems from the fact that directors are required to serve their own company rather than the group as a whole. If directors of a guarantor company focus on the interests of the group and these do not coincide with the interests of their company, the guarantee may be tainted by breach of duty. Yet another potential pitfall is that if the solvency of the guarantor company is in doubt, the guarantee may be vulnerable under provisions of the Insolvency Act 1986 concerned with preferences and transactions at an undervalue.[136]

Alternatives to lifting the veil: tort claims against other companies

In particular circumstances a parent company may be jointly liable in tort with a subsidiary, or sister subsidiaries may be joint tortfeasors. Whether liability can be spread around a corporate group in this way depends on the application of the ordinary principles of the law of tort for the determination of liability. Sole personal liability at parent level may also arise on occasion, as where, for example, a parent company has deceived someone into contracting with its subsidiary by issuing spurious information about it or where it has such *de facto* control over the subsidiary's operations that it can be said to owe a duty of care to persons affected by its actions.[137] An example of tort liability within a corporate group is provided by *Stocznia Gdanska SA v Latvian Shipping Co Latreefer Inc*.[138]

---

[134] [1989] 1 WLR 379, CA. See also *Re Atlantic Computers plc* [1995] BCC 696.

[135] In *Wake v Renault (UK) Ltd* 15 Tr L 514, The Times 1 August 1996, Robert Walker J noted that a comfort letter, even though not legally binding, may not be pointless since it may have important practical consequences: for instance in enabling a subsidiary company to borrow on more favourable terms than might otherwise be available, or in enabling auditors to sign off accounts on a going concern basis.

[136] Insolvency Act 1986, ss 238–41. The application of s 238 (transactions at undervalue) in the context of intragroup guarantees is considered by R Parry, *Transaction Avoidance in Insolvencies* (OUP, 2001) ch 4.

[137] See *Lubbe v Cape plc* [2000] 4 All ER 268, HL, which involved asbestos-related tort claims against a parent company on the grounds that it failed to take proper steps to ensure that proper working practices were followed and proper safety precautions observed throughout the group, and that it was in breach of a duty of care to employees of its subsidiaries and to persons living in the area of their operations. The decision of the House of Lords related to conflict of laws issues on the appropriate forum for the hearing of the claim.

[138] [2001] 1 Lloyd's Rep 537, affirmed [2002] 2 Lloyd's Rep 436, CA.

The defendant parent company arranged for the claimant shipyard to build vessels for one of its subsidiary companies, which was a specially incorporated Liberian subsidiary with directors provided by an independent Isle of Man service company. The market later declined and the parent and subsidiary sought unsuccessfully to renegotiate the contract. Eventually the subsidiary breached the contract by indicating that it could not meet obligations to make instalment payments. This led to much complex litigation including a tort action against the parent for inducing breach of contract by its subsidiary. The Court held that the mere refusal of a parent to fund a subsidiary where there was no obligation to do so did not amount to an actionable direct inducement. Even though not funding the subsidiary meant that it could not meet its obligations, there was no instruction by the parent company to the subsidiary to break its contract and therefore nothing that could be characterized as a direct inducement. The mere fact that the subsidiary was a wholly owned subsidiary controlled by its parent did not enable the Court to draw the inference that the directors of the subsidiary simply did as they were told and treated requests from the parent as if they were instructions that had to be carried out. However, the parent was held liable in tort because it had used unlawful means by breaking certain of its own contractual obligations indirectly to induce breaches of the shipbuilding contract between its subsidiary and the yard.

A parent company which appoints its employees to serve as directors of its subsidiary companies is not vicariously liable for breaches of duty by those directors.[139]

Alternatives to lifting the veil: Insolvency Act 1986

The preceding paragraphs demonstrate that British law permits the shifting of the responsibility for the debts of a failed company onto its parent or other members only in limited circumstances. A number of the provisions of the Insolvency Act 1986 are also relevant to the problem of potential abuse of limited liability within the corporate group. The route favoured in the Insolvency Act is to augment the assets of the failed company rather than to shift its liabilities onto other members of its corporate group but, in broad terms, asset-augmentation and liability-shifting mechanisms can be regarded as serving the same underlying purposes.

Under section 213 of the Insolvency Act 1986, if it appears that any business of a company that is in the process of being wound up has been carried on with intent to defraud creditors or for any fraudulent purpose, the court, on the application of the liquidator, may declare that persons who were knowingly party to the carrying-on of the business in that manner are to be liable to make such contributions to the company's assets as the court thinks proper. A parent company could, depending on the facts, be knowingly a party to the carrying-on of the business of an insolvent subsidiary. However, a further requirement for liability to arise under

---

[139] *Kuwait Asia Bank EC v National Mutual Life Nominees Ltd* [1991] 1 AC 187, PC.

this section is the presence of fraud. Fraud in this context means 'actual dishonesty, involving real moral blame'[140] and that can be difficult to establish.[141]

Section 214 of the Insolvency Act 1986 allows the court to order persons who knew or ought to have concluded that the company had no reasonable prospect of avoiding insolvent liquidation to contribute to the assets of a company in liquidation unless those persons can establish that they took every step that ought to have been taken with a view to minimizing the potential loss to the company's creditors. The judgment standards under this section are based on objective criteria rather than personal morality and honesty: a person is to be judged on the basis of his own knowledge, skill, and experience and also the knowledge, skill, and experience that could reasonably be expected of someone carrying out his functions in relation to the company.[142] For liability under section 214 to arise it must be shown that at the date of actual liquidation the company was in a worse position than it would have been if trading had ceased at the time it is contended it should have done. The appropriate comparison is between the net deficiency in the assets of the company as at the date at which it was contended that trading should have ceased and the date at which trading did in fact cease.[143] The amount of the contribution required of a director who is found to have engaged in wrongful trading is in the court's discretion; it has been said that the section is primarily compensatory rather than penal and that therefore the prima facie appropriate amount is the amount by which the company's assets can be said to have been depleted by the director's conduct.[144]

Section 214 of the 1986 Act applies only to the directors of the failed company. Directors for this purpose include *de facto* directors, who are persons who act as directors but who have not been formally appointed.[145] A substantial shareholder who intervenes directly in running the affairs of the company runs the risk of being held to be a *de facto* director, and this represents a legal risk for parent companies.[146] It is also possible for wrongful trading liability to attach to shadow directors, ie, persons on whose instructions or directions the actual directors[147] are accustomed to act.[148] A parent company could potentially be caught as a shadow

[140]   *Re Patrick and Lyon Ltd* [1933] 1 Ch 786.

[141]   *Re Augustus Barnett & Son Ltd* (1986) 2 BCC 98,904 where an attempt to make a parent company liable under the then equivalent of s 213 failed.

[142]   Insolvency Act 1986, s 214(4).

[143]   *Re Continental Assurance Co of London plc* [2001] BPIR 733; *Re Marini Ltd* [2004] BCC 172.

[144]   *Re Produce Marketing Consortium Ltd* (1989) 5 BCC 569.

[145]   *Re Hydrodam (Corby) Ltd* [1994] BCC 161; *Secretary of State for Trade and Industry v Tjolle* [1998] 1 BCLC 333; *Re Richborough Furniture Ltd* [1996] 1 BCLC 507; *Secretary of State for Trade and Industry v Hollier* [2007] BCC 11; *Ultraframe (UK) Ltd v Fielding* [2006] FSR 17, para 1254.

[146]   *Secretary of State for Trade and Industry v Jones* [1999] BCC 336, 349–50.

[147]   Including *de facto* directors: *Re Hydrodam (Corby) Ltd* [1994] BCC 161.

[148]   Insolvency Act 1986, s 251. The meaning of the definition of shadow director was considered by the Court of Appeal in *Secretary of State for Trade and Industry v Deverell* [2001] Ch 340, CA, where Morritt LJ summarized the law in a series of propositions.

director. Four facts must be established in a shadow directorship allegation: (1) the identity of the actual directors; (2) that the alleged shadow director directed at least the governing majority[149] of the actual directors how to act in relation to the company or was one of the persons who did so; (3) that those directors acted in accordance with such directions; and (4) that they were accustomed so to act.[150] Relationships can be structured so as to minimize the risk of one party being held to be a shadow director of another: for example, a provider of finance to an ailing company should impose conditions on its offer of finance which the company is free to accept, rather than lending the money with instructions as to how it is to be used, because the former structure sits more comfortably with the principle that a lender is entitled to lay down terms relating to the running of the business in the absence of which it would not be prepared to lend without constituting itself a shadow director.[151] Whether a parent company is a shadow director of its subsidiary will depend on the factual relationship between them.[152] It must be shown that it was the regular practice of the subsidiary board to follow directions from the parent.[153]

Sections 238 and 239 of the Insolvency Act 1986 allow for the restoration of positions that would have existed had a failed company not entered into transactions at an undervalue or given voidable preferences. Orders under these sections may include requiring transferred property or its proceeds to be vested in the company.[154] These sections are of general application but conditions that trigger grounds for an order may be more easily satisfied in the group context than in some other situations because of certain presumptions and longer time limits that apply where parties are connected to each other.[155] The rules on transactions at an undervalue and on preferences thus act as a check on the freedom to move resources around a corporate group on non-commercial terms contrary to the interests of the creditors of specific companies within the group.[156]

There is an express exclusion of parent companies from the category of shadow director in respect of certain provisions of the Companies Act 2006 (see Companies Act 2006, s 251) but there is no such exemption under the Insolvency Act 1986.

[149] *Re Unisoft Group Ltd (No 2)* [1994] BCC 766, 775; *Ultraframe (UK) Ltd v Fielding* [2005] FSR 17, para 1272.

[150] *Re Hydrodam (Corby) Ltd* [1994] BCC 161.

[151] *Ultraframe (UK) Ltd v Fielding* [2005] FSR 17, para 1269.

[152] *Shadow Directorships* (Financial Law Panel) (1994). In an Australian case the factual evidence indicated that a 42% shareholder controlled the affairs of a company to such an extent that it was liable under a provision extending liability to a person in accordance with whose directions or instructions the directors were accustomed to act: *Standard Chartered Bank v Antico* (1995) 18 ACSR 1, NSW SC.

[153] *Re Unisoft Group Ltd (No 2)* [1994] BCC 766; *Secretary of State for Trade and Industry v Becker* [2003] 1 BCLC 555. DD Prentice, 'Corporate Personality, Limited Liability and the Protection of Creditors' in R Grantham and C Rickett (eds), *Corporate Personality in the 20th Century* (Hart, 1998) 99, 115–18.

[154] Insolvency Act 1986, s 241.

[155] ibid s 240.

[156] R Parry, *Transaction Avoidance in Insolvencies* (OUP, 2001) 83–4 (intra-group guarantees as transactions at undervalue). Also note Parry, ibid, 238–9, considering the potential usefulness of

Is the law on corporate groups deficient?

In the major economies of the world, including that of the UK, company law developed originally in relation to companies which had shareholders who were human beings and it was then applied by extension to companies whose share capital was owned by other companies.[157] Whether that extension, which permits corporate groups to exploit multiple tiers of limited liability, demands a specific response within company and insolvency law, in particular to provide explicitly for enterprise-based rather than entity-based liability to creditors is a much debated issue,[158] on which lawmakers around the world have taken different views.[159]

Within the UK, the policy debate has shifted noticeably in recent years. Debate during the 1980s tended to suggest that corporate groups presented serious problems for creditors that demanded an interventionist legislative solution. That British law could be deficient in not making special provision for group liability was judicially acknowledged.[160] An important contribution to this debate was the report of the Cork Committee, which reviewed insolvency law and practice in the UK in the early 1980s.[161] The Committee noted that 'some of the basic principles of company and insolvency law fit uneasily with the modern commercial realities of group enterprise'. Intra-group transfers of assets at an undervalue, lending between group companies on other than commercial terms, gratuitous guarantees by one group company of another group company's debts, and intra-group dividends paid without reference to the cash needs of the paying company were identified as the type of transactions that gave rise to concern.[162] Despite its concern and its acknowledgement that the law was defective,[163] the Committee mostly refrained from making detailed recommendations. It outlined a number of justifications for its tentative stance.[164]

Insolvency Act 1986, s 423 (transactions defrauding creditors) where assets have been transferred around a corporate group deliberately to put them out of reach of creditors.

[157] JE Antunes, *Liability of Corporate Groups* (Kluwer, 1994) 30–4; A Muscat, *The Liability of The Holding Company for the Debts of its Insolvent Subsidiaries* (Dartmouth, 1996) ch 4.

[158] PI Blumberg, *The Multinational Challenge to Corporation Law: The Search for a New Corporate Personality* (OUP, 1993) ch 11. The author advocates a general regime of enterprise law which would include, but not be limited to, enterprise liability. See also, PI Blumberg, 'The American Law of Corporate Groups' in J McCahery, S Piccoitto, and C Scott (eds), *Corporate Control and Accountability* (Hart, 1993) 305, but contrast DD Prentice, 'Some Comments on the Law Relating to Corporate Groups' in ibid, 371; A Muscat, *The Liability of the Holding Company for the Debts of its Insolvent Subsidiaries* (Dartmouth, 1996) ch 7.

[159] RR Kraakman, P Davies, H Hansmann, G Hertig, KJ Hopt, H Kanda, and EB Rock, *The Anatomy of Corporate Law* (OUP, 2004) 85–7.

[160] *Re Southard & Co Ltd* [1979] 1 WLR 1198, CA; *Re Augustus Barnett & Son Ltd* (1986) 2 BCC 98,904, 98,908. See also in Australia *Qintex Australia Finance Ltd v Schroeders Australia Ltd* (1990) 3 ACSR 267, NSW SC ComD; *Re Spargos Mining NL* (1990) 3 ACSR 1, WA SC.

[161] *Insolvency Law and Practice* (Cmnd 8558, 1982) ch 51.

[162] ibid para 1922.

[163] ibid para 1926.

[164] ibid para 1934.

First, an alteration of the law so as to make a parent company liable for its insolvent subsidiary's debts would introduce a difference between types of shareholders (corporate or individual) with regard to the fundamental principle of limited liability. That could affect entrepreneurial activity as it might deter a prosperous company from embarking upon new ventures. Secondly, the Committee was concerned about the problems of allocating and apportioning liability. This concern had a number of facets: determining precisely what relationship between companies should trigger financial responsibility; the extent to which there might be financial responsibility for companies that were only partly-owned subsidiaries, and, if so, whether the parent could have any claims against the minority shareholders; whether financial responsibility for an insolvent subsidiary should lie only with its parent or with all the companies in the group; and to what extent there should be parental or group liability for debts incurred by an insolvent subsidiary at a time when it was not a member of the group. Thirdly, the Committee was also concerned about the foreign element, ie the extent to which, if at all, there should be parental or group liability for the debts of an insolvent foreign corporation. Fourthly, there were questions about the position of existing long-term creditors of companies when any changes in the law were introduced; the creditors of, say, a parent company, would be adversely affected by a law which made the parent responsible for the debts of a subsidiary unless complex transitional arrangements could be devised to prevent the legislation operating retrospectively to the detriment of those existing creditors. Taking all these factors into account, the Committee concluded that the implications of a change to some form of group enterprise liability would spread throughout company law and that a fundamental change to company law could not properly be introduced by means of proposals to change insolvency law. The Committee called for a wide review of the whole issue of group enterprise liability with a view to the introduction of reforming legislation within the foreseeable future.

By the 1990s, however, things had changed. In part led by the work of the Cork Committee, the law restricting certain forms of abuse of limited liability had been tightened up, especially with the enactment of wrongful trading liability in section 214 of the Insolvency Act 1986 and a more wide-ranging directors' disqualification regime in the Company Directors Disqualification Act 1986. These changes closed some perceived gaps in the regulatory framework and they helped to set the scene for a significant shift in the emphasis of the policy debate. Promoting enterprise and investment were the themes that dominated the company law reform debate during the second half of that decade and into the new century that preceded the Companies Act 2006. Promoting rescue, rather than sorting out the consequences of financial failure, became increasingly influential in discussion about the philosophy underpinning insolvency law.[165] Although risks that people faced in dealing with businesses in corporate form were not

---

[165] V Finch, 'The Recasting of Insolvency Law' (2005) 68 MLR 713.

ignored, clamping down on the freedom to establish a number of linked limited liabilities entities or restricting significantly the advantages of operating a business in that way never took hold as ideas that required close examination. There was no significant outcry against the Company Law Review Steering Group's strongly-stated view that there was no merit in imposing a more integrated regime on groups of companies because such a regime would take away flexibility in the way businesses organized themselves and would strike at the limited liability basis for company law.[166] Nor was there a significant outcry against its refusal to propose reform in the controversial area of parent company liability for its subsidiaries' torts.[167] In fact the Company Law Review Steering Group seemed more concerned to facilitate corporate groups by allowing the parent of a wholly-owned subsidiary formally to elect to guarantee the obligations of that subsidiary, with the effect that, for as long as the election remained in force, that subsidiary would enjoy specified exemptions from the requirements of the companies legislation. However, that proposal did not attract support and it was not included in the final reform package.[168]

The problem of the insolvent subsidiary can be sketched in emotive terms:

A parent company may spawn a number of subsidiary companies, all controlled directly or indirectly by the shareholders of the parent company. If one of the subsidiary companies, to change the metaphor, turns out to be the runt of the litter and declines into insolvency to the dismay of its creditors, the parent company and other subsidiary companies may prosper to the joy of the shareholders without any liability for the debts of the insolvent company.[169]

However, there is a danger of overestimating the problem by overlooking commercial considerations and creditor protection mechanisms that are in the general law. In many cases, a prosperous parent company will not abandon a failing subsidiary and its creditors, even though it could do so as a matter of law, because it is anxious not to damage the commercial reputation of the group or its credit rating.[170] There are detailed rules in company law that seek to protect creditors by requiring companies to maintain their capital, which apply to corporate groups as well as to individual companies. These rules are problematic and, as will be argued in Part II of this book, there are good grounds for saying that they should be abandoned because they do more harm than good, but, so long as they remain,

---

[166] Company Law Review Steering Group, 'Modern Company Law For a Competitive Economy: Completing the Structure', URN 00/1335, paras 10.19–10.20.

[167] ibid paras 10.58–10.59. However, for a view that too little attention was given to this issue: PT Muchlinski, 'Holding Multinationals to Account: Recent Developments in English Litigation and the Company Law Review' (2002) 23 *Company Lawyer* 168.

[168] Company Law Review Steering Group, 'Modern Company Law For a Competitive Economy: Final Report', URN 01/942, paras 8.23–8.28.

[169] *Re Southard* [1979] 1 WLR 1198 CA.

[170] T Hadden, *The Control of Corporate Groups* (Institute of Advanced Legal Studies, 1983) 23–4; KJ Hopt, 'Legal Issues and Questions of Policy in the Comparative Regulation of Groups' [1996] *I Gruppi di Società* 45.

they cannot be overlooked in addressing the question of whether the law should do more to respond to the 'problem' of corporate groups. Another important consideration is that many creditors can protect themselves by contract and, for them at least, there is no need for the law to adopt a paternalistic stance. To the extent that responsibility for the failure of a subsidiary can be placed on the shoulders of the subsidiary's directors, they will be liable to contribute to its assets and, depending on the coverage of directors' liability insurance policies and indemnity arrangements, this may augment the assets available for distribution by the insolvency practitioner quite significantly. The 'shadow directorship' concept has at least the potential to bring parent companies within the scope of personal liability to contribute to the assets of a failed subsidiary in circumstances where it has controlled its operations. General directors' duties and the special liabilities that can arise in insolvency situations can have a significant deterrent effect. Insolvency rules on preferences and on transactions at an undervalue, as well as equitable principles that facilitate the tracing of misappropriated assets including unlawful dividends, are mechanisms that can be used to reverse the movement of assets around a corporate group without due regard to the separate entity status of the various companies. Although not concerned directly with asset-augmentation, laws that permit the state to disqualify directors who have participated in wrongful or fraudulent trading or who have shown themselves to be unfit to be concerned in the management of a company,[171] reinforce the seriousness of the obligations on directors and act as incentives to pay proper attention to circumstances where preferring group interests to those of individual corporate entities could be a breach of duty.

Yet, notwithstanding the need to recognize that there is indeed much regulation that operates as a check on abuse within corporate groups, the fact remains that in the absence of contractual guarantee obligations, a shadow directorship relationship, a tort claim, or an agency or analogous relationship, under British law a parent company is free to walk away: where the debts of the subsidiary are of such magnitude as to threaten the solvency of the parent, the advantages of abandonment may outweigh the damage to the reputation of the group. Substantive consolidation, whereby assets of companies that are in law separate legal entities may be pooled, is not part of British law.[172] Nor is equitable subordination, whereby intragroup debts are subordinated to other debts of the insolvent entity.[173] Depending on your policy stance, this is either a deficiency in

---

[171] Company Directors Disqualification Act 1986.

[172] V Finch, *Corporate Insolvency Law Perspectives and Principles* (CUP, 2002) 411–13. cf the New Zealand Companies Act 1993, s 271 which provides for the court to order the pooling of assets of related companies where it considers it just and equitable to do so (applied in *Mountfort v Tasman Pacific Airlines of NZ Ltd* [2006] 1 NZLR 104, H Ct Auckland) and the Republic of Ireland Companies Act 1990, ss 140–141, which are in broadly similar terms to the New Zealand legislation (see G McCormack, 'Ireland: Pooling of Assets and Insolvency in Ireland' (1992) 13 Company Lawyer 191).

[173] V Finch, *Corporate Insolvency Law Perspectives and Principles* (CUP, 2002) 410–11.

the law or a consequence of adherence to the principle of limited liability which should be accepted because, in overall terms, the economic advantages of permitting free access to limited liability outweigh the problems and it is therefore appropriate not to draw the regulatory regime too tightly in case this inhibits value-creating entrepreneurial activity.

It is increasingly likely that the policy debate about the regulation of corporate groups will be influenced by developments at the EU level because the creation and functioning of groups of companies are matters that are on the agenda for Community-wide company law.[174] In not having specific substantive group laws in either its legislation or its case law, British law is notably different from that in some other major Member States of the EU.[175] This is significant because, although the European Commission is now using the rhetoric of facilitation and promotion of efficiency and competitiveness in describing the aims of company law,[176] all of which sounds very familiar to British ears, the variety of approaches to group law at Member State level indicates that a range of policy stances is likely to feed into EC legislative initiatives and suggests a high likelihood of an eventual outcome that could require Britain to change its approach in certain important respects. An important structural difference is also noteworthy. In Continental Europe, it is common to find listed companies that are partly-owned subsidiaries, which is not the case in the UK. Subsidiaries with minority shareholders, and especially those that are listed, give rise to a wider range of policy concerns than wholly-owned subsidiaries, because minority shareholders, corporate governance, and investor protection issues must be considered as well as the interests of creditors, and those issues may be regarded as giving rise to more pressing concerns than creditor-related matters.[177]

The most prominent European example of special laws on corporate groups is found in Germany. Under the German *Konzernrecht* a parent and its subsidiaries may conclude an enterprise contract. This allows the parent to direct the running of the group on an enterprise basis but only at the price of providing indemnities for losses stemming from the running of the business in the interests of the group

---

[174] KJ Hopt, 'Legal Issues and Questions of Policy in the Comparative Regulation of Groups' [1996] *I Gruppi di Società* 45; C Windbichler, 'Corporate Group Law for Europe: Comments on the Forum Europaeum's Principles and Proposals for a European Corporate Group Law' (2000) 1 *European Business Organization Law Review* 165; European Commission, 'Report of the High Level Group of Company Law Experts on a Regulatory Framework for Company Law in Europe' (Brussels, November 2002) ch V.

[175] On the relevant German provisions: F Wooldridge, *Groups of Companies The Law and Practice in Britain, France and Germany* (Institute of Advanced Legal Studies, 1981).

[176] European Commission, 'Modernising Company Law and Enhancing Corporate Governance in the European Union—A Plan to Move Forward' (COM (2003) 284).

[177] E Wymeersch, 'Do We Need a Law on Groups of Companies?' in KJ Hopt and E Wymeersch (eds), *Capital Markets and Company Law* (OUP, 2003) 573; C Windbichler, 'Corporate Group Law for Europe: Comments on the Forum Europaeum's Principles and Proposals for a European Corporate Group Law' (2000) 1 *European Business Organization Law Review* 165; KJ Hopt, 'Legal Issues and Questions of Policy in the Comparative Regulation of Groups' (1996) *I Gruppi di Società* 45.

rather than on an entity basis. This type of special arrangement for corporate groups is formal and arises only where the operators of a group choose to opt into it. Experience has shown it to be unpopular and it is little used. German law also has special standards for *de facto* groups, whereby a parent company can be held liable to compensate subsidiaries which it has caused to act in a manner contrary to the subsidiaries' own interests. However, satisfying the conditions for this liability to arise has proved to be difficult. One group of distinguished commentators has suggested that the German rules on indemnification are not taken seriously.[178] Elsewhere, the German law has been said to be based on a valid theoretical concept but to be unworkable in practice.[179]

The German model initially carried much weight in discourse at the EU level on Community-wide company law. The draft Ninth Directive on company law[180] proposed the introduction of a regime in Member States whereby, broadly, corporate groups could choose between a form of integrated operation which would entail group liability, or a form of operation in which the financial and managerial independence of the companies within the group would have to be respected and there would be no group liability.[181] The draft, which was loosely based on German law,[182] received a hostile reception when it was introduced, and that proposal has not since been pursued.

In 2003, the European Commission ruled out as unnecessary the enactment of an autonomous body of law specifically dealing with groups.[183] Its preference was for better financial and non-financial information about corporate groups to be mandated. It also suggested that Member States should be required to provide for a framework rule for groups that would allow those concerned with the management of a company belonging to a group to adopt and implement a coordinated group policy, provided that the interests of that company's creditors were effectively protected and that there was a fair balance of burdens and advantages over time for that company's shareholders. In broad terms, this proposal amounted to an endorsement of the '*Rozenblum*' doctrine by the Commission. The '*Rozenblum*' doctrine is derived from a decision of the French criminal courts whereby, under certain conditions, it is considered to be legitimate for the directors of subsidiaries to act in the overall interest of the group. [184] The conditions in

[178] Rr Kraakman, P Davies, H Hansmann, G Hertig, KJ Hopt, H Kanda, and EB Rock, *The Anatomy of Corporate Law* (OUP, 2004) 86–7.

[179] Wymeersch (n 177 above) 573, 588.

[180] Commission Document III/1639/84-EN.

[181] T Hadden, 'Insolvency and the Group—Future Developments' in RM Goode (ed), *Group Trading and the Lending Banker* (Chartered Institute of Bankers,1988) 101, 103–8.

[182] On which see: KJ Hopt, 'Legal Elements and Policy Decisions in Regulating Groups of Companies' in CM Schmitthoff and F Wooldridge (eds), *Groups of Companies* (Sweet & Maxwell, 1991) ch V, and F Wooldridge, *Groups of Companies The Law and Practice in Britain, France and Germany* (Institute of Advanced Legal Studies, 1981).

[183] European Commission, 'Modernising Company Law and Enhancing Corporate Governance in the European Union—A Plan to Move Forward' (COM (2003) 284) 18–20.

[184] From the decision of Cour de Cassation, 1985 *Revue des Sociétés* 648.

French law for the safe harbour are: (1) the firm structural establishment of the group; (2) the existence of a coherent group policy; and (3) an equitable distribution of the revenue and costs of the business among the members of the group.[185] It has been said of the French position that no group transaction is forbidden so long as there is some 'quid pro quo', though not necessarily an exact counterbalance.[186] However, support provided by a group company must not exceed what can reasonably be expected from it, so that where support is beyond the provider's financial capacity, it will be considered unlawful.[187] The Commission saw the introduction of such a rule as an important step towards improved business efficiency and competitiveness, but it stressed that appropriate safeguards would have to be carefully designed. The Commission's stated intention in 2003 was for a proposal for a framework Directive to this effect to be presented in the medium term. However, this proposal and other related ideas, such as the possibility of introducing a Community consolidated approach to group insolvencies,[188] do not appear to have received much attention since then, which suggests that they may have been sidelined.[189]

---

[185] Kraakman *et al* (n 178 above) 86–7.

[186] Wymeersch (n 177 above) 573, 591.

[187] E Wymeersch, 'Conflicts of Interest in Financial Services Groups' (forthcoming 2008, *Journal of Corporate Law Studies*).

[188] By the High Level Group: European Commission, 'Report of the High Level Group of Company Law Experts on a Regulatory Framework for Company Law in Europe' (Brussels, November 2002) 98.

[189] T Baums, 'European Company Law Beyond the 2003 Action Plan' (2007) 8 *European Business Organization Law Review* 144.

3

Capital Structure—Fundamental Legal, Accounting, and Financing Considerations

Scope of this chapter

The legal rules governing the financing of companies are the primary focus of this book. As a prelude to the more detailed examination that follows in later chapters, the purpose of this chapter is to outline the basic components of the capital structure of a company and to consider, in a rudimentary way, some of the factors that may be taken into account by the managers of a company when making financing choices. Simple illustrations of the way in which financing choices have to be recorded in a company's accounts are provided. A company's accounts play a key role in determining compliance with legal requirements on corporate capital. By giving historical information about previous financing choices and the performance of the company, the accounts also provide important investment information.

There are basically three ways for a company to finance its operations: share issues, debt, and retained profits. In an introductory exposition such as this, it is convenient to take the simplest type of share and to compare its standard features with those of the simplest type of debt instrument. This should not be allowed to obscure the great flexibility that exists in practice with regard to the characteristics of financial instruments issued by companies. It is possible to issue shares which, by their terms of issue, deviate significantly from the standard case, to structure debt so as to mimic the characteristics of share capital, and to devise instruments which combine some of the features of share capital and of debt. Devising innovative financial instruments that tap into particular investor preferences in changing market conditions is a significant part of corporate finance advisory activity.

Share capital terminology

There are many different types of share, including ordinary shares, preference shares, and redeemable preference (or ordinary) shares. The ordinary share is the most straightforward type of share.

The *allotted share capital* of a company is the amount of share capital that has been allotted by a company at any time. This amount may also be described as the company's *issued share capital*. Allotted share capital/allotted shares and issued share capital/issued shares are not precisely synonymous terms but, save for certain specific contexts where the differences may matter (such as the interpretation of a tax concession available in respect of 'issued' share capital), they can, and frequently are, used interchangeably. The terms *shareholder* and *member* are also often used interchangeably even though, again, there are certain technical differences between them.[1] The same is true of *equity share capital*: this term carries a precise meaning in particular contexts (such as that of the Companies Act 2006)[2] but it is often used in a looser sense to mean the same as share capital or, in the shortened form of *equity*, to mean share capital, other undistributable reserves and retained earnings.

A company limited by shares, whether public or private, is formed by one or more persons subscribing their names to a memorandum of association and complying with the requirements of the Companies Act 2006 with regard to registration.[3] The effect of these requirements is that the minimum number of allotted (or issued) shares in a company limited by shares is one. Prior to the Companies Act 2006, one-member, one-share public companies were not possible because the minimum requirement was for at least two members, each of whom had to agree to take at least one share. There is no regulation of the minimum overall amount of a private company's allotted share capital but for a public company there is a minimum of £50,000.[4]

Shares must have a *par* (or nominal) value ascribed to them in the statement of capital that a company must file with the registrar of companies on formation and whenever its capital is altered thereafter.[5] The par value sets the minimum allotment price.[6] Shares may be allotted at a price that is more than their par value. The difference (if any) between the par value of a share and the allotment price is known as a *share premium*.

Shares may be allotted on a fully, partly, or nil paid basis.[7] The amount paid up in respect of the par value of shares (ie excluding premiums) represents a company's *paid up share capital*. Where shares are allotted otherwise than on a fully-paid basis, payment dates may be set by the terms of allotment or the company's constitution (ie its articles of association); alternatively, it may be left to the

---

[1] Companies Act 2006, s 112 defines who are the members of a company.

[2] ibid s 548. This definition generally excludes preference shares, except where such shares are also participating with respect to dividends or/and capital. Another context where 'equity' carries a technical meaning is in accounting: see International IAS 32, *Financial Instruments: Disclosure and Presentation* and IAS 39, *Financial Instruments: Recognition and Presentation*. Depending on their specific terms, preference shares may be classified as equity instruments or financial liabilities for accounting purposes.

[3] Companies Act 2006, s 7.

[4] ibid ss 761 and 763.

[5] ibid s 10 refers to the statement of capital that must be filed on formation.

[6] ibid s 580.

[7] These, and other terms mentioned in this paragraph, are considered in more detail in ch 4 below.

discretion of the directors to call for payment in accordance with the articles. A company's *called up share capital* is made up of the share capital that has been paid up plus any amounts in respect of share capital (ie excluding premiums) that have been called up or are due on specified future dates. Allotted share capital which has not been called up is *uncalled share capital*.

In respect of private companies, company law in the UK does not require a specific minimum amount of share capital actually to be invested in the business before trading commences. In recent years, this feature of the law has put the UK at a competitive advantage compared to other European countries whose laws impose minimum capital requirements on private companies because it means that businesses can incorporate relatively cheaply in the UK and then operate elsewhere in the Community under EC Treaty freedoms in respect of cross-border activities.[8] To the extent that there is a direct *ex ante* constraint on UK private companies trading on minimal amounts of share capital, it is lending practice rather than law: banks may be reluctant to lend to a private company if its proprietors have not themselves demonstrated their confidence in the company's prospects by taking the risk of investing a substantial amount in its share capital. UK law relies more on *ex post* constraints: should a company that has started trading with an inadequate equity capital base fail, its financing structure may be a factor for the court to take into account in proceedings against its directors.[9]

The position is different in relation to public companies, which are required to have a paid up share capital of at least £12,500 before they start trading.[10] Whilst not completely trivial, this is hardly a significant amount. More powerful factors in determining the size of a public company's equity capital base stem from commercial pressures to maintain a balance between debt and equity ('gearing' or 'leverage') that is acceptable to lenders and investors.

Accounting for an allotment of shares

When a company allots shares for cash at their par value, this will be recorded as an increase in the company's current assets and as an increase in share capital.[11] In numerical terms, it will look like Table 3.1 below. The amount shown in a company's accounts as its share capital is subject to the legal rules on maintenance of capital.[12] The maintenance of capital principle operates as a trade-off for limited

---

[8] See further ch 4 below.

[9] *Re Purpoint Ltd* [1991] BCC 121, 127 *per* Vinelott J.

[10] This requirement follows from the combination of the minimum capital requirement of £50,000 (Companies Act 2006, s 761) and the rule that shares in public companies must not be allotted except as paid up at least as to one-quarter of nominal value (Companies Act 2006, s 586): ie 50,000/4 = 12,500.

[11] This discussion is in relation to ordinary shares or other shares that for accounting purposes are classified as equity instruments. The position is more complex in relation to shares that for accounting purposes are classified as financial liabilities: P Holgate, *Accounting Principles for Lawyers* (CUP, 2006) 151–4.

[12] Discussed in ch 7 below.

liability: shareholders cannot be held liable to contribute to the company's assets for more than they have undertaken to subscribe in respect of their shares, but in return the amounts subscribed must be maintained. 'Maintenance' in this context essentially means 'not returned to the shareholders'.[13] It is not a breach of the maintenance of capital principle for a company's share capital to be wiped out by improvident trading or bad investment decisions, although such events may trigger insolvency proceedings in relation to the company.

When shares are allotted at a premium to their par value, the share premium must be credited to a separate account, as illustrated by Table 3.2 below.

Table 3.1. Accounting for an allotment of shares at par value

Pre-allotment of new shares		
Assets	£m	£m
Cash	5,000	5,000
Financing		
Share capital	1,000	
Reserves	4,000	5,000
Post-allotment of 10m new £1 shares at par to investors who pay cash		
Assets		
Cash	5,010	5,010
Financing		
Share capital	1,010	
Reserves	4,000	5,010

Table 3.2. Accounting for an allotment of shares at a premium

Pre-allotment of new shares		
Assets	£m	£m
Cash	8,000	8,000
Financing		
Share capital	2,000	
Other reserves	6,000	8,000
Post-allotment of 10m new £1 shares at £2 per share		
Assets		
Cash	8,020	8,020
Financing		
Share capital	2,010	
Share premium	10	
Other reserves	6,000	8,020

---

[13] *Trevor v Whitworth* (1887) 12 App Cas 409, HL, 414 *per* Lord Herschell; this analysis is echoed by Lord Watson at 423–4.

With only a few exceptions, sums credited to a share premium account are subject to the maintenance of capital principle in the same way as paid up share capital.[14]

Characteristics of ordinary shares

The standard characteristics of an ordinary share relate to entitlements in respect of dividends, capital growth, and participation in internal governance through voting.[15]

Dividends

Dividends are distributions to shareholders that are made out of the company's distributable profits. A company that does not have profits available for distribution cannot pay dividends. Moreover, even where distributable profits are available, the holders of ordinary shares have no absolute entitlement to demand that dividends be paid. The payment of dividends is governed by a company's articles, which normally authorize the directors to pay interim dividends at their discretion where they consider that this is justified by the company's profits, and provide for final dividends to be declared by the shareholders in general meeting on the basis of a recommendation from the directors. As a matter of legal theory, it is possible for a company to pay dividends on its ordinary shares which fluctuate widely from year to year. It is also open to a company not to pay any dividends at all and to plough back the entire profits into the future funding of its operations. Both of these possibilities give way, in practice, to commercial considerations which may, depending on its nature or the sector in which it operates, require a company to pay steady dividends out of its distributable profits in order to satisfy the expectations of investors.[16] Dividends are paid out of a company's post-tax profits.

Capital gains and risk

When a company is wound up, the holders of its ordinary shares are entitled to any surplus that remains after all the liabilities have been paid. This means that the ordinary shareholders of a company may be described as its 'residual claimants' or, in legal terms, as its owners. The entitlement to eventual capital gains

---

[14] Companies Act 2006, Pt 17, ch 7. The implications of this are discussed further in ch 4 below.

[15] The financial incidents of ordinary shares are considered in more detail in ch 6 below. This chapter provides an overview.

[16] See further ch 9 below.

is reflected in the price at which its shareholders can sell their shares during the life of the company. On the other hand, however, as residual claimants or owners, investors in ordinary shares assume significant risks because they are the last to be paid in a winding up and, hence, will be the first to absorb any shortfall in the company's assets. Investors in ordinary shares will expect a return that is adequate to compensate them for the risk that they will not be repaid in the event of winding up.

Voting rights

Ordinary shares usually entitle their holders to one vote per share. It is possible to have non-voting ordinary shares or ordinary shares which carry multiple votes but their distorting effect on the operation of the market for corporate control (ie voting control of the company does not necessarily follow from acquiring the majority in number of its shares) and on corporate governance mechanisms, which are based on the control that shareholders can exercise through their votes, means that weighted voting shares are unpopular with institutional investors in the UK.[17] Participants in quasi-partnership type companies or joint venture companies may favour multiple voting rights as a means of entrenching their original bargain. One familiar form of multiple voting provision used for entrenchment purposes is a clause that is triggered by a proposal to remove a shareholder from the office of director and which provides that, in that event, the votes attaching to the shares held by that shareholder will be multiplied to an extent that is sufficient to defeat the motion.[18]

Debt finance terminology

A company can borrow from banks or other lenders or can tap the capital markets by issuing debt securities to investors. The raising of capital by an issue of debt securities is sometimes described as direct financing because the company appeals directly to investors; bank borrowing is in turn described as indirect financing because the bank stands between the company and the providers of the funds, namely the bank's depositors and persons from whom it has raised capital via the capital markets.

---

[17] See generally Institutional Shareholder Services, Shearman & Sterling and European Corporate Governance Institute, 'Report on The Proportionality Principle in the European Union' (May 2007) (study commissioned by the European Commission) available at <http://www.ecgi. org/osov/documents/final_report_en.pdf> (accessed December 2007). Issues relating to 'one share—one votes (the 'proportionality principle') are considered further in ch 13 below.

[18] This is commonly described as a *Bushell v Faith* clause after the House of Lords decision that sanctioned it: [1970] AC 1099, HL.

There are many different types of debt instrument that companies use to raise funds from the capital markets. The terminology used to describe debt instruments tends to be driven more by market practice than by legal definition and is thus liable to fluctuate from market to market and from time to time in response to practical developments. Markets devise terms to distinguish debt securities by reference to certain key characteristics such as duration (for example the term 'commercial paper' is commonly used to describe short-term debt securities, whilst long-term debt securities are often called 'bonds') and whether they are secured (sometimes described as 'debentures') or unsecured (often known as 'loan stock'). Terminological variety is a particular feature of the markets in specialist debt securities which are normally bought and traded in by limited numbers of expert investors.

The term *debenture* also crops up in the context of bank financing for companies. Here it tends to be used to describe a loan which is secured on the company's property. In confining the use of the term debenture to secured loans, practice is narrower than legal usage. There is no exhaustive legal definition of the term debenture[19] but a commonly cited description is that it encompasses any document which creates or acknowledges a secured or unsecured debt.[20]

Borrowing from banks and other lenders and issuing debt securities to investors are not the only ways in which companies can raise external non-equity finance to fund their operations. Companies can obtain short-term trade credit by acquiring goods on credit terms; sellers may supply goods on an open account or may require assurance as to payment in the form of documentary credits issued by banks and/or security by means of provisions that reserve title to the goods in the seller until payment.[21] Other asset financing mechanisms include finance leases, hire purchase, and arrangements such as 'repos', which are transactions in which a company sells assets but with an option to re-acquire them, that in functional or economic terms are the same as loans but which are in a different legal category.[22] In addition there are many types of receivables financing that companies can use to improve their cash flow by enabling them to obtain funds

---

[19] Companies Act 2006, s 738 lists various instruments which are debentures but the list is not closed. The absence of a precise definition has given rise to few practical problems: *Re SH & Co (Realisations) 1990 Ltd* [1993] BCC 60, 67.

[20] *Levy v Abercorris Slate and Slab Co* (1887) 37 Ch D 260. See also *Edmonds v Blaina Furnaces Co* (1887) 36 Ch D 215; *Lemon v Austin Friars Investment Trust Ltd* [1926] 1 Ch 1, CA; *Knightsbridge Estates Trust v Byrne* [1940] AC 613, HL; *R v Findlater* [1939] 1 KB 594, CCA; *NV Slavenburg's Bank v Intercontinental Natural Resources Ltd* [1980] 1 All ER 955.

[21] On retention of title (RoT) clauses generally, see G McCormack, *Secured Credit under English and American Law* (CUP, 2004) ch 6.

[22] Asset sales achieve the same economic effect as secured loans but avoid the Companies Act 2006 requirements for the registration of charges. An attempt to avoid the registration requirements by labelling a structure as a sale will not work if the legal substance of the arrangement is in fact a secured loan: *Welsh Development Agency v Export Finance Co Ltd* [1992] BCC 270, CA. On repos see further, Law Commission, *Registration of Security Interests: Company Charges and Property Other Than Land* (Law Com CP No 164, 2002) para 6.38.

more quickly than through awaiting payment from customers for goods supplied on credit. One type of receivables financing is debt factoring, where receivables (trade debts) are sold to a factor which then collects the debts, either on a recourse basis (where the factor has recourse to the company should customers fail to pay) or a non-recourse basis (where the factor in effect provides bad debts protection); another is block discounting, where debts are sold for an immediate cash payment by the discounter but ordinarily the company continues to collect the debts, acting as agent for the discounter.[23] Certain types of businesses are not thought suitable for receivables financing: it is useful for businesses operating in sectors that generate trade debtors, such as manufacturing and wholesale distribution, but less so for businesses that sell to the general public or otherwise for immediate settlement.[24] Reasons of space preclude separate consideration of asset and trade financing in this book.[25]

Characteristics of simple debt

Interest

The rate of interest payable in respect of a loan is determined by the contract between the company and the lender. The rate of interest may be fixed or may be floating and, as such, liable to be adjusted in specified circumstances. Unlike dividends, interest is normally payable whether or not the company makes profits. Interest is deductible from the company's pre-tax profits and thus goes to reduce the profits on which the company is liable to pay tax. The favourable tax treatment is one factor that makes debt a potentially cheaper source of finance for a company than share capital.

Capital gain and risk

A creditor is entitled to the repayment of the principal amount of the loan at the end of its term, but this is normally the limit of the creditor's claim against the company. Creditors do not share in a company's capital growth. The opportunity for capital gains for investors in debt securities lies in exploiting differences between the yield on the securities, measured by reference to their cash flows in the form of interest payments and principal repayment at maturity, and the interest rates prevailing in the market. Where the yield on debt securities is higher

---

[23] Law Commission, *Registration of Security Interests: Company Charges and Property Other Than Land* (Law Com CP No 164, 2002) paras 6.24–6.29.

[24] Competition Commission, 'The Supply of Banking Services by Clearing Banks to Small and Medium-sized Enterprises' (2002) paras 3.111–3.117.

[25] See RM Goode, *Commercial Law* (Penguin, 3rd edn, 2004); LS Sealy and RJA Hooley, *Commercial Law Text, Cases and Materials* (OUP, 3rd edn, 2003).

than market interest rates, an investor may be able to sell the securities at a premium to their face value and thereby obtain a capital gain.

Providers of debt finance rank above shareholders for repayment in the event of winding up. There is also a ranking order between debts depending on whether they are secured or unsecured and, if secured, the type of security. Certain types of debt are given a preferential ranking status by the insolvency legislation,[26] whilst others are deferred.[27] Priority over share capital in winding up is another factor that reduces the cost of debt finance in comparison to share capital: providers of debt finance accept less risk and that is reflected in the return that the company has to pay for financing in this form. However, in a highly leveraged firm, low ranking holders of debt occupy a residual position akin to that of shareholders because they will be first to absorb losses after the equity has been exhausted.

Control

Covenants, which are contractual restrictions in the terms on which debt capital is provided, are in a broad sense the debt finance equivalent to the control that shareholders are entitled to exercise via the votes attaching to their shares. The precise extent of the restrictions imposed contractually through covenants is fact-specific and dependent on a range of variables, including the length of the period for which the finance is to be available, whether it is privately negotiated or is raised directly from the capital markets, and whether it is secured or unsecured. General economic conditions are also relevant, as evidenced by 'covenant lite' financing transactions entered into in 2006–07, a period of great buoyancy in credit markets.[28] Covenants may include limitations on the company's borrowing levels, restrictions on the payment of dividends, negative pledge clauses whereby the company promises not to grant any new security on its property, and provisions restricting disposals of the company's property or major changes in the nature of its business.[29]

Hybrid securities in outline

A hybrid security combines some of the features generally associated with share capital with some of those of debt capital.[30] It can also be described as a form of

---

[26] Insolvency Act 1986, Sch 6 sets out the categories of preferential debt.

[27] ibid s 74(2)(f) (sums due to a member of the company). This section was considered in *Soden v British & Commonwealth Holdings plc* [1998] AC 298, CA and HL.

[28] G Moore, 'Europe's Second Cov-lite Loan' (2007) 26(5) *International Financial Law Review* 8.

[29] See further chs 11 and 15 below.

[30] R McCormick and H Creamer, *Hybrid Corporate Securities: International Legal Aspects* (Sweet & Maxwell, 1987).

mezzanine finance, occupying a mid-way position between debt and equity. A preference share is a form of hybrid security. Preference shares differ from ordinary shares in that they carry the right to a fixed annual dividend and/or to a return of a fixed principal amount. Preference shares normally carry limited voting rights. The fixed dividend and/or principal is payable in priority to the return on ordinary shares but (unless the terms on which the preference shares are issued otherwise provide) there is no right to participate over and above the fixed amount. The fixed return and the priority to ordinary shares are characteristics that resemble loan capital. Nevertheless, preference shares are still at law shares, although whether for accounting purposes they are equity instruments or financial liabilities depends on their specific terms. The legal constraints that flow from the maintenance of capital principle apply as much to preference shares as they do to ordinary shares: thus dividends on preference shares can be paid only from distributable profits and, accordingly, unlike interest, will not be paid if the company does not have these profits (but so long as the entitlement is cumulative it can be carried forward until such time as the company does have distributable profits); and holders of preference shares rank below creditors for the purposes of repayment.

A more sophisticated version of a preference share, is the convertible preference share which, in addition to the rights of a normal preference share, also entitles the holder at some point in the future to convert it into another security such as an ordinary share in the company or in its holding company. A convertible preference share combines the benefits of being preferential (in particular ranking ahead of ordinary shares for dividends and for repayment of capital) with the opportunity to share, via conversion, in capital growth, which is a key benefit associated with ordinary shares.

Debt capital can also be raised on terms that provide for the investor to be able to convert the debt into a share (of the borrower company or some other company) at some later date. This is described as convertible debt. Similar to a convertible debt security is a debt instrument with an attached warrant. The warrant gives the holder the option to subscribe shares. The debt-plus-warrant structure differs from convertible debt in that exercise of the warrant does not bring the debt instrument to an end, whereas the debt instrument disappears when a conversion right is exercised. The characteristic shared by convertible debt securities and warrants, and which makes them both hybrid securities, is that, unlike straight debt, they offer their holder the opportunity to participate in capital growth.

Another form of debt that is regarded as being hybrid is subordinated debt. Broadly speaking, when debt is subordinated its terms include provision for the principal amount of the loan (and sometimes interest as well) not to be repaid until some or all of the company's other debts have been paid in full. To compensate for the subordination, a company may have to pay a higher rate of interest than it would pay on its unsubordinated debt. To enhance the attractiveness of the investment opportunity for investors still further, it may also have to offer share options or conversion rights. Subordinated debt is similar to share capital in that it ranks for payment behind other debts and, if share options or conversion rights are attached, it offers the opportunity to participate in capital growth. Yet it remains debt on which interest may be payable even if the company does not have distributable profits and, prior to conversion, it ranks higher on the repayment ladder than share capital.[31]

Valuation of securities[32]

Shares

The value of a share ultimately comes down to what someone is willing to pay for it, and this can depend on precisely what it is that the purchaser seeks to acquire. Thus, a bidder who wants to take over a company may have to pay more for its shares than an investor who seeks to acquire a small parcel of its shares, the difference in price here being the premium that the bidder has to pay for control. Valuation is not an exact science but where shares are quoted, the starting point in any valuation process is to look at the price at which they are trading in the market. For some unquoted companies it may be possible to arrive at an estimate of the value of their shares based on empirical evidence of the market value of shares in analogous quoted companies. The market price of shares may then be compared with their value on the basis of other methods of valuation. This comparison may, in different contexts, assist professional investment analysts in arriving at their recommendations on whether to buy or sell securities, and enable bidders to determine the control premium they are prepared to pay. Other valuation techniques must necessarily be used to value the shares of unquoted companies where there are no appropriate quoted comparators.

The main methods of valuing shares otherwise than at the price at which they are trading in the market are set out below. All of these methods have limitations and some are more appropriate than others for particular purposes. Where they involve assumptions or projections, there is scope for different valuers to take different views. This means that the sensible course for, say, a potential bidder, is to

---

[31] *Collins v G Collins & Sons* (1984) 9 ACLR 58, NSW SC EqD illustrates this point. A corporate rescue scheme involving the subordination of certain debts was not approved by the court but, because of the technical differences between share capital and loan capital, it was prepared to sanction an alternative arrangement in which the relevant debts would be converted into preference shares. Query, however, whether it would be possible to structure subordinated debt which ranks behind preference shares. In principle, an arrangement whereby receipts in respect of subordinated debt are turned over to the preference shareholders should be possible but, depending on the structure used, this type of arrangement could raise financial assistance concerns or might be vulnerable as an indirect unlawful return of capital.

[32] HS Houthakker and PJ Williamson, *The Economics of Financial Markets* (OUP, 1996) ch 6; RA Brealey, SC Myers, and F Allen, *Principles of Corporate Finance* (McGraw-Hill, 8th edn, 2005) ch 4; SA Ross, RW Westerfield, and BD Jordan, *Corporate Finance: Core Principles and Applications* (McGraw-Hill, 2006) chs 4–7.

use a combination of valuation methodologies in order to derive a valuation range in respect of a target company.[33]

Net asset value

A valuation based on net asset value involves dividing the total market or book value of the company's net assets by the number of shares in issue. Where the book values of the company's assets are out of date, it may be necessary to conduct a revaluation exercise in order to bring these into line with market values. This method of valuation is the primary tool for valuing property companies. It is inappropriate where much of the value of the business is attributable to factors that do not appear in the balance sheet, such as the skills of the staff of an advertising or design company.

Dividend valuation

The principle underlying the dividend valuation method is that the value of a share lies in the flow of income that an investor can expect from it during its life, including any dividend paid on the liquidation of the company. Although the return to the holder of a share from time to time comes in the form of dividend plus the capital gain on the disposal of the share, the price that a purchaser is willing to pay for that share is based on expectation of future dividends, with the result that it is the value of the stream of dividends over the life of the share that represents its value. Dividend valuation methodology arrives at the present value of a share by looking at the expected flow of dividends during the life of the company and discounting future returns to reflect the time value of money and the risk that the expected cash flows may not in fact be forthcoming.

Free cash flow valuation

Instead of looking at just one component of the return to shareholders (ie dividends), the free cash flow valuation method proceeds on the basis that the company's entire free cash flow (ie its income remaining net of all operating costs and investment outlays) belongs to the shareholders. Discounted cash flow methodology involves discounting future cash flows at an appropriate discount rate and relies upon projections of future cash flows.

Debt securities

The value of a debt security lies in the present-day value of the stream of income payable in respect of the security. In the case of a simple debt security which has

---

[33] In a different context, note *Re Macro (Ipswich) Ltd* [1994] BCC 781, where the court employed both net-asset and dividend-yield methods of valuation as the basis for arriving at the price at which a minority holding in a private company should be bought out under (now) Companies Act 2006, s 994. Generally, on the valuation of shares in unquoted companies, see N Eastaway, H Booth, and K Eames, *Practical Share Valuation* (Butterworths, 4th edn, 1998).

a fixed interest rate and a fixed maturity date, its value is thus the discounted value of the interest that is payable during the life of the loan and of the principal amount that is repayable on maturity.

Cost of capital

The preceding discussion about valuation of shares and debt securities glossed over a fundamentally important point, namely, the appropriate discount rate to apply when determining the present value of expected future cash flows. The rate that is used must account for the time value of money and must reflect the risk that is inherent in any expectation of payments to be made in the future. A key element, therefore, is the valuation of risk. There are two forms of risk that are present in investing in corporate securities: risks relating to the particular companies whose securities are included in a portfolio (specific risks) and risks stemming from factors, such as the potential for changes in fiscal policy or interest rates, that are generally applicable (systematic risk). Portfolio theory dictates than an investor can eliminate specific risks by forming a diversified portfolio of investments in which risks attaching to particular securities are counterbalanced by the characteristics of other securities.[34] On this basis, it is only for systematic risk that investors can properly expect to receive compensation from the companies whose securities they hold. Accordingly, it is the valuation of systematic risk that is the focus of concern.

The Capital Asset Pricing Model (CAPM) is the most widely used technique for measuring systematic risk in equity investment and, hence, for estimating investors' required rate of return. In broad terms, the CAPM assesses the required rate of return on an equity investment by reference to the risk-free rate of return available to an investor, the premium required by investors to compensate them for the general systematic risk of investing in the equity market, and the undiversifiable systematic risk of a particular investment relative to the equity market. Although no investment is entirely risk-free, the rates of return on government securities (gilts) are the closest available comparator. The premium that investors require for holding a fully diversified portfolio of equity securities is determined by looking at the difference between historical gross returns on the equity market and on risk-free investments in gilts. The undiversifiable risk inherent in holding a particular share is known as its beta. Equity betas are calculated by reference to their historical returns and the corresponding returns on the market.

In theory, the CAPM can also be used to assess the required rate of return on debt securities but debt betas are not readily available. Instead, the rate of return required by investors in debt securities tends to be determined by reference to the rate of return on the existing debt securities of the company and of similar issuers. A similar process, involving examination of the company's borrowing history

---

[34] H Markowitz, 'Portfolio Selection' (1958) 7 *Journal of Finance* 77.

and comparison with analogous companies, may be used in determining the rate of return on debt finance provided by banks or other lenders.

The returns required by the providers of a company's share capital and debt constitute its cost of capital. The company's cost of capital is a driving factor in decisions on whether to invest in new projects because these will only be worthwhile investments where they are expected to generate returns at least equal to the company's cost of capital. Put another way, the company's cost of capital represents the cut-off rate for new projects. The average rate of a company's cost of capital is determined by the cost of its capital weighted by the proportion of funding obtained from each source (weighted average cost of capital, or 'WACC').

Capital structure

In modern economics literature, the analysis of corporate capital structures usually starts with the Modigliani-Miller (MM) theorem as a benchmark.[35] The main elements of the original MM theory are that (a) the total value of a company is independent of its capital structure, and (b) the cost of a company's equity capital is a linear increasing function of its debt to equity ratio, keeping the overall cost of capital constant. In other words, increasing the amount of debt would lead to an offsetting increase in the cost of equity and vice versa.[36] This theorem as to the irrelevance of financial leverage was developed on the basis of certain restrictive assumptions, including the absence of taxes and insolvency and transaction costs, and the existence of perfect capital markets in which all investors have equal access to information. Much of the subsequent literature has re-evaluated MM with more realistic assumptions.[37] Once the assumptions on which the original theory was based are relaxed, in particular to take into account the fact that interest is tax deductible whereas dividends are not, it appears that it may be possible to add some debt to a company's capital structure without affecting the expected return to shareholders. Against this, the relaxation of the assumption of no insolvency costs points away from reliance on debt because, the greater the proportion of debt, the more likely it is that the company will default and enter

---

[35] F Modigliani and MH Miller, 'The Cost of Capital, Corporation Finance and the Theory of Investment' (1958) 48 *American Economic Review* 433. For an appraisal of the theorem and some of the literature spawned by it, see MH Miller, 'The Modigliani-Miller Propositions After Thirty Years' (1988) 2 *Journal of Economic Perspectives* 99 and the other symposium papers published in that edition of the journal. Another overview that provides an introduction to decades of research on capital structure is SC Myers, 'Capital Structure' (2001) 15 *Journal of Economic Perspectives* 81. For a major review of the literature, see also M Harris and A Raviv, 'The Theory of Capital Structure' (1991) 46 *Journal of Finance* 297.

[36] RJ Gilson and RR Kraakman, 'The Mechanisms of Market Efficiency Twenty Years Later: The Hindsight Bias' (2003) 28 *Journal of Corporation Law* 715, 719.

[37] The original authors themselves relaxed some of the original assumptions in later papers: eg F Modigliani and MH Miller, 'Corporate Income Taxes and the Cost of Capital: a Correction' (1963) 53 *American Economic Review* 261.

into one of the corporate insolvency procedures within the framework of insolvency law. These procedures are costly to implement and, as the risk of insolvency grows with the addition of more and more debt to a company's capital structure, this can eventually outweigh the tax benefit of debt. The upshot of these competing considerations is that the addition of debt to a company's capital structure will be beneficial up to the point where the tax savings resulting from debt are eclipsed by the costs of financial distress. On that basis, the focus then shifts to the making of a trade-off between the benefits of debt and the expected costs of financial distress to determine the optimal long-term target capital structure. Subsidiary questions about the design of particular securities and about the public (capital markets) and private (banks) sources from which external finance may be available also assume considerable importance.

The trade-off theory of optimal capital structure implies that the correct mix of debt and equity for any particular company is dependent on a range of variables, including its age, its size, and the nature of its business and assets. Where companies are incorporated is another relevant variable because differences in applicable legal, tax, and institutional regimes can be expected to have some impact.[38] Gearing ratios do in fact vary across industries in ways that are broadly consistent with the theory: companies with steady cash flows or readily realizable assets, such as utility companies, tend to have higher gearing ratios;[39] and companies with relatively few current tangible assets but with considerable future growth prospects, such as exploration companies, tend to have lower gearing ratios, as do innovative technology companies where the reliability of profit growth is uncertain.[40] Some country-by-country differences can also be discerned.[41] At particular times—such as when a substantial new investment project is undertaken—there may temporarily be an abnormally high reliance on debt finance but some empirical evidence suggests that high gearing levels do not persist and that there is a strong reversion in leverage over the longer term as companies take steps to reduce their indebtedness.[42] However, evidence on the speed with which firms adjust towards target leverage does not all point in the same direction.[43]

[38] F Bancel and UR Mittoo, 'Cross-Country Determinants of Capital Structure Choice: A Survey of European Firms' (2004) 33(4) *Financial Management* 103.

[39] SC Myers, 'Capital Structure' (2001) 15 *Journal of Economic Perspectives* 81, 82–4.

[40] ibid.

[41] F Degeorge and EG Maug, 'Corporate Finance in Europe: A Survey', ECGI—Finance Working Paper No 121/2006, (23 March 2006) available at SSRN <http://ssrn.com/abstract=896518>; Bancel and Mittoo (n 38 above) 103. Differences in accounting rules complicate the process of attempting country-by-country comparative studies of capital structure.

[42] C Mayer and O Sussman, 'A New Test of Capital Structure', CEPR Discussion Paper No 4239 (February 2004) available at SSRN <http://ssrn.com/abstract=509022>; P Bunn and G Young, 'Corporate Capital Structure in the United Kingdom: Determinants and Adjustment' (August 2004). Bank of England Working Paper No 226 (August 2004) available at SSRN <http://ssrn.com/abstract=641281>.

[43] R Huang and JR Ritter, 'Testing Theories of Capital Structure and Estimating the Speed of Adjustment' (26 July 2007) available at SSRN <http://ssrn.com/abstract=938564>. Forthcoming in *Journal of Financial and Quantitative Analysis*.

More generally, the trade-off theory does not fully explain real-life capital structures because in fact many profitable companies operate with much lower levels of tax-deductible debt than the theory would predict.[44]

A different point of view on corporate capital structures is provided by the 'pecking order' theory.[45] The basis of the pecking order theory is that asymmetric information between managers and investors gives rise to mispricing risks, which vary in scale depending on the information sensitivity of the financial instrument in question and which are therefore more severe in relation to equity than to debt. 'Good' managers will seek to minimize the risk of mispricing so as to maximize value and therefore will opt for forms of financing that are least affected by problems of asymmetric information. This implies a 'pecking order' capital structure in which internally-generated funds are preferred to external sources of finance and, as between external sources, debt is preferred to new equity.[46] Evidence of large projects being primarily financed externally from debt is consistent with the pecking order theory's identification of a preference for debt over equity but, at the same time, evidence that firms do not exhaust internal resources before turning to external sources to finance such projects is not consistent with the theory.[47] Nor does the pecking order theory explain evidence of reversions to initial capital structures in the longer term.[48]

While the trade-off and pecking order theories of capital structure both have some explanatory power, neither provides all the answers. The same can also be said of other theories on corporate capital structure that have developed alongside the two main theories or as refinements of them. One such theory, which is associated with the trade-off theory, is based on 'agency costs'. There are agency costs in corporate finance that flow from the potential conflicts of interest between debt and equity investors and also from the absence of a perfect alignment between managers' and investors' interests.[49] When considering from an agency cost perspective the trade-offs involved in using debt as a source of finance, it becomes necessary to add to the financial distress side of the equation the costs associated with risks that managers will prefer the interests of shareholders to those of creditors by transferring value from one group to the other or by engaging in excessive risk-taking. Agency cost analysis of the implications of conflicts of interest between debt and equity investors may be a factor that helps to explain why many companies operate with more conservative debt ratios than would be warranted by comparing the benefits of interest tax shields against the costs involved in

---

[44] SC Myers, 'Capital Structure' (2001) 15 *Journal of Economic Perspectives* 81, 88–91.
[45] SC Myers, 'The Capital Structure Puzzle' (1984) *Journal of Finance* 575; SC Myers and NS Majluf, 'Corporate Financing and Investment Decisions When Firms Have Information Investors Do Not Have' (1984) 13 *Journal of Financial Economics* 187.
[46] Myers (n 44 above) 92–3.
[47] Mayer and Sussman (n 42 above).
[48] ibid.
[49] M Jensen and W Meckling, 'Theory of the Firm: Managerial Behavior, Agency Costs and Ownership Structure' (1976) 3 *Journal of Financial Economics* 305.

insolvency procedures.[50] On the other side of the equation, however, debt can be beneficial when it is examined through the lens of the misalignment between managers' and investors' interests because it acts as a discipline on management by forcing firms to commit cash to debt interest payments; as such, it reduces opportunities for managers to use the free cash flow to engage in 'empire building' for their own reputational advantage or in other activities that benefit themselves rather than investors.[51] From this perspective, some of the explanation for why managers do not exploit the tax advantages of debt as fully as the trade-off theory would imply may lie in their reluctance to submit to the disciplining effect of adding more debt to the capital structure.[52]

Yet another line of analysis suggests a 'market timing' theory of capital structure, which is to the effect that firms' capital structures can be understood as the cumulative result of efforts to time the equity market—ie to issue shares when market prices are high and to repurchase them when market values are low.[53] The market timing theory posits that financing decisions that depend on the time-varying relative costs of equity and debt have long-lasting effects on capital structure because the observed capital structure at any given date is the outcome of prior period-by-period securities issuance decisions.[54]

Despite considerable advances made by a rich body of literature, it is widely acknowledged that corporate capital structure decisions involve complex, multi-dimensional problems that are not yet fully understood and explained. Thus it has been said that: 'In any case, understanding the determinants of the evolution of capital structure is arguably the most important unresolved question in corporate finance, and only time and additional empirical work will tell where the answer lies.'[55] According to an empirical study involving a comprehensive survey of corporate financing decision-making in UK listed companies, published in 2006, firms were heterogeneous in their capital structure policies: about half of the firms sought to maintain a target debt level, consistent with trade-off theory, but 60 per cent claimed to follow a financing hierarchy, consistent with pecking order theory.[56] These two theories were not viewed by respondents as either mutually exclusive or exhaustive.

---

[50] Myers (n 44 above) 98.

[51] MC Jensen, 'Agency Costs of Free Cash Flow, Corporate Finance and Takeovers' (1986) 76(2) *American Economic Review* 323.

[52] Myers (n 44 above) 99.

[53] M Baker and J Wurgler, 'Market Timing and Capital Structure' (2002) 57 *Journal of Finance* 1.

[54] R Huang and JR Ritter, 'Testing Theories of Capital Structure and Estimating the Speed of Adjustment' (26 July 2007) available at SSRN <http://ssrn.com/abstract=938564>.

[55] ibid.

[56] V Beattie, A Goodacre, and SJ Thomson, 'Corporate Financing Decisions: UK Survey Evidence' (2006) 33(9) & (10) *Journal of Business Finance & Accounting* 1402. See also F Degeorge and EG Maug, 'Corporate Finance in Europe: A Survey', ECGI—Finance Working Paper No 121/2006 (23 March 2006) available at SSRN: <http://ssrn.com/abstract=896518>; F Bancel and

Sources of corporate finance in the UK

Smaller companies are heavily dependent on internal sources of finance and bank finance is their main source of external finance.[57] The external sources of finance available to small and medium-sized businesses is an issue that has been the focus of concern in a number of official reports stretching back many years.[58] The providers of debt finance to smaller firms currently operate in a quite concentrated industry, which was last investigated by the UK Competition Commission in 2002.[59] The Commission found that the cost and availability of lending in general were not a problem but it did identify factors indicating a market lacking effective competition among suppliers. As a consequence of that investigation, the clearing banks were required to give certain undertakings that were intended to remedy excessive profits and prices and to encourage price competition. However, in 2007, after a review by the Office of Fair Trading, some of these undertakings were relaxed in response to identified changes in the market that had improved the level of competition.[60]

External equity plays only a small role in the financing of small businesses generally.[61] Whether, or to what extent, the explanation for this lies in an 'equity gap' market failure—ie lack of access to an appropriate level of equity financing—as opposed to reluctance on the part the founders of such businesses to give up a share of ownership, is not entirely clear but the possibility of there being a market failure in the equity financing of technology-based small and medium-sized enterprises (SMEs) has been recognized.[62] In 2005, the government conducted 'A Mapping Study of Venture Capital Provision to SMEs in England', in which it sought to map out the provision of venture capital to SMEs in England, 'venture capital' being defined in this study to mean not only investment provided in the earlier stages of a company's life, and particularly in technology-oriented

UR Mittoo, 'Cross-Country Determinants of Capital Structure Choice: A Survey of European Firms' (2004) 33(4) *Financial Management* 103.

[57] M Lund and J Wright, 'The Financing of Small Firms in the United Kingdom' (May 1999) *Bank of England Quarterly Bulletin* 195.

[58] *Report of the Committee to Review the Functioning of Financing Institutions* (Cmnd 7937, 1980) which, in app 2, sets out the conclusion and summary of recommendations from the Committee's interim report on the financing of small firms (Cmnd 7503, 1979). Earlier reports on the financing of British industry also noted the particular difficulties faced by small firms: *Report of the Committee on Finance and Industry* (Cmnd 3897, 1931) (Macmillan Report); *Report of the Committee on the Workings of the Monetary System* (Cmnd 827, 1959) (Radcliffe Report); *Report of the Committee of Inquiry on Small Firms* (Cmnd 4811, 1971) (Bolton Report). A general review of the financial structure of small and medium-sized enterprises (SMEs) is provided by A Hughes, 'Finance for SMEs: A UK Perspective' (1997) 9 *Small Business Economics* 151.

[59] Competition Commission, 'The Supply of Banking Services by Clearing Banks to Small and Medium-sized Enterprises' (2002).

[60] OFT, 'SME Banking' (Report, August 2007).

[61] Lund and Wright (n 57 above) 199.

[62] ibid 200–1.

sectors (as the term is now widely understood), but also all forms of private equity provision to SMEs, regardless of stage or sector. The survey found that there had been dramatic growth in the previous ten years in the levels of venture capital and private equity activity in the UK and elsewhere in continental Europe but concluded that it remained the case that there were still sectors, stages, and regions of the economy that did not have access to an adequate supply of venture finance.[63] External equity finance is more important for technology-based small firms than for the sector generally.[64]

Survey data suggests that access to debt finance is not a major problem for smaller quoted companies in aggregate.[65] Banks are the main source; smaller quoted companies do not generally have access to bond markets because of their size.[66] Although there are concerns that access to equity financing could be more difficult because of secondary market illiquidity in the shares of smaller companies, lack of interest in such shares from the investment management and investment analyst communities, and owners' unwillingness to dilute equity stakes, recent data does not support the view that there are major barriers to raising equity finance for the broad majority of smaller quoted companies.

Large, profitable companies have the biggest range of available financing options. The trade-off theory may suggest a positive relationship between profitability and gearing because there is a low risk of financial distress and the tax benefits of debt should increase as profits rise.[67] The agency costs theory would also appear to point in the same direction because of the disciplining effect of debt servicing commitments and of restrictive covenants.[68] On the other hand, the pecking order theory would suggest a negative relationship because highly profitable companies will have less need than other companies for any type of external finance.[69] Survey data indicates a sharp rise in UK corporate gearing between 1999 and 2002, with rises in gearing being concentrated among the largest and most profitable companies.[70]

[63] DTI, 'A Mapping Study of Venture Capital Provision to SMEs in England' (DTI, Small Business Service, October 2005) para 2.1.

[64] P Brierley and P Bunn, 'The Determinants of UK Corporate Capital Gearing' (Autumn 2005) *Bank of England Quarterly Bulletin* 356, 363; P Brierley, 'The Financing of Technology-based Small Firms: A Review of the Literature' (Spring 2001) *Bank of England Quarterly Bulletin* 201.

[65] P Brierley and M Young, 'The Financing of Smaller Quoted Companies: A Survey' (Summer 2004) *Bank of England Quarterly Bulletin* 160. This survey defines SQCs to include non-financial companies with a full listing on the London Stock Exchange with a market capitalization below that of companies in the FTSE 350 index and those companies quoted on AIM.

[66] A Kearns and JE Young, 'Provision of Finance to Smaller Quoted Companies: Some Evidence from Survey Responses and Liaison Meetings' (Spring 2002) *Bank of England Quarterly Bulletin* 26.

[67] P Brierley and P Bunn, 'The Determinants of UK Corporate Capital Gearing' (Autumn 2005) *Bank of England Quarterly Bulletin* 356, 362.

[68] ibid.

[69] ibid. See also RG Rajan and L Zingales, 'What Do We Know About Capital Structure: Some Evidence From International Data' (1995) 50(5) *Journal of Finance* 1421.

[70] Brierley and Bunn (n 67 above) 362.

Securities markets

In broad terms, the securities markets comprise domestic and international markets for the issuance and trading of equity and debt securities and related financial instruments. Issuance is 'primary' market activity and trading is 'secondary' market activity. Secondary market activity is largely outside the scope of this book.

The Bank for International Settlements (BIS) publishes quarterly statistics on securities markets, broken down into three segments: international debt securities; international equities; and domestic debt securities. The BIS definition of international securities (as opposed to domestic securities) is based on three major characteristics of the securities: the location of the transaction, the currency of issuance, and the residence of the issuer. International issues comprise all foreign currency issues by residents and non-residents in a given country and all domestic currency issues launched in the domestic market by non-residents. In addition, domestic currency issues launched in the domestic market by residents are also considered as international issues if they are specifically targeted at non-resident investors.[71] Domestic debt securities are defined as those that have been issued by residents in domestic currency (with a few exceptions) and targeted at resident investors.[72] Tables 3.3 and 3.4 below, are taken from the BIS statistics; they provide an idea of the size and level of activity in the debt and equity international securities markets. According to the BIS statistics, amounts outstanding on domestic debt securities issued by UK resident corporate issuers at September 2006 fell just short of US$23 billion.[73]

It is not essential for a company that is in search of capital from the domestic or international securities markets to do so via a formally organized stock exchange or other trading facility. However, admission of securities to trading on an exchange or other trading system may offer significant benefits, including access to bigger pools of capital, better liquidity, and an enhanced corporate profile.

The Main Market of the London Stock Exchange is the UK's most prestigious organized securities market.[74] It is open to UK companies and also to companies from other countries. Companies can list different types of shares and debt securities on the Main Market. Other financial instruments can also be listed, including securitized derivatives and securitized commodities. The market now has a

---

[71] BIS, 'Guide to the International Financial Statistics', (BIS Papers No 14 Febuary 2003) section III, para 1.1.

[72] ibid, section III, para 3.1.

[73] BIS. *Quarterly Review* (March 2007), Table 16B (Domestic debt securities).

[74] This section on the Main Market is based on information on the London Stock Exchange's website, in particular its publication 'A Guide to the Main Market', see <http://www.londonstock exchange.com/en-gb/> (accessed December 2007).

Table 3.3. International debt securities—corporate issuers

By nationality of issuer
In billions of US dollars

Countries	Amounts outstanding				2005	2006	Net issues			
	Dec 2004	Dec 2005	Sep 2006	Dec 2006			Q1 2006	Q2 2006	Q3 2006	Q4 2006
All countries	**1,608.9**	**1,544.9**	**1,770.8**	**1,887.1**	**52.8**	**248.2**	**68.9**	**57.1**	**42.3**	**79.9**
Developed countries	**1,457.5**	**1,380.8**	**1,590.2**	**1,692.4**	**38.4**	**219.0**	**64.0**	**52.9**	**35.4**	**66.7**
Australia	17.2	15.4	16.3	17.0	-0.8	0.8	-0.1	0.4	0.2	0.3
Austria	11.4	15.6	17.5	19.4	5.9	2.2	0.3	0.7	-0.1	1.3
Belgium	11.4	8.9	9.8	13.0	-1.2	3.1	0.8	0.3	-0.7	2.8
Canada	100.1	99.3	98.0	101.4	-0.3	1.5	-1.1	-3.4	2.5	3.4
Denmark	16.1	16.6	16.7	16.6	2.7	-1.6	-0.0	-0.4	-0.6	-0.7
Finland	17.1	13.6	16.4	15.9	-1.7	1.0	-0.2	2.1	0.1	-1.0
France	271.8	246.3	266.8	280.1	8.9	7.1	-3.6	8.4	-1.0	3.3
Germany	95.3	89.1	110.3	110.7	5.8	11.2	1.8	14.0	-0.9	-3.7
Greece	9.5	8.9	10.3	14.6	0.6	4.7	—	0.8	—	3.9
Iceland	1.4	1.3	1.6	1.8	-0.0	0.4	0.1	-0.0	0.3	0.1
Ireland	9.1	8.4	10.2	10.0	0.2	1.0	-0.1	-0.1	1.6	-0.4
Italy	66.2	50.9	55.8	59.9	-7.2	3.3	-0.2	-0.2	1.7	2.0
Japan	63.3	58.9	59.1	59.8	2.1	0.3	0.6	0.6	-1.7	0.8
Luxembourg	4.4	3.6	3.7	3.9	-0.5	0.0	0.8	-0.7	-0.1	0.0
Netherlands	59.9	52.2	55.7	61.0	-1.2	3.9	2.0	-1.3	-0.3	3.5
New Zealand	2.6	2.4	2.7	2.8	-0.1	0.3	-0.2	0.4	0.0	0.1
Norway	20.0	18.5	20.0	20.4	-0.2	1.0	-0.4	-0.3	1.7	-0.1
Portugal	5.3	5.5	5.5	9.0	1.0	2.8	-0.6	0.4	-0.2	3.2
Spain	27.6	24.6	40.0	41.7	-0.3	14.2	7.1	4.2	2.5	0.4
Sweden	18.3	18.5	16.7	18.0	2.4	-2.2	0.3	-3.1	-0.1	0.7
Switzerland	8.6	8.2	8.8	9.0	0.3	0.4	-0.3	0.0	0.6	0.0
United Kingdom	218.2	202.8	248.3	259.4	4.9	34.6	16.6	1.3	14.2	2.4
United States	402.5	411.4	499.9	547.0	16.9	129.3	40.4	28.8	15.5	44.5

Continued

Table 3.3. (Continued)

| | By nationality of issuer
In billions of US dollars | | | | | | | | | |
| | Amounts outstanding | | | | Net issues | | | | | |
Countries	Dec 2004	Dec 2005	Sep 2006	Dec 2006	2005	2006	Q1 2006	Q2 2006	Q3 2006	Q4 2006
Offshore centres	**26.9**	**27.3**	**28.6**	**29.0**	**0.8**	**1.3**	**0.2**	**0.8**	**0.0**	**0.3**
Aruba	—	—	—	—	—	—	—	—	—	—
Bahamas	0.9	0.9	0.7	0.7	—	-0.1	—	-0.1	—	—
Bermuda	0.2	0.6	0.6	0.5	0.4	-0.1	—	—	—	-0.1
Cayman Islands	—	—	—	—	—	—	—	—	—	—
Hong Kong SAR	15.5	15.5	15.0	15.2	0.1	-0.4	0.2	-0.5	-0.2	0.1
Lebanon	0.0	0.0	—	—	—	-0.0	—	—	-0.0	—
Netherlands Antilles	—	—	—	—	—	—	—	—	—	—
Panama	0.2	0.3	0.3	0.3	0.2	—	—	—	—	—
Singapore	10.0	10.0	11.8	12.2	0.1	2.0	-0.0	1.5	0.3	0.3
West Indies UK	0.1	0.1	0.1	0.1	0.0	0.0	—	—	—	0.0
Developing countries	**124.5**	**136.7**	**152.1**	**165.7**	**13.7**	**27.9**	**4.8**	**3.3**	**6.9**	**12.9**
Africa & Middle East	**11.6**	**13.2**	**19.0**	**26.4**	**1.8**	**13.1**	**2.4**	**1.2**	**2.4**	**7.1**
Israel	5.6	4.8	6.3	6.0	-0.8	1.1	1.4	0.1	—	-0.4
Qatar	1.6	3.8	5.9	5.9	2.2	2.1	-0.0	0.7	1.5	—
South Africa	3.9	4.1	5.1	5.6	0.4	1.4	1.1	0.2	-0.1	0.2
Tunisia	—	—	—	—	—	—	—	—	—	—
United Arab Emirates	0.5	0.5	1.3	8.3	—	7.7	—	0.3	0.5	7.0
Asia & Pacific	**62.7**	**68.3**	**74.1**	**75.8**	**6.1**	**7.3**	**0.5**	**1.6**	**3.5**	**1.6**
China	1.5	1.0	1.1	1.1	-0.5	0.2	—	0.2	-0.1	0.1
India	4.1	6.7	12.0	12.7	2.5	6.0	2.5	2.2	0.5	0.7
Indonesia	0.1	0.3	0.2	0.2	0.2	-0.1	—	-0.1	—	—
Malaysia	7.3	6.4	6.8	6.0	-0.8	-0.5	-0.1	-0.1	0.5	-0.8
Philippines	4.7	5.0	4.5	4.8	0.3	-0.1	0.0	-0.2	-0.2	0.3
South Korea	22.7	25.5	27.9	28.2	3.2	2.5	0.1	0.6	1.5	0.2

Taiwan, China	19.5	19.3	16.6	17.1	-0.2	-2.2	-2.0	-0.7	-0.0	0.5
Thailand	2.4	3.8	3.5	3.6	1.4	-0.2	-0.0	-0.3	0.0	0.1
Europe	**12.2**	**13.2**	**14.6**	**16.4**	**1.3**	**2.8**	**0.3**	**0.4**	**0.5**	**1.6**
Croatia	0.4	0.3	0.0	0.2	-0.1	-0.1	—	—	-0.3	0.2
Cyprus	0.1	0.1	0.1	0.1	—	—	—	—	—	—
Hungary	—	0.9	1.2	1.3	0.9	0.3	0.3	—	—	—
Poland	0.4	0.3	0.3	0.4	—	—	—	—	—	0.9
Russia	7.7	8.5	9.2	10.1	0.8	1.7	0.1	0.4	0.2	-0.2
Slovakia	0.7	0.6	0.7	0.5	—	-0.2	—	—	—	0.1
Turkey	0.4	—	0.3	0.3	-0.4	0.3	—	—	0.3	—
Latin America & Caribbean	**37.9**	**42.1**	**44.4**	**47.1**	**4.5**	**4.8**	**1.5**	**0.1**	**0.5**	**2.6**
Argentina	4.3	3.8	3.7	3.9	-0.5	0.1	—	-0.2	0.1	0.2
Brazil	10.7	10.8	13.4	13.3	0.2	2.4	1.3	0.5	0.7	-0.1
Chile	6.8	7.2	6.4	6.9	0.5	-0.4	-0.7	0.2	-0.4	0.5
Colombia	0.9	0.9	1.0	1.0	-0.0	0.1	—	0.1	—	—
Mexico	14.6	18.4	18.2	19.8	3.9	1.4	0.4	-0.6	-0.0	1.6
Peru	—	—	—	—	—	—	—	—	—	—
Uruguay	—	—	—	—	—	—	—	—	—	—
Venezuela	0.3	0.3	0.3	0.3	—	0.1	0.1	0.0	0.0	0.0

Source: Bank for International settlements, *Quarterly Reivew* (March 2007), Table 12C. Reproduced with permission of the BIS <http://www.bis.org>.

Table 3.4. Announced international equity issues

Countries	2004	2005	2006	By nationality of issuer In billions of US dollars								
				Q4 2004	Q1 2005	Q2 2005	Q3 2005	Q4 2005	Q1 2006	Q2 2006	Q3 2006	Q4 2006
All countries	219.4	307.8	377.9	70.9	66.0	60.9	73.8	107.1	71.4	102.6	70.9	133.0
Developed countries	160.8	212.4	227.6	50.5	50.8	39.8	49.4	72.4	46.2	65.8	41.0	74.5
Australia	7.1	7.5	10.0	1.6	1.4	0.9	1.9	3.4	1.7	1.8	0.9	5.7
Austria	5.0	3.9	12.1	3.0	0.2	2.1	0.1	1.5	4.2	5.6	0.1	2.2
Belgium	5.0	2.7	2.9	1.2	0.4	1.1	—	1.2	0.7	0.0	1.6	0.6
Canada	10.8	12.1	5.9	5.5	4.9	2.7	2.4	2.1	1.8	1.6	0.2	2.3
Denmark	3.7	0.7	3.4	1.0	—	0.1	0.1	0.5	0.5	0.0	0.1	2.8
Finland	1.6	4.4	1.9	0.9	1.4	2.0	0.4	0.7	0.7	0.1	—	1.1
France	27.5	35.6	34.5	7.7	6.2	6.4	7.5	15.5	8.9	10.7	2.7	12.1
Germany	16.8	30.1	25.4	7.6	6.3	6.2	9.2	8.4	5.2	5.6	8.6	6.0
Greece	1.5	5.1	3.7	0.7	0.7	0.6	2.8	1.0	0.8	1.3	0.1	1.5
Iceland	1.5	0.7	1.2	0.9	—	—	—	0.7	0.3	—	—	0.9
Ireland	1.7	1.4	2.3	0.1	0.2	0.3	0.6	0.2	0.6	0.1	0.9	0.7
Italy	16.2	19.4	11.3	7.5	3.2	4.2	5.6	6.4	2.3	5.1	0.8	3.0
Japan	8.0	9.9	11.8	2.0	3.0	0.2	1.8	4.9	4.0	0.1	3.1	4.6
Luxembourg	3.0	0.9	0.4	0.9	—	—	0.9	—	0.4	—	—	—
Netherlands	6.8	13.9	9.6	2.1	5.6	1.8	2.7	3.7	0.6	4.9	2.0	2.1
New Zealand	0.2	0.2	—	0.0	0.1	—	0.0	0.0	—	—	—	—
Norway	3.7	5.4	7.1	0.2	2.9	0.7	0.4	1.4	2.3	3.0	0.9	0.9
Portugal	1.3	1.4	1.6	0.8	0.1	—	1.3	—	—	0.7	—	0.9
Spain	6.5	8.1	8.0	1.1	2.0	0.6	4.9	0.5	—	1.5	1.3	5.1
Sweden	5.4	2.6	3.8	2.1	0.8	0.5	0.4	1.0	0.7	1.2	0.3	1.5
Switzerland	4.2	6.0	14.0	1.0	0.2	0.6	1.5	3.8	1.3	6.0	0.5	6.2

	C1	C2	C3	C4	C5	C6	C7	C8	C9	C10	C11	C12
United Kingdom	21.4	34.6	41.9	2.3	9.8	7.2	3.8	13.7	7.8	8.4	14.1	11.6
United States	1.7	5.9	14.7	0.4	1.3	1.7	1.0	1.9	1.6	7.9	2.6	2.6
Offshore centres	**12.4**	**18.1**	**25.1**	**5.7**	**2.7**	**3.6**	**2.3**	**9.4**	**4.0**	**6.4**	**5.3**	**9.3**
Bahamas	—	—	0.1	—	—	—	—	—	—	—	—	0.1
Bahrain	—	0.1	0.4	—	—	—	—	0.1	—	—	—	0.4
Bermuda	2.2	3.9	2.0	0.7	0.6	0.4	0.2	2.7	0.6	0.7	0.8	0.0
Cayman Islands	—	0.0	1.2	—	—	0.0	—	—	—	0.0	—	1.2
Hong Kong SAR	7.4	7.5	16.0	3.3	1.5	0.9	1.2	4.0	1.3	4.3	3.3	7.2
Lebanon	—	0.8	0.2	—	—	—	—	0.8	0.2	—	—	—
Panama	—	0.4	0.2	—	—	—	—	0.4	—	0.2	—	—
Singapore	2.8	3.6	4.4	1.7	0.6	0.5	1.0	1.4	1.9	0.9	1.3	0.3
West Indies UK	—	—	0.1	—	—	—	—	—	—	—	—	0.1
Developing countries	**46.2**	**77.3**	**125.2**	**14.7**	**12.5**	**17.5**	**22.1**	**25.2**	**21.1**	**30.3**	**24.6**	**49.3**
Africa & Middle East	**4.8**	**5.0**	**5.0**	**1.3**	**1.2**	**0.8**	**0.7**	**2.3**	**3.0**	**0.7**	**0.3**	**1.1**
Egypt	0.1	0.7	0.7	0.1	—	0.2	—	0.5	0.3	0.4	—	—
Israel	1.5	2.0	0.6	0.2	1.1	0.2	0.3	0.4	0.2	0.1	—	0.2
Jordan	—	0.3	—	—	—	—	—	0.3	—	—	—	—
South Africa	1.9	1.0	2.4	—	—	0.3	0.3	0.5	2.1	—	0.1	0.1
United Arab Emirates	0.2	0.8	0.8	—	0.2	—	—	0.7	—	0.1	0.0	0.7
Asia & Pacific	**33.6**	**56.9**	**82.5**	**8.7**	**8.6**	**13.8**	**15.4**	**19.1**	**11.1**	**24.0**	**11.0**	**36.4**
China	18.1	26.9	50.3	4.9	2.2	8.0	4.3	12.4	3.1	16.8	5.3	25.1
Georgia	—	—	0.2	—	—	—	—	—	—	—	—	0.2
India	4.6	8.6	10.1	0.7	3.1	2.5	1.1	1.9	2.3	2.0	0.7	5.2

Continued

Table 3.4. *(Continued)*

| | | | | **By nationality of issuer** In billions of US dollars | | | | | | | | |
Countries	2004	2005	2006	Q4 2004	Q1 2005	Q2 2005	Q3 2005	Q4 2005	Q1 2006	Q2 2006	Q3 2006	Q4 2006
Indonesia	0.8	1.0	0.8	0.2	0.2	0.1	0.8	—	—	0.1	0.2	0.5
Kazakhstan	—	0.2	4.1	—	—	—	—	0.2	—	—	2.4	1.7
Malaysia	0.9	1.4	0.8	0.2	0.2	0.2	0.4	0.6	0.0	—	0.3	0.4
Pakistan	—	—	0.9	—	—	—	—	—	—	—	—	0.9
Philippines	0.1	0.9	1.5	0.1	0.9	—	—	—	0.5	0.2	0.4	0.4
South Korea	4.6	9.7	7.5	0.5	0.5	1.6	3.8	3.7	4.1	2.7	0.2	0.5
Taiwan, China	3.4	7.9	3.8	1.3	1.4	1.4	4.8	0.2	0.8	0.8	1.4	0.8
Thailand	1.1	0.3	2.1	0.9	0.1	0.0	0.2	0.0	0.1	1.3	0.1	0.6
Europe	**5.4**	**10.1**	**23.9**	**3.9**	**2.1**	**2.1**	**3.3**	**2.6**	**2.8**	**2.3**	**10.2**	**8.6**
Croatia	—	—	0.2	—	—	—	—	—	—	—	—	0.2
Cyprus	—	0.3	1.2	—	—	—	—	0.3	0.2	—	0.1	0.8
Czech Republic	0.2	0.3	0.3	—	—	0.1	0.2	—	—	—	—	0.3
Hungary	0.8	0.0	—	0.5	—	—	0.0	—	—	0.0	—	—
Poland	0.9	1.0	0.8	0.7	0.1	0.4	0.4	0.1	0.2	0.0	0.1	0.5
Romania	—	—	0.2	—	—	—	—	—	—	0.0	—	0.2
Russia	2.5	6.5	19.6	2.2	1.7	1.2	2.6	0.9	2.3	1.5	10.0	5.9
Turkey	1.0	1.5	1.5	0.4	0.2	0.3	0.1	0.9	0.1	0.7	—	0.7
Latin America & Caribbean	**2.4**	**5.3**	**13.8**	**0.9**	**0.5**	**0.9**	**2.7**	**1.3**	**4.3**	**3.3**	**3.1**	**3.2**
Argentina	—	—	0.9	—	—	—	—	—	0.9	—	—	—
Brazil	2.0	2.8	10.9	0.9	0.5	0.5	1.2	0.6	2.4	3.1	2.9	2.4
Chile	0.3	0.6	—	—	—	—	0.2	0.4	—	—	—	—
Mexico	0.2	2.0	1.5	—	0.0	0.3	1.3	0.3	1.0	0.1	0.2	0.2
Peru	—	—	0.6	—	—	—	—	—	—	—	—	0.6

Source: Bank for International settlements, *Quarterly Review* (March 2007), Table 18. Reproduced with permission of the BIS <http://www.bis.org>.

combined capitalization of over £4.3 trillion. In 2006, there were 83 new issues on the Main Market, raising over £18.8 billion and 712 further issues raising more than £14.5 billion. The Alternative Investment Market (AIM) is the London Stock Exchange's second-tier market. It describes itself as 'the world's leading market for smaller, growing companies from all over the world'.[75] Since its establishment in 1995, AIM has attracted over 2,100 companies, which between them have raised over £2.2 billion. AIM has a strong international focus. Compared to the Main Market, AIM has less stringent admission criteria and less wide-ranging continuing obligations. The London Stock Exchange also operates the Professional Securities Market (PSM), which is a market that enables domestic and overseas companies to raise capital through the issue of specialist securities, such as debt, convertibles, and depositary receipts, to professional or institutional investors.[76] The regulatory requirements governing the PSM are different from those for the Main Market and AIM because they are tailored for a specialist, professionals-only market segment.

The London Stock Exchange does not have a complete monopoly on securities market infrastructure provision in the UK. Another provider is the PLUS Markets Group, which provides primary and secondary equity market services.[77] The 'PLUS-quoted' primary market competes with AIM by specializing in smaller and mid-cap companies, domestic and international. As of mid-2007, it quoted around 180 companies with a combined market capitalization of over £2.4 billion. The 'PLUS-listed' market is a new market, launched in July 2007, that is intended to compete with the Main Market of the London Stock Exchange and is thus aimed at issuers of securities seeking a full listing.

Efficient capital markets

Efficient capital markets theory underpins the conventional understanding of the pricing of securities in financial markets.[78] In general terms, the theory is concerned with whether prices at any point in time 'fully reflect' available information.[79] Ever since a classic review published in 1970, it has been usual to distinguish between three degrees of efficiency: weak-form efficiency, semi-strong-form efficiency, and strong-form efficiency.[80] In a weak-form efficient

---

[75] This section on AIM is based on information on the London Stock Exchange website, in particular its publication, 'AIM—the most successful growth market in the world', from which the quotation is taken.

[76] This section on the PSM is based on information on the London Stock Exchange's website.

[77] Information on the PLUS Markets is taken from the PLUS Group website <http://www.plusmarketsgroup.com> (accessed December 2007).

[78] For an overview of the literature on this topic, see HS Houthakker and PJ Williamson, *The Economics of Financial Markets* (OUP, 1996) 130–40.

[79] EF Fama, 'Efficient Capital Markets: A Review of Theory and Empirical Work' (1970) 25 *Journal of Finance* 383.

[80] ibid.

market, the current prices of securities reflect all relevant historical information. A semi-strong efficient capital market is one where prices adjust rapidly in response to information as soon as it becomes available. A strong-form efficient capital market is one where the prices reflect all relevant information, including information that has not yet been made public. Empirical research supports weak-form efficiency and semi-strong efficiency as explanations of how securities markets actually work in major jurisdictions, with the semi-strong version being the one that is most favoured.[81] That markets do not normally conform to the strong-form efficiency hypothesis is demonstrated by the (illegal) profits that can be made by insider trading: the opportunity for profit exists because market prices have not yet absorbed the information that has not been made public or, to put it another way, because the market is not conforming to the model of strong-form efficiency.

The efficient capital market hypothesis provides the intellectual context for disclosure-oriented securities regulation.[82] It has been said that: 'Almost all issues are discussed against the background of market efficiency: whether issuers should be required to make duplicative disclosures; whether company insiders should be permitted to speak privately with institutional investors and analysts; and how damages can be inferred from stock price movements. Market efficiency and the mechanisms of market efficiency factor into all of these policy debates—and quite appropriately.'[83] Yet the hegemony of the efficient capital market hypothesis has not gone completely unquestioned. A distinction is now often drawn between *informational* efficiency and *fundamental* efficiency, by which is meant that prices represents the best current estimate of the present value of the future cash flows associated with a security. If prices in an informationally efficient market are inaccurate in a fundamental sense, this implies a potential problem with regard to allocative efficiency, meaning that scarce resources may fail to be allocated to their most productive use.[84] The trend for economists to incorporate behavioural sciences into their work has also cast a deep shadow over the efficient capital markets hypothesis because that hypothesis does not capture socio-psychological factors that may lead investors to engage in irrational trading activities that affect share prices.[85] Although supporters of the efficient capital markets

---

[81] EF Fama, 'Efficient Capital Markets: II' (1991) 46(5) *Journal of Finance* 1575.

[82] RJ Gilson and RR Kraakman, 'The Mechanisms of Market Efficiency' (1984) 70 *Virginia Law Review* 549, 550.

[83] HE Jackson, 'To What Extent Should Individual Investors Rely on the Mechanisms of Market Efficiency: A Preliminary Investigation of Dispersion in Investor Returns' (2003) 28 *Journal of Corporation Law* 671.

[84] Although some contend that the connection between prices in the public trading markets for stocks and the allocation of real resources is a weak one, and that stock markets may have far less allocative importance than has generally been assumed: L Stout, 'The Unimportance of Being Efficient: An Economic Analysis of Stock Market Pricing and Securities Regulation' (1988) 87 *Michigan Law Review* 613.

[85] FB Cross and RA Prentice, *Law and Corporate Finance* (Edward Elgar, 2007) ch 3 provides an overview of behavioural analysis of law and corporate finance. See further, A Shleifer, *Inefficient Markets* (OUP, 2000).

theory contend that arbitrage will quickly eliminate pricing inaccuracies caused by investor irrationality, others point out that arbitrage is risky, subject to limitations, and that even professional investors cannot be relied upon to act with perfect rationality.[86] The deep debate on these issues makes it hard now to claim, as was done in 1978, that 'there is no other proposition in economics which has more solid empirical evidence supporting it than the efficient market hypothesis'.[87] It is open to question whether securities regulatory policy design has kept pace with this debate or whether it remains rooted in assumptions that arguably have been shown to be too simplistic to be wholly convincing as explanations for how securities markets operate. However, since there is overwhelming empirical evidence that share prices react quickly, in the expected direction, to the release of information, overall the theory of efficient capital markets continues to contribute usefully to the analytical framework.

Measuring and assessing financial performance—company accounts

The definition of a semi-strong efficient capital market as one in which market prices shift rapidly in response to new information as soon as it becomes public, puts the spotlight onto the operation of processes whereby information is conveyed to the market and then impounded into prices. It has been said that: 'Since efficiency in the capital market depends on the distribution of information, it is ultimately a function of the cost of information to traders. The lower the cost of particular information, the wider will be its distribution, the more effective will be the capital market mechanism operating to reflect it in prices, and the more efficient will be the market with respect to it.'[88] Mandatory disclosure obligations eliminate the repetitive costs of individual acquisition of information by each market participant and, as such, they can be regarded as an efficiency-enhancing mechanism.[89] Regular reporting of financial performance is the central mandatory disclosure obligation to which companies are subject. This section therefore provides an overview of the UK mandatory financial disclosure obligations for companies and of the institutional framework within which they operate.

---

[86] A Shleifer and L Summers, 'The Noise Trader Approach to Finance' (1990) 4 *Journal of Economic Perspectives* 19 (stressing limits on arbitrage).

[87] MC Jensen, 'Some Anomalous Evidence Regarding Market Efficiency' (1978) 6 *Journal of Financial Economics* 95.

[88] RJ Gilson and RR Kraakman, 'The Mechanisms of Market Efficiency' (1984) 70 *Virginia Law Review* 549, 593.

[89] ibid 597–601.

Statutory financial disclosure framework for UK companies

The directors of every company must prepare accounts for the company for each of its financial years.[90] Before approving the accounts, the directors must be satisfied that they give a true and fair view of the assets, liabilities, financial position, and profit or loss of the company.[91] The accounts may be prepared in accordance with the Companies Act or in accordance with international accounting standards/international financial reporting standards (IAS/IFRS).[92] Companies Act accounts comprise a balance sheet as at the end of the relevant financial period and a profit and loss account covering that period.[93] These fundamental statutory requirements are amplified by accounting standards, which include a requirement for a cash flow statement.[94] Companies Act accounts are drawn up in accordance with the Act[95] and UK Generally Accepted Accounting Principles (UK GAAP), for which responsibility lies with the Accounting Standards Board (ASB).[96] The ASB favours the strategy of achieving the convergence of UK GAAP with IAS/IFRS.[97] A complete set of IAS/IFRS financial statements comprises a balance sheet, an income statement, a statement of changes in equity over the period, a cash flow statement, and notes.[98] International Accounting Standards and International Financial Reporting Standards are the responsibility of the International Accounting Standards Board (IASB).[99]

Subject to certain exemptions, directors of parent companies must also prepare consolidated group accounts for each year.[100] As a matter of European law, the consolidated group accounts of an issuer with securities admitted to trading on a 'regulated market' must be drawn up in accordance with IAS/IFRS.[101]

---

[90] Companies Act 2006, s 394.

[91] ibid s 393.

[92] ibid s 395.

[93] ibid s 396.

[94] FRS 1, *Cash Flow Statements*.

[95] Detailed requirements are to be set out in Regulations made under Companies Act 2006, ss 396 (individual accounts) and ss 404 (group accounts). See The Small Companies and Groups (Accounts and Directors' Report) Regulations 2008, SI 2008/409 and The Large and Medium-sized Companies and Groups (Accounts and Reports) Regulations 2008/410.

[96] Companies Act 2006, s 464 makes provision for a body or bodies to be prescribed for the purposes of issuing accounting standards. This section is a re-enactment of an equivalent provision in the Companies Act 1985. The ASB is the prescribed body under. The Accounting Standards (Prescribed Body) Regulations 2005, SI 2005/697.

[97] ASB, 'UK Accounting Standards: A Strategy For Convergence With IFRS', Discussion Paper (March 2004); ASB, 'Accounting Standard-setting in a Changing Environment: The Role Of The Accounting Standards Board', Exposure Draft (March 2005).

[98] IAS 1, *Presentation of Financial Statements*.

[99] Standards issued by the IASB are designated International Financial Reporting Standards but earlier pronouncements made by a predecessor body that remain in force are designated International Accounting Standards.

[100] Companies Act 2006, s 399.

[101] Regulation (EC) 1606/2002 of the European Parliament and of the Council of 19 July 2002 on the application of international accounting standards [2002] OJ L/243. This requirement is directly applicable in the UK. Companies Act 2006, s 403(1) notes its impact.

This requirement is applicable to issuers on the London Stock Exchange's Main Market and on the PLUS-listed Market, as these are both 'regulated' markets, but not directly to issuers on AIM or PLUS-quoted, which are 'exchange-regulated markets'. (However, under the rules governing admission to trading on AIM, there is a requirement for AIM companies incorporated in EEA countries to prepare and present their annual consolidated accounts in accordance with IAS/IFRS.[102]) The group accounts of other companies may be drawn up as Companies Act group accounts or as IAS/IFRS group accounts.[103] The financial statements required to be included in Companies Act or IAS/IFRS accounts are the same as for individual accounts but on a consolidated rather than an individual basis. The individual accounts of a parent company and each of its subsidiary undertakings must all be prepared using the same reporting framework except where there are good reasons not to do so.[104]

In addition to the accounts, the directors of a company must prepare a directors' report for each financial year of the company.[105] For a parent company that prepares group accounts, the directors' report must be a consolidated report.[106] Except for companies that are subject to a special regime for small companies, the directors' report must contain a business review providing a fair review of the company's business and a description of the principal risks and uncertainties facing it.[107] The prescribed contents of business reviews are more detailed for quoted companies than for unquoted companies.[108] A 'quoted company' for the purposes of the accounting requirements of the Companies Act 2006, includes companies whose equity share capital has been admitted to the London Stock Exchange's Main Market, or any other EEA market for officially listed securities, or which are admitted to dealing on the New York Stock Exchange or NASDAQ.[109] The directors of a quoted company are also required to prepare a directors' remuneration report for each financial year of the company.[110]

Subject to certain exemptions (including exemptions for small companies and dormant companies) annual accounts must be independently audited.[111] The auditor's report must state clearly whether, in the auditor's opinion, the annual accounts give a true and fair view, have been properly prepared in accordance with the relevant financial reporting framework, and have been prepared in accordance with the Companies Act 2006 and the IAS Regulation, where that

---

[102] AIM *Rules*, r 19.
[103] Companies Act 2006, s 403(2).
[104] Companies Act 2006, s 407.
[105] ibid s 415.
[106] ibid s 415.
[107] ibid s 417.
[108] ibid s 417(5).
[109] ibid s 385.
[110] ibid s 420.
[111] ibid s 475.

is applicable.[112] The auditor must also state whether, in his or her opinion, the information given in the directors' report (including the business review) is consistent with the accounts.[113] For quoted companies, the auditor's report must include a report on the auditable part of the directors' remuneration report and must state whether it has been properly prepared.[114]

The process under the Companies Act 2006 for putting annual accounts and reports into the public domain is that they must be sent to every shareholder and debenture holder, and every other person who is entitled to receive notice of the general meetings.[115] The Companies Act 2006 makes provision for documents and other information to be validly sent in hard copy form, in electronic form, or by being made available on a website.[116] Quoted companies must, in addition, make their annual accounts and reports available on a website which is accessible by the general public and not just members and debenture holders.[117] There is also provision for summary financial statements to be sent to shareholders, debenture holders, and other entitled persons instead of the full accounts and reports but the full accounts and reports must be sent to any such person who so requests.[118] Public (but not private) companies must then within a specified period lay their accounts and reports before a general meeting.[119] Finally, all limited companies must file their annual accounts and reports with the registrar of companies.[120] Exactly what has to be filed depends on the type of company:[121] there is provision for small and medium-sized companies to file abbreviated accounts but unquoted companies (that are not SMEs) must file the full accounts and directors' and auditor's[122] reports, and quoted companies must, in addition, file the directors' remuneration report.

The time limits for fulfilment of these requirements are important because a big time-lag is likely seriously to diminish the value of the information provided by the accounts. Under the Companies Act 2006, the time limit within which a public company must lay its accounts before the general meeting and then file them with the registrar is six months from the end of the relevant accounting reference period.[123] For private companies the time period for delivery of accounts

---

[112] Companies Act 2006, s 495.
[113] ibid s 496.
[114] ibid s 497.
[115] ibid s 423.
[116] ibid ss 1144–1148 and Schs 4–5.
[117] ibid s 430. Access can be restricted so far as necessary to comply with any enactment or regulatory requirement (in the UK or elsewhere): ibid s 430(3)(b).
[118] ibid s 426.
[119] ibid s 437.
[120] ibid s 441.
[121] ibid ss 444–448.
[122] Unless an exemption from auditing requirements applies and has been relied upon: ibid s 446(2).
[123] ibid s 442.

to the registrar is nine months.[124] Even though the publication timescales were shortened by the Companies Act 2006, they still remain quite generous.

Additional financial disclosure framework under FSA *Disclosure and Transparency Rules*

The EC Transparency Obligations Directive requires Member States to impose disclosure requirements in relation to annual accounts, half-yearly financial reports, and interim financial statements (which are broadly equivalent to quarterly reports).[125] The UK fulfils this Community obligation via the FSA *Disclosure Rules and Transparency Rules* (*DTR*) The *DTR* apply (with some exemptions) to issuers whose transferable securities are admitted to trading on a 'regulated market' and whose 'home State' is the UK. 'Regulated market' and 'home State' are regulatory concepts with considerable significance in EC securities law. For the purposes of this chapter, it can suffice to note that companies incorporated in the UK that have their equity share capital admitted to trading on the Main Market of the London Stock Exchange (which is a regulated market) are subject to the *DTR* financial disclosure rules but AIM and Plus-quoted companies, even if UK incorporated, are not; this is because AIM and the PLUS-quoted Market are 'exchange-regulated', rather than 'regulated', markets.

Under the *DTR*, audited annual reports must be published within four months of the year end (rather than the more generous six months permitted by the Companies Act 2006).[126] Annual reports must contain a statement from each responsible person within the issuer that to the best of his or her knowledge the financial statements give a true and fair view and the management report includes a fair review of performance together with a description of principal risks and uncertainties.[127] Half-yearly financial reports (which need not be audited) must be made public as soon as possible, but no later than two months after the end of the period to which the report relates.[128] The contents of half-yearly reports are prescribed in outline by the *DTR* as comprising a condensed set of financial statements, an interim management report, and responsibility statements.[129] In addition, in a period between ten weeks after the beginning, and six weeks before the end of each six-month period, an issuer must make public a statement by its management that provides an explanation of material events and transactions and their impact on its financial position, and also a general description

---

[124]   ibid s 442.
[125]   Directive (EC) 2004/109 of the European Parliament and of the Council of 15 December 2004 on the harmonisation of transparency requirements in relation to information about issuers whose securities are admitted to trading on a regulated market and amending Directive (EC) 2001/34, [2004] OJ L390/38, Arts 4–6.
[126]   *DTR* 4.1.3.
[127]   *DTR* 4.1.12.
[128]   *DTR* 4.2.2.
[129]   *DTR* 4.2.3. See also IAS 34, *Interim Financial Reporting*.

of its financial position and performance during the relevant period.[130] Interim management statements need not be audited and there is no requirement for the inclusion of responsibility statements.

The *DTR* also address the process whereby information is disseminated to the public.[131] All regulated information must be disseminated in a manner ensuring that it is capable of reaching as wide a public as possible, and as close to simultaneously as possible throughout the EEA. It must also be communicated to the media in unedited full text (save for annual financial reports which can, generally, be edited). When regulated information is disclosed it must at the same time be filed with the FSA.[132] However, there is no requirement in the *DTR* for financial statements to be sent directly to shareholders (or others).

Market efficiency (and investor protection) aims underpin the Transparency Obligations Directive. Its first recital declares that:

Efficient, transparent and integrated securities markets contribute to a genuine single market in the Community and foster growth and job creation by better allocation of capital and by reducing costs. The disclosure of accurate, comprehensive and timely information about security issuers builds sustained investor confidence and allows an informed assessment of their business performance and assets. This enhances both investor protection and market efficiency.

These sentiments owe much to the intellectual framework provided by the efficient capital markets theory.

Additional financial disclosure framework for other publicly traded companies

The rules of the market on which a company's securities are admitted to trading may impose financial disclosure obligations in addition to those under the general law. Under the AIM *Rules for Companies*, for example, AIM companies must prepare half-yearly reports, which must be published without delay and in any event not later than three months after the end of the relevant period.[133] The information contained in a half-yearly report must include at least a balance sheet, an income statement, and a cash flow statement. The half-yearly report must be presented and prepared in a form consistent with that which will be adopted in the company's annual accounts. AIM companies are not required to publish public quarterly reports or other interim financial statements. PLUS-quoted Market companies are subject to a similar obligation with regard to half-yearly reports and they must announce final results within five months of year end.[134]

---

[130] *DTR* 4.3.
[131] *DTR* 6.3.
[132] *DTR* 6.2.2.
[133] AIM *Rules*, r 18.
[134] PLUS Market *Rules for Issuers*, rr 30–31.

PART II
LEGAL CAPITAL

4

Formation of Share Capital

Scope of this part

This part of the book is concerned with legal capital. Legal capital is a broad concept that embraces the rules relating to the raising of capital through share issuance, the maintenance of share capital, and the returning of value to shareholders in circumstances that do not infringe the maintenance of capital requirements. This chapter deals with 'pay in' rules, ie the regulation of the amount of share capital that is put into a company and the forms of consideration that a company can accept in return for its shares. The basic idea that underpins the pay in rules is that investors should in fact put into the company the amount in cash or non-cash consideration that they have agreed to invest in return for their shares. However, the rules in the Companies Act 2006 that give effect to this straightforward principle are quite complex, especially for public companies where they implement requirements derived from the EC Second Company Law Directive.[1]

Minimum price of individual shares: par values

Every share in a limited company having a share capital must have a fixed nominal or par value.[2] An allotment of a share that does not have a fixed nominal value is void and, in the event of a purported allotment, criminal sanctions attach to every officer of the company who is in default.[3] The par value must be a monetary amount but it does not have to be an amount that is capable of being paid in legal tender.[4] This means that it can be a fraction or percentage of a monetary amount. The par value of any one share cannot be stated in two currencies—ie a share cannot have a par value of, say, US$1 or £1—but different shares in the same

---

[1] Council Directive (EEC) 77/91 as regards the formation of public limited liability companies and the maintenance and alteration of their capital [1977] OJ L26/1 ('Second Company Law Directive').

[2] Companies Act 2006, s 542.

[3] ibid s 542(2) and (4)–(5).

[4] *Re Scandinavian Bank Group plc* [1987] 2 All ER 70, [1987] BCC 93.

company can have par values stated in different currencies.[5] The nominal value of the shares taken on formation is part of the information that must be included in the statement of capital that is filed with the registrar when a new company is incorporated.[6] The statement of capital gives a snapshot of the company's share capital at the point in time to which it relates. Elsewhere in the Companies Act 2006, there are obligations to file an updated statement of capital when the share capital is altered, such as when new shares are allotted.[7]

There is no prescribed minimum par value in respect of the shares of public or private companies and thus any monetary amount can be selected for this purpose. To encourage liquidity, the ordinary shares of public companies tend to have low par values, such as 25p or lower. Liquidity is generally a less important issue in relation to the shares of a private company and larger par values, typically £1, are common. That it is for companies themselves to fix the par values of their shares softens considerably the impact of the seemingly mandatory rule that par values must be stated.

The legal consequence of giving a par value to a share is that this is the minimum price at which shares of that class can be allotted.[8] However, shares can, and often are, allotted at a price in excess of their par value. When this occurs, shares are said to be allotted at a premium. When the par value requirement was first established in British law it was thought to be important because it allowed creditors to ascertain the fixed and certain amount of capital that they were entitled to regard as their security.[9] However, ever since the 1940s, when rules were adopted that required companies to treat all amounts raised through share issuance as if they were capital, the significance of par values as a measure of the creditors' security disappeared because from that point onwards premiums as well as nominal amounts were to be counted as part of that security.

The concept of the par value of share capital might have significance if it gave some indication of the market value of a company's assets. However, it usually does not and instead may be a source of confusion. Where shares are issued at a premium, this creates an imbalance from the outset: an issue of 100,000 £1 shares at a premium of £1 each, gives the company a cash asset of £200,000 but the nominal value of its share capital (assuming no other issues) is £100,000. As time goes on, the overall net worth of the company and the value of individual shares in the company depend on the success of the company's business ventures and also on general economic factors. In practice, the par value of a share commonly bears little relation to the price at which it trades in the market.

---

[5] Companies Act 2006, s 542(3), which is consistent with earlier authority: *Re Scandinavian Bank Group plc* [1987] 2 All ER 70, [1987] BCC 93. This is subject to rules on denomination of minimum capital: Companies Act 2006, s 765 discussed below.

[6] Companies Act 2006, ss 9–10.

[7] ibid s 555 (return of allotments).

[8] ibid s 580. This statutory rule applies to all companies limited by shares. For public companies it gives effect to the Second Company Law Directive, Art 8.1.

[9] *Ooregum Gold Mining Co of India v Roper* [1892] AC 125, 133–4, HL.

Par value requirements have been criticized frequently by review bodies. In 1945, as part of a general review of company law, the Cohen Committee reported that it saw much logic in the arguments put forward in support of having shares of no par value but because there was no public demand for, and considerable opposition to, the proposal, as well as some concerns about possible abuse, it refrained from recommending any change.[10] Less than ten years later, in 1954, a Board of Trade Committee under the chairmanship of Mr Montagu Gedge QC reported specifically on the question of whether shares with no par values should be allowed.[11] On this occasion, the Committee found that there was general support for the proposal[12] and it recommended that shares with no par value should be permitted. The Gedge Committee accepted the following advantages claimed for no par value shares.

(1) They represent the share for what it is—a fraction or aliquot part of the equity—and they do not import a notional token of value.
(2) As there is no nominal capital and the share has no nominal value, they make it impossible to relate a dividend to a nominal capital and thus avoid a potential source of misunderstanding and misrepresentation.[13]
(3) It is the capital employed and not the paid up share capital which is the true value of the undertaking; an ordinary share of no par value does not purport to be anything but a share of the equity.
(4) Where shares do not have par values, capital reorganizations are simplified.
(5) Shares of no par value would in certain cases facilitate the raising of additional equity capital. The par value rules can hinder a company in financial difficulties that wants to raise new share capital where the par value of these shares is greater than the amount that anyone would be willing to pay for them.

The Gedge Committee acknowledged the need for safeguards against abuse but concluded that, provided the whole of the proceeds of any issue of shares having no par value were treated as capital money and not as distributable reserves, the position would be neither more nor less open to abuse than in respect of shares having a par value. The Jenkins Committee, in 1962, also recommended that

---

[10] *Report of the Committee on Company Law Amendment* (Cmd 6659, 1945). Previous company law amendment committees had also considered the issue: Wrenbury Committee (Cd 9138, 1918) and Greene Committee (Cmd 2657, 1926). For a detailed historical review of the debate in the UK on no par value shares, see C Noke, 'No Value in Par: a History of the No Par Value Debate in the United Kingdom' (2000) 10 *Accounting, Business & Financial History* 13.

[11] *Report of the Committee on Shares of No Par Value* (Cmd 9112, 1954).

[12] It was, however, opposed by the General Council of the Trades Union Congress: *Report of the Committee on Shares of No Par Value* (Cmd 9112, 1954) paras 29–31. Also, a minority report annexed to the main report recorded one member of the committee's opposition to the proposal.

[13] Articles normally provide for dividends to be paid on the amount paid up on shares. Where, as is the usual case, shares are fully paid up, the dividend is usually declared as a monetary amount per share (ie the amount available for distribution is divided by the number of shares in issue).

legislation should be introduced to permit shares with no par values.[14] This Committee went one step further than the Gedge Committee by recommending that no par value preference shares, as well as no par value ordinary shares, should be permitted. Despite this support in principle for reform, an attempt to include provision for no par value shares in the Companies Act 1967 failed.

The Company Law Review Steering Group that spearheaded the review that led to the Companies Act 2006 returned to the issue. By 1999, when the Steering Group issued its first consultation specifically on the issue, the UK was already lagging behind other parts of the common law world, where the trend of permitting no par value shares, and in some cases positively abolishing the concept of par value in its entirety, had already become firmly established. For example, section 38 of the New Zealand Companies Act 1993 provides in simple, uncompromising terms that 'a share must not have a nominal or par value'. Reform to similar effect was introduced in Australia in 1998: section 254C of the Corporations Act 2001 now states succinctly that shares of a company have no par value. The Steering Group recommended that the UK should move to this position but only for private companies.[15] The reason for the limitation was that its hands were tied in relation to public companies because Article 8 of the Second Company Law Directive requires public companies to attribute par values to their shares. Although Article 8 provides a no par share alternative, this alternative, which is based on a Belgian model, is unattractive because in essence it retains much of the distinction between par value and premium.

In the end, the proposal to abandon par values for private companies did not make it into the Companies Act 2006. Consultation revealed concern that having different regimes for private and public companies in this respect could act as a barrier to growth, as it could complicate the process of conversion from a private to a public company.[16] The long overdue full-scale reform to remove an anachronism must therefore await change at the European level. A working group established by the European Commission under its Simpler Legislation for the Internal Market (SLIM) project with the remit of examining the Second Company Law Directive concluded, in 2000, that the suggestion to introduce no par value shares was worthy of further study.[17] This view was endorsed by the High Level Group of Company Law Experts which was set up by the European

---

[14] *Report of the Company Law Committee* (Cmnd 1749, 1962) paras 32–34.

[15] Company Law Review Steering Group, 'Modern Company Law for a Competitive Economy—Company Formation and Capital Maintenance', URN 99/1145, para 3.8.

[16] Company Law Review Steering Group, 'Modern Company Law for a Competitive Economy—Capital Maintenance: Other Issues' (June 2000) para 9 notes this concern and other more technical points raised in the consultation exercise. The decision to drop the proposal is noted at Company Law Review Steering Group, 'Modern Company Law for a Competitive Economy—Completing the Structure', (URN 00/1335), para 7.3.

[17] 'Recommendations by the Company Law Slim Working Group on the Simplification of the First and Second Company Law Directives: Conclusions submitted by the Company Law Slim Working Group' available at <http://ec.europa.eu/internal_market/company/docs/official/6037en.pdf> (accessed October 2007).

Commission in September 2001 to make recommendations on a modern regulatory framework in the EU for company law.[18] In its final report, the High Level Group recommended that the accommodation of no par value shares within the Second Company Law Directive should be further reviewed.[19] Simplification, and even possible repeal, of the Second Company Law Directive remains under consideration at the European level.[20] However, in February 2008, as this book was going to press, the European Commission published the results of an independent study by the accountancy firm KPMG into the feasibility of an alternative to the Directive and announced that, based on the study, it had decided against proposing any reforms.[21]

Abolition of par values would have ramifications for existing rights in contracts, deeds, and other instruments that are determined by reference to par values but suitable transitional provisions could be enacted to minimize the upheaval.[22]

Minimum capital

Company formation requirements mean that there must be at least one person who agrees to become a member of the company and, in the case of a company that is to have a share capital, to take at least one share.[23] As we have seen, the allotment price of any shares taken on formation must be not less than their par value but the founders can fix the par value at whatever level they choose. In the case of a private company a share can be allotted on a nil paid, partly paid, or fully paid basis. The combination of these rules means that there is no legal bar in the UK to a private company starting to trade with little or no equity actually invested in the business. The position is different elsewhere in Europe as many countries impose in their national laws minimum capital requirements on their equivalents to British private limited companies.[24] As of 2005, countries that required substantial (€10,000+) minimum amounts of paid up share capital on formation of a private limited company were as shown in Table 4.1.

---

[18] High Level Group of Company Law Experts, 'A Modern Regulatory Framework for Company Law in Europe' (Final Report, Brussels, November 2002) 1. (Heremafter: 'High Level Group, Report').

[19] High Level Group, Report, 82–83.

[20] European Commission, 'Communication on a Simplified Business Environment for Companies in the Areas of Company Law, Accounting and Auditing' (COM (2007) 394).

[21] KPMG, *Feasibility Study on Capital Maintenance* (published by European Commission, February 2008).

[22] Company Law Review Steering Group, 'Modern Company Law for a Competitive Economy—Capital Maintenance: Other Issues' (June 2000), paras 13–21.

[23] Companies Act 2006, s 8.

[24] M Becht, C Mayer, and HF Wagner, 'Where Do Firms Incorporate?',. ECGI—Law Working Paper No 70/2006 (September 2006) available at SSRN <http://ssrn.com/abstract=906066>. Table 6 indicates the minimum capital requirements for private and public limited liability companies in the 25 EU Member States and Norway at the time of the study.

Table 4.1. Minimum capital requirements

Country	Minimum capital (€)	Paid up capital (€)
Austria	35,000	17,500
Denmark	16,800	16,800
Germany	25,000	12,500
Greece	18,000	18,000
Hungary	12,170	12,170
Luxembourg	12,500	12,500
Netherlands	18,000	18,000
Poland	12,460	12,460
Sweden	10,650	10,650

Source: Adapted from Table 6 of M Becht, C Mayer, and HF Wagner, 'Where Do Forms Incorporate?', ECEI—Law Working Paper No 70/2006.

In a series of important decisions, the European Court of Justice (ECJ) has established that it is not a fraud or a breach of EC Treaty freedoms for the founders of a business to incorporate a private company in a Member State that does not impose minimum capital requirements in order to bypass such requirements in the domestic laws of the Member State in which the controllers of the business are located and where the company is intended wholly or mainly to trade. The breakthrough decision, *Centros Ltd v Erhvervs- og Selskabsstyrelsen*,[25] involved a British company, Centros, that never traded in the UK and whose controllers were Danish residents. The decision to use a British company as the corporate vehicle was driven by the difference in approach to minimum capital between the UK and Denmark. The ECJ held that it was contrary to EC law for Erhvervs- og Selskabsstyrelsen (a Danish authority) to refuse to register in Denmark a branch of Centros.

In *Kamer van Koophandel en Fabrieken voor Amsterdam v Inspire Art Ltd*,[26] which again involved a British limited company which was used to conduct business in another Member State that had substantial minimum capital requirements for private companies in its domestic law (the Netherlands), the ECJ confirmed that it was immaterial, having regard to the application of the rules on freedom of establishment, that a company was formed in one Member State only for the purpose of establishing itself in a second Member State, where its main, or even entire, business was to be conducted. The reasons for which a company chose to be formed in a particular Member State were, save in the case of fraud, irrelevant with regard to application of the rules on freedom of establishment. The fact that a company was formed in a particular Member State for the sole purpose of enjoying the benefit of more favourable legislation did not constitute abuse even if that company conducted its activities entirely or mainly in a second state. In this case the ECJ determined that it was contrary to EC law for the Netherlands

---

[25] C-212/97, [1999] ECR I-1459.
[26] Case C-167/01, [2003] ECR I-10155.

to seek to restrict the exercise of freedom of secondary establishment by a British company by requiring it to comply with requirements of Dutch law relating to minimum capital and directors' liability.

In the period immediately after *Centros* there was a noticeable trend for small firms to opt for incorporation as a British private limited company even though, in terms of the residence of their directors and owners and the location of their main centre of activity, their nationality was that of another EU Member State. An empirical study of UK incorporations between 1997 and 2005 found that between 2002 and 2005 over 55,000 new UK private limited companies were set up from other EU Member States.[27] Using statistical analysis, the study established a link between the outflow of private limited companies to the UK from a number of EU Member States and minimum capital requirements and other incorporation costs in those states. In absolute numbers, firms obtaining *Centros*-style incorporations after 2002 came mainly from Germany, the Netherlands, and France. Germany and the Netherlands, were among the countries that, at the time of the study, imposed substantial minimum capital requirements on private limited companies. France also did so until 2003, when it reformed its law so as to cancel the mandatory minimum capital requirement for private companies.[28] The study noted that, after that change in its laws, France experienced much lower outflows. Thereafter, Germany and the Netherlands also reconsidered their position. In May 2006, the German Federal Ministry of Justice issued a preliminary draft proposal for a reform of the law on limited liability companies that included a measure to reduce the statutory minimum capital from €25,000 to €10,000, of which €5,000 would actually have to be paid up on incorporation.[29] In November 2006, the Dutch Council of Ministers approved a Bill to simplify Dutch private company law and sent it to the Council of State for advice. The Bill, expected to become law in 2007–8, will abolish the minimum capital requirement along with other formalities for setting up a Dutch private company.[30]

It is possible to characterize the post-*Centros* developments in Europe as an example of regulatory competition at work. Regulatory competition is a theoretical model in which states are seen as suppliers in a competitive product market, with the product being regulation, and market participants who choose between different sets of national law are regarded as the consumers of the product.

[27] Becht, Mayer and Wagner (n 24 above).

[28] I Urbain-Parléane, 'Working Group on the Share Capital in Europe—French Answers to the Questionnaire', in M Lutter (ed), *Legal Capital in Europe*, a special volume of the European Company and Financial Law Review (2006), 480.

[29] On the progress of this proposal see U Noack and DA Zetzsche, 'Germany's Corporate and Financial Law 2007: (Getting) Ready for Competition', CBC-RPS No 0028 (June 2007) available at SSRN <http://ssrn.com/abstract=986357>.

[30] <http://www.ez.nl/content.jsp?objectid=150533> (accessed December 2007). On the background to the proposals in the Bill, see H-J de Kluiver and SFG Rammeloo, 'Capital and Capital Protection in the Netherlands: A Doctrine in Flux' in Lutter (ed) (n 28 above) 558.

A precondition to the operation of regulatory competition is that the consumers must have freedom of choice: this was supplied by the ECJ in the *Centros* case, which put beyond doubt the legal validity of corporate mobility with regard to incorporation. Theorists suggest that regulatory competition is a reliable mechanism to enable policymakers to discover what people actually want.[31] It is evident from recent experience that mandatory minimum capital requirements are not in line with the preferences of many founders of businesses in corporate form—but what of people who deal with them? On this matter, the ECJ has made it clear that there is nothing about minimum capital requirements that can be regarded as a public interest justification for Member States to restrict Treaty freedoms by imposing them on companies incorporated elsewhere in the Community that are operating in their territory: protection for those dealing with such companies is provided instead under the company laws of the country of incorporation. Applying regulatory competition reasoning, we can thus conclude that national lawmakers have learnt from real experience that minimum capital requirements are not worth keeping, have incorporated that discovery into their policy formation process, and are amending their laws in order to maintain international competitiveness.

At the moment, the position for public companies is quite different from that in relation to private companies because all EU incorporated public companies are subject to a minimum capital requirement derived from Article 6 of the Second Company Law Directive. The amount of the minimum capital as specified in the Directive is not less than €25,000.[32] The UK 'over-implements' the Directive by specifying a minimum allotted capital requirement of £50,000 in nominal value or its euro equivalent, which on current exchange rates, would be considerably more than €25,000. Newly-formed public companies are required to have an allotted capital of at least this amount before they can obtain the trading certificate that allows them to do any business or exercise any borrowing powers.[33] Having an allotted capital of at least that amount is also a condition that must be satisfied before a private company can re-register as a public company.[34] However, not all of the £50,000 in nominal value needs to be paid up at the time of obtaining a trading certificate or, as the case may be, re-registration. The rules relating to payment for shares in a public company include a requirement that at least one-quarter of the nominal value must be paid up on allotment,[35] so the minimum amount that must actually be put in is £12,500 (50,000 x ¼).

---

[31] JM Sun and J Pelkmans, 'Regulatory Competition in the Single Market' (1995) 33 *Journal of Common Market Studies* 67, 82- 8.

[32] Second Company Law Directive, Art 6 in its original form referred to 25,000 European units of account (ECUs). The ECU was replaced by the euro for the purposes of Community legislation including the Second Directive with effect from 1 January 1999.

[33] Companies Act 2006, s 761.

[34] ibid ss 90–91.

[35] ibid s 586. There is an exception for shares allotted in pursuance of an employees' shares scheme (s 586(2)) but such shares do not count for the purposes of the minimum capital requirement

Denomination of minimum capital

By way of a qualification to the general freedom with regard to having a multi-currency share capital,[36] the minimum share capital requirement must be satisfied by reference either to allotted share capital denominated in sterling or to allotted share capital denominated in euros (but not partly in one and partly in the other).[37] In determining whether a company has satisfied the minimum capital requirement, no account is to be taken of any of its allotted share capital that is denominated in a currency other than sterling or, as the case may be, euros.[38] Once a company has obtained its trading certificate or re-registered, it can subsequently redenominate its share capital, including that part of it that constituted its minimum capital, into any other currency.[39] In several respects these requirements with regard to minimum capital are more flexible than was the case prior to the Companies Act 2006. By expressly permitting sterling or its euro equivalent and allowing redenomination, the 2006 Act departs from some very cautious interpretations of Article 6 of the Second Company Law Directive, which were to the effect that it could oblige the UK to require public companies to have and retain a tranche of their capital denominated in sterling in order to satisfy the minimum capital requirement. Yet, even though the Companies Act 2006 strips the minimum capital requirement down to a relatively unburdensome form, the position remains unsatisfactory because it forces public companies that do not want to have a tranche of sterling or euro denominated shares to go through a series of procedural steps that are of no apparent substantive benefit to anyone in order eventually to achieve that result.

Why might a company want to have a share capital denominated in a currency other than sterling or in a mixture of currencies, of which sterling is only one? One reason, which was relevant in *Re Scandinavian Bank Group plc*,[40] where the pre-2006 Act position was considered, is capital adequacy considerations.[41] Banks and other financial firms are subject to capital adequacy requirements that measure their capital against their assets. Where the capital and the assets are expressed in different currencies, the proportion of capital to assets may be eroded simply through exchange rate fluctuations. This problem can be eliminated by matching the denomination of the capital to that of the assets.

unless they have actually been paid up to at least one-quarter of their nominal value and any premium (s 761(3)). The same requirements apply to private companies seeking to re-register as public companies: ibid s 91(1)(b) and (2)(b).

[36] See ibid s 542(3).

[37] ibid s 765.

[38] ibid s 765(3).

[39] The redenomination procedure is contained in Companies Act 2006, ss 622–628. Note also ibid s 766.

[40] [1987] 2 All ER 70, [1987] BCC 93.

[41] N Daubney and N Cannon 'Converting to Multi-currency Share Capital in the UK' (1987) 6(5) *International Financial Law Review* 7.

All companies, including those that are not subject to capital adequacy requirements, face a similar problem if they have covenanted in loan agreements or other
contractual documents to maintain certain debt to equity ratios and the debt
and equity are denominated in different currencies. Companies in this position
may want to match the denomination or denominations of their capital to that
of their debts. A company may also want to have a multi-currency share capital
in order to attract foreign investors, or to encourage foreign vendors to accept the
company's shares as consideration.[42] More generally, companies with extensive
international operations may wish to have a multi-currency share capital in order
to match their capital base to their international earnings, to facilitate the raising
of capital from international equity markets or to reflect their status as significant
international businesses.[43]

Is any valuable purpose served by minimum capital requirements?

The thinking behind mandatory minimum capital requirements is that they are
intended to protect creditors by ensuring that companies have some substance
behind them in the form of permanent equity capital that cannot be withdrawn
at will by the shareholders. However, a simple rule such as that in the Second
Company Law Directive in reality fails to deliver meaningful creditor protection because it is not tailored to the financial needs of specific companies and
does nothing to prevent capital being lost in the course of business.[44] The High
Level Group of Company Law Experts that, in 2002, advised the European
Commission on European company law reform, explicitly noted the limitations
of the Second Company Law Directive in this respect: that Group concluded that
the only function actually performed by the minimum capital requirement was
to deter individuals from 'lightheartedly starting a public limited company'.[45]

It is not difficult to think of ways in which minimum capital requirements
could be reinforced with a view to increasing their effectiveness as a creditor protection mechanism but the potential negative consequences of imposing more
stringent capital requirements also need to be kept in mind. For instance, one
apparently straightforward reinforcement step would be to increase the amount

---

[42] The use of foreign currency denominated shares for this purpose is discussed by D Lewis,
'Foreign Currency Share Capital' (1993) 4(10) Practical Law for Companies 23.

[43] These were among the factors identified as being reasons to consider redenomination in
response to the introduction of the euro: DTI, 'The Euro: Redenomination of Share Capital',
Consultative Document, (1998) para 1.6; G Yeowart, 'The Equity Markets and Company Share
Capital: Planning for the Euro' [1998] 8 *Journal of International Banking Law* 269; C Proctor,
'Share Capital and the Euro' (1998) 9(3) *Practical Law for Companies* 17.

[44] The role of minimum capital requirements as a creditor protection mechanism is much discussed. Recent discussions include: W Schön, 'The Future of Legal Capital' (2004) 5 *European
Business Organization Law Review* 429; M Miola, 'Legal Capital and Limited Liability Companies:
the European Perspective' (2004) 4 *European Company and Financial Law Review* 413.

[45] High Level Group, Report (n 18 above) 82.

of mandatory minimum capital. However, if the level were to be set too high, that could operate as a barrier to growth and entrepreneurship and could impede competition. To minimize that risk, policymakers contemplating the imposition of higher minimum capital requirements for companies generally, would need to take on the complex task of designing a carefully calibrated set of requirements that achieved a degree of commensurability between the specific risks undertaken by individual companies and the amount of capital that each of them was required to hold. Whilst it is certainly possible for policymakers to do this, as is demonstrated by the sophisticated and complex capital adequacy frameworks within which banks and other financial institutions must operate, it could involve a huge investment in regulatory design and in the establishment of an accompanying supervisory regime, as well as very significant compliance costs for the regulated entities. An outlay of this magnitude may be justifiable where the soundness and stability of the financial system are at stake but few would regard it as being an acceptable price to pay to counter the risks that creditors face in dealing with limited liability commercial companies. That there are market mechanisms whereby creditors can influence the amount of permanent equity capital invested in a company should not be overlooked, nor should the fact that the market can operate much more flexibly than any regulatory regime could ever be designed to do (although this is not to deny that market mechanisms have imperfections too).[46] Companies in different sectors and at different stages of their development will have different financing needs and the ratio of debt to equity in their capital structure will represent the cumulative effect of financing arrangements entered into over time by reference to their then current stage of development and market conditions at that time. For instance, companies at an early stage of development that have few physical assets to offer as collateral to banks and no credit ratings to access bond markets, are likely to have to rely heavily on equity to finance their business.

Another option for reinforcement of minimum capital requirements would be to require capital to be topped up by an injection of fresh equity when it is no longer represented by assets. The Second Company Law Directive does not contain a requirement to this effect and there is none in the UK Companies Act 2006. All that the Directive does is to require that in the event of a serious loss of subscribed capital, a general meeting of shareholders must be called to consider whether the company should be wound up or any other measures taken.[47] As this requirement is applied in the UK, the obligation to hold a meeting is triggered only when the net assets of a public company have fallen to half or less of the value of the nominal value of its capital.[48] As such, it is likely to operate

[46] Ch 7 below, discusses further the interplay between the market and regulation in creditor protection.

[47] Second Company Law Directive, Art 17 and Companies Act 2006, s 656.

[48] s 656 refers to 'called up' share capital and the definition of called up share capital (s 547) points towards the conclusion that this does not include share premiums.

only in very extreme circumstances when a company's financial difficulties may already be becoming obvious, thus rendering redundant any disclosure functions that the obligation to convene a shareholders' meeting might serve, and the location of real decision-making power about its future may well have already shifted from the shareholders to the creditors. Some European countries go further and impose 'recapitalize or liquidate' obligations.[49] However, such rules have to be viewed with caution from a policy perspective because they are liable to distort corporate rescue efforts and have the potential to be used opportunistically in situations where shareholders are in dispute with each other, as one group could manipulate things to dilute the control of another group that cannot afford to contribute to the recapitalization.[50]

Rather than pondering on ways in which minimum capital requirements could be made more effective, it is more in line with current policy thinking in the UK, and increasingly in continental Europe generally,[51] to suggest that minimum capital has lost credibility as a creditor protection mechanism and that for public companies either it should be abolished outright or left to wither away gradually by not adjusting the amount in line with inflation so that over time the amount that needs to be invested becomes increasingly trivial.[52] Moreover, the option of applying a new pan-European minimum capital requirement to private companies now appears to be dead for all practical purposes, given that it is directly contrary to the policies that Member States are adopting within their domestic laws. In declining to accept arguments that sought to justify national minimum capital requirements on public interest grounds, the ECJ, in the *Centros* line of cases, has made it impossible to argue that minimum capital is an indispensable cornerstone of creditor protection and has indicated that, in so far as creditor

[49] M Miola, 'Legal Capital Rules in Italian Company Law and the EU Perspective' in M Lutter (ed), *Legal Capital in Europe*, a special volume of the European Company and Financial Law Review (2006) 515, 527–8 (discussing the Italian rule and describing it as less strict than that elsewhere, eg France). Spain also has stringent recapitalize or liquidate rules: JME Irujo, 'Capital Protection in Spanish Company Law' in Lutter (ed) (above) 582, 593–4.

[50] L Enriques and J Macey, 'Creditors Versus Capital Formation: The Case Against the European Legal Capital Rules' (2001) 86 *Cornell Law Review* 1165.

[51] However, note a recent German study that suggests that from a legal policy point of view, a reasonable increase of the minimum capital as an allowance for inflation must be considered with regard to possible revision of the Second Company Law Directive: H Eidenmüller, B Grunewald, and U Niack, 'Minimum Capital in the System of Legal Capital' in Lutter (ed) (n 49 above) 17, 40. Yet these authors do not appear to have a strong conviction about the practical merits of mandatory minimum capital: 'it must be stressed that the symbolic significance of this issue for the (supposed) modernisation of corporate law far exceeds its economic relevance' (at 30). Some other contributors to the same volume also express views that are moderately in favour of retention of mandatory minimum capital requirements: see, eg A Kidyba, S Soltysiński, and A Szumański, 'A Report on Selected Aspects of Legal Capital under Polish Code of Commercial Companies' Lutter (ed) (above) 597, 618.

[52] High Level Group, Report (n 18 above) 82 inclines towards the 'do nothing' option. Compare J Rickford (ed), 'Reforming Capital: Report of the Interdisciplinary Group on Capital Maintenance' [2004] *European Business Law Review* 919, 931 n 33: 'In our view useless provisions are always worth repealing' (Jonathan Rickford was a member of the High Level Group).

protection is part of company law's role, the requisite level of protection can be delivered in other ways.

Allotted, issued, and equity share capital

This section considers the interpretation of the terms 'allotted' and 'issued' and outlines key procedural formalities that are associated with the share allotment and issuance process.

Allotted share capital

References in the Companies Acts to 'allotted share capital' are to shares of a company that have been allotted.[53] Generally the term allotment when used in respect of shares is not a term of art.[54] In *Spitzel v The Chinese Corporation Ltd*[55] Stirling J answered the general question 'What is an allotment of shares?' by saying: 'Broadly speaking, it is an appropriation by the directors or the managing body of the company of shares to a particular person.' In *Nicol's Case*[56] Chitty J, however, equated allotment with the forming of a binding contract to take shares. The key distinction between these two interpretations is that appropriation could take place before a contract is concluded: it could happen when an offer to subscribe for shares is accepted but before the acceptance is communicated so as to form a contract, or it could even take place before acceptance where, as in a rights issue, the directors resolve that certain shares are to be allotted to particular persons and make an offer of those shares.[57] In line with the view that allotment may take place before there is a binding contract to take shares is *Re The Saloon Stream Packet Co Ltd, Fletcher's Case*,[58] where three stages in a contract to take shares were identified, namely an application for shares, an allotment and, finally, communication of and acquiescence in the allotment. In relation to timing, for the purposes of the Companies Acts a share in a company is taken to be allotted when a person acquires the unconditional right to be included in the company's register of members in respect of it.[59] A right to be included in the company's register of members would usually be derived from a contract to take shares. A contract

[53] Companies Act 2006, s 546(1)(b).
[54] *Re Florence Land and Public Works Co, Nicol's case* (1885) 29 Ch D 421, Ch D and CA, 427 *per* Chitty J; *Re Ambrose Lake Tin and Copper Co (Clarke's Case)* (1878) 8 Ch D 635, CA; *Re Compania de Electricidad* [1980] 1 Ch 146, 182; *Whitehouse v Carlton Hotel Pty Ltd* (1987) 70 ALR 251, H Ct of Aust, 271 *per* Brennan J.
[55] (1899) 80 LT 347.
[56] *Re Florence Land and Public Works Co, Nicol's case* (1885) 29 Ch D 421, Ch D and CA.
[57] *Spitzel v Chinese Corp Ltd* (1899) 80 LT 347; *Re Compania de Electricidad* [1980] 1 Ch 146, 182.
[58] (1867) 17 LT 136. See also *Re Scottish Petroleum Co* (1883) 23 Ch D 413, CA.
[59] Companies Act 2006, s 558.

to take shares is in essence no different from any other contract and the normal contractual rules, including those of offer and acceptance, apply. Accordingly, it would be possible for an offer of shares to be withdrawn before a contract is formed by communication of acceptance.

One case where a person may acquire the right to be included in the company's register of members otherwise than by contract is in a bonus issue of shares.[60] A bonus issue of shares means an issue of new shares to the existing shareholders where the subscription price is met by the company out of funds which it is permitted to apply for that purpose. In *Re Cleveland Trust plc* [61] Scott J held that the relationship between company and shareholder vis-à-vis an authorized bonus issue may not be strictly contractual; but unless the issue is for some reason fundamentally flawed,[62] the person to whom the shares are offered, or the person to whom he has renounced the offer, acquires a right to be included in the company's register of members in respect of the bonus shares.

Authority to allot shares

Issues relating to the authority of directors to allot shares and the pre-emption rights of existing shareholders in respect of any new share issue are considered in chapter 5 below.

Registration of allotment and return of allotments

A company is obliged to register an allotment of shares as soon as practicable and in any event within two months after the date of allotment.[63] Non-compliance with this obligation constitutes a criminal offence by the company and every officer who is in default.[64]

Under section 555 of the Companies Act 2006, within one month after the making of an allotment, a limited company must deliver to the registrar of companies for registration a return of the allotment which notifies details of the allotment, again under penalty under criminal sanctions attaching to the company and defaulting officers in the event of non-compliance.[65] The return must be accompanied by a statement of capital stating with respect to the company's share capital at the date to which the return is made up:

---

[60] The term 'issue' is used here because 'bonus issue' is common parlance. It is not meant to have any particular technical significance.

[61] [1991] BCLC 424, 434–5.

[62] As it was in the *Cleveland* case where the purported issue was held to be void for mistake. *Cleveland* was applied in *EIC Services Ltd v Phipps* [2005] 1 All ER 338, CA where a bonus issue was held to be void for mistake.

[63] Companies Act 2006, s 554.

[64] ibid s 554(3).

[65] ibid s 557.

(1) the total number of shares of the company;

(2) the aggregate nominal value of those shares;

(3) for each class of shares:

    (a) prescribed particulars of the rights attaching to the shares,

    (b) the total number of shares of that class, and

    (c) the aggregate nominal value of shares of that class, and

(4) the amount paid up and the amount (if any) unpaid on each share (whether on account of the nominal value of the share or by way of premium).[66]

Issued share capital and issued shares

References in the Companies Act 2006 to 'issued share capital' are to shares of a company that have been issued.[67] What constitutes the issue of a share? In *Levy v Abercorris Slate and Slab Co*,[68] a case that concerned an issue of debentures, Chitty J said:[69] '"issued" is not a technical term, it is a mercantile term well understood'. This comment is equally applicable to an issue of shares. It is very common in practice for the terms 'issued' and 'allotted' to be used interchangeably, as if they meant the same thing and as if both events happened at precisely the same time. However, since the word 'issued' takes its colour from the context in which it is used, in particular situations it may be used to mean something different from 'allotted'. In particular, in certain contexts a share which has been allotted may not be regarded as an issued share. The converse is generally not true—a share is normally taken to be issued at some point after it has been allotted; exceptionally, however, in *Mosely v Koffyfontein Mines Ltd*,[70] a case which concerned the construction of articles of association dealing with increase of share capital, Farwell LJ put the order of the three separate steps in the life of a new share as being creation, issue, and allotment.[71]

In *Ambrose Lake Tin and Copper Co (Clarke's Case)*[72] a reference in the Companies Act 1867 to the issue of shares was taken to mean something different from, and later than, their allotment. Also, in various cases concerned with construction of tax legislation employing the term, the term 'issue' has been interpreted to mean something other than, and subsequent to, allotment.[73] But what does 'issued'

---

[66] ibid s 557(4).

[67] ibid s 546(1)(a).

[68] (1887) 37 Ch D 260.

[69] At 264. See also *Spitzel v Chinese Corp Ltd* (1899) 80 LT 347; *National Westminster Bank plc v IRC* [1995] 1 AC 119, HL.

[70] [1911] 1 Ch 73, CA.

[71] At 84. See also *Whitehouse v Carlton Hotel Pty Ltd* (1987) 70 ALR 251, H Ct of Aust, 271 *per* Brennan J.

[72] (1878) 8 Ch D 635.

[73] eg *Oswald Tillotson Ltd v IRC* [1933] 1 KB 134, CA; *Brotex Cellulose Fibres Ltd v IRC* [1933] 1 KB 158; *Murex Ltd v Commissioners of Inland Revenue* [1933] 1 KB 173.

mean where it is used to mean something other than 'allotted', and where issue is thought to be subsequent to allotment? Again the answer to this question ultimately depends on the context in which the term is used[74] but a view that has attracted considerable support is that the distinction between allotment and issue of a share mirrors that between being a shareholder and being a member of a company. A person to whom a share has been allotted may be a shareholder[75] but that person does not become a member until registered as such on the company's register of members.[76] A shareholder is entitled to dividends in respect of the shares but rights such as attending meetings and voting on resolutions are membership rights which are held by members and not by mere shareholders.[77] Thus in *Oswald Tillotson Ltd v IRC*[78] the Court of Appeal equated the word 'issue', as used in certain tax legislation, with the creation of a registered shareholder. In *Agricultural Mortgage Corp v IRC*[79] Walton J, at first instance, and Goff LJ in the Court of Appeal, also inclined to the view that for the purpose of certain tax legislation 'issue' took place on registration.[80] The meaning of 'issue' for the purpose of certain tax legislation was considered by the House of Lords in *National Westminster Bank plc v IRC*.[81] As in the earlier tax cases, it was held that issue followed allotment and was completed by the entry of the names of the holders of the shares on the company's register of members. Lord Lloyd (in the majority) agreed that the interpretation of the term depended on its context and considered that the interpretation favoured by the majority was appropriate for the context of company law.

Except in this section (or where specifically indicated) the common practice of using the terms 'issued' and 'allotted' interchangeably is adopted in this chapter and elsewhere in this book.

Equity share capital

For the purposes of the companies legislation, 'equity share capital' means issued share capital excluding any part of that capital that, neither as respects dividends nor as respects capital, carries any right to participate beyond a specified amount in a distribution.[82]

---

[74] In *Central Piggery Co Ltd v McNicoll* (1949) 78 CLR 594, H Ct of Aust, 599 Dixon J interpreted the word 'issue' to mean a step after allotment whereby the shareholder is put in control of the shares allotted.
[75] ibid 599 *per* Dixon J.
[76] For registration as a member, see Companies Act 2006, s 112.
[77] *Spitzel v Chinese Corp Ltd* (1899) 80 LT 347.
[78] [1933] 1 KB 134, CA.
[79] [1978] Ch 72, CA.
[80] 'Or possibly some other act' 85 *per* Walton J, or 'the issue of a certificate' 101 *per* Goff LJ. However, the view that a share is only issued when registration *and* the issue of a share certificate takes place has been rejected: *Re Heaton's Steel and Slab Co (Blyth's Case)* (1876) 4 Ch D 140, CA explaining *Re Imperial River Co (Bush's Case)* (1874) 9 Ch App 554, CA; *Re Ambrose Lake Tin and Copper Co (Clarke's Case)* (1878) 8 Ch D 635, CA.
[81] [1995] 1 AC 119, HL.
[82] Companies Act 2006, s 548.

Payment for shares

Introduction

The next part of this chapter is concerned with the rules governing payment for shares. This is a very detailed and complex area of company law, especially for public companies where the forms of consideration that they may accept for their shares are very closely regulated. These rules are intended to protect creditors and shareholders against companies accepting consideration that is in fact worth less than the issue price of their shares.[83] It is debatable whether such extensive regulation of public company share capital as is now contained in the companies legislation is necessary or desirable, but many of the requirements are derived from the Second Company Law Directive and, barring changes at the European level, this precludes meaningful change to the domestic law. In 2006, certain modest changes were made to the Second Directive in the interests of simplification and modernization but the revising Directive largely left it to Member States to decide whether to apply the revised rules.[84] In February 2007, the UK announced that it did not intend to implement the relatively limited changes permitted by the amending Directive. Its view was that the relaxation of the requirements might provide some additional degree of flexibility for companies but that it would also increase legislation in an already complex area of company law. After consultation, the government changed its position slightly and indicated that it would make a few modest changes permitted by the amending Directive.[85] However, in overall terms, its preference remained to wait for a more fundamental review into alternatives to the capital maintenance regime established by the Second Directive.[86]

Paid up share capital

A company's paid up share capital means the amount of capital money it has received in respect of its issued shares. Unless the context indicates otherwise,

---

[83] Second Company Law Directive (EEC) 77/91 [1977] OJ L26/1 provides: 'whereas in order to ensure minimum equivalent protection for both shareholders and creditors of public limited companies, the co-ordination of national provisions relating to their formation, and to the maintenance, increase or reduction of their capital is particularly important'.

[84] Directive (EC) 2006/68 of the European Parliament and of the Council of 6 September 2006 amending Council Directive (EEC) 77/91 as regards the formation of public limited liability companies and the maintenance and alteration of their capital [2006] OJ L264/32.

[85] By a written Ministerial Statement: *Hansard*, HC, vol 462, col 23WS (26 June 2007).

[86] DTI, 'Implementation of Companies Act 2006 Consultative Document' (February 2007) paras 6.8–6.26. On the European simplification agenda, see European Commission, 'Communication on a Simplified Business Environment for Companies in the Areas of Company Law, Accounting and Auditing' (COM (2007) 394).

it does not include share premiums.[87] As noted earlier, there is no minimum amount that must be paid up on the allotment (or issue) of a share in a private company. Except for shares allotted in pursuance of an employees' share scheme, public companies must not allot a share except as paid up at least as to one-quarter of its nominal value and the whole of any premium on it.[88] If a share is allotted in contravention of this requirement, the allottee is liable to pay the minimum amount the company should have received (less any amount actually paid), with interest.[89] Subsequent holders of a share allotted in breach of this rule may also incur liability.[90] Subsequent holders (but not original allottees) may apply to court to be relieved of their liability.[91]

Called up share capital

Called up share capital means so much of a company's share capital as equals the aggregate amount of the calls made on its shares (whether or not those calls have been paid), together with;

(1) any share capital paid up without being called; and
(2) any share capital to be paid on a specified future date under the articles, the terms of allotment, or any other arrangements for payment of those shares.[92]

It is common for shares to be issued fully paid. This means that, in the ordinary case, the amount of a company's called up share capital will thus equal that of its paid up share capital. However, the called up share capital could be a larger amount where shares are issued partly paid. For example, where shares are issued on a partly paid basis and the terms of the allotment provide for payment of the balance by instalments, limb (2) of the definition above would mean that the outstanding amount of the capital that remains to be paid is included in the company's called up share capital. Note that the definition refers only to 'share capital'. Share premiums are not part of the share capital and therefore the share premium account does not constitute part of the called up capital.

Cash consideration for shares

A share is deemed to be paid up in cash or allotted for cash if the consideration is:

---

[87] This follows from Companies Act 2006, s 610(4) which requires the share premium account to be treated *as if it were* part of the paid up share capital (emphasis added).

[88] This rule is derived from the Second Company Law Directive, Arts 9 and 26.

[89] Companies Act 2006, s 586(3). In the case of an allotment of bonus shares, this liability does not apply except where the allottee knew or ought to have known of the contravention (s 586(4)).

[90] Companies Act 2006, s 588.

[91] ibid s 589.

[92] ibid s 547.

(1) cash received by the company;
(2) a cheque received by the company in good faith which its directors have no reason for suspecting will not be paid;
(3) a release of a liability of the company for a liquidated sum;
(4) an undertaking to pay cash to the company at a later date; or
(5) payment by some other means giving rise to a present or future entitlement (of the company or of a person acting on the company's behalf) to a payment, or a credit equivalent to payment, in cash.[93]

It is expressly provided that 'cash' in this context includes foreign currency.[94] Also expressly stated in the legislation is that the payment of cash, or any undertaking to pay cash, to any person other than the company is a form of non-cash consideration.[95]

Case law has shed some further light on the meaning of cash in this context. It has been held that an undertaking to pay cash at a later date in (4) means an undertaking given to the company in return for the allotment; it does not include the assignment of a pre-existing debt to the company as consideration for the allotment.[96] The scenario of a company that acquires assets on credit and then pays for them by allotting shares to the vendor has also been judicially considered. Because 'cash' includes the release of a liability for a liquidated sum, the shares would prima facie be allotted for cash in this case. In *Re Bradford Investments plc (No 2)*[97] Hoffmann J, referring to this type of situation, commented: 'I would not wish to give the impression that an artificial resort to two documents instead of one could be used to avoid the provisions [requiring independent valuation of non-cash consideration for shares].'[98] However, whilst the courts may be expected to be vigilant to ensure that statutory requirements are not evaded, where there is no question of the two stages of the transaction being artificial or a sham, it appears that the shares will be treated as having been allotted for cash.[99]

Shares must not be issued at a discount

Shares may not be allotted at less than their par value. Originally this rule was established by case law[100] and it is now enshrined in section 580 of the

---

[93] ibid s 583(3). The Secretary of State may by order provide that particular means of payment specified in the order are to be regarded as falling within (5) (s 583(4)).

[94] ibid s 583(6).

[95] ibid s 583(5).

[96] *System Controls plc v Munro Corporate plc* [1990] BCC 386.

[97] [1991] BCC 379.

[98] Independent valuation requirements are considered further below.

[99] *Re Harmony and Montague Tin and Copper Mining Co, Spargo's Case* (1873) 8 Ch App 407, CA.

[100] *Ooregum Gold Mining Co of India v Roper* [1892] AC 125, HL; *Re Eddystone Marine Insurance Co* [1893] 3 Ch 9 CA; *Welton v Saffery* [1897] AC 299, HL.

Companies Act 2006.[101] If the rule is contravened, the allottee is liable to pay the company an amount equal to the amount of the discount, together with interest.[102] Subsequent holders of shares that were allotted at less than par may also be liable to pay up the shares in full.[103] Section 589 of the Companies Act 2006, which permits applications to court for relief from liability arising from failure to comply with certain of the requirements of the Act regarding the allotment of shares, does not apply in the case of the liability of the allottee to pay the amount of the discount, but subsequent holders may apply for relief from this liability. The directors who authorized the allotment at a discount may also be liable to the company for breach of duty.[104] A contract to allot shares at a discount at a later date is void and cannot be enforced by either party.[105]

The no-discount rule and convertible securities

In *Mosely v Koffyfontein Mines Ltd*[106] the Court of Appeal analysed a proposal to issue convertible debentures at a discount to their par value where the debentures could immediately be converted into fully paid shares having a par value equal to the par value of the debentures. The Court of Appeal held that the issue of the debentures on the proposed terms was open to abuse as it could be used to circumvent the no-discount rule and, on that basis, granted an injunction to restrain the making of the issue. Cozens-Hardy LJ expressly left open the question of a debenture issued at a discount to its par value which conferred a right at some future date to demand a fully paid share in exchange for the par value of the debenture.[107] This situation is different from that where debentures issued at a discount are immediately convertible into fully paid shares having a par value equal to the par value of the debentures: in the former case the discount can be explained because it represents the investors' return without which, they would (presumably) have demanded a higher rate of interest; in the latter case it is difficult to find any explanation for the discount other than it being a backhanded way of allowing shares to be allotted at a discount. So interpreted, the decision in the *Mosely* case does not prevent the issue of convertible debentures at a discount where the conversion right is not immediately exercisable. There can be no hard and fast rule governing the length of time that would have to elapse between issue of the debentures and permitted exercise of the conversion rights. It would presumably depend on whether there is a genuine reason for the discount: if there is, even a short delay might suffice.

---

[101] For public companies this implements Second Company Law Directive, Art 8.
[102] Companies Act 2006, s 580(2).
[103] ibid s 588.
[104] *Hirsche v Sims* [1894] AC 654, PC.
[105] *Re Almada and Tirito Co* (1888) 38 Ch D 415, CA.
[106] [1904] 2 Ch 108, CA.
[107] [1904] 2 Ch 108, CA, 120.

When shares are allotted on conversion of convertible debentures, are they allotted for cash? Ultimately the answer to this question depends on the conversion mechanism in the terms of the debentures. In the *Mosely* case Vaughan-Williams LJ thought that shares allotted upon conversion of convertible debentures were allotted for money's worth,[108] but Cozens-Hardy LJ explained the conversion as involving the cancellation of a liquidated debt.[109] Where the issuer of the convertible securities and of the shares into which they convert is the same company, an allotment of shares in exchange for the release of the liquidated debt represented by the convertibles would be an allotment for cash according to the definition of that term in section 583(3)(c) of the Companies Act 2006.

Companies sometimes issue preference shares, or other shares carrying special rights, that are convertible at some point in the future into ordinary shares either of the same company or of another company in its group. A subscriber for shares does not become a creditor in respect of the amount subscribed and the conversion of a share would not constitute the release of a liability of the company for a liquidated sum. The conversion terms may provide for a return of capital to the shareholders (perhaps by the redemption of their shares) and subsequent application of the redemption proceeds in the subscription of new ordinary shares and, in that case, the conversion would involve an allotment of new shares for cash consideration.

The no-discount rule and underwriting commissions

A company is permitted, to a limited extent,[110] to use capital to pay underwriting commissions. This would permit, for example, the use of £2 per £100 subscribed for new £1 shares to pay a 2 per cent commission to the underwriters of the issue, provided this is consistent with the company's articles. If no subscribers can be found for the shares so that the underwriter has to take them itself this means, in effect, that for an issue of shares having an aggregate par value of £100 the underwriter only has to pay £98. This scenario is sometimes said to be an exception to the rule that shares may not be issued at a discount. This is a convenient shorthand but the strict technical position is that the company and the underwriter have mutual obligations—the underwriter to pay the full subscription money and the company to pay the commission—and to the extent of the level of the commission these obligations cancel each other out.[111]

---

[108] ibid 116.

[109] ibid 119.

[110] Companies Act 2006, ss 552–553. The payment must be authorized by the articles and must not exceed 10% of the issue price of the shares or the amount or rate authorized by the articles, whichever is the less. The use of capital in this way is sanctioned by the Second Company Law Directive, Art 8(2).

[111] *Metropolitan Coal Consumers Association v Scrimgeour* [1895] 2 QB 604, CA. The Court of Appeal had no doubt that using capital to pay commissions did not infringe the rule prohibiting the issue of shares at a discount.

Regulation of non-cash consideration for shares

Section 582(1) of the Companies Act 2006 provides that shares of public and private companies may be paid up either in money or in money's worth (including goodwill and know-how). There is one exception: shares taken by a subscriber to the memorandum of a public company must be paid up in cash.[112]

At common law, despite stressing the importance of the maintenance of capital doctrine as a device for protecting creditors and shareholders, the courts were reluctant to examine the adequacy of non-cash consideration for shares. In *Re Wragg Ltd*[113] the Court of Appeal accepted that the no-discount rule applied where a company allotted shares in consideration for the acquisition of property. But:

> ... if, however, the consideration which the company has agreed to accept as representing in money's worth, the nominal value of the shares be a consideration not clearly colourable nor illusory, then, in my judgement, the adequacy of the consideration cannot be impeached ... unless the contract can also be impeached; and I take it to be the law that it is not open to a [petitioner], unless he is able to impeach the agreement, to go into the adequacy of the consideration to show that the company have agreed to give an excessive value for what they have purchased.[114]

The Court of Appeal's approach in *Re Wragg Ltd* followed dicta in the opinions of the House of Lords in *Ooregum Gold Mining Co of India v Roper*[115] and also decisions in earlier cases[116] that established that a court could not interfere merely on the grounds that a company had, by issuing shares, overpaid for property and that only a dishonest or colourable transaction would allow the court to intervene.

Whether the consideration is colourable or illusory is one of fact to be decided by reference to the facts of each case.[117] Consideration that is clearly bad, such as past consideration[118] or consideration which permits an obvious money measure to be made showing that a discount was allowed,[119] will not be allowed to stand. The courts will not necessarily insist on a separate action to impeach a transaction involving the allotment of shares if the facts which go to establish that it is a colourable transaction are sufficiently plain to demonstrate that such an action would be little more than a technicality.[120] However, notwithstanding these

---

[112] Companies Act 2006, s 584.

[113] [1897] 1 Ch 796, CA.

[114] At 836 *per* ALS Smith LJ; see also at 830 *per* Lindley LJ.

[115] [1892] AC 125, HL.

[116] Cited in the judgments in *Re Wragg* [1897] 1 Ch 796, CA. See also *Re Theatrical Trust Ltd* [1895] 1 Ch 771.

[117] *Re Innes & Co Ltd* [1903] 2 Ch 254, CA, 262 *per* Vaughan Williams LJ.

[118] *Re Eddystone Marine Insurance Co* [1893] 3 Ch 9, CA (although in Scotland past consideration for shares has been accepted: *Park Business Interiors Ltd v Park* [1990] BCC 914, Court of Session, Outer House).

[119] *Re Theatrical Trust Ltd* [1895] 1 Ch 771.

[120] *Re White Star Line Ltd* [1938] 1 Ch 458.

cases, an overall assessment is that attempts to demonstrate that an agreement to issue shares in return for payment in kind rather than cash should be set aside as colourable or illusory have not often succeeded.[121]

Where shares of a public company are allotted for a non-cash consideration, the traditional reluctance to interfere has been replaced by stringent statutory rules derived from the Second Company Law Directive. Some of the requirements applicable to public companies are also relevant to a private company that is hoping to convert to a public company because the conversion may not proceed if those requirements have not been observed in respect of share issues in the period leading up to the proposed conversion.[122] The structure of the Second Directive is to prohibit forms of non-cash consideration for shares in a public company that are thought to be incapable of economic assessment,[123] namely undertakings to do work or perform services and long-term undertakings, and to permit other forms of non-cash consideration subject to independent valuation requirements. In the Companies Act 2006 the outright prohibitions are in chapter 5 of Part 17, whilst the independent valuation requirements are in chapter 6 of Part 17.

Public companies must not accept an undertaking to do work or perform services as consideration for shares

Under section 585 of the Companies Act 2006[124] a public company is prohibited from accepting in payment up of its shares, or any premium on them, an undertaking given by any person that he or another person should do work or perform services for the company or any other person. If a company accepts such an undertaking in payment up of its shares or any premium on them, the holder of the shares when they or the premium is treated as paid up (in whole or in part) by the undertaking is liable to pay to the company in respect of those shares an amount equal to the amount treated as paid up by the undertaking, together with interest.[125] The enforceability of the undertaking is unaffected.[126] Subsequent holders of the shares may also incur liability.[127] It is open to any person who is liable as a

---

[121] As noted in *Pilmer v Duke Group Ltd (in liquidation)* [2001] 2 BCLC 773, H Ct Aust, para 35.

[122] Companies Act 2006, s 93.

[123] Second Company Law Directive, Art 7. Technically Art 7 applies only to subscribed capital, which does not include share premiums. The Companies Act 2006 does not draw this distinction in its implementation of the rule.

[124] This section [over-]implements Second Company Law Directive, Art 7 with respect to premiums, as noted immediately above.

[125] Companies Act 2006, s 585(2).

[126] ibid s 591.

[127] ibid s 588.

result of a breach of the rule against such undertakings being an acceptable form of consideration for shares in a public company, to apply to the court for relief.[128]

A holder of shares for the purposes of this rule includes a person who has an unconditional right to be included in the register of members in respect of the shares or to have an instrument of transfer of them executed in his favour.[129] If shares are allotted as fully paid in return for an undertaking by the allottee, or another person, to do work or to perform services, liability under this rule will attach to the allottee. However, if the shares are allotted on a partly paid basis (which would be rare in practice) and the company later accepts from their then holder an undertaking to do work or perform services in payment up of the shares, that person would then incur liability under the statutory rule but previous holders of the shares, including the original allottee, would not incur statutory liability.

Public companies must not accept undertakings to be performed in the future as consideration for their shares

In addition to the absolute bar on accepting undertakings to do work or perform services in consideration for their shares, public companies are also restricted with regard to accepting other types of undertaking as consideration for their shares. Under section 587 of the Companies Act 2006 a public company must not allot shares as fully or partly paid up (as to their nominal value or any premium on them) otherwise than in cash if the consideration for the allotment is, or includes, an undertaking which is to be, or may be, performed more than five years after the date of the allotment.[130] The effect of contravening this rule is that the allottee is still liable to pay to the company an amount equal to the amount treated as paid up by the undertaking, with interest at the appropriate rate.[131] The enforceability of the undertaking is not affected.[132] Subsequent holders of the shares may also incur liability.[133] It is open to any person, whether allottee or subsequent holder, who incurs liability resulting from a contravention of the ban on long-term undertakings being good consideration for shares in a public company, to apply to court for relief under section 589 of the Companies Act 2006.

The prohibition in section 587 of the Companies Act 2006 extends to the variation of a contract where, had the varied terms been the original terms, the contract would have contravened the section.[134] Also caught is the case where a share is allotted in consideration of an undertaking which is to be performed within five

---

[128] Companies Act 2006, s 589.
[129] ibid s 585(3) and s 588(3).
[130] This rule is derived from Second Company Law Directive, Arts 9.2 and 27.1.
[131] ibid s 587(2).
[132] ibid s 591.
[133] ibid s 588.
[134] ibid s 587(3).

years of the allotment where the undertaking is not actually performed within the period allowed by the contract: at the end of the period allowed by the contract, the allottee then becomes liable to pay the company the amount which was treated as paid up by the undertaking, with interest.[135] Subsequent holder liability and applications to court for relief provisions apply here just as they would to a straightforward contravention of the section.

Valuation of non-cash consideration for shares in a public company

Section 593 of the Companies Act 2006 imposes a general requirement for independent valuation of any non-cash consideration for shares in a public company. A public company must not allot shares as fully or partly paid up (as to their nominal value or any premium on them) otherwise than in cash, unless the consideration has been independently valued and a valuation report has been made to the company in the six months preceding the allotment.[136] A copy of the valuation report must be sent to the proposed allottee before the allotment.[137] A copy of the valuation report must also be delivered to the registrar of companies when the company files the return of allotment of the shares required by section 555 of the Act.[138] The requirement for independent valuation of non-cash consideration is derived from the Second Directive.[139] However, the UK goes further than is strictly necessary to implement EC law because it applies the valuation requirement in respect of premium as well as nominal value, whereas the Directive is concerned with nominal value only.

The details of the valuation and report required by section 593 of the Companies Act 2006, are set out in sections 596 and 1149 to 1153.[140] The company must appoint as the independent valuer a person who would be qualified to be its auditor; it may appoint its current auditor.[141] The independent valuer so appointed may delegate the task of carrying out the valuation,[142] but has a non-delegable duty to produce a report stating a range of matters including a description of the consideration, the method used to value it, and the date of the valuation.[143] The independent valuer and the delegate (if any) are entitled to require from the officers of the company such information and explanations as they think necessary to enable them to carry out their responsibilities.[144] The sanction for knowingly

---

[135] ibid s 587(4).
[136] ibid s 593(1)(a)–(b).
[137] ibid s 593(1)(c).
[138] Companies Act 2006, s 597.
[139] This implements Second Company Law Directive, Arts 10 and 27.2.
[140] In *Re Ossory Estates plc* (1988) BCC 461, 463 Harman J described these requirements as 'curious and arcane'.
[141] Companies Act 2006, ss 1150–1151.
[142] ibid s 1150.
[143] ibid s 596.
[144] ibid s 1153.

or recklessly making a misleading, false, or deceptive statement in response to a proper inquiry is imprisonment, or a fine (or both).[145]

If the valuation requirements are not complied with, penal liability can attach to the allottee and also to subsequent holders of the shares. Even though the allottee may have duly conveyed assets of considerable value to the company, if the assets have not been duly valued, he can still be required to pay an amount equal to the aggregate of the nominal value and share premium that was treated as paid up by the non-cash consideration, together with interest. This liability attaches where the requirements for valuation have not been complied with and either (a) the allottee has not received the valuer's report; or (b) he knew or ought to have known that what has occurred amounted to a contravention of the statutory requirements relating to the valuation process.[146] Subsequent holders of shares allotted in contravention of the section 593 requirement of the Companies Act 2006 for independent valuation may also incur statutory liability.[147] However, there is the possibility of applying to court to be relieved of liability.[148]

The broad legislative policy underlying the penal liability that attaches to allottees and subsequent holders of shares in a public company that have been allotted for a non-cash consideration which has not been valued is to prevent public companies from issuing shares at a discount.[149] The liability is harsh because, prima facie, allottees can be required to pay twice over, once in cash and once in money's worth. Subsequent holders are also in what appears to be an invidious position because they can be obliged to pay for the shares in cash even though the company may have already received, from someone else, valuable non-cash consideration in respect of them. This harshness is mitigated by section 606 of the Companies Act 2006, which allows the court to grant relief from liability in certain circumstances. The onus is on the person, whether allottee or subsequent holder, seeking relief to apply to the court, and the burden is on the applicant to satisfy the court that a case for relief is made out.[150] The circumstances in which the court may grant relief are considered in a later section of this chapter.

There are two important statutory exemptions from the general rule requiring non-cash consideration for the shares of public companies to be independently valued. These are the *takeover* exemption and the *mergers* exemption, considered below.[151] It is also expressly provided in section 593(2) of the Companies Act 2006, presumably for the avoidance of doubt, that bonus issues fall outside the valuation requirements. In addition to the statutory carve-outs, it may be possible

---

[145] Companies Act 2006, s 1153(2) and (4).
[146] ibid s 593(3).
[147] ibid s 605.
[148] ibid s 606.
[149] *Re Bradford Investments plc (No 2)* [1991] BCC 379.
[150] ibid 383.
[151] Companies Act 2006, ss 594–595.

to structure transactions so as to fall outside the valuation rules, for example by the company agreeing to purchase an asset for cash and the vendor then agreeing to release the company from its obligation to pay for the asset in return for an allotment of shares.[152] It has been suggested that use of such structures means that in practice the valuation requirements are relatively easy to avoid.[153] However, the possibility that such structures might not withstand close judicial scrutiny cannot be completely discounted as there is undoubtedly room in this context for a court to look through an artificial arrangement.[154] One basis on which a court can depart from the legal form of a transaction is where it is a fraud or a sham but it is quite hard to persuade an English court to intervene on this ground. Another basis is where, as a matter of statutory interpretation, the particular provision in question requires (or permits) the court to look beyond its immediate legal form to its economic substance in order to ensure that the underlying statutory purpose is met.[155] A composite two-stage transaction designed to avoid the statutory valuation requirement could be vulnerable on this ground.[156] Since the requirement is derived from an EC Directive, views from elsewhere in Europe are worth noting. For example, there is a noticeable contrast between the view expressed by some British commentators on the ease with which the valuation requirement can be evaded and the position under German law, where the well-established doctrine on hidden contributions in kind is intended to prevent avoidance of the rules through the use of composite transactions.[157]

Takeover exemption

For the takeover exemption to apply there must be an arrangement providing for the allotment of shares in a public company ('company A') on terms that the whole or part of the consideration for the shares allotted is to be provided by the transfer to that company (or the cancellation) of some or all of the shares of another company ('company B') (or of a class of shares in that company).[158] The arrangement must allow for participation by all of the holders of the shares in company B (or, where the arrangement is in respect of a class of shares, all of the holders of the shares in that class) save that, for this purpose, shares held by the offeror company or by its nominees, or by other companies in its group or by their

---

[152] The shares are allotted for cash in this case because 'cash' includes the release of a liability for a liquidated sum (Companies Act 2006, s 583(3)(c)).

[153] J Rickford (ed), 'Reforming Capital: Report of the Interdisciplinary Group on Capital Maintenance' [2004] *European Business Law Review* 919, 935.

[154] *Re Bradford Investments plc (No 2)* [1991] BCC 379.

[155] J Vella, 'Departing From the Legal Substance of Transactions in the Corporate Field: the Ramsay Approach Beyond the Tax Sphere' [2007] *Journal of Corporate Law Studies* 243.

[156] ibid.

[157] A Pentz, H-J Priester, and A Schwanna, 'Raising Cash and Contributions in Kind When Forming a Company and for Capital Increases', in M Lutter (ed), *Legal Capital in Europe*, a special volume of the *European Company and Financial Law Review* (2006), 42, 52–3.

[158] Companies Act 2006, s 594.

nominees, are ignored.[159] Shares allotted 'in connection with'[160] an arrangement satisfying these criteria are exempt from the usual valuation requirements. This exemption is apt to cover takeover situations where the consideration offered to the shareholders of the target is, or includes, shares in the offeror. However, its scope arguably extends beyond straightforward share-for-share allotments of this sort. Since the exemption applies to allotments 'in connection with' qualifying arrangements, it is possible to argue that no valuation is required so long as the assets to be acquired in exchange for shares include the entire share capital of another company. Applying this line of argument, it appears that a public company could avoid the valuation requirements in circumstances where it uses its shares as consideration for the acquisition of non-cash assets of substantial value by the simple expedient of ensuring that the assets acquired include the entire share capital of a company, even though the value of that company may be insignificant in relation to the overall size of the transaction. However, again, there is a possibility that the exemption, which is derived from the Second Directive,[161] would be interpreted purposively by a court so as to limit its scope.

Mergers exemption

For the purposes of this exemption, a merger means a proposal by one company to acquire all the assets and liabilities of another company in exchange for the issue of shares or other securities of the first company to the shareholders of the other company.[162] Shares allotted by a company in connection with such a merger are not subject to the valuation requirement.[163] Again, this exemption is derived from Article 27 of the Second Directive, which allows a Member State to provide an exemption for an allotment 'to give effect to a merger'.

Relaxation of the independent valuation requirement by the 2006 amending Directive

The 2006 Directive makes it possible for Member States to lift the requirement for independent valuation of non-cash consideration for shares in a public limited company in certain circumstances. These circumstances include where the consideration in question is transferable securities that are valued by reference to the price at which they have been trading on a regulated market or assets that have been subject to a recent independent expert's report or valuation for the purpose of audited accounts. The Directive is limited in its deregulatory effect, however, because instead of the independent valuation obligation there is a requirement for publication of various

---

[159] Companies Act 2006, s 594(5).
[160] ibid s 594(1).
[161] Second Company Law Directive, Art 27.
[162] Companies Act 2006, s 595(2).
[163] ibid s 595.

matters (including a description of the consideration, its value and, where applicable, the source of valuation, and a statement that no new 'qualifying circumstances' affecting value have occurred since the valuation). In addition, shareholders holding at least 5 per cent of issued share capital can still request an independent expert's report. The UK government took the view that it was not worthwhile to take advantage of the option provided by the amending Directive in this respect.[164]

Liability of subsequent holders

Generally speaking, where there is a breach of any of the statutory rules relating to payment for shares (ie the no-discount rule (section 580); the work/services undertaking rule for plc shares (section 585); the one-quarter paid up rule for plc shares (section 586); the long-term undertaking rule for plc shares (section 587); the valuation requirement for plc shares (section 593)), statutory liability attaches to subsequent holders of the shares as well as to the original allottee or person who is holding the shares at the time when the liability first arises.[165] Subsequent holders are jointly and severally liable with any other person so liable. A 'holder' of shares for the purpose of subsequent holder liability includes a person who has an unconditional right to be included in the company's register of members in respect of the shares or to have an instrument of transfer of the shares executed in his favour.[166] In *System Controls plc v Munro Corporate plc*[167] a company contracted to allot shares and fulfilled its obligation by issuing a renounceable letter of allotment. Hoffmann J held that the person in whose favour the letter had been renounced was a holder of the shares for the purposes of these sections.

Subsequent holders escape liability if they are purchasers for value who, at the time of the purchase, did not have actual notice of the contravention, or are persons who derive title to the shares (directly or indirectly) from such a person.[168] In the *System Controls* case the subsequent holder was not exempt where it knew that the allotment had been effected without valuation, even though it might have been unaware of the need for such a valuation to be obtained; Hoffmann J held that actual notice in this context meant notice of the facts and need not extend to an appreciation that they constituted a contravention.

Relief from liability

With two exceptions, those who incur liability by reason of a breach of the statutory rules relating to payment for shares can apply to court to be relieved from

---

[164] DTI, 'Implementation of Companies Act 2006 Consultative Document' (February 2007) paras 6.8–6.26.
[165] Companies Act 2006, ss 588 and s 605.
[166] ibid ss 588(3) and s 605(4).
[167] [1990] BCC 386.
[168] Companies Act 2006, ss 588(2) and ss 605(3).

liability. The exceptions relate to the no-discount rule and the one-quarter paid up rule for plcs where the allottee cannot apply to be relieved of the obligation to pay to the company an amount equal to the discount or the minimum amount, plus interest. However, it appears that a subsequent holder of a share that was allotted in breach of either of these rules may be relieved of liability.[169] It is for the person seeking to be relieved of liability to make the application to court rather than for the company to apply to court for the imposition of liability. The applicant may seek to be relieved of the liability that arises under the companies legislation as a consequence of the fact that there has been a breach of the statutory rules or of a liability arising from any undertaking given to the company in or in connection with payment for the shares.[170] Contractual undertakings remain enforceable notwithstanding a breach of the statutory rules regarding payment for shares.[171]

Relief from liability must be granted only where and to the extent that it appears to the court just and equitable to do so.[172] In making its determination, the court must have regard to two overriding principles:[173]

(1) that a company which has allotted shares should receive money or money's worth at least equal in value to the aggregate of the nominal value of those shares and the whole of any premium or, if the case so requires, so much of that aggregate as is treated as paid up; and

(2) subject to this, that where a company would, if the court did not grant the exemption, have more than one remedy against a particular person, it should be for the company to decide which remedy it should remain entitled to pursue.

In *Re Bradford Investments plc (No 2)*[174] Hoffmann J said that the designation of (1) above as an overriding principle did not mean that the court would not have jurisdiction to grant an exemption unless it was satisfied that the company had received assets worth at least the nominal value of the allotted shares and any premium. However, it did mean that very good reasons would be needed before the court could accept that it would be just and equitable to exempt an applicant from liability in circumstances where the company had not received sufficient value in respect of its shares.

In determining whether it would be just and equitable to grant relief on an application for relief from liability under the Companies Act 2006, the court must take into account the following:

---

[169] ibid s 589(1).
[170] ibid ss 589(2) and 606(1).
[171] ibid ss 591 and 608.
[172] ibid ss 589(3)–(4) and 606(2)–(3).
[173] ibid ss 589(5) and 606(4).
[174] [1991] BCC 379, 384.

(a) whether the applicant has paid, or is liable to pay, any amount in respect of any other liability arising in relation to the shares under any of the relevant sections, or of any liability arising by virtue of any undertaking given in or in connection with payment of those shares;

(b) whether any person other than the applicant has paid or is likely to pay (whether in pursuance of an order of the court or otherwise) any such amount; and

(c) whether the applicant or any other person has performed in whole or in part, or is likely so to perform, any such undertaking, or has done or is likely to do any other thing in payment or part payment of the shares.[175]

Where the application is for relief from liability arising by virtue of an undertaking given to the company in, or in connection with, payment for shares, the court can grant an exemption only if and to the extent that it appears just and equitable to do so having regard to:

(1) whether the applicant has paid or is liable to pay any amount in respect of any liability arising in relation to the shares under any of the relevant provisions of the Companies Act; and

(2) whether any person other than the applicant has paid or is likely to pay (whether in pursuance of order of the court or otherwise) any such amount.[176]

The burden is on the applicant to satisfy the court that a case for relief exists.[177] In *Re Ossory Estates plc*,[178] where the company had already re-sold at substantial profits properties which had been acquired in consideration for the allotment of shares and there was clear evidence that the vendor had so far complied with all of the undertakings arising from the conveyancing transactions and was likely to continue so to comply, Harman J was satisfied that a case for relief had been made out. However, in *Re Bradford Investments plc (No 2)*[179] the applicants were unable to establish that the assets transferred in consideration for shares had any net value and accordingly it was held that there was no case for relief.

Criminal liability for breach of rules relating to payment for shares

It is a criminal offence for a company to contravene any of the statutory rules relating to payment for shares. The company and any officer of it who is in default are liable to a fine.[180]

---

[175] Companies Act 2006, ss 589(3) and 606(2).
[176] ibid ss 589(4) and 606(3).
[177] *Re Bradford Investments plc (No 2)* [1991] BCC 379.
[178] (1988) 4 BCC 461.
[179] [1991] BCC 379.
[180] Companies Act 2006, ss 590 and 607.

Share premiums

The next part of this chapter looks at rules relating to share premiums. These rules would disappear under a no par value shares regime since, in that event, all value put into a company in return for an issue of its shares would simply be subject to the same rules.

Determining the issue price

Shares can be issued at a price that is higher than their nominal or par value, with any excess over the nominal value of the share being known as a share premium. It falls to the directors, as part of their general managerial power, to fix the price at which shares are allotted. Directors' duties serve as a safeguard against directors acting quixotically in setting issue prices. It has been judicially stated that directors have a prima facie duty to obtain the best price that they can for new share issues.[181] Rights issues are often made at a discount to the prevailing market price of the company's shares which is greater than is necessary to take account of the fact that the rights issues will increase the number of shares in the market. The purpose of the discount is to ensure the popularity of the issue and to prevent a commercially unacceptable proportion of it being left with the underwriters. Occasionally companies dispense with underwriting altogether and make the issue at a very substantial discount to the prevailing market price. In *Shearer v Bercain Ltd*[182] it was accepted that directors could legitimately offer a discount in order to ensure the success of a rights issue.

Treatment of share premiums

Sums representing share premiums must be accounted for in a share premium account and, save for certain specified purposes, they must be treated as if they were part of the company's paid up share capital.[183] A rule to this effect was introduced into the domestic legislation following a recommendation from the Cohen Committee, which reported in 1945.[184] Prior to this change in the law, share premiums were seen as distributable and thus could be used for paying dividends or for writing off losses.[185]

---

[181] *Lowry v Consolidated African Selection Trust Ltd* [1940] AC 648, HL, 479 *per* Lord Wright; *Shearer v Bercain Ltd* [1980] 3 All ER 295, 307–8.

[182] [1980] 3 All ER 295.

[183] Companies Act 2006, s 610.

[184] *Report of the Committee on Company Law Amendment* (Cmd 6659, 1945) para 108.

[185] MV Pitts, 'The Rise and Rise of the Share Premium Account' (2000) 10 *Accounting, Business & Financial History* 317.

The Second Company Law Directive does not require share premiums to be treated in the same way as share capital and it is thus open to the UK government to change the treatment of share premiums for both private and public companies in its domestic law.[186] The Companies Act 2006 presented an opportunity to do so but it was not taken. The possibility of deregulation free from Directive constraints with regard to the treatment of share premiums came to prominence only rather late in the policy formation process relating to the Companies Act 2006, by which time the agenda was more or less set and the government had decided to defer radical reform relating to legal capital except in certain specific areas until reform of the Second Directive had been thoroughly considered at the European level. Such is the degree of divergence between Member States in the treatment of share premiums in their national laws that it has been said of the law relating to share premiums in Europe that it has applied 'scant regard to any coherent or rational philosophy'.[187]

Permissible uses for share premiums

Sums representing share premiums represent a valuable source of corporate finance and they may be used by a company to fund its business operations in the same way as any other finance that is available to it. In addition, the Companies Act 2006 authorizes the use of share premiums in a few other circumstances, and to this limited extent the treatment of share premiums differs from that in relation to share capital. The Companies Act 2006 narrowed the circumstances in which special use may be made of special premiums.[188]

Bonus issues

The share premium account may be applied by the company in paying up unissued shares to be allotted to members as fully paid shares.[189] Thus, if a company has issued 100 shares of £1 each at a premium of £1 per share, so that its share capital is £100 and it has a share premium account of £100, it may then issue a further 100 shares to its existing shareholders on the basis that the shares are to be issued fully paid by application of the share premium account; the end result is that the share premium account is reduced to zero but the company's paid up share capital increases to £200. As far as individual shareholders are concerned the total value of their capital contribution remains constant but the investment is made potentially more liquid by being represented by two shares, each of which

---

[186] J Rickford (ed), 'Reforming Capital: Report of the Interdisciplinary Group on Capital Maintenance' [2004] *European Business Law Review* 919, 939–41.

[187] ibid 941.

[188] This narrowing of the permissible uses for share premiums broadly followed recommendations made by the Company Law Review Steering Group, 'Company Formation and Capital Maintenance', URN 99/1145, para 3.21.

[189] Companies Act 2006, s 610(3).

has a lower individual value than the one share held before the bonus issue. A bonus issue does not result in undistributable reserves leaving the company to the detriment of its creditors.

This statutory authorization in respect of the payment up of bonus shares from share premiums is limited to issues of fully paid bonus shares, and does not extend to issues of partly paid bonus shares or to issues of debentures. The authorization to use the share premium account in this way can be exploited by companies that want to return surplus cash to their shareholders. An established method of doing this is for the company to make a bonus issue of a class of shares that is fully paid up by application of the share premium account and then to redeem or buy back those shares in accordance with the relevant provisions of the Companies Act 2006.[190] Share buy-backs are considered in chapter 8 below.

Expenses and commissions on an issue of shares

Where a company has made an issue of shares at a premium, it may write off the expenses of that issue and any commission paid on that issue against the sum transferred to the share premium account in respect of that specific issue.[191] What would be included within the category of 'expenses of the issue' has not attracted judicial scrutiny but there is some guidance in accounting standards.[192] Expenses incurred by a company in order to put itself in the position to issue securities—such as restructuring costs—are unlikely to be included.[193]

Share premiums and non-cash consideration

Until 1980 it was unclear whether a company had to create a share premium account whenever it issued shares for a non-cash consideration that was more valuable than the nominal value of the issued shares. In *Henry Head & Co Ltd v Roper Holdings Ltd*[194] a holding company acquired two companies by means of a share-for-share exchange. The actual value of the shares acquired was much greater than the nominal value of the shares issued as consideration and the directors of the holding company were advised that they had to account for this excess by crediting it to a share premium account. This advice was upheld by the court. Notwithstanding this ruling, some practitioners continued to believe that the obligation to create a share premium account in this type of situation could be avoided.[195] The arguments on which that practice was based were finally

---

[190] T Scott, 'Returning Value to Shareholders. Options for Companies' (1997) 8(3) *Practical Law for Companies* 19.
[191] Companies Act 2006, s 610(2).
[192] P Holgate, *Accounting Principles for Lawyers* (CUP, 2006) 149–150.
[193] ibid.
[194] [1952] Ch 124.
[195] For an account of the development of market practice and corresponding regulation in relation to share premiums, see C Napier and C Noke, 'Premiums and Pre-Acquisition Profits: The Legal and Accounting Professions and Business Combinations' (1991) 54 MLR 810.

considered by the court in *Shearer v Bercain Ltd*.[196] Essentially, those arguments were: (a) it was for the company to determine the terms of issue and it was not obliged to obtain a premium merely because investors might be willing to pay it; and (b) if the sale and purchase agreement provided for the assets to be sold at a price equal to the par value of the shares to be issued as consideration, there was no obligation on the company to create a share premium account.

Walton J rejected these arguments. In his view it was the prima facie duty of directors to obtain the best possible price for the shares.[197] Furthermore, the obligation to create a share premium account was not optional and could not be avoided by stating that the shares were issued at their nominal value; if the assets acquired in consideration of the issue of shares had an actual value greater than the nominal value of the consideration shares then, irrespective of the terms on which those shares had been issued, the company was subject to a mandatory requirement to create a share premium account.

As a result of the decision in *Shearer v Bercain Ltd*, pressure was brought to bear on Parliament to provide some relief from the obligation to create a share premium account. This was done in the Companies Act 1981 and the relevant reliefs are now to be found in sections 611 (group reconstruction relief) and 612 (merger relief) of the Companies Act 2006.

Group reconstruction relief

This relief applies where the issuing company:

(a) is a wholly-owned subsidiary of another company (the 'holding company'); and

(b) allots shares to its holding company or another wholly-owned subsidiary of its holding company in consideration for the transfer of non-cash assets to the issuing company—these assets may be assets of any company in the group comprising the holding company and all its wholly-owned subsidiaries.[198]

Where the shares in the issuing company are issued at a premium there is no obligation to carry the premium to a share premium to the extent that it exceeds what is referred to as the minimum premium value.[199]

The minimum premium value means the amount by which the base value of the consideration for the shares allotted exceeds the nominal value of the shares.[200] The base value of the consideration is determined as follows. First, the base value of the assets transferred (BVA) must be established: this is the cost

---

[196] [1980] 3 All ER 295.
[197] Following Lord Wright in *Lowry (Inspector of Taxes) v Consolidated African Selection Trust Ltd* [1940] AC 648, HL.
[198] Companies Act 2006, s 611(1).
[199] ibid s 611(2).
[200] ibid s 611(3).

of those assets to the transferor company or, if less, the amount at which those assets are recorded in the transferor's books immediately before the transfer.[201] Secondly, the base value of the liabilities of the transferor that are assumed by the issuing company (BVL) must be ascertained: this value is taken to be the amount at which the liabilities are stated in the transferor company's accounting records immediately before the transfer.[202] The base value of the consideration is BVA minus BVL. The Companies Act 2006 permits any amount over the minimum premium value to be disregarded in determining the amount at which any shares or other consideration provided for the shares issued is to be included in the company's balance sheet.[203] However, it should be noted that it is open to question whether this option is compatible with international financial reporting standards.[204]

Merger relief

Merger relief is available in circumstances where one company acquires the share capital of another company by issuing its shares to the shareholders of the target company. In those circumstances, provided certain conditions are satisfied, there is no statutory obligation to credit to a share premium account the amount by which the value of the acquired shares exceeds the nominal value of the shares issued by way of consideration.[205] Instead this amount can be credited to a merger reserve, which, unlike a share premium account, is realizable in certain circumstances.[206] A merger reserve is optional so far as the companies legislation is concerned. The Companies Act 2006 provides further that any amount not included in the issuing company's share premium account may also be disregarded in determining the amount at which the acquired shares (or other consideration) are shown in the issuer's balance sheet.[207] However, for companies that draw up their individual accounts in accordance with international financial reporting standards, this optionality may not be available because of requirements in these standards for assets to be shown at their fair value, which means that it may be necessary to recognize a 'merger reserve' corresponding to the difference between the fair value of the assets and the nominal value of the consideration shares.[208]

---

[201] Companies Act 2006, s 611(5)(a).

[202] ibid s 611(5)(b).

[203] ibid s 615.

[204] On the interrelationship with the IFRS, see ICAEW and ICAS, 'Distributable Profits: Implications of Recent Accounting Changes', TECH 02/07, para 6.105. See further below in the discussion of merger relief and the need to create a merger reserve.

[205] Companies Act 2006, s 612.

[206] ICAEW and ICAS, 'Guidance on the Determination Of Realised Profits and Losses in the Context of Distributions Under the Companies Act 1985', TECH 7/03, Appendix B, para 9. D Sonter and D Williams, 'IFRS and Accounting Changes' (2006) 17(3) *Practical Law for Companies* 33, 40.

[207] Companies Act 2006, s 615.

[208] ICAEW and ICAS, '*Distributable Profits: Implications of Recent Accounting Changes*' TECH 02/07, para 6.105. Sonter and Williams (n 206 above) 41.

The precise conditions which must be satisfied in order for merger relief to apply are that the issuing company must secure at least a 90 per cent equity holding in another company, and this holding must be secured pursuant to an arrangement[209] providing for the allotment of equity shares in the issuing company on terms that the consideration for the allotted shares is to be provided by the issue or transfer to the issuing company of equity shares in the other company; or by the cancellation of any such shares not held by the issuing company.[210] Thus if a company seeks to acquire all of the equity shares in a target company and offers the shareholders in the target its equity shares in exchange for each of the target's equity shares, merger relief will be available if and when the issuer acquires 90 per cent of the target's equity pursuant to the arrangement. Equity shares for this purpose are issued shares except those that neither as respects dividends nor as respects capital carry any right to participate beyond a specified amount in a distribution.[211] If a target company's equity share capital is divided into different classes of shares (for example ordinary shares which are fully participating as to both dividends and capital and preference shares which are fully participating as to dividend but participating only for a fixed amount in any capital distribution), for merger relief to apply the conditions must be satisfied separately in respect of each class.[212] If non-equity shares of the target are also included in the arrangement, the acquisition of those shares does not go towards satisfying the conditions but, if the conditions are otherwise satisfied, merger relief is extended to any shares allotted in return for the non-equity shares of the target.[213]

What is meant by securing 'at least a 90 per cent equity holding in another company in pursuance of... an arrangement' is amplified by section 613 of the Companies Act 2006. The issuing company[214] must end up holding equity shares in the target of an aggregate nominal value equal to 90 per cent or more of the nominal value of the target's total equity share capital. However, whilst the holding must be arrived at as a consequence of an acquisition or cancellation of target company shares pursuant to the arrangement, it is not necessary for all, or indeed any, of the shares comprising the issuing company's holding of target company shares to be acquired pursuant to the arrangement.[215] Thus if the issuing company holds a number of target company shares prior to entering into an arrangement to issue its own shares in consideration for the cancellation of target company shares and, as a result of such cancellation, the size of the issuing company's original holding becomes equal to 90 per cent or more of the nominal

---

[209] As defined in Companies Act 2006, s 616(1).
[210] ibid s 612(1).
[211] ibid ss 616(1) and 548.
[212] ibids 613(4).
[213] ibid s 612(3).
[214] Shares held by the issuing company's holding company or subsidiary, or by other subsidiaries of its holding company, or by its or their nominees, are to be regarded as held by the issuing company (Companies Act 2006, s 613(5)).
[215] ibid s 613(3).

value of the target's (diminished) equity share capital, merger relief conditions will have been satisfied. Similarly, where the arrangement is effected by means of a share-for-share exchange, the shares acquired by the issuing company pursuant to the exchange can be added to its prior holding of target company shares in order to ascertain whether the 90 per cent condition has been met.

The conditions for merger relief to apply do not preclude the acquirer from offering the target company's shareholders a mixed consideration, which is partly in the form of shares and partly in the form of cash or other assets. To the extent that shares of the acquirer are issued by way of consideration, merger relief can apply in respect of those shares.

The operation of merger relief can be illustrated by the following example.

Company A makes a successful bid for 100% of the equity of Company B, which consists of 400 million equity shares of 25p nominal value. The consideration is an issue to Company B's shareholders of 300 million equity shares in Company A, each of these shares having a nominal value of 5p and a fair value of £3. The transaction meets the conditions for statutory merger relief. Company A records the acquisition of B at fair value.

Company A's balance sheet after the transaction is as follows:

Assets	£m
Investment in Company B	900
Other assets	440
Liabilities	
Creditors	(100)
Provisions	(40)
Net assets	1,200
Capital and reserves	
Ordinary shares of 5p each (120 existing + 15 new)	135
Merger reserve (£2.95 x 300m)	885
Profit and loss reserve	180
	1,200

Importance of group reconstruction and merger relief

Why are group reconstruction and merger relief important? One reason relates to pre-acquisition profits of a target company and whether they can be made available for distribution by the acquirer. If the target company has distributable profits it is, of course, free to declare a dividend after the acquisition in favour of its new parent company. However, a further two-part question is whether the acquirer, the new parent company, is then able to treat that dividend as (a) a profit that is (b) realized and therefore available for distribution to its shareholders. Historically, UK accounting practice permitted distributions by a subsidiary to be recognized as a realized profit in the accounts of its parent provided that the dividend was received in the form of qualifying consideration[216] and the parent was able to conclude that there was no impairment to the carrying value of its investment in the subsidiary resulting from the distribution.[217] However, under international financial reporting standards the position is different because dividends from the pre-acquisition reserves of a subsidiary must be recognized as a reduction of the cost of the investment. To the extent that dividends received are accounted for as a reduction in the cost of investment, they are not treated as accounting profits at all. However, to the extent that the acquisition of the subsidiary benefited from merger relief or group reconstruction relief, the receipt by the parent of such a dividend in the form of qualifying consideration will result in the realization of an equivalent amount of the related merger reserve.[218]

Other reliefs

The Secretary of State is empowered to make provision, by statutory instrument, for further relief from the requirement to create a share premium account in relation to premiums other than cash premiums, or for restricting or modifying any of the reliefs provided by the Companies Act itself.[219]

Other capital contributions

The Privy Council has held that there is nothing in the company law of England to render ineffective an agreement to finance a company by means of capital contributions without a formal allocation of shares.[220] Where shareholders of a company agree to increase its capital in this way, the amount invested becomes, like share premium, part of the owners' equity.[221] The Companies Act 2006 does not expressly envizage this type of financing arrangement and there is no specific statutory obligation requiring the filing of a statement of capital when capital is invested in this way.

Stock

This is really little more than a footnote to the chapter, as in recent times it has been rare for UK companies to convert their shares into stock and the Companies

---

[216] Accounting guidance establishes generally that the primary criterion for a profit to be regarded as realized is for it to result from a transaction where the consideration received by the company is a 'qualifying consideration', such as cash: TECH 7/03, paras 16–18.

[217] ICAEW and ICAS, 'Distributable Profits: Implications of Recent Accounting Changes', TECH 02/07, para 6.108. The remainder of this paragraph draws heavily on TECH 02/07, paras 6.108–6.115.

[218] See further ch 9 below.

[219] Companies Act 2006, s 614.

[220] *Kellar v Williams* [2000] 2 BCLC 390, PC.

[221] ibid.

Act 2006 removes the possibility of doing so in future.[222] Historically, stock was thought to have two advantages over shares. First, it is possible to deal in fractions of stock but it is not possible to deal in fractions of shares. This advantage is, however, more theoretical than real. The market might want to be able to trade in a fraction of a share because the price of the whole unit is high. However, rather than converting its shares into stock, the company can meet this demand by sub-dividing its existing shares into new shares with lower par values than those which they replace. The second supposed advantage of stock is that stock does not have to be numbered. This makes stock administratively more convenient than shares, where a numbering obligation prima facie applies.[223] However, where all of the issued shares of a class are fully paid and rank *pari passu* for all purposes, none of those shares need thereafter have a distinguishing number so long as it remains fully paid and ranks *pari passu* for all purposes with all shares of the same class for the time being issued and fully paid up.[224] It is uncommon for shares to be issued on a partly paid basis, which means that advantage can normally be taken of this exception. In 1962, the Jenkins Committee expressed the view that since the 1948 Companies Act had introduced the exception allowing fully paid shares not to be numbered, the advantages of converting from shares to stock had become negligible. The Committee recommended that references to stock should be eliminated from the companies legislation.[225] The Companies Act 2006 does not go quite so far but the remaining references to stock in the legislation are there simply to cater for the possibility that a few companies may still have stock in their capital structure. The 2006 Act retains the power that was also in predecessor legislation for companies to reconvert stock into shares.[226]

---

[222] Companies Act 2006, s 540(2).
[223] ibid s 543(1).
[224] ibid s 543(2).
[225] *Report of the Company Law Committee* (Cmnd 1749, 1962) para 472.
[226] Companies Act 2006, s 540(3).

5

Share Allotments

Scope of this chapter

This chapter is concerned with internal corporate governance regulation in relation to share issuance activity. As a general rule, the management of a company's affairs is under the overall responsibility of its board and shareholders do not have a direct say in managerial decisions. Shares issues are an exception to this general rule because this is an area where potential agency problems between controllers (either managers or majority shareholders) and non-controllers are particularly significant. If left unregulated, there would be scope for controllers to use share issuance powers in ways that could adversely affect the interests of existing non-controlling shareholders in four key ways: (1) by effecting a transfer of wealth to new investors; (2) by diluting voting strength; (3) by distorting the operation of the market for corporate control or otherwise undermining mechanisms that are meant to promote managerial accountability to shareholders; (4) by being an instance of opportunistic exploitation of minority shareholders through misuse of majority shareholder power. Whilst the potential for abuse is held in check by directors' duties, in particular the proper purposes doctrine,[1] and statutory protection of minorities against unfair prejudice,[2] lawmakers at both the national (UK) and regional (EU) levels have seen fit to intervene more specifically by means of rules that empower shareholders by giving them a say in decisions to raise new finance through share issuance and protect minorities against controllers through mandatory pre-emption rights in favour of all shareholders.

The policy considerations in this area are complex. On the one hand, there are serious agency concerns that need to be addressed but, on the other, there is the obvious danger of undermining legitimate corporate financing objectives by imposing requirements that are too stringent. Paul Myners, the author of a report

---

[1] Codified as Companies Act 2006, s 171.
[2] ibid s 994.

on the topic that was commissioned by the UK government, described the competing tensions as follows:[3]

Shareholders need to know that they are protected from any unwelcome dilution of their investment. And public companies need to be able to raise new money through the capital markets in as cheap and efficient a way as possible in order to grow and develop. Neither of these statements is particularly contentious—indeed they may appear self-evident. And yet the question of whether shareholders' pre-emption rights adversely impact on a company's ability to raise cash through the issuance of new shares is a complex and tricky issue.

The concerns can take on a different emphasis depending on the particular corporate ownership structure (ie whether closely-held, dominated by a substantial shareholder but with some dispersed shareholders, or fully dispersed and with management in effective control). Differences in the ownership structures of publicly listed companies in Europe, especially the fact that the widely dispersed shareholder model is relatively uncommon outside the UK,[4] complicate the task of developing coherent policies at the European level. Furthermore, the contrast between Europe, where pre-emption rights are mandatory, and the US, where the principle of pre-emption has largely withered away as a form of shareholder protection, suggests that there is no single universally correct policy response to the agency conflicts that are inherent in share issuance activity.[5]

The Companies Act 2006 provided an opportunity for the UK to re-examine its approach to internal corporate governance-oriented regulation of share issuance and to simplify it in certain respects, particularly in relation to private companies. At the time of the last major revamp of the relevant law in the area in 1980, when the UK implemented the Second Company Law Directive, the new requirements that were enacted to meet Community obligations were largely added to the existing body of law without close examination of whether they made any of the established domestic rules effectively redundant. That (overdue) inquiry was finally conducted prior to the 2006 Act. Also, with the benefit of hindsight the decision made in 1980 to extend requirements that, under Community law, were mandatory only for public companies to private companies as well came to be seen as a defective policy choice in certain respects because it meant that bureaucratic procedures prima facie applied to situations where often they were not needed because the directors and shareholders were the same people, or at least closely connected groups. The 2006 Act learns from this experience.

---

[3] P Myners, 'Pre-emption rights: Final Report', URN 05/679 (February 2005) 3, available at <http://www.berr.gov.uk/files/file28436.pdf> (accessed September 2007).

[4] RJ Gilson, 'Controlling Shareholders and Corporate Governance: Complicating the Comparative Taxonomy' (2006) 119 *Harvard Law Review* 1641.

[5] Myners (n 3 above) 16 notes that the UK and US systems both 'work' despite their differences.

Policy arguments and responses

Wealth transfers

When a company issues new shares it usually does so at a larger discount to the price at which its existing shares are trading in the secondary market than is required to reflect the increase in the number of issued shares. The extra discount element is intended to encourage investors to acquire the new shares. Although directors have a duty to obtain the best price available for new shares,[6] it is justifiable for them to sanction a discount in order to ensure the success of a new issue.[7] If the discount element involved in a new issue of shares is not offered to existing shareholders this will result in the short term in an erosion in the value of their investment, as the following simplified example illustrates.[8]

A shareholder owns 100 XYZ plc shares currently trading at £1.85 each. The value of the holding is £185. XYZ raises share capital by an issue of new shares which increases its share capital by 10 per cent. The new shares are offered to the market for subscription at £1.50 each.

The value of the shares in the company as a result of the issue is:

$(10 \times 1.50 + 100 \times 1.85)/110$ = £1.818
Value of holding = $100 \times £1.818$ = £181.80

Shareholder has lost over £3 in value.

Had the shareholder had been given the right to subscribe for a proportion of the new shares (one new share for every ten shares held) and had it taken up those rights, paying £15 to do so, the position would have been as follows:

Value of holding $110 \times £1.818$ = £200
Shareholder's position $(200–15)$ = £185

Shareholders may not wish to, or may lack the funds to be able to, take up all or part of the shares that are offered to them on a pre-emptive basis. This possibility can be accommodated in a way that is protective of shareholders' interests by structuring the right to acquire the new shares at a discount as a tradable right in itself. In a conventionally structured rights issue the offer is made in the form of a provisional allotment letter (PAL); the PALs are in renounceable form and can be traded on a nil paid basis. The expected value of rights to acquire the shares can, using the same example, be calculated very roughly as the difference between the issue price of the new shares and the expected share price after issue, ie 32p.

---

[6] *Shearer v Bercain* [1980] 3 All ER 295.

[7] ibid 307.

[8] This problem was perceived in early US decisions developing the concept of pre-emption rights: HS Drinker, 'The Pre-emptive Right of Shareholders to Subscribe New Shares' (1930) 43 *Harvard Law Review* 586. More recent expressions of this view can be found in the 'ABI/NAPF Joint Position Paper on Pre-emption, Cost of Capital and Underwriting' (July 1996); R Hinkley, D Hunter, M Whittell, and M Ziff, *Current Issues in Equity Finance* (ACT Publications, 1998) ch 4.

Provided the shareholder is able to sell those rights at a price at least equivalent
to their expected value (which should be feasible so long as the reaction of the
market to the issue is favourable and the shares trade after the announcement at a
price at or above the theoretical ex-rights price) the shareholder's position should
not be adversely affected. The following example illustrates.

A shareholder sells eight of its subscription rights for £2.56 and takes up the balance of
the entitlement for two of those rights, paying £3 to do so, the eventual outcome for the
shareholder is again unchanged because:
    Value of holding 102 x £1.818   = £185.44
    Shareholder's position 185.44–3 + 2.56 = £185.00

In effect, the shareholder in the example sells part of the entitlement to fund
the acquisition of the remaining part, a process that is sometimes described in
practice as 'tail swallowing'. The example obviously ignores tax and dealing costs
incurred in selling nil paid rights and taking up the balance of the entitlement
and also market fluctuations in share prices but it serves nevertheless to demonstrate the importance of pre-emption rights from the viewpoint of investors.
From the company's viewpoint, by respecting pre-emption rights it secures the
advantage of being able to offer new shares at a substantial discount and possibly
therefore dispensing with underwriting and its associated costs.[9]

    Should the law intervene to protect shareholders against the risk of value trans-
fers by making pre-emption rights mandatory? One counter-argument is that
it is an unduly short-term perspective to focus on the transfer of value resulting from the discount element in a new issue and that the longer-term financial interests of a company and its shareholders may be better served by allowing
it more flexibility in the methods of raising capital. There are various facets to
this argument. An issue of shares to a group of investors not limited to existing
shareholders has the advantage of broadening the investor base in the company's
shares, which may in the longer term open up further new sources of funding for
the company. The ability to appeal to investors in jurisdictions outside those of
the existing shareholders is one particular aspect of this analysis.[10] The costs and
timescales involved in making an offer on a pre-emptive basis can also be compared unfavourably with a placing to external investors. Timing considerations
have particular significance for growing companies in volatile market segments
because of their immediate capital requirements and the particularly unstable
nature of capital market conditions relating to them.[11]

    [9] Myners (n 3 above) 19.
    [10] Pre-emption Rights' (1987) 27(4) *Bank of England Quarterly Bulletin* 545, 547; E Haggar,
'Issuing Abroad is a Risky Venture' (1993) 108 *Corporate Finance* 22; E Haggar, Who Needs US
Investors?' (1997) 148 *Corporate Finance* 42. The 'ABI/NAPF Joint Position Paper on Pre-emption,
Cost of Capital and Underwriting' (July 1996) para 2.2 argues that potential new investors can
always buy shares in the market and should not have preferential access to new and usually cheaper
shares. Further, it suggests that long experience demonstrates that shares placed at a discount with
new investors overseas usually flow back to their domestic market.
    [11] Myners (n 3 above) 19.

Protection against dilution

This argument for regulatory intervention in relation to share issuance is based on the idea of the shareholders' ownership rights: their proportionate share of the ownership of the company should not be diluted without their consent. Again there is a counter-argument: to the extent that investors are concerned about holding an investment in a certain proportion of the share capital, they can always acquire shares in the market to maintain their holding.[12] However, this counter-argument is not wholly persuasive. It clearly has no application in relation to companies whose shares are not openly traded.

Distortion of market for corporate control or other unconstitutional behaviour by directors

Another argument in favour of shareholder authorization requirements and pre-emption rights in respect of new share issues is that they help to curb unconstitutional behaviour by the directors of a company that is the target of a takeover bid, because they prevent the management from facilitating or blocking the bid by, as appropriate, issuing shares to a favoured bidder or to shareholders opposed to the bid. The counter-argument here is that directors are subject to general duties to promote the success of their company and to use their powers only for proper purposes.[13] As a number of cases clearly demonstrate, it is an improper and unconstitutional use of power to issue shares so as to influence the outcome of a bid.[14] The issue for debate is thus whether general duties, supplemented by the requirements of the Takeover Code, amount to an adequate constraint on the perceived abuse or whether it is necessary in addition for there to be specific controls in the form of shareholder authorization requirements and pre-emption rights.

Abuse of majority shareholder power

Where control of a company lies with a majority shareholder rather than with its directors, minority shareholders are in a particularly vulnerable position because the majority shareholders may put pressure on the directors to exercise share issuance or other capital structuring powers in ways that are unfair to the interests of minority shareholders. Anti-dilution concerns may have particular resonance in this context, for example in a company where the majority shareholders control sufficient votes to pass ordinary but not special resolutions, since a non-pre-emptive offering in this case could dilute the minority down to a level

---

[12] 'Pre-emption Rights' (1987) 27(4) *Bank of England Quarterly Bulletin* 545, 547.
[13] Companies Act 2006, ss 171–172.
[14] *Hogg v Cramphorn Ltd* [1967] Ch 254; *Bamford v Bamford* [1970] Ch 212, CA; *Howard Smith Ltd v Ampol Petroleum Ltd* [1974] AC 821, PC.

below that needed to block special resolutions.[15] Yet, in responding to majority/minority agency concerns, the law needs to be careful not to overprotect minorities by giving them powers that, in effect, allow them to hold the majority to ransom. Majority rule is a fundamentally important principle that runs through company law and any qualification to it needs to be carefully designed. The principle that no shareholder has the absolute right to expect their interest to remain constant forever is also well established in British law,[16] although it is relevant to note that an Advocate-General to the European Court of Justice has described the shareholders' right to retain unchanged their proportional share of their holding in the capital as being a right that is inherent in being a shareholder.[17]

Policy responses

The discussion in the immediately preceding paragraphs points towards the following considerations that are relevant to the shaping of a policy response. First, there can be no question of giving minority shareholders an absolute veto over new share issues as that could be commercially disastrous. Therefore, if shareholders are to be specifically empowered to authorize share issues, this should be by way of a requirement for shareholder consent by means of either a simple or a super majority. To be consistent with the general law, this means either an ordinary resolution passed with a majority of the votes cast or a special resolution passed with at least 75 per cent of the votes cast. Secondly, and for the same reasons, rights of pre-emption in favour of existing shareholders should have an inbuilt waiver mechanism that can be activated by a simple or super majority vote of the shareholders and the rights should be structured so as to permit a company to offer shares to external investors if, or to the extent that, existing shareholders decline to take up their pre-emptive entitlements. Thirdly, acceptance of the first two considerations necessarily implies that minority shareholders will be vulnerable to the exercise of majority power, so policymakers have to be comfortable that the general law on directors' duties and shareholder remedies provides adequate protection against abuse. Fourthly, procedural aspects of shareholder empowerment and pre-emption rights need close attention to ensure that these are as streamlined as they possibly can be while still meeting their intended policy goals.

These policy considerations are evident in the legal framework now contained in the Companies Act 2006. That framework is examined next.

---

[15] In *Re a company (No 005134 of 1986), ex p Harries* [1989] BCLC 383 a minority holding was diluted from 40% to 4%.

[16] *Mutual Life Insurance Co of New York v Rank Organisation Ltd* [1985] BCLC 11.

[17] Case C-42/95 *Siemens AG v Henry Nold* [1996] ECR I-6017, Opinion of Advocate General Tesauro, para 15.

Shareholder empowerment under the Companies Act 2006

Section 549(1) of the Companies Act 2006 provides that the directors of a company must not exercise any power of the company (a) to allot shares in the company, or (b) to grant rights to subscribe for, or to convert any security into, shares in the company, except in accordance with section 550 (private company with single class of shares) or section 551 (authorization by company). It is a criminal offence for a director knowingly to contravene or to permit or authorize a contravention of the section but nothing in the section affects the validity of an allotment.[18] If, in addition to failing to comply with the section, the directors act in breach of their general duties in making an allotment, its validity may be contested on that ground.[19]

The special authorization requirements imposed by this section apply to the allotment of all types of share, including ordinary, preference, and redeemable shares, save for shares allotted in pursuance of an employees' share scheme.[20] They also apply to the allotment of hybrid instruments such as warrants to subscribe for shares or bonds that are convertible into shares, save for allotments related to employees' share schemes.[21] However, where the allotment of a hybrid instrument has been duly authorized, the special authorization requirements do not apply to the subsequent allotment of shares on the exercise of subscription or conversion rights.[22]

Private company with a single class of shares

The position under the Companies Act 2006 in relation to a private company with a single class of shares is permissive: the directors may exercise allotment powers except to the extent that they are prohibited from doing so under the company's articles.[23] Requiring private companies that have a straightforward capital structure to opt into restrictions via their articles represents a policy reversal because under the Companies Act 1985, as in force immediately before the 2006 Act, special authorization requirements for share issues applied to all companies but private companies (and not only those with a single class of shares) were permitted to opt out under certain conditions and subject to certain alternative requirements. In fact policy in relation to the placing of the boundary line between the directors' constitutional sphere of action and that of the shareholders

---

[18] Companies Act 2006, s 549(4)–(6).
[19] *Hogg v Cramphorn* [1967] Ch 254; *Bamford v Bamford* [1970] Ch 212, CA; *Howard Smith Ltd v Ampol Ltd* [1974] AC 821, PC.
[20] Companies Act 2006, s 549(1)–(2).
[21] ibid s 549(1)–(2).
[22] ibid s 549(3).
[23] ibid s 550.

with regard to authority to allot shares in private companies has fluctuated quite a lot in recent years. Until 1980, the companies legislation was silent on authority to allot shares and this was left for companies to determine for themselves in their articles of association. The standard position was for the power to allot shares to be part of directors' general managerial powers. Directors' fiduciary duties served as the principal constraint against abuse of power. The Companies Act 1980 introduced a requirement for share allotments to be authorized by the shareholders in general meeting.[24] For public companies this implemented Article 25 of the Second Company Law Directive, which provides that 'any increase in capital must be decided upon by the general meeting'.[25] The Second Company Law Directive applies only to public companies but the UK government chose initially to apply the new requirements also to private companies. The Companies Act 1980 was consolidated into the Companies Act 1985 without substantive change.[26] However, the policy choice with respect to private companies was subsequently revisited and the 'opt out' regime for private companies was inserted into the Companies Act 1985 by the Companies Act 1989.[27] The issue was reviewed again in the general review of company law that preceded the Companies Act 2006. The Company Law Review Steering Group concluded that the imposition of special requirements subject to an opt-out regime did not reflect the needs and practice of most private companies.[28] It recommended that statutory requirements for shareholder authorizations of share allotments should not apply to private companies, save for private companies with more than one class of share in order to prevent unauthorized change in the relative power of different classes of shares.[29] The Companies Act 2006 gives effect to this recommendation.

Authorization by company

The Companies Act 2006, section 551 regulates the exercise of share allotment powers by public companies and private companies with more than one class of shares. Its scope also extends to private companies with a single class of shares but as an alternative to the more relaxed procedure in Companies Act 2006, section 550 that private companies can be expected to use in the ordinary case.

---

[24] Companies Act 2006, s 14.

[25] The purpose of Art 25 is to provide a minimum level of protection to shareholders in all of the Member States: Joined Cases C-19/90 and C-20/90 *Karella v Karellas* [1991] ECR I-2691. See also Case C-381/89 *Syndesmos Melon tis Eleftheras Evangelikis Ekklisias* [1992] ECR I-2111; Case C-441/93 *Panagis Pafitis v Trapeza Kentrikis Ellados AE* [1996] ECR I-1347.

[26] Companies Act 1985, s 80.

[27] ibid s 80A, inserted by Companies Act 1989, s 115(1), as from 1 April 1990.

[28] 'Modern Company Law for a Competitive Economy: Final Report', URN 01/942 para 4.5.

[29] ibid. An allotment of new shares may affect rights, eg by diluting existing voting control, but for the purposes of determining whether there is a variation of rights for which a specific class consent is required a distinction is drawn between a change to the right itself and a change to the enjoyment of the right. On class rights see further ch 6.

Section 551 provides that the directors of a company may exercise a power of the company to allot shares or to grant rights to subscribe for or to convert any security into, shares in the company if they are authorized to do so by the company's articles or by resolution of the company. This requirement is similar in substance to the equivalent provision in the Companies Act 1985,[30] although there are some changes of detail. Before the 2006 Act, it was common practice in public companies for authorization to be given by an ordinary resolution passed at the annual general meeting, although some companies adopted a composite approach whereby the articles contained parts of the authority that were unlikely to change from year to year and the resolution that was passed each year simply updated the amount of shares or other securities to which the authorization related. None of the changes in the Companies Act 2006 would, in itself, appear to necessitate a change of practice in this respect.

An authorization under section 551 may be general or for a particular exercise of power and it may be unconditional or subject to conditions.[31] The maximum amount of shares that may be allotted under the authorization and its expiry date must be stated in the resolution.[32] In relation to the grant of rights to subscribe for, or to convert any security into, shares in the company, the maximum amount of shares that may be allotted under the authorization means the maximum amount of shares that may be allotted pursuant to the rights.[33] The requirement to state an amount may preclude the use of a formula. According to guidance issued by the Association of British Insurers the maximum amount of capital specified in an authorization (other than that which is reserved for issue in connection with contractual conversion rights or options) should not exceed one-third of the issued ordinary share capital by reference to the total issued ordinary share capital shown in the last annual report and accounts or date used in compliance with disclosure under the FSA[34] *Listing Rules* or, if less, the unissued ordinary share capital.[35] The guidance pre-dates the Companies Act 2006 and its second limb (unissued share capital) is now meaningless because there is no longer a legal concept of share capital that has been created but not yet issued. Pending revision of the guidance to reflect the Companies Act 2006, the limit of one-third of the existing issued ordinary share capital can presumably continue to be regarded as a reliable guide to institutional investors' expectations with regard to the content of authorizations under section 551. The maximum duration of an authorization is five years.[36] Authorizations may be renewed for further periods not exceeding

[30] See Companies Act 1985, s 80.
[31] Companies Act 2006, s 551(2).
[32] ibid s 551(3).
[33] ibid s 551(6).
[34] The Financial Services Authority, which is the UK's financial (including securities) regulator.
[35] 'Directors' Powers To Allot Shares' (1995, amended 2002), at <http://www.ivis.co.uk/pages/framegu.html> (accessed September 2007).
[36] Companies Act 2006, s 551(3).

five years and they may be revoked at any time by an ordinary resolution.[37] In practice, authorizations are often updated annually to keep pace with developments in the company's capital over the course of the year and its changing needs. The directors may continue to exercise powers after an authorization has expired if (a) the shares are allotted, or the rights are granted, in pursuance of an offer or agreement made by the company before the authorization expired, and (b) the authorization allowed the company to make an offer or agreement which would or might require shares to be allotted, or rights to be granted, after the authorization had expired.[38]

Statutory pre-emption rights under the Companies Act 2006

Mandatory pre-emption rights are enshrined in chapter 3 of Part 17 of the Companies Act 2006. The basic structure of chapter 3 of Part 17 is that, save for three main exemptions,[39] pre-emption rights apply in relation to all allotments of ordinary shares or rights to subscribe for, or to convert securities into, ordinary shares of the company by public and private companies. However, pre-emption rights can be disapplied and, in the case of a private company, completely excluded. It is worthwhile to note that pre-emption rights apply in relation to private companies, even those that have only one class of shares, unless positive steps are taken to opt out. Since pre-emption rights are a safeguard against dilution, which is a particular risk that minority shareholders in small closely-held companies face should the personal relationships between those involved in the company begin to break down, it may be thought appropriate for the law to proceed on the basis that pre-emption rights apply unless there is a positive decision of the shareholders to the contrary. The Companies Act 2006 re-enacts the substance of the statutory pre-emption regime that was previously in the Companies Act 1985[40] and, before that, in the Companies Act 1980,[41] but with a considerable number of drafting changes. For public companies, the provisions on pre-emption rights in the companies legislation fulfil the UK's obligation to implement Article 29 of the Second Company Law Directive, which requires shares to be offered on a pre-emptive basis to shareholders. Prior to the UK's accession to the Community, the companies legislation did not impose pre-emption rights but there was such a requirement under listing rules for companies that were listed on the London Stock Exchange.

---

[37] ibid s 551(4)–(5). Revocation by ordinary resolution is possible even where it amends the company's articles (s 551(8)).

[38] ibid s 551(7).

[39] ibid ss 564 (bonus shares), 565 (non-cash issues), and 566 (employees' share schemes). (Note also Companies Act 2006, s 576, not considered further in this chapter, which provides savings for certain older pre-emption procedures.)

[40] Companies Act 1985, s 89.

[41] Companies Act 1980, s 17.

Pre-emption rights in relation to 'allotments' of 'equity securities': definitions

Statutory pre-emption rights under chapter 3 of Part 17 of the Companies Act 2006 apply in relation to allotments of 'equity securities'. Equity securities are defined as (a) ordinary shares in the company, or (b) rights to subscribe for, or to convert securities into, ordinary shares in the company.[42] 'Ordinary shares' are shares other than shares that, as respects dividends and capital, carry a right to participate only up to a specified amount in a distribution.[43] Preference shares would usually fall outside this definition but in a special case where the shares have a right to participate fully in respect of dividend or capital (or both) in addition to capped preferential entitlements, they would be ordinary shares for this purpose. This definition of ordinary shares is relevant both to the determination of when a pre-emptive offer must be made and to the identification of the existing shareholders who are entitled to have such an offer made to them.

An 'allotment' includes (a) the grant of a right to subscribe for, or to convert any securities into, ordinary shares in the company, and (b) the sale of ordinary shares in the company that immediately before the sale are held by the company as treasury shares.[44] Where statutory rights of pre-emption apply in relation to the grant of subscription or conversion rights, they do not apply in relation to the allotment of shares pursuant to those rights.[45] In other words, the procedures do not have to be followed twice.

The operation of the statutory pre-emption rights procedure

Section 561 of the Companies Act 2006 obliges a company that is proposing to allot new equity securities to offer the securities first to its existing holders of ordinary shares (disregarding the company in respect of shares held by it as treasury shares)[46] on the same or more favourable terms than they would be offered to others. The pre-emptive offer to each ordinary shareholder must be of a proportion of the new equity securities that is as nearly as practicable equal to the proportion in nominal value held by that shareholder of the ordinary share capital of the company (disregarding treasury shares).[47] The record date for determining the shareholders entitled to be made an offer and their proportional entitlements may be chosen by the company but it must be a date falling in the period of twenty-eight days immediately before the date of the offer.[48] Holders of options or

---

[42] Companies Act 2006, s 560(1).
[43] ibids 560(1).
[44] ibid s 560(2).
[45] ibid s 561(3).
[46] ibid s 561(4)(a).
[47] ibid s 561(1)(a) and (4)(b).
[48] ibid s 574.

convertible debt securities are not holders of ordinary shares and therefore are not within the group of persons to whom the offer must be made. Nor are the holders of non-participating preference shares. Before the company can allot securities otherwise than pursuant to the pre-emptive offer,[49] the period during which any such offer may be accepted must have expired or the company must have received notice of the acceptance or refusal of every offer so made.[50] The minimum statutory period of the pre-emptive offer is twenty-one days.[51] Section 562(5) of the Companies Act 2006 specifically states that the period begins with the date on which the offer is sent or supplied (in the case of an offer made in hard copy form), the date when the offer is sent (in the case of an offer in electronic form), or the date of publication (in the case of an offer made by publication in the Gazette); it is not necessary to delay starting the clock until after receipt of the offer (which was thought to be the position in relation to the equivalent regime in the Companies Act 1985).

The minimum time period for acceptances is an issue that has attracted policy attention. In specifying twenty-one days the Companies Act 2006 goes beyond what is required to implement Article 29 of the Second Company Law Directive, which requires a period of not less than fourteen days from the date of publication of the offer or from the date of dispatch of the letters to the shareholders.[52] The mandatory duration of the offer period has potentially adverse consequences for companies that need to raise capital quickly. The Myners Review of pre-emption rights found that one area of almost complete consensus among respondents was that it would be desirable to streamline the issuance process[53] and the amount of time that needed to be spent on a rights issue was a particular concern.[54] Pre-emption rights were also addressed in the general company law review that preceded the Companies Act 2006 and a reduction of the statutory minimum period to not less than fourteen days, in line with the Directive, was recommended.[55] Although the Companies Act 2006 does not implement this recommendation, section 562(6) makes provision for the Secretary of State to adjust the offer period by regulations, subject to the fourteen-day minimum required by the Directive. This rather indirect response reflects a general decision by the government in relation to parts of the law that were liable to be affected by the outcome of an ongoing debate at the European level on the future of the Second Company Law

---

[49] ibid s 561(2) allows the company within the time limit to allot securities that have been offered to a holder of ordinary shares or anyone in whose favour the shareholder has renounced the right to their allotment. The 'offer' mentioned in s 561(2) appears to mean the pre-emptive offer required by s 561(1).

[50] ibid s 561(1)(b).

[51] ibid s 562(5).

[52] Art 29(3).

[53] P Myners, 'Pre-emption rights: Final Report', URN 05/679 (February 2005) 33.

[54] ibid.

[55] 'Modern Company Law for a Competitive Economy: Final Report', URN 01/942 para 7.31.

Directive to wait for the European position to become clearer before making significant changes.[56]

The mechanics of the statutory pre-emption rights offer process are that an offer must be made to the holders of ordinary shares in hard copy or electronic form.[57] If the holder (a) has no registered address in a European Economic Area (EEA) state and has not given to the company an address in an EEA state for the service of notices on him, or (b) is the holder of a share warrant, the offer may be made by causing it, or a notice specifying where a copy of it can be obtained or inspected, to be published in the London Gazette.[58] Sending UK offer documentation into other countries is potentially problematic because the distribution of such documents may contravene the securities laws of those jurisdictions unless they are in a form that complies with the local law and any requisite approvals under that law have been obtained. The foreign law elements of the offer may add further to the time and costs involved in the offer process. The Gazette route offers a way round this problem. The distinction drawn between the EEA and third countries, which is new in the Companies Act 2006, reflects the fact that foreign securities laws are less of a problem within the EEA than outside because it is possible under EC prospectus laws to passport public offer prospectuses that are approved in one state into other states without compliance with additional 'local' laws.[59] Moreover, as discussed later in this chapter, companies that are fully listed may have no option but to distribute rights issue documentation to shareholders throughout the EEA because they are subject to FSA requirements (implementing EC transparency laws) that mandate equality of treatment for all shareholders and effective dissemination of information on a Community-wide basis. For companies to which EC prospectus and transparency laws do not apply (for example an unlisted company with relatively modest financing needs that can be accommodated within an exemption from prospectus requirements), the direct and indirect costs associated with sending offer documentation into other EEA countries may render the Companies Act 2006 pre-emption rights regime unattractive and may constitute a reason to consider disapplication or exclusion of that regime.

The Companies Act 2006 does not require offers to be made in the form of renounceable letters of allotment. This is, however, a requirement under the FSA *Listing Rules* in respect of rights issues by fully-listed issuers: for the purposes of the *Listing Rules,* a rights issue means an offer to existing holders to subscribe or purchase further securities in proportion to their holdings made by means of the issue of a renounceable letter (or other negotiable document) which may be

---

[56] Appendix to the Twenty-Sixth Report of the Delegated Powers and Regulatory Reform Committee (November 2006) (Supplementary memorandum by the Department of Trade and Industry).

[57] Companies Act 2006, s 562(2).

[58] ibid s 562(3).

[59] See ch 14 below.

traded (as 'nil paid' rights) for a period before payment for the securities.[60] The *Listing Rules* require an offer relating to a rights issue to remain open for acceptance for at least twenty-one days.[61]

Consequences of non-compliance

Failure to comply with the statutory pre-emption rights procedures results in the company and every officer of it who knowingly authorized or permitted the contravention being jointly and severally liable to compensate any person to whom an offer should have been made for any loss, damage, costs, or expenses which the person has sustained or incurred by reason of the contravention.[62] A two-year cut-off point applies to the bringing of claims for compensation under this section.[63] Failure to comply with the statutory pre-emption procedures does not in itself invalidate an allotment of shares but in appropriate cases the court may exercise its power under section 125 of the Companies Act 2006 to rectify the register of members by removing the names of persons to whom shares have been wrongly allotted. This was done in *Re Thundercrest Ltd*[64] where the court rectified the register of members of a small private company in order to remove the names of directors of the company to whom shares had been allotted in breach of the statutory pre-emption rights. The directors were the persons responsible for the breach and the court considered that not rectifying the register in those circumstances would have enabled the directors to profit from their own wrongdoing.

When pre-emption rights do not apply

The pre-emption rights procedures do not apply in relation to the allotment of bonus shares,[65] equity securities paid up, wholly or partly, otherwise than in cash,[66] and securities under an employees' share scheme.[67] The exemption for allotments for non-cash consideration calls for particular comment.

The fact that pre-emption rights do not apply to non-cash allotments facilitates share-for-share takeovers and other transactions in which companies use their shares as a form of currency for an acquisition.[68] However, the exemption can be used in more ingenious ways that, arguably, could be viewed as artificial

---

[60] FSA, *Handbook*, Glossary Definitions.
[61] *LR* 9.5.6.
[62] Companies Act 2006, s 563.
[63] ibid s 563(3).
[64] [1995] BCLC 117.
[65] Companies Act 2006, s 564.
[66] ibid s 565.
[67] ibid s 566.
[68] HS Drinker, 'The Pre-emptive Right of Shareholders to Subscribe to New Shares' (1930) 43 *Harvard Law Review* 586, 607.

structures that are designed to avoid the statute and whose legality is therefore open to question. The first such structure is the 'vendor placing'. In a vendor placing, the purchaser technically allots new shares to the vendor as consideration for the asset acquired, thereby coming within the non-cash exemption from pre-emption rights, but the new shares are then immediately sold in the market on the vendor's behalf with the result that the vendor receives the cash proceeds of the new issue. The ultimate outcome is thus that the vendor receives cash in return for the asset it has sold without the company having to go to its shareholders for it or for permission to raise it on a non pre-emptive basis. As Paul Myners has explained:[69] 'Mechanisms have therefore evolved to ensure that on a vendor placing the vendor bears no pricing risk, does not need to be a party to any legal agreements in relation to the placing and avoids the risk of being charged stamp duty on the transaction. The vendor receives the certainty of cash but with all the risk of execution being borne by the company.'

Even though there is a degree of artificiality about this two-stage process, it can be argued that vendor placings are close enough to the purpose that underlies the exemption, the facilitation of acquisitions, to make them acceptable. The company's balance sheet is expanded through the purchase of valuable assets and in that way each investor's stake in the enterprise is maintained.[70] Furthermore, the decision to acquire specific business assets is, within appropriate limits, a matter of management and board judgment.[71] Certainly, vendor placings are not regarded as controversial in practice provided institutional investors' views with regard to their structure are taken into account. Institutional investors take the view that existing shareholders are entitled to expect a right of clawback (ie a right for existing shareholders to subscribe for a share of an issue at the pre-agreed price)[72] for any issues of significant size or which are offered at more than a very modest discount to market price. It is generally expected that a vendor placing involving more than 10 per cent of issued equity share capital or a discount greater than 5 per cent will be placed on a basis which leaves existing shareholders with a right to claw back their pro rata share of the issue if they so wish.[73]

A vendor placing implies the need for a vendor. One step beyond the vendor placing is the 'cashbox' structure where a third party vendor has no direct involvement in the contractual structure. In a cashbox structure, the company in need of funds (Issuer) establishes a Newco and an offer of Newco ordinary and preference shares is made to an intermediary bank. The bank gives an undertaking

---

[69] 'The Impact of Shareholders' Pre-Emption Rights on a Public Company's Ability to Raise New Capital An Invitation to Comment from Paul Myners' , 39, at <http://www.berr.gov.uk/files/file13422.pdf> (accessed September 2007).

[70] ibid 25.

[71] ibid 25.

[72] Pre-emption Group, 'Statement of Principles on Pre-emption', definitions.

[73] ibid para 18 (with respect to price restrictions). See also 'The Impact of Shareholders' Pre-Emption Rights on a Public Company's Ability to Raise New Capital An Invitation to Comment from Paul Myners' (n 69 above) 12.

to pay the subscription price (X). The bank then agrees to transfer the Newco ordinary and preference shares to Issuer in consideration for the allotment of shares in Issuer to placees found by the bank. The placing made by the Issuer is thus an issue for non-cash consideration. The bank then pays X to Newco and the Issuer can thereafter extract it, for example by redeeming the preference shares or by an intra-group loan.[74] Cashbox structures tend to be utilized in conjunction with an acquisition.[75] Were a cashbox structure to be used to raise finance otherwise than in conjunction with an acquisition, it could provoke a negative reaction from institutional investors.[76] Moreover, it is possible that it could be held to be inconsistent with pre-emption rights employing a purposive acquisition-oriented interpretation of the exemption for non-cash issues.

Disapplication of pre-emption rights: all companies

All companies, both public and private, can disapply pre-emption rights by a provision to that effect in their articles or by a special resolution.[77] This disapplication procedure operates by reference back to the authorization mechanisms under section 551 of the Companies Act 2006. First, where directors are generally authorized for the purposes of section 551, pre-emption rights may be disapplied by the articles or by special resolution for all allotments pursuant to that authorization or the directors may be authorized to apply them to such allotments with such modifications as the directors may determine.[78] Secondly, where directors are generally or specifically authorized for the purposes of section 551, pre-emption rights may be disapplied by special resolution in relation to a specified allotment or may be applied to such an allotment with such modifications as may be specified in the resolution.[79] Special procedural requirements apply in relation to the obtaining of a special resolution in the second case.[80] A disapplication ceases to have effect when the section 551 authorization to which it relates is revoked or expires:[81] this means that the maximum period of a pre-emption rights disapplication under this procedure is five years. If a section 551 authorization is renewed, the disapplication may also be renewed for a period not longer than the renewed authorization.[82]

---

[74] M Wippell and A Stuart, 'Cash Box Structures: Uses and Implications' (2004) 16(6) *Practical Law for Companies* 37.

[75] 'The Impact Of Shareholders' Pre-Emption Rights On A Public Company's Ability To Raise New Capital An Invitation To Comment From Paul Myners' (n 69 above) 40.

[76] ibid.

[77] Companies Act 2006, ss 570–571.

[78] ibid s 570.

[79] ibid s 571.

[80] ibid ss 571(5)–(7) and 572.

[81] ibid ss 570(3) and 571(3).

[82] ibid ss 570(3) and 571(3).

Disapplications for the purposes of making a rights issue or open offer

One of the superficially surprising features of UK corporate finance practice relating to publicly quoted companies is that it is common to disapply statutory pre-emption rights in relation to rights issues and open offers, which are a variant form of pre-emptive offering. This practice prompts an obvious question: why disapply statutory pre-emption rights in relation to rights issues when the purpose of the statutory rights is exactly what is involved in a rights issue, namely the offering of new securities on a proportionate basis to existing shareholders? The key to solving this apparent puzzle lies in the detail of the statutory requirements, which can be inflexible in certain respects.

Fractions

Shareholders may have a technical entitlement to fractions of a share (for example a shareholder who holds seven shares will be technically entitled to a fraction of a share where the basis of the rights issue is that there will be one new share for every five shares held). Before the introduction of statutory pre-emption rights, the practice was to aggregate and sell the right to such fractions for the benefit of the company as soon as practicable after commencement of dealings in the new shares. This practice is not possible under section 561 of the Companies Act 2006 because it requires the company to make an offer which is as nearly as practicable in proportion to shareholders' existing holdings. It is practicable for fractions to be rounded up or down to the nearest whole number and it seems, therefore, that a company must do this in order to comply with the statutory requirements. This means that it may be practically impossible for the company to raise a round sum and the company loses the benefit that it would otherwise have had from the sale of the fractions. Disapplying statutory pre-emption rights enables fractions to be sold for the company's benefit; disapplication resolutions routinely authorize the directors to aggregate them and to sell them in the market for the benefit of the company. The disapplication of pre-emption rights for the purposes of dealing with fractions is expressly mentioned in the FSA *Listing Rules*.[83]

Overseas shareholders

Sending rights issue documentation to shareholders in other jurisdictions can be problematic because the distribution of such documents may contravene the securities laws of those jurisdictions unless the documents are in a form which complies with the local law and any requisite approvals under that law have been obtained. Although the Companies Act 2006 makes provision for this situation by allowing companies to publish offers to overseas shareholders outside the EEA by means of a notice in the London Gazette, resolutions disapplying statutory

---

[83] *LR* 9.3.12(2)(a).

pre-emption rights commonly permit the directors to make such arrangements as they think fit with regard to overseas shareholders who would, apart from such arrangements, be entitled to participate in a rights issue. In practice, this means that overseas shareholders in jurisdictions where the relevant securities laws could be infringed by the offer of new shares may be excluded from the offer and, instead, new shares representing their entitlements may be sold on the market when dealings in the new shares commence, with the net proceeds of such sales being sent to them. For listed companies this practice is envisaged by the FSA *Listing Rules*[84] but it needs also to be considered in relation to the FSA *Disclosure Rules and Transparency Rules*, which provide for equality of treatment of shareholders in the same position.[85] It may be possible to argue that shareholders in countries with onerous securities laws are not in the same position as other shareholders. This argument is supported by *Mutual Life Insurance Co of New York v The Rank Organisation Ltd*[86] where the exclusion of shareholders holding 53 per cent of the company's equity who were resident in the US and Canada from a rights issue was challenged as a breach of the contract between the company and its members contained in the articles. Specifically, it was alleged that the exclusion was contrary to a provision in the articles which required the company to treat all shareholders of the same class equally. Goulding J rejected the challenge for the following reasons: the directors had acted bona fide in the company's interests in making the allotment; the US and Canadian shareholders had not been treated unfairly since their exclusion from the right to acquire the new shares did not affect the existence of their shares or the rights attached to them; there was no suggestion that the terms of the offer were improvident; no shareholder in the company had the right to expect his interest to remain constant forever; and, the reason for the exclusion of the North American shareholders was because of a difficulty relating to their own personal situation.

The nature of the statutory contract formed by a company's articles is somewhat obscure and the extent to which the courts will enforce provisions contained in those documents is uncertain.[87] Partly for these reasons, contractual actions have tended to be eclipsed in recent years by actions under section 994 of the Companies Act 2006, which permits members of a company to seek relief from unfairly prejudicial conduct.[88] However, it is uncertain whether overseas investors

---

[84] *LR* 9.3.12(2)(b).

[85] *DTR* 6.1.3.

[86] [1985] BCLC 11.

[87] It has generated extensive academic debate, including the following articles: K W Wedderburn, 'Shareholders' Rights and the Rule in *Foss v Harbottle*' [1957] CLJ 194; GD Goldberg, 'The Enforcement of Outsider Rights under Section 20 of the Companies Act 1948' (1972) 35 MLR 362; GN Prentice, 'The Enforcement of "Outsider" Rights' (1980) 1 *Company Law* 179; R Gregory, 'The Section 20 Contract' (1981) 44 MLR 526; GD Goldberg, 'The Controversy on the Section 20 Contract Revisited'(1985) 48 MLR 158; RR Drury, 'The Relative Nature of a Shareholder's Right to Enforce the Company Contract' [1986] CLJ 219.

[88] The range of remedies open to the court on a successful petition under Companies Act 2006, s 994 is an important factor which encourages shareholders to seek relief under this section in

who are excluded from a rights issue for the reasons that the court found persuasive in the *Mutual Life* decision would fare any better if they brought a claim under this section, at least where they are located outside the EEA. In the *Mutual Life* decision Goulding J said that the exclusion was not unfair. This was followed in *Re BSB Holdings Ltd (No 2)*[89] where, in reaching the conclusion that a complex capital reorganization was not unfairly prejudicial to the petitioner, Arden J expressly adopted as applicable to the case in hand three of the reasons given by Goulding J in the *Mutual Life* decision as indicating an absence of unfairness: (1) the restructuring did not affect the existence of the petitioner's shares or the rights attaching to them; (2) the terms on which a rights issue which was part of the restructuring was made were not improvident; and (3) the petitioner did not have any overriding right to obtain shares.

With regard to overseas shareholders who are located within the EEA, the position requires slightly closer examination. The achievement of an integrated internal securities market is a major policy goal for the Community and there is now a large body of EC law, implemented into British domestic law, that is intended to facilitate and support its development. One part of relevant EC law makes it easier to make cross-border offers within the EEA by harmonizing prospectus disclosure requirements and providing a passporting facility whereby prospectuses that have been approved by the issuer's home state securities regulator are valid for use throughout the Community.[90] EC prospectus laws apply in relation to all public offers (subject to certain exemptions) and not only to those in respect of securities that are to be admitted to trading on a 'regulated market' (such as the Main Market of the London Stock Exchange but not its junior market, the Alternative Investment Market (AIM), which for the purposes of securities laws is an 'exchange-regulated' market). Another part of EC law addresses transparency and disclosure obligations for issuers that are admitted to trading on a regulated market. An aspiration that informs and shapes the transparency rules is that access for investors to information about issuers should be more organized at a Community level in order actively to promote integration of European capital markets.[91] There is a specific obligation in relation to information requirements for issuers to ensure equal treatment for all holders of shares who are in the same position.[92] Regulated information must be disclosed on a non-discriminatory basis through the use of such media as may reasonably be relied upon for the effective dissemination of information to the public throughout the

preference to other claims that may be open to them: see, Law Commission, *Shareholder Remedies A Consultation Paper* (Law Com CP No 142, 1996) paras 20.2–20.4.

[89] [1996] 1 BCLC 155.

[90] See further ch 13 below.

[91] Directive (EC) 2004/109 of the European Parliament and of the Council of 15 December 2004 on the harmonisation of transparency requirements in relation to information about issuers whose securities are admitted to trading on a regulated market and amending Directive (EC) 2001/34 [2004] OJ L390/38, rec 25.

[92] Transparency Obligations Directive, Art 17.

Community.[93] These requirements are reflected in the FSA *Disclosure Rules and Transparency Rules* for issuers admitted to trading on a regulated market which, as well as providing for equality of treatment for all holders of shares who are in the same position,[94] require regulated information to be disseminated in a manner ensuring that it is capable of being disseminated to as wide a public as possible, and as close to simultaneously as possible in the home Member State and in other EEA states.[95] Excluding overseas shareholders located in EEA states outside the UK from participation in a pre-emptive offering would not sit comfortably with the policy goals that underlie the pan-European framework. Furthermore, to the extent that EC law facilitates cross-border securities issuance activity within the EEA by providing passporting mechanisms for documentation, this makes it hard to rely on difficulties in complying with foreign laws as a factor in determining the fairness of excluding overseas shareholders located in the EEA from participation in a pre-emptive offering. As a matter of practice, the UK regulator, the FSA, normally expects all shareholders in EEA jurisdictions to be included in offers by companies that are subject to its *Disclosure Rules and Transparency Rules* because of the EC prospectus passporting arrangements.

Open offers

An open offer is a variant form of pre-emptive offer sanctioned by the FSA *Listing Rules*.[96] An open offer is defined as an invitation to existing holders to subscribe for or purchase securities in proportion to their holdings, which is not made by means of a renounceable letter (or other negotiable document). The fact that the offer is not made by means of a renounceable letter distinguishes the open offer from a rights issue. A further difference, and the one that makes it necessary to disapply statutory pre-emption rights, is in relation to the duration of the offer: open offers are not subject to the twenty-one-day minimum offer period. The timetable for an open offer must be approved by the recognized investment exchange on which the issuer's securities are traded.[97]

Disapplications for non pre-emptive offers

UK companies that are listed on the Main Market of the London Stock Exchange are expected to take account of the *Statement of Principles on Pre-emption* when they approach their shareholders for permission to disapply pre-emption rights. The *Statement* is an attempt to achieve a compromise between the desire of companies to have flexibility in the methods of raising capital which are open to them and institutional investors' interests in protecting pre-emption rights.

---

[93] ibid Art 21.
[94] *DTR* 6.1.3.
[95] *DTR* 6.3.4.
[96] FSA, *Handbook*, Glossary Definitions. On open offers see *LR* 9.5.7–9.5.8.
[97] *LR* 9.5.7.

The *Statement*, which has been adopted by the major investment management trade associations,[98] does not have legal force. It works by providing companies with an assurance that their major shareholders will, in principle, be favourably disposed towards a proposed disapplication of pre-emption rights so long as it is within limits specified in the *Statement*. The *Statement* is not intended to be inflexible: companies can still seek disapplications in circumstances falling outside the specified limits but early dialogue with shareholders will be of particular importance in such cases. According to the *Statement*, critical considerations in non-routine cases are likely to include: the strength of the business case; the size and stage of development of the company and the sector within which it operates; the stewardship and governance of the company; other financing options; the level of dilution of value and control for existing shareholders; the proposed process following approval; and contingency plans in case the request is not granted.

Under the *Statement* a request for disapplication of pre-emption rights will generally be regarded as routine provided it seeks permission to offer non-pre-emptively no more than 5 per cent of ordinary share capital in any one year. Companies are also expected to have regard to cumulative limits. A company should not without (a) suitable advance consultation and explanation or (b) the matter having been specifically highlighted at the time at which the request for disapplication was made, issue more than 7.5 per cent of the company's ordinary share capital for cash other than to existing shareholders in any rolling three-year period. The *Statement* also addresses pricing:

Companies should aim to ensure that they are raising capital on the best possible terms, particularly where the proposed issue is in the context of a transaction likely to enhance the share price. Any discount at which equity is issued for cash other than to existing shareholders will be of major concern. Companies should, in any event, seek to restrict the discount to a maximum of 5 per cent of the middle of the best bid and offer prices for the company's shares immediately prior to the announcement of an issue or proposed issue.[99]

Accountability in respect of how power to issue shares non-pre-emptively is also provided for: 'Once a request to disapply pre-emption rights has been approved, shareholders expect companies to discharge and account for this authority appropriately. It is recommended that the subsequent annual report should include relevant information such as the actual level of discount achieved, the amount raised and how it was used and the percentage amount of shares issued on a non-pre-emptive basis over the last year and three years.'[100]

---

[98] The Association of British Insurers (ABI), the National Association of Pension Funds (NAPF) and the Investment Management Association (IMA).

[99] Pre-emption Group, *Statement of Principles on Pre-emption*, para 18.

[100] ibid para 20.

Disapplication or exclusion of pre-emption rights: private companies

The articles of a private company may exclude the statutory pre-emption rights regime, either generally or in relation to allotments of a particular description.[101] This power to exclude pre-emption rights is not limited to companies with one class of shares.

With respect to disapplication, the procedure considered in the previous section is applicable to private companies. In addition, another provision of the Companies Act 2006 provides for the directors of a company with only one class of shares to be given power by the articles or by a special resolution of the company to allot equity securities of that class as if statutory pre-emption rights did not apply or applied with such modifications as the directors may determine.[102] Unlike the general disapplication route, disapplications under this provision are not tied to an allotment authorization under section 551 of the Companies Act 2006 (as none is required) and so need not be limited in duration to a maximum of five years.

Other formalities in relation to share allotments

A company must register in its books an allotment of shares as soon as practicable and in any event within two months after the date of the allotment.[103] Failure to comply constitutes a criminal offence by the company and every officer who is in default.[104] This requirement was introduced by the Companies Act 2006. Within one month of making an allotment of shares, a limited company must deliver to the registrar of companies a return of the allotment accompanied by a statement of capital.[105] The officers of the company who are in default in respect of this delivery requirement (but not the company itself) are liable to criminal sanctions.[106] Any person liable for the default can apply to court for relief and the court, if satisfied that the omission was accidental or inadvertent or that it is just and equitable to grant relief, may make an order extending the time for delivery of the document for such period as the court thinks proper.[107] Responsible officers (but not the company itself) also commit a criminal offence if they fail to comply with the obligation to issue share certificates within two months after allotment where it is applicable.[108]

---

[101] Companies Act 2006, s 567.
[102] ibid s 569.
[103] ibid s 554(1).
[104] ibid s 554(3)–(4).
[105] ibid s 555.
[106] ibid s 557.
[107] ibid s 557(3).
[108] ibid s 769.

6

Shares

The legal nature of a share

There is no comprehensive legal definition of a share[1] but in *Borland's Trustee v Steel*[2] Farwell J described a share in the following terms:

A share is the measure of a shareholder in the company measured by a sum of money, for the purposes of liability in the first place, and of interest in the second, but also consisting of a series of mutual covenants entered into by all the shareholders inter se. The contract contained in the articles is one of the original incidents of the share. A share is not a sum of money... but is an interest measured by a sum of money and made up of the various rights contained in the contract.

This description makes it clear that a shareholder is an investor: she pays a sum of money in the hope of earning a return. The shareholder's financial interest is in the company itself and it does not amount to a direct interest in the company's assets. These assets belong to the company, which is a separate legal person. Thus in *Macaura v Northern Assurance Co Ltd*[3] it was held that a shareholder did not have an insurable interest in the company's property.[4]

The financial rights or expectations associated with an investment in shares are discussed in detail in the first part of this chapter. The starting point, in outline, is that an investor in shares makes a permanent investment in a company in return for an expectation of a financial return in the form of dividends and capital growth. Capital growth may be realized by selling the shares to a third party or by waiting for the company to distribute surplus assets or to be wound up, at which point any surplus that remains after all of the debts have been discharged will be shared out among the shareholders. While more sophisticated arrangements that depart from this simple model and result in complex capital structures

---

[1] RR Pennington, 'Can Shares in Companies be Defined?' (1989) 10 *Company Lawyer* 140.

[2] [1901] 1 Ch 279, 288. This description was cited with approval in *IRC v Crossman* [1937] AC 26, HL, 66 *per* Lord Russell of Killowen.

[3] [1925] AC 619, HL.

[4] See also *Bank voor Handel en Scheepvaart NV v Slatford* [1953] 1 QB 248, CA (property held by a Dutch limited company bank with Hungarian shareholders did not fall within the scope of a provision concerned with property 'belonging to or held or managed on behalf of' a Hungarian); *John Foster & Sons Ltd v IRC* [1894] 1 QB 516, CA (conveyance of property from individuals to a company in which they held all of the shares was liable to stamp duty).

in which different shares carry different entitlements are possible, it is important to bear in mind from the outset that the terms on which a company raises capital in return for shares are always bounded by mandatory company law rules on maintenance of capital that restrict distributions to shareholders.[5]

Incidents of shares: dividends and capital

What financial entitlements do investors in shares acquire? The position of holders of ordinary shares

An ordinary share is the default share in the sense that the rights attached to ordinary shares are those that attach to all shares unless contrary provision is made when particular shares are issued or by subsequent variation of the rights attaching to particular shares. A company that wants to issue shares with different rights must have power to that effect in its constitution so as to displace the presumption that all shareholders are to be treated equally.[6] In commercial terms, ordinary shares are the 'equity' or 'risk' capital, with which is associated the greatest opportunity for capital growth but also the most financial exposure if the business is unsuccessful.

A key distinctive feature of the financial rights attaching to an ordinary share is that, in respect of both income and capital, the return to the holder is not fixed: dividends may vary depending upon the profitability of the company, and the ultimate capital return may be greater than the amount that was originally invested. The open-ended nature of the investment expectations serves to distinguish ordinary shares from non-participating preference shares, which in respect of dividends and capital enjoy a priority to ordinary shares, but only for a fixed amount. This description of the nature of the financial rights attaching to an ordinary share would not be accurate in a company that has deferred or founders shares because, in that case, the ordinary shareholders would receive only a fixed return and the balance would go to the holders of the deferred/founders shares. Deferred/founders shares are now rarely encountered and they are not discussed further in this work. A further fundamental incident of an investment in ordinary shares is that the holders' claims on the company assets are last in the queue so that if the company has insufficient assets to meet all of the claims against it, the ordinary shareholders will thus be the first to absorb the loss.

Among themselves, the holders of ordinary shares are entitled to share equally in dividends and in capital distributions. This simple statement is as much as needs to be said in the straightforward, and most common, case where shares are

---

[5] See chs 7 and 9 below.
[6] *Campbell v Rofe* [1933] AC 98, PC; *British and American Trustee and Finance Corp v Couper* [1894] AC 399, HL, 416 *per* Lord Macnaghten.

paid up in full:[7] the distribution available can simply be divided by the number of shares in issue in order to arrive at each shareholder's entitlement. The position is more complicated where there are partly paid shares because in that situation it becomes necessary to ask whether it is their nominal value or the amounts paid up on them that is to be taken as the basis for determining the return. For example, if a company has 10 ordinary shares with a nominal value of £1 each, 5 of which have paid up in full and 5 of which have been paid up as to 50p, using nominal values, the return on each share out of a total distribution of £100 would be £10 but, using paid up amounts, it would be £13.33 on the shares that have been paid up in full and £6.66 on the partly paid shares.

The company's articles of association may include express provision for these matters. Where the articles or the terms of issue of the shares are silent, certain default rules established by case law apply.

Default capital rights of ordinary shares

The seminal case on the default rule applicable in respect of the distribution of any surplus that remains after paid up capital has been repaid is *Birch v Cropper*.[8] In this case it was held by the House of Lords that any such surplus is distributable equally among the ordinary shareholders in proportion to the nominal value of their shares. Lord Macnaghten explained:[9] 'Every person who becomes a member of a company limited by shares of an equal amount[10] becomes entitled to a proportionate part in the capital of the company and, unless it be otherwise provided by the regulations of the company, entitled, as a necessary consequence, to the same proportionate part in all of the property of the company, including its uncalled capital.'

Default dividend rights of ordinary shares

The default rule established by case law is that entitlement to dividend distributions is based on the nominal value of the shares held by each shareholder.[11] This rule can be displaced: if so authorized by its articles, a company can pay a dividend in proportion to the amount paid up on each share rather than its nominal

---

[7] Paid up share capital means the amount of the nominal share capital that has been paid to the company and it does not include share premiums: see ch 4 above. It would not be feasible to measure an ordinary shareholder's entitlement to income and capital by reference to an amount which included a share premium paid when the share was first subscribed. Over time, it is likely that various share issues at different prices will have taken place and it would normally be impossible to trace back to the initial price at which a share was allotted because fully paid shares are not numbered and have no other individual distinguishing mark.

[8] (1889) 14 App Cas 525, HL. The default loss-sharing rule is also based on nominal values (*Re Hodges' Distillery, ex p Maude* (1870) 6 Ch App 51, CA) but this can be displaced by articles of association (*Re Kinatan (Borneo) Rubber Ltd* [1923] 1 Ch 124).

[9] (1889) 14 App Cas 525, HL, 543.

[10] 'Amount' in this context clearly means nominal amount: *Re Driffield Gas Light Co* [1898] 1 Ch 451.

[11] *Oakbank Oil Co v Crum* (1882) 8 App Cas 65, HL.

amount.[12] If the ordinary shares in a company are all fully paid, the dividend can be expressed simply as the amount available for distribution to the holders of the ordinary shares divided by the number of shares in issue.

Dividends must be paid in cash unless the articles otherwise provide.[13] It is usual for articles to make provision for the payment of dividends in kind.

The holder of an ordinary share does not have an absolute right to claim dividends in the way that a provider of debt finance could claim to be contractually entitled to receive interest. Dividend entitlements depend on articles of association which, in the standard case, distinguish between 'final' dividends declared by the shareholders in general meeting and 'interim' dividends paid on the authority of the board. In *Potel v IRC*[14] Brightman J outlined the entitlement of shareholders to dividends in the following terms:

i.   If a final dividend is declared, a date when such dividend shall be paid can also be specified.[15]
ii. If a final dividend is declared by a company without any stipulation as to the date of payment, the declaration of the dividend creates an immediate debt.[16]
iii. If a final dividend is declared and is expressed to be payable at a future date a shareholder has no right to enforce payment until the due date for payment arrives.[17]
iv. In the case of an interim dividend which the board has resolved to pay, it is open to the board at any time before payment to review the decision and resolve not to pay the dividend.[18] The resolution to pay an interim dividend does not create an immediate debt.
v.   If directors resolve to pay an interim dividend they can, at or after the time of such resolution, decide that the dividend should be paid at some stipulated future date. If a time for payment is so prescribed, a shareholder has no enforceable right to demand payment prior to the stipulated date.

The six-year limitation period in respect of an unpaid dividend runs from the date when it is declared or any later date for payment.[19]

A shareholder is a creditor in respect of a dividend that has been declared but not paid by the due date for payment.[20] However, when a company is in liquidation any sum due to a member of the company by way of dividend is deemed not to be a debt of the company in a case of competition between the member to whom it is due and any other creditor of the company who is not a member of a

---

[12] Companies Act 2006, s 581(c).
[13] *Wood v Odessa Waterworks Co* (1889) 42 Ch D 636.
[14] [1971] 2 All ER 504.
[15] *Thairwall v Great Northern Rly Co* [1910] 2 KB 509.
[16] *Re Severn and Wye and Severn Bridge Rly Co* [1896] 1 Ch 559.
[17] *Re Kidner* [1929] 2 Ch 121.
[18] *Lagunas Nitrate Co Ltd v Schroeder & Co and Schmidt* (1901) 85 LT 22.
[19] *Re Compania de Electricidad de la Provincia de Buenos Aires* [1980] 1 Ch 146, not following *Re Artisans' Land and Mortgage Corp* [1904] 1 Ch 796. Money due from a member to the company is now regarded as an ordinary contract debt rather than a specialty debt (Companies Act 2006, s 33(2)) with the consequence that the ordinary contractual limitation period applies.
[20] *Re Compania de Electricidad de la Provincia de Buenos Aires* [1980] 1 Ch 146.

company. Any such sum is to be taken into account for the purpose of the final adjustment of the rights of the contributories among themselves.[21]

In *Evling v Israel & Oppenheimer*[22] the dividend entitlement attaching to particular shares was exceptional in that dividends were expressed to be payable without declaration. Eve J held that the petitioning shareholder was entitled to a declaration as to his rights in the profits of the company but noted that the action could not fairly be said to be an action to recover a dividend. The difficulty that perhaps concerned Eve J in expressing this reservation is that there could be circumstances where a dividend, payable without declaration, has become payable in accordance with its terms but the company is unable to pay under the general law because it has insufficient distributable profits. The solution to this problem arrived at in an Australian case was to suspend the right to payment until there were sufficient distributable profits.[23] This probably represents the position under English law but the matter is not covered by authority.

What financial entitlements do investors in shares acquire? The position of holders of preference shares

A preference share is a share that, in respect of dividends and/or capital, enjoys priority, for a limited amount, over the company's ordinary shares. The precise extent of the priority is a matter of construction of the rights attached to the shares. It is not sufficient simply to designate shares as preference shares because that expression has no precise meaning. The preferential rights that are to be attached to the shares must be spelt out precisely as they will not be implied. Once the preferential entitlements are specified, there are certain secondary presumptions that apply unless contrary provision is made. The settling of the rights attaching to preference shares is a domestic matter in which neither creditors (unless they have specifically bargained for this) nor the outside public have an interest.[24]

As a matter of company law, preference shares are subject to the rules on maintenance of capital in the same way as ordinary shares. This means that dividends cannot be paid except from distributable profits and capital must not be returned otherwise than in accordance with reduction of capital procedures that are sanctioned by the companies legislation. For accounting purposes, however, many types of preference share are likely to meet the definition of financial liabilities and

---

[21] Insolvency Act 1986, s 74(2)(f). *Soden v British & Commonwealth Holdings plc* [1998] AC 298, HL.

[22] [1918] 1 Ch 101.

[23] *Marra Developments Ltd v BW Rofe Pty Ltd* [1977] 1 NSWLR 162, NSW Common Law Division.

[24] *Birch v Cropper* (1889) 14 App Cas 525, HL.

to be accounted for as such rather than as equity.[25] It is a matter of construction whether an issue of preference shares would be regarded as a borrowing for the purposes of borrowing limits in articles of association or loan agreements.

Default capital rights of preference shares

There is a presumption that all shares rank equally with regard to any distribution of assets.[26] Accordingly, any priority intended to be attached to a preference share must be expressly stated.[27] In particular, it is not to be presumed from the fact that a share has attached to it a preferential right in respect of dividend, that there is also a preferential entitlement in respect of capital.[28]

Where a preferential entitlement in respect of capital is specified, is that exhaustive or is there also an entitlement in participate *pari passu* in the distribution of any surplus? In *Scottish Insurance Corp v Wilsons & Clyde Coal Co Ltd*[29] the articles provided that in the event of winding up, preference stock ranked before ordinary stock to the extent of repayment of the amounts called up and paid thereon. The House of Lords held that this amounted to a complete statement of the rights of the preference shares in the winding up and that they did not carry the further entitlement to share in any assets remaining after repayment of the capital paid up on the ordinary shares. Observations of Lord Macnaghten in *Birch v Cropper*[30] that had suggested that preference shares were entitled to share in surplus assets unless their terms contained an express and specific renunciation of that right were not followed.[31] Where it is claimed that preference shares are participating with regard to the distribution of a surplus, the onus is therefore on the person making that claim to point to some provision in the company's constitution or terms of issue that confers an entitlement to share in any surplus assets.[32]

In *Re Saltdean Estate Co Ltd*[33] the articles provided that preference shares carried an entitlement to priority in respect of capital on a winding up, but that those shares were not to share in surplus assets remaining after all capital had been repaid. The articles were silent with regard to the position of preference shares in

---

[25] See further IAS 32, *Financial Instruments: Disclosure and Presentation*; ICAEW and ICAS, 'Distributable Profits: Implications of Recent Accounting Changes', TECH 02/07, paras 5.1–5.87.

[26] *HSBC Bank Middle East v Clarke* [2006] UKPC 31, para 26; *Welton v Saffery* [1897] AC 299, HL, 309 *per* Lord Watson; *Birch v Cropper* (1889) 14 App Cas 525, HL.

[27] *Re London India Rubber Co* (1869) LR 5 Eq 519.

[28] *Birch v Cropper* (1889) 14 App Cas 525, HL.

[29] [1949] AC 462, HL.

[30] *Birch v Cropper* (1889) 14 App Cas 525, HL, 546 *per* Lord Macnaghten.

[31] *Scottish Insurance Corp v Wilsons & Clyde Coal Co Ltd* [1949] AC 462, HL, 490 *per* Lord Normand.

[32] *Re National Telephone Co* [1914] 1 Ch 755, Ch D; *Re Isle of Thanet Electricity Supply Co Ltd* [1950] Ch 161, CA. In *Dimbula Valley (Ceylon) Tea Co Ltd v Laurie* [1961] Ch 353 preference shares were held to be participating and therefore entitled in a winding up to share in surplus assets remaining after all capital in respect of preference and ordinary shares had been repaid.

[33] [1968] 1 WLR 1844.

the event of a reduction of capital. Buckley J held that their position in a reduction of capital mirrored the rights that would apply in a winding up and that,
accordingly, the first class of capital to be repaid was the class comprising the
preference shares. The decision in *Re Saltdean Estate Co Ltd* was approved by the
House of Lords in *House of Fraser plc v ACGE Investments Ltd*[34] although, in
this case, the position was less uncertain because the articles expressly provided
that the rights attached to the preference shares on a return of capital otherwise
than on winding up were the same as the rights that they enjoyed on a winding
up. Lord Keith of Kinkel thought fit to quote from Buckley J's judgment in the
Saltdean case, including the following passage:[35]

> It has long been recognised that, at least in normal circumstances, where a company's
> capital is to be reduced by repaying paid-up share capital in the absence of agreement of
> the sanction of a class meeting to the contrary, that class of capital should first be repaid
> which would be returned first in a winding-up of a company... The liability to prior
> repayment on a reduction of capital, corresponding to their right to prior return of capital
> in a winding-up... is part of the bargain between the shareholders and forms an integral
> part of the definition or delimitation of the bundle of rights which make up a preferred
> share.

Lord Keith described this as 'an entirely correct statement of the law'.[36]

Spens *formula*

A term, sometimes known as a 'Spens formula', is commonly attached to preference shares. The essence of the Spens formula is that, on a repayment of capital
in a liquidation or on a reduction of capital, the holders of the preference shares
are entitled to a premium if, during a defined period prior to the repayment,
the shares have been standing in the market at a figure in excess of par. The premium is usually ascertained by reference to the average middle-market quotation
in excess of par during the relevant period, subject to adjustments to take account
of any accrued arrears of dividend that are reflected in the market price of the
shares.

Default dividend rights of preference shares

Whether a preference share carries a preferential right to dividends as well as capital is a matter of construction of the terms of the share. There is no presumption
that a share which carries a preferential right in respect of one financial aspect of
shareholding (whether it be dividend or capital) also carries a preferential right in

---

[34] [1987] AC 387, HL.
[35] *Re Saltdean Estate Co Ltd* [1968] 1 WLR 1844, 1849–50.
[36] *House of Fraser plc v ACGE Investments Ltd* [1987] AC 387, HL, 393. See also *Re Hunting plc*
[2005] 2 BCLC 211. Note *Re Northern Engineering Industries plc* [1994] BCC 618, CA where the
articles made special provision with regard to the rights of the preference shares.

respect of the other.[37] Commonly, however, preference shares carry preferential rights in respect of both dividends and capital.

A preferential dividend is commonly expressed as a specified percentage of the nominal value of the share; sometimes, however, it can be expressed as a specified percentage of the amount paid up on the share. Preferential dividends are usually expressed to be payable only when declared[38] but, if no dividend is declared in one year (or the dividend which is declared does not fully satisfy the preference shareholders' entitlements), it is presumed that the amount which is not paid is to be carried forward into subsequent years.[39] This well-established presumption that preferential dividends are cumulative can be displaced by provision to that effect in the company's constitution or in the terms of issue.[40]

Once the specified preferential dividend has been paid, can preference shareholders invoke the equality principle so as to rank equally with the ordinary shareholders in respect of any further distribution of profits? This question was answered in the negative in *Will v United Lankat Plantations Co.*[41] The shares in question had the right to a preferential dividend of 10 per cent and the House of Lords held that, as a matter of construction, that was the sum total of the holder's entitlement to dividends in respect of those shares. Articles or terms of issue could provide for preference shares to be participating with ordinary shares in respect of general dividends in addition to a fixed preferential dividend, although a provision to that effect would be relatively unusual. In commercial terms, companies and investors tend to regard preference shares as being akin to debt in the sense that the return paid to the investors is expected to be fixed or capped; if it is intended to give the investor the right to participate, that may be achieved alternatively by attaching a right to convert the preference share into an ordinary share at some later date.

Enfranchisement when preferential dividends are in arrears

Under the general law, a company cannot pay a preferential dividend if it does not have sufficient distributable profits available for that purpose. In such circumstances, the holder of a preference share cannot sue for breach of contract in the way that a creditor could sue in the event of a company failing to pay interest when due. The way in which the interests of preference shareholders are protected in circumstances such as these is for articles to make provision for them to become entitled to participate in the internal governance of the company's affairs.

Preference shares are typically issued on terms specifying that they carry no or very limited voting rights in normal circumstances and only become fully

---

[37] *Birch v Cropper* (1889) 14 App Cas 525, HL.

[38] *Bond v Barrow Haematite Steal Co* [1902] 1 Ch 362.

[39] *Henry v Great Northern Rly* (1857) 1 De G&J 606, 44 ER 858; *Webb v Earle* (1875) LR 20 Eq 556.

[40] *Staples v Eastman Photographic Materials Co* [1896] 2 Ch 303, CA.

[41] [1914] AC 11, HL.

enfranchised when the preferential dividend is in arrear. Provided the drafting of the articles follows the usual form, exemplified by *Re Bradford Investments plc*[42] where the articles specified dates on which preferential dividends were deemed to be payable and provided for enfranchisement of the shares when the dividend had not been paid in full for six months or more after the due date for payment,[43] the dividend may be in arrear either because the company has chosen not to declare a dividend, even though sufficient distributable profits to cover that dividend are available, or because the requisite distributable profits are not available. This wording ensures that preference shares become enfranchised in either case and leaves no room for the argument that the dividend cannot be said to have become payable because of the lack of available distributable profits; Hoffmann J noted in the *Bradford* case that, with this wording, it is 'really beyond argument' that the preference shareholders become entitled to vote in these circumstances.

Payment of accumulated unpaid preferential dividends

Where cumulative preferential dividends have been in arrear for some time but distributable profits subsequently become available or the company goes into liquidation, special rules govern the entitlement of the holders of the shares in respect of those dividends. When a cumulative preference dividend is finally declared, the whole of the accumulated amount is payable to the persons who are the holders of the preference shares at that time and it does not have to be apportioned between them and the other persons (if any) who held the shares during the time when the dividends were not declared.[44] Where preference shares of the same class have been issued over a period of time and the cumulative preferential dividend has not been declared over that period, the correct approach with regard to distributing any profits that do become available is to distribute them rateably among the shareholders according to the amount of dividend that has accumulated on each of the shares.[45] Where a company is in liquidation or is making a reduction of capital involving repayment, it is a question of the construction of the articles whether undeclared preference dividends are payable.[46] However, express provision is often made in articles or terms of issue for the payment in a winding up or reduction of capital of a sum equal to the amount of preference dividends (whether declared or not) on preference shares calculated up to the date of the winding up or of repayment of the capital in priority to any payment to ordinary shareholders.[47]

---

[42] [1990] BCC 740.

[43] This is a customary provision, the practice of inserting it having developed after it was held in *Re Roberts & Cooper Ltd* [1929] 2 Ch 383 that, without such provision, preferential dividends which had not been declared could not be said to be in arrear.

[44] *Re Wakley* [1920] 2 Ch 205.

[45] *First Garden City Ltd v Bonham-Carter* [1928] 1 Ch 53.

[46] *Re EW Savory Ltd* [1951] 2 All ER 1036.

[47] eg see *Re Wharfedale Brewery Co Ltd* [1952] Ch 913.

What financial entitlements do investors in shares acquire?
The position of holders of redeemable shares

Redeemable shares are shares issued on terms that provide for the company to redeem the shares at some point in the future. Both ordinary and preference shares can be issued on a redeemable basis provided certain conditions set out in chapter 13 of Part 18 of the Companies Act 2006 are complied with in connection with the issue. Companies were first allowed to issue redeemable preference shares by the 1929 companies legislation, and in 1981 the permission was extended so as to allow ordinary shares also to be issued on that basis. The background to the changes made by the 1981 legislation included a report by a committee under the chairmanship of Sir Harold Wilson that highlighted the difficulties faced by smaller companies in raising share capital[48] and a government report on the purchase by a company of its own shares.[49]

An issue of redeemable shares allows a company to raise short-term capital. The reasons for seeking short-term capital in this form may vary from company to company. Smaller companies may favour redeemable shares because they ensure that any loss of control resulting from an issue of shares to outsiders is only temporary. Being able to offer either ordinary or preference shares on a redeemable basis gives such companies the flexibility to appeal to the widest possible range of potential investors; and, for their part, investors may be more willing to invest in redeemable shares than they would have been to invest in non-redeemable ordinary or preference shares of a company whose shares are not actively traded and for which there is no ready market. For a company whose shares are actively traded, giving potential investors a way of realizing their investment would tend to figure less prominently as a reason for issuing redeemable shares. When larger companies issue redeemable shares, they tend to be non-participating redeemable preference shares carrying a preferential entitlement in respect of dividends and capital. From an economic terms perspective, an issue of redeemable preference shares on such terms is very similar to raising fixed-rate, fixed-term debt financing.

Section 684 of the Companies Act 2006 allows a company to issue redeemable shares except where, or to the extent that, this is excluded or restricted by its articles of association. To avoid the situation of a company being left with no permanent share capital, no redeemable shares may be issued at a time when there are no issued shares of the company which are not redeemable.[50]

Section 685 of the 2006 Act permits the directors to determine the terms, conditions, and manner of redemption of shares if they are authorized to do so by the company's articles or by a resolution of the company. This approach represents

---

[48] Committee to Review the Functioning of Financial Institutions, *Interim Report on the Financing of Small Firms* (Cmnd 7503, 1979) para 17.

[49] Department of Trade, *The Purchase by a Company of its Own Shares* (Cmnd 7944, 1980).

[50] ibid s 684(4).

a departure from the previous position under the Companies Act 1985, which provided for the redemption of shares to be effected on such terms and in such manner as might be provided by the company's articles. The correct construction of this provision was a matter of some dispute because it was unclear whether the company's articles could give a measure of discretion to the directors with regard to the detailed aspects of the redemption, such as the redemption price and the date of redemption, or whether it required those details to be set out specifically in the articles. The Companies Act 2006 clarifies the position in favour of a flexible approach.

The financial terms of redeemable shares may include a provision for the payment of a redemption premium, ie an amount greater than the par value of the shares.

There are detailed rules concerning the financing of redemptions. Redeemable shares may be redeemed out of distributable profits of the company, or out of the proceeds of a fresh issue of shares made for the purpose of the redemption.[51] Redemption premiums must be paid from distributable profits, except that in respect of redeemable shares that were issued at a premium, redemption premiums may be paid out of the proceeds of a fresh issue of shares up to an amount equal to the aggregate of the premiums received by the company on the issue of the shares redeemed, or the current amount of the company's share premium account, whichever is the less.[52] Private companies are also permitted, subject to certain conditions, to redeem shares out of capital.[53] These requirements are considered further in chapter 8 below.

Incidents of shares: transferability

A share is a chose in action.[54] Its transferability depends on the company's articles of association.[55] Transfer restrictions are commonly included in the articles of private companies, for example a right of pre-emption in favour of the remaining shareholders or a power for the directors to refuse to register a transfer to a person of whom they do not approve. The purpose of such restrictions is not hard to detect: it is to prevent control of the company passing outside a limited circle.[56] To be fully listed, shares must be free from any restriction on the right of transfer (except any restriction imposed for failure to comply with a notice under

---

[51] ibid s 687(2).
[52] ibid s 687(3)–(4).
[53] ibid s 687(1).
[54] *Colonial Bank v Whinney* (1886) 11 App Cas 426, HL.
[55] Companies Act 2006, s 544.
[56] Until 1980 there was an obligation on private companies to include restrictions on share transfers in their articles.

provisions of the Companies Act 2006 relating to company investigations).[57] The regulator, the Financial Services Authority (FSA), may in exceptional circumstances modify or dispense with this rule if it is satisfied that the power to restrict transfers would not disturb the market in those shares.[58]

Incidents of shares: voting rights

The default position is one vote per share unless the articles make contrary provision.[59] Ordinary shares normally follow the default position, although it is possible to have non-voting ordinary shares and ordinary shares that carry multiple votes generally or in particular circumstances.[60] Preference shares normally carry only limited voting rights but the shares may become fully enfranchised if the preference dividend is in arrear for longer than a specified period. A preference dividend that is not paid because the company has insufficient distributable profits is in arrear for this purpose if the articles provide a payment date and that date is past.[61]

The juridical nature of the relationship between a company and its registered shareholders

By virtue of section 33 of the Companies Act 2006, a contractual relationship subsists between a company and its members and also between its members amongst themselves.[62] The persons who are members of a company are the subscribers to its memorandum whose names must be entered as such in the company's register of members and those persons who agree to become members of

---

[57] *LR* 2.2.4.

[58] *LR* 2.2.6.

[59] Companies Act 2006, s 284.

[60] For detailed studies examining departures from the one share, one vote (proportionality) principle, see Institutional Shareholder Services, Shearman & Sterling and European Corporate Governance Institute, 'Report on The Proportionality Principle in the European Union' (May 2007) available at <http://www.ecgi.org/osov/documents/final_report_en.pdf> (accessed December 2007); Deminor Rating, 'Application of the One Share—One Vote Principle in Europe', available at <http://www.abi.org.uk/BookShop/ResearchReports/DEMINOR_REPORT.pdf> (accessed December 2007).

[61] *Re Bradford Investments plc* [1990] BCC 740.

[62] Authorities on the contract between the company and its members include: *Oakbank Oil Co v Crum* (1882) 8 App Cas 65, HL; *Welton v Saffery* [1897] AC 299, HL; *Hickman v Kent or Romney Marsh Sheepbreeders Association* [1915] 1 Ch 881; *Bratton Seymour Service Co Ltd v Oxborough* [1992] BCC 471, CA. Authorities on the contract between the members among themselves include: *Wood v Odessa Waterworks Co* (1889) 42 Ch D 636, 642; *Rayfield v Hands* [1960] Ch 1. On the history of the statutory contract: Law Commission, *Shareholder Remedies A Consultation Paper* (Law com CP No 142, 1996) paras 2.6–2.8.

the company and whose names are entered on the register of members.[63] The terms of the statutory contract constituted by section 33 are contained in the company's constitution, and mainly in the articles. Articles of association are a commercial document and, within the confines of the language used, are to be construed in a manner giving them reasonable business efficiency in preference to a result which would or might prove unworkable.[64] The parol evidence rule generally precludes reference to a prospectus or listing particulars accompanying an issue of shares to determine their terms;[65] however, the parol evidence rule can be displaced, for example, where it can be shown that the prospectus contains a collateral contract.[66]

The statutory contract is of a special kind, its distinctive features being outlined by Steyn LJ in *Bratton Seymour Service Co Ltd v Oxborough*[67] as follows:

(i)   it derives its binding force not from a bargain struck between the parties but from the terms of a statute;

(ii)   it is binding only insofar as it affects the rights and obligations between the company and the members acting in their capacity as members;

(iii) it can be altered by a special resolution without the consent of all the contracting parties;

(iv)   it is not defeasible on the grounds of misrepresentation, common law mistake, mistake in equity, undue influence or duress; and

(v)   it cannot be rectified on the grounds of mistake.

To this list can be added the decision in *Bratton Seymour* itself: a term cannot be implied to articles of association from extrinsic circumstances on the grounds of business efficacy but this does not prevent the implication of a term purely from the language of the document itself.[68]

A further distinctive feature of the statutory contract is that not all of the provisions of the constitution can be enforced. There are two limitations. First, only those rights and obligations in the constitution that affect members in their capacity as members can be enforced as part of the section 33 contract.[69] Thus if

---

[63] Companies Act 2006, s 112. The agreement to become a member need not be contractual: *Re Nuneaton Borough Association Football Club* (1989) 5 BCC 377.

[64] *Holmes v Keyes* [1959] 1 Ch 199, CA, 215 *per* Jenkins LJ; *BWE International Ltd v Jones* [2004] 1 BCLC 406, CA; *Hunter v Senate Support Services Ltd* [2005] 1 BCLC 175.

[65] *Baily v British Equitable Assurance Co Ltd* [1906] AC 35, HL.

[66] *Jacobs v Batavia and General Plantations Trust Ltd* [1924] 2 Ch 329, CA.

[67] [1992] BCC 471, CA, 475 *per* Steyn LJ.

[68] See also *Stanham v NTA* (1989) 15 ACLR 87, NSW SC EqD, 90–1 *per* Young J; *Towcester Racecourse Co Ltd v The Racecourse Association Ltd* [2003] 1 BCLC 260.

[69] *Hickman v Kent or Romney Marsh Sheepbreeders Association* [1915] 1 Ch 881; *Beattie v E & F Beattie Ltd* [1938] 1 Ch 708, CA. There is extensive academic literature debating the proposition that a member should be able to enforce all articles of association (see in particular KW Wedderburn, 'Shareholders' Rights and the Rule in *Foss v Harbottle*' [1957] CLJ 193; GD Goldberg, 'The Enforcement of Outsider Rights under Section 20 of the Companies Act 1948' (1972) 33 MLR 362; GN Prentice, 'The Enforcement of Outsider Rights' (1980) 1 *Company Lawyer* 179; R Gregory, 'The Section 20 Contract' (1981) 44 MLR 526; GD Goldberg, 'The Controversy on the Section 20 Contract Revisited' (1985) 48 MLR 121; and RR Drury, 'The Relative Nature of a

an article purports to give someone the right to hold or make appointments to an office or position in the company, such as company solicitor[70] or director,[71] those articles will not ordinarily be enforceable as part of the statutory contract. Secondly, even a failure to comply with a provision of the constitution which does affect members in their capacity as members does not necessarily entitle an aggrieved party to seek a contractual remedy. The court will not act in vain, and if the failure amounts simply to a procedural irregularity, the court will stand back and allow the company to take steps to remedy the position itself. What amounts to a procedural irregularity has to be considered on a case-by-case basis as there is little consistency in the reported decisions.[72]

A member may seek a declaration or an injunction against the company for breach of the statutory contract.[73] In *Hunter v Senate Support Services Ltd*[74] flawed decisions by directors of a company in respect of the exercise of power in the company's articles to forfeit shares for non-payment of calls were held to be in breach of the claimant's individual rights as a shareholder. The directors' decision to forfeit the claimant's shares was therefore held to be voidable at the instance of the claimant and the resolutions to that effect were to be set aside.

It is possible that a member may be able to claim damages from the company for breach of the statutory contract. Section 655 of the Companies Act 2006 provides that a person is not debarred from obtaining damages or other compensation by reason only of his holding or having held shares in the company. This reverses the decision of the House of Lords in *Houldsworth v City of Glasgow Bank*[75] where it was held that a person who had been induced to take shares in a company by a fraudulent misrepresentation could not claim damages for deceit whilst he remained a shareholder. However, whilst the reversal of the *Houldsworth* decision opens up the possibility of a damages claim, there is no clear authority

---

Shareholder's Right to Enforce the Company Contract' [1986] CLJ 219. However, although there is a House of Lords decision which, on its facts, supports the proposition that members should be able to enforce all articles (*Quin & Axtens Ltd v Salmon* [1909] AC 442, HL), when specifically required to consider the point, the courts have tended to adopt a more restrictive approach and the accepted view is as stated by Steyn LJ in the *Bratton Seymour* decision.

[70] *Eley v Positive Government Security Life Assurance Co Ltd* (1875–6) 1 Ex D 88, CA.

[71] *Browne v La Trinidad* (1887) 37 Ch D 1, CA.

[72] eg of *MacDougall v Gardiner* (1876) 1 Ch D 13, CA where the court refused to declare that a poll was improperly refused and *Pender v Lushington* (1877) 6 Ch D 70 where a failure to allow certain votes to be cast was held to be remediable by way of injunction. On the same side of the line as the *MacDougall* decision are cases such as *Normandy v Ind Coope & Co Ltd* [1908] 1 Ch 84 (inadequate notice of general meeting) and *Devlin v Slough Estates Ltd* [1983] BCLC 497 (allegedly defective accounts). Cases on the *Pender* side of the line include *Kaye v Croydon Tramways Co* [1898] 1 Ch 358, CA (notice of meetings) and *Henderson v Bank of Australasia* (1890) 45 Ch D 330 (moving amendments to resolutions).

[73] *Pender v Lushington* (1877) 6 Ch D 70; *Johnson v Lyttle's Iron Agency* (1877) 5 Ch D 687, CA; *Wood v Odessa Waterworks Co* (1889) 42 Ch D 636.

[74] [2005] 1 BCLC 175.

[75] (1880) 5 App Cas 317, HL.

establishing that damages may be claimed for breach of the statutory contract and, given the special nature of this contract, it should not be assumed that damages would necessarily be available. In any event, circumstances where damages for breach of the statutory contract would be more than nominal would probably be rare.

Since the statutory contract is bilateral, the company is entitled to seek contractual remedies against members who are in breach of, or may be proposing to breach, the contractual provisions of the constitution.[76]

Until the decision in *Rayfield v Hands*[77] there was a residual doubt regarding whether individual members could sue each other directly for breach of the statutory contract. Dicta in *Wood v Odessa Waterworks Co*[78] supported the view that such actions were permissible, but a comment (in a dissenting judgment) in *Welton v Saffery*[79] suggested that all actions in respect of the statutory contract had to be mediated through the company. In the *Rayfield* decision this comment was described as 'somewhat cryptic'[80] and it was held that, even where the company was not joined as a party to the action, petitioning members were entitled as against fellow members to a contractual remedy. The circumstances where a member might wish to sue fellow members for breach of the statutory contract are likely to be fairly limited. It is perhaps more likely that disputes between members that involve allegations relating to breach of the statutory contract would be ventilated through a claim for relief from unfair prejudice under section 994 of the Companies Act 2006.

The rather anomalous nature of the statutory contract and the uncertainty about which rights are enforceable and which are not were considered in the review that preceded the Companies Act 2006. The Company Law Review Steering Group was against simple re-enactment of the equivalent position in the Companies Act 1985[81] but, save for a substantive amendment affecting limitation periods and some drafting improvements, this is what was done. The government's view was that it was not convinced that there was anything better and clearer that could replace the established approach; it was wary of imposing radical solutions where it was not sure how much of a problem there really was in practice and, for that reason, the effect of a company's constitution was not an area in which it wanted to introduce substantive changes.[82]

---

[76] *Hickman v Kent or Romney Marsh Sheepbreeders Association* [1915] 1 Ch 881, 897.
[77] [1960] Ch 1.
[78] (1889) 42 Ch D 636.
[79] [1897] AC 299, HL, 315 *per* Lord Herschell.
[80] [1960] Ch 1, 5.
[81] Companies Act 1985, s 14. 'See Modern Company Law for a Competitive Economy: Completing the Structure', URN 00/1335, para 5.64 and 'Modern Company Law for a Competitive Economy: Final Report', URN 01/942, paras 7.33–7.40.
[82] Lord Sainsbury, *Hansard*, HL vol 678, col GC37 (30 January 2006).

Variation of rights attaching to shares

The general rule governing the alteration of rights attaching to shares that are contained in the company's articles is that they can be changed by special resolution of the company.[83] This general rule is subject to two qualifications. First, the power to alter rights by special resolution may be removed or restricted by a provision in the articles for entrenchment. Secondly, where a company's capital structure comprises more than one type of share, further consents in addition to the special resolution may be required because rights attaching to a class of share are specially protected and, generally speaking, can be changed only with the consent of the class.

Provision for entrenchment

A provision for entrenchment is a provision in the articles to the effect that specified provisions of the articles may be amended or repealed only if conditions are met or procedures are complied with that are more restrictive than those applicable in the case of a special resolution.[84] A provision for entrenchment may only be made in the company's articles on formation or by an amendment of the company's articles agreed to by all the members of the company.[85] A provision for entrenchment does not prevent amendment of the company's articles by agreement of all the members of the company or by order of a court or other authority having relevant authority.[86] Absolute entrenchment—no alteration in any circumstances, ever—is not possible.

Where there is a proposal to change a provision in the articles that sets out a right attaching to a particular class of shares, it is likely that a class consent will need to be obtained as well as the special resolution of the general meeting to alter the articles. The mechanism for alteration of the class right may itself be contained in the articles. Is this a provision for entrenchment? On one interpretation, it may be possible to regard a provision in the articles providing for the variation of class rights as a 'condition' or 'procedure' that is more restrictive than in the case of a special resolution, depending on how the provision is drafted.[87] However, if that view is correct, a consequence flowing from it is that companies may not be able to include certain types of variation of rights procedures in their articles

---

[83] Companies Act 2006, s 21.
[84] ibid s 22(1).
[85] ibid s 22(2).
[86] ibid s 22(3)–(4).
[87] However, if the provision provides simply for the obtaining of a special resolution of the class in accordance with normal procedures for special resolutions (see Companies Act 2006, s 283(1), which defines special resolutions including special resolutions of a class of members), the point does not arise because the procedure is not more restrictive than in the case of a special resolution.

post-formation otherwise than with the unanimous consent of the members. This view does not appear to be what is intended: the official Explanatory Notes on the Companies Act 2006 suggest that the variation of class rights procedure and a provision for entrenchment are different things.[88] On this basis, a mechanism for the variation of class rights can be added to articles post-formation without necessarily commanding the unanimous approval of all of the members.

A class of shares

Section 629(1) of the Companies Act 2006 provides that for the purposes of the Companies Acts shares are of one class if the rights attached to them are in all respects uniform.[89] A general statutory definition of a class of shares is new.[90] The statement of capital that a company must file on its formation and after changes in its capital structure must include for each class of shares: (a) prescribed particulars of the rights attached to the shares, (b) the total number of shares of that class, and (c) the aggregate nominal value of shares of that class, and (d) the amount to be paid up and the amount (if any) to be unpaid on each share (whether on account of the nominal value of the share or by way of premium).[91]

A class of shares—some clear cases

There is no doubt that shares that have different rights attached to them are in different classes. This is clear from section 629 of the Companies Act 2006, and it was also the position established by earlier case law.[92] There are endless ways in which the rights attaching to shares could differ, but obvious examples of shares in different classes are preference and ordinary shares,[93] redeemable shares and non-redeemable shares,[94] and convertible shares and those which are not convertible. Preference shares carrying different rights to dividend and/or capital would be treated as being in different classes from each other; although one case

---

[88] Para 937. Notes are available at <http://www.opsi.gov.uk/acts/en2006/ukpgaen_20060046_ en.pdf> (accessed December 2007).

[89] But rights attached to shares are not regarded as different from those attached to other shares by reason only that they do not carry the same rights to dividends in the 12 months immediately following allotment (s 629(2)).

[90] Other sections of the Companies Act 2006 that refer to classes of shares and to which this definition is therefore relevant, include ss 334, 352, and 359 (application of provisions relating to shareholder meetings to class meetings); s 550 (power of directors to allot shares etc: private company with only one class of shares); s 569 (disapplication of pre-emption rights: private company with only one class of shares); and ss 947–985 (the takeover 'squeeze-out' and 'sell-out' provisions).

[91] See eg Companies Act 2006, s 10, which details the contents of the statement of capital filed on formation.

[92] *Cumbrian Newspapers Group Ltd v Cumberland & Westmorland Herald Newspaper & Printing Co Ltd* [1987] Ch 1, 15.

[93] *Scottish Insurance Corp Ltd v Wilsons & Clyde Co Ltd* [1949] AC 462, HL; *White v Bristol Aeroplane Co* [1953] Ch 65, CA.

[94] *TNT Australia v Normandy Resources NL* [1990] 1 ACSR 1, SA SC.

on the interpretation of an investment clause of a settlement refers to 'sub-classes' of shares,[95] the concept of a sub-class is meaningless in relation to variation of rights procedures.

These examples focus on the financial aspects of shares but differences in the rights attaching to shares that result in the existence of separate classes of shares for the purposes of variation of rights procedures need not necessarily be financial. Thus, for instance, ordinary shares carrying limited or enhanced voting rights would comprise a class of shares separate from ordinary shares carrying a right to one vote per share. Non-voting or limited-voting ordinary shares are not common in listed companies but are often used in quasi-partnership companies or joint venture companies in order to give effect to the particular arrangements between the parties. Another familiar provision in the articles of joint venture companies is for the shares held by each of the joint venturers to be designated as 'A' shares, 'B' shares, 'C' shares, and so forth; each group of shares enjoys the same rights save that only the holder of the A shares can appoint an A director, and likewise with the other designated shares. The purpose of these arrangements is to ensure that each joint venturer has the right to appoint one member of the board; the effect of the arrangements is to create separate classes of shares.

Golden shares

Special rights may be attached to particular shares for so long as those shares are held by a named individual. In the UK during the 1980s this type of right was included in the articles of association of some privatized companies at the time when the businesses were first transferred from state to private ownership.[96] The government retained some control over the businesses for a period of time by taking a share (known as a 'golden share'), to which were attached certain rights such as the right to cast the majority of the votes on a poll at general meetings of the company in the event that any person offered to acquire more than 50 per cent of the ordinary shares; but the articles provided for the determination of these rights in the event of the sale of the golden share by the government.[97] In *Cumbrian Newspapers Group Ltd v Cumberland & Westmorland Herald Newspaper & Printing Co*[98] Scott J considered that the fact that the special rights would determine in the event of a transfer of the shares did not prevent the golden share from forming a special class. The reasoning on this point does not appear to be

---

[95] *Re Powell-Cotton's Resettlement* [1957] 1 Ch 159.

[96] C Graham, 'All that Glitters—Golden Shares and Privatised Enterprises' (1988) *Company Lawyer* 23.

[97] The practice of including golden shares is now liable to be held to be in breach of EC principles relating to free movement of capital: Case C-463/00 *European Commission v Spain (supported by United Kingdom intervening)* and Case C-98/01 *European Commission v United Kingdom* [2003] All ER (EC) 878. See also Case C-112/05 *European Commission v Germany*, decision October 2007.

[98] [1987] Ch 1.

undermined by the adoption of the statutory definition of a class of shares in section 629 of the Companies Act 2006.

Rights conditional on holding a specified percentage shareholding

In the *Cumbrian Newspapers* case the articles conferred on a named individual the right to appoint a director, conditional upon that individual holding not less than 10 per cent in nominal value of the company's issued shares. This type of provision differs from the golden share structure because, although the right is dependent on holding a certain proportion of the company's shares, it is not attached to any particular shares. It was held that the special rights granted by the defendant's articles were rights that, although not attached to any particular shares, were conferred on the claimant in its capacity as a shareholder in the company and were attached to the shares for the time being held by the claimant without which it was not entitled to the rights; and that accordingly the claimant had 'rights attached to a class of shares'. This controversial decision depended closely on the wording of particular sections of the legislation in force at the time (Companies Act 1985). The Companies Act 2006 differs from the 1985 legislation in significant material respects in relation to this matter and it is open to question whether rights of the *Cumbrian Newspapers* type are still to be regarded as giving rise to a class of shares. However, nothing was said explicitly in the parliamentary process leading up to the enactment of the Companies Act 2006 to suggest that a narrowing of the category of class rights to exclude *Cumbrian Newspaper*-style rights was intended.

Shares with different par values

In *Greenhalgh v Arderne Cinemas Ltd*[99] the company's share capital included ordinary shares with a par value of 50p (converting the relevant amount to decimals) and ordinary shares with a par value of 10p. It did not fall to the Court of Appeal to decide the point but Lord Greene MR indicated that he was inclined to agree with the view of the first instance judge, Vaisey J,[100] that the 10p shares formed a separate class from the 50p shares for the purpose of an article concerned with variation of rights attaching to a class of shares. The nominal value of the shares in a class is one of the matters that must be stated in any statement of capital filed under the Companies Act 2006.

Shares on which different amounts have been paid up

It could happen that different amounts are paid up in respect of shares that have the same par value. If, say, some shares are fully paid and some are partly paid,

---

[99] [1946] 1 All ER 512, CA.

[100] [1945] 2 All ER 719. It must be noted that the authorities that 'fortified' Vaisey J in his conclusion were scheme of arrangement cases: *Sovereign Life Assurance Co v Dodd* [1892] 2 QB 573, CA and *Re United Provident Assurance Co Ltd* [1910] 2 Ch 477. These cases may proceed on a different basis because consideration of economic interests as well as technical rights is permissible under Companies Act 2006, Pt 26, which governs schemes of arrangement.

does this give rise to two separate classes of shares? It is true to say that a person holding fully paid shares may be able to enjoy rights under the articles that a holder of partly paid shares does not enjoy—for example, assuming the articles follow the normal form, the fully paid shares will be freely transferable but the partly paid shares are likely to be subject to restrictions on transfer. Yet this difference is rooted in a factual matter, not a lack of uniformity in formal rights. Rather than viewing the shares as being in different classes (if the only difference between them is with regard to amounts paid up), it seems preferable to say that the rights attaching to them are in all respects uniform but the extent to which they can be actually enjoyed is fact-dependent. In the context of a scheme of arrangement under the companies legislation, shareholders holding partly paid shares have been held to constitute a separate class of members from shareholders holding fully paid shares,[101] but, since the courts can consider economic interests as well as rights in that context, this decision is not determinative in relation to other provisions that are concerned with more formal procedures and rights.

When class distinctions matter

In *Greenhalgh v Arderne Cinemas Ltd*[102] it was accepted that shares could be in different classes for some purposes and in the same class for others. It is suggested that the way in which this should be understood is that it is only in respect of certain matters that class distinctions need to taken into account. For example, in a company whose capital structures comprises two classes of ordinary voting shares (say A shares and B shares), the holders of the A shares and B shares may be entitled to vote on ordinary governance matters, such as re-appointment of directors, as if they were a single undivided class but on a matter that would involve a variation of rights attaching to either the A or B shares a separate class consent may be required. This example, however, prompts the following questions: When does a proposal involve a variation of rights attached to a class of shares? Are all constitutional changes variations of the rights attached to a class of shares or only some of them? What is the position where the economic value of rights is eroded or otherwise affected but the formal rights remain the same? These questions are considered next.

Variation of class rights

The Companies Act 2006 contains a special procedure for the variation of class rights. Rights attached to a class of a company's shares may only be varied in accordance with a provision in the articles for the variation of those rights or, if there is no such procedure, in accordance with a procedure in the Act itself.[103]

---

[101] *Re United Provident Assurance Co Ltd* [1910] 2 Ch 477.
[102] [1945] 2 All ER 719, [1946] 1 All ER 512, CA.
[103] Companies Act 2006, s 630. There is an equivalent procedure for variation of class rights in companies without a share capital (s 631).

What is a right attached to a class of shares for this purpose?

There are three possible ways of interpreting the concept of a right attached to a class of share for the purposes of variation of class rights procedures. The broadest interpretation is that once a company's share capital is divided into more than one class, all of the rights that flow from holding a share in the company—ie all the rights under the statutory contract—are 'rights attached to a class of shares'. However, that interpretation that would mean that all changes to the articles that modify the statutory contract would need to be regarded as a variation of class rights to which special protections apply; the principle of majority rule, which in relation to articles of association means that they can be altered by special resolution, would be very significantly curtailed. It has never been seriously maintained that the class rights protection procedure gives minorities such an extensive power of control over constitutional changes. In *Hodge v James Howell & Co Ltd* Jenkins LJ said: 'In general, one expects to find ordinary shares entitled to the whole of the profits and surplus assets remaining after preferences attached to any other class of shares are satisfied, and this residual right is not generally regarded as a special right or privilege or class right attached to the ordinary shares for the purposes of a modification of rights clause.'[104] Something more than the division of the capital into more than one class is required for rights attached to those shares to be regarded as class rights for the purposes of a modification of rights clause and, it is suggested, for the statutory procedure for the variation of class rights.

What is the something more? References to 'special' rights might be taken to suggest exclusivity[105] but it is apparent from the authorities that a right can be a right attached to a class of shares for the purposes of a variation of rights procedure even where it is common to more than one class: in *Greenhalgh v Arderne Cinemas Ltd*[106] voting rights that were common to two classes of shares were regarded as rights attached to a class of shares for the purposes of variation procedures (although the decision in the case was that there was in fact no variation of rights). Although there is no authority precisely on the point, the cases appear to proceed on the assumption that any rights that are exclusive to a particular class are rights attached to a class of shares but that, in addition, dividend and capital rights, rights to vote, and rights relating to protection of class rights[107] are rights

---

[104] [1958] CLY 446, CA.

[105] *Cumbrian Newspapers Group Ltd v Cumberland & Westmorland Herald Newspaper & Printing Co Ltd* [1987] Ch 1, 15. See also *Re John Smith's Tadcaster Brewery Co Ltd* [1953] Ch 308, CA, 319–20 *per* Jenkins LJ.

[106] [1945] 2 All ER 719, [1946] 1 All ER 512, CA. Also note *Re Old Silkstone Collieries Ltd* [1954] 1 Ch 169, CA where two classes of preference shares were entitled to participate in a compensation scheme to be established under nationalization legislation. This entitlement though common to the two classes was held to be a special right that triggered a protective procedure under the company's articles relating to variation of class rights.

[107] Companies Act 2006, s 630(5) expressly provides that any alteration of a variation of rights clause in articles, or the insertion of such a clause into articles, is itself to be treated as a variation of rights attached to a class of shares.

attached to a class of shares even when they are not exclusive and the same rights may also attach to other classes of share.

In essence, what is in issue in this debate about the interpretation of the expression 'rights attached to a class of shares' is the extent to which minority interests are entitled to protection. Investors in share capital take the risk that the rights which they acquire under the company's constitution by virtue of becoming members of the company will be changed by a resolution of the shareholders in general meeting; typically such rights are in the articles and, under section 21 of the Companies Act 2006, they can be changed by a special resolution (75 per cent of those voting) of the shareholders in general meetings. Where, however, a right attached to a class of shares is involved, this power to alter the articles is qualified by a procedure that requires the consent of a specified majority of the class also to be obtained. The more broadly the expression 'rights attached to a class of shares' is interpreted, the more protection is afforded to minorities, and vice versa. The law needs to achieves a balance that is consistent with rational expectations. Rights that rational investors would regard as fundamental to the investment—ie, financial return and voting entitlements—should be treated as deserving of special protection even where they are not enjoyed by one class only, but more general rights derived from the articles should be capable of being changed more easily under the general power to alter articles without requiring compliance with the variation of class rights procedures. Whilst uncertainty remains, in practice it would thus be prudent for companies to assume that proposals to vary dividend, capital, or voting rights attaching to a class of shares would vary class rights even where the same rights are attached to more than one class of shares.

What is a 'variation' of a right attached to a class of shares?

Articles of association that contain procedures for the variation of class rights may specify what, for the purpose of those articles, is meant by the term 'variation'; in that case whether a particular proposal is a variation requires close examination of the construction of the particular articles. Section 630 of the Companies Act 2006 also makes provision for variation of rights attached to a class of shares to cover cases where the company's articles do not make provision for variation (and to provide certain minority protection and procedural requirements that are generally applicable). For the purposes of the statutory variation procedure, and also (unless the context otherwise requires) in relation to provisions for the variation of rights contained in articles, references to variation are to be read as including 'abrogation'.[108]

Straightforward examples of variations of class rights would include reducing the rate of a preferential dividend or decreasing the number of votes attached to a share. Since variation includes abrogation, removing a right to a preferential

---

[108] Companies Act 2006, s 630(6).

dividend would also amount to a variation of class rights. In *Re Schweppes Ltd*[109] it was held that an issue of ordinary shares did not vary the class rights of existing ordinary shares, nor those of existing preference shares. An issue of preference shares ranking *pari passu* with existing preference shares was held not to vary the class rights of the existing preference shares in *Underwood v London Music Hall Ltd*.[110] In *Dimbula Valley (Ceylon) Tea Co Ltd v Laurie*[111] the rights attached to preference shares included the right to participate in a winding up rateably with the ordinary shares in all assets remaining after paying creditors, costs, arrears of preference dividend, and repayment of all paid up capital. It was held that a bonus issue of shares did not vary this entitlement to participate even though it might reduce individual shareholders' share of the surplus available on liquidation.

The distinction implicit in the *Dimbula* decision between varying a right and affecting the enjoyment of a right was developed in a trio of cases decided by the Court of Appeal in the 1940s and 1950s. In *Greenhalgh v Arderne Cinemas Ltd*[112] the Court of Appeal held that in respect of a share capital divided into 50p and 10p shares (using decimal equivalents for the sake of simplicity), a proposal to sub-divide the 50p shares into 10p shares did not amount to a variation of the class rights of the original 10p shares even though, as a result of the sub-division, the application of the provision in the articles which provided for each share (regardless of par value) to have one vote meant that the voting strength of the holders of the original 10p shares would be greatly diminished. Formally the rights attaching to the 10p shares were unchanged and it was simply that, through sub-division, those shareholders who could previously cast one vote in respect of each 50p share now could cast five, with a resulting diminution in the effectiveness of the votes cast by the holders of the original 10p shares. Lord Greene MR also commented on what the position might have been if the proposal had been to give the 50p shares five votes per share, rather than to sub-divide them. In that case, his Lordship considered that the rights attaching to the 10p shares might well have been varied because one of the rights attaching to those shares was that they should have voting powers *pari passu* with the other ordinary shares.[113]

The articles in the *Greenhalgh* decision imposed a special procedure to be followed on a 'variation' of rights. In *White v Bristol Aeroplane Co Ltd*[114] the relevant articles contained a more elaborate provision stipulating a procedure that was to be followed where rights attaching to a class of shares were to be 'affected, modified, varied, dealt with or abrogated in any manner'. The company's share capital comprised preference shares and ordinary shares and it proposed to increase its share capital by issuing new preference shares ranking *pari passu* with the existing

---

[109] [1914] 1 Ch 322 CA.
[110] [1901] 2 Ch 309.
[111] [1961] 1 Ch 353.
[112] [1946] 1 All ER 512, CA.
[113] ibid 515.
[114] [1953] 1 Ch 65, CA.

preference shares and new ordinary shares ranking *pari passu* with existing ordinary shares. The question considered by the Court of Appeal was whether this
clause applied on the basis that the rights of the existing preference shares would
be 'affected' by a new issue of *pari passu* shares. The court held that the rights
would not be affected and that, accordingly, the procedure did not apply. The
reasoning was that after the issue the rights attaching to the existing preference
shares would, in formal terms, be precisely the same as they had been before the
issue, the only change being in the enjoyment of, and the capacity to make effective, the voting rights attached to the shares.

In *Re John Smith's Tadcaster Brewery Co Ltd*[115] the Court of Appeal again
restricted the application of special procedures for the variation of rights. In this
case it was held that an issue of new ordinary shares did not 'affect' the voting
rights attaching to preference shares so as to trigger special procedures under the
company's articles. Evershed MR went so far as to express some dissatisfaction
with the prolix drafting of variation of rights procedures in articles of the kind in
question in *White v Bristol Aeroplane Co Ltd* and the particular case before him,
commenting: 'it is perhaps unfortunate that those responsible for drafting these
regulations seem apt . . . to string together words without pausing to reflect what
their joint or separate significance might be'.[116] Evershed MR also sought to justify the court's restrictive stance by pointing out that a loose interpretation of a
word such as 'affect' would mean that any activity on the part of the directors
in pursuance of their powers which could be said to affect or touch the value of
the preference shares would be rendered ineffective unless the special protective
procedures were adhered to—a result which, in his Lordship's view, would be
absurd.[117]

The distinction between varying a right and affecting the enjoyment of a right
is now well established although on which side of the line a particular series of
events falls can still be a disputed point.[118] It is justifiable for the special protection afforded to minorities by class rights protections to be kept within strict
limits so as avoid situations where the holders of a class of shares could hold an
effective veto over virtually all of the company's activities.[119] Yet some of the cases
seem to verge on an excessively restrictive interpretation of clauses that purport to
extend variation procedures to situations where class rights are affected and such
narrowness may be thought to defeat reasonable expectations.[120] As a matter of
drafting, it is clear that if it is intended that proposals such as that involved in the
White case should be subject to variation procedures, those procedures must be

---

[115] [1953] Ch 308, CA.
[116] ibid 312.
[117] ibid 316–17.
[118] eg *Re Smiths of Smithfield Ltd* [2003] BCC 769, especially para 57.
[119] RR Pennington, *Company Law* (Butterworths, 7th edn, 1995) 283.
[120] Criticisms were voiced before the House of Lords in *House of Fraser plc v ACGE Investments
Ltd* [1987] AC 387, HL but the House of Lords, in line with the earlier cases, adopted a narrow
approach.

carefully drafted such as by providing that an issue of new shares ranking *pari passu* with existing shares will be a variation of class rights. Most favourable to the holders of a class of shares would be a provision drafted in general terms, such as one which provides for the protective procedure to apply where rights are 'affected as a business',[121] but, from the company's perspective, a general formula such as this would probably be unacceptably vague and unpredictable.

There is one situation where there is a possibility of the literal approach not being followed in respect of articles that provide for protection in the event of class rights being 'affected'. This stems from a dictum in Evershed MR's judgment in *White v Bristol Aeroplane Co Ltd* where he said that:

> ...a resolution aimed at increasing the voting power of the ordinary stockholders by doubling it, so giving them twofold their present power, without altering any other of the privileges or rights attached to any class, might be said to be something so directly touching the position, and therefore the rights, of the preference stockholders...albeit that there was no variation of their own individual rights.[122]

The context for this statement was that Evershed MR used this example to demonstrate that meaning could be given to the term 'affected' as distinct from 'variation'. However, he emphasized that he was not deciding the point and it is therefore uncertain how much weight should be attached to this comment. Departing from the literal rule for this particular case would seem to have little merit and would serve only to create further complexity and anomaly in this already difficult area. However, applying normal principles, if the articles provide for two classes of shares to have *pari passu* voting rights and there is a subsequent proposal to increase the voting rights of one class, that would vary the *pari passu* voting right of the other class.[123]

Variation of rights by enhancement

Are class rights varied if the rights attached to that class are enhanced in some respect, for instance if the rate of a preferential dividend is increased or if the number of votes attached to a share is multiplied? A dictum in *Dimbula Valley (Ceylon) Teas Co Ltd v Laurie*[124] suggests that increasing rights is a reinforcement rather than a variation of those rights but, in principle, it is difficult to see why the mere fact of a change being beneficial rather than adverse should preclude it from amounting to a variation of class rights. Notably, although the point was not specifically addressed, *Rights and Issues Investment Trust Ltd v Stylo Shoes Ltd*[125] proceeded on the assumption that an alteration increasing the voting rights attached to a class of shares required the consent of the relevant class. In *Unilever (UK)*

---

[121] As discussed in *White v Bristol Aeroplane Co* [1953] Ch 65, CA, 80 *per* Evershed MR.
[122] ibid 76–7.
[123] *Greenhalgh v Arderne Cinemas Ltd* [1946] 1 All ER 512, CA.
[124] [1961] 1 Ch 353, 374.
[125] [1965] 1 Ch 250.

Holdings Ltd v Smith (Inspector of Taxes),[126] in considering tax issues relating to an alteration to the rights attaching to shares the Court of Appeal was of the view that the same test must apply whether the suggested alteration took the form of a restriction or an enhancement of rights.

The procedure for variation of class rights

In addition to the normal corporate consents required to change the company's constitution, the variation of rights attached to a class of shares also requires the consent of the class obtained in accordance with provisions in the company's articles for the variation of rights or, where the articles contain no such provision, in accordance with the statutory procedure in the companies legislation. The variation of rights procedure in the Companies Act 2006 is considerably simpler than the equivalent procedure in the Companies Act 1985. This is one of the consequences that follows from the simplification of the law on company constitutions by that Act, in particular the recharacterization of the memorandum as a historical formation document only; the option of setting out rights attached to shares in the memorandum rather than the articles is no longer available.[127]

The statutory procedure for the variation of a right attached to a class of shares is that:

(1) the holders of three-quarters in nominal value of the issued shares of that class (excluding treasury shares) must consent in writing to the variation; or
(2) a special resolution passed at a separate general meeting of the holders of that class must sanction the variation.[128]

Class meetings for a variation of class rights are governed by the procedural requirements applicable to company meetings generally (with appropriate modifications) except that: (a) the necessary quorum at any meeting (other than an adjourned meeting) is two persons holding, or representing by proxy, at least one-third in nominal value of the issued shares of the class in question (excluding treasury shares), and at an adjourned meeting one person holding shares of the class in question or his proxy; and (b) any holder of shares of the class in question present may demand a poll.[129] It is for the chairman of a class meeting to regulate its conduct but prima facie the meeting should be attended only by the members of the class so that they have an opportunity to discuss the matter privately and without their discussion being overheard by members of other classes.[130] Where rights attached to a class of shares are varied, the company must, within one month from the date when the variation is made, deliver to the registrar a notice giving particulars of the variation.[131]

---

[126] [2003] STC 15, 76 TC 300, para 56.
[127] See Companies Act 2006, s 8.
[128] ibid s 630(4).
[129] ibid s 334, especially s 134(4)–(6).
[130] *Carruth v Imperial Chemical Industries Ltd* [1937] AC 707, HL.
[131] Companies Act 2006, s 637.

Voting to alter class rights—a fettered power?

It is well established that a vote attached to a share is a property right to be exercised as its owner thinks fit.[132] In principle, a shareholder cannot be compelled to vote, nor can he be held to account for the way in which he chooses to exercise his vote. A line of authorities, however, imposes a qualification: in certain circumstances the courts will deny effect to a resolution if the shareholders who supported it were, in some sense, exercising their power inappropriately. Although some of the language in relevant judgments may suggest otherwise,[133] denying effect to a resolution is not the same thing as imposing a duty on the shareholders to vote in a particular way—shareholders may please themselves, knowing that even though the court may deny effect to their decisions, they will not be held to have breached a duty, or be liable to pay compensation, to anyone who may be aggrieved by their actions.[134] However, rational shareholders would want to avoid the trouble and expense of voting in circumstances where that vote may later be held to be ineffective by a court. Accordingly, if they vote at all, they may consider themselves to be under a practical, if not a legal, duty to cast their votes in a manner that will withstand judicial scrutiny.

A class consent to the variation of rights attached to the shares comprising the class is one of the situations where the courts have been prepared to deny effect to the decision of the majority of the class. In *British American Nickel Corp Ltd v O'Brien*[135] the company proposed a scheme for the reconstruction of the company involving mortgage bonds being exchanged for income bonds. The proposal was passed at a meeting of the mortgage bondholders but the sanction would not have been obtained but for the support of the holder of a large number of bonds who had been given an incentive to support the scheme that was not made available to other bondholders and which was not disclosed. The Privy Council held that the resolution was invalid, one reason for this invalidity being that the bondholder who had been given the incentive had not treated the interest of the whole class of bondholders as the dominant consideration. Viscount Haldane, delivering the judgment, explained the principle applied by the court:[136]

There is, however, a restriction of such powers, when conferred on a majority of a special class in order to enable that majority to bind a minority. They must be exercised subject to a general principle, which is applicable to all authorities conferred on majorities of classes enabling them to bind minorities; namely, that the power given must be exercised for the purpose of benefiting the class as a whole, and not merely individual members only.

---

[132] Leading authorities are *Pender v Lushington* (1877) 6 Ch D 70; *Northern Counties Securities Ltd v Jackson & Steeple Ltd* [1974] 1 WLR 1133; *North-West Transportation Co Ltd v Beatty* (1887) 12 App Cas 589, PC.

[133] eg *British American Nickel Corp v O'Brien* [1927] AC 369, PC, 378 *per* Viscount Haldane.

[134] LS Sealy, 'Equitable and Other Fetters on a Shareholder's Freedom to Vote' in NE Eastham and B Krivy (eds), *The Cambridge Lectures 1981* (Butterworths, 1982) 80.

[135] [1927] AC 369, PC.

[136] ibid 371.

This principle was applied by Megarry J in *Re Holders Investment Trust Ltd*[137] where trustees who were the holders of the majority of the preference shares in a company had supported a proposal to convert the preference shares into loan stock. The trustees also held the majority of the company's ordinary shares and the evidence indicated that they had acted throughout on the basis of what was in the interests of trust (which, of course, as trustees they were obliged to do) and had not applied their minds to the question of what was in the interests of the preference shareholders as a class. In these circumstances, Megarry J held that the sanction given by the preference shareholders as a class was not effective.

Statutory protection of minorities in a class

Under Section 633 of the Companies Act 2006, shareholders have the right to apply to court to have a variation of class rights cancelled. There are certain requirements that must be satisfied in order to bring a claim under this provision and it is therefore limited in its effect. To have standing to bring a claim under this section, the petitioner or petitioners must hold not less in the aggregate than 15 per cent of the issued shares of the class in question. The petitioner or petitioners must not have consented to or voted in favour of the resolution for the variation; shareholders who have simply changed their minds may not invoke section 633. The application must be made within twenty-one days after the date on which the consent was given or the resolution was passed. If a claim is properly brought, the variation has no effect until it is confirmed by the court. The court may disallow the variation if it is satisfied, having regard to all the circumstances of the case, that the variation would unfairly prejudice the shareholders of the class represented by the applicant; if the court is not so satisfied, it must confirm the variation. The court's decision is final. A copy of the court's order must be filed with the registrar of companies.[138]

The remedy under section 633 of the Companies Act 2006 overlaps with the unfair prejudice remedy in section 994 of that Act. The general unfair prejudice remedy does not have a threshold condition in relation to a minimum shareholding nor does it impose a strict time limit within which claims must be brought. The court has considerable remedial flexibility under section 994 of the Companies Act 1985, which is in distinct contrast to the position under section 633 of the 2006 Act, where the court is empowered only to disallow the variation.

Class rights and reduction of capital

Cases concerning reduction of capital provide further examples of judicial consideration being given to the question of what constitutes a variation of rights attaching to a class of shares. Reductions of capital in accordance with section

---

[137] [1971] 1 WLR 583.
[138] Companies Act 2006, s 635.

645 of the Companies Act 2006 are subject to the approval of the court. Whilst some older cases establish that the court has jurisdiction to approve a reduction of capital notwithstanding that it is not in precise conformity with class rights,[139] more recent authority has described separate class consents as a 'prerequisite' of a proposed reduction of capital involving a variation of class rights and held that the court has, accordingly, no jurisdiction to confirm the reduction in the absence of such approval.[140] The view that the court does not have jurisdiction to override class right is consistent with section 641(6), which makes the statutory reduction procedures subject to any provision of the company's articles restricting or prohibiting the reduction of capital. The new procedure in the Companies Act 2006 for private companies to reduce their capital out of court by means of a special resolution of the shareholders supported by a solvency statement from the directors does not make specific reference to class rights.[141] However, since section 630 of the Companies Act 2006 makes it clear that rights attached to a class of shares can only be varied in accordance with the specified procedure, it is difficult to see how any out of court reduction of capital that involves a variation of class rights could validly proceed in the absence of appropriate class consents.

In determining whether a reduction of capital would vary the rights attached to a class of shares, the starting point is the company's articles of association or terms of issue of the shares, as these may make specific provision in relation to the situation.[142] For example, in *Re Northern Engineering Industries plc*[143] the articles provided that any reduction of capital would be a variation of the class rights of the preference shares and an attempt to limit the application of this provision on the basis of an argument that 'reduction' for this purpose did not include cancellation of the preference shares was rejected. If the articles or terms of issue do not make provision, the position is that the various classes of shares are to be treated as they would be treated in the event of a winding up. What this means is that if a company's share capital comprises ordinary shares and preference shares carrying a right to priority as to return of capital (but no right to share in any surplus remaining after payment of creditors, costs, accrued unpaid dividends on preference shares (if any), and the return of paid up capital), a reduction of share capital involving the return of capital is effected in accordance with class rights where

---

[139] *British and American Trustee and Finance Corp v Couper* [1894] AC 399, HL.

[140] *Re Northern Engineering Industries plc* [1993] BCC 267. See also on the importance of class rights in reduction of capital situations: *Bannatyne v Direct Spanish Telegraph Co* (1887) 34 Ch D 287, CA, 300 *per* Cotton LJ; *Re Chatterley-Whitfield Collieries Ltd* [1948] 2 All ER 593, CA (affirmed *sub nom Prudential Assurance Co Ltd v Chatterley-Whitfield Collieries Ltd* [1949] AC 512, HL).

[141] Companies Act 2006, ss 642–644.

[142] A provision dealing with return of capital 'on a winding up or otherwise' will be taken to refer to repayment of capital in accordance with Companies Act 2006, s 645: *House of Fraser plc v ACGE Investments Ltd* [1987] AC 387, HL.

[143] [1993] BCC 267.

the preference shares are paid off first[144]—they would rank before the ordinary shares on a winding up. Conversely, where the reduction involves cancellation of nominal share capital as a result of losses, it is the ordinary shares (which would bear this loss in the event of winding up) that must be cancelled first.[145]

It is clear from the case law that the payment off and cancellation of non-participating preference shares as outlined in the last paragraph does not abrogate, affect, modify, or deal with the rights attached to those shares. In *Re Saltdean Estate Co Ltd*[146] Buckley J explained that the rights were not abrogated; rather, by paying off the preference shares first, the company was giving effect to the priority right attached to those shares. In *House of Fraser plc v ACGE Investments Ltd*[147] Lord Keith of Kinkel amplified this explanation. Paying off preference shares that were entitled to priority on a winding up or otherwise, gave effect to the entitlement and did not abrogate it; and the reduction did not 'modify, commute, affect or deal with' the rights attached to the shares within the meaning of the company's articles because those words all contemplated that, after the transaction, the shareholders in question would continue to hold some rights, albeit of a different nature from those that they previously held. The payment off and cancellation of non-participating preference shares extinguishes any further entitlement to whatever fixed divided was previously attached to those shares.[148] It is not a variation of class rights to extinguish this entitlement; rather, this is something that the holders of the shares must be taken to have agreed to as a necessary consequence of their right to priority on a return of capital.[149]

Where a company's share capital consists of ordinary shares and preference shares that have a priority right in respect of dividends (calculated by reference to paid up amounts) but which rank *pari passu* with the ordinary shares in respect of capital, any reduction of capital must, to conform to class rights, be spread equally across both classes. A reduction involving capital repayment or cancellation will thus result in a reduction of the amounts paid up on both classes of shares, but the effect on the continuing enjoyment of the priority dividend right will be especially significant: although the rate of the dividend will remain the same, the amount that the holders of the shares actually receive will be potentially significantly less because of the reduction of the principal amount on which that dividend is based. In line with the restrictive approach that characterizes case law

---

[144] *Re Chatterley-Whitfield Collieries Ltd* [1948] 2 All ER 593, CA (affirmed *sub nom Prudential Assurance Co Ltd v Chatterley-Whitfield Collieries Ltd* [1949] AC 512, HL); *Scottish Insurance Corp v Wilsons & Clyde Coal Co Ltd* [1949] AC 462, HL; *Re Saltdean Estate Co Ltd* [1968] 1 WLR 1844; *House of Fraser plc v ACGE Investments Ltd* [1987] AC 387, HL.

[145] *Re Floating Dock of St Thomas Ltd* [1895] 1 Ch 691.

[146] [1968] 1 WLR 1844.

[147] [1987] AC 387, HL. See also *Re Hunting plc* [2005] 2 BCLC 211; *Re Peninsula and Oriental Steam Navigation Co* [2006] EWHC 389 (Ch).

[148] *Re Chatterley-Whitfield Collieries Ltd* [1948] 2 All ER 593, CA (affirmed *sub nom Prudential Assurance Co Ltd v Chatterley-Whitfield Collieries Ltd* [1949] AC 512, HL).

[149] *House of Fraser plc v ACGE Investments Ltd* [1987] AC 387, HL.

relating to the interpretation of the term 'variation', a reduction in the amount of dividend actually received resulting not from a direct adjustment to the rate of dividend but indirectly from a reduction of the principal amount by reference to which it is calculated is not, in itself, regarded as a variation of class rights.[150]

Class rights and redemption of shares/share buy-backs

Class rights issues similar to those in reduction of capital situations can also arise in relation to share buy-backs and redeemable shares. Even where a redemption is funded from distributable reserves, from the investor's perspective its investment in the company's capital is returned and thus questions about priority entitlements in respect of capital repayments are relevant.

In determining whether a repurchase of shares or issue of redeemable shares constitutes a variation of rights attached to a class of shares the starting point is, again, the articles of association or the terms of issue of existing shares. For example, the terms on which preference shares are issued may expressly anticipate further issues of redeemable issues and specify whether or not those issues will constitute a variation of the rights of the preference shares. Where no such provision is made and the company has issued preference shares that are entitled to priority on a winding up or any return of capital, a subsequent issue of redeemable shares would constitute a variation of the class rights of the existing preference shares since, on redemption, capital could be returned first to the holders of the redeemable shares. Even if the terms of the preference shares simply provide for priority on a winding up and are silent with regard to returns of capital, the analysis should be the same by extension of the decisions on reduction of capital where the court held that it is to be implied that the position corresponds to the rights on winding up unless otherwise stated. Where there are preference shares that are entitled to priority on a return of capital in a winding up or otherwise, it would be a variation of their class rights for the company to purchase ordinary shares before the preference shares have been paid off unless (as is often the case) the terms on which the preference shares were issued expressly sanctioned share buy-backs of ordinary shares.

---

[150] *Bannatyne v Direct Spanish Telegraph Co* (1887) 34 Ch D 287, CA; *Re Mackenzie & Co Ltd* [1916] 2 Ch 450. See also *Adelaide Electric Co Ltd v Prudential Assurance Co* [1934] AC 122, HL where the rate of dividend was unchanged but, because of a change in the place of payment and currency of payment (from English pounds to Australian pounds), shareholders actually received a much smaller amount. The House of Lords held that there was no variation of class rights. This case again illustrates the restrictive approach of the courts, but the decision does turn on the interpretation of 'pound' as used in the company's articles. A change of currency that is not within the scope of the language used in the articles could, it is suggested, constitute a variation of class rights.

7

Maintenance and Reduction of Capital

Protection of creditors' interests: introduction

In modern systems of corporate regulation, the benefits to shareholders and controllers that flow from limited liability are counterbalanced by provisions that seek to protect creditors' interests. The main corporate regulatory strategies for the protection of creditors' interests are: mandatory disclosure rules, especially in relation to financial performance; detailed legal capital rules that throughout the life of a company govern the maintenance of its share capital and other quasi-capital reserves; and broad solvency-based standards underpinned by personal liability attaching to directors or controllers. These strategies can operate independently of each other or can be complementary, such as where mandatory financial statements are used as the basis for measuring compliance with legal capital rules.

UK company law, in common with that in all other EU Member States, still contains many detailed rules on the maintenance of capital, some of which are mandatory under the EC Second Company Law Directive;[1] elsewhere in the economically developed world, however, many countries have moved away from these rules in favour of more open-textured solvency-based standards.[2] There is a lively and detailed European debate on options for reform, which has gathered pace since landmark decisions of the European Court of Justice that held that certain detailed legal capital rules in national laws could not be justified by reference to public interest imperatives[3] and which has deepened more recently, as changes in accounting have

---

[1] Second Council Directive 77/91 on co-ordination of safeguards which, for the protection of the interests of members and others are required by Member States of companies within the meaning of the second paragraph of Article 58 of the Treaty, in respect of the formation of public limited companies and the maintenance and alteration of their capital with a view to making such safeguards equivalent [1977] OJ L26/1 ('Second Company Law Directive').

[2] G Hertig and H Kanda, 'Creditor Protection' in RR Kraakman, P Davies, H Hansmann, G Hertig, KJ Hopt, H Kanda, and EB Rock, *The Anatomy of Corporate Law: A Comparative and Functional Approach* (OUP, 2004) ch 4.

[3] Case C-212/97 *Centros Ltd v Erhvervs- og Selskabsstyrelsen* [1999] ECR I-1459; Case C-208/00 *Überseering BV v Nordic Construction Co Baumanagement GmbH (NCC)* [2000] ECR I-09919; Case C-167/01 *Kamer van Koophandel en Fabrieken voor Amsterdam v Inspire Art Ltd* [2003] ECR I-10155. See also Case C-411/03 *Reference for a preliminary ruling from the Landgericht Koblenz in proceedings against SEVIC Systems AG* [2005] ECR I-10805.

shifted the emphasis of financial disclosure from informing creditors to informing investors and, as a result, put in question the usefulness of published accounts as the yardstick for determining compliance with legal capital rules.[4]

Policymakers appear to be edging towards dismantling the detailed legal capital rules, although the pace of change at the European level is quite conservative, reflecting the fact that there is still a considerable divergence of views in Europe on fundamental questions about the role of company law, as opposed to insolvency law, in addressing creditors' interests and on whether this is an area where pan-European regulatory harmonization is appropriate in any event. The issues are complex and policymakers are aware that they require a nuanced and careful response. Although the Second Company Law Directive was amended in 2006,[5] the changes made were so slight as to prompt the remark from a leading commentator that: 'The revision of the Second company law directive has not even started.'[6] Thereafter, the Commission commissioned the accountancy firm KPMG to write a feasibility study on alternatives to the Second Directive and possible reform of the Directive was mentioned in the context of the Commission's general 'Better Regulation' agenda to simplify the regulatory environment for businesses.[7] The UK is among the Member States that favour significant reform, a stance that is reflected in the Companies Act 2006, which moves towards greater reliance on solvency standards, although it does not go quite as far as would be permissible without breaching EC law.[8] For those who favour radical reform, the findings of the KPMG study—published in February 2008 as this book was going to press—that the Second Directive is a flexible instrument, that compliance costs associated with it are limited, and that it does not cause significant operational problems for companies, and the Commission's decision, in response to the study, not to propose any follow-up measures or further changes, will come as a disappointment.[9]

Questioning the value of the legal capital doctrine

The essence of the legal capital doctrine is that share capital and certain other reserves must not be paid out to shareholders except in tightly constrained

---

[4] EV Ferran, 'The Place for Creditor Protection on the Agenda for Modernisation of Company Law in the European Union' [2006] *European Company and Financial Law Review* 178.

[5] Directive (EC) 2006/68 of the European Parliament and of the Council of 6 September 2006 amending Council Directive (EEC) 77/91 as regards the formation of public limited liability companies and the maintenance and alteration of their capital [2006] OJ L264/32.

[6] E Wymeersch, 'Reforming the Second Company Law Directive' (November 2006) available at SSRN <http://ssrn.com/abstract=957981>.

[7] European Commission, 'Communication on a simplified business environment for companies in the areas of company law, accounting and auditing' (COM (2007) 394).

[8] See the rejection of a solvency-based regime for determining the ability of a private company to pay dividends discussed further in ch 9 below.

[9] KPMG, *Feasibility Study on Capital Maintenance* (published by European Commission, February 2008).

circumstances. The payout constraint is expressed in the following way in Article 15(1)(a) of the Second Company Law Directive: 'Except for cases of reductions of subscribed capital, no distribution to shareholders may be made when on the closing date of the last financial year the net assets as set out in the company's annual accounts are, or following a distribution would become, lower than the amount of the subscribed capital plus those reserves which may not be distributed under the laws or the statutes.'

The effect of this is that only that portion of the net assets that exceeds the capital and undistributable reserves can be paid out to shareholders, notwithstanding that from a solvency perspective, which tests ability to pay debts as they fall due and/or by reference to the overall net asset position (total assets less total liabilities, not treating share capital as a liability), the company might well have capacity to make larger payouts without threatening its creditors' expectations of repayment. Article 15 carves out reductions of subscribed capital but under other provisions of the Directive these are subject to other formal requirements with regard to shareholder resolutions and the oversight of the court in relation to creditor protection.[10] As further exemplified by the Second Company Law Directive, the payout constraints that form the centrepiece of the legal capital doctrine may be reinforced by rules relating to the raising of capital, including minimum capital requirements and rules regulating the types of consideration that can be accepted in return for shares, and by requirements relating to share buy-backs and other corporate actions that could be indirect forms of payout to shareholders.

A large body of literature has grown up in which many failings of legal capital as a creditor protection device are outlined.[11] The criticisms (which are not necessarily always entirely consistent with each other) include the following:

(1) legal capital rules are crude mechanisms that fail to protect creditors because they are poorly designed;
(2) legal capital rules are unsophisticated and their intended protective effect is nullified by the efforts of astute legal and financial professionals who, with relative ease, can devise schemes to bypass the rules;
(3) legal capital rules impose costs that are not outweighed by their benefits;

---

[10] Arts 30–33.
[11] The literature includes: JA Armour, 'Share Capital and Creditor Protection: Efficient Rules for a Modern Company Law' (2000) 63 MLR 355; J Armour, 'Legal Capital: An Outdated Concept?' (2006) 7 *European Business Organization Law Review* 5; L Enriques and JR Macey, 'Creditors Versus Capital Formation: The Case Against the European Legal Capital Rules' (2001) 86 Cornell Law Review 1165; F Kübler, 'The Rules of Capital Under Pressure of the Securities Markets' in KJ Hopt and E Wymeersch (eds), *Capital Markets and Company Law* (OUP, 2003) 95; J Rickford (ed), 'Reforming Capital. Report of the Interdisciplinary Group on Capital Maintenance' (2004) 15 *European Business Law Review* 919; EV Ferran, 'Creditors' Interests and "Core" Company Law' (1999) 20 *Company Lawyer* 314; EV Ferran, 'The Place for Creditor Protection on the Agenda for Modernisation of Company Law in the European Union' [2006] *European Company and Financial Law Review* 178.

(4) legal capital rules distort corporate finance decisions by preventing some economically worthwhile transactions or other steps;
(5) creditors can protect themselves and there is no need for mandatory rules of company law to perform that function;
(6) creditor protection should be addressed primarily through insolvency rather than company law; and
(7) flexible *ex post* standards are inherently preferable to rigid *ex ante* rules.

On the other hand, counterarguments put forward by defenders of legal capital include:[12]

(1) legal capital provides preventive protection;
(2) legal capital has the same effect as a covenant with all the creditors and is thus of value to weaker creditors who cannot negotiate covenants for themselves— furthermore, for all creditors, it avoids the transaction costs involved in negotiating contractual protection;
(3) legal capital rules prevent the plundering of a company, especially after a takeover;
(4) restrictions on distributions protect the management against pressure from shareholders;
(5) distributions limited by legal capital have a more long-term effect than a short-term solvency test;
(6) a credible shift to greater reliance on solvency tests would require major expansion of liability rules for management and much more rigorous enforcement; and
(7) legal capital is deeply rooted in the Continental European legal culture and any change would entail massive upheaval, with associated adaptation costs, for uncertain benefits.

The interests of long-term creditors are a particular sticking-point in considering options for change. Solvency-based standards operate by requiring the directors of a company to take a view on the company's solvency and to assume personal liability for that view. Solvency tests can be drafted in different ways but typically would require directors to certify that the company is solvent at the time of the payout and for some time thereafter. Since it is not feasible to expect directors to assume personal responsibility for the performance of the company long into the future (when they may no longer be in charge of directing its affairs), a limited time horizon, such as twelve months, is appropriate for the prospective limb of the solvency test. Yet long-term liabilities cannot be ignored completely and how they are to be taken into account by directors in determining solvency for the

---

[12] This list is drawn from the executive summary by Marcus Lutter of an Expert Group on 'Legal Capital in Europe' that was published as a special issue of the European Company and Financial Law Review: M Lutter (ed), *Legal Capital in Europe* (De Gruyter Recht, 2006).

specified period (such as one year) is a complex and controversial issue.[13] When the possibility of shifting to a payout regime for dividends based on a solvency test was considered in the UK for private companies (which are not within the scope of the Second Company Law Directive) in the reform exercise that preceded the Companies Act 2006, there was concern that the way in which the proposed solvency test was drafted provided only an assurance of short-term solvency and that this was not a sufficient guarantee of a company's ability to meet its long-term debts, and therefore did not provide adequate protection for creditors. This concern was voiced in the Parliamentary debate on the Companies Bill where a spokesman for the government noted that:

The solvency test proposed in the amendment would only require the directors to consider debts falling due in the next year, thus allowing the company to pay a dividend even though it had long term liabilities—such as for pensions—exceeding its assets. Directors would still, of course, need to consider their general duties under Chapter 2 of Part 10 of the [. . . Act], but there is a real question as to whether this would be sufficient protection for long term creditors.[14]

One approach with regard to incorporating longer-term considerations into a time-limited solvency test is to require directors to take account of long-term liabilities in determining their company's solvency but this leaves considerable discretion with directors as to the weight they attach to long-term liabilities. Another approach is to require directors to determine solvency specifically by reference to an accounts-based balance sheet test of an excess of assets over liabilities but this leads back to the problem that financial statements drawn up under accounting rules that were not designed with creditors' interests primarily in mind are not necessarily a reliable yardstick.[15]

To some extent British policy views, as reflected in the recent legislation, on the adequacy of solvency tests from a creditor protection perspective give an impression of inconsistency: though rejected in the context of dividends, a solvency-based regime for reductions of capital by private companies was adopted in the Companies Act 2006 and that Act also continues a regime first enacted in predecessor legislation whereby private companies can use capital to fund share buy-backs so long as solvency requirements are satisfied.[16] This inconsistency is odd given that, in economic terms, dividends, reductions of capital, and share buy-backs are simply different methods of returning value to shareholders. However,

---

[13] J Rickford, 'Legal Approaches to Restricting Distributions to Shareholders: Balance Sheet Tests and Solvency Tests' (2006) 7 *European Business Organization Law Review* 135; W Schön, 'Balance Sheet Tests or Solvency Tests—or Both' (2006) 7 *European Business Organization Law Review* 181; W Schön, 'The Future of Legal Capital' (2004) 5 *European Business Organization Law Review* 429.

[14] Lord Sainsbury, *Hansard*, vol 680, col GC48 (20 March 2006).

[15] Rickford (n 13 above).

[16] Companies Act 2006, s 714.

even though the end result may appear somewhat anomalous,[17] there are several background factors that influenced the government's hesitancy with regard to moving to a solvency test for the determination of private companies' dividend-paying capacity and which provide some explanation for it: the proposal surfaced quite late in the reform process and the government was not sure that important questions of principle had been fully addressed;[18] in so far as the pressure for change was linked to developments in accounting, there was a case for waiting to see the practical impact of new accounting rules;[19] and, even though EC law did not preclude changes in the law relating to private companies, there was thought to be some merit in not rushing ahead of EU-level initiatives on reform of the Second Company Law Directive that might, in due course, overtake national level developments and permit a comprehensive, coherent reform of the rules on dividends for both public and private companies.[20] With the decision by the European Commission in February 2008 not to propose any changes to the Second Directive, this may come to be seen as a missed opportunity.

The development of the maintenance of capital regime in the UK

In *Trevor v Whitworth*[21] Lord Watson explained that the law prohibits:

. . . every transaction between a company and a shareholder, by means of which the money already paid to the company in respect of his shares is returned to him, unless the Court has authorized the transaction. Paid up capital may be diminished or lost in the course of the company's trading; that is a result which no legislation can prevent; but persons who deal with, and give credit to a limited company, naturally rely upon the fact that the company is trading with a certain amount of capital already paid, as well as upon the responsibility of its members for the capital remaining at call; and they are entitled to assume that no part of the capital which has been paid into the coffers of the company has been subsequently paid out, except in the legitimate course of its business.

Similarly in *Guinness v Land Corporation of Ireland*[22] Cotton LJ noted that paid up capital could not be returned to shareholders because that would 'take away

---

[17] In fact anomalies in the legal procedures governing these variant mechanisms can be found in the laws of many countries: Rickford (n 13 above) 144–5.

[18] Lord Sainsbury, *Hansard*, vol 680, col GC 48 (20 March 2006).

[19] ibid.

[20] The Appendix to the 'Twenty-Sixth Report of the Delegated Powers and Regulatory Reform Committee' (November 2006) contains a memorandum from the relevant government department (then the Department of Trade and Industry (DTI), now the Department for Business, Enterprise and Regulatory Reform (BERR)) explaining its policy of not making changes to the law in respect of private companies until the position in Europe becomes clearer.

[21] (1887) 12 App Cas 409, HL, 423–4.

[22] (1882) 22 Ch D 349, CA, 375. See also *Verner v General and Commercial Investment Trust* [1894] 2 Ch 239, CA, 264 *per* Lindley LJ; *Ammonia Soda Co Ltd v Chamberlain* [1918] 1 Ch 266, CA, 292 *per* Warrington LJ; *Hill v Permanent Trustee Co of New South Wales Ltd* [1930] 720, PC, 731 *per* Lord Russell of Killowen.

from the fund to which the creditors have a right to look as that out of which they are to be paid'.

The common law rule prohibiting the return of capital is now reinforced by statutory rules relating to distributions and to reduction of capital. Under Part 23 of the Companies Act 2006, distributions of the company's assets to members must be made only out of profits available for the purpose. 'Profits available for the purpose of a distribution' is a precise statutory concept under Part 23 but, broadly speaking, it excludes share capital and other quasi-capital reserves. Part 23 and its effect are examined separately in chapter 9 below. A reduction of capital is not a distribution for the purposes of Part 23.[23] Reductions of capital are regulated instead by chapter 10 of Part 17 of the 2006 Act and are permissible only when confirmed by the court or, in the case of a private company, when supported by a solvency statement given by the directors. The two statutory procedures for the reduction of capital are considered in detail later in this chapter.

Application of the common law rule prohibiting the return of capital to shareholders

Notwithstanding the intervention of statute, the courts continue sometimes to use the common law rule prohibiting the return of capital as the basis for looking through to the substance of corporate actions, howsoever labelled, and striking down those that are inappropriate in the sense that they amount to a fraud on the company's creditors. In the words of Pennycuick J in *Ridge Securities Ltd v IRC*[24] that are frequently cited in this context, the operative principle is that:

The corporators may take assets out of the company by way of dividend or, with leave of the court, by way of reduction of capital, or in a winding up. They may of course acquire them for full consideration. They cannot take assets out of the company by way of voluntary disposition, however described, and, if they attempt to do so, the disposition is ultra vires the company.

The approach of the courts is illustrated by the following cases.

In *Re Halt Garage (1964) Ltd*[25] a family company was owned and managed by a husband and wife team. The company continued to pay the wife as a director of the company even after it had become apparent that she was seriously ill and would never again play an active role in the management of the company. The company later went into liquidation and, on the application of the liquidator, Oliver J held that the amount of remuneration so paid exceeded what could be regarded as a genuine exercise of the power to pay remuneration. To the extent that

---

[23] Companies Act 2006, s 829(2)(b)(ii).

[24] [1964] 1 WLR 479, 495.

[25] [1982] 3 All ER 1016. See also *Ridge Securities Ltd v IRC* [1964] 1 All ER 275; *Jenkins v Harbour View Courts Ltd* [1966] NZLR 1, NZ CA; *Redweaver Investments Ltd v Lawrence Field Ltd* (1990–91) 5 ACSR 438, NSW EqD.

the payments exceeded genuine remuneration for the holding of the office of director, they were repayable to the liquidator because they amounted to a disguised return of capital. The test of 'genuineness' for distinguishing between proper transactions and disguised gifts to shareholders from capital is more interventionist than a test based solely on honesty. In the *Halt Garage* case it was accepted that a payment could amount to a disguised gift from capital even where the good faith of the directors (in the sense of absence of fraudulent intent)[26] was not in doubt. The mere fact that a company has transacted on terms which appear to the court to be somewhat generous to the other party will not suffice for a transaction to be treated as a disguised gift from capital; but evidence of patently excessive or unreasonable terms will cast doubt on the genuineness of that transaction.[27]

In *Aveling Barford Ltd v Perion Ltd*[28] the claimant company, at a time when it had no distributable profits, sold some of its property at a price considerably lower than that at which it had been valued by an independent valuer. The purchaser was a company, Perion Ltd, which was controlled by Dr Lee, who was also the controller of the vendor company. Within a year Perion Ltd re-sold the property for a significant profit. The liquidator of Aveling Barford successfully sought to recover the proceeds of sale on the grounds that Perion Ltd held it on constructive trust. The court held that Dr Lee had breached his fiduciary duty to Aveling Barford by selling the property at such a low price and that since Perion Ltd had known of the facts which made this transaction a breach of duty it was liable as a constructive trustee. Hoffmann J dealt with the argument that, if there had been a breach of fiduciary duty by Dr Lee, it was unchallengeable because it had been done with the consent of the shareholders of Aveling Barford by holding that the transaction was not a genuine exercise of the company's power under its memorandum to sell its assets, and that it amounted to an unlawful return of capital which could not be validated by shareholder authorization or ratification. In this case, the purchaser company was not itself a shareholder in the vendor company, although both companies shared the same controller. Hoffmann J held that the fact that the transaction was in favour of a company controlled by, rather than directly to, Dr Lee was irrelevant because the real purpose of the transaction was to benefit Dr Lee. The facts thus fell within the scope of the rule prohibiting the return of capital to shareholders because, by an indirect route, that was exactly the result in that case.[29]

---

[26] [1982] 3 All ER 1016, 1043. See also *Re National Funds Assurance Co* (1878) 10 Ch D 118, 128 *per* Jessel MR.

[27] [1982] 3 All ER 1016 Ch, 1041.

[28] 1989] BCLC 626. See also *Hickson Timber Protection Ltd (in receivership) v Hickson International plc* [1995] 2 NZLR 8, NZ CA, noted RI Barrett, 'Diversion to Shareholders of Proceeds of Sale of Corporate Asset' (1996) 70 ALJ 43; R Grantham, 'Corporate Groups and Informality' [1995] NZLJ 176.

[29] The High Court of Australia has held that a scheme from which shareholders benefit indirectly can amount to an unlawful return of capital: *Australasian Oil Exploration Ltd v Lachbery* (1958) 101 CLR 119, H Ct of Aust.

An indirect return of capital was also in issue in *Barclays Bank plc v British & Commonwealth Holdings plc*[30] where a group of banks, acting through a corporate vehicle, was required to buy a company's redeemable preference shares in the event of the company failing to redeem those shares in accordance with their terms. The company gave financial covenants to the banks so that, if it found itself unable to redeem its preference shares, it would also be in breach of covenant to the banks. The economic effect of the arrangement was that the banks had to pay for the shares but could then prove in the company's liquidation as creditors for the amount that they had paid for the shares as the sum due for breach of contract. This arrangement was held to amount to an indirect return of capital, contrary to *Trevor v Whitworth*,[31] on the basis that the rule in that case was wide enough to catch an agreement which was only likely to be called upon in the event of the company's insolvency, and which enabled shareholders in that event to obtain from third parties a payment in an equivalent amount to the payment due from the company, and for the third parties thereupon to become entitled as creditors to seek repayment from the company. Had the decision been otherwise, the effect would have been to allow a claim by one group of shareholders to be converted into a claim by creditors ranking before general shareholders' claims and equally with other creditors.

An unlawful return of capital is *ultra vires*

In the quotation from the *Ridge Securities* case above, Pennycuick J describes the disposition as being *ultra vires* the company. *Ultra vires* is an appropriate term in this context because the disposition is contrary to what companies are permitted to do under the general law. Thus in *MacPherson v European Strategic Bureau Ltd*[32] an arrangement involving payments to shareholders that were described as payments for consultancy services, which was entered into at a time when the company was insolvent, was held to be *ultra vires* because, according to Chadwick LJ (emphasis added):[33]

In my view, to enter into an arrangement which seeks to achieve a distribution of assets, as if on a winding up, without making proper provision for creditors is, itself, a breach of the duties which directors owe to the company; *alternatively, it is ultra vires the company*. It is an attempt to circumvent the protection which the 1985 Act aims to provide for those who give credit to a business carried on, with the benefit of limited liability, through the vehicle of a company incorporated under that Act.

---

[30] [1995] BCC 19 (affirmed [1995] BCC 1059, CA) following *Re Walters' Deed of Guarantee* [1933] Ch 321.
[31] (1887) 12 App Cas 409, HL.
[32] [2000] 2 BCLC 683, CA.
[33] At para 48.

Buxton LJ agreed:

> It would need a considerable degree of cynicism to think that an arrangement whereunder the corporators depart with the future income leaving the creditors with the debts is for the benefit of the company, even if the beneficiaries hold the whole of the interest in the company; and for the reasons set out by Chadwick LJ such an arrangement is without question *ultra vires* the company.[34]

Ultra vires, in this sense, is to be distinguished from *ultra vires* in the sense of actions falling outside the scope of a company's stated objects. Historically, the *ultra vires* rule in the latter sense was used by the courts as a creditor protection device, in addition to the rule prohibiting the return of capital to shareholders. Thus in *Trevor v Whitworth* Lord Herschell said:[35]

> The capital may, no doubt, be diminished by expenditure upon and reasonably incidental to all the objects specified. A part of it may be lost in carrying on the business operations authorised. Of this all persons trusting the company are aware, and take the risk. But I think they have a right to rely, and were intended by the Legislature to have a right to rely, on the capital remaining undiminished by any expenditure outside these limits, or by the return of any part of it to the shareholders.

At the time when *Trevor v Whitworth* was decided, having stated objects that defined the limits of a company's capacity was one of the fundamental tenets of company law: anything that fell outside the objects was *ultra vires* and void. The modern position is very different. In practice, companies tend to have very wide objects and the Companies Act 2006 finally takes this practice to its endpoint by permitting, for the first time, unrestricted objects.[36] Where objects are stated they 'do not need to be commercial; they can be charitable or philanthropic; indeed, they can be whatever the original incorporators wish, provided that they are legal. Nor is there any reason why a company should not part with its funds gratuitously or for non-commercial reasons if to do so is within its declared objects.'[37] Furthermore, even if a company has restricted objects under its constitution, the validity of an act done by the company cannot be called into question on the ground of lack of capacity by reason of those restricted objects.[38] Whilst constitutional restrictions may limit internally the authority of directors to act on the company's behalf, externally the Companies Act 2006 protects outsiders (as did predecessor companies legislation) by providing that in favour of a person dealing with a company in good faith, the power of the directors to bind the company or authorize others to do so is deemed to be free of any such constitutional

---

[34] At para 60.
[35] (1887) 12 App Cas 409, HL, 415. Also 424 *per* Lord Watson and 433 *per* Lord Macnaghten.
[36] Companies Act 2006, s 31.
[37] *Re Horsley & Weight Ltd* [1982] Ch 442, CA. See also *Rolled Steel Products (Holdings) Ltd v British Steel Corp* [1986] Ch 246, CA.
[38] Companies Act 2006, s 39.

limitation.[39] A person deals with a company for this purpose if he is a party to any transaction or other act to which the company is a party;[40] the inclusion of other acts indicates that this protection is not limited to commercial transactions. The net result of all of this is that the *ultra vires* rule, in the sense that is related to constitutional limitations, no longer plays a meaningful creditor protection role.

Gratuitous dispositions to third parties and directors' duties

Gratuitous dispositions otherwise than to, or for the benefit of, shareholders by definition fall outside the scope of the prohibition on returning capital to shareholders but they are, of course, subject to the general framework of company law as well as to provisions of the insolvency legislation relating to voidable preferences and transactions at an undervalue.[41] In *Barclays Bank plc v British & Commonwealth Holdings plc*[42] it was asserted at first instance that there is a fundamental principle of company law established by the cases that no company may make truly gratuitous dispositions of its assets. The judge accepted as correct a submission from counsel that the principle that a company cannot make a gratuitous disposition of its assets save either for the benefit of its business or out of distributable profit with the approval of its shareholders applied very widely. However, in so far as this assertion of a fundamental principle appears to relate to corporate capacity to dispose of assets it is not consistent with other authority that supports the view that a company *can* give away its assets, provided this is permitted by its constitution:[43] the principle, such as it is, is defeasible at the option of the company. Moreover, where a company's constitution restricts gratuitous dispositions, such dispositions may stand where the recipients can claim the benefit of the statutory protection for outsiders mentioned in the previous paragraph.

The principle relating to gratuitous dispositions of assets may be more accurately regarded nowadays as a constraint on directors in the exercise of their powers.[44] Under the Companies Act 2006 directors must act to promote the success of their company for the benefit its members,[45] subject to a duty developed by case law for directors of insolvent (or nearly insolvent companies) to consider creditors'

---

[39] ibid s 40.
[40] ibid s 40(2)(a).
[41] In particular, Insolvency Act 1986, ss 238–239.
[42] [1995] BCC 19 (affirmed [1995] BCC 1059, CA).
[43] In particular *Brady v Brady* [1988] BCLC 20, 38 *per* Nourse LJ.
[44] *ANZ Executors & Trustee Co Ltd v Qintex Australia Ltd* (1990–1) 2 ACSR 676 where McPherson accepted that it was *ultra vires* in the sense of abuse of power rather than corporate capacity that was relevant in answering the question whether a disposition of the property of the company was made for the benefit and to promote the prosperity of the company. A similar distinction is drawn in *Rolled Steel Products (Holdings) Ltd v British Steel Corp* [1986] Ch 246, CA. See also *MacPherson v European Strategic Bureau Ltd* [2000] 2 BCLC 683, CA.
[45] Companies Act 2006, s 172.

interests.[46] Under the Companies Act 2006, directors must also act in accordance with the company's constitution and must only exercise powers for the purposes for which they are conferred.[47] For directors to make a gratuitous disposition of assets otherwise than for the benefit of the company would be a breach of these statutory and (in respect of having regard to creditors' interests) common law duties.[48] It is generally possible for shareholders to ratify breaches of duty by directors[49] but this rule is subject to exceptions.[50] One exception is that shareholder ratification is not effective in relation to a transaction that constitutes a fraud on a company's creditors[51] and this exception would catch gratuitous dispositions made in breach of duty at a time when a company is insolvent.[52] Although the boundaries of what can (and cannot) be ratified are not entirely clear, in principle the exception should also catch gratuitous dispositions in breach of duty that are funded from undistributable reserves, even though overall solvency may not be in doubt, because shareholders are not empowered to sanction gifts from capital otherwise than in accordance with the prescribed statutory procedures for reduction of capital.[53]

Reduction of capital under the statutory procedures

A limited company having a share capital can reduce its capital only in accordance with prescribed statutory procedures. Section 641(1)(b) of the Companies Act 2006 provides a procedure for court-approved reductions of capital, which can be used by all limited companies that have a share capital. In addition, section 641(1)(a) introduces a new procedure for private companies only, whereby

---

[46] ibid s 172(3) and *West Mercia Safetywear Ltd v Dodd* [1988] BCLC 250. This duty is also recognized in a line of Commonwealth authority including: *Kinsela v Russell Kinsela Pty Ltd (in liq)* (1986) 4 NSWLR 722; *Spies v R* (2000) 201 CLR 603, 636, H Ct Aust; *Nicholson v Permakraft (NZ) Ltd* [1985] 1 NZLR 242, NZ CA. The Canadian Supreme Court has held that directors of a company in the zone of insolvency do not owe a fiduciary duty directly to creditors: *Peoples Department Store v Wise* [2004] 3 SCR 461; R Flannigan, 'Reshaping the Duties of Directors' (2005) 84 *Canadian Bar Review* 365. On the fluctuating situation in US law, see HTC Hu and JL Westbrook, 'Abolition of the Corporate Duty to Creditors' (2007) 107 *Columbia Law Review* 1321; SM Bainbridge, 'Much Ado about Little? Directors' Fiduciary Duties in the Vicinity of Insolvency' (2007) 1 *Journal of Business and Technology Law* 335; RB Campbell and CW Frost, 'Managers' Fiduciary Duties in Financially Distressed Corporations: Chaos in Delaware (and Elsewhere)' (2007) 32 *Journal of Corporation Law* 491.

[47] Companies Act 2006, s 171.

[48] However, note Companies Act 2006, s 247 which overrides s 172 to the extent of authorizing directors to make provision for employees on the cessation or transfer of the company's business.

[49] ibid s 239.

[50] *Aveling Barford Ltd v Perion* [1989] BCLC 626, 631. Companies Act 2006, s 239(7) provides that the section does not affect any rule of law as to acts that are incapable of being ratified by the company.

[51] *Rolled Steel Products Ltd v British Steel Corp* [1986] Ch 246, CA, 296 *per* Slade LJ.

[52] *West Mercia Safetywear Ltd v Dodd* [1988] BCLC 250.

[53] *Re George Newman and Co* [1895] 1 Ch 674.

they can reduce their capital on the basis of a directors' statement of solvency and court approval is not required. The new procedure is not made available to public companies because of complications stemming from the UK's obligation to implement Community law. Articles 30 to 34 of the Second Company Law Directive regulate reductions of capital by public companies. Article 32 provides that creditors whose claims pre-date the publication of the decision to reduce capital are entitled to have the right to obtain security for their claims. Furthermore, the reduction cannot proceed until the creditors have obtained satisfaction or a court has decided that their application should not be acceded to.

Why reduce capital?

A company may find itself in a position where it has assets that are excess to the needs of its business. For example, a rationalization programme may lead a company to decide to sell off certain divisions of the company's business in order to concentrate on its core activities. The cash generated by selling off the divisions may then not be needed by the company to finance what has become a smaller business. A reduction of capital is one of the methods whereby the company may return this surplus to its shareholders.[54] Other ways of returning value to shareholders are share buy-backs (considered in chapter 8 below) and special dividends (considered in chapter 9 below). The choice between the different methods of returning value will be affected by a range of considerations, including the differences in the tax treatment of the various options and the varying opportunities they offer for managing the shareholder base. Reductions of capital and buy-backs, but not dividends, can be used to reduce the number of shares in issue. As between reductions and buy-backs, a difference, which may be crucial in some circumstances, is that the reduction of capital procedure has an expropriatory dimension—ie it has the potential to be used to pay off shareholders against their wishes—whereas buy-backs are only possible where there are willing sellers.

Another situation where a company may want to reduce its capital is where the share capital recorded in the company's books is no longer reflected by the assets of the company because of trading or other losses that the company has suffered.[55] In this situation the company may want to cancel part of its stated capital without making any payment to its shareholders in order to restore reality to its balance sheet position. If a company in this position did not reduce its capital it would have to make good the losses before it could resume paying dividends to its shareholders.

A third situation in which a reduction of capital may be appropriate is where the company wants to refinance by paying off a relatively expensive form of

---

[54] eg *Wilsons & Clyde Coal Co Ltd* [1949] AC 462, HL; *Prudential Assurance Co Ltd v Chatterley-Whitfield Collieries Co Ltd* [1949] AC 512, HL.

[55] eg *Re Jupiter House Investments (Cambridge) Ltd* [1985] BCLC 222, [1985] 1 WLR 975.

financing and replacing it with cheaper financing from a different source. Another is where the company wishes to convert an undistributable reserve, such as a share premium account, into a reserve that may be capable of being regarded as distributable.[56]

Forms of reduction of capital sanctioned by the Companies Act 2006

Section 641(3) of the Companies Act 2006 allows a limited company with a share capital to reduce its share capital in any way in accordance with the prescribed statutory procedures. In particular, but without prejudice to the general nature of the power, the company may:[57]

(1) extinguish or reduce liability on any of its shares in respect of share capital not paid up;
(2) either with or without extinguishing liability on any of its shares, cancel any paid up share capital that is lost or unrepresented by available assets; or
(3) either with or without extinguishing liability on any of its shares, pay off any paid up share capital that is in excess of the company's wants.

Limitation on use of solvency statement reduction of capital procedure

Generally speaking, a private company can choose between the court approval procedure and the solvency statement procedure. However, there is one qualification: the solvency statement reduction of capital procedure may not be used if as a result of the reduction there would no longer be any member of the company holding shares other than redeemable shares. This qualification ensures that private companies cannot rely on relatively informal methods to reduce their capital to zero and that this must be overseen by the court. Many reductions of capital do involve the momentary reduction of capital to zero immediately followed by an increase in capital in a recapitalization.[58]

The court approval procedure

Special resolution of the shareholders

The first step in a reduction of capital under the court approval procedure is the passing of a special resolution in accordance with the procedure for special resolutions generally.[59] The resolution may be passed as a resolution passed at a meeting or, in the case of a private company, as a written resolution. A special resolution

---

[56] As in *Re Ransomes plc* [1999] 1 BCLC 775 (affirmed [1999] 2 BCLC 591, CA).
[57] Companies Act 2006, s 641(4).
[58] eg *Re MB Group plc* [1989] BCC 684.
[59] Companies Act 2006, s 283.

may not provide for a reduction of capital to take effect later than the day on which it has effect in accordance with the 2006 Act.[60]

The oversight of the court in respect of creditors' interests

After the resolution has been passed, the company must then apply to court for an order confirming the reduction.[61] The court has a discretion regarding whether to confirm a reduction and on what terms, provided that statutory requirements in respect of creditors are satisfied.[62] These statutory creditor protection requirements apply, unless the court otherwise directs, where the reduction involves diminution of liability in respect of unpaid share capital or the payment to a shareholder of any paid up share capital.[63] They also apply in other types of reduction if the court so directs[64] but this would be unusual.[65]

The key statutory creditor protection requirement is that every creditor who would be entitled to prove in the company's liquidation is also entitled to object to the reduction of capital.[66] The court must settle a list of creditors who are entitled to object.[67] The statutory procedure for drawing up the list of creditors is underpinned by criminal sanctions: an officer of the company commits an offence if intentionally or recklessly he conceals the name of a creditor entitled to object to the reduction or misrepresents the nature or amount of the debt or claim of any creditor, or if he is knowingly involved in any such concealment or misrepresentation.[68] If a creditor whose name is entered on the list does not consent, this blocks the court from confirming the reduction unless it is satisfied that the creditor's debt or claim has been discharged, determined, or secured.[69] The court may dispense with a creditor's consent if the company secures payment of the creditor's debt or claim by appropriating the amount of the debt or, where the debt or claim is not admitted and the company is not willing to provide for it in full, or it is contingent or not ascertained, an amount fixed by the court.[70]

In practice, reductions of capital are typically structured with in-built creditor protection with a view to persuading the court to order the dis-application of the statutory protections where they would otherwise apply. One such form of in-built creditor protection is for the company to demonstrate that it has, and

---

[60] ibid s 641(5).
[61] ibid s 645(1).
[62] *British and American Corp v Couper* [1894] AC 399, HL, 403–6 *per* Lord Herschell LC; *Poole v National Bank of China* [1907] AC 229, HL, 239 *per* Lord Macnaghten.
[63] Companies Act 2006, s 645(2)–(3).
[64] ibid s 645(4).
[65] *Re Meux's Brewery Ltd* [1919] 1 Ch 28 provides a rare example.
[66] Companies Act 2006, s 646.
[67] ibid s 646(2).
[68] ibid s 647.
[69] ibid s 648(2).
[70] ibid s 646(4)–(5).

after the reduction will continue to have, sufficient cash and readily realizable investments to pay all of its existing creditors, including its contingent creditors. Another is for the company to arrange for a bank to guarantee repayment of its creditors' debts. The court will also dispense with the statutory creditor protection requirements where, or to the extent that, creditors have already consented to the reduction. Widespread use of these various established mechanisms means that it is uncommon, in practice, for reductions of capital to involve inquiries into creditors' interests.

The oversight of the court in respect of shareholders' interests

Although not specifically mentioned in the Companies Act 2006, it is clear from case law that a court which is asked to confirm a reduction of capital will also be concerned to ensure that shareholders are properly treated. The court seeks to apply broad standards of fairness, reasonableness, and equity.[71] It will be concerned to see that the shareholders had the matter properly explained to them so that when it came to the general meeting at which they passed the special resolution they were fully informed about what they were doing.[72] The court will also be concerned to see that the reduction has a discernible purpose and, in establishing this, the applicant company has a duty of full and frank disclosure to the court.[73]

Where a company's share capital is divided into more than one class of shares, it is possible that a reduction of capital may impinge on class rights. Section 630 of the Companies Act 2006 provides that rights attached to a class of shares may *only* be varied in accordance with procedures specified in that section and does not make provision for any reduction of capital procedures to override. In spite of this, some cases relating to the court approval reduction of capital procedure establish that the court does have jurisdiction to confirm any type of reduction notwithstanding that it involves a departure from the legal rights of the classes for the court's power to confirm a reduction is perfectly general.[74] However, in *Re Northern Engineering Industries plc*[75] Millett LJ described separate class consents of the preference shareholders as a 'prerequisite' of a proposed reduction of capital involving a variation of class rights and held that the Court had, accordingly, no jurisdiction to confirm the reduction in the absence of such approval. The position must be regarded as uncertain but it may be noted that the view that the court does not have jurisdiction to override class right is consistent with section 641(6) of the Companies Act 2006, which makes the court approval and solvency statement statutory reduction of capital procedures subject to any

---

71 *Scottish Insurance Corp v Wilsons & Clyde Coal Co Ltd* [1949] AC 462, HL.
72 *Re Ratners Group plc* [1988] BCLC 685, 688.
73 *Re Ransomes plc* [1999] 2 BCLC 591, CA.
74 eg *British and American Corp v Couper* [1894] AC 399.
75 [1994] BCC 618, CA.

provision of the company's articles restricting or prohibiting the reduction of capital because it is in the articles that rights attaching to a class of share are usually specified.

Where the company's share capital comprises ordinary shares and preference shares with rights to a preferential dividend at a specified rate and priority with regard to the return of capital but no further rights to participate and no special terms deeming a reduction of capital to be a variation of class rights,[76] it accords with the class rights of the preference shares to repay those shares first on a reduction of capital.[77] The holders of the preference shares cannot therefore prevent the company from paying them off and refinancing more cheaply from an alternative source. The converse in respect of entitlements applies in a reduction of capital involving no repayment but merely a cancellation of shares: it accords with their respective class rights for the ordinary shares, rather than the preference shares, to absorb this loss.[78]

A class consent to a reduction of capital involving a variation of class rights may not be effective if those who voted in favour did not act in the interests of the class as a whole. In *Re Holders Investment Trust Ltd*[79] a class meeting of preference shareholders approved a reduction of capital that varied their class rights but this approval was held to be ineffective because the majority preference shareholders were held to have acted in what they considered to be their own best interests without asking themselves what was in the interests of the class as a whole. However, it is obviously difficult for the court to scrutinize too closely the motives that lead to votes being cast in any particular way and it is questionable how far this intervention by the court is compatible in any event with the principle that a vote attaching to a share is a right of property which the shareholder is free to exercise as he or she thinks fit.

General powers of the court

The court can confirm a reduction on such terms and conditions as it thinks fit. The court may order that the fact of reduction be indicated by the company adding to its name as its last words the phrase 'as reduced' for a specified period.[80] The court may also order the company to publish the reasons for the reduction of capital or such other reasons in regard to it as the court thinks expedient, with a view to giving proper information to the public, and (if the court thinks fit) the causes which led to the reduction.[81]

[76] On special provisions such as this see *Re Northern Engineering Industries plc* [1994] BCC 618, CA.

[77] *Scottish Insurance Corp v Wilsons & Clyde Coal Co Ltd* [1949] AC 462, HL; *Re Saltdean Estate Co Ltd* [1968] 1 WLR 1844; *House of Fraser plc v ACGE Investments Ltd* [1987] AC 387, HL.

[78] *Re Floating Dock of St Thomas Ltd* [1895] 1 Ch 691.

[79] [1971] 1 WLR 583.

[80] Companies Act 2006, s 648(4).

[81] ibid s 648(3).

Registration

A copy of the order of the court, together with a statement of capital (approved by the court) setting out details of the company's altered share capital must be registered with the registrar of companies.[82] The registrar must certify registration of the order and statement of capital and this certificate is conclusive evidence that all the requirements of the Act with respect to the reduction of capital have been complied with and that the company's altered share capital is as stated in the statement of capital.[83] Notice of the registration must be published in such manner as the court may direct.[84] The reduction of capital takes effect ordinarily on the registration of the order and statement of capital but where the reduction of capital forms part of a scheme of arrangement under Part 26 of the Companies Act 2006, it takes effect either on delivery of the order and statement of capital to the registrar or, if the court so orders, on the registration of the order and statement.[85] The provision on when reductions of capital that are part of a scheme take effect was introduced by the Companies Act 2006 to provide more flexibility and to address problems identified in the review process about timing in schemes being outside the company's control.

Where allotted capital is reduced below the authorized minimum

Where a reduction of capital would bring the allotted share capital below the authorized minimum for a public company (currently set at £50,000), the normal procedures for registration of the reduction are qualified. The registrar must not register the reduction whilst the company remains a public company unless the court otherwise directs.[86] The company should re-register as a private company. There is a special expedited procedure for the re-registration of a public company in these circumstances where the court oversees constitutional changes to be made in connection with the re-registration and a special resolution of the shareholders is not required.[87]

Effect of a court-approved reduction of capital

The effect of a reduction of capital is to relieve a member of the company (past or present) of any liability in respect of any share to any call or contribution exceeding the amount that remains unpaid on the share calculated by reference to the statement of capital showing the altered share capital.[88] This is qualified in one

[82] Companies Act 2006, s 649(1)–(2).
[83] ibid s 649(5)–(6).
[84] ibid s 649(4).
[85] ibid s 649(3).
[86] ibid s 650.
[87] ibid s 651. The normal re-registration procedure, in Companies Act 2006, ss 97–101, requires a special resolution.
[88] ibid s 652.

respect in order to protect creditors who, by reason of their ignorance of the proceedings or of their nature and effect, were not entered on the list of creditors. If, after the reduction of capital, the company is unable to pay the amount of such a creditor's debt or claim, members of the company at the time the reduction took effect are then liable to contribute for the payment of that debt or claim an amount not exceeding that which they would have been liable to contribute if the company had commenced to be wound up on the day before that date.[89]

Pre-Companies Act 2006 guidance from accounting bodies provided that, where a reduction or cancellation of capital under the court approval procedure resulted in a credit to reserves, that reserve was treated as a realized profit except to the extent that, and for as long as, the company had undertaken that it would not treat the reserve arising as a realized profit, or where the court had directed that it must not be treated as a realized profit.[90] Section 654 of the Companies Act 2006 makes provision for this guidance to be put onto a statutory footing. Section 654(1) states that a reserve arising from a reduction of capital is not distributable subject to any provision made by order under the section. Regulations made under that section provide that the prohibition in the section does not apply in relation to a reserve arising from a court-approved reduction of capital and that such a reserve is to be treated for the purposes of Part 23 (distributions) as a realized profit except where the order of the court provides otherwise.[91]

Reduction of capital under the solvency statement procedure: private companies only

Special resolution of the shareholders and class consents

A special resolution is also required under the solvency statement procedure.[92] For the reasons discussed above in relation to court-approved reductions of capital, class consents should be obtained where a reduction of capital is structured in such a way as to constitute a variation of class rights.

Solvency statement

The special resolution must be supported by a solvency statement made by the directors not more than fifteen days before the date of the special resolution.[93]

---

[89] ibid s 653.

[90] ICAEW and ICAS, ' Guidance on the Determination of Realised Profits and Losses in the Context of Distributions under the Companies Act 1985', TECH 07/03 (March 2003).

[91] The Companies (Share, Share Capital and Authorised Minimum) Regulations 2008, SI 2008/(draft), reg 9.

[92] Companies Act 2006, s 641(a).

[93] ibid s 642(1).

The solvency statement must be made available to members when they vote on the resolution. Where the resolution is proposed as a written resolution, a copy of the solvency statement must be sent to every eligible member at or before the time when the proposed resolution is sent or submitted.[94] Where the resolution is to be proposed at a meeting, a copy of the solvency statement must be made available for inspection by members of the company throughout the meeting.[95] Failure to observe the procedural requirements to make the solvency statement available to members will not affect the validity of the special resolution.[96] The sanction is that defaulting officers of the company commit an offence if they deliver a solvency statement to the registrar that was not provided to the members.[97] Furthermore, if directors choose to propose a resolution for the reduction of capital without making the solvency statement available, they run the risk of the resolution being vetoed by members.

Contents of solvency statement

A solvency statement for the purposes of the reduction of capital procedure is a statement that each of the directors (a) has formed the opinion, as regards the company's position at the date of the statement, that there is no ground on which the company could then be found to be unable to pay (or otherwise discharge) its debts and (b) has also formed the opinion that the company will be able to pay (or otherwise discharge) its debts as they fall due during the year immediately following that date.[98] If it is intended to wind up the company within twelve months of the date of the statement, the prospective opinion in (b) is modified and must relate to ability to pay debts in full within twelve months of the commencement of the winding up.[99] In forming those opinions, the directors must take account of all of the company's liabilities, including any contingent or prospective liabilities.[100] However, it is to be noted that for the purposes of the prospective opinion required by limb (b) (where there is no intention to wind up the company) that, whilst account must be taken of all liabilities, ultimately all the directors need be satisfied of in order to give the opinion is that debts can be paid as they fall due during that year. The solvency statement must be in the form that is to be prescribed under section 1167 of the Companies Act 2006.[101] The solvency statement must be made by all the directors of a company. A director who is unable or unwilling to join in the making of a solvency statement would have to resign or be removed from office before that procedure can be used.

---

[94] Companies Act 2006, s 642(2).
[95] ibid s 642(3).
[96] ibid s 642(4).
[97] ibid s 644(7).
[98] ibid s 643(1).
[99] ibid s 643(1)(b)(i).
[100] ibid s 643(2).
[101] ibid s 643(3).

Sanctions in respect of false solvency statements

Making a statutory statement without having reasonable grounds for the opinions expressed in it is a criminal offence for which the maximum punishment is imprisonment for up to two years.[102] The Companies Act 2006 does not specify civil sanctions for making a false or inaccurate solvency statement. Since the provision of a defective solvency statement would mean that the statutory procedures for a lawful reduction of capital have not been followed, the common law rules that the reduction is void,[103] that the responsible directors are in breach of their duties to the company,[104] and that recipient shareholders may be held liable to repay any capital that has been distributed to them[105] presumably apply. A reduction of capital by paying off paid up share capital is not a distribution for the purposes of Part 23 of the Companies Act 2006[106] and therefore the statutory remedy in that Part for unlawful distributions does not apply.[107]

Registration requirements relating to the solvency statement procedure

The special resolution for reduction of capital must be delivered to the registrar within fifteen days after it is passed or made in accordance with the general procedures governing the delivery of special resolutions.[108] In addition, the solvency statement and a statement of capital must also be delivered to the registrar within fifteen days of the passing of the resolution.[109] The registrar must register these documents on receipt and the resolution does not take effect until those documents are registered.[110] There must also be delivered to the registrar, within the same time period, a statement by the directors confirming that the solvency statement was made not more than fifteen days before the date on which the resolution was passed and was properly provided to members.[111] These various registration obligations are underpinned by criminal sanctions[112] but it is expressly provided that the validity of a resolution for reduction of capital is not affected by compliance failures.[113]

---

[102] ibid s 643(4)–(5).
[103] *MacPherson v European Strategic Bureau Ltd* [2000] 2 BCLC 683, CA.
[104] *Aveling Barford Ltd v Perion Ltd* [1989] BCLC 626.
[105] *Re Halt Garage (1964) Ltd* [1982] 3 All ER 1016.
[106] Companies Act 2006, s 829(2)(b).
[107] ibid s 847.
[108] ibid ss 29–30.
[109] ibid s 644.
[110] ibid s 644(3)–(4).
[111] ibid s 644(5).
[112] ibid s 644(8)–(9).
[113] ibid s 644(6).

Effect of a reduction of capital under the solvency statement procedure

After a reduction the members cease to be liable for calls or other contributions as regards the amount by which the nominal amount of their shares has been reduced.[114]

As yet there is no guidance from the accounting professional bodies on when a credit to reserves that results from a reduction of capital under the solvency statement procedure is to be treated as a realized profit. The prima facie statutory rule is that the reserve is not distributable but this is subject to provision that may be made by order under section 654 of the Companies Act 2006. The Regulations provide that a reserve arising from a reduction under the solvency statement procedure is not within the prima facie prohibition to the extent that the reserve is treated as a realized profit and, to that extent, it is to be treated for the purposes of Part 23 (distributions) as realized.[115]

Exceptional reduction of capital procedures

Reduction of capital following redenomination of shares

The Companies Act 2006 allows companies to redenominate their share capital.[116] The redenomination process may result in shares that are denominated in awkward fractions of the new currency and, in that case, companies may wish to nominalize the share capital in order to achieve shares with nominal values that are in whole units of the new currency. Companies can achieve this result by increasing the nominal value of the shares (with a capitalization of reserves up to the amount by which the capital is increased). Alternatively, the 2006 Act introduces a new procedure whereby a company can reduce its share capital (but not its overall undistributable reserves) in order to adjust the nominal value of redenominated shares to obtain more suitable values.[117] This special procedure requires a special resolution of the company but neither a solvency statement from the directors nor court approval is required. The amount by which a company's share capital is reduced must be transferred to a redenomination reserve, which may be applied in paying up fully paid bonus shares but which must otherwise be treated as if it were part of the company's share capital.[118] A reduction of capital in connection with redenomination must be notified to the registrar and, in the usual

---

[114] Companies Act 2006, s 652.
[115] The Companies (Share, Share Capital and Authorised Minimum) Regulations 2008, SI 2008/(draft), reg 9.
[116] Companies Act 2006, s 622.
[117] ibid s 626.
[118] ibid s 628.

way, the notification must be accompanied by a statement of capital.[119] Where a public company reduces its share capital under this procedure and the effect of the reduction is that the nominal value of the company's allotted share capital is less than the authorized minimum for a public company, the company must re-register as a private company within one year of the date when the resolution under section 626 is passed.[120]

Reduction of capital pursuant to an order of the court

Various sections of the Companies Act 2006 empower the court to grant remedial orders providing for the purchase by the company of the shares of any member and for a consequential reduction of the company's capital.[121]

Reduction of capital in respect of forfeited or acquired shares

A public company that forfeits shares for non-payment of calls or instalments pursuant to its articles or accepts shares surrendered in lieu of forfeiture must either dispose of such shares, or cancel them and diminish the amount of the share capital by their nominal value within three years.[122] The steps to cancel the forfeited or surrendered shares and to diminish the share capital figure can be taken by the directors without recourse to the general reduction of capital procedures.[123] This dispensation also applies where a public company acquires any of its own fully paid shares otherwise than for valuable consideration or has a beneficial interest in shares acquired by a nominee or other person in circumstances where the company is required either to dispose of the shares or to cancel them.[124] However, where shares are bought back or redeemed in accordance with the main statutory procedures governing redeemable shares and share buy-backs, the consequential adjustments to share capital and other undistributable reserves are governed by their own dedicated statutory framework.[125]

---

[119] ibid s 627.

[120] The Companies (Share, Share Capital and Authorised Minimum) Regulations 2008, SI 200/(draft), regs 4–8. An expedited procedure for re-registration as a private company is available in these circumstances (ibid).

[121] Companies Act 2006, s 996(2)(e) (relief from unfairly prejudicial conduct), s 98(5) (relief in respect of re-registration of a public company as a private company), s 721(6) (relief in respect of a redemption or purchase of shares from capital by a private company), and s 759(5) (relief in respect of breach of the prohibition of public offers of securities by a private company).

[122] Companies Act 2006, s 662.

[123] Companies Act 2006, s 662(4).

[124] Companies Act 2006, s 662.

[125] Companies Act 2006, Pt 18, chs 3–7. See further ch 8.

8

Share Buy-backs and Redeemable Shares

Introduction

The Companies Act 2006 contains a general rule prohibiting the acquisition by limited companies of their own shares[1] but the impact of this ban is attenuated by other provisions in the Act whereby they are permitted to purchase their own shares and also to issue redeemable shares.[2] The law has been progressively relaxed over the years so as to extend the range of financing options available to the corporate sector and to increase flexibility but the statutory powers whereby buy-backs and redeemable shares are permitted remain subject to restrictions that are intended to prevent abuse that would prejudice creditors or discriminate against groups of shareholders.

Arguments for and against allowing companies share buy-back/redeemable share issuance powers[3]

To attract external investors

A company whose shares are not actively traded is not an attractive investment prospect to external investors because of the risk of being permanently locked into that investment. Whilst the other existing shareholders are the persons who are most likely to be interested in acquiring the shares of an investor who wants to leave the company, and indeed they may have pre-emption rights in respect of the shares under the company's articles, their personal circumstances may be such that they are unwilling or unable to commit more of their own resources to an investment in the company. The risk of being locked into an investment in shares that are not actively traded is lessened if the company is able to act as

---

[1] Companies Act 2006, s 658.

[2] The maintenance of capital rules do not apply to unlimited companies but they are subject to the distribution rules in Companies Act 2006, Pt 23. This means that unlimited companies can purchase their own shares but must finance this from distributable profits as defined by Pt 23.

[3] IM Ramsay and AS Lamba, 'Share Buy-backs: An Empirical Investigation', Research Report, Centre for Corporate Law and Securities Regulation, University of Melbourne (May 2000). available at SSRN <http://ssrn.com/abstract=227930> or DOI <10.2139/ssrn.227930>.

an alternative purchaser and, by being able to offer this possibility, smaller companies may find it easier to raise share capital from external sources than would otherwise be the case.

Redeemable shares offer the most comfort to external investors who are concerned about becoming locked into their investment; although investors are not absolutely guaranteed the return of their capital, since this will depend on the company having available funds at the time of redemption, by holding redeemable shares they are, broadly speaking, assured of an exit from the company provided it remains prosperous.[4]

To facilitate exit

Being able to sell the shares back to the company also offers a way of unlocking the investment made by a proprietor of a small business who subsequently wishes to retire. The estate of a dead shareholder may similarly benefit from the company being able to purchase the shares. Where the management of a smaller company is paralysed because of a dispute between its proprietors, for the company to buy one faction's shares may be a way of resolving the deadlock without recourse to litigation (probably a petition under section 994 of the Companies Act 2006 for relief from unfair prejudice).

To structure a temporary loss of control

By issuing redeemable shares the controllers of a company can raise share capital without a permanent dilution of their controlling stake.

To return value to shareholders

Buying back shares is a way of returning to shareholders surplus cash (sometimes termed 'free cash flow') that the company itself is unable to invest efficiently in profitable investment projects. A buy-back of shares can prove to be a particularly useful application of surplus cash because it can have a positive impact on some of the performance ratios that are commonly used by analysts and investors to assess corporate performance. The performance of a listed company is commonly assessed by reference to its earnings per share, ie the profits which are attributable to equity shareholders divided by the number of equity shares in issue. Buying back shares will improve this figure provided the positive effect of the reduction

---

[4] Arrangements whereby a company tries to guarantee that investors in its redeemable shares will obtain a capital payment when the shares are due to be redeemed even though the company itself may be insolvent (eg by arranging for a third party to buy the shares in that event) need to be examined closely for potential maintenance of capital and financial assistance concerns. See *Barclays Bank plc v British & Commonwealth Holdings plc* [1995] BCC 19 (affirmed [1995] BCC 1059, CA).

in the number of shares is not outweighed by the negative effect on the company's profits of the loss of interest on the cash used to finance the buy-back. Certain companies, in particular property and investment companies, are also commonly measured by the yardstick of net assets per shares, ie the net assets divided by the number of equity shares in issue. Again, a buy-back of shares can improve this figure.

Although it was the 1981 companies legislation that first permitted UK companies to purchase their own shares, it was not until the 1990s that this method of returning value to shareholders came to be extensively used in UK market practice.[5] This was a time when factors such as the ending of recession and the existence of a largely dormant takeover market combined to create a build-up of surplus cash in the corporate sector. New trends in techniques for returning value, which were strongly influenced by tax considerations,[6] brought share buy-backs into vogue.

To give information signals

A buy-back of shares by a company can serve as a mechanism for delivering credible information signals to the market in that it can be used to demonstrate that its management considers its share price to be undervalued.

To achieve a target capital structure

A company may choose to buy back its shares in order to achieve a target capital structure. For example, a company may want to eliminate a particular class of shares and replace it with another class of shares with special rights or with ordinary shares. Or, it may want to increase financial leverage by replacing expensive share capital with cheaper debt. The company will need to consider the ramifications of a buy-back for the percentage holdings of the remaining shareholders. A particular point to note is that if the company is officially listed it must ensure that it can still comply with the requirement of the *Listing Rules* that a sufficient number of shares must be distributed to the public, with 25 per cent of the shares taken to be sufficient for this purpose.[7]

---

[5] Other methods include special dividends (see ch 9 below), formal reductions of capital and schemes of arrangement (see ch 7 above). See generally, T Scott, 'Returning Cash to Shareholders. Options for Companies' (1997) 8(3) *Practical Law for Companies* 19.

[6] J Tiley, 'The Purchase by a Company of Its Own Shares' [1992] *British Tax Review* 21; S Edge, 'Do We Have an Imputation System on Not?' (1996) 375 *Tax Journal* 2; S Edge, 'The Background to the Introduction of Schedule 7' [1997] *British Tax Review* 221; PR Rau and T Vermaelen, 'Regulation, Taxes and Share Repurchases in the United Kingdom' (2002) 75 *Journal of Business* 245.

[7] *LR* 6.1.19. This rule is a requirement for admission to listing in respect of equity securities and it is provided as a continuing obligation that a listed company must comply with *LR* 6.1.19 at all times: *LR* 9.2.15.

To expand the range of financing options

Redeemable shares are a type of hybrid security: they are shares but the fact that they are to be repaid on or by a specified date is a feature that makes them akin to impermanent debt finance. As such, the power to issue redeemable shares adds to the range of financing options available to the corporate sector and thus enhances flexibility.

To buy back redeemable shares at a discounted price

Early repurchase of redeemable shares that are trading at a discount to their redemption price can enhance efficiency by enabling the issuer to retire those securities at a price that is lower than it would have pay on redemption.

To facilitate the organization of employee share schemes

Another advantage claimed for allowing companies to purchase their own shares is that this can facilitate the operation of an employee share scheme by assuring employees of a purchaser for their shares when they leave the company. In larger companies it is common for employee share schemes to be operated through a trust and for the trustees to buy the shares of employees who are leaving the company, but for the company to be able to buy back the employee shares is an alternative that can be more straightforward and which can therefore make the establishment of employee share schemes less of a burden for smaller companies.

To achieve an informal reduction of capital

A redemption or repurchase of shares could be used by a company in order to reduce its share capital without the need for court approval and the obligation to observe the other formalities attending a conventional court-approved reduction of capital under the Companies Act 2006. Historically, the potential for creditors to be prejudiced by an informal reduction of capital was a key objection to allowing companies to buy back their own shares. In *Trevor v Whitworth*[8] the House of Lords relied on infringement of the maintenance of capital principle as the main reason for coming to the conclusion that the purchase by a company of its own shares was unlawful. However, as doubts have grown about the value of legal capital as a creditor protection mechanism, objections to buy backs that are rooted in this concern have receded.

---

[8] (1887) 12 App Cas 409, HL.

To defend against a takeover or deal with dissident shareholders

A buy-back may be viewed as a useful defensive mechanism in a takeover situation by, for example, reducing the number of shares potentially available to a hostile bidder. The controllers of a company may also welcome the flexibility of buy-back powers that enable them to negotiate an exit for troublesome shareholders by buying them out at a favourable price. On the other hand, however, giving the management of a company threatened with a takeover free rein to buy back shares as a defensive tactic could enable management to entrench themselves in position and thereby impede the efficient functioning of the market for corporate control. The use of buy-back powers in order to deal with dissenting shareholders is also potentially open to abuse.

The argument that a company ought to be able to purchase its own shares in order to buy out shareholders whose continued presence in the company was undesirable was accepted in some nineteenth-century cases[9] but it found little favour in the House of Lords in *Trevor v Whitworth*. Lord Macnaghten stated:[10]

But I would ask, Is it possible to suggest anything more dangerous to the welfare of companies and to the security of their creditors than such a doctrine? Who are the shareholders whose continuance in a company the company or its executive consider undesirable? Why, shareholders who quarrel with the policy of the board, and wish to turn the directors out; shareholders who ask questions which it may not be convenient to answer; shareholders who want information which the directors think it prudent to withhold. Can it be contended that when the policy of directors is assailed they may spend the capital of the company in keeping themselves in power, or in purchasing the retirement of inquisitive and troublesome critics?

The constitutional function of the directors in a conventionally structured company is to manage the company and it is beyond their powers to seek to control the ownership of its shares. Allowing a company to purchase its own shares could be open to abuse because directors could, by offering an exceptionally favourable price, use the power to secure their own control by getting rid of troublesome or disaffected shareholders who might otherwise have been tempted to make a takeover bid or to accept another's bid. The directors of a company might also be tempted to pay too much for the company's shares in order to favour a selling shareholder who has a special connection to the company, such as one of its original proprietors who is retiring from the company after many years of service. If a company were to pay an unjustifiably high price for the shares, this wealth transfer would be detrimental to its remaining shareholders and, potentially, its creditors.

---

[9]   eg *Re Dronfield Silkstone Coal Co* (1881) 17 Ch D 76, CA.
[10]   (1887) 12 App Cas 409, HL, 435.

To stabilize the share price

A company may want to have the power to buy its own shares in order to bolster or stabilize their market price. However, whilst this can be presented as an argument in favour of share buy-backs, allowing a company to be able to buy its own shares to bolster or stabilize the price at which they are trading in the market also raises concerns about market abuse. For the company to use its own money to bolster or stabilize its share price is open to the obvious objection that this practice could mislead the investing public about the value of the company's shares and could create a false market in those shares.[11] Yet, if the risk of market manipulation were the only argument against permitting companies to buy back their own shares, it would be doubtful whether this would justify a specific company law ban on the practice because market abuse is in any event regulated by the UK's regulator of financial markets, the Financial Services Authority (FSA), which can impose administrative sanctions on perpetrators of market abuse and also seek criminal sanctions.[12]

Consideration by review bodies

Following the Report of the Greene Committee in 1926,[13] section 18 of the Companies Act 1928 first allowed companies to issue redeemable preference shares subject to safeguards that were intended to preserve the amount of the company's share capital. The Jenkins Committee, which reviewed the position in 1962, compared the limited power allowed to British companies with the freedom enjoyed by US companies to repurchase shares, and acknowledged the usefulness of the US position with regard to such matters as employee share schemes and the unlocking of investment in small companies.[14] The Committee thought that if British companies were to be given a wider power to purchase their own shares it would be necessary to introduce stringent safeguards to protect creditors and shareholders but that it would be possible to devise effective safeguards and that they would not be unduly complicated. However, it refrained from recommending the general abrogation of the rule that a company could not purchase its own shares because it had received no evidence that British companies needed the power and because it identified serious tax disadvantages in selling shares back to the company rather than to a third party.

At the end of the 1970s, the problems in raising capital encountered by smaller companies were the subject of a review by a Committee under the chairmanship

---

[11] *General Property Co Ltd v Matheson's Trustees* (1888) 16 R 82 Ct of Sess.
[12] Financial Services and Markets Act 2000, Pt 8 (administrative penalties for market abuse) and s 397 (criminal sanctions for misleading statements and practices).
[13] *The Report of the Committee on Company Law* (Cmd 2657, 1926) para 28.
[14] *Report of the Company Law Committee* (Cmnd 1749, 1962) paras 167–169.

of Sir Harold Wilson. In its Interim Report on the *Financing of Small Firms* this Committee suggested that consideration should be given to permitting such companies to issue redeemable equity shares as a means of raising capital without parting permanently with family control.[15] During Parliamentary debates on the Bill which became the Companies Act 1980, it was indicated that the government attached high priority to relaxing the general prohibition on companies purchasing their own shares. This was then followed by the publication by the relevant government department of a consultative document on *The Purchase by a Company of its Own Shares*, which was written by Professor Gower.[16] In the consultative document, Professor Gower recommended that companies should be allowed to issue redeemable equity shares and that consideration should be given to the possibility of permitting public and private companies to repurchase their own shares.[17] He outlined safeguards intended to ensure that capital would be maintained despite repurchase or redemption of shares but, in relation to private companies, he further recommended that consideration be given to allowing them to reduce their capital by repurchasing or redeeming shares.

Powers broadly in line with those recommended for consideration by Professor Gower were enacted in the Companies Act 1981, later consolidated into the Companies Act 1985.

The next step in the process of gradual relaxation of the rules relating to share buy-backs was taken in relation to treasury shares. At the time of the Gower review in 1980, the mood was against allowing companies to purchase own shares, hold them in 'treasury', and then resell them. In 1998, however, the government returned to this issue and published a new consultative document seeking views on whether there should be a change in the law to permit treasury shares.[18] This time, the response was favourable and in 2003 the Companies Act 1985 was amended to introduce a limited power for companies to have treasury shares.[19] In principle, treasury shares give companies additional flexibility with regard to the management of their capital structure because the shares can be re-sold without having to go through the full range of formalities that apply to new share issues. However, in fact, the amending provisions that introduced treasury shares included a requirement for the resale of treasury shares to be subject to pre-emption rights in favour of existing shareholders, and this had the effect of reducing flexibility. A significant practical benefit resulting from the introduction of treasury shares is that the shares can be used to satisfy entitlements under employee share schemes.[20]

---

[15] Cmnd 7503 (1979).
[16] Cmnd 7944 (1980).
[17] Ibid para 67 (Conclusions).
[18] DTI, 'Share Buybacks: A Consultative Document' (1998).
[19] The changes were introduced by the Companies (Acquisition of Own Shares) (Treasury Shares) Regulations 2003, SI 2003/1116.
[20] V Knapp, 'Treasury Shares: The Practicalities' (2004) 15(2) *Practical Law for Companies* 15.

Perhaps because it had been officially reviewed on several occasions in the relatively recent past, the law relating to share buy-backs and redeemable shares was not a particularly controversial area in the context of the general review of British company law that preceded the Companies Act 2006. Chapters 3 to 7 of Part 18 of that Act, which contain the enabling provisions that empower limited companies to issue redeemable shares and to purchase their own shares, are largely restated versions of the previous law, with only limited substantive change.

The European dimension

Before turning to the detail of the Companies Act 2006, it is necessary also to mention the European dimension.

The Second Company Law Directive[21] does not require Member States to have laws permitting companies to issue redeemable shares or to repurchase shares but those Member States that do have such enabling provisions in their company laws must observe the conditions imposed by the Directive. The core provision is Article 19.1, which, as amended in 2006,[22] provides that own share acquisitions must be subject to the following conditions:

(a) authorization must be given by the general meeting, which shall determine the terms and conditions of such acquisitions, and, in particular, the maximum number of shares to be acquired, the duration of the period for which the authorization is given, the maximum length of which shall be determined by national law without, however, exceeding five years, and, in the case of acquisition for value, the maximum and minimum consideration.

(b) the acquisitions, including shares previously acquired by the company and held by it, and shares acquired by a person acting in his own name but on the company's behalf, may not have the effect of reducing the net assets below the amount of distributable reserves; and

(c) only fully paid up shares may be included in the transaction.

Members of the administrative or management body must satisfy themselves that, at the time when each authorized acquisition is effected, the conditions referred to in points (b) and (c) are respected.

In addition, Article 19.1 (as amended) gives Member States the option of applying any of the following conditions:

(i) that the nominal value or, in the absence thereof, the accountable par of the acquired shares, including shares previously acquired by the company and held by it, and shares acquired by a person acting in his own name but on the company's behalf,

---

[21] Second Company Law Directive (EEC) 77/91, [1977] OJ L26/1.

[22] By Directive (EC) 2006/68 of the European Parliament and of the Council of 6 September 2006 amending Council Directive (EEC) 77/91 as regards the formation of public limited liability companies and the maintenance and alteration of their capital [2006] OJL 264.

may not exceed a limit to be determined by Member States. This limit on the number of shares acquired and held in treasury may not be lower than 10 per cent of the subscribed capital;

(ii) that the power of the company to acquire its own shares, the maximum number of shares to be acquired, the duration of the period for which the power is given and the maximum or minimum consideration must be laid down in the statutes or in the instrument of incorporation of the company;

(iii) that the company must comply with appropriate reporting and notification requirements;

(iv) that certain companies, as determined by Member States, may be required to cancel the acquired shares provided that an amount equal to the nominal value of the shares cancelled must be included in a reserve which cannot be distributed to the shareholders, except in the event of a reduction in the subscribed capital. This reserve may be used only for the purposes of increasing the subscribed capital by the capitalization of reserves;

(v) that the acquisition shall not prejudice the satisfaction of creditors' claims.

Prior to the amendments made in 2006, Article 19.1 stipulated that the period of authorization granted by the general meeting for own share purchases could not exceed eighteen months and that the amount of shares bought back and held in treasury could not exceed 10 per cent of the subscribed capital. These conditions were relaxed because it came to be accepted that they were too rigid and that they inhibited useful share buy-back programmes.[23] A further change effected by the 2006 amendments is that the list of mandatory and additional optional conditions to which own share purchases can be made subject is now exhaustive. Article 19.1 now also expressly provides that the powers conferred are without prejudice to the principle of equal treatment of all shareholders who are in the same position, and to Directive (EC) 2003/6 of the European Parliament and of the Council of 28 January 2003 on insider dealing and market manipulation (market abuse).

The 2006 changes to the Second Company Law Directive came too late to be reflected in the Companies Act 2006 as originally enacted but an amending power in that Act provides a mechanism for introducing them into British law.[24] The British government was inclined initially against making any changes in response to the amending Directive because it considered that the Act was already compliant with the mandatory requirements of the Directive and its preference was to wait for the outcome of a more fundamental review of legal capital taking place at the European level rather than to tinker with domestic law to

---

[23] The Company Law SLIM Working Group on the Simplification of the First and Second Company Law Directives recommended these changes, which were then endorsed by a High Level Group that reviewed aspects of EC company law on behalf of the European Commission: European Commission, 'Report of the High Level Group of Company Law Experts on a Regulatory Framework for Company Law in Europe' (Brussels, November 2002) 84–5.

[24] Companies Act 2006, s 737.

implement relatively limited optional amendments.[25] However, after a round of consultation, the government indicated that it would think further about introducing an amendment to take advantage of the abolition of the 10 per cent cap in the Directive on the acquisition and holding in treasury of own shares.[26]

General statutory rule in the Companies Act 2006 against a company acquiring its own shares

The thrust of *Trevor v Whitworth*[27] is now embodied in section 658 of the Companies Act 2006, which provides that a limited company must not acquire its own shares, whether by purchase, subscription, or otherwise. If a company purports to act in contravention of this rule it is liable to a fine and every officer of the company who is in default is liable to imprisonment or a fine, or both; and the purported acquisition is void. The general prohibition is, however, qualified by section 659 of the Companies Act 2006, which provides exceptions to the general rule as follows.

Under section 659 a limited company may acquire any of its own fully paid shares otherwise than for valuable consideration. This does not infringe the Second Company Law Directive because Article 20(1)(c) provides that Member States are not obliged to apply Article 19 to fully paid up shares acquired free of charge Other exceptions to the general rule stated in section 659, and which are also sanctioned by the Second Company Law Directive, are:[28]

(1) the acquisition of shares in a reduction of capital duly made;
(2) the purchase of shares in pursuance of court orders made under certain sections of the Companies Act 2006; and
(3) the forfeiture of shares, or the acceptance of shares surrendered in lieu, in pursuance of the articles, for failure to pay any sum payable in respect of the shares.

In *Acatos and Hutcheson plc v Watson*[29] the High Court was asked to rule on whether the purchase by a company of another company whose sole asset was a substantial holding of shares in the purchasing company would infringe the prohibition that is now contained in section 658 of the Companies Act 2006. Lightman J held that the proposed acquisition would not amount to a side-stepping of the

---

[25] DTI, 'Implementation of the Companies Act 2006: A Consultative Document' (February 2007) ch 6.
[26] The government's brief response to the consultation (URN No 07/1300) is at *Hansard*, HC vol 462, col 23 WS (26 June 2007).
[27] (1887) 12 App Cas 409, HL.
[28] Companies Act 2006, s 659(2).
[29] [1994] BCC 446.

prohibition which the court would prevent by lifting the veil between the purchaser and the target company. In reaching this conclusion, Lightman J followed three Australian cases that had adopted the same approach.[30] He noted that the opposite conclusion would enable companies to protect themselves from becoming the target of a takeover bid simply by acquiring some of the predator's shares, a result which he characterized as 'absurd'. Lightman J also drew support from what is now section 136 of the Companies Act 2006 (prohibition on subsidiary being a member of its holding company), which recognizes the possibility that a company may acquire shares in a company that later becomes its holding company; in that event, the subsidiary may continue to hold the shares but may not exercise any votes attaching to them.

Also of note in this context is section 660 of the Companies Act 2006, which specifically regulates the subscription or acquisition of shares in a limited company by a nominee of that company. Subject to limited qualifications, where shares are issued to a nominee of a limited company or are acquired by a nominee from a third person as partly paid up, then, for all purposes the shares are to be treated as held by the nominee on his own account and the company is to be regarded as having no beneficial interest in them.

In circumstances where a company is permitted to acquire its own shares, it must then observe any statutory limitations on what it can do with the shares so acquired. Relevant limitations are determined by reference to the method of acquisition.[31]

Share buy-backs—authorizations required by the Companies Act 2006

A limited company having a share capital may purchase its own shares provided that it abides by the requirements of the legislation and subject to any restriction or limitation in its articles.[32] That the 2006 Act provides that companies can buy back shares unless their articles provide otherwise is a reversal of the position under the previous companies legislation, which was that specific constitutional authorization via the articles was required.

The Companies Act 2006 gives effect to the requirement in Article 19 of the Second Company Law Directive for buy-backs to be authorized by the general meeting. The details of the statutory shareholder authorization requirements

---

[30] *August Investments Pty Ltd v Poseidon Ltd* (1971) 2 SASR 71, SA SC-FC, noted H Leigh French, 'Exceptions to Self-Purchase of Shares' (1987) 8 *Company Lawyer* 88; *Dyason v JC Hutton Pty Ltd* (1935) 41 ALR 419, V SC; *Trade Practices Commission v Australian Iron & Steel Pty Ltd* (1990) 22 FCR 305.
[31] Companies Act 2006, ss 662–669 deal with cancellation of shares in a public company held by or for the company.
[32] Companies Act 2006, s 690.

are different depending on whether the buy-back is to be a 'market' or an 'off-market' purchase.

Market purchase

A market purchase by a company of its own shares means a purchase made on a recognized investment exchange (RIE) provided that the shares are subject to a marketing arrangement on that exchange.[33] The FSA is responsible for the recognition and supervision of recognized investment exchanges under the Financial Services and Markets Act 2000.[34] All FSA-regulated RIEs, other than those that are overseas investment exchanges, are recognized investment exchanges for the purposes of the buy-back requirements in the Companies Act 2006.[35] Officially listed shares (such as shares admitted to trading on the listed segment of the London Stock Exchange) are automatically treated as being subject to a marketing arrangement.[36] Otherwise, shares admitted to trading on a recognized investment exchange are subject to a marketing arrangement if the company has been afforded facilities for dealing in those shares to take place on the exchange without prior permission from the exchange and without limit as to the time during which those facilities are to be available.[37] This would encompass, for example, shares that are admitted to trading on the Alternative Investment Market.

Ordinary or special resolution?

Section 701 of the Companies Act 2006 provides that the shareholder authorization required in respect of an on-market purchase of shares is a resolution, which implies an ordinary resolution. In practice, listed companies which take power to purchase their own shares commonly do so by special resolution in order to comply with recommendations from the Association of British Insurers (ABI), the representative body of a major group of institutional investors.[38] An important feature of an on-market authority, whether in the form of an ordinary or a special resolution, is that it can be a general authority not linked to any particular purchase of shares.[39] The authority must, however (and as required by the Second Company Law Directive), specify limits with regard to the maximum number of shares authorized to be acquired and the maximum and minimum prices which may be paid for the shares.[40] Such prices may be fixed or may be determined by

---

[33] Companies Act 2006, s 693(4).
[34] Financial Services and Markets Act 2000, Pt 18.
[35] Companies Act 2006, s 693(5).
[36] ibid s 693(3)(a).
[37] ibid s 693(3)(b).
[38] The ABI has not published formal guidelines on this subject but its views are public and well-known. A statement of these views is available at <http://www.ivis.co.uk/pages/framegu.html> (accessed October 2007).
[39] Companies Act 2006, s 701(2).
[40] ibid s 701(3).

reference to a formula, provided this is without reference to any person's discretion or opinion.[41] The authorizing resolution must also state the date on which it is to expire, which (since the 2006 Act was drawn up on the basis of the unamended requirements of Article 19 of the Second Company Law Directive), must be not later than eighteen months after the date when the resolution is passed.[42] The ABI currently favours annual renewal of the authority and, because of this, it is the practice in some companies for a resolution to this effect to be passed regularly at their annual general meeting (AGM). With regard to amount, the ABI has said that, assuming the company is trading normally, authority to purchase up to 5 per cent of the ordinary share capital is unlikely to cause concern but regard will be had to the effect on gearing, etc where larger amounts of capital are involved. There is some reluctance to accept own share purchase powers over share capital in excess of 10 per cent of the issued ordinary share capital. As a consequence, in practice, it is usual for companies to seek a general authority to purchase up to 10 per cent at each AGM. A further ABI expectation is that the company should undertake only to exercise the power if to do so will result in an increase in earnings per share (or asset value per share in the case of property companies or investment trusts) and is in the best interests of shareholders generally.

The Companies Act 2006 provides for a resolution authorizing a market purchase of shares to be varied, revoked, or renewed by ordinary resolution.[43] Provided this is permitted by the resolution, a company may, after the expiry of an authority, complete a purchase of shares arising from a contract entered into before the authority expired.[44]

Off-market purchase

A purchase of shares that is not a market purchase is an off-market purchase. The Companies Act 2006 requires off-market purchases of shares to be approved by special resolution and in this case a general authorization is not acceptable.[45] The shareholders must approve specifically either the terms of the proposed contract by which the shares are to be purchased before it is entered into or the contract must provide that no shares may be purchased until its terms have been authorized by a special resolution of the company.[46] The contract may be a straightforward share purchase contract or a contract under which the company may (subject to any conditions) become entitled or obliged to purchase shares.[47] An example of such a contract would be an option contract under which the company is entitled to call for the shares in specified circumstances.

---

[41] ibid s 701(7).
[42] ibid s 701(5).
[43] ibid s 701(4).
[44] ibid s 701(6).
[45] ibid s 694.
[46] ibid s 694(2).
[47] ibid s 694(3).

A resolution approving an off-market purchase of own shares will not be effective if any shareholder holding shares to which the resolution relates exercised the voting rights carried by those shares in voting on the resolution and the resolution would not have been passed if he had not done so.[48] Where the resolution is proposed as a written resolution, any member holding shares to which the resolution relates is not an eligible member.[49] In the case of a resolution passed at a shareholders' meeting, the contract (or a written memorandum of its terms if it is not in writing) must be available for inspection by members of the company both at the company's registered office for not less than fifteen days ending with the date of the meeting at which the resolution is passed and also at the meeting itself.[50] Where a private company uses the statutory written resolution regime to pass a resolution authorizing an off-market purchase of its own shares, the requirement for the contract (or its terms) to be available for inspection by members is necessarily varied to provide that details must have been supplied to each member before he signed the resolution.[51] The names of all of the selling shareholders must always be disclosed.[52]

Non-compliance with the publicity requirements in respect of the details of the contract renders any resolution which is passed invalid.[53] The disclosure requirements are aimed at preventing directors entering into arrangements to buy back favoured members' shares at especially favourable terms or otherwise abusing their powers. The requirement of equal treatment for shareholders is expressly backed by Article 42 of the Second Company Law Directive. However, it has been held that failure to comply with the requirement to make available the contract or a memorandum containing its terms is a formality for the benefit of shareholders only and is therefore capable of being waived if they all agree.[54]

A special resolution authorizing an off-market purchase of shares may, in the case of a private company, be of unlimited duration but, given that the contract terms must be authorized before it is entered into or the contract must be made conditional on the passing of an authorizing resolution, it is reasonable to expect that the time gap will usually be fairly short. A resolution passed by a public company must state when the authority conferred by the resolution is to expire and the expiry date must be not later than eighteen months after the passing of the resolution.[55]

---

[48] Companies Act 2006, ibid s 695(3).
[49] ibid s 695(2).
[50] ibid s 696(2)(b).
[51] ibid s 696(2)(a).
[52] ibid s 696(3)–(4).
[53] ibid s 696(5).
[54] *Kinlan v Crimmin* [2007] BCC 106, citing *BDG Roof-Bond Ltd v Douglas* [2000] 1 BCLC 401.
[55] Companies Act 2006, s 694(5). This time limit is consistent with the unamended Second Company Law Directive, Art 19.

A special resolution authorizing an off-market purchase of shares can be varied, revoked, or renewed by special resolution.[56] Any variation in the terms of the contract by which the shares are to be purchased must be approved by special resolution before it is agreed to by the company, and the rules on eligibility to vote on the resolution and with regard to the disclosure to members of the proposed variation track those for authorization of the original contract.[57]

Generally speaking, the authorization and other procedural requirements in respect of share buy-backs are mandatory.[58] This means that they must be complied with even in circumstances where all of the shareholders would be willing to waive them and, if they are not, the purported acquisition is void in accordance with section 658 of the Companies Act 2006.[59] It has been held that these requirements are to be viewed in this way because their purpose extends beyond protection of the existing shareholders and encompasses protection of creditors' interests, and possibly also wider public interests.[60] However, particular provisions are for the protection of shareholders only, and in respect of those provisions it is open to the shareholders acting unanimously to waive compliance.[61]

Other statutory restrictions on the terms and manner of buy-backs

A company must not purchase its own shares where to do so would result in there being no member of the company holding shares other than redeemable shares or shares held as treasury shares.[62] The purpose of this requirement is to ensure that a company does not bring its existence to an end through buy-backs and later redemptions. Shares may not be bought back unless they are fully paid (so that the valuable asset represented by uncalled capital is not lost) and the shares must be paid for on purchase.[63] The requirement for shareholders to be paid off at once ensures that members cannot be pressurized into accepting terms under which they are required to sell and thus lose their rights as members immediately but are not compensated for this for some considerable time. However, having to find all of the purchase money up front rather than agreeing to deferred payment by

---

[56] Companies Act 2006, s 694(4).
[57] ibid ss 697–699.
[58] *Re RW Peak (Kings Lynn) Ltd* [1998] 1 BCLC 193.
[59] ibid, as explained in *Wright v Atlas Wright (Europe) Ltd* [1999] 2 BCLC 301 CA, 310–15 *per* Potter LJ. Note Companies Act 2006, s 696(5).
[60] *Wright v Atlas Wright (Europe) Ltd* (n 59 above) 204–5.
[61] *Kinlan v Crimmin* [2007] BCC 106 (sanctioning waiver in relation to what is now Companies Act 2006, s 696(2)).
[62] ibid s 690.
[63] ibid s 691. See *Pena v Dale* [2004] 2 BCLC 508; *Kinlan v Crimmin* [2007] BCC 106.

instalments may pose a difficulty to smaller companies and may inhibit the use of the buy-back power.

There is some support for the view that a company can pay for shares that it is buying back either in cash or by a transfer of assets.[64]

Accounting for a share buy-back

Share buy-backs have implications for shareholder funds. The purchase price can be met from distributable reserves, in which case, in accounting terms, the reduction in the company's cash or other assets represented by the purchase price will be matched by a reduction in distributable reserves.[65] Alternatively, the proceeds of a fresh issue of shares can be used provided that the issue was made for the purpose of financing the purchase.[66] Any premium payable on purchase must be paid out of distributable profits, save that where shares were issued at a premium, the company may pay a premium on redemption out of the proceeds of a fresh issue of shares up to an amount equal to the lesser of the aggregate of the premiums received by the company on the issue of the shares repurchased and the current amount of the company's share premium account (including any premium in respect of the new shares).[67]

When shares are purchased they must be treated as cancelled and the amount of the company's issued share capital must be diminished by the nominal value of those shares accordingly, save to the extent that those shares are allowed to be held as treasury shares.[68] Where shares are cancelled as a result of a buy-back from distributable reserves, an amount equivalent to the nominal value of those shares must be credited to a capital redemption reserve, which is to be treated as if it were share capital with the one exception that it may be used to pay up fully paid bonus shares.[69] This requirement, which is subject to a special regime for private companies considered later in this chapter, ensures that the company's overall undistributable reserves remain intact and prevents buy-backs being used to effect informal reductions of capital. Where, or to the extent that, a buy-back is made from the proceeds of a fresh issue of shares made specifically for that purpose, it is only necessary to credit the capital redemption reserve with the amount (if any) by which the aggregate amount of the proceeds is less than the aggregate nominal value of the shares redeedmed or purchased.[70] In effect, the new capital

---

[64] *BDG Roof-Bond Ltd v Douglas* [2000] 1 BCLC 401 but on the facts there was actually money consideration for the shares.

[65] Companies Act 2006, s 692(2)(a)(i).

[66] ibid s 692(2)(a)(ii).

[67] ibid s 692(2)(ii).

[68] ibid s 706(b).

[69] ibid s 733.

[70] ibid s 733(3).

raised from the share issue takes the place of the amount repaid; creditors are not prejudiced because the fresh issue was made specifically for the purposes of the buy-back and not as an injection of new equity finance.

The accounting implications of these rules are illustrated by the following simplified examples.

A buy-back from distributable reserves of 1 million shares of nominal value £1 each for £1.3m:

	Before £000	Issue £000	Purchase £000	Maintain capital £000	After £000
Cash	3,800		(1,300)		2,500
Net assets	3,800		(1,300)		2,500
Capital and reserves					
Share capital: £1 ordinary shares	2,000			(1,000)	1,000
Share premium account	400				400
Capital redemption reserve				1,000	1,000
Share capital + undistributed reserves	2,400				2,400
Profit and loss account reserve	1,400		(1,300)		100
	3,800		(1,300)	—	2,500

As in the example above, save that there is an issue of 500,000 new shares at par of £1 each for the purposes of financing the purchase:

	Before £000	Issue £000	Purchase £000	Maintain capital £000	After £000
Cash	3,800	500	(1,300)		3,000
Net assets	3,800	500	(1,300)		3,000
Capital and reserves					
Share capital: £1 ordinary shares	2,000	500		(1,000)	1,500
Share premium account	400				400
Capital redemption reserve				500	500
Share capital + undistributed reserves	2,400	500	(500)		2,400
Profit and loss account reserve	1,400		(800)		600
	3,800	500	(1,300)	—	3,000

Treasury shares[71]

Treasury shares are own shares that are purchased by a company with the company then being entered in the register of members in respect of them for reasons of transparency.[72] For own shares to be treated as treasury shares, the purchase must be made out of distributable profits and the shares must be 'qualifying shares', which means that they must be officially listed under Part 6 of the Financial Services and Markets Act 2000 (such as shares admitted to trading on the Main Market of the London Stock Exchange), admitted to trading on AIM admitted to listing in an EEA state or traded on an EEA regulated market.[73] The current maximum permissible holding of treasury shares (derived from the unamended Second Company Law Directive) is 10 per cent of the nominal value of the issued share capital or, where the share capital is divided into shares of different classes, the maximum holding in respect of any class is 10 per cent of the nominal value of that class.[74] If the limit is exceeded, the acquisition is not void under section 658 of the Companies Act 2006 but the company must dispose of or cancel the excess shares within twelve months.[75]

During the period that own shares are held in treasury, the company may not exercise any rights in respect of them, such as a right to attend or vote at meetings, and no dividends may be paid in respect of them.[76] However, bonus shares may be allotted in respect of them and where they are redeemable shares, the redemption obligation may be honoured.[77]

A company that has treasury shares may deal with them by disposing of them[78] or cancelling them.[79] 'Disposal' in this context means selling the shares for a cash consideration or transferring them for the purposes of, or pursuant to, an employees' share scheme.[80] When treasury shares are sold and the proceeds are equal to or less than the price paid for them by the company, they are treated as a realized profit but where the proceeds exceed the price that the company paid for them the excess must be credited to the share premium account.[81] When treasury shares are cancelled, the amount of the share capital is reduced accordingly by

---

[71] G Morse, 'The Introduction of Treasury Shares into English Law and Practice' [2004] JBL 303.

[72] Companies Act 2006, s 724.

[73] ibid s 724(2). Regulated market is defined in Companies Act 2006, s 1173.

[74] ibid s 725.

[75] ibid s 725(3)–(4).

[76] ibid s 726(2)–(3).

[77] ibid s 726(4).

[78] ibid s 727. On notification relating to disposal (Companies Act 2006, s 728).

[79] Companies Act 2006, s 729. Cancellation will be required if shares cease to qualifying shares but suspension of listing or trading does not of itself mean that shares cease to be qualifying (s 729(2)–(3)). On notifications relating to cancellation (Companies Act 2006, s 730).

[80] ibid s 727. On cash consideration (s 727(2)).

[81] ibid s 731.

the nominal amount of the share cancelled[82] and an equivalent amount must be transferred to the capital redemption reserve.[83]

Buy-back of own shares out of capital: private companies only

Under certain conditions, private companies are allowed to reduce their capital by purchasing shares. These conditions are intended to protect creditors from the risks that lie in permitting companies to use their capital in this way. They are also designed to protect members of the company.

Recourse can only be had to the company's capital where there is a shortfall after the available profits and the proceeds of any fresh issue made for the purpose of the purchase have been applied.[84] The amount of capital that the company can use to make up the shortfall is referred to as the 'permissible capital payment'.[85] The available profits of the company for this purpose are determined first by reference to the company's accounts but the amount so determined must then be reduced by the amount of any lawful distributions and other specified payments made by the company after the date of the relevant accounts.[86] If the permissible capital payment, together with the proceeds of any fresh issue of shares, is less than the nominal value of the shares purchased, the difference must be credited to the capital redemption reserve[87] but, if it is greater, the capital redemption reserve, share premium account, share capital account, or revaluation reserve may be reduced by the excess amount.[88] These rules can be illustrated by the following simplified example.

A private company has the following balance sheet:

	£000
Cash	2,400
Net assets	2,400
Capital and reserves	
Share capital: £1 ordinary shares	2,000
Profit and loss account	400
	2,400

Assuming all conditions and formalities have been met, the company redeems 1 million shares for £1.3m and no fresh issue of shares is to be made.

---

[82] ibid s 729(4).
[83] ibid s 733(4).
[84] ibid s 710.
[85] ibid s 710.
[86] ibid ss 711–712.
[87] ibid s 734(2) and (4).
[88] ibid s 734(3) and (4).

(a) What is the Permissible Capital Payment (PCP)?

	£000
Price of purchase	1,300
Less: proceeds of fresh issue	0
Less: balance on distributable reserves	(400)
PCP	900

(b) The balance sheet of the company after the transaction.

	Before £000	Purchase £000	Maintain capital £000	After £000
Cash	2,400	(1,300)		(1,100)
Net assets	2,400	(1,300)		
Capital and reserves				
Share capital: £1 ordinary shares	2,000		(1,000)	1,000
Capital redemption reserve			100	100
Share capital + undistributed reserves	2,000	(900)		1,100
Profit and loss account reserve	400	(400)		—
	2,400	(1,300)	—	1,100

There are various procedural formalities associated with a payment out of capital.[89] These include a requirement for the directors of the company to file a statutory statement as to the solvency of the company.[90] The statement must specify the amount of the permissible capital payment and must state that, having made full inquiry into the affairs and prospects of the company, the directors have formed the opinion:

(1) that immediately following the payment out of capital, there will be no grounds on which the company could then be found to be unable to pay its debts (taking into account contingent and prospective liabilities); and
(2) that, prospectively, having regard to their intentions with regard to the management of the company and the amount and character of the financial resources which in their view will be available to the company throughout the year following the date on which the payment is made, the company will be able to continue to carry on its business as a going concern (and will accordingly be able to pay its debts as they fall due).[91]

---

[89] Companies Act 2006, s 713.
[90] ibid s 714.
[91] ibid s 714(2)–(3).

There are criminal sanctions for making a statement without having reasonable grounds for the opinion expressed in it.[92] The directors' statement must have annexed to it a report from the company's auditor indicating that he has inquired into the company's affairs, checked that the permissible capital payment has been properly determined, and is not aware of anything to indicate that the directors' opinion is unreasonable in all the circumstances.[93] The directors' statement, and the accompanying auditor's report, must be made available to members prior to their vote on whether to approve the payment from capital.[94] The directors' statement and auditor's report must be kept available at the registered office for a specified period for inspection by any member or creditor.[95] Delivery of a copy of the statement and accompanying report to the registrar is also required.[96]

The payment must be approved by a special resolution of the shareholders passed on or within the week immediately following after the date on which the directors made their statement.[97] This resolution is ineffective if any member of the company holding shares to which the resolution relates votes on it and the resolution would not have been passed if he had not done so.[98] The fact that the company has passed a special resolution for payment out of capital must be publicized by a notice in the London Gazette.[99] A notice to the same effect must also be published in an appropriate national newspaper unless the company gives such notice in writing to each of its creditors.[100]

Within five weeks of the passing of a special resolution approving a payment from capital for the purchase of shares, an application may be made to court by any creditor of the company and by any member other than one who consented to or voted in favour of the resolution.[101] On the hearing of an application the court may adjourn the proceedings to give the parties an opportunity to come to an arrangement for the purchase of the interests of dissentient members or for the protection of dissentient creditors, as the case may be. Subject to that, on the hearing of the application the court is required to make an order on such terms and conditions as it thinks fit either confirming or cancelling the resolution. The court order can provide for the purchase by the company of the shares of any member and for the reduction accordingly of the company's capital. To allow for the possibility of an application to court being made, the payment out of capital must be made no earlier than five weeks after the date of the special resolution but

---

[92] ibid s 715.
[93] ibid s 714(6).
[94] ibid s 718.
[95] ibid s 720.
[96] ibid s 719(4).
[97] ibid s 716.
[98] ibid s 717(3). Where the resolution is passed by means of a written resolution, a member who holds shares to which the resolution relates is not an eligible member (s 712(2)).
[99] ibid s 719(1).
[100] ibid s 719(3).
[101] ibid s 721. The rest of this paragraph outlines requirements of this section.

it must also be no later than seven weeks after that date unless the court orders otherwise.[102]

Section 76 of the Insolvency Act 1986 is relevant where a company is being wound up and it has previously made a payment out of capital to purchase its own shares. If (a) the aggregate amount of the company's assets and the amounts paid by way of contribution to its assets (apart from this section) is insufficient for the payment of its debts and liabilities and the expenses of the winding up, and (b) the winding up commenced within a year of the date on which the relevant payment was made, the person from whom the shares were purchased and the directors who signed the statutory statement as to the company's solvency are prima facie personally liable to contribute to the company's assets to enable that insufficiency to be met. The former member who sold his shares is liable to contribute an amount not exceeding so much of the relevant payment as was made by the company in respect of his shares. The directors are jointly and severally liable with that person to contribute that amount but a director can escape this liability by showing that he had reasonable grounds for forming the opinion as to the company's solvency set out in the statement.

Statutory modification of contractual matters relating to share buy-backs

The consequences of a company failing to complete its bargain to purchase shares are dealt with by section 735 of the Companies Act 2006. The company is not liable in damages in that event but this is without prejudice to any other right that the shareholder may have; the shareholder may thus seek specific performance of the contract, but the court must not grant this if the company shows that it is unable to meet the costs of redeeming or purchasing the shares in question out of distributable profits. The winding up of the company does not necessarily preclude enforcement of a contract to purchase shares, but payment of the sums due under any such contract ranks behind the ordinary debts and liabilities of the company and any sums due in satisfaction of preferred rights attaching to other shares.

The rights of a company under a contract to purchase its own shares cannot be assigned.[103]

FSA regulatory requirements relating to share buy-backs

The purchase of its own securities by a listed company is regulated by the FSA *Listing Rules* as well as by the general law.[104] Included in the *Listing Rules* are

---

[102] Companies Act 2006, s 723.
[103] ibid s 704.
[104] *LR* 12.

provisions relating to the price paid for own shares.[105] The general requirement is that unless a tender offer is made to all holders of a class, purchases by a listed company of less than 15 per cent of any class of its equity shares (excluding treasury shares) pursuant to a general authority granted by shareholders, may only be made if the price to be paid is not more than the higher of (a) 5 per cent above the average market value of the company's equity shares for the five business days prior to the purchase and (b) the higher of the price of the last independent trade and the highest current independent bid on the trading venues where the purchase is carried out.[106] Purchases of 15 per cent or more of any class of equity shares (excluding treasury shares) must be by way of a tender offer to all shareholders of that class.[107] A tender offer is defined by the *Listing Rules* as an offer by a company to purchase all or part of a class of securities at a maximum or fixed price (that may be established by means of a formula) that is: (a) communicated to all holders of that class by means of a circular or advertisement in two national newspapers; (b) open to all holders of that class on the same terms for at least seven days; and (c) open for acceptance by all holders of that class pro rata to their existing holdings. So far as timing is concerned, the *Listing Rules* generally prohibit buy-backs during prohibited periods (ie periods immediately prior to the announcement of financial results or periods when there exists inside information in relation to the company),[108] although there are some exceptions.[109] Additional requirements may apply where the vendor of the shares that are to be bought back is a related party.[110] The *Listing Rules* also require that the circular accompanying the buy-back resolution must include a statement of the directors' intentions about using the buy-back authority and, in particular, whether the company intends to cancel the shares or hold them in treasury.[111]

Care must also be taken to ensure that a share buy-back programme does not give rise to concerns with regard to market abuse. There is a specific safe harbour in EC law for share buy-back programmes and, provided the conditions associated with this safe harbour are adhered to, the programme will not amount to market abuse.[112]

---

[105] *LR* 12.4.

[106] *LR* 12.4.1.

[107] *LR* 12.4.2.

[108] *LR* 9 Annex 1, the Model Code, para 1(e).

[109] *LR* 12.2. See also *LR* 12.6, which bans (subject to exceptions) sales or transfers of treasury shares during prohibited periods.

[110] *LR* 12.3.

[111] *LR* 13.7.1(a) and (c) .

[112] FSMA 2000, s 118A(5)(b); Commission Regulation (EC) 2273/2003 of 22 December 2003 implementing the Market Abuse Directive a regards exemptions for buy-back programmes and stabilisation of financial instruments [2003] OJ L336/33; and FSA *Handbook*, MAR 1, Annex 1.

Takeover Code implications of share buy-backs

The City Code on Takeovers and Mergers contains certain rules relating to the purchase by a company of its own shares. The Code is of relevance mainly in relation to offers for UK incorporated public companies, although its exact scope is wider than this and includes, for example, some offers for private companies. The Code provides, in Rule 37.1, that when a company redeems or purchases its own voting shares, any resulting increase in the percentage of shares carrying voting rights in which a person or group of persons acting in concert is interested will be treated as an acquisition for the purpose of the mandatory bid obligation in Rule 9 of Code, which is triggered when the threshold of a 30 per cent holding is crossed. However, the Panel will normally waive any resulting obligation to make a general offer unless the person holding that proportion of voting rights is a director, or the relationship of that person with any one or more of the directors is such that the person is, or is presumed to be, acting in concert with any of the directors. The Takeover Panel, which administers the Code, will expect the waiver to have been approved by a vote of independent shareholders and it must be consulted in advance in any case where Rule 9 may be relevant. Rule 37.3 addresses the use of the buy-back power as a defensive measure by a target in a takeover situation. This reinforces the general prohibition in the Code on directors of a target company taking frustrating action without the approval of the shareholders in general meeting.[113] During the course of an offer, or even before the date of an offer if the board of the offeree company has reason to believe that a bona fide offer may be imminent, no redemption or purchase by the target company may be made unless it is approved by the shareholders in general meeting. Where it is felt that the redemption or purchase is in pursuance of a contract entered into earlier or another pre-existing obligation, the Panel must be consulted and its consent to proceed without a shareholders' meeting obtained.

The authorizations required for an issue of redeemable shares

A limited company which has a share capital is permitted by section 684 of the Companies Act 2006 to issue redeemable shares. In the case of a private company there is now no requirement for the articles to authorize the issue of redeemable shares, although articles may exclude or restrict this power.[114] This contrasts with the position under the Companies Act 1985, where authorization in the articles was required. The requirement for articles to authorize the issue of

---

[113] City Code, Rule 21.
[114] Companies Act 2006, s 684(2).

redeemable shares continues to apply in relation to public companies.[115] Section 684(1) permits the issuance of shares which are to be redeemed or are liable to be redeemed at the option of the company or of the shareholder. Any class of shares may be issued as redeemable. However, a company must not issue redeemable shares at a time when there are no issued shares of the company that are not redeemable: in other words, a company may not redeem itself out of existence.[116]

Prior to the Companies Act 2006, there was uncertainty about whether the details of the terms and manner of redemption had to be specified precisely in the articles or whether it was sufficient for the articles simply to state that these details were to be fixed by the directors at the time when the shares were actually issued. The latter interpretation was preferable from the viewpoint of flexibility in that it allowed for fine-tuning of the terms on which shares were to be issued to reflect the market conditions at the time of issue. However, it was unclear whether it could be adopted (at least in relation to public companies) because of a reference in Article 39 of the Second Company Law Directive to the terms and manner of redemption being 'laid down' in the company's statutes or instrument of incorporation. Section 685 of the Companies Act 2006 resolves the issue in favour of a broadly flexible approach by permitting the directors to fix the terms, conditions, and manner of redemption provided that they are authorized to do so by the company's articles or by a resolution of the company. This provision applies to both public and private companies. Where the directors are so authorized, they must determine the terms, conditions, and manner of redemption before the shares are allotted and these details must be disclosed in a statement of capital.[117] Where the directors are not so authorized, the terms, conditions, and manner of redemption must be stated in the company's articles.[118]

Other requirements of the Companies Act 2006 relating to redemption of redeemable shares

The statutory framework governing the financing of a redemption of redeemable shares follows the same pattern as that which applies in relation to share buy-backs. Thus redeemable shares may only be redeemed out of distributable profits or the proceeds of a fresh issue of shares made for the purpose of the redemption.[119] This is subject to the qualification that, in the circumstances considered earlier in relation to buy-backs, a private company may use its capital to redeem its shares.[120] Any redemption premium should usually be paid from distributable

---

[115] ibid s 684(3).
[116] ibid s 684(4).
[117] ibid s 685(3).
[118] ibid s 685(4).
[119] ibid s 687(2).
[120] ibid s 687(1).

profits, but if the shares were issued at a premium the proceeds of a fresh issue can be applied for this purpose up to the aggregate of the premiums so received or the current amount of the company's share premium account, whichever is the less.[121] Only fully paid redeemable shares can be redeemed and the shares must be paid for on redemption unless the redemption terms provide for payment on a later date.[122] Redeemed shares must be cancelled, which has the effect of reducing the company's issued share capital; they may not be held in treasury.[123] Notice must be given to the registrar of companies of the redemption and cancellation of redeemable shares.[124]

If a company fails to redeem redeemable shares in accordance with their terms, the holder may seek specific performance but not damages.[125] The court must not grant an order for specific performance if the company shows that it is unable to meet the costs of the redemption from its distributable profits.[126]

Class rights issues relating to share buy-backs and redeemable shares

Where a company's share capital comprises more than one class of shares, a proposal to buy back shares may amount to a variation of class rights. If it does, an appropriate class consent must be obtained in addition to the corporate consents considered in this chapter. Likewise, an issue of redeemable shares may vary the class rights of existing preference shares which are entitled to priority on any return of capital and, again therefore, class consents may be required.[127] The Association of British Insurers recommends that class meeting consent to a buy-back of shares should be obtained in any case where a company has preference shares. This is a general recommendation and is not limited to instances where the buy-back would amount to a variation in the rights attaching to the preference shares.

Share buy-backs and redeemable shares and protection of minorities

It would be open to a shareholder who objects to any aspect of the capital reorganizations discussed in this chapter to seek relief under section 994 of the

---

[121] Companies Act 2006, s 687(3)–(4).
[122] ibid s 686.
[123] ibid s 688.
[124] ibid s 689.
[125] ibid s 735.
[126] ibid s 735.
[127] On class rights generally, see ch 6 above.

Companies Act 2006, on the ground that the action amounts to unfairly prejudicial conduct. An unsuccessful claim arising from a proposal to buy back shares
is *Rutherford, Petitioner*,[128] a decision of the Scottish Court of Session (Outer
House). The company proposed to buy back a 33 per cent interest in the company's shares. The purpose of this acquisition was to satisfy the view of most of
the shareholders of the company that shareholdings should be widely spread and
that there should be no dominant block of shares available to encourage individual shareholders to acquire a controlling interest. The petitioner averred that the
company was proposing to pay too much for the shares because it was proposing
to offer 64p per share even though the shares were trading in the market at 19p.
The Court held that a prima facie case to this effect was not established on the
facts, concluding that the transactions in which the shares had traded at around
19p probably involved small blocks of shares and that the value of the dominant
block of shares would be likely to be materially more valuable. In this context, it
was held to be relevant that there was known to be an investment trust that was
willing to pay up to 72p per share for a controlling interest in the company. Also,
the proposed share purchase was designed to stabilize the management of the
company which, the court concluded, might well elevate the price of the shares.
The Court held further that the petitioner would face problems in establishing
the second claim, namely that the company was not in a position to fund the purchase and that interest payments on borrowings to finance the acquisition would
exceed the company's annual profits. Thirdly, although the petitioner might further wish to allege that the purchase would have the effect of discouraging the
investment trust which was willing to pay a premium for a controlling interest,
the Court thought that if this was what the majority of the shareholders wanted,
it would be a fine question whether the petitioner's decreased chance of securing
an offer from that bidder could be described as unfair. Taking all these factors
into account in determining the balance of convenience, the Court refused to
grant the interdict (injunction) sought by the petitioner.

---

[128] [1994] BCC 876.

9

Distributions to Shareholders

Investor expectations

Established canons of corporate finance are that shareholders in widely-owned companies where dividends have been paid in the past are conservative in their dividend expectations: they expect to continue to receive regular dividends in respect of their shares, that those dividends will be smoothed over time, and that any increases will reflect underlying longer-term prospects for the business.[1] Recent empirical work has confirmed that these principles are still supported by market practice: dividend conservatism is prevalent and only firms that are confident about the prospects for sustainable earnings growth tend to consider increasing dividends.[2] One factor that has changed in recent years is that it has become more common for companies to return value to shareholders by means of share buy-backs. Some substitution of repurchases for dividend increases has been identified in the US.[3] A decrease in the overall number of firms paying dividends that was evident during the 1980s and 1990s[4] may have been linked to the availability of share buy-backs as an alternative payout mechanism.[5] In the UK, share buy-back programmes by large companies have become common (a trend linked to

[1] J Lintner, 'Distribution of Incomes of Corporations Among Dividends, Retained Earnings, and Taxes' (1956) 46(2) *American Economic Review* 97.
[2] A Brav, JR Graham, R Campbell, CR Harvey, and R Michaely, 'Payout Policy in the 21st Century' (2005) 77 *Journal of Financial Economics* 483. European managers broadly agree in that they try to smooth dividends from year to year and avoid reducing dividends: F Bancel, UR Mittoo, and N Bhattacharyya, 'Cross-Country Determinants of Payout Policy: A Survey of European Firms' (2004) 33 *Financial Management* 103.
[3] G Grullon and R Michaely, 'Dividends, Share Repurchases and the Substitution Hypothesis' (2002) 57(4) *Journal of Finance* 1649. But evidence suggests that a different position obtains elsewhere: CA Brown and JW O'Day, 'The Dividend Substitution Hypothesis: Australian Evidence' (June 2006) available at SSRN <http://ssrn.com/abstract=911508>.
[4] Noted by E Fama and K French, 'Disappearing Dividends: Changing Firm Characteristics or Lower Propensity to Pay?' (2001) 60 *Journal of Financial Economics* 3. But the aggregate amount of dividends paid by industrial firms increased over the period, both in nominal and in real terms: H DeAngelo, L DeAngelo, and DJ Skinner, 'Are Dividends Disappearing? Dividend Concentration and the Consolidation of Earnings' (2004) 72 *Journal of Financial Economics* 425. Since 2000, a rebound of conventional dividend policies has been detected: B Julio and D Ikenberry, 'Reappearing Dividends' (2004) 16(4) *Journal of Applied Corporate Finance* 89.
[5] A Brav, JR Graham, R Campbell, CR Harvey, and R Michaely, 'Payout Policy in the 21st Century' (2005) 77 *Journal of Financial Economics* 483. F Allen and R Michaely, 'Payout Policy'

changes in the applicable taxation rules).[6] Share buy-backs are more flexible than dividends because they have not become associated with raised expectations with regard to future payouts.[7] As such they can be a useful mechanism for returning to shareholders cash surpluses that arise from time to time.

Dividend policy

Dividend policy—why companies choose to initiate dividend payouts, the factors that explain the level of payout, the reasons for increasing or cutting the payout level—has been described as one of the most thoroughly researched issues in modern finance.[8] Yet despite the intense attention it has received, there has yet to emerge a theory that is fully consistent with real-life dividend policy.[9] The following paragraphs outline key lines of inquiry in the literature exploring determinants of payout policy.

Dividend policy and market value

A foundation of modern corporate finance theory is that in frictionless markets dividend policy should not affect the overall market value of a company's shares.[10] The theory is based on the fact that shares give their holders the right to share in capital growth as well as in whatever income is distributed by the company from time to time. Shares will have a higher capital value where the company retains the profits and invests them in new profitable ventures than they would have if the company distributed those profits by way of dividend and then raised further capital to fund the new venture by an issue of new shares. An investor who wants cash can always sell his shares to realize a capital gain instead of relying on the company to pay him a dividend. The theory implies that dividend policy should be a simple matter of paying out the residual cash flow after decisions on investment opportunities have been made.

However, real markets are not frictionless and there are various practical difficulties with this theory. It ignores the transaction costs involved in buying and selling shares and the differing tax treatment of dividends and capital gains on

in G Constantinides, M Harris, and R Stulz, (eds), *Handbook of Economics of Finance* (North-Holland, Amsterdam, 2002), 337, 404–20.

[6] D Oswald and S Young, 'Cashing In On Share Buybacks' (November 2003) *Accountancy* 55.
[7] ibid (in relation to the UK); Brav *et al* (n 5 above) (in relation to the US).
[8] WL Megginson, *Corporate Finance Theory* (Addison Wesley, 1997) 353.
[9] MW Faulkender, TT Milbourn, and AV Thakor, 'Does Corporate Performance Determine Capital Structure and Dividend Policy?' (9 March 2006) available at SSRN <http://ssrn.com/abstract=686865>: F Bancel, UR Mittoo, and N Bhattacharyya, 'Cross-Country Determinants of Payout Policy: A Survey of European Firms' (2004) 33 *Financial Management* 103.
[10] MH Miller and F Modigliani, 'Dividend Policy, Growth and the Valuation of Shares' (1961) 34 *Journal of Business* 411.

the disposal of shares.[11] It assumes the existence of a liquid market for the shares which may not in fact exist. It also assumes that new investments will be perfectly reflected in the company's share price. However, although, in theory, the effect of low dividends in the early years of a project should be counterbalanced by the expected higher dividends in future years where shares are valued on the basis of their expected future dividend yield, in practice, investors may view the future gains that may result from new projects funded from retained earnings as more risky than dividends paid here and now and may, as a result, undervalue the shares of a company that pays out a low level of dividends.[12] The theory also excludes the possibility of investor irrationality: irrespective of the value maximizing arguments, shareholders may simply prefer to receive steady dividends than to have to sell part of their shareholding in order to generate cash.[13]

Once the restrictive assumptions on which the 'irrelevance' theory was first developed are relaxed, it becomes evident that dividend policy can affect the overall value of a company's shares.[14] Empirical data indicates that corporate managers do not behave as the 'irrelevance' theory would predict and that they will pass up positive investment opportunities or borrow to fund them before cutting dividends because of the adverse impact that taking that step will have on the share price.[15] Real-world dividend policy is that maintaining the dividend level is a priority on a level with investment decisions rather than being secondary to them. A consequence is that dividends are path dependent, with the level of payouts by a firm in any given period being constrained by its previous payout policy.

Dividend policy, information asymmetries, and signalling

Dividends can perform an information function: paying healthy, consistent dividends in an environment shaped by conservatism is a way of indicating to investors who are not directly involved in managing a company that its management has long-term confidence in the business and its prospects.[16] If managers choose

---

[11] If income gains are taxed more heavily than capital gains a generous dividend policy can reduce shareholder wealth: MJ Brennan, 'Taxes, Market Valuation and Corporate Financial Policy' (1970) *National Tax Journal* 417; MH Miller, 'Behavioral Rationality in Finance: The Case of Dividends' (1986) 59(4.2) *Journal of Business* S451.

[12] MJ Gordon, 'Dividends, Earnings and Stock Prices' (1959) 41 *Review of Economics and Statistics* 99; S Keane, 'Dividends and the Resolution of Uncertainty' (1974) *Journal of Business Finance and Accounting* 389.

[13] F Allen and R Michaely, 'Payout Policy' in G Constantinides, M Harris and R Stulz, (eds), *Handbook of Economics of Finance* (North-Holland, Amsterdam, 2002) 337, 399–404 consider investor irrationality as a factor affecting payout policy.

[14] ibid 376–7.

[15] A Brav, JR Graham, R Campbell, CR Harvey, and R Michaely, 'Payout Policy in the 21st Century' (2005) 77 *Journal of Financial Economics* 483.

[16] WL Megginson, *Corporate Finance Theory* (Addison Wesley, 1997) ch 8; S Bhattacharya, 'Imperfect Information, Dividend Policy and the "Bird in the Hand" Fallacy' (1979) *Bell Journal of Economics* 259. This is not a particularly recent phenomenon: JB Baskin and PJ Miranti, *A History*

to increase the level of dividend, that is liable to be interpreted not just as an indication of the company's past profitability but also as a sign of greater dividend-paying capacity in the future. Conversely, a dividend cut may be taken as an indicator of long-term problems within the company rather than as a temporary blip in profitability or liquidity.[17]

Viewed in this way, dividends act as a counterweight to the information asymmetries between managers and investors. Some academics have developed the idea of dividends as an information-conveying mechanism to suggest that managers may use dividend policy to signal the strength of their company and to distinguish it from competitors, the underlying reasoning being that weaker competitors will not be able to afford to take that step because of the longer-term expectations associated with paying a generous dividend in one period.[18] However, recent scholarship casts doubt on whether signalling to investors is a significant determinant of corporate dividend policy.[19] One US study found that dividends were mainly paid by major companies that already enjoyed significant coverage from analysts and journalists.[20] Companies of such prominence are unlikely to have much need to use financial decisions to communicate to investors. The authors of the study concluded that it is 'possible that signalling motives may be important on the margin for some prominent dividend-paying firms' but that 'it is hard to envision plausible scenarios in which a material portion of aggregate dividends reflects signaling motives'.[21] Another study, which examined managers' opinions and the motives underlying their companies' dividend policy, found that managers regarded payout policy as performing an information-conveying function but that it was 'rarely thought of as a tool to separate a company from competitors'.[22]

Dividend policy and agency costs

The standard way of looking at the internal structure of a company from an economic perspective is to regard it as a 'nexus of contracts'[23] between the shareholders,

of Corporate Finance (CUP, 1997) 86–7 discussing dividends as a source of information in the period up to the early 18th century.

[17] JR Woolridge and C Ghosh, 'Dividend Cuts: Do They Always Signal Bad News' (Winter 1986) *Midland Corporate Finance Journal* 20; J Tirole, *The Theory of Corporate Finance* (Princeton University Press, 2006) 257.

[18] Bhattacharya (n 16 above) 259; MH Miller and K Rock, 'Dividend Policy under Asymmetric Information'(1985) 40 *Journal of Finance* 40, 1031; K John and J Williams, 'Dividends, Dilution, and Taxes: A Signaling Equilibrium' (1985) 40(4) *Journal of Finance* 1053. F Allen and R Michaely, 'Payout Policy' in G Constantinides, M Harris, and R Stulz, (eds), *Handbook of Economics of Finance* (North-Holland, Amsterdam, 2002) ch 7 provides a review of the signaling literature.

[19] Allen and Michaely (n 18 above) ch 7 provides a general survey of the literature.

[20] H DeAngelo, L DeAngelo, and DJ Skinner, 'Are Dividends Disappearing? Dividend Concentration and the Consolidation of Earnings' (2004) 72 *Journal of Financial Economics* 425.

[21] ibid 453.

[22] A Brav, JR Graham, R Campbell, CR Harvey, and R Michaely, 'Payout Policy in the 21st Century' (2005) 77 *Journal of Financial Economics* 483.

[23] FH Easterbrook and DR Fischel, 'The Corporate Contract' (1989) 89 *Columbia Law Review* 1416.

who provide the capital, and the managers, who are engaged as agents[24] of the shareholders to manage the business on their behalf. Where the managers and the shareholders do not comprise broadly the same group of people, an agency conflict arises: the shareholders fund the business but do not manage it; the managers run the business but they lack the incentive to maximize profits over the longer term and are liable instead to act in their own self-interest.[25] The agency conflict produces 'agency costs', meaning that, because of the divergence between shareholders' interests and managers' interests, investors will pay less for shares in companies where shareholding is widely dispersed and management is the responsibility of a few individuals. It follows that to improve the price which investors are willing to pay for its shares, the managers of a company should do all that they can to reduce agency costs.

Agency cost analysis suggests that companies should pay high dividends and, where necessary, raise finance from other sources: this will reduce agency costs because equity investors have the security of knowing that management will have had to expose their business record and their plans for the future to the scrutiny of lenders or to the market, and may have had to submit to restrictive covenants in order to secure the funds.[26] In Easterbrook's words: 'expected, continuing dividends compel firms to raise new money in order to carry out their activities. They therefore precipitate the monitoring and debt-equity adjustments that benefit stockholders.'[27]

There is some evidence to support the hypothesis that mitigating agency problems is significant as a determinant of dividend policy.[28] Even though it has

---

[24] In legal terms, the directors are the agents of the company, not of the shareholders: *Automatic Self-Cleansing Filter Syndicate Co Ltd v Cuninghame* [1906] 2 Ch 34, CA.

[25] On the problem of agency conflicts and agency costs generally, see M Jensen and W Meckling, 'Theory of the Firm: Managerial Behavior, Agency Costs and Ownership Structure' (1976) 3 *Journal of Financial Economics* 305; EF Fama, 'Agency Problems and the Theory of the Firm' (1980) 88 *Journal of Political Economy* 288.

[26] M Jensen, 'Agency Costs of Free Cash Flow, Corporate Finance and Takeovers' (May 1986) 76 *American Economic Review* 323; FH Easterbrook, 'Two Agency-Cost Explanations of Dividends' (1984) 74 *American Economic Review* 650; RC Clark, *Corporate Law* (Little, Brown, 1986) 598–9. A draconian proposal following this line of reasoning is that companies should be legally obliged to pay out all or a designated portion of earnings as dividends: K Brewster, 'The Corporation and Economic Federalism' in ES Mason (ed), *The Corporation in Modern Society* (CUP, 1959) 72. A more moderate proposal is that there should be greater mandatory disclosure of the way in which management arrives at the company's dividend policy: V Brudney, 'Dividends, Discretion and Disclosure' (1980) 66 *Virginia Law Review* 85.

[27] FH Easterbrook (n 26 above). See also R La Porta, F Lopez de Silanes, A Shleifer, and RW Vishny, 'Agency Problems and Dividend Policies Around the World' (2000) 55 *Journal of Finance* 1. For a review of the literature on agency problems-related explanations of dividends see F Allen and R Michaely, 'Payout Policy' in G Constantinides, M Harris, and R Stulz, (eds), *Handbook of Economics of Finance* (North-Holland, Amsterdam, 2002) ch 7.

Cheffins has suggested that dividend policies contributed to the separation of ownership and control in Britain that occurred from the 1940s onwards: BR Cheffins, 'Dividends as a Substitute for Corporate Law: The Separation of Ownership and Control in the United Kingdom' (2006) 63 *Washington and Lee Law Review* 1273.

[28] H DeAngelo, L DeAngelo, and RM Stulz, 'Dividend Policy, Agency Costs, and Earned Equity', NBER Working Papers 10599 (June 2004) available at SSRN <http://ssrn.com/abstract=558747>.

been found that corporate managers do not regard dividend policy as a means of imposing discipline on themselves,[29] in practice, the probability of paying dividends increases with the amount of earned equity in the capital structure and this can be explained by saying that it is a response to the agency problems that would loom large for high-earning companies if they retained earnings and thereby increased opportunities for managers to engage in activities that benefited themselves more than their shareholders.[30] However, it is also possible to find evidence that is inconsistent with this hypothesis.[31]

A recent line of scholarship on agency costs suggests two models in which dividend policy is associated with the quality of legal protection for shareholders: the 'outcome' model, which associates high dividends with high quality legal protections because shareholders are able exert pressure on the managers to disgorge cash; and the 'substitute' model, which associates high dividends with low quality legal protections because managers want to build a good reputation with investors.[32] However, the significance of shareholder protection laws as a determinant of dividend policy is controversial.[33]

Dividend policy and managerial-shareholder agreement levels

A new line of inquiry in dividend policy scholarship may develop from a recent paper suggesting that the degree of agreement (or disagreement) between managers and shareholders is an economically important determinant of dividend policy.[34] The idea is that strong corporate performance will deepen shareholder confidence in management and make it less expensive for managers to make financial policy choices that increase the managers' control, such as a low level of payouts. The authors of this theory contend that empirical data supports their view that firms with greater agreement between managers and shareholders display significantly lower dividend payout ratios. They suggest that agreement level analysis provides a possible explanation of why a company like Microsoft paid no dividends for many years but later decided to commence payouts.

---

[29] A Brav, JR Graham, R Campbell, CR Harvey, and R Michaely, 'Payout Policy in the 21st Century' (2005) 77 *Journal of Financial Economics* 483.

[30] DeAngelo, DeAngelo, and Stulz (n 28 above).

[31] See the literature review in MW Faulkender, TT Milbourn, and AV Thakor, 'Does Corporate Performance Determine Capital Structure and Dividend Policy?' (9 March 2006) available at SSRN <http://ssrn.com/abstract=686865>. See also the survey of European managers' views by F Bancel, UR Mittoo, and N Bhattacharyya, 'Cross-Country Determinants of Payout Policy: A Survey of European Firms' (2004) 33 *Financial Management* 103, which finds little support for the agency theory.

[32] R La Porta, F Lopez de Silanes, A Shleifer, and R Vishny, 'Agency Problems and Dividend Policies Around the World' (2000) 55 *Journal of Finance* 1.

[33] Bancel *et al* (n 31 above) do not find a systematic relation between quality of legal systems and dividend policies.

[34] Faulkender, Milbourn, and Thakor (n 31 above).

Regulation of dividend policy decisions

An overview of the regulatory response to agency problems relating to shareholders

The commercial necessity of meeting investors' expectations with regard to dividends limits the opportunity for managerial abuse of the power to control dividend policy. Failure to meet shareholders' expectations will have a negative effect on share price and may put the company into the frame as a potential takeover target. The finance director and others most closely associated with the policy may be criticized and their job security put at risk. Yet, even though these market pressures are powerful, they do not entirely eliminate the risk of managerial abuse because it may be possible for directors to satisfy investor expectations by paying a reasonable dividend in circumstances where the company's performance and the investment opportunities available to it would warrant a different level of payout. The directors may decide to retain profits to expand the company's business into new ventures for reasons that are more to do with the enhancement of their personal reputation resulting from the growth of the company than with the benefits that may ultimately flow to the shareholders from the company from those new investments.[35] Equally, directors may decide to pay out excessive dividends because of short-term personal considerations, rather than because they genuinely believe this to be in the company's interests.

Systems of company law and corporate governance employ various strategies to bolster market-based controls of the director-shareholder agency problems that arise in classic form in the context of corporate distributions. One is to give shareholders a say in distribution decisions. Shareholder involvement in distribution decisions is not compulsory in the UK under the general law but the norm is for companies to include requirements to this effect in their internal constitutions.[36] The procedure for the declaration and payment of dividends is set out in the articles of association and these usually provide for final dividends to be declared by shareholders in general meeting on the recommendation of the directors and for interim dividends to be paid by the directors without reference to the shareholders for approval. Articles usually provide that shareholders cannot declare a dividend in excess of the amount recommended by the directors, and

---

[35] The argument that management will pursue policies for the purposes of self-aggrandisement rather than shareholder wealth maximization is described as the 'managerialist theory': ES Herman, *Corporate Control, Corporate Power* (CUP, 1981) 9–14; R Marris, *The Economic Theory of Managerial Capitalism* (Free Press of Glencoe, 1964). For discussion of its application to dividend policy, see V Brudney, 'Dividends, Discretion and Disclosure' (1980) 66 *Virginia Law Review* 85, 95; DR Fischel, 'The Law and Economics of Dividend Policy' (1981) 67 *Virginia Law Review* 699, 710–14; MC Jensen, 'Eclipse of the Public Corporation' (Sept–Oct 1989) *Harvard Business Review* 61.

[36] See The Companies (Model Articles) Regulations 2007, SI 2007/(draft).

apart from contested takeover or other exceptional circumstances where tactical disputes over directors' dividend recommendations may arise between majority and minority shareholders,[37] shareholders can be expected generally to be disinclined to opt for a lesser amount. This means that the shareholders' decision to approve final dividends can appear to be little more than a rubber stamp but the fact that the shareholders do at least have the opportunity formally to review dividend recommendations and to require directors to justify them may have a disciplining effect.

It would be open to companies to vest more direct control in shareholders via their articles—for example giving shareholders the power to exceed the amount of payout recommended by the directors—but this could be unwise as it could result in important managerial decisions that have ramifications for share price being taken by an inexpert, ill-informed group. Moreover, its success in addressing managerial-shareholder agency conflicts could be outweighed by its adverse effects with regard to majority-minority agency issues where problems could be intensified as majority shareholders might force through excessive dividends that would then make it difficult for the company to pursue profitable business opportunities that would be beneficial for minority shareholders. The basic structure of the large company is that shareholders leave it to the directors, as a concentrated, focused, and expert group, to manage the business; where the shareholders are dissatisfied the answer, ultimately, is for them to replace the directors rather than themselves to assume direct managerial control. The Companies Act 2006 allows shareholders to vote directors out of office by an ordinary resolution.[38] This important provision helps to ensure that directors focus on shareholders' interests rather than their own.

Another strategy for controlling agency problems is the governance mechanism of appointing independent non-executive directors to the board. Non-executive directors have much greater access than the shareholders in general meeting to information about the company's financial position and prospects, and are much better placed to impose pressure on the executive directors and senior management to justify their dividend policy. The Combined Code on Corporate Governance, which is applicable to all fully listed UK companies (although they may choose to deviate from it on a comply or explain basis), provides as a main principle that a board should include a balance of executive and non-executive directors (and in particular independent non-executive directors) and as a specific code provision that, except for smaller companies, at least half the board, excluding the chairman, should comprise non-executive directors determined by the board to be independent.[39]

---

[37] As in the factual background to *Re Astec (BSR) plc* [1999] BCC 59 where a majority shareholder, which was seeking to acquire the remainder of the shares, opposed the board's dividend recommendation.

[38] Companies Act 2006, s 168.

[39] Combined Code, A.3.2.

All directors, executive and non-executive, are constrained by the duties attaching to their office. If directors were to manipulate the dividend policy to serve private interests rather than those of the members generally, that would amount to a breach of their statutory duties to promote the success of the company and to avoid conflicts of interest.[40] Directors' duties, which are owed to the company rather than to the shareholders directly, have a deterrent effect even though there are various factors that can be expected to operate so as to restrict the number of cases where action is actually taken. First, the powerful market and commercial constraints on dividend policy limit the scope for abuse and, hence, for legal dispute.[41] Secondly, the masking effect of a policy of paying dividends which are sufficient to satisfy investor demands even though the company's business and prospects would justify higher levels, means that it may be difficult to detect and prove wrongdoing.[42] Thirdly, even if an action did reach the courts, it is likely that, in the absence of evidence demonstrating a clear conflict of interests, the court would be reluctant to second-guess the directors' business judgment about dividend policy,[43] a reluctance that would be entirely appropriate given the complexity and commercial sensitivity of the issue.[44] As well as these factors, there are also considerations that inhibit the incidence of intra-corporate litigation generally, such as the formidable legal and procedural hurdles that have to be overcome by shareholders who seek to bring derivative actions, the availability of active stock markets on which shares can be sold thereby giving dissatisfied shareholders an alternative to pursuing grievances through the courts, and the unattractive prospect of the commencement of an action attracting media coverage that is damaging to the company's commercial interests. Since 2006, the derivative action has been set out in statute[45] rather than in obscure and often difficult to understand case law but it is not clear whether this clarification of the law will lead to the derivative action becoming a more actively used mechanism of corporate governance control.

There is also the possibility that a policy of paying low dividends (or, as the case may be, excessive dividends) could be challenged as amounting to unfairly prejudicial conduct. Section 994 of the Companies Act 2006 allows a shareholder to petition the court for relief where the affairs of the company are being conducted in an unfairly prejudicial manner. To succeed in a section 994 petition, a shareholder must ordinarily show that there has been some breach of the terms on which he agreed (contractually or otherwise) that the affairs of the company

---

[40] Companies Act 2006, Pt 10, ch 2.

[41] DR Fischel, 'The Law and Economics of Dividend Policy' (1981) 67 *Virginia Law Review* 699, 715–16.

[42] *Re a Company, ex p Glossop* [1988] 1 WLR 1068, 1076.

[43] *Burland v Earle* [1902] AC 83, PC.

[44] *Miles v Sydney Meat Preserving Co Ltd* (1912) 12 SR (NSW) 98, 103 *per* AH Simpson, CJ in E; Fischel (n 41 above) 715–16; V Brudney, 'Dividends, Discretion and Disclosure' (1980) 66 *Virginia Law Review* 85, 103–5.

[45] Companies Act 2006, Pt 11.

should be conducted or some use of the rules in a manner which equity would regard as contrary to good faith.[46] It has been judicially stated that a useful question to ask, in relation to unfair prejudice complaints, is whether the exercise of the power or rights in question would involve a breach of an agreement or understanding between the parties which it would be unfair to allow a member to ignore.[47] Mere disappointment that investment or involvement in the company has not turned out as had been hoped does not suffice.

The need to show breach of an agreement or an inequitable use of power restricts the scope for shareholders to use unfair prejudice petitions to complain about dividend policy. Shareholders in UK companies have no absolute entitlements to dividends. Their legal rights depend on the terms on which the shares were issued and the company's constitution. The standard constitutional position is that shareholders are only entitled to such dividends as may be declared by the shareholders in general meeting or as may be paid by the directors. This means that even though a company's dividend policy may not be to the liking of shareholders, it will not ordinarily be possible to show that it is in breach of an agreement. Yet the courts have left open the possibility of dividend policy being held to be unfairly prejudicial conduct in particular circumstances.[48] The circumstances in which this is most likely are where an agreement or understanding, which is in addition to the formal constitutional documents, has not been respected. Since shareholders in public companies with outside investors are entitled to proceed on the footing that the company's public documents provide a complete account of the shareholders' rights,[49] side agreements are not significant in that context. However, in a smaller company it may be possible for a shareholder to show that there was an agreement or understanding, perhaps driven by fiscal considerations, on how profits would in fact be distributed and that there is unfair prejudice because that understanding has not been followed. *Irvine v Irvine*[50] illustrates the potential for the unfair prejudice remedy to operate in small company contexts. In this case the business was a group of companies that had been run over many years by two brothers who were equal shareholders. After the death of one them, his widow and a family trust, of which she was one of the trustees, petitioned for relief as minority shareholders on the grounds that the surviving brother had procured the payment to himself of excessive remuneration and that, as a result, the shareholders had received no or inadequate dividends. The evidence was that during the twenty-two years or so that the brothers ran the business, the entire annual profits had been extracted and divided between them, apart from amounts needed for tax, regulatory, and other immediate business concerns. There had

[46] *O'Neill v Phillips* [1999] 1 WLR 1092, HL.
[47] *Grace v Biagioli* [2006] 2 BCLC 70, CA.
[48] *Re a Company, ex p Glossop* [1988] 1 WLR 1068; *Re Sam Weller & Sons Ltd* [1990] 1 Ch 682.
[49] *Re Blue Arrow plc* [1987] BCLC 585, 590 *per* Vinelott J; *Re Leeds United Holdings plc* [1996] 2 BCLC 545, 559 *per* Rattee J; *Re Astec (BSR) plc* [1998] 2 BCLC 556, 588 *per* Jonathan Parker J.
[50] [2006] EWHC (Ch) 1875.

been no dividend policy and dividends had been paid only in four years. Instead, profit extraction had been effected by whatever means the firm's accountants advised to be fiscally advantageous. The court agreed that the surviving brother had paid himself excessively and that, taking into account the historic policy of extracting all profits apart from the bare minimum needed for the business, this prevented the minority shareholders from receiving their proper share of the profits through dividend payments. Unfair prejudice having been so established, the majority shareholder was ordered to buy out the shares of the minority.

Dividend policy could conceivably form the basis for a shareholder petition under the Insolvency Act 1986 for the company to be wound up on the grounds that it is just and equitable to do so.[51] In one case it was said that if it were to be proved that directors had resolved to exercise their powers to recommend dividends to a general meeting, and thereby prevent the company in general meeting declaring any dividend greater than that recommended, with intent to keep moneys in the company so as to build a larger company in the future and without regard to the right of members to have profits distributed so far as was commercially possible, the directors' decision would be open to challenge; and that if it were proved that the board of directors had habitually so exercised its powers, that could justify the making of an order for winding up on the just and equitable ground.[52] However, winding up is a remedy of the last resort, as no court will lightly pass a death sentence on a viable business.[53]

There is a very detailed statutory framework now in the Companies Act 2006 governing the funds from which distributions can be made and the financial disclosure requirements that must be satisfied in respect of them. This form of regulation is mainly associated with creditor-protection goals, and it is considered in more detail in that context later in this chapter, but it is relevant to note here that it also has a shareholder-protection dimension in that it can operate so as to prevent excessive payouts being made to satisfy the preferences of controlling shareholders. Controlling shareholders are less commonly found in UK listed companies than elsewhere in the world (apart from the US) but they are not wholly unknown and they can certainly be found in unquoted and private companies.

An introduction to the regulatory response to agency problems in relation to creditors

Agency problems also arise as between creditors and the controllers of a company, whether they be its directors or its dominant shareholder(s), because excessive payouts are liable to undermine a company's financial position to the detriment of its creditors. However, the extent to which it is appropriate to emphasize

---

[51] Insolvency Act 1986, s 122(1)(g). *Ebrahimi v Westbourne Galleries Ltd* [1973] AC 360, HL.
[52] *Re a Company, ex p Glossop* [1988] 1 WLR 1068, 1075.
[53] *Re Guidezone Ltd* [2000] 2 BCLC 321.

creditor protection as part of the functions of company law is a matter for considerable debate. One reason for thinking that it is not appropriate to shape company law too much around the needs of creditors is that they (or at least those with commercial muscle) can protect themselves contractually. Loan agreements between sophisticated lenders and companies often contain covenants restricting dividends. Another reason for caution is that insolvency law is designed to address creditors' interests, including the interests of creditors who are unable to protect themselves contractually and, save perhaps for some specific rules that might apply in the period when companies are in serious financial difficulties and potentially heading towards insolvency, it is therefore duplicative and perhaps damaging to worthwhile economic activity for company law to take on that role as well. We return to these issues after we have considered in more detail the current company rules restricting distributions that have a strong creditor-protection focus.

Statutory regulation of distributions

Part 23 of the Companies Act 2006 (sections 829 to 853) regulates distributions by public and private companies. In summary, Part 23 provides that a company can only lawfully make distributions out of profits available for the purpose. It defines distributable profits and requires the availability of distributable profits to be supported by the distributing company's financial statements. The requirements for public companies are stricter than those for private companies. So far as public companies are concerned, Part 23 gives effect to Article 15 of the Second Company Law Directive,[54] which restricts distributions by public companies. The UK, along with other EU Member States, has extended broadly the same rules to private companies.

It fell originally to the courts to develop distribution rules out of the principle of maintenance of capital[55] but the detailed statutory code that now operates has been in place from 1980, although it has been amended from time to time since then. The statutory code is without prejudice to the maintenance of capital principle, which continues therefore to play a role in this area. It is open to companies to supplement the statutory code in their internal constitutions. As we have seen, it is usual for articles of association to regulate the procedure for the declaration and payment of dividends.

---

[54] Second Council Directive (EEC) 77/91 on co-ordination of safeguards which, for the protection of the interests of members and others are required by Member States of companies within the meaning of the second paragraph of Article 58 of the Treaty, in respect of the formation of public limited companies and the maintenance and alteration of their capital with a view to making such safeguards equivalent [1977] OJ L26/1 ('Second Company Law Directive').

[55] EA French, 'The Evolution of the Dividend Law of England' in WT Baxter and S Davidson (eds), *Studies in Accounting* (ICAEW, 3rd edn, 1977); BS Yamey, 'Aspects of the Law Relating to Company Dividends' (1941) 4 MLR 273.

What is a 'distribution'?

In Part 23 a distribution means 'every description of distribution of a company's assets to its members, whether in cash or otherwise' subject to four exceptions.[56] The exceptions are:

(1) an issue of shares as fully or partly paid bonus shares;
(2) the reduction of share capital by extinguishing or reducing the liability of any of the members on any of the company's shares in respect of share capital not paid up, or by paying off share capital;
(3) the redemption or purchase of any of the company's own shares out of capital (including the proceeds of a fresh issue of shares) or out of unrealized profits in accordance with the provisions of the Act governing redemption and purchase of shares;
(4) a distribution of assets to members of the company on its winding up.

All kinds of cash and non-cash (sometimes described as *in specie*) dividends are thus within the statutory code. A type of dividend that was in vogue for a period during the 1990s is a 'special' dividend, which in substance is an interim dividend paid by the directors in accordance with the normal procedure in the articles.[57] The label 'special' is important in commercial terms because it signals that the dividend is meant to be a 'one-off', either as a stand-alone step or in combination with a restructuring of the share capital, and should not be seen as indicating the start of a more permanent increase in the level of payout. However, the label carries no significance so far as the application of the Part 23 statutory code is concerned: special dividends are subject to it as much as (and to no greater extent than) any other type of dividend.

While there is no doubt that all types of dividend are distributions, more complicated characterization questions can arise in relation to corporate actions that do not follow the procedure for dividends but which result in cash or other assets that belonged to the company ending up in the hands of shareholders. Examples of situations where these complex questions can arise are transfers of assets between companies in a corporate group and the payment of remuneration to directors who are also shareholders. Dispositions of property or payments to persons who happen to be shareholders of a company are not distributions by reason only of the fact of that relationship, even where the amount of the disposition or payment is in proportion to the amount of the shareholdings.[58] Accordingly, many transactions between companies and shareholders will unquestionably be outside the scope of the law relating to distributions. In *Ridge Securities Ltd v*

---

[56] Companies Act 2006, s 829.

[57] The decline of the special dividend is examined in H DeAngelo, L DeAngelo, and DJ Skinner, 'Special Dividends and the Evolution of Dividend Signaling' (2000) 57 *Journal of Financial Economics* 309.

[58] *MacPherson v European Strategic Bureau* [2000] 2 BCLC 683 CA, 702 *per* Chadwick LJ.

IRC[59] the distinction between permissible and impermissible (because caught by the law on distributions) transactions was explained in the following terms: 'The corporators may take assets out of the company by way of dividend or, with leave of the court, by way of reduction of capital, or in a winding up. They may of course acquire them for full consideration. They cannot take assets out of the company by way of voluntary disposition, however described, and, if they attempt to do so, the disposition is ultra vires the company.'

Difficulties arise where the company appears to have overpaid for what it received or to have been underpaid for what it delivered because this suggests the possibility of a disguised distribution. The courts disregard the form of a transaction where it is a sham but this power is only used in quite narrow circumstances.[60] Significantly, however, the courts have been willing to recharacterize some corporate transactions as distributions even where they are not shams. This is demonstrated by *Aveling Barford Ltd v Perion Ltd*[61] where an intra-group sale of assets at less than their market value was held to be in law a sale rather than a sham but it was still an unlawful distribution because it infringed the rule that capital may not be returned to shareholders. Similarly, in *MacPherson v European Strategic Bureau Ltd*,[62] where a so-called payment for consultancy services was in issue, the Court of Appeal held that it was not necessary to categorize the provision as a sham but that it was an unlawful distribution because it was *ultra vires* the company to seek to distribute assets to shareholders without making proper provision for creditors.

The Part 23 definition of 'distribution' is very wide: apart from the four specified exceptions, every description of distribution of a company's assets is caught. In spite of this, there remains a noticeable tendency for the courts to decide cases involving undervalue transactions or other alleged disguised distributions by reference to common law principles on maintenance of capital and directors' duties, rather than on the basis that they are in breach of the statutory code. This is particularly evident in the *MacPherson* case where Chadwick LJ, who gave the leading judgment, specifically commented that the problem with the consultancy services payment arrangement was not that it contravened the statutory code but that it exceeded the powers of the company and of the directors. However, it is clear that the statutory and common law regimes overlap. One of the important changes to the statutory code, which was made by the Companies Act 2006, clarifies the operation of the statutory regime in relation to transfers of assets at less than market value.[63] This change was in response to the decision in *Aveling Barford Ltd v Perion Ltd*,[64] which had created difficulties for the statutory regime

---

[59] [1964] 1 All ER 275, 288 *per* Pennycuick J.
[60] *Snook v London and West Riding Investments Ltd* [1967] 2 QB 786, CA, 802 *per* Diplock LJ.
[61] [1989] BCLC 626.
[62] [2000] 2 BCLC 683, CA.
[63] Companies Act 2006, s 845.
[64] [1989] BCLC 626.

even though it was decided on the basis of the common law maintenance of capital principle.[65]

Profits available for distribution

The profits of a company that are available for distribution are defined in the Companies Act 2006 as its accumulated realized profits, so far as not previously utilized by distribution or capitalization, less its accumulated realized losses, so far as not previously written off in a reduction or reorganization of capital duly made.[66] No distinction is drawn between revenue profits and losses (profits and losses from trading) and capital profits and losses (profits and losses on the disposal of fixed assets) for this purpose. Losses incurred in previous years, so far as not previously written off, must be taken into account in determining the amount of distributable profits.[67] On the other hand, retained distributable profits from earlier years can be carried forward and used to pay dividends in years when the company makes a loss, so long as the loss is not so large as to wipe out the retained distributable reserves.

When fixed assets are revalued, increases in value are unrealized profits and they are not normally available for distribution.[68] Instead, they appear in the company's balance sheet as an undistributable reserve. A significant exception to this rule arises where a company makes a distribution of, or including, a non-cash asset. Any part of the amount at which the asset is shown in the relevant accounts which is an unrealized profit is to be treated as a realized profit for the purposes of determining the lawfulness of the distribution and complying with Companies Act accounting requirements.[69] Companies must pay dividends in cash unless dividends in kind are authorized by the articles.[70] Such authorization is commonly included.

Depreciation charges in respect of assets are taken into account as realized losses in determining the profits available for distribution.[71] There is a special rule for depreciation charges in respect of revalued assets where the revaluation has given rise to an unrealized profit. The Companies Act 2006 allows the difference between the depreciation charge on the revalued amount and the depreciation charge on the original amount to be treated as a realized profit.[72]

---

[65] See ch 7 above.

[66] Companies Act 2006, s 830(2).

[67] This reverses the common law position: *Lee v Neuchatel Asphalte Co* (1889) 41 Ch D 1, CA; *Ammonia Soda Co v Chamberlain* [1918] 1 Ch 266, CA.

[68] This reverses the common law position where unrealized profits on fixed assets could be distributed: *Dimbula Valley (Ceylon) Tea Co Ltd v Laurie* [1961] Ch 353.

[69] Companies Act 2006, s 846.

[70] *Wood v Odessa Waterworks Co* (1889) 42 Ch D 636.

[71] Companies Act 2006, s 841. Depreciation did not have to be charged under the common law rules: *Lee v Neuchatel Asphalte Co* (1889) 41 Ch D 1, CA.

[72] Companies Act 2006, s 841(4) and (5).

Additional requirement for public companies

For public companies there is the further requirement that a distribution may only be made when the amount of its net assets is not less than the aggregate of its called up share capital and undistributable reserves and only if, and to the extent that, the distribution does not reduce the amount of those assets to less than that aggregate.[73] This additional requirement gives effect to Article 15(1)(a) of the Second Company Law Directive, which states that 'no distribution to shareholders may be made when . . . the net assets are, or following such distribution would become, lower than the amount of the subscribed capital plus those reserves which may not be distributed under the law or the statutes'.

'Net assets' for this purpose means the aggregate of the company's assets less the aggregate of its liabilities.[74] A company's 'undistributable reserves' comprise: (1) the share premium account, (2) the capital redemption reserve, (3) the amount by which accumulated unrealized profits exceed accumulated unrealized losses, and (4) any other reserve which the company is prohibited from distributing by any enactment or by its articles.[75] The effect of this restriction can be illustrated by the following example.

Say a company has net assets of £10 million, a share capital of £3 million, share premium account of £6 million, unrealized losses of £2 million, and distributable profits of £3 million. If the company is private, it can distribute the full amount of the distributable profits: £3 million. However, if the company is public, it must also meet the balance sheet test. Its undistributable reserves are its share capital (£3 million) and its share premium account (£6 million). The profits available for distribution are therefore only £1 million.

In effect, what the net asset test, as embodied in section 831 does, is to require public companies to take unrealized losses into account in determining the maximum amount available for distribution.

The impact of section 831 has received attention in the context of International Financial Reporting Standards (IFRS) (previously International Accounting Standards (IAS)). Under IAS 32, *Financial Instruments: Presentation*, in accounts drawn up in accordance with the IFRS reporting framework certain preference shares must be shown as liabilities rather than as part of the share capital, which is their legal form. As liabilities, in accounting terms they have the effect of reducing net assets by the amount at which they are so presented in the accounts. This could appear to mean that, for the purposes of company law, dividend-paying capacity is reduced by that amount. However, the interpretation that prevailed in guidance issued by accounting bodies is that an amount that is shown as a liability in the accounts in respect of preference shares is also to be regarded as excluded from undistributable reserves for the purposes of section 831. Therefore

---

[73] ibid s 831.
[74] ibid s 831(2).
[75] ibid s 831(4).

the net effect is that the presentation of preference shares as liabilities does not reduce the amount of distributable reserves.[76]

Relevant accounts

The amount of a distribution which may be made is to be determined by reference to the company's financial position as stated in its relevant accounts.[77] It is individual company accounts rather than group accounts that are relevant for this purpose.[78] The company's last annual accounts will usually constitute the 'relevant accounts'.[79] These accounts must have been properly prepared in accordance with the requirements of the Companies Act 2006 or have been so prepared but for immaterial matters.[80] If the auditors have qualified their report on the accounts, they must also state in writing whether they consider the matter in respect of which the report is qualified to be material for determining the legality of the distribution.[81] If the last annual accounts do not show adequate reserves to cover a proposed distribution, the company can produce interim accounts and justify the distribution by reference to those accounts.[82] Generally, the interim accounts must enable a reasonable judgment to be made as to the company's financial position[83] but there are more detailed requirements in respect of interim accounts prepared for a proposed distribution by a public company.[84]

Choice of accounting regulatory framework

A company's individual accounts by reference to which a proposed dividend is to be justified may be drawn up in accordance with either the UK's accounting rules (UK Generally Accepted Accounting Principles or 'UK GAAP') or with the IFRS.[85] This optionality is in contrast to the position with regard to consolidated accounts, where it is mandatory for EU companies that have their securities admitted to trading on an EU regulated market to use IFRS.[86] Notwithstanding a trend for convergence of UK GAAP towards IFRS,[87] at least for an interim

---

[76] ICAEW and ICAS, 'Distributable Profits: Implications of Recent Accounting Changes', TECH 2/07, paras 5.24–5.30. This is a jointly issued technical release.

[77] Companies Act 2006, s 836(1).

[78] ibid s 837(1).

[79] ibid s 836(2).

[80] ibid s 837(2).

[81] ibid s 837(4).

[82] ibid s 836(2).

[83] ibid s 838(1).

[84] ibid s 838(2)–(6).

[85] ibid s 395.

[86] Regulation (EC) 1606/2002 of the European Parliament and of the Council of 19 July 2002 on the application of international accounting standards [2002] OJ L243/1. In the UK, unlisted groups have the option to produce their consolidated accounts under either UK GAAP or IFRS.

[87] P Holgate, *Accounting Principles for Lawyers* (CUP, 2006) 14.

period certain aspects of IFRS may lead to a less favourable result than UK GAAP so far as the determination of accounting profits is concerned, which has potentially adverse ramifications for the determination of profits that, as a matter of company law, are available for distribution. The threat to dividend-paying capacity presented by IFRS is a disincentive to switching to that system in respect of individual accounts even though, for companies that are subject to mandatory obligations regarding use of IFRS for consolidated accounts, it is clearly not ideal to maintain two different systems for financial records. There is a prima facie rule to the effect that financial reporting within a corporate group must be consistent, ie the individual accounts must all be prepared using the same financial reporting framework,[88] but this does not apply where there are 'good reasons for not doing so'[89] and, moreover, where the parent company's accounts (group and individual) are prepared in accordance with IFRS, the rule does not apply to require the subsidiaries to adopt that framework.[90]

Accounting profits and profits available for distribution

It is important to note that whilst the amount of profits available for distribution is derived from accounts, accounting profits and distributable profits do not necessarily equate to each other. One potential source of divergence stems from the fact that modern accounting frameworks increasingly permit reporting entities to account at fair value (which is, broadly, current market value) for certain assets. Where assets are recorded at fair value, changes in their value may be taken through the profit and loss account or income statement but these fluctuations may not always be 'realized', as that concept is understood for the purposes of the legal rules.[91] The legal rules give prominence to the accounting concept of prudence, which implies conservatism in the recognition of profits so that assets and income are not overstated (and also that liabilities are not understated), but the concept has become less significant for accounting purposes. At a fundamental level, there is a deepening divergence between the underlying aims of accounting regulation, which are to provide financial statements that provide information that is useful to investment decisions, and the distribution rules, which are concerned with capital maintenance and creditor protection. This divergence means that the numbers yielded by application of the accounting requirements may be increasingly inappropriate for the purposes of rules that are intended to protect creditors. In some circumstances, moreover, changes in accounting may lead to significant changes in the measurement of a company's assets or liabilities that

---

[88] Companies Act 2006, s 407(1).
[89] ibid s 407(1).
[90] ibid s 407(5).
[91] Holgate (n 87 above) 171.

could have adverse ramifications for dividend-paying capacity. This was an issue of real concern to many companies in 2005, when the accounting treatment of pension fund deficits was revised.[92] That companies could be constrained from paying dividends, not because their economic performance has declined but simply because of developments in the accounting measurement of that performance, is controversial and it has led to growing pressure to break the link between accounts and dividend-paying capacity in some way that instead determines capacity by reference to solvency, although no generally agreed consensus has emerged as yet on the details of how to do so.[93]

Generally accepted principles with respect to the determination of realized profits or losses

Section 853(4) of the Companies Act 2006 provides that references to 'realised profits' and 'realised losses' in relation to a company's accounts are to such profits or losses of the company as fall to be treated as realized in accordance with principles generally accepted at the time when the accounts are prepared, with respect to the determination for accounting purposes of realized profits or losses. In the UK, a leading role in establishing these 'generally accepted principles' is played by the Institute of Chartered Accountants in England and Wales (ICAEW) and the Institute of Chartered Accountants of Scotland (ICAS).

In March 2003, the Institutes issued guidance on the determination of realized profits under UK GAAP, which revised and updated guidance published previously in 1982 (TECH 7/03).[94] This was followed, in 2007 by guidance on the implications of recent accounting changes (in particular the transition to IFRS) for distributable profits (TECH 2/07):[95] TECH 2/07 supplements and in certain respects amends TECH 7/03. There are also a number of other such papers that provide guidance on certain specific matters.[96]

---

[92] Under UK GAAP, FRS 17, *Retirement Benefits* came fully into force in 2005. IAS 19, *Employee Benefits* is the IRFS equivalent. A prominent casualty was British Airways, which was unable to pay a dividend in 2005 despite an increase in operating profit, because its £1.4bn pension deficit effectively wiped out its distributable reserves.

[93] E Ferran, 'The Place for Creditor Protection on the Agenda for Modernization of Company Law in the European Union' (2006) 2 *European Company and Financial Law Review* 178. The Federation of European Accountants (FEE) has produced a thoughtful paper that suggests a persuasive solvency-based test: FEE, 'Discussion Paper on Alternatives to Capital Maintenance Regimes' (September 2007). This paper is discussed further at the end of the chapter.

[94] 'Guidance on the determination of realised profits and losses in the context of distributions under the Companies Act 1985', Texh 7/03.

[95] 'Distributable Profits: Implications of Recent Accounting Changes', TECH 7/03.

[96] TECH 2/07, para 2.5 lists the various technical releases and indicates that a consolidation in due course is intended.

TECH 7/03

The Guidance notes that under UK GAAP,[97] it is generally accepted that profits are to be treated as realized only when realized in the form of 'cash or of other assets the ultimate cash realization of which can be assessed with reasonable certainty'. The first of a series of examples of realized profits provided in the Guidance is a profit arising from a transaction where the consideration received by the company is 'qualifying consideration'.[98] The Guidance states that qualifying consideration comprises:[99]

(1) cash;
(2) an asset that is readily convertible to cash;[100]
(3) the release, or the settlement or assumption by another party, of all or part of a liability of the company, unless:
   (a) the liability arose from the purchase of an asset that does not meet the definition of qualifying consideration and has not been disposed of for qualifying consideration, and
   (b) the purchase and release are part of a group or series of transactions or arrangements that fall within paragraph 12 of the guidance;[101]
(4) an amount receivable in any of the above forms of consideration where:
   (a) the debtor is capable of settling the receivable within a reasonable period of time, and
   (b) there is a reasonable certainty that the debtor will be capable of settlement, and
   (c) there is an expectation that the receivable will be settled.[102]

Whereas the Guidance is quite lengthy on what a profit is and when it is to be regarded as realized, the definition of a realized loss is more succinct: the main stipulation provides that losses should be regarded as realized losses except to the extent that the law, accounting standards, or the Guidance provide otherwise.[103]

TECH 7/03, as originally drafted, provided for certain limited circumstances in which profits arising from the use of the mark to market method of accounting (ie accounting for marketable securities at their market value and recognizing gains and losses in the accounts as they arose rather than waiting for the asset to

---

[97] FRS 18, *Accounting Policies.*
[98] TECH 7/03, para 16(a).
[99] TECH 7/03, para 16, as amended by TECH 2/07.
[100] TECH 7/03, para 19 and paras 35–40O, as amended by TECH 2/07.
[101] TECH 7/03, para 12 is concerned with linked transactions. It provides: 'In assessing whether a company has a realised profit, transactions and arrangements should not be looked at in isolation. A realised profit will arise only where the overall commercial effect on the company satisfies the definition of realised profit set out in this guidance. Thus a group or series of transactions or arrangements should be viewed as a whole, particularly if they are artificial, linked (whether legally or otherwise) or circular.'
[102] TECH 7/03, para 18.
[103] TECH 7/03, para 17.

be sold) were to be treated as realized profits. One of the most significant consequences of TECH 2/07 is that it amends TECH 7/03 to broaden the circumstances in which realized profits may arise from fair value accounting (which has a similar meaning to marking to market).[104] That accounting practice may evolve is anticipated by section 853(4) of the Companies Act 2006 in its reference to profits and losses that fall to be treated as realized in accordance with principles generally accepted *at the time when the accounts are prepared*.

TECH 2/07

Under the IFRS, the range of assets in respect of which 'fair value' accounting is permitted is extended to include financial instruments (including derivatives), commodities, investment property, and biological assets.[105] In response to this, TECH 2/07 amended TECH 7/03 to encompass within the concept of 'realized', profits and losses resulting from the recognition of changes in fair values, in accordance with relevant accounting standards, to the extent that they are readily convertible to cash.[106] TECH 2/07 inserts into TECH 7/03 a considerable amount of guidance on what 'readily convertible to cash' means[107] but cautions that it is for the directors of any particular company to consider their own company's facts and circumstances in determining whether an accounting profit arising through changes in fair value is readily convertible into cash.[108]

Dividend payment procedure

The declaration of a final dividend is a standard part of the business at the AGMs of companies. If, between the date when the notices are despatched and the holding of the meeting, it is discovered that the last annual accounts were not properly prepared then, unless the irregularity is immaterial, the dividend cannot lawfully be declared because, unless the accounts have been properly prepared they cannot be 'relevant accounts' for the purposes of Part 23 of the Companies Act 2006.[109] The shareholders cannot sue the company for a dividend that has been recommended but not declared, because a final dividend does not become a debt payable to shareholders until it has been declared.[110] The board's decision to pay an interim dividend does not give rise to a debt and that decision can therefore be reversed at any time before payment.[111] Under UK GAAP, historically, dividends

[104] TECH 2/07, para 3.1.
[105] TECH 2/07, para 3.2.
[106] TECH 7/03, para 10, inserted by TECH 2/07, para 3.8.
[107] TECH 7/03, para 19 and paras 35–40O, as amended by TECH 2/07.
[108] TECH 7/03, para 3.17 (as amended).
[109] Companies Act 2006, ss 837–839.
[110] *Bond v Barrow Haematite Steel Co* [1902] 1 Ch 353; *Re Accrington Corp Steam Tramways Co* [1909] 2 Ch 40.
[111] *Lagunas Nitrate Co v Schroeder & Co and Schmidt* (1901) 85 LT 22.

relating to an accounting period, but declared after the balance sheet date, used to be recognized as a liability even if the approval of that dividend took place after the balance sheet date. Under IFRS and current UK GAAP,[112] however, proposed dividends do not meet the definition of a liability until such time as they have been declared, and in the case of the final dividend, approved by shareholders at the annual general meeting.

Shares in quoted companies are traded either cum-dividend or ex-dividend. If a share is acquired at a cum-dividend price that means that the purchaser is entitled to the dividend. Conversely, an ex-dividend price means that the vendor keeps the dividend. In the absence of any contrary provision in the company's articles, it is the person who is the registered holder of the share on the date of the declaration of a final dividend or payment of an interim dividend who is entitled to the dividend.[113] However, articles commonly authorize the board to select a date (the record date) for the payment of dividends. Shareholders on the register on the selected date receive the dividend, which means that the share price goes ex-dividend on that date.

Dividends are paid on the nominal value of the shares unless the articles otherwise provide.[114] The effect of this is that the holder of a partly paid share of a particular class would receive the same amount of dividend as the holder of a fully paid share of that class. Companies can change the position in their articles and it is commonly provided that dividends are to be calculated and paid on the amounts paid up on shares rather than their nominal value. For quoted companies the point is largely theoretical, however, because shares in such companies are normally issued on a fully paid basis.

Unlawful distributions

When is a distribution unlawful?

A dividend or other distribution may be unlawful because it is not covered by distributable reserves or because of a failure to comply with the requirements of the companies legislation for the distribution to be justified by reference to properly prepared company accounts that give a true and fair view of the financial position of the individual distributing company. A company's power to pay dividends (or make other distributions) is linked to and controlled by the very detailed codes for accounts[115] and failure to comply with the statutory requirements is not a mere procedural irregularity that the courts will readily overlook.

---

[112] IAS 10 and FRS 21.

[113] *Re Wakley, Wakley v Vachell* [1920] 2 Ch 205, CA; *Godfrey Phillips Ltd v Investment Trust Corp Ltd* [1953] Ch 449.

[114] *Oakbank Oil Co Ltd v Crum* (1882) 8 App Cas 65, HL.

[115] *Bairstow v Queens Moat House plc* [2001] 2 BCLC 531, CA, para 31 *per* Robert Walker LJ.

In *Precision Dippings Ltd v Precision Dippings Marketing Ltd*[116] the legality of a dividend paid by a subsidiary to its parent company was challenged on the grounds that a statutory requirement to obtain a statement from the auditors on the materiality of a qualification in the accounts in relation to the dividend had not been satisfied. The claim was thus not that the dividend *had* been paid otherwise than from distributable reserves; rather it was that the company had failed to do all that it was required to do by the companies legislation to demonstrate that the dividend was permissible. The Court of Appeal rejected the argument that the company's failing was a mere procedural irregularity. Dillon LJ, giving the judgment of the court, stated that the relevant provisions of the companies legislation constituted a major protection to creditors and that the shareholders were not free to waive or dispense with those requirements. The Court of Appeal left open the question of whether anything could be done to restore the situation in a solvent company, for example the production of an auditors' statement after the event because that situation did not arise on the facts. In *Bairstow v Queens Moat House plc*[117] the Court of Appeal returned to the issue of distributions that could not be justified by reference to the relevant accounts. In this case over several years the company paid dividends that exceeded its distributable reserves, as disclosed in its relevant individual accounts. For some of the years in dispute, the accounts were also defective because they failed to give a true and fair view of the financial position. However, there were significant distributable reserves in the corporate group as a whole. This led counsel for the directors to argue that any breaches of the companies legislation could be regarded as technical, that they could be waived by the shareholders, and that the action of the parent company in declaring dividends in excess of its own distributable reserves must be taken to have amounted to the informal declaration of sufficient dividends from its wholly-owned subsidiaries. These arguments were rejected: the failure was not a procedural irregularity; it could not be waived; and the directors could not go behind the individual accounts that they had prepared and laid before the general meeting.

The importance of proper accounting records is reinforced by a distinction that has emerged from recent cases. Whereas a dividend is entirely unlawful if the relevant accounts fail to give a true and fair view, it has been held that a dividend that exceeds the amount available for distribution based on relevant accounts that are in proper order is only unlawful to the extent of the excess.[118]

---

[116] [1986] Ch 447, CA.

[117] [2001] 2 BCLC 531, CA.

[118] *Re Marini Ltd* [2004] BCC 172, distinguishing *Inn Spirit Ltd v Burns* [2003] BPIR 413, where it was held that it was not arguable that liability to repay an unlawful dividend was limited to any excess over the amount at which a lawful dividend might have been declared, on the grounds that this was a case where a dividend had been paid without regard for the need for accounts showing a true and fair view of the financial position.

Other restrictions on dividends

Notwithstanding that a company's relevant accounts are in order and it is evident from them that the company has healthy distributable reserves, it is not necessarily the case that the directors can safely proceed to pay or recommend the payment of a dividend. The Companies Act 2006 makes it clear that the statutory regime is not exhaustive and that other rules of law restricting distributions are also applicable.[119] So too are provisions of a company's articles restricting distributions.[120] If, for instance, the company's financial position has deteriorated significantly since the accounts were prepared, there is a possibility that the payment of a dividend in those circumstances could infringe the still extant common law principle not to make distributions from capital or could be held to be a fraud on the company's creditors. Directors will thus need to check that the proposed dividend is still permissible taking into account changes in the company's financial position since the relevant accounts were published. Their decision will need to be made within the framework of the general duties that they owe to their company.

An issue that has acquired particular significance in recent years because of the many changes in accounting related to the transition to IRFS and the project to converge UK GAAP towards IFRS is the effect of the introduction of a new accounting standard.[121] Guidance from the Accounting Institutes is that although the effect of the new accounting standard may be to reduce or even to eliminate a company's net realized profit, this will not render unlawful a dividend already made and there is no retrospective effect on a proposed final dividend for a period preceding the adoption, so long as the dividend was provided for in the statutory accounts for that period. For example, for a company with a 31 December year-end and adopting IFRS in its individual account for the first time in 2005, the effect of adoption is not relevant when considering the lawfulness of a proposed final dividend for 2004 that is included in the 2004 accounts (and, as was permitted by the then current UK GAAP, recognized as a liability in the 2004 accounts). However, any interim dividend paid during 2005 would have to have regard to the effect of the adoption of IFRS even though the 'relevant accounts' may still be those for 2004 prepared under UK GAAP. The Guidance suggests that the directors may, as an exercise of appropriate care and skill, wish to prepare interim accounts drawn up under IRFS to check that the dividend remains permissible and would not infringe common law maintenance of capital principles.

Liability consequences of unlawful dividends

The payment of unlawful dividends has serious consequences for the directors and potentially also for the recipient shareholders.

---

[119] Companies Act 2006, s 851.
[120] ibid s 852.
[121] This paragraph draws heavily on TECH 2/07, paras 6.22–6.33.

Directors' liability

Directors have traditionally been regarded as stewards of the company's property and trustee-like responsibilities have been held to attach to them in this role.[122] At common law it was regarded as a breach of the trustee-like obligations of directors to pay a dividend out of capital.[123] The common law liability of directors to account for dividends paid from capital is sometimes referred to as the principle in *Flitcroft's Case*. The principle in *Flitcroft's Case* has been held to apply also to failures to comply with requirements of the companies legislation with regard to distributions being based on accounts that give a true and fair view of the company's financial position.[124] The principle has also been held to be applicable to solvent as well as to insolvent companies, with the reasoning underlying this being that the regulatory regime for distributions is intended to protect shareholders as well as creditors.[125]

In some of the older cases, the liability of directors to account for unlawful dividends was expressed in very strict terms: 'as soon as the conclusion is arrived at that the company's money has been applied by the directors for purposes which the company cannot sanction it follows that the directors are liable to repay the money, however honestly they may have acted'.[126] The view that prevailed, however, was that directors would not be held liable where they acted under an honest and reasonable belief that the facts justified the payment.[127] Accordingly, directors could escape liability where dividends were paid on the basis of accounts that were later found to have been defective provided that they had no reason to doubt the integrity, skill, and competence of those responsible for the production of the accounts.[128]

Directors' duties have been codified by the Companies Act 2006. There is no statutory duty that is the direct equivalent of directors' trustee-like duties of stewardship developed in cases such as *Flitcroft's Case* but they appear to be subsumed within the duty in section 171 of the Companies Act 2006 to exercise powers only for the purposes for which they were conferred, since directors' powers in

---

[122] *Bairstow v Queens Moat House plc* [2001] 2 BCLC 531, CA, para 53. It is only in some respects that the position of a director is equated to that of a trustee. See LS Sealy, 'The Director as Trustee' [1967] CLJ 83.

[123] *Re Exchange Banking Co, Flitcroft's Case* (1882) 21 Ch D 519, CA; *Re Sharpe* [1892] 1 Ch 154, CA.

[124] *Precision Dippings Ltd v Precision Dippings Marketing Ltd* [1986] Ch 447, CA.

[125] *Bairstow v Queens Moat House plc* [2001] 2 BCLC 531, CA, para 44 *per* Robert Walker LJ.

[126] *Re Sharpe* [1892] 1 Ch 154, CA, 165–6 *per* Lindley LJ.

[127] *Dovey v Cory* [1901] AC 477, HL, where a director escaped liability for an unlawful dividend because he had no reason to doubt the company officials on whom he relied. The cases supporting the strict approach and the approach whereby honest and reasonable directors escape liability are reviewed by Vaughan Williams J at first instance in *Re Kingston Cotton Mill Co (No 2)* [1896] 1 Ch 331, affirmed [1896] 2 Ch 279, CA.

[128] For a modern application of these principles see *Hilton International Ltd v Hilton* [1989] 1 NZLR 442, NZ H Ct: directors who did not obtain a proper set of accounts were held liable to refund the amount of the dividend.

respect of distributions are necessarily constrained by what is permissible under the general law, and the statutory duty of care and skill under section 174 of the 2006 Act.

The civil consequences of a breach of the codified general duties (including the duties under sections 171 and 174) are the same as would apply if the corresponding common law rule or equitable principle applied.[129] In *Bairstow v Queens Moat House plc*[130] it was held that directors who acted deliberately and dishonestly were liable to account in full for unlawful dividends paid out of company funds that were in their stewardship. The Court of Appeal indicated that in circumstances of deliberate wrongdoing there was no room for the argument that the company had suffered no compensatable loss because dividends could have been declared and paid in a lawful manner by first paying up distributable profits from the subsidiaries.[131] However, it left open the possibility of a more lenient approach to directors who were in breach of their stewardship duties merely through imprudence.[132]

Directors are only liable to account for *unlawful* dividends. It has been held that a dividend that is paid on the basis of proper accounts that give a true and fair view but which exceeds available distributable reserves is only unlawful to the extent of the excess and the liability of the directors is therefore limited to that amount.[133]

A director who has been held to be in breach of duty can apply to court to be relieved of liability on the grounds that he acted honestly and reasonably, and that having regard to all the circumstances of the case (including those connected with his own circumstances), he ought fairly to be excused.[134] Since honesty and reasonableness are factors that are relevant in the first place to the determination of a director's liability for unlawful dividends, there may be little need (or room) for discretionary relief to operate in this context, although in a recent case the court indicated that it would have been willing to grant relief to directors who had acted on professional advice had it been necessary to do so.[135] It is also open to a director to pre-empt liability proceedings by applying for discretionary relief where he has reason to apprehend that a claim will or might be made against him but this provision is not much utilized in practice.

Shareholder liability

Shareholders who receive an unlawful distribution may be liable to repay it. There is statutory liability under section 847 of the Companies Act 2006, which applies

---

129 Companies Act 2006, s 178.
130 [2001] 2 BCLC 531, CA.
131 At paras 49–53.
132 At para 54.
133 *Re Marini Ltd* [2004] BCC 172.
134 Companies Act 2006, s 1157.
135 *Re Marini Ltd* [2004] BCC 172. It was not necessary to do so because, to the extent that the court would have been willing to grant relief, the dividend was held to be lawful.

where a distribution, or part of one, is made in contravention of the Act. If, at the time of the distribution, the member knows or has reasonable grounds for believing that it is so made, he is liable to repay it (or that part of it, as the case may be) to the company. It used to be thought that statutory liability required more than fact-based knowledge but in *It's a Wrap (UK) Ltd v Gula*[136] the Court of Appeal held that it was not a precondition of statutory liability that the recipient shareholder must be shown to have had knowledge or reasonable grounds for belief that the distribution contravened the law. The Court of Appeal interpreted the statutory liability in the light of Article 16 of the Second Company Law Directive, to which it gave effect. According to the Court, on its true interpretation, Article 16 meant that a shareholder was liable to return a distribution if he knew or could not have been unaware that it was paid in circumstances amounting to a contravention of the Second Directive, whether or not he knew of those legal restrictions.

Statutory liability is without prejudice to any other liability that may arise. A shareholder who receives an unlawful dividend may also incur personal liability in equity for knowing receipt of property that has been disposed of in breach of duty.[137] Recipient liability thus depends on a breach of duty by the directors, and on the recipient being aware of the factual circumstances amounting to the breach of trust but the recipient does not need to be aware of the law.[138] According to a leading case on recipient liability, the test for knowledge in such a claim is whether the defendant's knowledge made it unconscionable for him to retain the benefit of the receipt.[139] However, in *It's a Wrap (UK) Ltd v Gula* Arden LJ noted that the authorities under the general law on distributions established that liability attached where the shareholder knew or ought to have known of the factual circumstances that made the distribution unlawful rather than where the shareholder had acted unconscionably.[140]

The statutory and equitable regimes overlap to a significant extent but there are some differences between them.[141] For instance, statutory liability is based on the fact that there has been a contravention of the 2006 Act and it need not

[136] [2006] BCC 626, noted J Payne, 'Recipient Liability for Unlawful Dividends' [2007] LMCLQ 7.

[137] *Precision Dippings Ltd v Precision Dippings Marketing Ltd* [1986] Ch 447, CA. On the elements of knowing receipt see *El Ajou v Dollar Land Holdings plc* [1994] 2 All ER 685, 700 *per* Hoffmann LJ: 'This is a claim to enforce a constructive trust on the basis of knowing receipt. For this purpose the plaintiff must show, first, a disposal of his assets in breach of fiduciary duty; secondly, the beneficial receipt by the defendant of assets which are traceable as representing the assets of the plaintiff; and thirdly, knowledge on the part of the defendant that the assets he received are traceable to a breach of fiduciary duty'.

[138] *Precision Dippings Ltd v Precision Dippings Marketing Ltd* [1986] Ch 447, CA; *It's a Wrap (UK) Ltd v Gula* [2006] 1 BCLC 143, CA, para 12 *per* Arden LJ.

[139] *Bank of Credit and Commerce International (Overseas) Ltd (in liquidation) v Akindele* [2001] Ch 437, CA.

[140] Citing in particular *Moxham v Grant* [1900] 1 QB 88, 69 LJQB 97, 7 Mans 65.

[141] For an account of some differences see *It's a Wrap (UK) Ltd v Gula* [2006] 1 BCLC 143, CA, para 12 *per* Arden LJ.

be shown that the directors were in breach of duty; in this respect the statutory liability regime is more stringent for shareholders. On the other hand, statutory liability is limited to contraventions of the Act: where a dividend is permissible according to the properly prepared, relevant accounts but a post-accounts downturn in the company's financial position has rendered it unlawful as infringing common law maintenance of capital principles, only recipient liability in equity appear to be relevant.

The knowledge requirements in both the statutory and equitable regimes will make it hard for a company to recover improperly paid dividends from outside shareholders but controlling shareholders and director-shareholders are more at risk. In the *Precision Dippings* case, for example, recovery was achieved in respect of an unlawful dividend paid by a subsidiary to its parent and in *It's a Wrap Ltd v Gula* unlawful dividends were recovered from persons who were both directors and shareholders. It has been argued that restitutionary strict liability, coupled with a change of position defence, would be a preferable mechanism for the recovery of unlawful dividends to personal equitable liability which is fault based, but the extension of restitutionary liability into this field is controversial.[142] Looking at the issue from a European standpoint, there is an argument for saying that since the European standard, as indicated by the Second Company Law Directive, is good faith/fault based there is good reason for the UK not to adopt a more stringent standard. Current government policy is not to gold-plate directives unless there are exceptional circumstances, justified by a cost benefit analysis and consultation with stakeholders.[143] This does not rule out the possibility of a more stringent liability standard being developed by the courts through the application of principles in the law of restitution but it suggests a reason for questioning the merits of doing so.

Directors' claims against recipient shareholders

Shareholders who benefit from an unlawful dividend may be in line to receive an unmeritorious windfall if the amount of the unlawful dividend is restored to the company by the directors and then distributed again lawfully to the same people. The Court of Appeal in *Bairstow v Queens Moat House plc*[144] briefly considered

---

[142] Arguments in favour are suggested by J Payne, 'Unjust Enrichment, Trusts and Recipient Liability of Unlawful Dividends' (2003) 119 LQR 583 but a contrary view is expressed in CH Tham, 'Unjust Enrichment and Unlawful Dividends: a Step Too Far?' [2005] CLJ 177. In *Bank of Credit and Commerce International (Overseas) Ltd (in liquidation) v Akindele* [2001] Ch 437, 456 Nourse LJ expressed the view that shifting the burden onto recipients to defend receipts either by a change of position or in some other way could be commercially unworkable and contrary to established principles whereby persons dealing with companies generally are not affected by irregularities that are internal to the corporate operations. In *Farah Constructions Pty Ltd and ors v Say-Dee Pty Ltd* [2007] HCA 22 the High Court of Australia rejected a restitutionary approach to recipient liability for breach of trust or fiduciary duty.

[143] Policy in this area is set by the Better Regulation Executive within the Cabinet Office. See <http://www.cabinetoffice.gov.uk/regulation/index.asp> (accessed December 2007).

[144] [2001] 2 BCLC 531, CA.

this 'double recovery' argument but denied its relevance to the question of whether the directors were liable in the first place. However, earlier authority recognizes that directors who are held personally liable in respect of an unlawful dividend may be able to seek an indemnity from those shareholders who received the payment with notice of the facts.[145]

Other issues

Scrip dividends

The articles of association of a company may permit shareholders to elect to take additional fully paid ordinary shares in the company in whole or in part in lieu of a cash dividend. A dividend in this form is known as a 'scrip dividend'. Scrip dividends enable shareholders to acquire additional shares without incurring dealing costs. Conceptually, a scrip dividend can be characterized either as a reinvestment of the cash amount of a dividend or as a bonus issue of shares. The reinvestment characterization is appropriate where shareholders make their election after the dividend has been declared. Because the electing shareholders release the company from the obligation to pay cash, the shares are allotted for cash for the purposes of the Companies Act 2006, with the consequence that the statutory pre-emption requirements are relevant.[146] For accounting purposes, the new shares are deemed to be paid up out of distributable reserves. The bonus issue characterization is appropriate where the shareholders' election is in place before the declaration of a dividend. There are advantages for the company in structuring its scrip dividends election procedures so that the elections precede the dividend. Shares allotted in satisfaction of elections timed in this way are not allotted for cash and therefore the statutory pre-emption requirements do not apply. Also, for accounting purposes, the shares are bonus shares and can be paid up from undistributable reserves, such as the share premium account, thereby preserving the distributable reserves for subsequent dividend payments.

Dividend reinvestment plans

Dividend reinvestment plans are like scrip dividends to the extent that they are a means whereby shareholders can acquire additional shares without having to pay the normal dealing costs, although an administration fee is usually charged. However, in a typically structured dividend reinvestment plan, the company does not allot new shares to shareholders who wish to take advantage of the scheme

---

[145] *Moxham v Grant* [1896] 1 Ch 685.
[146] Companies Act 2006, s 561.

but, instead, it arranges for their dividends to be invested in existing shares in the company that are trading in the market. Since there is no allotment of new shares, no issues with regard to pre-emption rights arise and the share purchases do not have any effect on the company's capital as recorded in its accounts. The fact that there is no dilution of the existing share capital means that there is no impact on the company's earnings-per-share or dividend-per-share ratios as there would be where there is extensive take up of scrip dividend alternatives.

Intra-group distributions

The operation of the law relating to distributions within a corporate group calls for special consideration under a number of headings.

Intra-group dividends and principles of realization

Whether a dividend received from a subsidiary is to be treated as a realized profit in the hands of its parent is a issue that is considered at some length in the guidance issued by the Accountancy Institutes. TECH 7/03 emphasizes substance over form: 'in assessing whether a company has a realized profit, transactions and arrangements should not be looked at in isolation'.[147] Circular transactions—where, for example, a subsidiary declares a dividend in favour of its parent and the parent immediately reinvests the dividend in the subsidiary—or artificial transactions—which could arise, for example, where an asset is purchased by a subsidiary from its parent to create a profit in the parent but there is an agreement to buy the asset back at a future date—may result in a dividend not giving rise to a realized profit in the hands of its parent.[148]

In accordance with the general rules, an intra-group dividend would need to be in the form of 'qualifying consideration' to be regarded as realized. Cash dividends clearly satisfy this requirement but a dividend *in specie* would require careful examination.

Intra-group dividends and dividend blocks

A further complication is that it is also necessary to consider the effect of an upstream dividend on the value of the investment in the subsidiary. An intra-group dividend that is in the form of qualifying consideration may not constitute a realized profit in the hands of its parent company if the effect of the dividend is to cause a diminution in the value of the parent company's investment in the subsidiary below its book amount. Under UK GAAP the impairment in value caused by an intra-group dividend is a matter of judgment, which must be applied on each occasion. Under IFRS the position is more rigid so far as concerns intra-group dividends paid from the pre-acquisition profits of an acquired subsidiary.

---

[147] TECH 7/03, para 12.
[148] These examples are drawn from TECH 7/03, Appendix A.

Here the position is that any dividend paid out of pre-acquisition profits must be treated as a reduction in the cost of investment and not treated as accounting profits at all, ie it is treated as a repayment of the original capital investment.[149] This creates a problem of 'dividend blocks' within a corporate group. However, a mitigating factor is that to the extent that the acquisition of the subsidiary benefited from merger relief or group reconstruction relief,[150] the receipt of a dividend from pre-acquisition profits in the form of qualifying consideration will result in the realization of an equivalent amount of the related merger reserve.[151] The following example illustrates the position:

Company P buys 100% of the share capital of Company S for £100m by means of a share-for-share exchange (involving P shares with a nominal value of £40m) which qualifies for merger relief. At the date of acquisition S has distributable reserves of £20m. If, in a subsequent year, S distributes that £20m to P, the following accounting will arise in P's accounts:

	Before dividend £m	After dividend £m
Investment in S	100	80
Cash	0	20
	100	100
Share capital	40	40
Merger reserve	60	40
Profit and loss reserve	0	20
	100	100

Had merger relief not been available in respect of the acquisition, the intra-group dividend would not have given rise to an accounting profit in the hands of the parent.

Intra-group transfers of assets at an undervalue

Transactions whereby assets are moved round corporate groups at their book value instead of their greater market value are commonplace. However, such transactions need to be structured with care so as to ensure that they do not infringe the statutory and common law principles relating to distributions. There is no doubt that a transaction in which assets are transferred by a subsidiary to its parent at less than their market value is within the scope of the law on

---

[149] IAS 27 and TECH 2/07, paras 6.108–6.115.
[150] For discussion of when merger relief is available, see ch 4 above.
[151] TECH 2/07, para 6.112.

distributions.[152] Furthermore, it is clear from *Aveling Barford Ltd v Perion Ltd*,[153] which involved a sale at an undervalue between companies that had the same controlling shareholder, that undervalue transactions between sister companies can also be distributions.

Where a company which does not have any distributable profits makes a distribution by way of a transfer of assets at an undervalue to an associated company, the transaction is an unlawful distribution contrary to Part 23 of the Companies Act 2006 and also an infringement of the common law maintenance of capital principle. This was the situation in the *Aveling Barford* decision itself, where the transferor company had an accumulated deficit on its profit and loss account and therefore was not in a position to make any distribution to its shareholders. The *Aveling Barford* case did not decide anything about the situation where a company has some positive distributable reserves but those reserves fall short of the difference between the price at which an asset is transferred (typically its book value) and its market value but it led to considerable uncertainty in practice about the lawfulness of those transactions. The concern focused essentially on the determination of the 'amount' of the distribution and the need for the distribution to be justified by reference to relevant accounts, as stipulated in section 836 of the Companies Act 2006: if the requisite amount was held to be the difference between the book and the market value of the asset, the transfer at book value would infringe the distribution rules to the extent not covered by distributable reserves (although the transferor would have the option of conducting a formal revaluation exercise to record the unrealized profit, which could then be added to distributable reserves under the exception for *in specie* dividends);[154] but if the 'amount' was held to be just the difference between the transfer price and book value (which, in the ordinary case, would be zero) no revaluation would be required and the transfer would be lawful. Section 845 of the Companies Act 2006 resolves the issue by providing that the amount of a distribution arising from a sale, transfer, or other disposition of assets by a company with profits available for distribution is zero so long as the amount or value of the consideration for the disposal is not less than the book value of the asset.

Reform

The Companies Act 2006 restates the law relating to distributions and helpfully clarifies some aspects of it (in particular, addressing the *Aveling Barford* problem). However, it does not effect radical change. There is now considerable discussion in Europe about the merits of abandoning rules that make certain

---

[152] *Ridge Securities Ltd v IRC* [1964] 1 All ER 275, 288.
[153] [1989] BCLC 626.
[154] Companies Act 2006, s 846.

reserves undistributable in favour of a regulatory approach that uses solvency tests to determine whether or not a distribution is permissible. This change would move the European position more into line with that of developed economies elsewhere in the world, and would address the increasingly awkward problems flowing from the links between the lawfulness of distributions and accounts that are drawn up under regulatory frameworks intended to serve different purposes. For the moment, the Second Company Law Directive precludes the full adoption of a solvency-based approach for public companies as a complete alternative to the existing regime.[155] The possibility of introducing an alternative solvency-based regime was explored by the European Commission, which commissioned a study by the accountancy firm, KPMG, on alternatives to the Second Directive. Based on the KPMG report, published in 2008 when this book was going to press, however, the Commission decided not to propose any changes to the Second Company Directive, although it noted that it was already possible for Member States to introduce solvency tests in addition to the Directive's requirements.[156]

It was open to introduce a solvency-based regime for private companies in the Companies Act 2006 and that possibility was discussed in the Parliamentary debates on the Bill but it was not adopted. A solvency-based system appears to give more discretion to directors and places considerable faith in the deterrent effect of the sanctions that would apply to directors who deliberately or negligently authorized distributions that were not supported by the company's financial position. How to accommodate long-term liabilities within a solvency-based system is another concern: when the issue was considered in Parliament, the government spokesperson was concerned that a solvency test that required directors to consider their company's solvency in the next year might be inadequate because it would leave no clear statutory rules to prevent the dissipation of assets needed for long-term obligations such as pensions.[157] Yet the fact that there are solvency-based mechanisms already in the companies legislation (including, since the Companies Act 2006, a procedure for private companies to reduce capital on the basis of a shareholder resolution and a directors' one-year solvency statement) indicates a gradual shifting of attitudes and gives credence to suggestions that concerns about maintaining a regulatory framework that promotes long-term corporate sustainability may not ultimately be an insurmountable barrier to the adoption of more flexible laws on distributions. The new explicit statutory duty on directors to have regard to the likely long-term consequences of their decisions

---

[155] Strictly interpreted, the Second Directive relates only to nominal share capital and it would therefore be possible for the UK to introduce for plcs a solvency-based system for distribution of share premiums. There appears to be little enthusiasm, however, for piecemeal reform.

[156] KPMG, *Feasibility Study on Capital Maintenance* (published by European Commission, February 2008).

[157] *Hansard*, HL, vol 682, cols 188–189 (16 May 2006) *per* Lord Sainsbury.

may be important in enhancing confidence in the robustness of the regulatory framework.[158]

A fully thought-through response to concerns about companies exploiting a less rigid distributions regime in ways that would fail to pay proper regard to long term liabilities was not possible because of the pressures of the Parliamentary timetable for the Companies Act 2006. However, enough was said in Parliament about the problems of the current regime to suggest that this is an issue that will not disappear from the policy agenda, either nationally or regionally, notwithstanding the European Commission's current unwillingness to put forward reform proposals.

Key voices within the accountancy profession, which plays a key role in administering the existing regime, are among those now pressing for change. In particular, in September 2007 the Federation of European Accountants (FEE) came out in favour of the introduction at the EU level of an optional alternative capital maintenance regime in the form of a solvency-based regime.[159] The FEE specifically addressed the question of what the directors' declaration of solvency would need to cover. It suggested both a 'snapshot' test and a 'forward looking' test, which it described in the following terms:

The **snapshot** test would help determine whether the proposed distribution would lead to a financial situation where liabilities exceeded assets, thus precluding the making of such distribution. This test would protect the interests of creditors since they are directly affected by the company's ability or otherwise to meet its long-term liabilities. A minimum requirement of the solvency-based system should be that distribution should not lead to a situation where liabilities exceeded assets under the measurement basis adopted. We consider that there are different options regarding the question of which values should be taken from the balance sheet or should be used for a net asset test:

Balance sheet test: values are directly derived from the balance sheet as drawn up under national GAAP or IFRS; and

Net asset test: the company could discharge its debts, ie, the directors would need to compare the value of the company's assets and the amount of the company's liabilities at that date with assets stated at no more than fair value or value in use.

The **forward looking** test would supplement the findings from the snapshot test. This test should be based on the financial position of the company and enhanced by a liquidity plan which included payments and receipts that are expected as sufficiently certain within the selected time horizon. The test could take a number of different forms:

A simple cash flow test covering only cash receipts and payments over a certain period of time;

A broader liquidity test, in addition, covering receivables and obligations that led to receipts and payments over a certain period of time; and

---

[158] Companies Act 2006, s 172(1)(a).

[159] FEE, 'Discussion Paper on Alternatives to Capital Maintenance Regimes' (September 2007) available at <http://www.fee.be/fileupload/upload/DP%20Alternatives%20to%20Capital%20 Maintenance%20Regimes%200709289200741923.pdf> (accessed December 2007).

A working capital test (including all short term assets and liabilities, such as inventories).

The FEE recognized that a crucial element of the forward looking test would be the time horizon used in its calculation. It commented:

The uncertainty of matters occurring or of the effects of payments in the future increases with the extension of the time horizon. However, a very short period may be of less or no protection for creditors of the company since they may also be directly interested in the company's ability to pay its debts later on in the future. FEE's view is that the proper length of the time horizon used for the forward looking test cannot be determined with a 'one size fits all' approach, but would have to be decided on a case by case basis. However a minimum time horizon could be put in place at EU level or Member State level. Should the EC set a minimum time horizon, this time horizon should be one year (which FEE considers the minimum level of protection for creditors). Individual Member States may set longer (than one year) minimum time horizons.

The FEE's thoughtful and detailed paper suggests that the technical hurdles involved in working out an effective solvency-based regime should not be insurmountable. It appears to move forward significantly the debate on the merits of adopting such a regime, at least as an alternative to that mandated by the Second Company Law Directive.

10

Financial Assistance

Prohibition on the giving of financial assistance—some preliminary issues

What is 'financial assistance' law?

The law on financial assistance is concerned with actions whereby a company financially supports the acquisition of its shares. In *Chaston v SWP Group plc*[1] Arden LJ used the phrase 'smoothed the path to the acquisition of shares' to describe a payment that was held to constitute financial assistance[2] and this phrase usefully encapsulates the essence of the law. The giving of financial assistance by public companies or their subsidiaries is generally prohibited, although there are certain exceptions. Since the coming into force of the Companies Act 2006, private companies are no longer caught by the ban (except where they are subsidiaries of public companies).

Legislative history

The giving of financial assistance was first made a specific statutory[3] offence by section 16 of the Companies Act 1928.[4] This was re-enacted without change as section 45 of the Companies Act 1929.[5] Loopholes emerged in the drafting of

---

[1] [2003] 1 BCLC 675, CA.

[2] At para 38.

[3] In *R v Lorang* (1931) 22 Cr App Rep 167, CCA this provision was described as declaratory and not as a new offence.

[4] On the statutory history of the ban generally: GR Bretten, 'Financial Assistance in Share Transactions' (1968) 32 *Conv* 6; GK Morse, 'Financial Assistance by a Company for the Purchase of its Own Shares' [1983] JBL 105; BG Pettet, 'Developments in the Law of Financial Assistance for the Purchase of Shares' [1988] 3 *Journal of International Banking Law* 96.

[5] It provided that: 'It shall not be lawful for a company to give, whether directly or indirectly, and whether by means of a loan, guarantee, the provision of security or otherwise, any financial assistance for the purpose of or in connection with a purchase made or to be made by any person of any shares in the company.'

that section[6] and it was redrafted in the Companies Act 1947 and then consolidated as section 54 of the Companies Act 1948. New companies legislation in the 1980s provided an opportunity to recast the prohibition on financial assistance and to clarify some of the difficulties that had been thrown up by cases and by the experience of the operation of section 54 of the Companies Act 1948 in practice.[7] A minor amendment was made in the Companies Act 1980 followed by a more wide-ranging revision in the Companies Act 1981. The Companies Act 1981 was later consolidated into the Companies Act 1985, with section 151 of that Act containing the basic prohibition and subsequent sections elaborating on its scope.

From the 1980s legislation onwards, the legislative history of the prohibition on financial assistance has been influenced by the Second Company Law Directive.[8] The Second Company Law Directive seeks to coordinate on a Community-wide basis the requirements for the formation of public companies and the maintenance and alteration of their capital. As an aspect of this, Article 23(1) of the Second Directive provides that, with certain exceptions, 'A [public] company may not advance funds, nor make loans, nor provide security with a view to the acquisition of its shares by a third party.' This limits what a Member State may provide in its domestic legislation with regard to permitted or prohibited financial assistance, in relation to public companies. To comply with Community obligations, domestic legislation must prohibit financial assistance by public companies at least to the extent that this is prohibited by Article 23(1), although that article sets only a minimum standard and Member States are free to impose more rigorous rules and requirements if they so desire.

Financial assistance law received attention in the review of company law that preceded the Companies Act 2006.[9] By removing private companies from the scope of the ban, that Act takes to its endpoint the policy, supported by the Jenkins Committee in 1962 and implemented to some extent in the Companies Act 1981, of having a more relaxed approach in relation to private companies.[10] However, the options for change so far as public companies were concerned were constrained by the need to comply with the Community obligation to implement Article 23.

---

[6] *Re VGM Holdings Ltd* [1942] 1 Ch 235, CA where it was held than the ban on financial assistance for the purchase of shares did not apply where the company provided financial assistance for the subscription of its shares. As a matter of construction the word 'purchase' could not be extended to include 'subscription'.

[7] Such as the views of members of the Court of Appeal in *Belmont Finance Corp v Williams Furniture Ltd (No 2)* [1980] 1 All ER 393, CA on transactions for full value and on transactions entered into for mixed purposes that including the giving of financial assistance.

[8] (EEC) 77/91 [1977] OJ L26/1.

[9] In particular Company Law Review, 'Developing the Framework', URN 00/656, paras 7.18–7.25.

[10] The Companies Act 1981 introduced the private company 'whitewash' regime whereby private companies were permitted to give financial assistance provided certain conditions (including a special resolution of the shareholders and a directors' statement of solvency) were fulfilled. A regime broadly to this effect had been recommended by the Jenkins Committee: *Report of the Company Law Committee* (Cmnd 1749, 1962) paras 178–179 and 187.

In the end the Companies Act 2006 makes few significant substantive changes to financial assistance law in relation to public companies and many of the difficulties and uncertainties that emerged in relation to the Companies Act 1985 thus continue to affect the law. The possibility of Article 23 being amended meaningfully at some point in the near future was a disincentive to grappling with the issues involved in a substantive rewrite in the Companies Act 2006.[11] Although some redrafting efforts were made, suggested revisions failed to attract government support because of doubt as to whether they would actually improve the position.[12]

Who is protected by the ban?

The ban on the giving of financial assistance is intended to protect company funds and the interests of shareholders in bid situations as well as the interests of creditors.[13] In the *Chaston* case[14] Arden LJ explained:

The general mischief, however, remains the same, namely that the resources of the target company and its subsidiaries should not be used directly or indirectly to assist the purchaser financially to make the acquisition. This may prejudice the interests of the creditors of the target or its group, and the interests of any shareholders who do not accept the offer to acquire their shares or to whom the offer is not made.

Why is the giving of financial assistance banned?

Objections to leveraged takeovers/buyouts

In *Re VGM Holdings Ltd*[15] Lord Greene MR explained the practices against which the ban on the giving of financial assistance is directed in the following terms:

Those whose memories enable them to recall what had been happening for several years after the last war will remember that a very common form of transaction in connection with companies was one by which persons—call them financiers, speculators, or what

---

[11] In the *White Paper* that preceded the Act the government indicated that rather than making technical changes it preferred to give priority to pressing for fundamental reform of the Second Company Law Directive: (Cm 6456, 2005) 43. However, if the quite feeble changes to the Second Directive (including to Art 23) made by Directive (EC) 2006/68 of the European Parliament and of the Council of 6 September 2006 amending Council Directive (EEC) 77/91 as regards the formation of public limited liability companies and the maintenance and alteration of their capital [2006] OJ 2006 L264/32 are anything to go by, significant reform at the European level may take a long time.

[12] *Hansard*, vol 680, GC col 24 (20 March 2006) and *Hansard*, HC vol 682, col 182 (16 May 2006).

[13] *Wallersteiner v Moir* [1974] 3 All ER 217, CA, 255 *per* Scarman LJ and 239 *per* Lord Denning MR.

[14] [2003] 1 BCLC 675, CA, para 31.

[15] [1942] Ch 235, CA, 239.

you will—finding a company with a substantial cash balance or easily realisable assets, such as war loan, bought up the whole, or the greater part, of the shares for cash, and so arranged matters that the purchase money which they then became bound to provide was advanced to them by the company whose shares they were acquiring, either out of its cash balance or by realization of its liquid investments. That type of transaction was a common one, and it gave rise to great dissatisfaction and, in some cases, great scandals.

This passage echoed comments that had appeared in the report of the Greene Committee, which had recommended that such practices should be against the law.[16]

Reporting in 1962, the Jenkins Committee on the reform of company law[17] also gave an example of the type of abuse that the prohibition of the giving of financial assistance was intended to correct:

If people who cannot provide the funds necessary to acquire control of a company from their own resources, or by borrowing on their own credit, gain control of a company with large assets on the understanding that they will use the funds of the company to pay for their shares it seems to us all too likely that in many cases the company will be made to part with its funds either on inadequate security or for an illusory consideration.

In *Wallersteiner v Moir*[18] Lord Denning MR summed up the perceived abuse succinctly, describing it simply as a 'cheat'.

Market manipulation

In some circumstances, the effect of giving financial assistance may be to boost the price of the shares of the company giving the assistance. An obvious example of this arises in a takeover situation where the consideration for the offer to the shareholders of the target takes the form of shares in the bidder and, to ensure that the price of those shares remains attractive, the bidder organizes a share-support operation in which purchasers of its shares are indemnified against any losses they may suffer as a result of their purchases. Looked at from this angle, the ban on the giving of financial assistance is closely connected to the rule whereby companies are prohibited from trading in their own shares.[19] The Greene Committee referred to the practice of 'share trafficking' when recommending that financial assistance should be prohibited.[20] In *Darvall v North Sydney Brick & Tile Co Ltd*,[21] an Australian case, Kirby P expressly stated that the purposes of the prohibition on financial assistance 'include the avoidance of the manipulation of the value of shares by companies and their officers dealing in such shares'.

---

[16] *Report of the Company Law Amendment Committee* (Cmd 2657, 1926) para 30.
[17] *Report of the Company Law Committee* (Cmnd 1749, 1962) para 173.
[18] [1974] 3 All ER 217, CA, 222.
[19] GR Bretten, 'Financial Assistance in Share Transactions' (1968) 32 Conv 6.
[20] *Report of the Company Law Amendment Committee* (Cmd 2657, 1926) para 30.
[21] (1989) 15 ACLR 230, NSW CA, 256 *per* Kirby J.

Unconstitutional conduct by management

Another reason for banning financial assistance is to prevent the management of a company from interfering with the normal market in the company's shares by providing support from the company's resources to selected purchasers. In this respect, the ban on financial assistance again complements the ban on a company purchasing its own shares, one purpose of which is to prevent the management of a company from seeking to influence the outcome of a takeover bid by purchasing its own shares.[22]

Maintenance of capital and 'detriment'

Financial assistance law overlaps with the maintenance of capital principle,[23] as can be seen by considering the example of an issuing company that uses its existing capital to provide funds to investors to subscribe for a new issue of its shares; in these circumstances the appearance of an injection of fresh equity is simply illusory. However, whilst it is conventional to deal with financial assistance as part of the maintenance of capital/legal capital principle, the scope of the ban on the giving of financial assistance extends far beyond actions that would also infringe the maintenance of capital principle. For example, it covers actions whereby a company uses its distributable reserves to support share acquisitions and is not limited to misuse of capital or other undistributable reserves. It can even extend to certain actions that do not deplete the assets of the company that provides the assistance: actual financial detriment is not necessarily required.[24] Where a company makes a gift to enable someone to purchase its shares, there is

---

[22] *Trevor v Whitworth* (1887) 12 App Cas 409, HL.

[23] C Proctor, 'Financial Assistance: New Proposals and New Perspectives' (2007) 28 *Company Lawyer* 3.

[24] *Chaston v SWP Group plc* [2003] 1 BCLC 675, CA, para 37 *per* Arden LJ. Accordingly, Lord Denning MR's description of financial assistance in *Wallersteiner v Moir* [1974] 3 All ER 217, CA, 239 ('You look to the company's money and see what has become of it. You look to the company's shares and see into whose hands they have got. You will then soon see if the company's money has been used to finance the purchase') should be read as merely one example of financial assistance and not as illustrative of the whole category: see JH Farrar and NV Lowe, 'Fraud, Representative Actions and the Gagging Writ' (1975) 38 MLR 455.
In Australia there was a competing line of authority on whether 'impoverishment' was a necessary element of financial assistance legislation based on the English model (which has since been overridden by more modern Australian legislation) but it has been stated judicially that the better view was that impoverishment was not a necessary element of the contravention: *Re HIH Insurance Ltd (in prov liquidation) and HIH Casualty and General Insurance Ltd (in prov liquidation); Australian Securities And Investments Commission v Adler* [2002] NSWSC 171, (2002) 41 ACSR 72, NSW Sup Ct EqD, para 363. In Singapore it has been said in relation to companies legislation based on the English model that the test is whether in the ordinary commercial sense the assets of the company have been used or put at risk in connection with the acquisition of its own shares: *PP v Lew Syn Pau and Wong Sheung Sze* [2006] SGHC 146, para 107.
Also BG Pettet, 'Developments in the Law of Financial Assistance for the Purchase of Shares' [1988] 3 *Journal of International Banking Law* 96, 100.

a clear immediate reduction in its resources. However, unlawful financial assistance can come in many forms and is not confined to simple situations where
the company makes a gift of the money which is to be used to buy its shares.
Also included within the prohibition are loans, security, guarantees, and indemnities. These types of unlawful financial assistance do not necessarily involve any
reduction in the company's assets at the time when they are given. For instance,
a loan does not involve any diminution in the lender's assets provided the borrower's credit is good and no provision against the likelihood of default has to be
made. A contingent obligation, such as a guarantee, does not reduce the assets of
the company unless some provision has to be made against the obligation being
enforced.[25] The granting of a security does not diminish or deplete the value of a
company's assets and merely restricts the company from using the proceeds of the
secured assets otherwise than in satisfaction of the secured debt.[26]

Is the ban on the giving of financial assistance justified?[27]

Technical problems

The law on financial assistance is notorious for being riddled with costly uncertainty, which results in the corporate sector spending a large amount each year
for legal advice on its potential impact on transactions. According to one estimate (which some market participants say is 'conservative'), transaction costs
related to dealing with financial assistance law are in the region of £20 million per
annum.[28] Whereas the costs associated specifically with financial assistance may
be a drop in the ocean in the context of multi-billion pound mega-transactions
involving publicly quoted companies, they will weigh more heavily in smaller
deals. Accordingly, it is not surprising that cost considerations were prominent
in the decision to abolish the ban on the giving of financial assistance by private
companies in the Companies Act 2006.[29] Underlying the decision to take this

---

[25] *Milburn v Pivot Ltd* (1997) 15 ACLC 1520 Fed Ct of Aust, 1546 *per* Goldberg J; *Lipschitz No
v UDC Bank Ltd* [1979] 1 SA 789, Sup Ct of SA, 800–1 *per* Miller JA.

[26] *Re MC Bacon Ltd* [1990] BCLC 324. This case concerned Insolvency Act 1986, s 238 (transactions at an undervalue). See also *Lipschitz No v UDC Bank Ltd* [1979] 1 SA 789, Sup Ct of SA,
800–1 *per* Miller JA.

[27] This section draws upon the following articles: E Ferran, 'Financial Assistance: Changing
Policy Perceptions but Static Law' [2004] CLJ 225; E Ferran, 'Simplification of European Company
Law on Financial Assistance' [2005] *European Business Organization Law Review* 93; E Ferran, 'The
Place for Creditor Protection on the Agenda for Modernisation of Company Law in the European
Union' [2006] *European Company and Financial Law Review* 178; E Ferran, 'Regulation of Private
Equity-Backed Leveraged Buyout Activity in Europe' (May 2007). ECGI—Law Working Paper
No 84/2007, available at SSRN <http://ssrn.com/abstract=989748>.

[28] Impact Assessment of the [draft] Companies (Shares, Share Capital and Authorised
Minimum) Regulations 2008 (Department for Business, Enterprise & Regulatory Reform,
2007).

[29] *White Paper* (Cm 6456, 2005) 41.

more radical step, as opposed to trying to address the problem by improving the drafting of the relevant provisions, was the recognition that, to the extent that the ban sought to achieve worthwhile policy objectives by curbing harmful practices, it was possible to control perceived abuses in other, more cost-effective, ways.

Policy concerns

Financial assistance law is intended to protect the interests of creditors and also to protect shareholders in takeover situations from abusive conduct by controllers.[30] On the surface, these are uncontroversial objectives that are familiar to any company lawyer. However, company law has a variety of goals and the aim of protecting people who deal with companies is not necessarily worthy of priority over all others. Contemporary thinking about the aims and objectives of company law have shifted away from prioritizing the protection of people who deal with companies (who can often protect themselves) to facilitating business activities so as to promote economic growth. From this perspective, financial assistance law is open to criticism for placing too much emphasis on protective functions and for making questionable policy choices on what constitutes 'abuse' from which protection is needed. In relation to creditors, for instance, the criticisms of the capital maintenance regime considered in chapter 7 above apply in this context but with enhanced force because, whereas the general regime controls distributions of assets representing capital and other undistributable reserves, financial assistance law goes further and prohibits the distribution of any assets to support the acquisition of shares. Indeed, financial assistance law extends even beyond this because certain forms of prohibited financial assistance do not require any depletion of assets at all.

As for what financial assistance protects against, the bristling hostility of the post-Second World War judiciary to leveraged financing of company acquisitions is at odds with the contemporary environment in which leveraged buyouts are commonplace and the mood has shifted from viewing them as invariably questionable transactions in which sharp operators play the market for corporate control with other peoples' money to seeing them in a more nuanced way as transactions that undoubtedly present some classic agency problems—managers who are liable to promote their own interests over those of the general body of shareholders; majority shareholders who are poised to exploit minorities; and controllers who may load their company with a heavy additional debt burden that could threaten the interests of the existing creditors and of employees—but which can also be economically worthwhile, value-producing activities.

There are difficult questions about the range of regulatory and governance strategies that can best address the agency problems inherent in highly leveraged transactions. This was recognized in the debate that preceded the Companies

[30] *Chaston v SWP Group plc* [2003] 1 BCLC 675, CA para 31.

Act 2006: the decision to abolish financial assistance law completely for private companies was taken not because British policymakers decided that there was no need for some protective regulatory intervention to achieve the goals that underpin financial assistance law but rather because they concluded that general company law on directors' duties and minority protection, takeover regulations, and insolvency laws could be relied upon instead to perform that function. Insolvency laws that allow for the unwinding of undervalue transactions made by companies in financial difficulties have particular significance in this context.[31] Whilst there is room for a difference of views on the effectiveness of these various strategies, all of them appear to be superior to financial assistance law, which is too blunt an instrument to address properly the various complex and multi-faceted concerns raised by such transactions.

The ban on financial assistance law is also an unnecessary appendage so far as it relates to concerns about market manipulation. These days, ensuring a clean and orderly securities market is rightly seen to be the province of securities regulation rather than company law. The Financial Services and Markets Act 2000 provides for draconian sanctions against those who engage in market abuse, including the possibility of unlimited administrative fines and criminal penalties.[32]

A further criticism of financial assistance law is that it often fails to achieve its goals (though this may be no bad thing in so far as a more effective ban could prevent worthwhile transactions from taking place). On the face of it, a rule that prohibits public companies from giving financial assistance for the acquisition of their shares, appears to strike at the heart of leveraged buyouts because the economic structure of these transactions depends on being able to use the acquired company's assets as security for the debt financing incurred to effect the acquisition and that is precisely what the ban appears to prohibit. Yet the European buyout market has flourished in recent years in spite of the pan-European ban on the giving of financial assistance.[33] How has this come about? The answer is simple: it has happened because the market has worked out ways round the law, with the consequence that financial assistance law has been reduced to the level of a hindrance rather than an insurmountable hurdle.

This is not to say, however, that financial assistance law has been made practically irrelevant and that there is no real need therefore to continue to press for its reform. Despite the growth in the leveraged buyout market, the European Private Equity and Venture Capital Association continues to regard dealing with the consequences of the rules on financial assistance as a significant challenge for

---

[31] Insolvency Act 1986, s 238 (undervalue transactions). DG Baird, 'Legal Approaches to Restricting Distributions to Shareholders: The Role of Fraudulent Transfer Law' (2006) 7 *European Business Organization Law Review* 199. Baird suggests a similarity between the prohibition on financial assistance and the operation of US fraudulent conveyance law in connection with LBO (ibid 201, note 6).

[32] Financial Services and Markets Act 2000, ss 123 and 397.

[33] L Enriques, 'EC Company Law Directives and Regulations: How Trivial Are They?' (2006) 7 *University of Pennsylvania Journal of International Economic Law* 1.

private equity investors and views countries with the least burdensome form of the rules as offering a much more favourable environment for buyouts, compared to countries with stricter prohibitions.[34] An emerging trend that is disquieting is of financial assistance law being used opportunistically by parties seeking to escape from obligations or to reverse the consequences of transactions they have undertaken, although in a number of cases the British courts have given short shrift to unmeritorious claims of this sort.[35] There is also concern about the potential for financial assistance law to be exploited in hostile takeover situations by the commencement of litigation as a tactical ploy, not necessarily with a view to winning the case but simply to hold up the transaction for long enough to undermine its commercial rationale.[36] Financial assistance is a good choice as a spoiler because the uncertainties surrounding it mean that it is likely to take the court a considerable amount of time to come to a conclusion.

Had the options for change in relation to public companies not been constrained by the Second Company Law Directive, it is very likely that the policy arguments would have been found persuasive in relation to public companies, with the consequence that financial assistance law would have been abolished outright for all companies, or at least reduced in scope and effect to a shadow of its former self.

Outline of the legal framework

The statutory provisions on financial assistance are now found in chapter 2 of Part 18 of the Companies Act 2006. This chapter is derived from chapter VI of Part V of the Companies Act 1985. Apart from changes resulting from the decision to exclude private companies (other than subsidiaries of public companies) from

---

[34] EVCA, 'Debt Financing Structures' (Special Paper, 2004) available at <http://www.evca.com/images/attachments/tmpl_9_art_69_att_857.pdf#search=%22EVCA%20financing%20structures%22> (accessed December 2007).

[35] *Chaston v SWP Group plc* [2003] 1 BCLC 675, CA is an example of an unmeritorious case succeeding (purchaser benefited from due diligence reports for which subsidiary of the target company paid but later sued successfully for breach of duty the former director of the subsidiary who had authorized the payment). See also *Re Hill and Tyler Ltd, Harlow v Loveday* [2005] 1 BCLC 41. But cf *Dyment v Boyden* [2004] 2 BCLC 423, affirmed [2005] 1 BCLC 163, [2005] BCC 79, CA (company could not get out of obligations under a lease by claiming it was unlawful financial assistance); *Anglo Petroleum Ltd v TFB (Mortgages) Ltd* [2007] BCC 407, CA (parties could not escape liabilities under a guarantee and security by pleading financial assistance law); and *Corporate Development Partners LLC v E-Relationship Marketing Ltd* [2007] EWHC 436 (Ch) (commitment to pay an introduction fee was not financial assistance and was therefore enforceable).

[36] E Ferran, 'Regulation of Private Equity—Backed Leveraged Buyout Activity in Europe' (May 2007). ECGI—Law Working Paper No 84/2007, available at SSRN <http://ssrn.com/abstract=989748> discusses the Gas Natural hostile bid for Endesa, where a suit was filed in the Spanish courts on grounds that included alleged contravention of the financial assistance prohibition, which led to the whole transaction being frozen by a preventive order for a considerable period of time.

the scope of the law on financial assistance, there are few differences of substance between the 2006 and 1985 Acts. Cases that interpreted and applied the version of financial assistance law that was contained in the Companies Act 1985 therefore continue to be relevant. It can also be useful to refer back to older cases that related to former legislation, in particular the Companies Act 1948 and foreign statutes that used the 1948 Act as a precedent but those authorities have to be read with some caution because of developments in the statutory framework since they were decided.

'Definition' of financial assistance

We now turn to a more detailed examination of the law. An obvious place to start this more detailed analysis is with the meaning of financial assistance. Perhaps surprisingly, the phrase 'financial assistance' is not defined by the legislation. Instead the Companies Act 2006 (following the same approach as predecessor legislation) merely lists the forms of financial assistance that are within the scope of the ban.[37] It has been suggested judicially that the legislature has thought it wise not to lay down a precise definition of financial assistance because of the risk that clever people would devise ways of defeating the purpose of the section while keeping within the letter of the law.[38]

'Financial assistance' is not a technical term

It has been said repeatedly in the relevant cases that the phrase 'financial assistance' does not have a technical meaning and that the frame of reference is the language of ordinary commerce. A statement by Hoffmann J in *Charterhouse Investment Trust Ltd v Tempest Diesels Ltd*[39] (a case on section 54 of the Companies Act 1948) is frequently cited:

The words have no technical meaning and their frame of reference is in my judgment the language of ordinary commerce. One must examine the commercial realities of the transaction and decide whether it can properly be described as the giving of financial assistance by the company, bearing in mind that the section is a penal one and should not be strained to cover transactions which are not fairly within it.[40]

---

[37] In *Barclays Bank plc v British & Commonwealth Holdings plc* [1995] BCC 19, 37 Harman J said that 'Companies Act 1985, s 152 [now Companies Act 2006, s 677] supplied the definition of "financial assistance" that was missing from the earlier legislation' but this view is not generally accepted.

[38] *Anglo Petroleum Ltd v TFB (Mortgages) Ltd* [2007] BCC 407, para 26 *per* Toulson LJ.

[39] (1985) 1 BCC 99, 544, 99,552.

[40] See also *Barclays Bank plc v British & Commonwealth Holdings plc* [1996] 1 BCLC 1, CA; *Chaston v SWP Group plc* [2003] 1 BCLC 675, CA; *MacNiven v Westmoreland Investments Ltd* [2003] 1 AC 311, HL; *MT Realisations Ltd (in liquidation) v Digital Equipment Co Ltd* [2003] 2 BCLC 117, CA; *Anglo Petroleum Ltd v TFB (Mortgages) Ltd* [2007] BCC 407.

In *Barclays Bank plc v British & Commonwealth Holdings plc*[41] the Court of Appeal emphasized that the assistance has to be financial in nature. An example of assistance that is not financial in nature is where a company permits a potential purchaser of its shares to inspect its books and records.[42] Another example is of covenants given by a target company to reassure the purchaser of its shares where it is not anticipated at the time of the covenants that there would be any liability thereunder.[43] However, the concept of financial assistance is not limited to financial support that helps directly or indirectly to pay for the shares; it embraces inducements to acquire shares and there is no necessity for the financial assistance to impact directly on the price of the target shares.[44] As noted earlier, even though the assistance must be financial, for most forms of proscribed financial assistance there is no requirement for the giving of it to deplete the assets of the company. With regard to timing, it is at the point when a company undertakes an obligation, rather than when it comes to be performed, that the existence or otherwise of financial assistance is to be tested.[45]

Recent cases applying the test of commercial substance and reality

Chaston v SWP Group plc[46] arose out of the acquisition of Dunstable Rubber Company Holdings Ltd by SWP Group plc, a listed company. The acquisition did not turn out well from the purchaser's viewpoint. At the time of the acquisition, Robert Chaston was a director of a subsidiary of the target company. The claim brought against Mr Chaston was that he had breached his fiduciary duties to the subsidiary by procuring, or conniving in, the giving of financial assistance for the purpose of the acquisition by the purchaser of the shares in its parent company. The alleged financial assistance was the incurring of liability by the subsidiary to pay the accountants' fees for the short and long form reports in respect of the transaction and/or the payment of those fees. The purchaser brought the claim as assignee from its subsidiary of all the claims it might have had against Mr Chaston. The Court of Appeal held that the payment of the fees by the subsidiary of the target passed the commercial substance and reality test for 'financial assistance': the vendor and the purchaser were relieved from any obligation to pay for the service provided by the accountants and the payment of the fees smoothed the path to the acquisition of the shares.

---

[41] [1995] BCC 1059, CA.

[42] *Burton v Palmer* (1980) 5 ACLR 481, NSW SC, 489 *per* Mahoney J.

[43] *Chaston v SWP Group plc* [2003] 1 BCLC 675, CA, para 43 *per* Arden LJ.

[44] *Chaston v SWP Group plc* [2003] 1 BCLC 675, CA, especially para 45 *per* Arden LJ. In so far as Laddie J at first instance in *MT Realisations Ltd (in liquidation) v Digital Equipment Co Ltd* [2002] 2 BCLC 688, Ch D took the opposite view, Arden LJ disagreed

[45] This was common ground between the counsel involved in *Parlett v Guppys (Bridport) Ltd* [1996] BCC 299, CA.

[46] [2003] 1 BCLC 675, CA.

On the other hand, the commercial substance and reality test was not passed in *MT Realisations Ltd (in liquidation) v Digital Equipment Co Ltd*.[47] This case concerned a transaction in which the purchaser acquired the share capital of the target, MT Realisations (MTR), for a nominal amount which, it was accepted, was a fair price for the shares. In a separate agreement the purchaser also agreed to pay the vendor £6.5 million in consideration of the assignment of a £8 million intercompany loan repayable on demand by MTR and associated security interests. The loan assignment agreement provided for the purchase price for the loan to be paid in instalments by the purchaser. The commercial effect of the loan assignment was to relieve the vendor of any credit exposure to its former subsidiary. In allowing the purchaser to pay for the assignment by instalments, the vendor instead assumed a new credit risk in relation to the purchaser. This structure was presumably helpful to the purchaser in that it meant that, at the time of completion, it did not have to raise finance to cover the full costs of the transaction. Subsequently, the purchaser was unable to meet its obligations to pay instalments due under the loan assignment. The arrangement was restructured at that point to provide for the set-off of any sums due from the vendor to MTR against the outstanding instalments of the purchase price due to be paid to the vendor by the purchaser under the loan assignment. When MTR later went into liquidation, its liquidator argued that the post-acquisition rescheduling of the purchaser's obligations under the loan assignment was prohibited financial assistance.

The Court of Appeal held that there was no financial assistance. Looked at commercially, there was no financial assistance in the rescheduling arrangement. Financial assistance did not exist in a vacuum, something had to be given to someone that they did not have already. The rescheduling did not give the purchaser any new rights against MTR and therefore no financial assistance had been given. Under the loan assignment the purchaser had already acquired an on-demand loan repayable by MTR and associated security. The purchaser could have required MTR to pay over any sums it received from the vendor (if need be, enforcing its security rights to recover its legal entitlement) and then used those sums to meet its own payment obligations under the loan assignment. The arrangement for sums due to MTR from the vendor to be set off against sums due to the vendor by the purchaser simply short-circuited the process. As a matter of commercial substance, the purchaser was exercising a pre-existing legal entitlement and was not receiving any form of financial assistance from the acquired company.

This test of discovering the commercial substance and reality of the facts was also taken as the starting point by the Court of Appeal in *Anglo Petroleum v TFB (Mortgages) Ltd*,[48] another case involving a post-acquisition financial restructuring that included new borrowings by the company that had been taken over,

---

[47] [2003] 2 BCLC 117, CA.
[48] [2007] BCC 407, CA.

which were secured by charges and a personal guarantee. When the lender sought to obtain repayment and/or to the enforce the security and guarantee, the target company and the guarantor advanced various arguments to the effect that the financing and related security arrangements were illegal and void because they infringed the ban on financial assistance. The Court of Appeal held that, while these arguments were 'ingenious', the commercial reality was that the target company and guarantor were seeking to avoid their liabilities to the funder for what was in essence a straightforward commercial loan by a strained reading of the statute.

The *Anglo Petroleum* decision suggests that the courts will take a robust attitude towards what they perceive to be unmeritorious attempts to exploit financial assistance law in order to escape liability. A number of other recent cases are to similar effect.[49] They are in contrast to the first instance decision in *Re Hill and Tyler Ltd, Harlow v Loveday*,[50] where the financing for the acquisition of shares included financial assistance in the form of a loan provided by the target company. The target company had raised the money for the loan by entering into a financing arrangement secured by a charge on its assets. It was held that as a matter of commercial reality and applying the concept of 'smoothing the path', the charge constituted financial assistance in circumstances where all the parties knew that the borrowed funds were to be used to finance the acquisition of shares. The court expressed the view that but for the use of the private company 'whitewash' procedure (a procedure under the Companies Act 1985 that enabled private companies in certain circumstances to give financial assistance that would otherwise have been prohibited),[51] the charge would have been illegal and unenforceable. This controversial decision was distinguished in the *Anglo Petroleum* case where the Court of Appeal determined that it was unnecessary to express any view as to its correctness.

Forms of financial assistance that are prohibited

The forms of financial assistance that are prohibited are set out in section 677 of the Companies Act 2006. They are as follows.

Financial assistance given by way of gift[52]

Any gift, irrespective of its size, either in absolute terms or as a percentage of the donor company's total assets, falls within this category. There is no *de minimis*

---

[49] *Dyment v Boyden* [2004] 2 BCLC 423, affirmed [2005] 1 BCLC 163 CA (company could not get out of obligations under a lease by claiming it was unlawful financial assistance); *Corporate Development Partners LLC v E-Relationship Marketing Ltd* [2007] EWHC 436 (Ch) (commitment to pay an introduction fee was not financial assistance and was therefore enforceable).

[50] [2005] 1 BCLC 41.

[51] This procedure is now abolished as it is no longer necessary.

[52] Companies Act 2006, s 677(1)(a).

exception and Article 23(1) of the Second Company Law Directive, in its current form, precludes the enactment of one for public companies. During the 1990s the option of introducing a *de minimis* exception for private companies was given serious consideration but that eventually gave way to the more radical policy choice for private companies to which the Companies Act 2006 gives effect.[53]

A gift is normally taken to mean a gratuitous transfer of the ownership of property.[54] In *R v Braithwaite*,[55] a case concerned with the interpretation of the Prevention of Corruption Act 1906, Lord Lane CJ said:[56] 'The word "gift" is the other side of the coin, that is to say it comes into play where there is no consideration and no bargain. Consideration deals with the situation where there is a contract or a bargain and something moving the other way.' However, in relation to the category of 'gift' in section 677(1)(a) of the Companies Act 2006, it has been held that an arrangement in which the amount payable by a company was greater than the value of the assets it was to acquire constituted a gift, to the extent of the overpayment.[57] This case was considered by the Court of Appeal in *Barclays Bank plc v British & Commonwealth Holdings plc*[58] where Aldous LJ, delivering a judgment with which the other members of the Court agreed, said that overpayments could be gifts depending on the circumstances of the case, and appeared to accept that in this context it was appropriate to look at the 'reality' of transactions rather than their form.

Charterhouse Trust Ltd v Tempest Diesels Ltd[59] concerned the reorganization of a corporate group prior to the disposal of one of the subsidiaries in the group. As part of this reorganization the subsidiary in question agreed to surrender certain tax losses. Hoffmann J held that the agreement to surrender tax losses had to be considered in conjunction with the transaction as a whole to determine where the net balance of financial advantage lay and that it could constitute the giving of financial assistance if it amounted to a net transfer of value which reduced the price that the purchaser had to pay for the subsidiary company. This case was decided under section 54 of the Companies Act 1948, which did not contain a list of the forms of financial assistance that were prohibited. This type of transaction could fall within the gift category provided this is construed in the extended sense as including arrangements in which the company gives more than it receives in return and is not limited to wholly gratuitous transactions.

---

[53] DTI, 'Financial Assistance by a Company for the Acquisition of Its Own Shares: Conclusions of Consultation' (1997) indicated that the DTI (now BERR) intended at that time to introduce a *de minimis* exemption for private company financial assistance based on a 3% of net assets test.

[54] *Customs and Excise Commissioners v Telemed Ltd* [1989] VATTR 238, 243 (appeal dismissed [1992] STC 89).

[55] [1983] 1 WLR 385, CA.

[56] At 391.

[57] *Plaut v Steiner* (1989) 5 BCC 352.

[58] [1995] BCC 1059, CA.

[59] (1983–85) 1 BCC 99,544.

It may even be possible to regard an issue of shares at a price that it is less than could otherwise have been achieved as a gift in this extended sense.[60] However, this would seem to be straining the category somewhat. It is not a gift within section 677(1)(a) of the Companies Act 2006 for a company to agree to issue warrants or options in return for a directorship.[61]

Financial assistance given by way of guarantee or security[62]

A company may be asked personally to guarantee borrowings that an acquirer of its shares has incurred in order to acquire the shares or it may be asked to grant security over the company's assets for that borrowing. Both of these transactions are straightforward examples of unlawful financial assistance within this category, as *Re Hill and Tyler Ltd, Harlow v Loveday*[63] illustrates. In this case, the purchaser borrowed money from a number of sources in order to acquire shares in the target. One of the sources was a director of the target company. The loan provided by the director was secured by a written guarantee and a charge given by the target company. There was no dispute that this guarantee and charge constituted financial assistance falling within the Act. More controversially, it was held that a charge given by the target company to secure funding obtained by it for the purposes of loaning it on to the purchaser to pay for the shares was also unlawful financial assistance within this category in circumstances where all the parties were aware of how the borrowed funds were to be used.

However, it is important to note that the mere fact that the arrangements for the acquisition of shares include the giving of security by the target in respect of its own indebtedness does not lead inevitably to the conclusion that there is unlawful financial assistance within the Act. The security may be outside the scope of the Act because, applying the commercial reality test, there is no financial assistance or because the required causal link between the financial assistance and the purpose for which it is given (considered later in this chapter) is not present. The particular factual circumstances therefore require close examination. This can be illustrated by reference to *Anglo Petroleum v TFB (Mortgages) Ltd*.[64] In this case the target company was indebted to its parent in the sum of £30 million. That indebtedness was apparently repayable on demand and carried interest at a commercial rate. The target entered into a compromise agreement with its parent in which it agreed a repayment schedule in respect of a portion of its outstanding indebtedness and to grant security over its assets in respect of that indebtedness. In return, the parent released and discharged the target from repayment of the

---

[60] On the possibility of a low subscription price for new shares being a form of financial assistance, see also *Milburn v Pivot Ltd* (1997) 15 ACLC 1,520 Fed Ct of Aust.

[61] *Oxus Gold plc (formerly Oxus Mining plc) v Templeton Insurance Ltd* [2006] EWHC 864 (Ch), para 184.

[62] Companies Act 2006, s 677(1)(b)(i).

[63] [2005] 1 BCLC 41.

[64] [2007] BCC 407, CA.

balance of the outstanding inter-company debt. On the same day the target was sold to the purchaser. A subsequent attempt to characterize the security as unlawful financial assistance failed since, as a matter of commercial reality, the security was the price the target had to pay for obtaining a reduction in its debt and was not financial assistance.

Financial assistance given by way of indemnity[65]

The term 'indemnity' is used in a technical sense in section 677 of the Companies Act 2006 and means a contract by one party to keep the other harmless against loss.[66] For a company, as part of a share-support operation, to undertake to make good any losses which investors in its shares may suffer as a result of having bought them would infringe this aspect of the ban on the giving of financial assistance.

A situation where indemnities are commonly given by companies to persons who acquire, or who may acquire, their shares is in the context of underwriting agreements. This type of indemnity differs from that considered in the previous paragraph in that it is an indemnity in respect of losses that the underwriter may incur arising from the underwriting process but not in respect of a fall in the share price, which is precisely the risk that the underwriter undertakes to bear. Section s 677(1)(b)(i) of the Companies Act 2006 expressly excludes indemnities that are in respect of the indemnifier's own loss or default, but indemnities in underwriting agreements may be more extensive. Where this is the case, there is a risk of the indemnity being challenged on financial assistance grounds. Again, however, it is important not to jump to the conclusion that an indemnity in an underwriting agreement that is not limited to the indemnifier's own loss or default is unlawful financial assistance. It may not be financial assistance at all because, as a matter of commercial reality, it is simply an element of the legitimate bargain that a company enters into as part of the process of raising capital by issuing shares to the market.

Financial assistance given by way of release or waiver[67]

The terms 'release' or 'waiver' relate to circumstances where a company relinquishes, or forbears from enforcing, rights that it has against another party. It is unclear whether contractual variations are within the scope of this category, although variation of a bilateral contract by mutual agreement of the parties is sometimes described as a waiver. Even if contractual variations can be regarded as waivers for this purpose, it may be that in many instances the new mix of benefits and burdens assumed by the parties to a varied contract will be such that it is not

---

[65] Companies Act 2006, s 677(1)(b)(i).
[66] *Yeoman Credit Ltd v Latter* [1961] 1 WLR 828, CA, 830 *per* Pearce LJ adopted in *Barclays Bank plc v British & Commonwealth Holdings plc* [1995] BCC 1059, CA.
[67] Companies Act 2006, s 677(1)(b)(ii).

possible to conclude that, as a matter of commercial reality, a company has given assistance of a financial nature.

Financial assistance given by way of loan[68]

For a company to lend money to finance the acquisition of its own shares is among the most blatant forms of financial assistance and where there is clear evidence that this has occurred the point is unlikely to be disputed.[69]

The usual meaning of the term 'loan' is that it is an advance of money on terms providing for repayment.[70] An arrangement whereby a company pays off a debt that has been incurred by a purchaser of its shares to a third party on terms providing for the purchaser later to reimburse the company is not a loan within this interpretation. A loan is also to be distinguished from a transaction whereby a company buys goods on credit. Provided the form of the transaction is not a sham and its terms are consistent with the label which the parties have attached to it, buying goods on credit, or against a post-dated debt, does not give rise to a lender-borrower relationship.[71]

Financial assistance given by way of any other agreement under which the obligations of the person giving the assistance are to be fulfilled at a time when, in accordance with the agreement, any obligation of another party to the agreement remains unfulfilled[72]

This is the category that would apply to such things as a tripartite arrangement whereby a company pays off the debts incurred by a purchaser of its shares against an undertaking from that person to repay at some later stage, or transactions whereby a company sells assets for deferred consideration or buys assets and pays for them in advance. If the purchaser of assets from a company were to issue loan notes or other debt securities in circumstances where there was an active market for those securities so that they could readily be converted into cash, it is conceivable that this would be regarded as falling outside the scope of the ban because the consideration which the company has received is as good as cash. The position would be different where the securities which are issued are not liquid, because there would then be a risk of the issuer being unable to meet its obligations.[73]

---

[68] ibid s 677(1)(c)(i).

[69] Re Hill and Tyler Ltd, Harlow v Loveday [2005] 1 BCLC 41.

[70] Chow Yoong Hong v Choong Fah Rubber Manufactory [1962] AC 209, PC, 216 per Lord Devlin; Vigier v IRC [1964] 1 WLR 1073, HL, 1084 per Lord Upjohn; Champagne-Perrier SA v HH Finch Ltd [1982] 3 All ER 713; Potts v IRC [1951] AC 443, HL.

[71] Chow Yoong Hong v Choong Fah Rubber Manufactory [1962] AC 209, PC; IRC v Port of London Authority [1923] AC 507, HL.

[72] Companies Act 2006, s 677(1)(c)(i).

[73] WJL Knight, The Acquisition of Private Companies and Business Assets (FT Law & Tax, 7th edn, 1997) 61 discusses this example.

Financial assistance given by way of novation of, or assignment of rights arising under, a loan or such other agreement[74]

When a contract is novated, the original agreement is discharged and is replaced by a new agreement between different parties. Novation acts as a mechanism whereby the burden of a contract can be transferred to another party. This is in contrast to assignment, which can be used to transfer rights but not liabilities.

Any other financial assistance given by a company the net assets of which are thereby reduced to a material extent[75]

This is a 'catch all' category for forms of financial assistance that reduce the assisting company's net assets to a material extent. It is pertinent to undervalue transactions and to arrangements under which companies pay fees in return for services. It was the form of financial assistance that was relevant in *Chaston v SWP Group plc*[76] where the company paid for the accountant's reports. The category is potentially applicable to break fees, which are arrangements between a bidder and a target whereby a fee is payable by the target if a specified event occurs that prevents the takeover from going ahead.

'Net assets' here means the aggregate amount of the company assets less the aggregate amount of its liabilities.[77] It is market, rather than book, values that are relevant.[78] There is no statutory definition of materiality in this context.[79] The materiality test is open to at least two distinct interpretations. One approach is to focus on the size of the reduction in percentage terms and to regard it as immaterial if it falls below a certain minimum threshold. The other approach is to look at the total amount involved and to regard it as material if it is a large number, even though it may represent a tiny reduction in the company's net assets based on a percentage test. Which (if either) of these alternative approaches is correct is not clear from the wording of the legislation. It is even possible that some form of combined method—in which the percentage reduction and the amount in absolute terms both feature as relevant considerations—could be held to apply. In *Parlett v Guppys Bridport Ltd*[80] it was said to be a question of degree and that there

---

[74] Companies Act 2006, s 677(1)(c)(ii). 'Such other agreement' is a reference back to the second limb of s 677(1)(c)(i).

[75] ibid s 677(1)(d)(i).

[76] [2003] 1 BCLC 675, CA.

[77] Companies Act 2006, s 677(2).

[78] This interpretation is based on a comparison between Companies Act 2006, ss 677(2) and 682(3)–(4). In *Parlett v Guppys (Bridport) Ltd* [1996] BCC 299, CA, it was common ground between counsel that it was market values that were relevant for the purposes of what is now Companies Act 1986, s 677(2). But Nourse LJ commented (at 305) that whilst it was easy to speak in the abstract about the difference between actual assets and liabilities and assets and liabilities as stated in accounting records, it was less easy to disassociate an actual asset or liability from the notion of what is or ought to be in the accounting records.

[79] That the fee payment in *Chaston* satisfied the materiality requirement was conceded by counsel: [2003] 1 BCLC 675, CA, para 12.

[80] [1996] 2 BCLC 34, CA.

was no rule of thumb as to materiality, such as a reduction of five per cent or more being material.[81] Extinguishing the assets will clearly suffice.[82] Notwithstanding the reluctance of the courts to endorse a rule of thumb, a practice has grown up of regarding agreements to pay fees capped at one per cent of the payer's value as generally immaterial. This practice has acquired a degree of regulatory endorsement in that Rule 21.2 of the City Code on Takeovers and Mergers allows inducement (break) fees subject to certain safeguards, one of which is that the fee must be *de minimis* (defined as 'normally no more than 1 per cent of the value of the offeree company calculated by reference to the offer price'). The Panel explicitly warns, however that its views in relation to such fees relate only to the Code and do not extend to requirements of the companies legislation.[83]

This is the one form of financial assistance where 'detriment', ie a depletion of the assets of the assisting company, is essential.[84]

Any other financial assistance given by a company which has no net assets[85]

This is also a catch-all category of financial assistance that is applicable only to companies that have no net assets. It differs from the previous category in that any financial assistance, even of a *de minimis* amount, is prohibited. Furthermore, detriment is not required—indeed, something that is positively beneficial to the assisting company, such as a loan by it on highly favourable terms, could constitutes unlawful financial assistance in this category.[86]

Circumstances in which the giving of financial assistance is prohibited

We now arrive at the heart of the ban on the giving of financial assistance. This is contained in section 678 of the Companies Act 2006[87] and is as follows:

(1) Where a person is acquiring or proposing to acquire shares in a public company, it is not lawful for that company, or a company that is a subsidiary of that company, to give financial assistance directly or indirectly for the purpose of the acquisition before or at the same time as the acquisition takes place.

...

(3) Where—
  (a) a person has acquired shares in a company, and

---

[81] At 35 *per* Nourse LJ.
[82] *MacPherson v European Strategic Bureau Ltd* [2000] 2 BCLC 683, CA.
[83] Rule 21.2, note 2.
[84] *Chaston v SWP Group plc* [2003] 1 BCLC 675, CA, para 41 *per* Arden LJ.
[85] Companies Act 2006, s 677(1)(d)(ii).
[86] *Chaston* (n 84 above) para 41.
[87] Note also Companies Act 2006, s 679, which relates to financial assistance given by a public company subsidiary of a private company.

(b) a liability has been incurred (by that or another person) for the purpose of the acquisition, it is not lawful for that company, or a company that is a subsidiary of that company, to give financial assistance directly or indirectly for the purpose of reducing or discharging the liability if, at the time the assistance is given, the company in which the shares were acquired is a public company.

Elements of these two provisions may be separated out for particular consideration.

An acquisition

The choice of the word 'acquisition' gives breadth to the scope of the ban because it ensures that it extends to issues of shares for non-cash consideration. This was not the case under section 54 of the Companies Act 1948, which referred to the purchase of, or subscription for, shares because the term 'subscription' has been held to mean taking shares for cash.[88] A purchase of shares for non-cash consideration is also an acquisition.[89]

Must an acquisition take place at some point in order for the prohibition to bite? On the one hand, it is possible to argue that financial assistance given in circumstances where an acquisition never takes place is not financial assistance given 'before' an acquisition, so it does not come within the scope of section 678(1) of the Companies Act 2006, (and section 678(3) being concerned with post-acquisition financial assistance is clearly inapplicable). On the other hand, the reference in section 678(1) to a 'proposed' acquisition of shares can be reading as meaning that it is not essential for an acquisition of shares ever to take place. The latter interpretation of the statute appears to have been adopted, without discussion of the point, in *Cox v Cox*,[90] where payments made by a company to a shareholder, who was in the process of divorcing her husband, another shareholder, were held to be unlawful pre-acquisition financial assistance in relation to the acquisition of the wife's shares by the husband notwithstanding that he had yet to acquire the shares by the time of the proceedings. This is also the view that underpins the legal analysis of break fees, which are fees that become payable in the event of a bid being aborted.

The ban relates only to an acquisition of shares

In *NZI Bank Ltd v Euro-National Corp Ltd*[91] it was held by the New Zealand Court of Appeal that providing money to acquire share options was not within the ban on the giving of financial assistance in the form of money for the acquisition

---

[88] *Government Stock and Other Securities Investment Co Ltd v Christopher* [1956] 1 All ER 490.
[89] *Plaut v Steiner* (1989) 5 BCC 352, decided under the Companies Act 1985, s 151, involved a share-for-share exchange.
[90] [2006] EWHC 1077 (Ch).
[91] [1992] 3 NZLR 528, NZ CA.

of shares imposed by section 62 of the New Zealand Companies Act 1955. Section 62 of the 1955 Act was based on section 54 of the English Companies Act 1948 and the wording of section 62 is sufficiently close to that of section 678 of the Companies Act 2006 to give this case some persuasive authority in relation to the interpretation of section 678. This line of reasoning suggests that financial assistance given in relation to the acquisition of debt securities that are convertible into shares should also fall outside the statutory ban. This is subject to the qualification that the court may look through formalities to substance where a structure has been adopted in order to evade the application of a statute or where, as a matter of statutory interpretation, a particular statute requires or permits it to do so.[92]

The ban applies only to public companies and their subsidiaries

As mentioned earlier in this chapter, the one big difference between section 678 of the Companies Act 2006 and its predecessor, section 151 of the Companies Act 1985, is that the ban now applies only in relation to public companies and their subsidiaries. This point is now given closer examination.

The status of the company whose shares are acquired

Under section 678 of the Companies Act 2006 the company whose shares are acquired must be a public company at the time when the assistance is given. This is straightforward in relation to pre-acquisition financial assistance and financial assistance that is contemporaneous with an acquisition (ie the situations covered by section 678(1)) but needed to be specifically addressed in relation to post-acquisition financial assistance (ie the situations covered by section 678(3)). The drafting of section 678(3) ensures that the ban on financial assistance does not affect refinancing activity relating to a public company that has been taken over, so long as the acquired company is re-registered as a private company before the refinancing takes place. This carve-out is of considerable practical importance as it enables participants in leveraged buyouts to achieve desired financial restructurings of acquired companies free of the constraints imposed by financial assistance law.

Under section 679 of the Companies Act 2006 there is a ban on financially assisting the acquisition of shares in a *private* company where the company providing the assistance is a public company subsidiary of that private company. This section largely mirrors section 678.

---

[92] *Barclays Bank plc v British & Commonwealth Holdings plc* [1995] BCC 1059, CA suggests that the courts can look to substance rather than form in applying the statutory provisions relating to financial assistance. See further J Vella, 'Departing from the Legal Substance of Transactions in the Corporate Field: the Ramsay Approach Beyond the Tax Sphere' [2007] *Journal of Corporate Law Studies* 243.

The status of the company providing the assistance

To come within section 678 of the Companies Act 2006, the company providing the assistance must be either a public company whose shares are acquired or a public or private company that is a subsidiary of the public company whose shares are acquired. To this extent, the ban on the giving of financial assistance continues to apply to private companies. (For the purposes of section 679 of the 2006 Act, the assisting company must be a public company subsidiary of the private company whose shares are acquired.)

Section 678 (and section of 679) of the Companies Act 2006 specify that the ban applies only to subsidiaries that are companies, thereby excluding foreign subsidiaries from their scope. This is a departure from the wording in section 151 of the Companies Act 1985, which, literally interpreted, did cover foreign subsidiaries, although case law established that a literal interpretation of the statute should not be adopted.[93] The revised drafting in the Companies Act 2006 in effect codifies the case law on the point. Whether a foreign subsidiary can lawfully give financial assistance will depend on the law of its place of incorporation. In some circumstances, the foreign subsidiary's actions may have implications for UK companies within the group: the hiving down of an asset by a British company to a foreign subsidiary in order to enable it to be made available to finance a contemplated acquisition of shares in the British company could be caught by section 678 (or section 679 as the case may be) as indirect provision of financial assistance by the British company.[94]

The acquirer of the shares

The ban applies to acquisitions of shares by natural persons or legal persons such as companies. Does it include acquisitions by the assisting company itself with the consequence that the ban is applicable in relation to share buy-backs (subject to any available exception)?[95] This is a controversial point on which different views are tenable. It may be that, as a matter of commercial reality, it is not financial assistance for a person to meet its own obligations from its own resources but, based on the current authorities, it is hard to be definite on this point. In *Chaston v SWP Group plc*[96] Arden LJ appeared to favour the view that an acquisition by a company of its own shares is potentially caught. However, in the Parliamentary debate on the Bill that became the Companies Act 2006, the

---

[93] *Arab Bank plc v Merchantile Holdings Ltd* [1994] Ch 71.

[94] As Millett J noted in the *Arab Bank* case.

[95] Companies Act 2006, s 681(2)(d). The existence of this exception could be taken to indicate that the legislature must have considered that an acquisition by a company of its own shares could, if not specifically excluded, fall within the scope of the ban on the giving of financial assistance. On the other hand, however, it could have been included simply for the avoidance of doubt (as can also be said about other exceptions in s 681).

[96] [2003] 1 BCLC 675, CA.

government spokesperson said that, in the government's view, the references to 'person' did not include the company itself and indicated that it did not read the relevant passage in Arden LJ's judgment as being inconsistent with that view.[97] The spokesperson further suggested that to include the company within the scope of person to whom the company could not give financial assistance would be 'at odds' with the Second Company Law Directive, which envisages a person being a third party and not the company itself. Whilst some weight can be placed on the statement in Parliament,[98] it should be noted that the reference to the Second Directive is not wholly persuasive as Article 23 does not appear to be a maximum harmonization measure and it is therefore open to Member States to enact in their domestic legislation a version of financial assistance law that goes further than the minimum necessary to implement the Directive.

Must the acquirer be known to the company providing the assistance at the time when the assistance is given?

This question could, for example, arise in circumstances where the management of a company decides that its business would be more effectively conducted if it were part of a larger group and engages an investment bank or other professional adviser to find a buyer for the company's shares. Agreements to pay fees are capable of falling within one the categories of financial assistance mentioned in section 677.[99] Can it be said that the ban on the giving of financial assistance does not apply because, at the time when the company agrees to pay the fee,[100] the company is unaware of the identity of any acquirer, or aspiring acquirer, of its shares? The answer to this question is not clear from the statute but some arguments may be advanced. The mere fact that there is no specifically identified purchaser by itself does not appear to take the situation outside the scope of the ban, which, as section 678(1)[101] indicates, extends to proposed acquisitions (which may never in fact take place). However, depending on the particular circumstances, it may be possible to argue that the agreement to pay the fees is too remote from any actual or proposed acquisition of shares to be capable of being regarded, as a matter of commercial reality, as financial assistance for the acquisition of shares. It may also be possible to argue that the company's actions were not causally linked in the way required by section 678 because they were not 'for

---

[97] *Hansard*, Standing Committee D, Session 2005–06, cols 856–857 (20 July 2006) *per* Vera Baird MP.

[98] Following the decision in *Pepper v Hart* [1993] AC 593, HL, if primary legislation is ambiguous or obscure, the courts may in certain circumstances take account of statements made in Parliament by Ministers or other promoters of a Bill in construing that legislation.

[99] ie any other financial assistance that reduces net assets to a material extent or by a company that has no net assets (Companies Act 2006, s 677(1)(d)).

[100] This, rather than the time when the money is actually paid, is the relevant time: *Parlett v Guppys (Bridport) Ltd* [1996] BCC 299, CA where this was common ground between the counsel in the case.

[101] As does Companies Act 2006, s 679(1).

the purpose' of an acquisition or proposed acquisition, though again this will depend on a close examination of the specific facts.

The assisted person—direct and indirect financial assistance

Unlawful financial assistance can be given directly, such as where the company whose shares are acquired, lends money to the purchaser to fund the acquisition, or indirectly, such as where the purchaser raises the purchase money from bank borrowings that are guaranteed by the company. The payment of the fees of professional advisers who advise on a share acquisition, such as the accountants in *Chaston v SWP Group plc*,[102] is another example of indirect financial assistance because the company's assumption of responsibility to pay the fees relieves the principals to the transaction of any obligation in that respect.

There can thus be no doubt that the fact that the vendor rather than the purchaser is the recipient of some action by a company does not preclude a finding that that action constitutes unlawful financial assistance.[103] Where, however, the action benefits only the vendor and is of no help whatsoever to the purchaser— for example where the target company pays the fees of advisers engaged to figure out how to sell the company at the most favourable price—it is open to question whether this is capable of being regarded as financial assistance within the scope of the Act. As Arden LJ noted in *Chaston v SWP Group plc*,[104] the general mischief that underlies financial assistance law is 'that the resources of the target company and its subsidiaries should not be used directly or indirectly *to assist the purchaser financially to make the acquisition*' (emphasis added). Where the vendor is the exclusive beneficiary of some action (and perhaps it has worked to the purchaser's disadvantage by making the acquisition more expensive to complete), this mischief is not present. However, on the current state of the authorities it is not possible to reach a confident conclusion that the purchaser must be assisted in some way (directly or indirectly) for the prohibition to bite.

In *Armour Hick Northern Ltd v Armour Hick Trust Ltd*[105] a subsidiary paid off a debt due from its immediate holding company to a major shareholder and that shareholder then sold its shares in the holding company to its other existing shareholders. It was held that the subsidiary's action was financial assistance to the vendor shareholder for the purpose of or in connection with the share purchase by the remaining shareholders because it was a voluntary payment without which the vendor shareholder would not have proceeded with the sale. This case was decided in relation to section 54 of the Companies Act 1948, which banned financial assistance in 'connection with' as well as 'for the purpose of' a purchase

---

[102] [2003] 1 BCLC 675, CA.
[103] *Armour Hick Northern Ltd v Whitehouse* [1980] 3 All ER 833, [1980] 1 WLR 1520.
[104] [2003] 1 BCLC 675, CA, para 31.
[105] [1980] 3 All ER 833, [1980] 1 WLR 1520.

of shares, but it continues to be cited as good authority for the proposition that financial assistance given to a vendor is within the scope of the ban, as currently formulated.[106] Since it was found that the acquisition would not have gone ahead but for the payment made by the subsidiary, it is possible to regard the *Armour Hick* case as being consistent with the proposition that the purchaser must benefit in some way from the action that is alleged to be unlawful financial assistance. As Rimer J noted in *Corporate Development Partners LLC v E-Relationship Marketing Ltd*,[107] the offending assistance given to the vendor 'was plainly directed at enabling the acquisition to happen'. However, a wider interpretation, namely, that any assistance to the vendor is caught irrespective of its impact on the purchaser, is also tenable. In practice, a cautious approach is warranted, given the draconian consequences of contravention of the ban on the giving of financial assistance.

The purpose(s) for which financial assistance is given

The causal link

The ban only applies to financial assistance given *for the purpose of* an acquisition (section 678(1)) or *for the purpose of* reducing or discharging a liability incurred *for the purpose of* an acquisition (section 678(3)).[108] 'Purpose' thus acts as the causal link between the financial assistance and the acquisition: simply coming within one of the categories of financial assistance mentioned in section 677 is not on its own enough and such assistance will only constitute a breach of section 678 if it is also assistance for a specified purpose. In relation to section 678(3), a person incurs a liability, *inter alia*, if he changes his financial position by making any agreement (enforceable or unenforceable) either on his own account or with any other person, or by any other means, and a company reduces or discharges such a liability by the giving of financial assistance if it is given wholly or partly for the purpose of restoring that person's financial position to what it was before the acquisition took place.[109]

In *Dyment v Boyden*[110] a partnership within a corporate shell was dissolved with one shareholder acquiring the holdings of the two other shareholders in the company and, in return, the departing shareholders taking exclusive ownership of the business premises that were then leased to the company at a rent of £66,000 per annum. Some time later, the shareholder who had remained with the company claimed that the real market rent for the property was £37,000 per annum,

---

[106] eg *Chaston v SWP Group plc* [2003] 1 BCLC 675, CA; *Anglo Petroleum Ltd v TFB (Mortgages) Ltd* [2007] BCC 407, CA.
[107] [2007] EWHC 436 (Ch), para 35.
[108] Likewise, Companies Act 2006, s 679.
[109] ibid s 683(2).
[110] [2005] 1 BCLC 163, CA.

not £66,000 per annum; that the difference of £29,000 per annum amounted to unlawful financial assistance given by the company; and that the lease was void and unenforceable with the result that no rent was ever properly payable under it. It was agreed that the additional £29,000 had the effect of reducing the company's net assets to a material extent. The Court of Appeal upheld the first instance decision that this arrangement was not unlawful financial assistance. Although it was an implied term of the agreement dissolving the partnership that the applicant should procure the company to enter into the lease, it could not properly be said that the obligation to procure the company's acceptance of the lease was undertaken for the purpose of the acquisition of the shares or that the company, by subsequently entering into the lease, had discharged a liability contrary to the Act. Applying the test of commercial substance and reality, the company's acceptance of the lease, although connected with the acquisition of the shares, could not fairly be said to have been 'for the purpose' of that acquisition, since the reality was that the company entered into the lease in order to obtain the premises that it needed in order to continue in business, and had agreed to pay an excessive rent because the owners of the freehold were in a position to exact a ransom for that property.

The causal link was also held to be missing in *Corporate Development Partners LLC v E-Relationship Marketing Ltd*.[111] In this case the defendant engaged the claimant to work on identifying possible target companies for it to acquire but, as things turned out, the defendant was itself taken over by another company to which it had been introduced by the claimant. In the period between the parties to the takeover being introduced to each other and the completion of that takeover, the consultancy agreement between the claimant and defendant was renegotiated and the revised agreement included provision for the defendant to pay a specified fee in the event of that takeover going ahead. The defendant subsequently attempted to use financial assistance law to escape its obligation to pay the fee, arguing that (a) the introduction effected by the claimant facilitated, or smoothed the path towards, an acquisition of its shares; (b) the payment commitment in the revised agreement was by way of a reward for that introduction; and (c) therefore the commitment—or payment if ultimately made—itself facilitated the acquisition and so amounted to the giving of unlawful financial assistance for the purpose of the acquisition. The Court held that the third proposition was wrong on its facts. Rimer J explained:[112]

Since CDP was playing no role in the negotiation of the acquisition—and was neither intended nor required to—the commitment to pay it the transaction fee was not going to, was not intended to and did not in fact assist or advance the acquisition at all. The payment commitment was not a condition of the takeover; it would not serve to reduce Red Eye's acquisition obligations by a single penny; and it was neither intended to, nor did

---

[111] [2007] EWHC 436 (Ch).
[112] At para 35.

it, smooth the path towards any ultimate acquisition. No doubt the reason for the commitment was because CDP had earlier introduced a party who might thereafter acquire E-RM; and it was intended to be by way of a financial reward to CDP for that introduction. But, for reasons given, the commitment was not entered into 'for the purpose' of such an acquisition.

Reference can also be made to the decision of the Court of Appeal in *Barclays Bank plc v British and Commonwealth Holdings plc*.[113] In that case the company, as part of a scheme whereby a shareholder took redeemable shares from it with an option to sell the shares to a third party if the company failed to redeem on the due date, covenanted with that third party to maintain a certain asset value. The company failed both to redeem the shares and to maintain that value. The shareholder exercised his option to sell and the third party sued the company for damages for breach of the covenant. One of the questions for the Court of Appeal was whether this covenant amounted to financial assistance for the acquisition of the shares, either by the shareholder or the third party. The Court of Appeal, upholding the decision of Harman J, held that the purpose of the covenant was to reassure the shareholder and that the covenant was a bona fide undertaking, the performance of which did not involve any financial assistance. This is not to say, however, that inducements, incentives, and concurrent benefits provided by target companies as part of a transaction in which their shares are acquired will necessarily always fail to satisfy the requirement for a causal link based on the purpose for which they are given.[114] Whether the required link exists depends on a close, fact-specific examination in each case.[115]

Mixed purposes

The purpose of assisting the acquisition of the shares or reducing or discharging a liability incurred for the purpose of an acquisition of shares need only be one of the purposes for which the financial assistance was given.[116] However, where there are mixed purposes, the financial assistance may be taken outside the scope of the prohibition if that purpose is subsidiary to another 'principal'

---

[113] [1996] 1 BCLC 1, CA.

[114] *Chaston v SWP Group plc* [2003] 1 BCLC 675, CA, para 43 *per* Arden LJ. In so far as the decision at first instance in *MT Realisations Ltd v Digital Equipment Co Ltd* [2002] 2 BCLC 688 suggests that an incentive that is part of a transaction for the acquisition of shares is not given for the purpose of the acquisition (paras 30–31 in particular) it must be treated with caution. The Court of Appeal upheld the decision but on different grounds: [2003] 2 BCLC 117, CA.

[115] Laddie J held that the purchaser's assumption of obligations to pay for the assignment of the loan (which the subsequent rescheduling agreement addressed) was not a liability incurred for the purpose of the acquisition of the shares. Although it was undoubtedly true that the loan assignment would not have gone through without the assignment of the shares, the loan assignment was properly to be characterized as something distinct from the acquisition, ie as an incentive connected to, but not for the purpose of, the sale of the shares.

[116] *Chaston v SWP Group plc* [2003] 1 BCLC 675, CA.

purpose[117] or is incidental to another 'larger' purpose,[118] provided that, in either case, the assistance is given in good faith in the interests of the assisting company. Discussion of the scope of the principal or larger purpose exception is dominated by the difficult decision of the House of Lords in *Brady v Brady*.[119]

Brady v Brady

This case concerned an arrangement that was put in place to break a deadlock in a group of family-run private companies where the businesses had become paralysed because of disputes between family members. The solution was to divide the businesses, which necessitated a complex series of transactions including the transfer of a significant portion of the company's assets in order to meet liabilities incurred in purchasing that company's shares. The transfer was undoubtedly financial assistance given for a requisite purpose and the issue before the courts was whether it could it be saved by the principal purpose or larger purpose exception. At first instance it was held that the giving of the financial assistance to reduce or discharge a liability related to the acquisition of shares was incidental to the larger purpose of the arrangement and fell within the exception. The Court of Appeal also thought that there were mixed purposes and that the principal purpose was not to facilitate the acquisition of shares but to enable the businesses to continue by ending the deadlock between the two principal shareholders but it held that the exception did not apply because the assistance had not been given in good faith in the interests of the company.[120] In the House of Lords, it was held that the good faith requirement was satisfied but that there was no principal or larger purpose that could be relied upon to save the transaction.

Lord Oliver (with whom the other members of the House of Lords agreed) said:[121]

... 'purpose' is, in some contexts, a word of wide content but in construing it in the context of the fasciculus of sections regulating the provision of finance by a company in connection with the purchase of its own shares there has always to be borne in mind the mischief against which section 151 [now s 678] is aimed. In particular, if the section is not, effectively, to be deprived of any useful application, it is important to distinguish between a purpose and the reason why a purpose is formed. The ultimate reason for forming a purpose of financing an acquisition may, and in most cases probably will, be more important to those making the decision than the immediate transaction itself. But... 'reason' [is not] the same as 'purpose'. If one postulates the case of a bidder for

---

[117] Companies Act 2006, s 678(2). See also ibid s 679(2).

[118] ibid s 678(4). See also ibid s 679(4).

[119] [1989] AC 755, HL. The decision has attracted considerable comment, much of it critical. See eg BG Pettet, 'Developments in the Law of Financial Assistance for the Purchase of Shares' [1988] 3 *Journal of International Banking Law* 96; R Greaves and B Hannigan, 'Gratuitous Transfers and Financial Assistance after *Brady*'(1989) 10 *Company Lawyer* 135; Polack, K, 'Companies Act 1985—Scope of Section 153' [1988] CLJ 359.

[120] [1988] BCLC 20, CA.

[121] [1989] AC 755, HL, 779–80.

control of a public company financing his bid from the company's own funds—the obvious mischief at which the section is aimed—the immediate purpose which it is sought to achieve is that of completing the purchase and vesting control of the company in the bidder. The reasons why that course is considered desirable may be many and varied. The company may have fallen on hard times so that a change of management is considered necessary to avert disasters. It may merely be thought, and no doubt would be thought by the purchaser and the directors whom he nominates once he has control, that the business of the company would be more profitable under his management than it was heretofore. These may be excellent reasons but they cannot, in my judgment, constitute a 'larger purpose' of which the provision of assistance is merely an incident. The purpose and the only purpose of the financial assistance is and remains that of enabling the shares to be acquired and the financial or commercial advantages flowing from the acquisition, whilst they may form the reason for forming the purpose of providing assistance, are a by-product of it rather than an independent purpose of which the assistance can properly be considered an incident.

This passage has become notorious among company lawyers because it has not proved easy to identify what counts as a principal or larger purpose as opposed to a 'mere' good reason for entering into a particular arrangement. Perhaps the most that can be said with certainty is that the House of Lords sent out a very strong signal that the term 'purpose' here is to be narrowly interpreted and therefore it should not be lightly assumed that a purpose-based exception is available.

Reversing Brady

For many years there have been calls for the purpose exception to be reformulated so as to remove its very narrow scope, as interpreted in the *Brady* case. During the 1990s it did appear to be the government's intention to reverse the effects of the *Brady* judgment by introducing a predominant reason test in place of the larger/principal purpose exception. Yet, when the opportunity to rewrite the exception in the Companies Act 2006 was presented, the government declined to do so. The explanation for this apparent volte-face emerged in discussion in Parliament on the Bill that became the Companies Act 2006: it was not that the government had changed its mind on the desirability of reversing the effect of the *Brady* case but rather that it had had second thoughts on whether it had yet hit upon a form of words that would achieve the desired effect. The government signalled that it remained prepared to consider a reworking of the provisions so as to have the intended effect of removing the very narrow scope of the purpose exceptions as interpreted in *Brady*, and indicated that new provisions could refer to concepts along the current lines or might be framed on an entirely different basis so long as they remained consistent with the implementation of Article 23 of the Second Company Law Directive.[122]

---

[122] *Hansard*, vol 680, GC col 24 (20 March 2006) and *Hansard*, HC vol 682, col 182 (16 May 2006).

Examples of a larger or principal purpose

For now, it remains necessary therefore to grapple with thorny questions on the scope of the purpose-based exception for which few definite answers are available.

An example of a principal purpose was given by Lord Oliver in *Brady v Brady*:[123]

The [principal purpose exception] envisages a principal and, by implication, a subsidiary purpose. The inquiry here is whether the assistance given was principally in order to relieve the purchaser of shares in the company of his indebtedness resulting from the acquisition or whether it was principally for some other purpose—for instance, the acquisition from the purchaser of some asset which the company requires for its business.

An example of an operative larger purpose is more difficult to formulate.[124] Even Lord Oliver in the *Brady* case acknowledged that the concept of a larger corporate purpose was not easy to grasp.[125] One situation that may yield an example is the case of a subsidiary company that provides funds to its parent company some years after its acquisition to effect a more efficient deployment of assets within the group or to improve the group's financial position. Should the parent use the funds so provided to repay a debt that was incurred for the purpose of acquiring the subsidiary, it is possible that the purpose of achieving that greater efficiency could be viewed as an operative larger purpose. What would distinguish these facts from those in *Brady*? A discernible difference between the two situations can be found by focusing attention on *corporate* purpose, as opposed to the purpose of individual shareholders or directors. A larger *corporate* purpose may have been what was lacking in the *Brady* case where the driving factor was the desire of the shareholders to ensure the survival of the businesses. This contrasts with the example of an intra-group transaction for which there may exist many legitimate corporate purposes that a company seeks to achieve by its participation.[126]

Good faith

The purpose exception is available only where there is an operative principal or larger purpose *and* the assistance is given in good faith in the interests of the company. In the *Brady* case Lord Oliver held that this phrase was a single, composite

---

[123] [1989] AC 755, HL, 779.
[124] Greaves and Hannigan (n 119 above) 139: 'it is difficult to envisage a situation where the section will be applicable'; Polack (n 119 above) 361: 'It may be that Lord Oliver's analysis has rendered [the larger purpose] ... exception virtually unattainable'.
[125] [1989] AC 755 HL, 779.
[126] This suggestion derives some support from the Irish case *CH (Ireland) Ltd v Credit Suisse Canada* [1999] 4 IR 542, HC, where it was held that the principal purpose for the giving of a guarantee was to secure continued financial assistance for the guarantor's corporate group rather than to provide financial assistance. As so interpreted, the facts disclosed a legitimate corporate purpose. However, other aspects of the arrangements between the parties amounted to unlawful financial assistance.

expression and that it postulated a requirement that those responsible for procuring the company to provide the assistance must act in the genuine belief that it is being done in the company's interest.[127] In the Court of Appeal[128] Nourse LJ had placed particular emphasis on how the scheme would affect the company's creditors and regarded it as fatal to the claim to rely on the exception that there was no evidence that the directors had considered the interests of the creditors; whilst the directors had acted in the interests of the shareholders, in not considering the creditors they had failed to act in the interests of the company. Lord Oliver disagreed with Nourse LJ's treatment of the evidence but accepted that the interests of the creditors had to be considered at the time when the financial assistance was given: the directors had to satisfy themselves at that time that the giving of the financial assistance would not impair the company's power to pay its debts as they fell due. In a case decided shortly after *Brady*,[129] it was held that where a company would have been insolvent if it had given the financial assistance, the good faith test could not be satisfied.

Unconditional exceptions

Section 681 of the Companies Act 2006 lists a number of specific matters that are not within the scope of the ban on the giving of financial assistance. This list of 'unconditional exceptions' is largely for the avoidance of doubt.[130] A common theme underlying many of the exceptions in this section is that they relate to matters that are regulated by other provisions of the Companies Act 2006 or the Insolvency Act 1986, and regulatory duplication or inconsistency is thus avoided.

Distributions

In *Re Wellington Publishing Co Ltd*[131] it was held that the payment of a dividend was not something which would ordinarily be regarded as the giving of financial assistance within the meaning of the New Zealand equivalent of section 54 of the English Companies Act 1948. Section 681(2)(a) of the Companies Act 2006 puts this beyond doubt by providing an exception for any distribution of a company's assets by way of dividend lawfully made or distribution made in the course of the company's winding up. This important exception facilitates the extraction of liquid funds from companies.

---

[127] [1989] AC 755, HL, 777–8.
[128] [1988] BCLC 20, CA.
[129] *Plaut v Steiner* (1989) 5 BCC 352.
[130] *Hansard*, Standing Committee A, Session 1980–81, col 301 (30 June 1981).
[131] [1973] 1 NZLR 133, NZ SC.

Bonus issues

Literally interpreted, an allotment of bonus shares could be an 'acquisition' but it would be outside the mischief that the ban on the giving of financial assistance is meant to address for bonus share issues to be included. Section 681(2)(b) provides an exception.

Other unconditional exceptions

The other matters listed in section 681 as following outside the scope of the ban are:

(1) any reduction of capital under chapter 10 of Part 17 of the Companies Act 2006;

(2) a redemption of shares under chapter 3 of Part 18 of the Companies Act 2006;

(3) a purchase of its own shares by a company under chapter 4 of Part 18 of the Companies Act 2006;

(4) anything done in pursuance of an order of the court under Part 26 of the Companies Act 2006 (order sanctioning compromise or arrangement with members or creditors); and

(5) anything done under an arrangement made in pursuance of section 110 of the Insolvency Act 1986 or the equivalent provision of the Insolvency (Northern Ireland) Order 1989;[132] and

(6) anything done under an arrangement made between a company and its creditors which is binding on the creditors by virtue of Part 1 of the Insolvency Act 1986 (voluntary arrangements) or the Northern Irish equivalent.[133]

Conditional exceptions

Section 682 of the Companies Act 2006 provides 'conditional exceptions' for loans in the ordinary course of a lending business and for certain arrangements to support the acquisition of shares by employees. These exceptions apply in favour of private companies as well as public companies but they operate more restrictively in relation to public companies. Since a private company is within the scope of financial assistance law only in relation to the giving of financial assistance for the acquisition of shares in a public company of which it is a subsidiary, the circumstances in which a private company will need to rely on these exceptions are limited.

---

[132] SI 1989/2405 (NI 19), art 96.
[133] Insolvency (Northern Ireland) Order 1989, SI 1989/2405 (NI 19), Pt 2.

The restrictive condition that must be satisfied where a public company seeks to rely on one of the these exceptions is that the financial assistance must not reduce the assisting company's net assets or, to the extent that it does, the financial assistance must be provided out of distributable profits.[134] For this purpose, net assets are calculated by looking at the amount by which the aggregate of the company's assets exceeds the aggregate of its liabilities, taking the amount of both assets and liabilities to be as stated in the company's accounting records immediately before the financial assistance is given.[135] In other words, it is book values as opposed to market values that must be considered. The term 'liabilities' includes an amount retained as reasonably necessary for the purpose of providing for any liability or loss which is either likely to be incurred, or certain to be incurred but uncertain as to amount, or as to the date on which it will arise.[136]

Prima facie a loan would not reduce the net assets of the lender company provided the borrower's credit is good and no provision against default has to be made. Similarly, with contingent liabilities such as guarantees and indemnities, if the contingency is so remote that in accounting terms it would be valued at nil, there will be no immediate reduction in net assets.

Exception for money-lending businesses

Article 23(2) of the Second Company Law Directive provides that Article 23(1) does not apply to 'transactions concluded by banks and other financial institutions in the normal course of business'. The domestic equivalent of this exception is section 682(2)(a) of the Companies Act 2006, which provides that the ban on the giving of financial assistance does not apply to the lending of money by a company in the ordinary course of business where the lending of money is part of the ordinary business of the company. Section 54 of the Companies Act 1948 had a similarly worded exemption which was considered by the Privy Council in *Steen v Law*[137] and given quite a narrow scope. Viscount Radcliffe, delivering the judgment of the Judicial Committee, commented that the exemption had to be read as:

... protecting a company engaged in money lending as part of its ordinary business from an infraction of the law, even though moneys borrowed from it are used and, perhaps, used to its knowledge, in the purchase of its own shares. Even so, the qualification is imposed that, to escape liability, the loan transaction must be made in the ordinary course of its business. Nothing, therefore, is protected except what is consistent with the normal course of its business and is lending which the company ordinarily practices... it is, on the other hand, virtually impossible to see how loans, big or small, deliberately

---

[134] Companies Act 2006, s 682(1)(b).
[135] ibid s 682(4)(a).
[136] ibid s 682(4)(b).
[137] [1964] AC 287, PC.

made by a company for the direct purpose of financing a purchase of its shares could ever be described as made in the ordinary course of business.

It is thus not sufficient that the company's ordinary business involves lending money; the particular loan must also be within the ordinary course of its business and, if it is a loan made specifically to finance an acquisition of its own shares, there is every likelihood that it will fail this test. Thus, in *Fowlie v Slater*[138] loans deliberately made by an investment bank for the purpose of financing the purchase of shares in its holding company were held to be special loans for special purposes. They could not be regarded as being within the ordinary course of business of the investment bank and, accordingly, they did not come within the exception.

Exception for employee share purchases

A number of overlapping exemptions are intended to allow companies to support employee share schemes and other acquisitions of shares by employees. Again, these exemptions exist against the background of a specific exemption in the Second Company Law Directive: Article 23(2) provides that Article 23(1) does not apply to transactions effected with a view to the acquisition of shares by or for the company's employees or the employees of an associate company.

The first exception, in section 682(2)(b) of the Companies Act 2006 relates to the provision by a company, in good faith in the interests of the company or its holding company, of financial assistance for the purposes of an employee share scheme.[139] This provision was first inserted into the companies legislation by the Companies Act 1989 in order to replace a more restrictively worded exception. Prior to the change made by the 1989 Act, the relevant exception allowed 'money' to be provided for the 'acquisition of fully paid shares' in the company. Other forms of financial assistance—such as guaranteeing the borrowings of the trust under which the employee share scheme was constituted—were not permitted. Also there was some doubt about whether money could be provided to cover the incidental costs of an acquisition as opposed to the cash consideration itself. Both of these limitations have now fallen away.

NZI Bank Ltd v Euro-National Corporation Ltd[140] involved an attempt to take advantage of the employee share scheme exception to the ban on the giving of financial assistance in the New Zealand companies legislation. The employee share scheme was to act as the conduit for the provision of financial assistance to certain major shareholders in the company, the aim of this being to avoid the likely effect on the company's share price if they sold their shares. The New

---

[138] Unreported but noted by K Walmsley, 'Lending in the "Ordinary Course of Business"' (1979) 129 NLJ 801.

[139] Employee share schemes are defined by Companies Act 2006, s 1165.

[140] [1992] 3 NZLR 528, NZ CA.

Zealand Court of Appeal held that it was necessary to examine what the directors were in truth endeavouring to achieve in setting up the employee share scheme so as to ensure that the exception was not being used to cover a financial engineering purpose for which it was never designed. It seems likely that the English courts would adopt a similarly inquiring approach in order to prevent manipulation or abuse of the exemption.

Section 682(2)(c) of the Companies Act 2006, authorizes the provision of financial assistance by a company for the purpose of, or in connection with, anything done by the company (or another company in the same group) for the purpose of enabling or facilitating transactions in shares in the first-mentioned company between, and involving the acquisition of beneficial ownership of, those shares by bona fide employees or former employees of that company (or another company in the same group) or their dependants, ie their spouses, civil partners, widows, widowers, surviving civil partners, and minor children and step children. For this purpose a company is in the same group as another company if it is a holding company or a subsidiary of that company, or a subsidiary of a holding company of that company.[141] The gist of this is clear: it is intended to allow companies to support internal share-dealing schemes. But the dual requirement—that only present or former employees (or connected persons) should be the beneficial participants and should be the only parties to transactions—appears to exclude common types of schemes where one of the parties to transactions can be a trust established for the benefit of employees and connected persons.

Section 682(2)(d) of the Companies Act 2006 relates to the making by a company of loans to persons other than directors employed in good faith by the company with a view to enabling those persons to acquire fully paid shares in the company or a holding company to be held by them by way of beneficial ownership. It has been held, in relation to an the equivalent section in New South Wales legislation, that this exception only applies if the sole or major purpose is to allow the employees to purchase shares. If the major purpose is to facilitate the change of control of a company then the exception does not apply.[142]

Criminal sanctions for unlawful financial assistance

A company commits an offence if it gives unlawful financial assistance and is liable to a fine.[143] Since the persons who are intended to be protected by the ban on the giving of financial assistance include the company that provides the assistance, the company's inclusion in the category of perpetrators of the crime

---

[141] Companies Act 2006, s 682(5).

[142] *Saltergate Insurance Co Ltd v Knight* [1982] 1 NSWLR 369.

[143] Companies Act 2006, s 680. According to s 680(2), any person who commits the offence is also liable to be imprisoned but clearly this does not make sense in relation to a company. cf Companies Act 1985, s 151 where the drafting was different and the point did not arise.

requires comment. The general question of when to impose corporate liability on a company was considered carefully in the Review that preceded the Companies Act 2006. The Review Steering Group suggested a presumption against imposing liability on the company where both (a) the act was capable of seriously damaging the company, and (b) making the responsible individuals criminally liable was likely to be a sufficient deterrent.[144] However, during the passage of the Bill that became the Companies Act 2006 the government indicated that it had chosen to adopt a different approach:

The general principle adopted as to whether a company should be liable for a breach of the requirements of Companies Acts is that where the only victims of the offence are the company or its members, the company should not be liable for the offence. On the other hand, where members or the company are potential victims, but not the only ones, then the company should be potentially liable for a breach. All the offences in the Companies Acts, both those in the Bill and those that remain in the 1985 Act, have been reviewed in the light of this principle.[145]

Since the prohibition on the giving of financial assistance is intended to protect creditors as well as shareholders and the company, it is therefore an example of conduct for which corporate criminal liability was not ruled out under the general principle.

Every officer of the company who is in default is also guilty of a criminal offence for which the penalty is imprisonment, up to a maximum of two years, or a fine or both.[146] The Review Steering Group considered decriminalizing some offences by directors, including the giving of financial assistance, and giving greater emphasis to administrative penalties.[147] Consultation elicited mixed views and in the end the Group recommended retention of criminal sanctions for financial assistance because it was not convinced that an approach based on civil penalties and the market abuse provisions of the Financial Services and Market Act 2000 would work.[148] According to the government spokesperson in the Parliamentary debate on the Bill that became the Companies Act 2006, it was appropriate to retain criminal sanctions for financial assistance because offences were less likely to be committed if they were backed up by criminal penalties. In the government's view, criminal sanctions were appropriate, proportionate, and essential for effective enforcement of breaches, but the underlying threat of prosecution enabled authorities to exercise a progressive approach to enforcement that secured compliance without prosecution.[149]

---

[144] Company Law Review, 'Final Report', URN 01/942, para 15.36.
[145] Explanatory Notes on the Companies Act 2006, paras 1433–1435.
[146] Companies Act 2006, s 680.
[147] Company Law Review, 'Completing the Structure', URN 00/1335, para 13.42.
[148] Company Law Review, 'Final Report', URN 01/942, para 15.18.
[149] *Hansard*, Standing Committee D, Session 2005–06, cols 858–860 (20 July 2006) *per* Vera Baird MP.

Civil consequences of unlawful financial assistance

The Companies Act 2006 does not refer to the civil consequences of unlawful financial assistance. These consequences are derived from case law and to examine them fully would take this discussion beyond the scope of this book and into an analysis of complex issues in the fields of equity, contract, and restitution where aspects of the law are still developing. It is not proposed here to attempt to give an exhaustive account of all of the remedies available in respect of, and other civil consequences of, transactions that are tainted by unlawful financial assistance. Instead, it suffices for the purposes of this book to indicate the main areas of concern and the issues that arise in relation to them.

The invalidity of the financial assistance transaction

Any security, guarantee, or other transaction constituting unlawful financial assistance is illegal and any obligations undertaken by the company providing the financial assistance are unenforceable.[150] An undertaking can be viewed as financial assistance even though it is without legal effect because, as Fisher J explained in *Heald v O'Connor*:[151] 'By the provision of a security . . . the company undoubtedly gives financial assistance to the purchaser of the shares whether the security is valid or not. All that is necessary to make the financial assistance effective is that the lender should believe the security to be valid and on the strength of it make the loan.' If all that has happened is that the company has undertaken some commitment which amounts to the giving of unlawful financial assistance, a declaration that the commitment is void may be the only remedy that the company needs. However, the position is more complicated if the company seeks to recover money or other property that it has parted with in purported performance of its contractual obligations. Although a person who parts with money or other property in the mistaken belief that he is contractually obliged to do so is normally entitled to a restitutionary claim, the general rule is that illegality operates as a defence to a restitutionary claim.[152] An exception to this rule allows the less guilty party to recover in certain circumstances. This exception has been held to apply where a contract is rendered illegal by a statute in order to protect a class of persons and the claimant is within the protected class. In one case it was held that a company providing financial assistance was not within the protected class and

---

[150] *Brady v Brady* [1989] AC 755, HL; *Selangor United Rubber Estates Ltd v Cradock* [1968] 2 All ER 1073, 1154; *Heald v O'Connor* [1971] 2 All ER 1105; *Dressy Frocks Pty Ltd v Bock* (1951) 51 SR (NSW) 390; *EH Dey Pty Ltd (in liquidation) v Dey* [1966] VR 464, Vic SC; *Shearer Transport Co Pty Ltd v McGrath* [1956] VLR 316, Vic SC. See also the obiter discussion in *Re Hill and Tyler Ltd, Harlow v Loveday* [2005] 1 BCLC 41, paras 65–70.

[151] [1971] 2 All ER 1105, 1109.

[152] G Virgo, *The Principles of the Law of Restitution* (OUP, 2nd edn, 2006) 168–9.

thus could not have a personal claim in respect of money that it had lent pursuant to a loan that constituted unlawful financial assistance.[153] The inclusion of the assisting company among the perpetrators of the crime of giving unlawful financial assistance has particular significance in this context.[154]

Validity of the acquisition of the shares

In *Carney v Herbert*[155] it was not disputed that unlawful financial assistance in the form of mortgages had been given in relation to the sale of shares. The issue was whether this illegality tainted the whole transaction or whether the illegal mortgages could be severed so as to leave the sale of the shares intact. The Privy Council held that severance was possible. Lord Brightman, giving the judgment of the Judicial Committee, stated:[156]

Subject to a caveat that it is undesirable, if not impossible, to lay down any principles which will cover all problems in this field, their Lordships venture to suggest that, as a general rule, where parties enter into a lawful contract of, for example, sale and purchase, and there is an ancillary provision which is illegal but exists for the exclusive benefit of the plaintiff, the court may and probably will, if the justice of the case so requires, and there is no public policy objection, permit the plaintiff if he so wishes to enforce the contract without the illegal provision.

In *Neilson v Stewart*[157] this dictum was quoted by Lord Jauncey in the House of Lords as authority for the proposition that a share transfer would normally be severable from surrounding unlawful financial assistance.[158]

Claims against directors

In *Wallersteiner v Moir*[159] Lord Denning MR said: 'Every director who is a party to a breach of [the ban on the giving of financial assistance] is guilty of a

---

[153] *Selangor United Rubber Estates Ltd v Cradock* [1968] 2 All ER 1073. The facts and decision in the *Selangor* case are analysed in detail by MR Chesterman and AS Grabiner, 'Sorting Out A Company Fraud' (1969) 32 MLR 328.

[154] GR Bretten, 'Financial Assistance in Share Transactions' (1968) 32 Conv 6, 12–15; R Barrett, 'Financial Assistance and Share Acquisitions' (1974) 48 ALJ 6, 8–11.

[155] [1985] 1 AC 301, PC.

[156] [1985] 1 AC 301, PC, 317.

[157] [1991] BCC 713, HL.

[158] Earlier cases supporting the possibility of severance, at least in some circumstances, are *Spink (Bournemouth) Ltd v Spink* [1936] Ch 544; *South Western Mineral Water Co Ltd v Ashmore* [1967] 2 All ER 953; *Lawlor v Gray* (1980) 130 NLJ 317, CA. See also the obiter discussion in *Re Hill and Tyler Ltd, Harlow v Loveday* [2005] 1 BCLC 41, para 79.

[159] [1974] 3 All ER 217, CA, 239. See also at 249 *per* Buckley LJ and 255 *per* Scarman LJ; *Steen v Law* [1964] AC 287, PC.

misfeasance and breach of trust; and is liable to recoup to the company any loss occasioned to it by the default.'

There were numerous other pre-codification of directors' duties cases that regarded participation in the giving of unlawful financial assistance by directors as a breach of trust or of fiduciary duty.[160] In *Steen v Law*[161] the Privy Council was of the view that where directors had given unlawful financial assistance in breach of their duty to the company, it was not a defence to plead merely that they acted in ignorance of the law.

Under the now codified general duties that directors owe to their company, a director who is party to a breach of the prohibition would presumably be held to be in breach of the duty in section 171 of the Companies Act 2006 to act in accordance with the company's constitution and only exercise powers for the purposes for which they are conferred. A director who is technically in breach of duty but not morally culpable may seek relief from the court on the grounds that he acted honestly and reasonably and having regard to all the circumstances of the case ought fairly to be excused.[162]

Liability of other parties

Third parties, such as lending banks, that are implicated in a scheme involving unlawful financial assistance (accessories) or who receive money or property from the company by reason of it (recipients) may also be personally liable to the company. Detailed analysis of the circumstances in which a company may have a claim against third parties shifts the focus from the relatively narrow confines of financial assistance law and into much broader fields of equity and restitution that are not explored in detail here. However, an outline is called for because these potential civil liabilities add significantly to the legal risks faced by lending institutions and other professionals involved in corporate finance transactions that raise financial assistance concerns.

Accessory liability

Traditionally called liability for 'knowing assistance', anyone who assists the directors to misapply company funds in the giving of unlawful financial assistance may be held personally liable to compensate the company.[163] The degree of knowledge needed to trigger this liability is a thorny question that has divided

---

[160] See eg *Belmont Finance Corp v Williams Furniture Ltd (No 2)* [1980] All ER 393, CA; *Karak Rubber Co v Burden (No 2)* [1972] 1 WLR 602 *Selangor United Rubber Estates Ltd v Cradock (No 3)* [1968] 1 WLR 1555; *Curtis's Furnishing Store Ltd v Freedman* [1966] 1 WLR 1219; *Steen v Law* [1964] AC 287, PC.

[161] [1964] AC 287, PC.

[162] Companies Act 2006, s 1157.

[163] *Belmont Finance Corp v Williams Furniture (No 2)* [1980] All ER 393, CA.

judicial opinion over many years.[164] In *Royal Brunei Airlines Sdn Bhd v Tan*[165] the Privy Council delivered a powerful restatement of the law. Lord Nicholls, giving the judgment, said, first, that the breach of trust or fiduciary obligation need not itself be either dishonest or fraudulent. So, in a case involving the giving of unlawful financial assistance by directors, it does not matter whether the directors are themselves acting fraudulently. Secondly, Lord Nicholls decided that to couch accessory liability in terms of knowledge was unhelpful and preferred the test of dishonestly procuring or assisting in the breach of trust or fiduciary obligation. Honesty in this context, said Lord Nicholls, was an objective standard and meant not acting as an honest person would act in the circumstances. However, the court would look at all the circumstances known to the accessory at the time, not to what a reasonable person would have known or appreciated, and regard could be had to the personal attributes of the accessory, such as his experience and intelligence, and the reason why he acted as he did. This was followed by the House of Lords in *Twinsectra Ltd v Yardley*[166] but, unfortunately, the majority of the House of Lords again muddied the waters by saying that a defendant would not be held to be dishonest unless it was established that his conduct had been dishonest by the ordinary standards of reasonable and honest people and that he himself had realized that by those standards his conduct was dishonest even though he might not have so regarded it himself. The second limb of this formulation attracted criticism because it appeared to suggest that a defendant who had a subjective belief that his conduct was not dishonest by ordinary standards would escape liability.[167] The Privy Council returned to the issue in *Barlow Clowes International Ltd (in liquidation) v Eurotrust International Ltd*[168] where the majority view in *Twinsectra* was 'explained' as not having this meaning: in considering whether a defendant's state of mind was dishonest, an inquiry into the defendant's view about standards of honesty was required; the defendant's knowledge of a transaction had to be such as to render his participation contrary to normally acceptable standards of honest conduct but there was no requirement that he should have had reflections about what those normally acceptable standards were. Some commentators have suggested that the Privy Council in the *Eurotrust* case in fact went beyond explaining the second limb in *Twinsectra* and actually excluded it.[169] It is evident from subsequent cases that the search

---

[164] *Baden Delvaux v Société Générale pour Favoriser le Développement du Commerce et de l'Industrie en France SA (Note)* [1993] 1 WLR 509; *Agip (Africa) Ltd v Jackson* [1991] Ch 547, CA; *Eagle Trust plc v SBC Securities Ltd* [1993] 1 WLR 484; *Cowan de Groot Properties Ltd v Eagle Trust plc* [1992] 4 All ER 488; *Polly Peck International plc v Nadir (No 2)* [1992] 4 All ER 700, CA.

[165] [1995] AC 378, PC.

[166] [2002] 2 AC 164, HL.

[167] TM Yeo and H Tijo, 'Knowing What is Dishonesty' (2002) 118 LQR 502.

[168] [2006] 1 WLR 1276, PC.

[169] M Conaglen and A Goymour, 'Dishonesty in the Context of Assistance—Again' [2006] CLJ 18; TM Yeo, 'Dishonest Assistance: Restatement From The Privy Council' (2006) 122 LQR 171. But see Sir Anthony Clarke, 'Claims Against Professionals: Negligence, Dishonesty and Fraud' [2006] 22 *Professional Negligence* 70. Other comments on the *Eurotrust* re-statement of

for clarity in this complex area of law remains rather elusive as uncertainty remains as to whether liability depends on the defendant being aware that he has transgressed ordinary standards of honest behaviour:[170] as one judge put it, 'the boundaries of dishonesty have been somewhat mobile over the last few years'.[171]

Recipient liability

Anyone who receives the funds of the company misapplied by the directors with knowledge of the breach may be held personally liable to the company. The degree of knowledge needed to trigger this liability, which is traditionally described as liability for knowing receipt, has also generated a considerable amount of case law and academic commentary.[172] The position was comprehensively reviewed by the Court of Appeal in *Bank of Credit and Commerce International (Overseas) Ltd v Akindele*.[173] The Court of Appeal in this case considered that there should be a single test to determine the requisite knowledge for liability for knowing receipt. That was whether the recipient's state of knowledge was such as to make it unconscionable for him to retain the benefit of receipt. Such a test, said the Court, would still involve difficulties of application but would simplify the issue and enable the courts to give common-sense decisions in a commercial context.[174]

The tort of conspiracy

A combination between a number of persons to procure a company to give unlawful financial assistance amounts to a conspiracy to effect an unlawful purpose. It has been held that the company that provides the financial assistance is not barred by reason of the fact that it is technically a party to the illegality from

the position include D Ryan, 'Royal Brunei Dishonesty: Clarity at Last' [2006] *Conveyancer and Property Lawyer* 188; N Kiri, 'Recipient and Accessory Liability—Where Do We Stand Now?' [2006] 21 *Journal of International Banking Law and Regulation* 611; JE Penner, 'Dishonest Assistance Revisited: Barlow Clowes International Ltd (In Liquidation) And Others v Eurotrust International Ltd' (2006) 20(2) *Trust Law International* 122.

[170] *Abou-Rahmah v Abacha* [2007] 1 Lloyd's Rep 115, CA. But see D Ryan, 'Royal Brunei Dishonesty: A Clear Welcome For Barlow Clowes' [2007] *Conveyancer and Property Lawyer* 168.

[171] *Mullarkey v Broad* [2007] All ER (D) 33 (Jul), Ch, Lewison J.

[172] The cases include *Belmont Finance Corp v Williams Furniture (No 2)* [1980] All ER 393, CA; *Selangor United Rubber Estates v Cradock (No 3)* [1968] 1 WLR 1555; *Karak Rubber Co v Burden (No 2)* [1972] 1 WLR 602; *Re Montagu's ST* [1987] Ch 264; *Polly Peck International plc v Nadir (No 2)* [1992] 4 All ER 769, CA; *El Ajou v Dollar Land Holdings plc* [1993] BCLC 735. Pre-*Akindele* commentary on knowing receipt liability includes the following chapters of WR Cornish, R Nolan, J O'Sullivan, and G Virgo (eds), *Restitution Past, Present and Future* (Hart, 1998): Sir Peter Millett, 'Restitution and Constructive Trusts' 199; AJ Oakley, 'Restitution and Constructive Trusts: A Commentary' 219; Lord Nicholls, 'Knowing Receipt: The Need for a New Landmark' 231; and C Harpum, 'Knowing Receipt: The Need for a New Landmark: Some Reflections' 247.

[173] [2000] 4 All ER 221, CA.

[174] Commentary on the decision in *Akindele* includes S Barkehall Thomas, '"Goodbye" Knowing Receipt. "Hello" Unconscientious Receipt' (2001) 21 OJLS 239; J Stevens, 'No New Landmark—An Unconscionable Mess in Knowing Receipt' (2001) 9 *Restitution Law Review* 99. See also PBH Birks, 'Knowing Receipt: Re Montagu's Settlement Trusts Revisited' (2001) 1 (2) *Global Jurist Advances*, article 2.

suing the conspirators in tort for compensation for loss suffered as a result of any such conspiracy.[175]

Disqualification

A person who is guilty of an indictable offence in connection with the management of a company is liable to be disqualified under section 2 of the Company Directors Disqualification Act 1986. Giving unlawful financial assistance is an indictable offence.[176] A director's failure to recognize that actions taken by the company amounted to the giving of unlawful financial assistance is also a factor that can be taken into account in disqualification proceedings on grounds of unfitness under section 6 of the Company Directors Disqualification Act 1986.[177]

Amending Directive

Article 23 of the Second Company Law Directive was amended in 2006.[178] A recital in the amending Directive provides that 'Member States should be able to permit public limited liability companies to grant financial assistance with a view to the acquisition of their shares by a third party up to the limit of the company's distributable reserves so as to increase flexibility with regard to changes in the ownership structure of the share capital of companies'. However, the recital also cautions that: 'this possibility should be subject to safeguards, having regard to this Directive's objective of protecting both shareholders and third parties'. When the detail of the substantive amendment is examined, it quickly becomes apparent that it delivers only a modest concession in favour of financial assistance. The amendment provides for a new gateway procedure whereby financial assistance can be given provided certain conditions are satisfied. The conditions, which are onerous, include: (1) ex ante shareholder approval for financial assistance on a transaction-by-transaction basis, which has been said to be 'unworkable in the context of most corporate transactions where financial assistance is an issue';[179] (2) investigation of the credit standing of counterparties, which could expose directors to the risk of personal liability;[180] and (3) a requirement for the company

---

[175] *Belmont Finance Corp v Williams Furniture Ltd* [1979] Ch 250, CA.

[176] Companies Act 2006, s 680.

[177] *Re Continental Assurance Co of London plc, Secretary of State for Trade and Industry v Burrows* [1997] 1 BCLC 48.

[178] By Directive (EC) 2006/68 of the European Parliament and of the Council of 6 September 2006 amending Council Directive (EEC) 77/91 as regards the formation of public limited liability companies and the maintenance and alteration of their capital [2006] OJ L264/32.

[179] DTI, 'Directive Proposals on Company Reporting, Capital Maintenance and Transfer of the Registered Office of a Company: A Consultative Document' (London, March 2005) para 3.4.2.

[180] ibid.

to include, among the liabilities in the balance sheet, a reserve, unavailable for distribution, of the amount of the aggregate financial assistance. It has been said that the provisions relating to the gateway procedure 'remain based on the largely false premise that financial assistance is an unacceptable practice'.[181]

The amendment is optional for Member States: they are permitted but not required to change their domestic legislation to make the gateway procedure available. At the time of writing, the British government has no intention to amend the Companies Act 2006 to include the gateway procedure and its preference is to press for more meaningful reform of the Second Company Law Directive.

---

[181] E Wymeersch, 'Reforming the Second Company Law Directive' (November 2006). Financial Law Institute Gent WP 2006–15, available at SSRN <http://ssrn.com/abstract=957981>.

PART III

DEBT CORPORATE FINANCE

11

Debt Corporate Finance—General Considerations

Scope of this part

Companies can raise debt finance by issuing debt securities (bonds) directly into the capital markets or by borrowing from banks or other lenders. Other financing mechanisms, such as invoice financing, factoring, and invoice discounting, can also be used to smooth out cash flow by providing short-term working capital in return for an assignment of receivables.[1] Most of the debt finance for small and medium-sized enterprises (SMEs) in the UK is provided by the banking sector.[2] Small quoted companies (SQCs) also depend heavily on the banks because their size and lack of credit ratings, in practice, tend to rule out access the bond markets at reasonable rates.[3] Large companies have more choices available to them.[4] Whether bank-based or market-based financing is better at financing industrial expansion and achieving the efficient allocation of capital resources is much debated but the evidence is inconclusive.[5]

---

[1] Invoice financing comes in two forms: factoring and invoice discounting. Both services normally provide finance against debtor balances outstanding. Factoring provides the additional advantage of a full sales ledger and collections service under which the Factor takes on the responsibility for the sales ledger. Under an Invoice Discounting service the company continues to administer the sales ledger and the service is usually undisclosed to customers. These definitions are taken from the website of the Factors and Discounters Association <www.factors.org.uk> (accessed November 2007). See also, A Hewitt, 'Asset Finance' (Summer 2003) *Bank of England Quarterly Bulletin* 207.

[2] Competition Commission, 'The Supply of Banking Services by Clearing Banks to Small and Medium-sized Enterprises' (2002).

[3] P Brierley and M Young, 'The Financing of Smaller Quoted Companies: a Survey' (Summer 2004) *Bank of England Quarterly Bulletin* 160.

[4] By way of comparison, a recent US study found debt financing to be the predominant source of new external funds for US corporations: firms with the highest credit quality borrow from public sources, firms with medium credit quality borrow from banks, and firms with the lowest credit quality borrow from non-bank private lenders: DJ Denis and VT Mihov, 'The Choice Among Bank Debt, Non-bank Private Debt, and Public Debt: Evidence From New Corporate Borrowings' (2003) 70 *Journal of Financial Economics* 3.

[5] T Beck and R Levine, 'Industry Growth and Capital Allocation: Does Having a Market- or Bank-based System Matter?' (2002) 64 *Journal of Financial Economics* 147.

This chapter examines general issues relating to unsecured debt corporate finance.[6] It concentrates mainly on traditional types of bank lending (overdrafts and term loans) but many of the issues discussed are relevant also to corporate bonds. Chapter 12 below, deals with issues that arise when debt finance is made available to companies on a secured basis. Also relevant is chapter 15 below, on corporate bonds.

Unsecured lending—overview

The terms on which a loan is made available depend on agreement between borrower and lender. Provided they refrain from agreeing to something that is illegal, conceptually impossible,[7] or contrary to public policy, the law will give contractual effect to whatever bargain the parties arrive at. This provides great scope for variety and innovation in the corporate debt sector. Studies of the negotiation process associated with determining the contents of documentation in the bank loan market in several countries with Anglo-American financing systems, indicate that the process can be intensely contentious and that a range of borrower-specific considerations (such as size, internal governance structure, ownership, management reputation, and business risk) and contract-specific characteristics (such as term and size of loan) act as determinants of the terms in any particular case.[8] Individual loan officers have considerable discretion to depart from standard form precedents to suit particular circumstances.[9]

The main terms of a loan are those governing the principal (the amount, the basis on which it is to be made available to the borrower, and the mechanisms for repayment) and the interest charges. A company may secure lending facilities on which it can draw from time to time, an agreed overdraft facility being a familiar

---

[6] Sections of this chapter are derived from E Ferran, 'The Place for Creditor Protection on the Agenda for Modernisation of Company Law in the European Union' [2006] *European Company and Financial Law Review* 178.

[7] But 'the courts should be very slow to declare a practice of the commercial community to be conceptually impossible': *Re Bank of Credit and Commerce International SA (No 8)* [1998] AC 214, HL, 228 *per* Lord Hoffmann.

[8] P Mather, 'The Determinants of Financial Covenants in Bank-Loan Contracts' [2004] *Journal of International Banking Law and Regulation* 33; JFS Day and PJ Taylor, 'Evidence on Practices of UK Bankers in Contracting for Medium-Term Debt' [1995] *Journal of International Banking Law* 394; JFS Day and PJ Taylor, 'Bankers' Perspectives on the Role of Covenants in Debt Contracts' [1996] Journal of International Banking Law 201–205; JFS Day and PJ Taylor, 'Loan Contracting by UK Corporate Borrowers' [1996] *Journal of International Banking Law* 318; JFS Day and PJ Taylor, 'Loan Documentation in the Market for UK Corporate Debt: Current Practice and Future Prospects' [1997] *Journal of International Banking Law* 7; RN Nash, JM Netter, and AB Poulsen, 'Determinants of Contractual Relations Between Shareholders and Bondholders: Investment Opportunities and Restrictive Covenants' (2003) 9 *Journal of Corporate Finance* 201.

[9] Mather (n 8 above) 36.

example of this type of lending arrangement,[10] or it may borrow a principal amount all at once or in agreed instalments. Interest will usually be charged on amounts borrowed and the company may also be required to pay commitment or negotiation fees in respect of lending facilities that have been made available. Interest rates may be fixed for the period of the loan or may be liable to be adjusted from time to time. An alternative to interest charges is for a company to borrow less than the stated principal amount of a loan on terms that oblige it to repay the full principal amount. In this case, the discount between the amount borrowed and the principal amount of the loan represents the return to the lender.[11]

The principal amount of a loan may be denominated in one currency or it may be divided into a number of portions, each of which is denominated in a different currency. Principal may be repayable on demand or may be lent to the company for a set term but with provision for early repayment and for termination by the lender upon the occurrence of specified events of default. The principal may be required to be repaid in one lump sum or the agreement may provide for repayment by instalments.

In addition to the core operative terms governing principal and interest, loan agreements commonly contain covenants by which the company undertakes to meet performance targets, to refrain from certain activities, and to provide the lender with information about its affairs. Covenants enable the lender to monitor the company while the debt is outstanding. Failure to comply with covenants will usually be an event of default that entitles the lender to terminate the loan. Other typical terms in loan agreements include conditions that must be satisfied before the company can obtain the money (or 'draw down' the funds, as this process is often referred to) and representations and warranties about the company and its affairs.

An individual bank or other lender may be unwilling to accept the whole of the risk involved in lending a very large sum of money to a company. In that event, provided the company is sufficiently creditworthy, it may still be able to obtain the required funds by entering into a syndicated loan agreement (secured or unsecured) with a number of financial institutions under which each participant in the syndicate contributes a part of the loan.[12] It is normally only the largest corporate borrowers that require syndicated loans. Sovereign states and other public authorities also enter into syndicated loans. In recent years the syndicated loan market (now increasingly known as the 'leveraged loan' market) has played a major role in providing the debt finance for leveraged buyout activity by private

---

[10] A more complex example is a revolving loan that enables the borrower to borrow, repay, and re-borrow up to a maximum amount. A revolving loan differs from an overdraft in that it is not current account financing (and is not repayable on demand as an overdraft normally is). An ordinary term loan may allow for early repayment but will not provide for re-borrowing.

[11] WL Megginson, *Corporate Finance Theory* (Addison-Wesley, 1997) 404–5.

[12] On syndicated loans generally, see PR Wood, *International Loans, Bonds, Guarantees, Legal Opinions* (Sweet & Maxwell, 2nd edn, 2007); R Cranston, *Principles of Banking Law* (OUP, 2nd edn, 2002) ch 2, V.

equity firms.[13] The emergence of sophisticated mechanisms for trading syndicated debt in the secondary market has facilitated this development.[14]

A company may also borrow from its directors or other insiders. This form of lending is most likely to be encountered in smaller or family-owned concerns where the directors and shareholders have a particularly strong personal interest in the company's affairs. Insider loans can give rise to particular points of note or concern. At one end of the spectrum, an insider loan may be made on much softer terms than would be available from a commercial lender—for example, the loan may be interest free or may be made on the basis that the lender is to be subordinated to some or all of the company's other creditors. The legal validity of contractual subordination of debts, which was once a matter of some uncertainty, is now clearly established.[15] At the other extreme, an insider may seek to exploit his position by requiring the company to accept exceptionally harsh or onerous terms, perhaps with a view to masking what is really an unlawful gift from capital by describing it as an 'interest charge'.[16]

Overdrafts

An overdraft is a form of debt financing provided through a customer's current account. An overdraft arises when a company draws on its current account to such an extent that a negative balance is produced. If the drawing that overdraws the account is met by the bank, the bank becomes the creditor of the company for the amount so overdrawn. An arrangement to overdraw up to a specified maximum amount would usually be agreed in advance between a company and its bank, and the company may be required to pay a commitment fee for this facility. There is no implied term in the banker–customer relationship that permits a customer to overdraw, with the consequence that, in the absence of agreement to the contrary, the bank is not bound to meet any drawing which is not covered

[13] U Axelson, T Jenkinson, PR Strömberg, and MS Weisbach, 'Leverage and Pricing in Buyouts: An Empirical Analysis', Swedish Institute for Financial Research Conference on The Economics of the Private Equity Market (August 2007) available at SSRN <http://ssrn.com/abstract=1027127>.

[14] S Drucker and M Puri, 'On Loan Sales, Loan Contracting, and Lending Relationships' (March 2007) available at SSRN <http://ssrn.com/abstract=920877>; Loan Market Association website <http://www.loan-market-assoc.com> (accessed November 2007). The LMA was established in December 1996 with the objective of fostering an environment that would facilitate the development of a secondary market for loans. It has supplied standard form documentation for secondary market trading activities.

[15] *Re SSSL Realisations (2002) Ltd* [2006] Ch 610, CA. At para 66 Chadwick LJ commented: 'It seems to me commercially important that, if group companies enter into subordination agreements of this nature with their creditors while solvent, they and the creditors should be held to the bargain when the event for which the agreement was intended to provide (insolvency) occurs'.

[16] See eg *Ridge Securities Ltd v IRC* [1964] 1 All ER 275.

R La Porta, F Lopez de Silanes, and G Zamarripa, 'Related Lending' (2003) 118(1) *Quarterly Journal of Economics* 231 reports that a study of bank lending to firms in Mexico found evidence to support the view that related lending is a manifestation of looting.

by funds in the account.[17] If a company makes an unauthorized drawing, this can be viewed conceptually as an offer by the company[18] and, if the bank meets the drawing, this constitutes an acceptance, thus forming a contract between the company and the bank in respect of the overdraft.[19] By honouring a cheque drawn on an overdrawn account, a bank is lending the sum in question to its customer and, as agent of the customer, paying that sum to the person in whose favour the cheque is drawn.[20]

Just as a bank must pay any sums standing to the credit of a current account to the company whenever it demands it,[21] an overdraft is normally repayable on demand.[22] Whatever its legal rights, as a matter of practice a bank would almost certainly exercise a degree of caution in demanding repayment of an overdraft in order to protect its commercial reputation:

... it is obvious that neither party would have it in contemplation that when the bank had granted the overdraft it would immediately, without notice, proceed to sue for the money; and the truth is that whether there were any legal obligation to abstain from so doing or not, it is obvious that, having regard to the course of business, if a bank which had agreed to give an overdraft were to act in such a fashion, the results to its business would be of the most serious nature.[23]

What is meant by 'on demand'? According to the English cases all that the bank is required to do is to give the company time to effect the mechanics of payment, such as by arranging for the transfer of funds from one account to another. The bank is not obliged to give the customer time to raise funds that it does not have at the time when the demand is made. In *Cripps (Pharmaceutical) Ltd v Wickenden*[24] the bank was held to be within its rights when it appointed a receiver to enforce its rights less than two hours after it had demanded repayment in circumstances

---

[17] *Cunliffe Brooks & Co v Blackburn Benefit Society* (1884) 9 App Cas 857, HL, 864 *per* Lord Blackburn; *Barclays Bank Ltd v WJ Simms Son & Cooke (Southern) Ltd* [1980] 1 QBD 699. An agreement to grant an overdraft may be inferred from a course of conduct: *Cumming v Shand* (1860) 5 H&N 95, 157 ER 1114.

[18] *Barclays Bank Ltd v WJ Simms Son & Cooke (Southern) Ltd* [1980] 1 QBD 699; *Cuthbert v Robarts Lubbock & Co* [1909] 2 Ch 226, CA, 233 *per* Cozens Hardy MR.

[19] *Barclays Bank Ltd v WJ Simms Son & Cooke (Southern) Ltd* [1980] 1 QBD 699.

[20] *Coutts & Co v Stock* [2000] 2 All ER 56.

[21] *Walker v Bradford Old Bank* (1884) 12 QBD 511, 516 *per* Smith J; *Joachimson v Swiss Banking Corp* [1921] 3 KB 110, CA.

[22] *Williams and Glyn's Bank v Barnes* [1981] Com LR 205, (1977–86) 10 Legal Decisions Affecting Bankers 220. The parties can agree otherwise but whether they have done so is a question of construction and it is not inconsistent for a bank to grant a facility that it is envisaged will endure for some time but with a term allowing it to call for repayment on demand: *Lloyds Bank plc v Lampert* [1999] BCC 507.

On the emergence in practice of committed one-year overdraft facilities see Competition Commission, 'The Supply of Banking Services by Clearing Banks to Small and Medium-sized Enterprises' (2002) para 3.92.

[23] *Rouse v Bradford Banking Co* [1894] AC 586, HL, 596 *per* Lord Herschell LC.

[24] [1973] 1 WLR 944.

where it was clear that the company did not have the money to pay. A delay of just one hour between the making of the demand and the sending in of the receivers has also been held to be justifiable.[25]

With regard to interest charges on an overdraft, it is usual for the interest to be calculated on the daily balance and then debited to the account on a periodic basis.[26] Once the interest has been debited to the account it is capitalized and thereafter interest is charged on an amount including the capitalized interest. The practice of charging compound interest on overdrafts is well established as a general banking usage, which will be implied into all contracts between banks and customers unless there is express provision to the contrary.[27] Banks can be expected usually to make express provision for compound interest charges and the practice of having the position clearly spelt out has received judicial endorsement: '[Banks] should make express provisions for compound interest in their contracts. Since the repeal of the Usury Acts there has been nothing to stop them.'[28]

When money is paid into a bank account that is overdrawn, unless the parties have reached a contrary agreement, it is treated as discharging the earlier debit items. Applying this rule to the following facts:

• 1 January, company's current account has a debit balance of £200,000
• 15 January, the company draws on the overdraft facility for a further £150,000
• 30 January, £250,000 is paid into the account

the position is that, first, the whole of the £200,000 that was outstanding on 1 January is to be regarded as having been repaid and, secondly, £50,000 of the amount borrowed on 15 January is also to be treated as having been repaid; the balance of the amount borrowed on 15 January remains outstanding. This rule of appropriation of payments was established in *Devaynes v Noble, Clayton's Case*[29] and it is commonly referred to as the rule in *Clayton's Case*. It can be relevant where, for example, a bank takes security for an existing overdrawn account and the company then continues to draw on, and make payments into, that account because under the insolvency legislation a security can be held to be invalid if it is given in respect of moneys previously advanced to the borrower. Unless displaced by agreement between the parties, the rule in *Clayton's Case* will determine

---

[25] *Bank of Baroda v Panessar* [1986] 3 All ER 751, noted JD Kay, ' "On Demand" Liabilities' [1986] *Journal of International Banking Law* 241 where reference is made to a number of Commonwealth cases which appear to be more generous to the borrower by allowing it a reasonable time to repay; *Sheppard & Cooper Ltd v TSB Bank plc* [1996] 2 All ER 654.

[26] *Reddie v Williamson* (1863) 1 Macph 228; *Parr's Banking Co Ltd v Yates* [1898] 2 QB 460, CA; *Yourell v Hibernian Bank Ltd* [1918] AC 372, HL, 385 *per* Lord Atkinson; *IRC v Holder* [1931] 2 KB 81, CA, 96 *per* Lord Hanworth MR and 98 *per* Romer LJ; *Paton v IRC* [1938] AC 341, HL.

[27] *National Bank of Greece SA v Pinios Shipping Co (No 1)* [1990] 1 AC 637, CA and HL.

[28] ibid CA and HL 659 *per* Lloyd LJ. Although the Court of Appeal's decision was reversed by the House of Lords, this comment is unaffected.

[29] (1816) 1 Mer 572, 35 ER 781.

whether the balance outstanding on the account at the time when the insolvency legislation falls to be applied represents new money advanced after the security was granted, in which case the security will be valid, or old money which had been lent to the company before the security was created, in which case the security may be invalid.[30]

Studies of different segments of the corporate sector establish that overdraft facilities are common but that active usage is less prevalent and that sometimes they are put in place only as a contingency. A Bank of England survey of SQCs, for instance, found that only 24 per cent of the firms with overdraft facilities were using at least half of them and some 42 per cent claimed to be making no use of them.[31] Among SMEs, in recent years there has been a shift away from overdraft financing in favour of term loans.[32] Alternative forms of asset finance, including invoice financing, leasing and hire purchase, and asset-based lending (which involve financiers taking ownership of assets and selling them to firms on credit terms) have also grown in significance.[33] British banks are sometimes criticized for favouring overdraft financing at the expense of longer-term, more stable financial support for the corporate sector, especially SMEs. However, it is debatable how far the incidence of overdraft financing reflects the preferences of those who run businesses, who may be attracted to overdraft financing because it is simple, flexible, and does not require them to surrender equity, and how far it is a function of a limited range of financing options that are offered by banks to smaller businesses and a preference among banks for on-demand financing.[34]

Term loans

Term loans are, as the name implies, loans for a specified period. A distinction is often drawn in practice between short-term loans (used to mean loans of up to one year), medium-term loans (between one and five years), and long-term loans (between five and ten years, or perhaps even longer).[35]

---

[30] See Insolvency Act 1986, s 245 and the application of the rule in *Clayton's Case* in *Re Yeovil Glove Co Ltd* [1965] Ch 148, CA.

[31] P Brierley and M Young, 'The Financing of Smaller Quoted Companies: a Survey' (2004) *Bank of England Quarterly Bulletin* 160, 163. See also A Kearns and J Young, Provision of Finance to Smaller Quoted Companies: Some Evidence from Survey Responses and Liaison Meetings' (2002) *Bank of England Quarterly Bulletin* 26.

[32] *Competition in UK Banking: A Report to the Chancellor of the Exchequer* (Cruickshank Report, 2000) para 5.26, available via <http://www.hm-treasury.gov.uk/documents/financial_services/banking/bankreview/fin_bank_reviewfinal.cfm> (accessed November 2007).

[33] A Hewitt, 'Asset Finance' (2003) *Bank of England Quarterly Bulletin* 207.

[34] J Charkham, *Keeping Good Company* (OUP, 1995) 297–8; A Hughes, 'The "Problems" of Finance for Smaller Businesses' in N Dimsdale and M Prevezer (eds), *Capital Markets and Corporate Governance* (Clarendon Press, 1994) 209; A Hughes, 'Finance for SMEs: A UK Perspective' (1997) 9 *Small Business Economics* 151.

[35] Terminological practice differs: eg P Brierley and M Young, 'The Financing of Smaller Quoted Companies: a Survey' (2004) *Bank of England Quarterly Bulletin* 160, 163 use 'short term' to mean

Principal

The core operative term of a term loan agreement is the one specifying the principal amount of the loan; the currency, or currencies, in which it is denominated; and the way in which it is to be made available to the borrower. The full amount of the loan may be made available to the borrower at one time or the agreement may provide for the borrower to be entitled to draw down successive tranches of the loan at, or by, specified times. The period during which the borrower is entitled to draw down (the 'availability period') may be limited so that, at the end of the period, the lender is no longer obliged to lend and any undrawn portion of the loan is no longer available to the borrower. With regard to repayment, the agreement may provide for repayment of the whole loan at one time (commonly known as bullet repayment) or for repayment in instalments over a period of time (sometimes described as amortized repayment). Where there is an instalment repayment obligation with a final instalment that is larger than earlier ones, this is sometimes described as a 'balloon' repayment. An instalment repayment obligation is a mechanism that can allow a lender to detect early signs of a borrower's financial difficulties.[36] The borrower may be granted an option to repay early and in any well-drafted agreement the lender will be entitled to demand early repayment in the event of the occurrence of any one of a number of specified events of default. Can the lender insert a term to the effect that the principal amount is to be repayable on demand? It has been held that a provision for on-demand repayment is not incompatible with the nature of a facility which it is envisaged by the lender and borrower will last for some time.[37] Where the lender is legally committed to a loan of a certain term (as opposed to the duration being merely a matter of looser expectations between the parties) it is a question of construction whether a provision for repayment on demand is repugnant to the lending agreement as a whole.[38] The alternative, and more conventional, mechanism in term loans for the protection of lenders' interests is through events of default, whose occurrence would trigger rights to accelerate repayment.

If a lender refuses to lend in breach of contract, the borrowing company is entitled to damages. If the company can secure broadly the same lending terms from another lender, the damages may be little more than nominal[39] but if, say, the first lender had agreed to an exceptionally low rate of interest, the damages could

---

less than 5 years by original maturity, 'medium term' to mean 6 to 10 years by original maturity and 'long term' to mean in excess of 10 years.

[36] WL Megginson, *Corporate Finance Theory* (Addison-Wesley, 1997) 405.

[37] *Lloyd's Bank plc v Lampert* [1999] BCC 507.

[38] *Williams & Glyn's Bank Ltd v Barnes* [1981] Com LR 205; *Titford Property Co Ltd v Cannon Street Acceptances Ltd* (unreported, 25 May 1975).

[39] The costs of negotiating a substitute loan may be recoverable: *Prehn v Royal Bank of Liverpool* (1870) LR 5 Exch 92.

be more substantial. In *South African Territories v Wallington*[40] the House of Lords refused to grant specific performance of a contract to lend money to a company. This ruling is consistent with the general rule that specific performance will not be ordered where damages are an adequate remedy,[41] but with this decision must now also be read section 740 of the Companies Act 2006. This provision, which was first introduced into the companies legislation after the *Wallington* decision,[42] provides that a contract with a company to take up and pay for debentures of a company may be enforced by an order for specific performance. The term 'debenture' has no hard and fast meaning,[43] although a commonly cited description is that it encompasses any document which creates or acknowledges a debt.[44] It is debatable whether a loan agreement can be said to create or acknowledge a debt because in normal circumstances the debt is not actually created until after the agreement is concluded and the money is advanced. Another view is that an instrument containing a promise to pay can be a debenture.[45] This description would catch a loan agreement since it contains a promise by the borrower to repay the principal and also, usually, a promise to pay interest at specified intervals. However, it is suggested that for the purposes of section 740 of the Companies Act 2006, the term 'debenture' should be more narrowly interpreted and should be limited to debt securities issued directly to investors and which can be traded by them.[46] This interpretation is based on the reference in that section to

[40] [1898] AC 309, HL. Also *Western Wagon and Property Co v West* [1892] 1 Ch 271, 275 *per* Chitty J; *Rogers v Challis* (1859) 27 Beav 175, 54 ER 68; *Sichel v Mosenthal* (1862) 30 Beav 371, 54 ER 932.

[41] G Jones and W Goodhart, *Specific Performance* (Butterworths, 2nd edn, 1996) 154–61 where the general principle is described as 'arguably too harsh' (at 155) and various recognized exceptions are discussed. See also ICF Spry, *Equitable Remedies* (LBC Information Services, 6th edn, 2001) ch 3; *Loan Investment Corporation of Australasia v Bonner* [1970] NZLR 724, PC, 741–2 *per* Sir Garwick Berwick (dissenting) where the possibility of an order for specific performance of an obligation to lend being granted in exceptional circumstances was envisaged.

[42] As Companies Act 1907, s 16.

[43] Companies Act 2006, s 738 lists various instruments which are debentures but does not contain an exhaustive definition of the term. This section does make clear that the term 'debenture' is not confined to secured loans. The courts have frequently acknowledged the absence of a precise definition: see eg *British India Steam Navigation Co v Commissioners of Inland Revenue* [1881] 7 QBD 165; *Knightsbridge Estates Trust Ltd v Byrne* [1940] AC 613 HL, 621 *per* Viscount Maugham; *NV Slavenburg's Bank v Intercontinental Natural Resources Ltd* [1980] 1 All ER 955, 976. The absence of a precise definition has given rise to few practical problems: *Re SH & Co (Realisations) 1990 Ltd* [1993] BCC 60, 67 quoting LBC Gower, *Principles of Modern Company Law* (Sweet & Maxwell, 5th edn, 1992) 379.

[44] *Levy v Abercorris Slate and Slab Co* (1887) 37 Ch D 260. See also *Edmonds v Blaina Furnaces Co* (1887) 36 Ch D 215; *Lemon v Austin Friars Investment Trust Ltd* [1926] 1 Ch 1, CA; *Knightsbridge Estates Trust v Byrne* [1940] AC 613, HL; *R v Findlater* [1939] 1 KB 594, CCA.

[45] *British India Steam Navigation Co v Commissioners of Inland Revenue* [1881] 7 QBD 165, 173 *per* Lindley J. The Court was required to determine whether the instrument was a debenture or a promissory note for stamping purposes.

[46] Tradability by itself does not provide the key to distinguishing between what is and is not within the scope of the term 'debenture' for the purposes of Companies Act 2006, s 740 since there are secondary markets in lenders' participations in loan agreements. On the secondary market in loan participations: J Barratt, 'Distressed Debt—The Sale of Loan Assets' [1998] *Journal of*

taking up and paying for debentures. Those words are apt to describe an investor's decision to acquire debt securities issued to the market but they do not easily fit a promise in a loan agreement to lend money. Also the context of the Part of the Companies Act 2006 in which section 740 appears suggests that it is concerned only with debt securities issued to investors and not with loan agreements negotiated between companies and banks or other lenders.[47]

It is unlikely that a borrower would not draw down the loan having gone to the trouble of arranging it. Should this occur, it will be a matter of construction to determine whether the borrower was obliged to draw down or had simply acquired an option to do so. Even if the borrower is in breach of contract, in accordance with the general principle that specific performance of contracts to lend money will not be ordered, the lender's remedy will lie only in damages and these are likely to be minimal.[48]

In the absence of any provision to the contrary, it is unclear whether a borrower can make early repayments of borrowed money[49] but express provisions regarding early repayment are commonly included. These provisions typically require the borrower to give notice of an intended early repayment and to make the repayment on a specified date, such as the last day of an interest period. Restrictions on early repayment are usually closely linked to the lender's own financing commitments. It is usual to provide that any amount pre-paid is to be applied to the repayment instalments in inverse order to their maturity. This has the effect of shortening the life of the loan.

Interest

In the absence of express agreement to the contrary or some course of dealing or custom to such effect, interest is not payable on a bank loan.[50] This point is of limited practical significance since loan agreements almost invariably make express provision for interest charges. Since the Usury Laws Repeal Act 1954, there is no statutory control with regard to interest rates charged to companies. The rate of interest may be fixed for the term of the loan or may be variable (or 'floating') over the life of the loan. It is theoretically possible to provide for interest to be variable

---

International Banking Law 50; S Drucker and M Puri, 'On Loan Sales, Loan Contracting, and Lending Relationships' (March 2007) available at SSRN <http://ssrn.com/abstract=920877>; Loan Market Association website <http://www.loan-market-assoc.com> (accessed November 2007).

[47] Contrast A Berg, 'Syndicated Lending and the FSA' (1991) 10(1) *International Financial Law Review* 27.

[48] *Rogers v Challis* (1859) 27 Beav 175, 54 ER 68.

[49] The Australian courts have held that a borrower does not have the right to repay early unless this is provided for expressly: *Hyde Management Services (Pty) Ltd v FAI Insurances* (1979–80) 144 CLR 541, H Ct of Aust. It has also been held in England that an issuer of debt securities cannot redeem them early unless the terms of issue provide for this: *Hooper v Western Counties and South Wales Telephone Co Ltd* (1892) 68 LT 78.

[50] *Chatham & Dover Rly v South East Rly* [1893] AC 429, HL.

entirely at the discretion of the lender, but borrowers with sufficient negotiating strength would be likely to resist agreeing to this degree of uncertainty. Floating-rate loan agreements commonly provide for the interest rate to be adjusted at specified intervals by reference to a formula which is intended to maintain the lender's return on the loan.

The money that a bank lends to its borrowing customers may be its own money (share capital and reserves) or it may be money which it has borrowed either from depositors (the relationship between banks and depositing customers being one of debtor and creditor) or from other lenders. Banks can borrow in the inter-bank market by taking in short-term deposits. Such deposits are made for short specific periods, typically three or six months and they bear interest at a fixed rate. LIBOR, the London Inter-Bank Offered Rate, denotes the rate at which such deposits are available from time to time in the London markets.[51] This is just one of the interest bases that may be used for calculating floating interest rates in loan agreements but it suffices for the purposes of illustration. Where a bank takes deposits in the inter-bank market and then makes a term loan to a borrower, there is an obvious mismatch between the bank's obligation to repay the deposit, in three or six months' time, and its rights to claim repayment in what may be many years' time: it has borrowed short to lend long. One of the ways of managing the consequences of this mismatch is for the bank to adjust the rate of interest that the borrower is required to pay to reflect LIBOR on each occasion when it is required to refinance in the inter-bank market. To achieve this, the agreement should provide for the borrower to pay interest at a rate equivalent to LIBOR from time to time plus an additional margin which is set at the outset and which is the bank's return on the transaction. This structure enables the bank to pass its funding costs through to the borrower.

There are various ways in which a lender may seek to protect its interests against the possibility of a borrower company failing to make an interest payment when it is due. Failure to pay any sum, representing either interest or principal, which is due and payable is the first event of default in a typical loan agreement. Such an agreement will provide that, upon the occurrence of an event of default, the lender is entitled to terminate the agreement; to demand repayment of principal, interest, and any other sums payable pursuant to the agreement; and to cancel any facilities that remain outstanding. The occurrence of an event of default thus does not, in the usual case, terminate the agreement automatically but it gives the

---

[51] The British Bankers Association (BBA) publishes a daily LIBOR rate (for details of how it is calculated and the publication process see <http://www.bba.org.uk/bba/jsp/polopoly.jsp?d=225&a=1416> (accessed November 2007)). According to the BBA, BBA LIBOR is the most widely used 'benchmark' or reference rate for short-term interest rates. It is, claims the BBA, the primary benchmark for short-term interest rates globally. It is used as the basis for settlement of interest rate contracts on many of the world's major futures and options exchanges (including LIFFE, Deutsche Term Börse, Chicago Mercantile Exchange, Chicago Board of Trade, SIMEX, and TIFFE) as well as most over the counter (OTC) and lending transactions.

lender an option to do so.[52] The courts have a jurisdiction to hold unenforceable a contractual term that amounts to a penalty clause intended to punish the party in breach. However, it is clear that a contractual provision that entitles the lender to terminate the agreement if the borrower fails to make an interest payment when due is not a penalty clause.[53]

The rules on penalty clauses also require examination in relation to provisions that seek to impose a higher rate of interest if the borrower defaults on making a payment when due. A penalty clause is to be distinguished from a provision for liquidated damages, which is valid. Into which category a particular agreement falls is a question of construction and the label attached by the parties is not conclusive.[54] In the leading case on penalties it was said that one of the indicia of a penalty was where the breach consisted only in not paying a sum of money and the sum stipulated was greater than the sum that ought to have been paid.[55] Concern that this could catch a provision for default interest led to the development of structures that achieved the same economic effect as default interest but adopted a different legal form. Such arrangements were held to be legally effective in a number of cases. Thus it was held that a provision specifying a high rate of interest and providing for it to be reduced to a lower rate in the event of punctual payment was effective even though there is no difference in substance between this and a default interest clause.[56] Another rather technical and fine distinction was upheld in *General Credit and Discount Co v Glegg*.[57] In this case the terms of an interest-bearing loan provided for repayment by instalments. If default was made in the payment of any instalment at the due date there was also to be paid a 'commission' of 1 per cent upon what ought to have been paid for every month or part of a month from the due date to the date of payment of such instalment. This arrangement was held to be a distinct, separate, substantive contract to pay something in the event of default and not an agreement in the nature of a penalty. The Court gave effect to the agreement as drafted and did not treat the commission simply as a device intended to allow the lender to increase the rate of interest on default.

A robust review of the effect of default interest clauses under English law finally took place in *Lordsvale Finance plc v Bank of Zambia*.[58] The Court held that a provision for default interest was not an invalid penalty where it operated only with

---

[52] This is in accordance with established general contractual principles: *Decro-Wall International SA v Practitioners in Marketing Ltd* [1971] 1 WLR 361, CA; *Photo Production Ltd v Securicor Transport Ltd* [1980] AC 827, HL.

[53] *Keene v Biscoe* (1878) 8 Ch D 201; *Wallingford v Mutual Society* (1880) 5 App Case 685, HL; *Oresundsvarvet Aktiebolag v Marcos Diamantis Lemos, The Angelic Star* [1988] 1 Lloyd's Rep 122, CA.

[54] *Dunlop Pneumatic Tyre Co Ltd v New Garage and Motor Co Ltd* [1915] AC 79, HL.

[55] ibid 87 *per* Lord Dunedin.

[56] *Wallingford v Mutual Society* (1880) 5 App Cas 685, HL, 702 *per* Lord Hatherley; *Herbert v Salisbury and Yeovil Rly Co* (1866) 2 LR Eq 221, 224 *per* Lord Romilly MR.

[57] (1883) 22 Ch D 549.

[58] [1996] QB 752.

effect from the event of default, provided that the increase in the interest rate was no more than sufficient to compensate the lender for its additional funding costs and the increased credit risk involved in lending to a defaulting borrower. Apparently inconsistent older cases[59] were distinguished on the grounds that they concerned default interest clauses that operated retrospectively as well as prospectively from the date of default. The *Lordsvale* decision clarifies English law and brings it into line with that in the US, Canada, and Australia.[60] The *Lordsvale* decision is part of a trend in the modern authorities, which is to the effect that the courts will not lightly hold a clause in a commercial document involving sophisticated parties who can be expected to look after themselves to be a penalty.[61] Even though a stipulated amount exceeds what would otherwise be payable under a contract, it will not be penal so long as its contractual purpose is compensatory rather than deterrent.[62]

Conditions precedent

A loan agreement may require the borrower to satisfy various conditions before it can draw down the funds. For example, the company may be required to supply the lender with copies of its constitutional documents and relevant board resolutions to enable the lender to check that the loan is duly authorized. This practice may not now be strictly necessary where the borrower is incorporated under the British companies legislation, given that lenders are largely protected against the lack of authorization by the provisions of the companies legislation[63] that operate in conjunction with established agency principles and with the rule of company law known as the internal management rule, which protects outsiders against internal irregularities (for example the lack of a quorum at relevant board meetings) unless they are put on notice to the contrary.[64] However, there is still something to be said for maintaining a policy of checking in advance that the loan is duly authorized because of the greater certainty that this affords;

---

[59] *Holles v Vyse* (1693) 2 Vern 289, 23 ER 787; *Hunter v Seton* (1802) 7 Ves 265, 32 ER 108. In *Herbert v Salisbury and Yeovil Rly Co* (1866) 2 LR Eq 221, 224 Lord Romilly MR said: 'but if the mortgage interest is at 4 per cent, and there is an agreement that if it is not paid punctually 5 or 6 per cent interest shall be paid, that is in the nature of a penalty which this Court will relieve against'.

[60] *Lordsvale Finance plc v Bank of Zambia* [1996] QB 752, 765–7.

[61] *Philips Hong Kong v A-G of Hong Kong* (1993) 61 BLR 49; *United International Pictures v Cine Bes Filmcilik VE Yapimcilik* [2004 1 CLC 491, CA; *Murray v Leisureplay plc* [2005] IRLR 946, CA.

[62] *Lordsvale Finance plc v Bank of Zambia* [1996] QB 752, 762, a passage cited with approval in *United International Pictures v Cine Bes Filmcilik VE Yapimcilik* [2004] 1 CLC 401 CA, para 13 *per* Mance LJ and in *Murray v Leisureplay plc* [2005] IRLR 946, CA, para 13 *per* Arden LJ, para 106 *per* Clarke LJ, and para 100 *per* Buxton LJ. See also *Euro London Appointments Ltd v Claessens International Ltd* [2006] 2 Lloyd's Rep 436, CA.

[63] Companies Act 2006, ss 39–40.

[64] *Royal British Bank v Turquand* (1865) 6 E&B 327, 119 ER 327; *Mahoney v East Holyford Mining Co* (1875) LR 7 HL 869.

whilst the statutory protections given to persons who deal with companies are now very extensive, there would be a risk that a borrower or its liquidator (insolvency being a particular situation in which a borrower may be especially keen to escape from its obligations) might seek to challenge their application in a particular case, thereby delaying repayment. Another common condition precedent is for the borrower to be required to confirm that no events of default have occurred and that the representations and warranties are true and accurate.

The lender is only obliged to make the funds available when the borrower has fulfilled the specified conditions precedent. Can the lender withdraw completely from the agreement before the borrower has had an opportunity to satisfy those requirements? This will depend on the construction of the agreement.[65] The cases indicate that the effect of including conditions precedent in an agreement can, depending on the drafting, include the following: (a) the agreement is not fully binding until the conditions are fulfilled and until then either party can withdraw with impunity;[66] (b) the main agreement is not binding but, so long as the events constituting the conditions precedent can still occur, one (or both) of the parties cannot withdraw;[67] (c) the main agreement is not binding but neither party must do anything to prevent the occurrence of the events[68] or one of the parties undertakes to make reasonable endeavours to bring about the events.[69]

Representations and warranties

Loan agreements commonly contain representation and warranties covering such matters as:

(1) the capacity of the company and the authority of its directors and officers to enter into the loan agreement;
(2) compliance with applicable laws and regulations;
(3) compliance with other contractual obligations of the company—the lender will be concerned to ensure that this loan will not, for example, trigger default under another loan agreement in which the company has covenanted to limit the amount of its borrowings;
(4) the accuracy of the information about the borrower that was supplied to the lender during the course of the negotiations, including confirmation that no facts or circumstances have been omitted so as to render the information that was supplied misleading;

---

[65] *Total Gas Marketing Ltd v Arco British Ltd* [1998] 2 Lloyd's Rep 209, HL; R Cranston, *Principles of Banking Law* (OUP, 2nd edn, 2002) 312–13.
[66] *Pym v Campbell* (1856) 6 E&B 370, 119 ER 903.
[67] *Smith v Butler* [1900] 1 QB 694, CA.
[68] *Mackay v Dick* (1881) 6 App Cas 251, HL.
[69] *Hargreaves Transport Ltd v Lynch* [1969] 1 WLR 215, CA.

(5) the financial position of the borrower—representations and warranties on this matter would commonly take the form of a statement from the borrower to the effect that its last audited accounts represent a true and fair view of its financial position and that there has been no material adverse change since they were prepared;

(6) claims against the borrower, ie whether any litigation is pending or threatened which might have a material adverse effect on the borrower or on its ability to perform its obligations under the loan agreement;

(7) whether any event of default has occurred;

(8) the existing security arrangements into which the borrower has entered, including hire purchase agreements, conditional sales, factoring agreements and guarantees.

If the borrower is a holding company, representations and warranties may also relate to the other companies in its group.

Representations and warranties perform an investigative function.[70] In the negotiations leading up to the signing of the loan agreement the borrower will need to disclose any information that is inconsistent with the representations and warranties that are to be included in the agreement or risk being held liable thereafter for breach. This helps to extend the lender's knowledge and understanding of the borrowing entity. The representations and warranties that are finally agreed seek to encapsulate the factual circumstances in reliance on which the lender makes its decision to lend. As such, the truth of the matters contained in the representations and warranties is likely to remain important to a lender throughout the life of a loan and for this reason it may require the borrower to repeat the representations and warranties at specified intervals. A situation in which a lender would be likely to attach particular importance to the repetition of representations and warranties is where the loan is to be available to the borrower in instalments: the lender may require the borrower to repeat the representations and warranties before each drawing is made. Repetition can be required at more frequent intervals, for example at the beginning of each interest period. The way in which repetition will normally be effected is by a provision in the loan agreement to the effect that there is deemed repetition at the specified intervals. Representations and warranties that are required to be repeated at specified intervals are sometimes described as 'evergreen'.

Under the general law relating to liability for statements, the term 'representation' is used to denote a statement of fact that induces an innocent party to enter into a contract and which, if it is later discovered to have been untrue, gives the innocent party a remedy for misrepresentation. A 'warranty' is a contractual statement that, if untrue, allows the innocent party to sue for breach of contract;

---

[70] PR Wood, *International Loans, Bonds, Guarantees, Legal Opinions* (Sweet & Maxwell, 2nd edn, 2007) ch 4.

generally,[71] 'warranty' is used in contradistinction to 'condition' to describe a term that, if breached, allows for a claim for damages but does not entitle the innocent party to terminate the agreement. The need for detailed analysis of these technicalities is avoided in well-drafted loan agreements which stipulate expressly the consequences of making a representation or warranty which is incorrect or, allowing some leeway to the borrower, which is incorrect in any material respect. If the making of an inaccurate representation or warranty constitutes an event of default, this will entitle the lender to call for repayment of the whole loan at once and to sue in debt for the amount due under the agreement if the borrower refuses to pay.

Covenants

The function of the covenants in a loan agreement is to seek to restrict the borrower in the conduct of its business and thus to give the lender some control over the way in which that business is managed. They aim to ensure that the borrower's credit rating does not decline whilst the loan is outstanding. Covenants divide, broadly, into things that the borrower promises to do (positive covenants) and things that it promises to refrain from doing (negative covenants).[72] The underlying aim is to ensure that the borrower remains able to fulfil its obligations under the loan and does not engage in conduct that would prejudice that ability. The inclusion of a range of financial covenants is a common feature of lending in the UK and Ireland.[73] Continental European lending practices have been less dependent on financial covenants historically but recent reviews indicate a trend towards greater use.[74] This occurrence is attributed to market integration and globalization pressures that are moving business practices towards Anglo-American models.[75]

Covenants commonly found in loan agreements include:

---

[71] The term 'warranty' can also be used to describe an agreement which is collateral to another contract between the same parties. Breach of a collateral warranty may lead to an action for damages or may be a ground on which the court refuses specific performance of the main contract. See generally KW Wedderburn, 'Collateral Contracts' [1959] CLJ 58.

[72] WLMegginson, *Corporate Finance Theory* (Addison-Wesley, 1997) 407. WW Bratton, 'Bond Covenants and Creditor Protection: Economics and Law, Theory and Practice, Substance and Process' (2006) 7 *European Business Organization Law Review* 39.

[73] J Day, P Ormrod, and P Taylor, 'Implications for Lending Decisions and Debt Contracting of the Adoption of International Financial Reporting Standards' [2004] *Journal of International Banking Law and Regulation* 475.

[74] ibid. Historically, German banks have tended to rely on contractual provisions giving them the right to ask for further security/collateral or to accelerate the maturity of a loan agreement if the financial condition of the debtor's business worsens substantially. It is consistent with British evidence to suggest that lenders are more relaxed about the degree of covenant protection they look for when their lending is secured: P Brierley and M Young, 'The Financing of Smaller Quoted Companies: a Survey' (2004) *Bank of England Quarterly Bulletin* 160.

[75] Day, Ormrod, and Taylor (n 73 above) 475.

(1) *Provision of information.* The borrower must supply the lender with copies of its annual audited accounts and interim financial statements (including consolidated accounts where relevant), any communications sent to the borrower's shareholders, and any other information that the lender reasonably requires.

(2) *Events of default.* The borrower must notify the lender of the occurrence of an event of default or of any other event which, with the giving of notice or passage of time, would constitute an event of default.

(3) *Working capital.* The borrower must ensure that its current assets exceed its current liabilities (or, where relevant, group assets and liabilities) by a specified multiple and that the ratio of current assets to current liabilities does not fall below a specified minimum.

(4) *Tangible net worth.* The borrower must ensure that its (or, where relevant, its group's) paid up share capital and reserves exceed a specified figure and that the ratio between total liabilities and total net worth (consolidated where appropriate) does not fall below a specified minimum.

(5) *Distributions.* The borrower must ensure that dividends and other distributions to shareholders do not exceed a specified percentage of the company's net profits.

(6) *Disposal of assets or change of business.* The borrower must not dispose of any substantial part of its undertaking or, except in the ordinary course of business, assets unless it has the lender's consent; similarly it must not, without the lender's consent, change the scope or nature of its business in a way that would have a material adverse effect on its business, assets, or financial condition; if the borrower is a holding company, it may be required to undertake to procure, so far as it is able to do so,[76] that other companies within its group also abide by this covenant but the covenant may be qualified so as to permit some intra-group transfers of assets.

(7) *Creation of security.* The borrower must not create any further security over the whole or any part of its undertaking or assets without the consent of the lender (and, where relevant, the borrower may be required to undertake to procure, so far as it can do so, that other companies in its group will also abide by this covenant); the covenant may extend to increasing the amount secured by existing securities, entering into hire purchase, conditional sales, factoring and similar agreements, and to the giving of guarantees.

The covenants that are actually included in a particular financing arrangement will depend on a number of factors including the negotiating strength of the borrowing company, the amounts involved (a lender which is advancing a relatively small amount may attach loss importance to covenants than a lender which is

---

[76] The extent of parent company control over the conduct of its subsidiaries' affairs and the dangers involved in having too much control (ie potential *de facto* or shadow directorship liability) are considered in ch 2 above.

taking a large exposure), the rate of interest (a high interest rate may compensate the lender for fewer covenants), the intended duration of the loan, whether it is to be secured or unsecured, and whether it is a bank loan or an issue of securities.[77] As noted earlier in this chapter, the process of agreeing the terms of a loan can be very contentious and it is typically the covenants that are the most heavily negotiated part of the documentation.[78] There are dangers (for the lender as well as the borrower) in having very restrictive covenants, as these could damage a borrowing company's potential for economic growth by preventing it from pursuing worthwhile investment and financing opportunities; in an extreme case, onerous covenants could even hinder efforts to rescue a borrowing company that is in serious financial difficulties.[79] Under the costly contracting hypothesis developed by Smith and Warner, companies will search for an optimal financing structure by comparing the benefits of affording control to lenders, via covenants, against the reduction of flexibility for the borrowing company so as to arrive at a value-maximizing set of borrowing terms.[80] Studies support the proposition that there is a trade-off between the costs imposed on borrowers when covenants are imposed and the benefits of restrictive covenants that reduce the scope for controllers of companies to behave opportunistically at creditors' expense.[81] There is evidence that the price impact of including covenants restricting investments and distributions can be economically significant.[82]

The potential problems that could result from very tight covenants arise most sharply in the context of bond issues because if bond covenants prove to be too restrictive, the process of obtaining a relaxation may be particularly cumbersome, time-consuming, and expensive, as it may require the convening of a special meeting of the holders of the securities for that purpose. It is easy to see why the process of renegotiating a loan agreement involving just a small number of parties is likely to be much more straightforward. Concern about potential

[77] WW Bratton, 'Bond Covenants and Creditor Protection: Economics and Law, Theory and Practice, Substance and Process' (2006) 7 *European Business Organization Law Review* 39 looks at US experience in using contractual covenant protection for creditors.

[78] See also RJ Lister, 'Debenture Covenants and Corporate Value' (1985) 6 *Company Lawyer* 209.

[79] PR Wood, *International Loans, Bonds, Guarantees, Legal Opinions* (Sweet & Maxwell, 2nd edn, 2007) ch 5; JJ Day and P Taylor, 'Evidence on the Practice of UK Bankers in Contracting for Medium-Term Debt' [1995] *Journal of International Banking Law* 394; J Day and P Taylor, 'Bankers' Perspectives on the Role of Covenants in Debt Contracts' [1996] *Journal of International Banking Law* 201. Wider considerations arising from market and economic conditions may also over time cause lenders to vary their perception of the importance of particular covenants: WW Bratton, 'Corporate Debt Relationships: Legal Theory in a Time of Restructuring' [1989] *Duke Law Journal* 135.

[80] CW Smith and JB Warner, 'On Financial Contracting: An Analysis of Bond Covenants' (1979) 7 *Journal of Financial Economics* 117.

[81] Recent examples are: S Chava, P Kumar, and A Warga, 'Managerial Moral Hazard and Bond Covenants' (26 May 2007) available at SSRN <http://ssrn.com/abstract=989342>; MH Bradley and MR Roberts, 'The Structure and Pricing of Corporate Debt Covenants' (13 May 2004) available at SSRN <http://ssrn.com/abstract=466240>.

[82] ibid.

future renegotiation difficulties is a factor that helps to explain why covenants in publicly issued bonds tend to be lighter than in privately negotiated debt financing arrangements[83] and to have more of a predictable, standardized character.[84] Bond issue covenants are considered further in chapter 15 below.

A boom in leveraged buyout activity in the 2000s led to the emergence of 'covenant lite' loan deals in which borrowers were not required to give significant covenants to maintain financial ratios and which had other borrower-friendly features such as clauses to the effect that a breach of covenant would not constitute an event of default unless it was repeated. This trend reached a high-water mark in the summer of 2007 but thereafter changing market conditions (commonly referred to as a 'credit crunch') led to indications that the tide was turning away from loan financing on bond-like covenant lite terms.[85]

Reporting covenants

Reporting covenants that require the borrower to supply the lender with copies of accounts and other information are important to the lender because they facilitate the task of monitoring the company's affairs on an ongoing basis. Information covenants supplement the disclosure of financial information and audit requirements of the companies legislation and securities regulation in that they are likely to be more extensive than those requirements and may require information to be updated more regularly or more promptly. It is clearly vital for a lender to have early notice of the occurrence of an event of default so that it can consider its position and it is not unreasonable to require the borrower to notify the lender when it is in default. A requirement to notify the lender of impending events of default may create some uncertainty.

Financial covenants

Financial covenants seek to ensure that the borrower's solvency will be maintained and that the borrower will not become too heavily dependent on debt finance: the thinking is that it will be able to pay its debts as they fall due (cashflow solvency) because its current assets comfortably exceed its current liabilities (the working capital covenant) and it will also be solvent in a balance sheet sense because its total assets easily exceed its total liabilities (the tangible net worth covenant). The effect of financial covenants may be to oblige a company to seek new equity capital for a new venture that it wants to pursue. The lender can argue that

[83] eg M Kahan and D Yermack, 'Investment Opportunities and the Design of Debt Securities' (1998) 14 *Journal of Law, Economics and Organization* 136 is a study finding that that high-growth companies tended to prefer conversion rights to covenants in their public market bond issues.

[84] I Ramsay and BK Sidhu, 'Accounting and Non-accounting Based Information Market for Debt: Evidence from Australian Private Debt Contracts' (1998) 38 *Accounting and Finance* 197.

[85] M Hitching and D O'Brien. 'Leveraged Lending Terms: a Less Brave New World?' (2007) 18(10) *Practical Law for Companies* 9.

this is reasonable on the grounds that, if the venture were to be financed by additional borrowed funds, this would dilute the value of each lender's claim in the event of failure putting the company's solvency at risk, but lenders would not reap the benefits of success since they do not share in capital growth.[86] Conversely it can be argued that overreliance on debt can result in companies rejecting potentially profitable opportunities because substantial benefits from those opportunities will accrue to lenders rather than to shareholders;[87] looked at in this way, covenants restricting borrowing may reduce the incentive to underinvest.[88]

Covenants restricting dividends are less common in European loan agreements than in US equivalents; one study found that dividend restrictions in debt contracts are an important factor for 42 per cent of US managers and for only 8 per cent of European managers.[89] Article 15 of the Second Company Law Directive imposes payout restrictions under the general law.[90] There is some suggestion that the lack of covenants restricting dividends in British[91] and German[92] loan documentation can be explained in terms of lenders being content with the position under the general law and seeing no need to follow US market practice, where dividend covenants are more common[93] but there are, broadly speaking, no such payout constraints under the general law.[94] How far the Second Directive can be

---

[86] DR Fischel, 'The Economics of Lender Liability' (1989) 99 *Yale Law Journal* 131.

[87] SC Myers, 'Determinants of Corporate Borrowing' (1977) 5 *Journal of Financial Economics* 147; R Sappideen, 'Fiduciary Obligations to Corporate Creditors' [1991] JBL 365.

[88] CW Smith and JB Warner, 'On Financial Contracting: An Analysis of Bond Covenants' (1979) 7 *Journal of Financial Economics* 117, 124.

[89] F Bancel, UR Mittoo, and N Bhattacharyya, 'Cross-Country Determinants of Payout Policy: A Survey of European Firms' (2004) 33 *Financial Management* 103.

[90] Second Council Directive (EEC) 77/91 on co-ordination of safeguards which, for the protection of the interests of members and others are required by Member States of companies within the meaning of the second paragraph of Article 58 of the Treaty, in respect of the formation of public limited companies and the maintenance and alteration of their capital with a view to making such safeguards equivalent [1977] OJ L26/1. Art 15 limits distributions to net profits accumulated since the company's incorporation and imposes the further restriction that distributions must not reduce net assets to an amount that is lower than subscribed capital and undistributable reserves.

[91] JFS Day and PJ Taylor, 'The Role of Debt Contracts in UK Corporate Governance' (1998) 2 *Journal of Management and Governance* 171.

[92] C Leuz, D Deller, and M Stubenrath, 'An International Comparison of Accounting-Based Pay-Out Restrictions in the United States, United Kingdom and Germany' (1998) 28 *Accounting and Business Research* 111; C Leuz, 'The Role of Accrual Accounting in Restricting Dividends to Shareholders' (1998) 7 *European Accounting Review* 579, 580; C Leuz and J Wüstemann, 'The Role of Accounting in the German Financial System', in P Krahnen and RH Schmidt (eds), *The German Financial System* (OUP, 2004) 450–81.

[93] A Kalay, 'Stockholder-Bondholder Conflict and Dividend Constraints' (1982) 10 *Journal of Financial Economics* 211; WW Bratton, 'Bond Covenants and Creditor Protection: Economics and Law, Theory and Practice, Substance and Process' (2006) 7 *European Business Organization Law Review* 39.

[94] Leuz, Deller, and Stubenrath (n 92 above) 111. The idea that regulation can substitute for covenants is explored in a range of different contexts: eg EL Black, TA Carnes, M Mosebach, and SE Moyer, 'Regulatory Monitoring as a Substitute for Debt Covenants' (2004) 37 *Journal of Accounting and Economics* 367 is a study examining whether banks substituted regulatory monitoring for covenants by investigating debt issues of 105 banks between 1979 and 1984, a period when monitoring increased.

regarded as playing a useful role because it mimics lenders' preference is a controversial issue. It is relevant to note that contractual debt financing terms can differ from case to case as a result of context-specific considerations, unlike legal capital rules that provide one rigid, universally applicable model, which cannot be adapted to different circumstances. The degree of flexibility and adaptability within contractual processes gives credence to the view that situations where the debt financing terms that are actually agreed in practice will bear close resemblance to the legal model are likely to be infrequent.[95]

An argument in favour of constraints on dividends is that they can encourage new investment by the company,[96] so that although shareholders may appear to lose out in the short term (in that the company's freedom to determine whether to distribute profits or to retain them for investment is restricted), such a covenant can operate to their benefit in the longer term where it results in enhanced capital growth. Balanced against this is the suggestion that if a covenant is unduly onerous so that management is required to retain more of the company's profits than it can prudently invest, this could result in investments being made in risky ventures with potentially adverse consequences for both lenders and shareholders.[97] Where a company has surplus retentions, it may be possible to use these to make early repayment of expensive or restrictive debt to the extent that this is permitted by the relevant debt financing terms.[98]

Disposals of assets covenant

A covenant restricting disposals of assets is intended to prevent asset-stripping, such as where property is sold by the borrowing company at a nominal price. Even disposals of assets at a fair market price could prejudice the lender because piecemeal sales of assets may generate significantly lower proceeds than a sale of all of the assets and undertaking of the business as a going concern. Where the borrower is a holding company, a transfer of assets between wholly-owned subsidiaries, even at a nominal value, does not prejudice the lender since the value remains within the group throughout. A transfer from the holding company borrower to another company in its group is, however, potentially prejudicial because it means that assets that would previously have been available to repay the borrower's creditors will be claimed first by the creditors of the transferee subsidiary. A transfer from a wholly-owned subsidiary to another group company that is not wholly owned could also be problematic in that the other shareholders in the

[95] L Enriques and J Macey, 'Creditors Versus Capital Formation: The Case Against the European Legal Capital Rules' (2001) 86 *Cornell Law Review* 1165, 1193.

[96] A Kalay, 'Stockholder—Bondholder Conflict and Dividend Constraints' (1982) 10 *Journal of Financial Economics* 211.

[97] RJ Lister, 'Debenture Covenants and Corporate Value' (1985) 6 Company Lawyer 209, 213; R Sappideen, 'Fiduciary Obligations to Corporate Creditors' [1991] JBL 365, 378.

[98] In the case of debt securities, the borrower may be required to make payments into a sinking fund which is to be used to buy back securities before they mature.

transferee company or undertaking will acquire an interest in the assets which ranks equally with that of the borrowing holding company. In effect, creditors of the holding company will be structurally subordinated. Hence, if the covenant is qualified so as to permit intra-group transfers, this will usually exclude transfers by the borrower itself and may also exclude or restrict transfers otherwise than between wholly-owned subsidiaries. A disposals covenant must necessarily be qualified so as to permit disposals of assets in the ordinary course of business. Disposals of insubstantial parts of the borrower's business and undertaking may also be permitted, although the introduction of a substance test may sow the seeds of potential future difficulties in interpretation and application.

Change of business covenant

A covenant requiring the borrower not to change its business or operations helps to preserve the identity of the borrower throughout the term of the loan. However, where, as is common, the covenant is qualified so as to restrict only changes that would have 'a material adverse effect' on its business, assets, or financial condition, interpretative uncertainties may complicate the process of monitoring compliance with this covenant.[99]

Negative pledge covenant

The purpose of a covenant whereby the company undertakes not to create new security interests or to increase the amount secured by existing securities is to ensure that the priority position of the lender does not change whilst the loan is outstanding. The lender does not want to find itself postponed to subsequent creditors and thereby subject to the risk that the borrower's assets will be exhausted before its turn to be paid. A covenant to this effect is commonly described as a 'negative pledge' covenant. Forms of negative pledge covenants can be found in both unsecured and secured loans but in this chapter the focus is solely on unsecured lending.[100] A typical clause would seek to prohibit quasi-securities (such as credit sales) as well as conventional security interests but the lender's attempts to produce an all-embracing clause may be defeated by the ingenuity of other corporate financiers who subsequently devise arrangements that perform the same economic function as a secured loan but which adopt a legal form that is not anticipated by the negative pledge covenant.

As with any other covenant, breach of a negative pledge covenant will be a breach of contract entitling the lender to contractual remedies. In a well-drafted

---

[99] In *Re IBP, Inc Shareholders' Litigation* [2001] WL 675339 (Del Ch 2001) the Delaware Court of Chancery held in the context of a merger agreement that a MAC event was something that produced 'a significant diminution of the value of the business entity as a whole'. However, this 'well meaning effort' to deal with ambiguity has attracted criticism: RJ Gilson and A Schwartz, 'Understanding MACs: Moral Hazard in Acquisitions' (2005) 21 *Journal of Law, Economics and Organization* 330.

[100] See ch 12 below, for negative pledges in secured lending.

loan agreement, the breach is likely to be an express event of default entitling the lender to terminate the agreement and to demand repayment of the principal and of any other sums that are outstanding. It is possible for a lender to seek an injunction to prevent a company from granting security in breach of a negative pledge covenant but practical difficulties in detecting whether or when a company proposes to do this are likely to preclude extensive successful recourse to this remedy.[101] Another equitable remedy is for the court to appoint a receiver but this remedy is generally only available to secured lenders, although the possibility of exercising this power in favour of an unsecured lender in the event of breach of a negative pledge in its favour was left open in one Australian decision.[102]

Does the breach of a negative pledge covenant by the granting of a subsequent security have any legal implications for the creditor in whose favour the offending security is created? In a broad sense, the answer to this question is yes, because a company that is in a position where it is prepared to break the terms of its existing financial facilities in this way is, inferentially, a company that is very likely to be in financial difficulties. The lender in whose favour the relevant security is created, in common with the company's other creditors, may thus soon find itself embroiled in the consequences of having advanced credit to an insolvent company. In particular, should the company enter into the insolvency procedures of administration or liquidation,[103] the security may be vulnerable under those provisions of the Insolvency Act 1986 that invalidate, or authorize the court to invalidate, security that was created in the twilight period of a company's solvency.[104]

A specific technical issue is whether the original unsecured lender in whose favour the negative pledge covenant was given may have a claim against the subsequent lender whose security[105] was created in breach of the covenant. The point of departure here is the privity of contract rule, which is to the effect that contracts cannot give rights to, or impose burdens on, persons who are not parties to them.[106] This rule is subject to various exceptions and qualifications, but the one that is particularly relevant in this context is the equitable principle in *de Mattos*

---

[101] An injunction for this purpose was granted in *Pullen v Abelcheck Pty Ltd* (1990) 20 NSWLR 732, discussed in JRC Arkins, '"OK—So You've Promised, Right?" The Negative Pledge Clause and the "Security" it Provides' [2000] *Journal of International Banking Law* 198.

[102] *Bond Brewing Holdings Ltd v National Australia Bank Ltd* (1989–90) 1 ACSR 445, Vic SC, App D and (1980–90) 1 ACSR 722, High Ct of Aust (refusing leave to appeal).

[103] Where a company's existing facilities contain cross-default clauses, the creation of security in breach of a negative pledge covenant in one agreement may mean that it is in default under all of them and therefore that all of its lenders can call for repayment. The domino effect of a cross-default clause thus increases the likelihood of the company being unable to pay its debts as they fall due, and that will form the basis for the making of an administration order or a winding-up order under Insolvency Act 1986. Cross-default clauses are discussed further later in this chapter.

[104] Especially Insolvency Act 1986, ss 245 (avoidance of certain floating charges) and 239 (preferences).

[105] Here this term is used loosely to include interests that perform the same economic function as a security but which are in a different legal form.

[106] Law Commission, 'Privity of Contract: Contracts for the Benefit of Third Parties', Report No 242 (1996) provides a general review of the law in this area.

v Gibson.[107] This principle is that where a person acquires property or an interest in property with knowledge of a previous contract affecting that property, he can be restrained by injunction from acting in a manner that is inconsistent with that contract.[108] The basis of this principle, its limits, and even whether it remains good law are issues on which the cases provide scope for different interpretations and for this reason it is unsurprising to discover that these are matters that have been extensively discussed by academic commentators.[109] One point on which there is broad agreement is that, even if it does survive as an extant legal principle, *de Mattos v Gibson* is subject to restrictive conditions that severely limit its application. In particular, it only operates against persons who know of the existence of the earlier covenant and knowledge in this context means actual knowledge of the prior rights.[110] Constructive knowledge—which can arise from the public filing of information—does not suffice and, in any case, negative pledge clauses in unsecured loan agreements are not subject to any general disclosure or registration requirement under British law that would fix the public with deemed knowledge of their terms. Thus, whilst there could be particular situations in which an original lender is able to prove that the security holder became aware of the existence of a prior negative pledge as part of the process of negotiating the terms of its secured financing, in many instances claims based on *de Mattos v Gibson* will fall at the first hurdle because relevant knowledge cannot be shown.

Even if the knowledge hurdle can be cleared, there remain formidable barriers to success in a claim by an unsecured holder of a negative pledge covenant that is based on *de Mattos v Gibson*. The principle operates where a person acquires property and *thereafter* seeks to deal with it in a manner that is inconsistent with an earlier contractual promise that was known about at the time of the acquisition. This wording is not apt to cover situations where security is created in breach of a negative pledge because, there, it is the very acquisition of the security interest in the property, rather than subsequent dealings with it, that infringes the earlier covenant. Following this line of analysis, breach of a negative pledge covenant may lie outside the scope of the *de Mattos v Gibson* principle altogether.

---

[107] (1858) De G&J 276, 282, [1843–60] All ER Rep 803, 805 *per* Knight-Bruce LJ. But the principle is not a panacea for outflanking the doctrine of privity of contract: *Law Debenture Corp v Ural Caspian Ltd* [1993] 2 All ER 355, 362 *per* Hoffmann LJ (sitting as an additional judge of the High Court). This decision was reversed on appeal ([1995] 1 All ER 157, CA) but on grounds that are not relevant to this point.

[108] *Law Debenture Corp v Ural Caspian Ltd* [1993] 2 All ER 355, 362 *per* Hoffmann LJ.

[109] S Worthington, *Proprietary Interests in Commercial Transactions* (Clarendon Press, 1996) ch 5 provides a detailed and careful review of the authorities and the different interpretations that have been ascribed to them by numerous commentators.

[110] *Swiss Bank Corp v Lloyds Bank Ltd* [1979] 1 Ch 548, 575 *per* Browne-Wilkinson J (varied on appeal but on other grounds [1982] AC 584, CA and HL). In the context of the economic tort of inducing breach of contract, actual knowledge can embrace a conscious decision not to inquire into the existence of a fact (turning a blind eye): *OBG LTD v Allan; Douglas v Hello! Ltd; Mainstream Properties Ltd v Young* [2007] 2 WLR 920, HL. The *de Mattos v Gibson* principle can be viewed as the equitable counterpart of the tort of inducing breach of contract (see *Swiss Bank Corp v Lloyds Bank Ltd* [1979] 1 Ch 548, 573).

In support of this viewpoint, it can be argued that the underlying purpose of the *de Mattos v Gibson* principle is to give bite to an undertaking by an acquirer of property to respect existing third party claims on that property; where security is taken in breach of an earlier negative pledge it is self-evidently not part of the bargain that the acquirer will abide by existing restrictions.[111]

As an alternative to the equitable *de Mattos v Gibson* principle, the lender whose negative pledge covenant has been breached has the possibility of a tort claim against the taker of the security.[112] To succeed in a claim based on the economic tort of inducing a breach of contract, the claimant must demonstrate that the defendant intentionally violated its contractual rights.[113] An inherent element of intentional violation is that the defendant must know that it is inducing a breach of contract.[114] Actual knowledge is required but this can embrace a conscious decision not to inquire into the existence of a fact or, putting it another way, turning a blind eye to the obvious.[115] In determining intention, the breach of contract must be the ends or the means to an end and not just a foreseeable consequence of certain actions.[116] Whether a lender that has provided a facility on the basis of a negative pledge which is later broken will be able to establish the elements of the tort will depend heavily on what it can discover about the disclosure process that preceded the subsequent secured loan agreement.

It is sometimes the case that negative pledge lenders attempt 'self-help' by including in their loan agreements a clause to the effect that the loan will become secured in the event of breach of the negative pledge. The legal effectiveness of this form of self-help is doubtful. First, a provision for automatic security may fail to result in a valid security because it does not define the subject-matter of the security with sufficient certainty.[117] Secondly, the security that springs into effect on breach of the negative pledge may not achieve the desired priority effect, ie to

---

[111] This places *de Mattos v Gibson* under the broader heading of prevention of unjust enrichment. For further development of this idea see Worthington (n 109 above) 102–5 and the sources cited there.

[112] Although *Swiss Bank Corp v Lloyds Bank Ltd* [1979] 1 Ch 548 may suggest that the *de Mattos v Gibson* principle is simply concerned with the granting of an equitable remedy to prevent the commission of a tort, it is also possible to regard that principle and tort claims as distinct: AP Bell, *Modern Law of Personal Property in England and Wales* (Butterworths, 1989) 210–16.

[113] *Lumley v Gye* [1843–60] All ER Rep 208; *OBG LTD v Allan* [2007] 2 WLR 920, HL. There is also the possibility of pursuing claims based on other economic torts such as conspiracy. See further J Stone, 'Negative Pledges and the Tort of Interference with Contractual Relations' [1991] *Journal of International Banking Law* 310.

[114] *OBG LTD v Allan* [2007] 2 WLR 920, HL; *Torquay Hotel Co Ltd v Cousins* [1969] 1 All ER 522, CA.

[115] *Torquay Hotel Co Ltd v Cousins* [1969] 1 All ER 522, CA, 530 *per* Lord Denning MR; *Emerald Construction Co Ltd v Lowthian* [1966] 1 WLR 691, CA, 700–1 *per* Lord Denning MR. In *OBG LTD v Allan* Lord Hoffmann referred to Lord Denning's views in *Emerald* and said that it was in accordance with the general principle of law that a conscious decision not to inquire into the existence of a fact is in many cases treated as equivalent to knowledge of that fact. Lord Hoffmann emphasized that it is not the same as negligence or even gross negligence.

[116] *OBG LTD v Allan* [2007] 2 WLR 920, HL.

[117] *National Provincial Bank v Charnley* [1924] 1 KB 431, CA.

rank ahead of the security created in breach of the negative pledge. According to the conventional view, an agreement that provides for security to take effect on fulfilment of a contingency (the contingency in this case being breach of the negative pledge) does not give rise to a security until that contingency is fulfilled.[118] Therefore, in order to win any priority battle that is governed by a 'first in time' rule, careful drafting is needed to ensure that the security comes into effect immediately prior to the creation of the security in breach of the negative pledge. There is some doubt as to whether drafting can in fact achieve this effect.[119] In *Smith (Administrator of Cosslett (Contractors) Ltd) v Bridgend County Borough Council*[120] Lord Scott suggested that a charge expressed to come into existence on the occurrence of an uncertain future event could, even prior to fulfilment of the contingency, count as a charge for some of the requirements relating to company charges[121] but the majority of the House agreed with Lord Hoffmann, whose speech did not make reference to this point. In *Re Spectrum Plus Ltd*[122] Lord Scott again mentioned the issue and suggested that a fixed charge expressed to come into existence on a future event in relation to a specified class of assets would in principle be categorized prior to the fulfilment of the contingency as a floating charge[123] but this remark was peripheral to the decision in the case. In neither case did Lord Scott consider previous authority to the effect that a contingent security is not a security until the contingency is fulfilled. In the absence of a full examination of the issues in a case decided squarely on the basis of the legal effect of a contingent security, the conventional view, based on clear authority, still stands.

The third problem with which a lender that is seeking to rely on a security arising automatically on breach of a negative pledge covenant must contend arises from registration requirements relating to company charges. Most forms of security must be registered within twenty-one days of creation in order to preserve their validity against other secured creditors and against the borrowing company, should it enter into the formal insolvency proceedings of administration or liquidation.[124] Under the conventional view of contingent securities, the period for registration runs from the fulfilment of the contingency and there is therefore

---

[118] *Re Gregory Love Ltd* [1916] 1 Ch 203.

[119] *Fire Nymph Products Ltd v The Heating Centre Pty Ltd* (1991–92) 7 ACSR 365, NSW CA recognizes that it is possible to achieve this order of events. This was a case involving automatic crystallization of a floating charge but the reasoning may be equally applicable to unsecured negative pledge lending, although this has been doubted: JRC Arkins, "'OK—So You've Promised, Right?' The Negative Pledge Clause and the "Security" it Provides' [2000] *Journal of International Banking Law* 198. On the priority of competing securities, see ch 12 below.

[120] [2002] 1 AC 336 HL.

[121] At para 63.

[122] *Re Spectrum Plus Ltd; National Westminster Bank plc v Spectrum Plus Ltd* [2005] 2 AC 680, HL.

[123] At para 107.

[124] Companies Act 2006, s 874.

an onus of considerable vigilance on the lender.[125] Lord Scott's alternative view would mean that the time period would run from the date of the original loan agreement but that would rather defeat the purpose of the lending being on an unsecured basis.

There are other problems too. It is not clear whether a contingent security has to be supported by fresh consideration provided at the time when the contingency is fulfilled.[126] Furthermore, the implications of the potential mismatch between the appearance that the loan is still unsecured and the reality that it has become secured are unexplored. All in all, the irresistible conclusion is that self-help through the mechanism of a provision for automatic security on breach of a negative pledge is highly unreliable. The negative pledge unsecured lender should accept at the negotiation stage that, for practical purposes, its remedies for default will lie only against the defaulting company, and should price its risk accordingly.[127]

Implied covenants

In addition to the terms expressly agreed by the parties, in theory terms may also be implied into their contractual relationship. Terms may be implied, in fact, on the basis that the parties must have intended to include them but simply omitted to state this expressly. In specific contexts terms may also be implied in law (for example in relation to contracts for the sale of goods under the Sale of Goods Act 1979) or as a matter of custom. The court's power to imply terms is limited and it cannot imply a term simply on the grounds that it would be reasonable to do so.[128] It is not the court's function to rewrite the parties' bargain but to give effect to it as they must have intended, and for this reason it is clearly impossible for the court to imply a term that is inconsistent with an express term. The detailed and extensive drafting of a typical loan agreement will usually leave little scope for the implication of terms. There is no general implied covenant of good faith and fair dealing in contractual matters under English law.[129]

---

[125] *Re Jackson and Bassford Ltd* [1906] 2 Ch 467, 476–7.
[126] J Maxton, 'Negative Pledges and Equitable Principles' [1993] JBL 458 argues that fresh consideration is needed but cf J Stone, 'The "Affirmative" Negative Pledge' [1991] *Journal of International Banking Law* 364.
[127] A McKnight, 'Restrictions on Dealing with Assets in Financing Documents: Their Role, Meaning and Effect' [2002] *Journal of International Banking Law* 193.
[128] *Liverpool City Council v Irwin* [1977] AC 239, HL.
[129] *Walford v Miles* [1992] 2 AC 128, HL. The US courts have closed the doors to good faith claims in bond contracts: WW Bratton, 'Bond Covenants and Creditor Protection: Economics and Law, Theory and Practice, Substance and Process' (2006) 7 *European Business Organization Law Review* 39.

Events of default

A well-drafted loan agreement will entitle the lender to accelerate the loan upon the occurrence of any one of a number of specified 'events of default'.[130] Common events of default include:

(1) the borrower's failure to pay any sum due and payable pursuant to the agreement;

(2) the borrower's breach of any other obligation or undertaking under the agreement;

(3) any representation or warranty proving to be incorrect (or, less severe, incorrect in a material respect);

(4) cross-default: the borrower's failure to pay or meet any other indebtedness or financial obligation when due;

(5) the commencement of the winding up of the borrower or of other insolvency or reorganization procedures;

(6) distress or execution being levied against any assets of the borrower;

(7) cessation of business by the borrower.

Where the borrower is a holding company, events of default may also relate to subsidiaries and subsidiary undertakings within its group. Grace periods of a number of days may be allowed to the borrower in respect of some or all of the events of default to give the borrower an opportunity to rectify the position before the lender can call in the loan, a concession that will be important to the borrower in relation to trivial or technical breaches.

When a borrower defaults, the lender, if the loan is typically drafted, will have an option whether to declare the loan due and this will not be an automatic consequence of the default.[131] Youard has explained why automatic acceleration would generally be unusual:[132]

... since the events of default (other than non-payment) simply amount to an informed guess by the parties at the time the loan is negotiated as to the events which might occur over the next (say) 10 years, and which would entitle the lender to call for immediate

---

[130] R Youard, 'Default in International Loan Agreements I and II' [1986] JBL 276 and [1986] JBL 378.

[131] In the event of any ambiguity, the courts will favour the interpretation that the lender has an option to accelerate and that this is not an automatic consequence of default: *Government Stock and Other Securities Investment Co v Manila Rly Co* [1897] AC 81, HL.

For interpretation of the contractual procedure to be followed upon the occurrence (or apparent occurrence) of an event of default in a bond issue, see *Law Debenture Trust Corp plc v Acciona SA* [2004] EWHC 270 (Ch); *Concord Trust v Law Debenture Trust Corp plc* [2005] 1 WLR 1591, HL; *Law Debenture Trust Corp plc v Elektrim Finance BV* [2005] EWHC 1999 (Ch); *Law Debenture Trust Corp plc v Concord Trust* [2007] EWHC 2255 (Ch). P Rawlings, 'The Changing Role of the Trustee in International Bond Issues' [2007] JBL 43; S Wright, 'Making Lenders Liable for Damage Caused by "Wrongful Acceleration" of Loans' (2006) 27 *Company Lawyer* 123.

[132] Youard (n 130 above) 278.

repayment, it would in normal circumstances be wholly inappropriate for the occurrence of those events to give rise to automatic acceleration.

The cross-default clause is especially noteworthy. Under this provision the lender is entitled to call in the loan in circumstances where the borrowing company has defaulted on its obligations *to someone else* even though (apart from the cross-default clause) the borrower may have met all of its obligations to this particular lender. The rationale of the cross-default clause is that any default is a sign of trouble in response to which the lender will want to be entitled to accelerate its claim to prevent other creditors stealing a march over it with regard to enforcement or with regard to renegotiation of terms. When a borrower is negotiating the events of default in one loan agreement, it will need to bear in mind that it may in the future enter into other loan agreements containing cross-default clauses, so that accepting very strict events of default on one occasion (for example no grace periods or no qualifications with regard to 'materiality') could be sowing the seeds of a later catastrophe because of the 'domino' effect of cross default. Also, the terms of any cross-default clause itself will need to be considered closely: if all of the borrower's obligations are included, it may find itself almost always technically in default and it may therefore press for a more limited clause that, perhaps, limits the cross default to failure to pay amounts exceeding a specified threshold figure or which is confined only to particular types of indebtedness.

Lenders tend to favour cross-default clauses that are drafted so as to come into effect when the relevant other indebtedness has become due or '*is capable of being declared due*'. The italicized words relate back to the fact that default does not, in normal practice, cause automatic acceleration of a loan. When a borrowing company defaults on one loan, instead of demanding repayment, the lender may seek to impose harsher terms on the borrower, with the threat of acceleration hovering in the background should the borrower fail to comply. If the borrower's other lenders have accepted cross-default clauses that only come into effect when borrowings become 'due', those lenders are in a weaker negotiating position (unless there have been separate defaults apart from the cross-default clause) because they cannot threaten to call in their loans under the cross-default clause as so drafted, and this may defeat the purpose of the clause which was to ensure equality among creditors.

Debt finance and corporate governance[133]

Although a single theory to explain corporate capital structures has not yet emerged, debt finance features prominently in the two models that dominate the

---

[133] See generally GG Triantis and RJ Daniels, 'The Role of Debt in Interactive Corporate Governance' (1995) 83 *California Law Review* 1073; BR Cheffins, *Company Law Theory, Structure and Operation* (OUP, 1997) 75–9.

literature: the trade-off theory[134] and the pecking order theory.[135] The dependence of the corporate sector on debt means that providers of debt finance are in a position to play a significant role in corporate governance by imposing constraints on managers.[136] They have the power to supply or to withhold finance and to stipulate the terms on which it is to be made available. In particular, covenants allow debt financiers a say in the way that borrowing companies conduct their affairs and events of default clauses provide them with the leverage to renegotiate for yet more stringent control of borrowers in financial difficulties. Should a company become unable to pay its debts, providers of debt finance move into a central corporate governance position because, in effect, they replace the shareholders as residual claimants on the firm's assets.[137] Corporate managers can send out positive signals by voluntarily committing to the discipline of legally enforceable debt servicing obligations and monitoring covenants.[138] Debt can thus mitigate the effects of agency and information problems within companies, although its constraining effect depends on the type of debt[139] and the intensity of monitoring activity by lenders.[140]

The contractual framework for monitoring by banks emerges from a process of contractual negotiation and is therefore liable to be affected by a range of variables, including the maturity and track record of the borrower, the size and duration of the financing, whether the financing is to be secured or unsecured, and broader competitive pressures. For instance, a small or recently formed company that has limited access to external sources of debt finance apart from banks may have no commercial alternative but to accept short-term loans or loans which are subject to detailed restrictive covenants.[141] Thus it has been said that: 'Bank power tends to be inversely related to borrower size, because the latter is closely

[134] That firms identify optimal leverage by weighing the costs (bankruptcy costs) and benefits (tax treatment) of additional debt: EF Fama and KR French, 'Financing Decisions: Who Issues Stock?' (2005) 76 *Journal of Financial Economics* 549, 549–50.

[135] That asymmetric information problems and transaction costs involved in the issuance of equity securities, lead firms to finance new investments first with retained earnings, then with debt, and only finally with outside equity: SC Myers, 'The Capital Structure Puzzle' (1984) 39 *Journal of Finance* 575.

[136] Triantis and Daniels (n 133 above) 1073.

[137] J Armour, B Cheffins, and DA Skeel, 'Corporate Ownership Structure and the Evolution of Bankruptcy Law: Lessons from the United Kingdom' (2002) 55 *Vanderbilt Law Review* 1699, 1722; DG Baird, 'The Uneasy Case for Corporate Reorganizations' (1986) 15 *Journal of Legal Studies* 127, 129–31.

[138] H Leland and D Pyle, 'Informational Asymmetries, Financial Structure, and Financial Intermediation' (1977) 32 *Journal of Finance* 371; SA Ross, 'The Determination of Financial Structure: the Incentive-signaling Approach' (1977) 8 *Bell Journal of Economics* 23.

[139] O Hart, *Firms. Contracts and Financial Structures* (Clarendon Press, 1995) ch 5.

[140] CR Harvey, KV Linsc, and AH Roper 'The Effect of Capital Structure when Expected Agency Costs are Extreme' (2004) 74 *Journal of Financial Economics* 3.

[141] M Middleton, M Cowling, J Samuels, and R Sugden, 'Small Firms and Clearing Banks' in N Dimsdale and M Prevezer (eds), *Capital Markets and Corporate Governance* (Clarendon Press, 1994) 141.

correlated with credit rating and available borrowing options.'[142] Bond market financing, which in practice is only accessible to larger companies, tends to be more standardized and covenants, which provide the basis for monitoring, tend to be quite limited in scope.

The actual process of monitoring has been described as 'the ongoing acquisition, processing, interpretation, and verification of information about the firm'.[143] The relationship between borrowing companies and their banks tends to be closer than that which exists between issuers and holders of their debt securities, giving banks informational advantages that should make them more efficient monitors.[144] The superiority of banks as monitors is further reinforced by the fact that even though bond issues often have trustees to represent the collective interests of the bondholders, standard documentation limits trustees' monitoring obligations by permitting them to assume that issuers are complying with their obligations and that there is no event of default, unless they have actual knowledge or express notice to the contrary.[145] Until a trustee has such knowledge or notice, normal monitoring practice involves simply receiving annual directors' certificates as to compliance with covenants and other bond issue terms, and reviewing issuers' annual accounts and other documents sent out to shareholders or creditors.[146] Even where an event of default has occurred, a trustee is usually permitted to refrain from taking action unless it has been indemnified by or on behalf of the holders against any resultant costs and liabilities.[147]

Naturally, the level of bank monitoring is driven by each bank's self-interest and is not an exercise in altruism, but its disciplining effect can yield benefits for other creditors, shareholders, and wider groups of stakeholders. This suggests that the policy framework should, broadly speaking, encourage diligent bank monitoring because of its positive externalities. On the other hand, there is the obvious danger that, as Triantis and Daniels put it, 'the bank also has incentives to use its considerable monitoring advantage and its leverage over firm decisions to enhance its position at the expense of other stakeholders'.[148] This indicates the need, in policy terms, for boundaries so as to limit the scope for banks to exploit their informational advantages. English law uses a range of mechanisms

---

[142] ES Herman, *Corporate Control, Corporate Power* (CUP, 1981) 122. See also D Lomax, 'The Role of the Banks' in Dimsdale and Prevezer (eds) (n 141 above) 161, 173–7 outlining differences in a clearing bank's relationships with small and larger businesses.

[143] Triantis and Daniels (n 133 above) 1073, 1079.

[144] ibid 1088–90.

[145] Financial Markets Law Committee, 'Trustee Exemption Clauses', Issue No 62 (May 2004) ch 3, available at <http://www.fmlc.org/papers/trustee_exemption_clauses_issue62.pdf> (accessed November 2007). This report fed into a project by the Law Commission (the law reform body for England and Wales), which consulted on trustee exemption clauses in 2003 and then reported on the matter in 2006: *Trustee Exemption Clauses* (Law Com Rep No 301, 2006). In its Report the Law Commission stepped back from recommending statutory intervention.

[146] Financial Markets Law Committee (n 145 above).

[147] ibid.

[148] Triantis and Daniels (n 133 above) 1073, 1091.

to rein in the potential for inter-stakeholder conflicts of this sort.[149] In particular, where monitoring shades into actually telling companies how to run their affairs, a bank runs the risk of being held liable as a *de facto* or a shadow director.[150] A *de facto* director is someone who undertakes the functions of a director, even though not formally appointed as such, and a person in that position is subject to the range of duties that apply to directors who have been formally appointed.[151] Generally, the risk of monitoring activity escalating to a level that would put a bank into this category is not significant. Where (as sometimes happens) a bank has the right to appoint a director to the board of a borrowing company, the individual appointed would, of course, be subject to directors' duties but the bank, as nominator, would not be vicariously responsible for that individual's actions nor, in the absence of fraud or bad faith, would it have direct personal responsibility to ensure that the duties are properly discharged.[152] A shadow director means a person in accordance with whose directions or instructions the directors of the company are accustomed to act.[153] A shadow director is someone who has real influence in the affairs of a company.[154] It is not necessary that such influence should be exercised over the whole field of its corporate activities[155] but there must be proof of a pattern of consistent conduct in which the actual directors (or at least the majority of them) act on the instructions or directions of the alleged shadow director.[156] Certain statutory duties apply to shadow directors, including the possibility of being held personally liable to make good losses incurred through wrongful trading.[157] A number of cases have considered the possibility that lenders might fall to be regarded as shadow directors[158] but the position that has emerged is that a bank must step outside the ordinary bank–customer

---

[149] As well as the potential directorial liability discussed in the text, other important constraints are provided by provisions of the insolvency legislation which allow for the invalidation of certain transactions in the period immediately before insolvency, which could be infringed, for instance, where, because of close relationships between a company and selected lenders, certain debts are repaid ahead of others or unsecured debts are converted into secured debts (Insolvency Act 1986, ss 238–239).

[150] The two categories are not necessarily mutually exclusive: *Secretary of State for Trade and Industry v Aviss* [2007] BCC 288, paras 88–89 commenting on *Re Hydrodam Ltd* [1994] 2 BCLC 180. The functions of a shadow director are different from those of a *de facto* director but the point being made in *Aviss* is that a person can be both simultaneously. See also D Noonan and S Watson, 'The Nature of Shadow Directorship: Ad Hoc Statutory Liability or Core Company Law Principle' [2006] JBL 763.

[151] *Ultraframe (UK) Ltd v Fielding* [2005] EWHC 1638, para 1254.

[152] *Kuwait Asia Bank EC v National Mutual Life Nominees Ltd* [1991] 1 AC 187, PC.

[153] Companies Act 2006, s 251, Insolvency Act 1986, s 251, and Company Directors Disqualification Act 1986, s 22. *Secretary of State for Trade and Industry v Deverell* [2001] Ch 340, CA; *Secretary of State for Trade and Industry v Becker* [2003] 1 BCLC 555.

[154] *Secretary of State for Trade and Industry v Deverell* [2001] Ch 340, CA, para 35 *per* Morritt LJ.

[155] ibid.

[156] *Secretary of State for Trade and Industry v Becker* [2003] 1 BCLC 555.

[157] Under Insolvency Act 1986, s 214.

[158] *Re a Company No 005009 of 1987* (1988) 4 BCC 424; *Re PTZFM Ltd* [1995] 2 BCLC 354; *Ultraframe (UK) Ltd v Fielding* [2005] EWHC 1638, para 1254.

relationship to be at risk of being held to be a shadow director.[159] Merely having a nominee director on a board does not make the appointor a shadow director.[160] It is established that a bank is entitled to keep a close eye on what is done with its money, and to impose conditions on its support for the company.[161] This does not mean that the bank is running the company or emasculating the powers of the directors, even if (given their situation) the directors feel that they have little practical choice but to accede to its requests.[162] When a bank follows the usual practice of requiring the borrower to give warranties about its present circumstances and covenants as to the conduct of its affairs and imposes conditions precedent before the funds can be accessed, and thereafter monitors compliance, it is not giving 'directions' or 'instructions' but is simply attaching terms and conditions to the provision and continuation of its financial support which, technically, the company is free to accept or reject.

Keeping on the right side of the line in the context of corporate rescue situations is especially challenging but also especially important because it is then that the potential for wrongful trading liability looms large as a legal risk.[163] In the UK, a movement away from debt collection to more monitoring and intervention to effect corporate turnaround has been identified.[164] This trend has been fostered by legislative changes designed to promote a 'rescue culture'.[165] Finch reports that the change in the focus of insolvency-related processes has brought a burgeoning group of turnaround specialists onto the scene to assist banks and companies in effecting turnarounds.[166] The development of a stronger rescue culture and of a healthy market for the supply of specialist turnaround services could be taken to indicate that the risk of shadow directorship liability is not excessive and that it may in fact be set at a level that fits reasonably well within a policy framework that aims to provide incentives for bank monitoring and early reaction to emerging problems but, at the same time, to curb opportunities for inter-stakeholder conflicts.[167]

---

[159] That the case law would evolve in this direction was predicted by a leading judge, writing extra judicially: Sir Peter Millett, 'Shadow Directorship—A Real or Imagined Threat to the Banks' [1991] Insolvency Practitioner 14.

[160] *Lord v Sinai Securities Ltd and ors* [2005] 1 BCLC 295.

[161] *Ultraframe (UK) Ltd v Fielding* [2005] EWHC 1638, para 1268. This was a submission by Counsel accepted 'in broad terms' by Lewison J.

[162] ibid.

[163] D Milman, 'Strategies for Regulating Managerial Performance in the "Twilight Zone"—Familiar Dilemmas: New Considerations' [2004] JBL 493, 495–6.

[164] V Finch, 'Doctoring in the Shadows of Insolvency' [2005] JBL 690.

[165] V Finch, 'Control and Co-ordination in Corporate Rescue' (2005) 25 *Legal Studies* 374; S Frisby, 'In Search of a Rescue Regime: The Enterprise Act 2002' (2004) 67 MLR 247; V Finch, 'The Recasting of Insolvency Law' (2005) 68 MLR 713.

[166] V Finch, 'Doctoring in the Shadows of Insolvency' [2005] JBL 690, 692.

[167] ibid 728–30.

12

Secured Debt

Advantages of being a secured creditor

This chapter is concerned with forms of real security that companies can give to lenders. A lender with a real security has control over the assets which form the security and is entitled to enforce its claims against those assets in the event of the company failing to meet its obligations to service and repay the debt. A lender can also take guarantees in respect of the company's indebtedness from third parties (for example from its directors or its parent company). Guarantees are sometimes described as personal security but in this chapter the term 'security' denotes a proprietary claim, ie a claim which involves rights in relation to a thing.[1] A guarantee is not a security as so defined because the creditor has only a personal claim against the guarantor.[2]

If a company becomes insolvent, its secured creditors are, generally speaking, in a much stronger position than its unsecured creditors. In insolvency, unsecured debts are governed by the *pari passu* rule, which means that if there are insufficient assets to meet all of the claims, they must abate rateably among themselves. The result of the application of the *pari passu* rule is that the company's pool of assets is distributed to its unsecured creditors in proportion to the size of their respective claims, and each of the creditors must bear a proportionate share of the shortfall. The *pari passu* rule is subject to various qualifications and exceptions.[3] For the purposes of this chapter, the most important qualification is that the rule has no application in relation to secured debts because proprietary rights acquired before insolvency are respected and not subjected to the collective procedures of insolvency law.[4] Avoiding the *pari passu* rule and ensuring priority over

---

[1] EI Sykes and S Walker, *The Law of Securities* (Law Book Company, 5th edn, 1993) 9.

[2] Unless, of course, the guarantor has given the creditor a mortgage, charge, or other form of security interest.

[3] In particular, the Insolvency Act 1986 creates a category of preferential debts which are to be paid before ordinary unsecured debts (and also before debts secured by a floating charge). See generally F Oditah, 'Assets and the Treatment of Claims in Insolvency' (1992) 108 LQR 459.

[4] *Sowman v David Samuel Trust Ltd* [1978] 1 WLR 22; *Re Potters Oils Ltd* [1986] 1 WLR 201. The importance of property rights in an insolvency context are discussed generally by RM Goode, 'Ownership and Obligations in Transactions' (1987) 103 LQR 433, 434–53.

unsecured creditors in the event of insolvency are compelling reasons for taking security.[5] This remains so even though insolvency legislation has intervened in certain respects so as to redistribute assets that are subject to a security back to unsecured creditors: such legislation erodes the advantages of being a secured creditor but it does not destroy them completely.[6] Redistributive insolvency legislation creates incentives for lenders to obtain forms of security that do not fall within its scope.[7]

More options are available to a secured creditor in the event of default by a borrower than are open to unsecured creditors. In a well-drafted loan agreement an unauthorized disposal of assets in breach of a covenant prohibiting or restricting disposals will be an event of default that entitles the lender, whether secured or unsecured, to accelerate the loan and demand repayment. However, if the loan is secured and the assets disposed of were part of the subject-matter of the security, the secured creditor may be able, subject to the protections afforded to persons who acquire property in good faith, for value, and without notice of competing interests, to follow the assets into the hands of the person who received them or to claim the proceeds of the disposal. An unsecured creditor does not have these rights.[8] In the event of default, a secured creditor may appoint a receiver to realize the security where the security provides for this or may petition the court for the appointment of a receiver (although such applications are now rare as lenders are normally adequately protected by their contractual powers of appointment). The court will not normally appoint a receiver on the application of an unsecured creditor.[9] Statute has recently intervened to limit the secured creditor's right to appoint a receiver—apart from certain special cases, the holder of a floating charge created or after 15 September 2003 cannot appoint an *administrative* receiver, ie a receiver or manager of the whole (or substantially the whole) of the company's property.[10] A secured creditor who before September 2003 could have appointed an administrative receiver, can now appoint an administrator[11] but

---

[5] *Insolvency Law and Practice* (Cmnd 8558, 1982) ch 34 (Report of the Review Committee under the Chairmanship of Sir Kenneth Cork) (here in after 'Cork Committee Report').

[6] J Armour, 'Should We Redistribute in Insolvency?' in J Getzler and J Payne (eds), *Company Charges: Spectrum and Beyond* (OUP, 2006) ch 9 discusses the redistributive effects of Insolvency Act 1986, ss 40, 175, 386 (preferential claims which are elevated above those of the holders of a floating charge), and 176A (which requires a prescribed part of the assets subject to a floating charge to be set aside for unsecured creditors).

[7] The story of charges on book debts, which is discussed later in this chapter, can be summed up as an attempt by lenders to create fixed charges so as to fall outside the ambit of redistributive insolvency legislation affecting floating charges.

[8] Apart from covenants or other contractual restrictions, an unsecured creditor has no standing to object to the way in which a borrower deals with its assets: *Re Ehrmann Bros Ltd* [1906] 2 Ch 697, CA.

[9] *Harris v Beauchamp Bros* [1894] 1 QB 802, CA.

[10] Defined by Insolvency Act 1986, s 29.

[11] Insolvency Act 1986, Sch B1, para 14.

administration, unlike receivership, is a collective insolvency procedure for the benefit of all creditors.[12]

Economic perspectives on secured debt[13]

There is at least the potential for a trade-off between the granting of security and the rates at which a company can borrow.[14] Because security puts its holder in an advantageous position in insolvency, it may enable the company to borrow from a particular lender which would otherwise have been unwilling to sanction the loan or, at least, to borrow at cheaper rates than that lender would otherwise have been willing to offer.[15] Improvements in interest charges may also be secured because of the monitoring costs savings of secured debt: instead of having to monitor the whole of the company's business through covenants, a secured creditor can simply check that the assets which are subject to its security have not been dissipated.[16] However, other unsecured creditors may demand higher interest to compensate them for the risk of being postponed to the secured debt in the event of the borrowing company's insolvency.[17] Likewise, reductions in monitoring costs so far as secured creditors are concerned have to be set against possible increases in unsecured creditors' monitoring costs; as one commentator has explained: 'the existence of security raises the expected cost of default for

[12] Ways in which this change in the law puts the charge holder into a less advantageous position include the following: the administrator has to act in the interests of the creditors as a whole rather than primarily in the interests of the charge holder; satisfying the charge holder's security ranks last in the hierarchy of objectives of an administration; and the new administration regime is more formal and elaborate than a receivership, and consequently slower and more expensive.

[13] JL Westbrook, 'The Control of Wealth in Bankruptcy' (2004) 82 *Texas Law Review* 795, 838–43 reviews the two decades of literature on this topic published in the US law reviews.

[14] However, empirical data does not unambiguously support the conclusion that loan interest margins and security are negatively correlated: SA Davydenko and JR Franks, 'Do Bankruptcy Codes Matter? A Study of Defaults in France, Germany and the UK', ECGI Finance Working Paper No 89(2005).

[15] In a perfectly competitive market, interest rates would rise with the degree of risk associated with a project. But information imbalances create market imperfections and the theory of credit rationing (J Stiglitz and A Weiss, 'Credit Rationing in Markets with Imperfect Information' (1981) 71 *American Economic Review* 393) suggests that for a given interest rate, debt may not be provided to all borrowers who want it: 'Competition in UK Banking: A Report to the Chancellor of the Exchequer' (Cruickshank Report, 2000), para 5.8, available at <http://www.hm-treasury. gov.uk/documents/financial_services/banking/bankreview/fin_bank_reviewfinal.cfm> (accessed November 2007).

[16] TH Jackson and AT Kronman, 'Secured Financing and Priorities Among Creditors' (1979) 88 *Yale Law Journal* 1143. But where the security is a floating charge this analysis breaks down because the essence of the floating charge is that it allows the debtor to continue to deal with its assets as if they were not subject to a security.

[17] A Schwartz, 'Security Interests and Bankruptcy Priorities: A Review of Current Theories' (1981) 10 *Journal of Legal Studies* 1; A Schwartz, 'The Continuing Puzzle of Secured Debt' (1984) 37 *Vanderbilt Law Review* 1051.

unsecured creditors by reducing the available asset pool and thus creates incentives for these parties to monitor more extensively'.[18]

Overall, secured debt will only be worthwhile where the additional price that unsecured creditors charge for lending to a company that has given security over its assets does not eclipse the savings that flow from the lower price charged on secured debt.[19] The existence of security can yield positive externalities for unsecured creditors because it prevents the borrowing company from disposing of its existing major assets and embarking on new and more risky ventures[20] and puts in place a focused monitor.[21] The presence of a powerfully secured lender may also facilitate efficient enforcement[22] or restructuring in times of financial distress.[23] In some instances, security may be given in return for an injection of debt finance that enables the company to stay afloat and avoid costly insolvency.[24] Such considerations suggest that the lower monitoring costs of secured creditors may not be entirely cancelled out by the higher monitoring costs incurred by unsecured creditors, with the result that raising part of its debt on a secured basis may have a beneficial overall effect on a company's cost of capital.

The efficiency case for secured debt, though much debated, remains, as Westbrook has said, incomplete and inconclusive.[25] Whilst it is true that in a perfect market, unsecured creditors would, after taking due account of positive externalities, accurately adjust the price of their debt to compensate for the additional risks inherent in lending to a borrower that has granted security over its assets, there are situations, such as involuntary credit or credit provided by

---

[18] Schwartz (1981) (n 17 above) 10. For variations on the 'monitoring' explanation of secured debt: S Levmore, 'Monitors and Freeriders in Commercial and Corporate Settings' (1982) 92 *Yale Law Journal* 49; RE Scott, 'A Relational Theory of Secured Financing' (1986) 86 *Columbia Law Review* 901, 925 *et seq.*

[19] JJ White, 'Efficiency Justifications for Personal Property Security' (1984) *Vanderbilt Law Review* 473; FH Buckley, 'The Bankruptcy Priority Puzzle' (1986) 72 *Virginia Law Review* 1393; H Kripke, 'Law and Economics: Measuring the Economic Efficiency of Commercial Law in a Vacuum of Fact' (1985) 133 *University of Pennsylvania Law Review* 929.

[20] Schwartz (n 18 above) 11; see also CW Smith and JB Warner, 'Bankruptcy, Secured Debt, and Optimal Capital Structure: Comment' (1979) 34 *Journal of Finance* 247; CW Smith and JB Warner, 'On Financial Contracting: An Analysis of Bond Covenants' (1979) 7 *Journal of Financial Economics* 117, 127 where the authors note advantages of secured debt but also point out that secured debt involves opportunity costs by restricting the firm from potentially profitable dispositions of assets which are subject to the security.

[21] TH Jackson and AT Kronman, 'Secured Financing and Priorities Among Creditors' (1979) 88 *Yale Law Journal* 1143, 1149–57.

[22] RE Scott, 'The Truth About Secured Lending' (1997) 82 *Cornell Law Review* 1436.

[23] J Armour, 'Should We Redistribute in Insolvency?' in J Getzler and J Payne (eds), *Company Charges: Spectrum and Beyond* (OUP, 2006) ch 9.

[24] F Oditah, *Legal Aspects of Receivables Financing* (Sweet & Maxwell, 1991) 14–18 (this provides a valuable discussion of the various economic theories used by commentators to explain secured debt); F Oditah, 'The Treatment of Claims in Insolvency' (1992) 108 LQR 459.

[25] JL Westbrook, 'The Control of Wealth in Bankruptcy' (2004) 82 *Texas Law Review* 795, 842. L LoPucki, 'The Unsecured Creditor's Bargain' (1994) 80 *Virginia Law Review* 1887; LA Bebchuk and JM Fried, 'The Uneasy Case for the Priority of Secured Claims in Bankruptcy' (1996) 105 *Yale Law Journal* 857.

unsophisticated lenders that lack the skills to price risk correctly, in which price adjustment may not occur. This suggests that security devices could be socially harmful because they may result in uncompensated risk falling on those creditors that are least well informed, least able to adjust loan terms, least protected in the insolvencies of their debtor companies, and least likely to be capable of absorbing financial shocks.[26] Empirical data on this issue is not conclusive but it has been argued that there is room for scepticism about whether the harmful effects of security outweigh its benefits.[27] Claims have been made for a growing international consensus that secured credit is a general social and economic good.[28]

Security has been said to be a signal of a company's creditworthiness[29] but the effectiveness of security as a signaller does not go unquestioned because there is some evidence that companies give security only when they are unable to borrow on an unsecured basis, so that whatever signal is sent out may be more negative than positive.[30] It is consistent with intuitive expectations for security to be more prevalent in relation to smaller, riskier companies where the likelihood of default is higher[31] and this is supported by empirical research showing that the principal users of secured debt are small and medium-sized firms.[32] There is evidence of a relative aversion for secured borrowing among smaller quoted companies (SQCs) but banks do tend to require security for companies of this size, especially on longer-term loans.[33] Very profitable SQCs are more able to borrow on an unsecured basis.[34] Most of large companies' debt is unsecured.[35] Special purpose vehicles (SPVs) for particular ventures often have complex financing structures that include various tiers of security.[36]

---

[26] V Finch, 'Security, Insolvency and Risk: Who Pays the Price' (199) 62 MLR 633, 668. LoPucki (n 25 above); 1887; Bebchuk and Fried (n 25 above).

[27] Armour (n 23 above) R Mokal, 'The Search for Someone to Save: A Defensive Case for the Priority of Secured Credit' (2002) 22 OJLS 687.

[28] G McCormack, 'The Priority of Secured Credit: An Anglo-American Perspective' [2003] JBL 389, 404–7 provides a review.

[29] A Schwartz, 'Security Interests and Bankruptcy Priorities: A Review of Current Theories' (1981) 10 *Journal of Legal Studies* 1, 14–21.

[30] See M Bridge, 'The *Quistclose* Trust in a World of Secured Transactions' (1992) 12 OJLS 333, 336–9.

[31] J Armour (n 23 above).

[32] Armour (n 23 above) reviews the data.

[33] P Brierley and M Young, 'The Financing of Smaller Quoted Companies: a Survey' (Summer 2004) *Bank of England Quarterly Bulletin* 160.

[34] ibid.

[35] MA Lasfer, *Debt Structure, Agency Costs and Firm's Size: An Empirical Investigation*, working paper, available at <http://www.staff.city.ac.uk/m.a.lasfer/wopapers/mez/debtStructure.pdf> (accessed November 2007); G McCormack, 'The Priority of Secured Credit: An Anglo-American Perspective' [2003] JBL 389, 404.

[36] PR Wood, 'Is the English Law of Security Interests Sleepwalking?' (2005) 20(6) *Butterworths Journal of International Banking and Financial Law* 211.

Policy—dominance of freedom of contract

English law allows companies to create a wide range of security interests, including security that extends to all of their assets. The prevailing policy stance is exemplified by a comment by Lord Hoffmann in a case that raised questions about the legal validity of a particular type of security arrangement: 'In a case in which there is no threat to the consistency of the law or objection of public policy, I think that the courts should be very slow to declare a practice of the commercial community to be conceptually impossible.'[37]

Through its flexibility and its ability to absorb and give effect to innovative structures, English law has played an important role in the development of business by providing security mechanisms that meet the needs of both the consumers and providers of capital.[38] Practitioners, rather than the legislature, have driven the law forward, with it falling to the courts to determine the legal effects of their efforts in instances of uncertainty. In areas of doubt, the courts have certainly not simply provided a rubber-stamp endorsement for whatever new structures and schemes emerge from the ingenious minds of corporate finance practitioners. Freedom of contract is bounded by what is legally possible[39] and where those limits have been exceeded the courts do not shy away from making a decision merely because it will disappoint practitioners and disrupt existing commercial arrangements.[40] Yet, taking a long-term view, it is fair to say that over the centuries the English courts have generally been supportive of transactional lawyers' efforts to mould and develop the law so as to provide cost-effective financing solutions for the corporate sector.[41] Within the limits of what is legally possible, the parties' freedom of contract is not constrained by additional considerations of public policy.[42]

---

[37] *Re Bank of Credit and Commerce International SA (No 8)* [1998] AC 214, HL, 228.

[38] *Buchler v Talbot* [2004] 2 AC 298, HL, para 2 *per* Lord Nicholls.

[39] F Oditah, 'Fixed Charges and Recycling of Proceeds of Receivables' (2004) 120 LQR 533, 537–8.

[40] *Re Spectrum Plus Ltd* [2005] 2 AC 680, HL (refusal by the House of Lords to overrule earlier inconsistent authority with prospective effect only so as not to disrupt existing security arrangements); *Smith (Administrator of Cosslett (Contractors) Ltd) v Bridgend County Borough Council* [2002] 1 AC 336, HL. (The fact that a standard form document had been used for many years without anyone thinking that it created a floating charge was not a reason for holding that this was not its legal effect; Lord Hoffmann said (at para 42): 'The parties cannot therefore be supposed to have intended to create such a charge. But the intentions of the parties, as expressed in the ICE form of contract, are relevant only to establish their mutual rights and obligations. Whether such rights and obligations are characterised as a floating charge is a question of law ... The answer to this question may come as a surprise to the parties but that is no reason for adopting a different characterisation.')

[41] R Nolan, 'Property in a Fund' (2004) 120 LQR 108.

[42] *Re ASRS Establishment Ltd (in administrative receivership and liquidation)* [2000] 2 BCLC 631, CA, 642.

This stance can prompt fairness-related concerns.[43] By readily accommodating the preferences of creditors for security, the law permits situations in which holders of security can step in and sweep off everything, leaving nothing for unsecured creditors including, in particular, a company's employees whose wages have not been paid.[44] Such concerns have attracted the attention of the legislature but the response thus far has not been to limit freedom of contract in the creation of security.[45] Instead, the legislature has intervened by means of mandatory disclosure requirements in the companies legislation, whereby most forms of security must be registered in order to protect their legal effectiveness,[46] and of provisions in the insolvency legislation that have redistributive effects in favour of unsecured creditors of an insolvent borrower. These include provision for security interests created in the twilight period leading up to a company's insolvency to be invalidated;[47] stipulation for certain employee claims to have a preferential status over debts secured by particular types of security;[48] and provision for a prescribed part of secured assets to be set aside for unsecured creditors.[49]

Consensual security interests

The scope of the term 'security interest' is a matter of some uncertainty but in *Bristol Airport plc v Powdrill*[50] counsel acting for one of the parties described real security in the following terms: 'Security is created where a person ("the creditor") to whom an obligation is owed by another ("the debtor") by statute

[43] V Finch, 'Security, Insolvency and Risk: Who Pays the Price' (199) 62 MLR 633, 660–7.

[44] *Re Spectrum Plus Ltd* [2005] 2 AC 680, HL, para 97 *per* Lord Scott. In *Salomon v A Salomon and Co Ltd* [1897] 2 AC 22, HL, 53 Lord Macnaghten described the sweeping effect of the floating charge as a 'great scandal'.

[45] In particular, calls for the outright abolition of the floating charge have generally not found favour: see the discussion in the Cork Committee Report (n 5 above), ch 36 and AL Diamond, 'A Review of Security Interests in Property' (1989) ch 16 (herein after 'Diamond Report'). Recent discussion on reforming the law of credit and security is surveyed at the end of this chapter.

[46] Companies Act 2006, Pt 25. In *Agnew v The Commissioner of Inland Revenue* [2001] 2 AC 710, PC, para 10 Lord Millett described the benefits of registration so far as the ordinary trade creditors were concerned as 'more theoretical than real'.

[47] Insolvency Act 1986, ss 239 (avoidance of voidable preferences) and ss 245 (invalidity of certain floating charges) are the key sections. These sections permit a retrospective review of security for a maximum period of 2 years prior to the commencement of liquidation or administration. If certain conditions are satisfied, the court can order the invalidation of a security on the grounds that it is a voidable preference. If certain conditions are satisfied, a floating charge created in the twilight period is automatically invalid under s 245. A security is not a transaction at an undervalue under Insolvency Act 1986, s 238 because there is no disposal of the company's property: *Re MC Bacon Ltd* [1990] BCC 78.

[48] Insolvency Act 1986, ss 40, 175, 386, and Sch 6.

[49] ibid s 176A; Insolvency Act (Prescribed Part) Order 2003, SI 2003/2097. See J Armour, 'Should We Redistribute in Insolvency?' in J Getzler and J Payne (eds), Company Charges: Spectrum and Beyond (OUP, 2006) ch 9; G McCormack, 'The Priority of Secured Credit: An Anglo-American Perspective' [2003] JBL 389, 416–19.

[50] [1990] Ch 744 CA, 760.

or contract, in addition to the personal promise of the debtor to discharge the obligation, obtains rights exercisable against some property in which the debtor has an interest in order to enforce the discharge of the debtor's obligation to the creditor.' Browne-Wilkinson V-C declined to hold that this was a comprehensive definition of security but confirmed that the description was certainly no wider than the ordinary meaning of the word. One way in which it may be too restrictive is that it fails to acknowledge that a third party may grant rights over its property by way of guarantee to secure the loan to the debtor.[51] The description does highlight the essence of security, namely, that it gives the creditor proprietary and not merely personal rights in respect of a debt.

The proprietary nature of security was emphasized by Lord Jauncey in *Armour v Thyssen Edelstahlwerke AG*:[52]

A right in security is a right over property given by a debtor to a creditor whereby the latter in the event of the debtor's failure acquires priority over the property against the general body of creditors of the debtor. It is of the essence of a right in security that the debtor possesses in relation to the property a right which he can transfer to the creditor, which right must be retransferred to him upon payment of the debt.

The focus of the discussion in this chapter is security interests created by agreement of the parties. Security interests can also arise by operation of law, an example being the vendor's lien on property sold which is to secure payment of the purchase price but these types of security are not considered further in this chapter.[53]

Grant and reservation—fundamental legal distinctions

An element of these descriptions of security that merits closer examination is the emphasis on the creditor *obtaining* rights and the debtor *granting* rights. An important distinction is conventionally[54] drawn in English law between being granted an interest to secure an obligation and reserving an interest for that purpose.[55] If, for example, a supplier sells goods to a customer on credit and title

---

[51] A guarantor can charge its property without giving a personal undertaking to pay: *Re Conley* [1938] 2 All ER 127 CA; *Re Bank of Credit and Commerce International SA (No 8)* [1998] AC 214, HL.

[52] [1990] 3 All ER 481, HL, 486.

[53] See S Worthington, *Proprietary Interests in Commercial Transactions* (Clarendon Press, 1996) Pt II.

[54] See RM Goode, *Legal Problems of Credit and Security* (Sweet & Maxwell, 3rd edn, 2003) 20–3; WJ Gough, *Company Charges* (Butterworths, 2nd edn, 1996) 3–4; and EI Sykes and S Walker *The Law of Securities* (Law Book Company, 5th edn, 1993) 3, 12–13. Contrast F Oditah, *Legal Aspects of Receivables Financing* (Sweet & Maxwell, 1991) 4–11 where it is argued that consensual security need not always lie in grant and that reservation can give rise to a security interest in law.

[55] A distinction clearly established by the House of Lords in *McEntire v Crossley Brothers Ltd* [1895] AC 457, HL.

to those goods passes, the seller, if it wants to be secured in respect of the credit which it has advanced, must take an interest in the purchaser's, or some other person's, property. An alternative course for the seller would have been to reserve title to the goods until payment had been effected. An effective retention of title clause[56] has the same economic effect as taking a security but it falls into a different legal category for the purpose of English law and, in particular, it does not require registration under the company charges provisions of the Companies Act 2006.[57] Furthermore, although this will depend on the precise wording of the provision in question, it may fall outside a covenant not to create future security that was previously given by the company. The fact that by fitting the arrangement into one legal category rather than another, even though the economic effect is the same in either case, is a feature of English law which is open to criticism, in that form is allowed to prevail over substance.[58] Transactions which are really very similar in nature are treated in different ways and this compartmentalization leads to complexity. However, counter-arguments are that English law's respect for the legal form of transactions, is one of the reasons for its popularity as the governing law for international financial transactions and that the benefits of having a flexible system that can be moulded to fit business needs should not be jeopardized.[59]

At intervals, various review bodies have proposed that English law should adopt a more flexible approach and that interests retained by the creditor should be treated as security interests in the same way as interests granted by the debtor.[60] The most recent airings for this idea were in two consultation papers published by the Law Commission in 2002 and 2004.[61] Treating proprietary interests reserved by the creditor in the same way as proprietary security interests granted by the debtor would bring English law more into line with article 9 of the US Uniform Commercial Code, where the term 'security interest' is defined broadly to include any 'interest in personal property or fixtures which secures payment or

---

[56] There is a considerable amount of case law on when such clauses will be effective, including *Aluminium Industrie Vaassen BV v Romalpa Aluminium Ltd* [1976] 1 WLR 676, CA; *Re Peachdart Ltd* [1984] Ch 131; *Hendy Lennox Ltd v Grahame Puttick Ltd* [1984] 1 WLR 485; *Clough Mill Ltd v Martin* [1985] 1 WLR 111, CA; *Armour v Thyssen Edelstahlwerke AG* [1990] 3 All ER 481, HL. Generally, on retention of title agreements, see G McCormack, *Reservation of Title* (Sweet & Maxwell, 2nd edn, 1995); S Wheeler, *Reservation of Title Claims: Impact and Implications* (Clarendon Press, 1991).

[57] *Clough Mill Ltd v Martin* [1985] 1 WLR 111, CA.

[58] RM Goode, 'The Modernisation of Personal Property Security Law' (1984) 100 LQR 234, 237–8; M Bridge, 'Form, Substance and Innovation in Personal Property Security Law' [1992] JBL 1.

[59] R Calnan, 'The Reform of Company Security Interests' (2005) 20(1) *Butterworths Journal of International Banking and Financial Law* 25.

[60] *Report of the Committee on Consumer Credit* (Cmnd 4596, 1971) paras 5.2.8–5.2.15 (herein after 'Crowther Report'); Diamond Report (n 45 above) paras 3.4–3.10.

[61] Law Commission, *Registration of Security Interests: Company Charges and Property other than Land* (Law Com CP No 164, 2002). Law Commission, *Company Security Interests, A Consultative Report,* (Law Com CP No 176, 2004).

the performance of an obligation' and it is clear that this encompasses retained interests as well as interests granted by the debtor. However, proposals to this effect are invariably controversial, with opponents raising technical objections as well as policy concerns about the potential adverse impact on English law's attractiveness to commerce. In 2005 the Law Commission withdrew its proposal to include title-retention devices such as finance leases, hire purchase, and conditional sale agreements within a new registration scheme but suggested that it would reconsider the issue at a later date.[62] There is scant indication that proposals for radical change will attract a consensus among interested groups or political support in the short to medium term.

There are two principles that limit the rule of English law that courts must respect the distinction between law and economics and give effect to the legal form of a transaction, notwithstanding that in economic terms it is the functional equivalent of another type of transaction that would attract a different legal treatment.[63] The first is the doctrine of 'shams'. Acts or documents are regarded as shams where the parties intend by means of those acts or documents to give to third parties or to the court the appearance of creating between the parties legal rights and obligations different from the actual legal rights and obligations (if any) which the parties intend to create.[64] An arrangement will not take legal effect in accordance with its appearance if, in fact, that appearance is a sham. The court will disregard the deceptive language by which the parties have attempted to conceal the true nature of the transaction into which they have entered and attempt by extrinsic evidence to discover what the real transaction was.[65] The doctrine of sham is not lightly invoked, however. A sham transaction has been said to be one in which there is a degree of dishonesty on the part of the parties, and the courts are generally slow to find dishonesty.[66] There is a very strong presumption that parties intend to be bound by the provisions of agreements into which they enter and intend the agreements they enter into to take effect.[67] An arrangement is not a sham merely because it is artificial or uncommercial.[68]

The second basis for disregarding the apparent form of a transaction is what may be described as the 'mislabelling' principle. Freedom of contract means that, generally speaking, contracting parties can grant each other whatever rights and obligations they like but the categorization of the transaction created by the

---

[62] Law Commission, *Company Security Interests* (Law Com Rep No 296, 2005) para 1.29.

[63] *Bank of Tokyo Ltd v Karoon* [1986] 3 All ER 468, CA, 486 *per* Goff LJ.

[64] *Snook v London & West Riding Investments Ltd* [1967] 2 QB 786 CA, 802 *per* Diplock LJ.

[65] *Orion Finance Ltd v Crown Financial Management Ltd* [1996] 2 BCLC 78 CA, 84 *per* Millett LJ.

[66] *National Westminster Bank plc v Jones* [2001] 1 BCLC 98, paras 39 and 46. Appeal dismissed [2001] EWCA Civ 1541.

[67] *National Westminster Bank v Jones* [2001] 1 BCLC 98, para 59.

[68] *Hitch v Stone (Inspector of Taxes)* [2001] EWCA Civ 63, [2001] STC 214, para 67 *per* Arden LJ; *National Westminster Bank v Jones* [2001] 1 BCLC 98, para 39.

chosen bundle of rights and obligations is a matter of law.[69] Whatever label the parties have put on their agreement is not conclusive and the court will recategorize it if its terms are inconsistent with the label that has been attached.[70]

Security interests are defeasible interests

An uncontroversial feature of a security interest is that it confers an interest in property that is defeasible or destructible on payment of the debt or performance of the obligation which was secured.[71] A borrower that gives security can always obtain the release of its property from the security by repaying the loan.[72] Subject to one exception, equity renders void any attempt to restrict the borrower's right to redeem a security.[73] The exception is contained in section 739 of the Companies Act 2006, which provides that a condition contained in debentures, or in a deed for securing debentures, is not invalid by reason only that the debentures are thereby made irredeemable or redeemable only on the happening of a contingency (however remote), or on the expiration of a period (however long), any rule of equity to the contrary notwithstanding. The term 'debenture' lacks a precise definition,[74] but it is clear that for the purposes of this section it includes a mortgage on land.[75] In practice, debentures that are described as 'perpetual' or 'irredeemable' may in fact give the company an option to redeem.

A security interest is an interest in the chargor's property to secure a debt

Two distinct issues arise under this heading. The first is that a security interest is inextricably linked with the debt for which it is security. It follows from this that

---

[69] *Agnew v The Commissioner of Inland Revenue* [2001] 2 AC 710, PC, para 32. This case concerned characterization of a charge as fixed or floating but the reasoning can be regarded as being of more general application and as being relevant to questions whether a transaction creates an absolute interest or a security: H Beale, M Bridge, L Gullifer, and E Lomnicka, *The Law of Personal Property Security* (OUP, 2007) 24.

[70] *Re George Inglefield Ltd* [1933] Ch 1, CA; *Re Curtain Dream plc* [1990] BCLC 925; *Welsh Development Agency v Export Finance Co Ltd* [1992] BCC 270, CA; *Orion Finance Ltd v Crown Financial Management Ltd* [1996] BCC 621, CA; *Re Bond Worth Ltd* [1980] Ch 228; *Borden UK Ltd v Scottish Timber Products Ltd* [1981] Ch 25, CA; *Pfeiffer E Weinkellerei-Weineinkauf GmbH & Co v Arbuthnot Factors Ltd* [1988] 1 WLR 150; *Tatung (UK) Ltd v Galex Telesure Ltd* (1989) 5 BCC 325.

[71] *Re Bond Worth Ltd* [1980] Ch 228, 248.

[72] *Re George Inglefield Ltd* [1933] Ch 1, CA, 27 *per* Romer LJ. This is one characteristic which can help to distinguish a mortgage or charge from a sale (ibid).

[73] The history of this rule of equity is traced by Viscount Haldane LC in *Kreglinger v New Patagonia Meat and Cold Storage Co Ltd* [1914] AC 25, HL. In this case the House of Lords confirmed that the rule applies to floating charges, thereby dispelling doubts raised by *De Beers Consolidated Mines v British South Africa Co* [1912] AC 52, HL.

[74] See ch 11 above.

[75] *Knightsbridge Estates Trust Ltd v Byrne* [1940] AC 613, HL.

a creditor cannot be said to have a security interest in property at any time when there is no outstanding debt. This situation could arise, for example, where the charge pre-dates the advance of the money or where it relates to a current account which fluctuates between being in credit and being overdrawn.

The second issue relates to the essential feature of a security interest that it gives the creditor an interest in the property of the person providing the security. This means that if the debtor[76] agrees to give security over property that it does not presently own but will acquire in the future, the creditor cannot be viewed as having a security interest in the debtor's property at the time when the agreement is concluded.[77] Adopting language that is familiar to that of US lawyers in the context of article 9 of the Uniform Commercial Code, the Crowther Committee, whose report containing a review of credit and security was published as a government command paper in 1971, described situations where there is an agreement for security but no outstanding loan, or where the security is not presently owned by the debtor, as being ones where the security interest has not 'attached' to the debtor's property:[78] 'The fact that there is an enforceable agreement which provides for a security interest is not by itself sufficient to make that security interest attach to a security, for the agreement may well have been entered into before the security was acquired by the debtor and/or before any advance has been made by the secured party.'

Even though attachment may not have taken place, the date of an enforceable agreement for security has considerable legal significance. It is the date from which the twenty-one-day registration period runs for the purposes of the registration requirements of the Companies Act 2006.[79] Also, as is clear from cases involving security on property not owned by the debtor at the time of the agreement but later acquired (commonly referred to as 'future property'), even though the security does not attach until the property is acquired, the creditor has more than a mere contractual right from the time when the agreement is concluded, which has important implications should the debtor become insolvent or grant someone else an interest in the same property, thereby creating a potential priority dispute.

Security on future property

The seminal authority on the effect of an agreement for security relating to future property is the decision of the House of Lords in *Holroyd v Marshall*.[80] The indenture between the lenders and the borrower in this case provided for the lenders

---

[76] As used here, this term is intended to include a third party provider of security by way of guarantee.

[77] There are some exceptions to the rule that a debtor cannot give a valid security over another's property but these exceptions are of limited significance: see RM Goode, *Legal Problems of Credit and Security* (Sweet & Maxwell, 3rd edn, 2003) 64.

[78] *Report of the Committee on Consumer Credit* (Cmnd 4596, 1971) para 5.6.4. See also Goode (n 77 above) ch II.

[79] Companies Act 2006, s 870.

[80] (1862) 10 HLC 191, 11 ER 999, [1861–73] All ER Rep 414, HL. This case did not lay down new doctrine but contains 'the mere enunciation of elementary principles long settled in Courts of

to have security on existing premises, machinery, and other implements owned by the borrower and also on 'all machinery, implements and things, which during the continuance of this security shall be fixed or placed in or about the said mill ... in addition to or substitution for the said premises or any part thereof'. When the borrower later defaulted on the loan, the lenders sold the machinery and effects that had been in existence at the date of the security agreement but this sale did not realize sufficient proceeds to discharge their loan. They therefore also sought to claim, as part of their security, machinery which had been added and substituted since the date of the security but this was also claimed by a judgment creditor. The question for the House of Lords was whether the lenders had an interest in the added and substituted machinery because, if they did, that machinery could not be taken in execution by the judgment creditor.

The House of Lords held that the lenders had an equitable interest and that their title therefore prevailed over the judgment creditor. Although the agreement to confer an interest in future property was void as law because there was nothing to convey,[81] in equity the agreement took effect so that as soon as the future property was acquired by the borrower and without the need for any new act on the part of the lenders, it became subject to the lenders' security. Lord Westbury LC said:[82]

But if a vendor or mortgagor agrees to sell or mortgage property, real or personal, of which he is not possessed at the time, and he receives the consideration for the contract, and afterwards becomes possessed of property answering the description in the contract, there is no doubt that a court of equity would compel him to perform the contract, and that the contract would in equity transfer the beneficial interest to the mortgagee or purchaser immediately on the property being acquired.

Holroyd v Marshall was considered and in some respects clarified by the House of Lords in the later case of *Tailby v The Official Receiver*.[83] Here a bill of sale assigned (among other things) all of the book debts due and owing or which might during the continuance of the security become due and owing to the mortgagor. It was held that this was effective to give the creditor an equitable interest in the book debts incurred after the date of the bill of sale. The respondent's argument that the description of the security was too vague to be effective (which had found favour in the Court of Appeal) was rejected. The House of Lords took the view that the Court of Appeal (and courts in some previous cases) had proceeded on a misapprehension of some observations of Lord Westbury in *Holroyd v Marshall* which had appeared to link the doctrine enunciated in that case to the class of circumstances in which a court of equity would grant specific

---

Equity': *Tailby v Official Receiver* (1888) 13 App Cas 523, HL, 535 *per* Lord Watson; see also 546 *per* Lord Macnaghten.

[81] *Robinson v Macdonnell* (1816) 5 M&S 228, 105 ER 1034.
[82] (1862) 10 HLC 191, HL, 211.
[83] (1888) 13 App Cas 523, HL.

performance.[84] Lord Macnaghten in particular sought to correct the misunderstanding. He explained that the principle of equity underlying *Holroyd v Marshall* was that equity considers as done that which ought to be done. This principle was independent of the rules relating to the granting of specific performance and applied where there was an agreement assigning future property for value, with the result that, provided the consideration had passed, the agreement was binding on the property as soon as it was acquired.[85]

Tailby v Official Receiver indicates that the principle enunciated in *Holroyd v Marshall* will apply where a person has agreed to give a security interest to a lender in the following circumstances:

(1) There is an agreement to confer the security interest on the lender: in *Holroyd v Marshall* this took the form of an agreement to assign by way of security whilst in *Tailby v Official Receiver* this took the form of a present assignment (by way of security) of future debts. As Lord Macnaghten stated, the principle gives effect to the parties' contractual intentions.

The truth is that cases of equitable assignment or specific lien, where the consideration has passed, depend on the real meaning of the agreement between the parties. The difficulty, generally speaking, is to ascertain the true scope and effect of the agreement.[86]

(2) The consideration for the security interest has been executed, ie the lender has advanced the money.

(3) The borrower has acquired an interest in property matching the description of the subject-matter of the security. The subject-matter of the security may be expressed in broad terms as in the *Tailby* case where it extended to all of the borrower's future book debts. Provided the clause identifying the subject-matter of the security is not so vaguely drafted as to make it impossible to ascertain to what it is applicable, the principle will apply. Two members of the House of Lords in the *Tailby* decision adverted to the possibility of equity denying effect to a purported equitable assignment on grounds of public policy where it included all of the present and future property of the person giving it and deprived that person of the power of maintaining himself but that possible limitation has not been applied in later cases.

The position of the creditor between the conclusion of the security agreement and the acquisition of the property by the debtor is demonstrated by *Re Lind*,

---

[84] ibid 529 *per* Lord Hershell, 535 *per* Lord Watson. The third judge, Lord Fitzgerald did not address the point (and he neither assented to nor dissented from the decision). The opinion of the remaining judge, Lord Macnaghten, is considered next.

[85] *Metcalfe v Archbishop of York* 1 My & Cr 547.

[86] *Tailby v Official Receiver* (1888) 13 App Cas 523, HL, 547. Contrast *Carr v Allatt* (1858) 27 LJ (Ex) 385 and *Brown v Bateman* (1866–7) LR 2 CP 272 with *Reeve v Whitmore* (1864) 33 LJ (Ch) 63, *Thompson v Cohen* (1871–2) LR 7 QB 527; *Cole v Kernot* (1871–2) LR 7 QB 534n; *Collyer v Isaacs* (1881) 19 Ch D 342, CA (as explained in *Re Lind* [1915] 2 Ch 345 CA, 362–3 *per* Swinfen Eady LJ).

Industrial Finance Syndicate Ltd v Lind.[87] Lind was presumptively entitled to a share in his mother's personal estate and he used this expectancy as security for two mortgages. Later, but before his mother's death, Lind became bankrupt and obtained his discharge. He then assigned his expectancy to a syndicate. On his mother's death, the two mortgagees claimed Lind's share of the estate in priority to the syndicate and the Court of Appeal upheld their claim. The discharge in bankruptcy had discharged Lind's personal obligations but the mortgagees had a stronger claim. Bankes LJ explained: 'it is true that the security was not enforceable until the property came into existence, but nevertheless the security was there';[88] and Phillimore LJ stated, 'it is I think well and long settled that the right of the assignee is a higher right than the right to have specific performance of a contract, that the assignment creates an equitable charge which arises immediately upon the property coming into existence'.[89] Earlier, apparently inconsistent, authority was explained and distinguished.[90]

The precise nature of the interest held by a lender with security over future property before the property has been acquired has never been defined but some of the consequences of *Re Lind* are reasonably clear. First, a lender which has security over future property ranks as a secured creditor in the chargor's liquidation and is not required to proceed as an unsecured creditor by submitting a proof. If the chargor company is in compulsory liquidation, the creditor can enforce its rights against the property when it is acquired without infringing section 127 of the Insolvency Act 1986, which renders void any disposition of the company's property after the commencement of the winding up.[91] The reason for this is that the creditor's interest in the property pre-dates the insolvency and there is therefore no disposition of the company's property at a vulnerable time. Secondly, for the purposes of priority rules which depend on order of creation, a security over future property is created when the agreement is concluded and not at the later date when the property is acquired. Thus, in the *Re Lind* decision itself, the mortgagees held interests that took priority over a later assignment.

The subject-matter of a security interest—forms of property that can be used as security

The previous section made the point that a chargor can grant security only over its own property but including property that it may acquire in the future. Here,

---

[87] [1915] 2 Ch 345, CA.
[88] ibid 374.
[89] ibid 365–6.
[90] *Collyer v Isaacs* (1881) 19 Ch D 342, CA.
[91] *Re Androma Pty Ltd* [1987] 2 Qd 134, Q FC. Although a decision on Australian legislation, the reasoning would seem to be equally applicable to the English statute.

the question is whether there is any limitation on the type of property owned by the chargor that can be used as security.

It is now clear that a company can use all of its present and future assets as security. Land, whether freehold or leasehold, and the fixtures and fittings attaching to it, tangible personal property such as the company's stock in trade and intangible personal property, including debts owing to the company and its intellectual property, can all be used as security.

The decision in *Re Charge Card Services Ltd*,[92] in which it was held that a chargor could not use debts as security in favour of a creditor which was itself the person that owed the debts to the company—ie that a chargor could not 'charge back' debts to the debtor—because a security in that form was 'conceptually impossible', sparked a decade of controversy. The matter was extensively debated in academic journals and elsewhere.[93] When an opportunity to consider the issue arose in *Re Bank of Credit and Commerce International SA (No 8)*,[94] the view that charge-backs were conceptually impossible was rejected by the House of Lords. Lord Hoffmann, who delivered the only reasoned speech, accepted that a charge-back lacked one of the regular features of a charge on debts—ie the chargee could not enforce the security by suing the debtor since the chargee could not sue itself—but held that the absence of this one feature did not preclude the existence of a charge. His Lordship emphasized that where there was no threat to the consistency of the law or objection of public policy, the courts should be very slow to declare a practice of the commercial community to be conceptually impossible. Although resolution of the charge-back issue was not essential to the decision in the case and Lord Hoffmann's views can therefore be regarded as technically obiter,[95] the point had been very fully argued before their Lordships and, for most practical purposes, the Opinion appears to put an end to the debate and confirm the validity of charge-backs as a form of security.[96]

Forms of consensual real security

Consensual real security is conventionally divided into four categories: pledge, lien, mortgage, and charge. Pledges and liens have limited practical significance

---

[92] [1987] Ch 150 (affirmed but without reference to the point relevant here [1989] Ch 497, CA).

[93] The leading proponent of the pro charge-back view was Philip Wood: see PR Wood, 'Three Problems of Set-off: Contingencies, Build-ups and Charge-Backs' (1987) 8 *Company Law* 262. Detailed analysis of the point is also to be found in PR Wood, *English and International Set-off* (Sweet & Maxwell, 1989) paras 5.134–5.181.

[94] [1998] AC 214, HL. G McCormack, 'Charge Backs and Commercial Certainty in the House of Lords' [1998] CFILR 111.

[95] A point made by RM Goode, *Legal Problems of Credit and Security* (Sweet & Maxwell, 3rd edn, 2003) 93–4. Goode had argued that charge-backs were conceptually impossible.

[96] On certain detailed questions that still remain, see H Beale, M Bridge, L Gullifer, and E Lomnicka, *The Law of Personal Property Security* (OUP, 2007) 107–8.

because they require the creditor to take some form of possession of the subject-matter of the security. The forms of security that are in more widespread use in corporate financing are mortgages and charges. The terms 'mortgage' and 'charge' are often used interchangeably but there are some technical distinctions between them. For the purposes of the registration requirements of the Companies Act 2006, the term 'charge' includes mortgages.[97]

Pledge and lien[98]

In a pledge, assets of the debtor are delivered to the creditor as security for the debt or other obligation.[99] The creditor is said to have a special interest in the pledged property and, if the debtor fails to pay the debt when due, the creditor can sell the pledged property and use the sale proceeds to discharge the debt whilst accounting to the debtor for any surplus.[100] This distinguishes the pledge from the lien, which at common law confers on the creditor a right to detain the debtor's property but no right of sale or disposition.[101] The creditor may use the pledged assets at its own risk. The creditor may also assign his interest as pledgee and may sub-pledge that interest.[102] The debtor is entitled to the immediate possession of the assets when he has paid the debt for which they were pledged and, if the goods have been sub-pledged, the sub-pledgee may be sued in conversion if he impedes the debtor from exercising this right. In these circumstances, the debtor can also sue the creditor for breach of the contract of pledge.[103]

A valid pledge requires an agreement between the debtor and creditor and also delivery of the assets which form the subject-matter of the security; agreement alone does not suffice.[104] In addition to actual delivery, the law has recognized constructive delivery as being effective for this purpose, an example of this being the delivery of the key to a warehouse in which goods are stored.[105] Negotiable instruments and securities, such as bearer bonds, can be pledged[106] but it has been held that the effect of depositing share certificates with a lender is to create an equitable mortgage rather than a pledge.[107] This distinction can be explained: delivery of bearer securities to a creditor constitutes delivery of the assets in the same way as delivery of goods; but delivery of share certificates, which are simply

[97] Companies Act 2006, s 861(5).

[98] Beale, Bridge, Gullifer, and Lomnicka (n 96 above) ch 3.

[99] *Coggs v Barnard* (1703) 2 Ld Raym 909, Ct of Kings Bench; *Haliday v Holgate* (1868) LR 3 Exch 299, Exch Chamber.

[100] *Re Hardwick, ex p Hubbard* (1886) 17 QBD 690, CA.

[101] *Donald v Suckling* (1866) LR 1 QB 585, 604, 610, 612.

[102] ibid.

[103] See further LS Sealy and RJA Hooley, *Commercial Law Text, Cases and Materials* (Butterworths, 3rd edn, 2003) 1038–52.

[104] *Official Assignee of Madras v Mercantile Bank of India Ltd* [1935] AC 53, PC.

[105] *Wrightson v McArthur and Hutchinsons (1919) Ltd* [1921] 2 KB 807.

[106] *Carter v Wake* (1877) 4 Ch D 605.

[107] *Harrold v Plenty* [1901] 2 Ch 314.

evidence of title to the shares,[108] does not amount to delivery of the shares and even the delivery of share certificates accompanied by executed share transfer forms does not complete delivery of the shares.[109]

A pledge requires agreement between debtor and creditor and there is no such thing as a pledge arising by operation of law. A common law lien can arise by operation of law[110] or by agreement. A lien is a limited form of security which entitles the creditor to hold the assets which are the subject-matter of the security but not to sell them.[111]

Mortgage

Leaving aside statutory intervention, a mortgage is a transfer of ownership, legal or equitable, as security for a debt or other obligation with an express or implied proviso for retransfer when the debt or obligation has been discharged.[112] A debtor may mortgage its own property as security but it is also possible for a third party to mortgage its property as security for another's debts and the third party need not itself undertake any personal obligation to pay.[113] Since 1926, mortgages of land have been subject to special statutory rules under which the creation of a mortgage does not involve a transfer of ownership. Mortgages of land and interests in land are not explored further in this chapter.

Also excluded from detailed discussion in this chapter are security interests in equitable property, such as beneficial interests under trusts. Although companies may hold equitable property, it is perhaps more common to think of the property that a company may use as its security as being property of which it is the legal owner, such as plant, machinery and equipment, stock in trade, intellectual property, book debts, and other receivables.

A legal mortgage of personal property requires the transfer to the creditor of the legal title to the assets that are to form the security. The form of the transfer depends on the nature of the assets in question. A legal mortgage of goods may be oral[114] or may be created by deed or by delivery of the goods. Whether a transaction involving the delivery of goods is a mortgage or a pledge depends on the

---

[108] Companies Act 2006, s 768. Cf Companies Act 2006, s 779(2), which is concerned with share warrants, title to which does pass by delivery.

[109] *London and Midland Bank Ltd v Mitchell* [1899] 2 Ch 161; *Stubbs v Slater* [1910] 1 Ch 632, CA. It is generally considered that legal title to shares passed only when the transferee is registered in the company's books as a member of the company: *Société Générale de Paris v Walker* (1885) 11 App Cas 20, HL, 28 *per* Lord Selborne; *Colonial Bank v Hepworth* (1887) 36 Ch D 36, 54.

[110] *Re Bond Worth Ltd* [1980] Ch 228, 250 *per* Slade J.

[111] *Hammonds v Barclay* (1802) 2 East 227, 102 ER 356; *Tappenden v Artus* [1964] 2 QB 185, CA. On liens see further Sealy and Hooley (n 103 above) 1053–68.

[112] *Santley v Wilde* [1899] 2 Ch 474, CA; *Noakes & Co Ltd v Rice* [1902] AC 24, HL, 28 *per* Earl of Halsbury LC.

[113] *Perry v National Provincial Bank of England* [1910] 1 Ch 464, CA; *Re Conley* [1938] 2 All ER 127 CA.

[114] *Newlove v Shrewsbury* (1888) 21 QBD 41, CA.

intention of the parties.[115] Generally, a legal mortgage of a chose in action, such as a debt, must comply with section 136(1) of the Law of Property Act 1925 and, as such, must be in writing with written notice to the debtor,[116] but particular types of choses in action are subject to special rules: a legal mortgage of shares requires the mortgagee to be registered in the company's register of members in respect of the shares;[117] and a legal mortgage of negotiable instruments, such as bearer securities, can be created simply by delivery of the relevant documents. Future property cannot be the subject of a legal mortgage.[118] An assignment of part of a debt cannot be brought within section 136(1) with the result that it is not possible to create a legal mortgage of part of a debt.[119]

An equitable mortgage involves the transfer to the creditor of equitable ownership subject to a proviso for redemption. An equitable mortgage of personal property can be created in various ways. For instance, a contract to give a legal mortgage on property can give rise in equity to an equitable mortgage when the requirements for a full legal mortgage (for example registration of the creditor in the company's register of members in the case of a legal mortgage of shares or compliance with the Law of Property Act 1925, section 136(1) in relation to the legal mortgage of a debt) have not been fulfilled.[120]

The debtor's continuing interest in mortgaged property stems from its entitlement to require the property to be reconveyed on the discharge of the secured debt or other obligation. This is known as the 'equity of redemption'. The equity of redemption survives default,[121] and late payment or performance will still entitle the mortgagor to redeem at least until such time as the creditor enforces its security by selling the secured assets or by foreclosure. Any provision in the terms of

---

[115] AP Bell, *Modern Law of Personal Property in England and Ireland* (Butterworths, 1989) 185; RW Ramage, 'Chattel Mortgages' (1971) 121 NLJ 291.

[116] Law of Property Act 1925, s 136(1) refers to 'absolute' assignments and provides that it does not apply to assignments purporting to be by way of charge only. An assignment by way of mortgage is considered to be absolute and not by way of charge only: *Burlinson v Hall* (1884) 12 QBD 347; *Tancred v Delagoa Bay Co* (1889) 23 QBD 239.

[117] *General Credit and Discount Co v Glegg* (1883) 22 Ch D 549 is an example of a legal mortgage of shares. It is generally considered that legal title to shares passed only when the transferee is registered in the company's books as a member of the company: *Société Générale de Paris v Walker* (1885) 11 App Cas 20, HL, 28 *per* Lord Selborne; *Colonial Bank v Hepworth* (1887) 36 Ch D 36, 54.

[118] *Holroyd v Marshall* (1862) 10 HLC 191; 11 ER 999, [1861–73] All ER Rep 414, HL; *Robinson v Macdonnell* (1816) 5 M&S 228, 105 ER 1034.

[119] *Durham Brothers v Robertson* [1898] 1 QB 765, CA; *Re Steel Wing Co Ltd* [1921] 1 Ch 349; *Earle v Hemsworth* (1928) 44 TLR 605; *Williams v Atlantic Assurance Co* [1933] 1 KB 81, CA. Although there are authorities to the contrary, so that the point may not be regarded as being definitively settled, the view expressed in the text is widely regarded as being the better view: OR Marshall, *Assignment of Choses in Action* (Pitman, 1950) 173–4. In *Norman v FCT* (1963) 109 CLR 9, High Ct of Aust, 29 Windeyer J stated that the earlier inconsistent decisions must be taken to be overruled.

[120] See further LS Sealy and RJA Hooley, *Commercial Law Text, Cases and Materials* (Butterworths, 3rd edn, 2003) ch 26.

[121] This was not always the case: see AWB Simpson, *A History of the Land Law* (Clarendon Press, 2nd edn, 1986) ch X.

a mortgage which purports to remove the mortgagor's right to redeem, or which would indirectly tend to have the effect of making the mortgage irredeemable, is regarded in equity as a 'clog' or 'fetter' on the equity of redemption and, as such, it is void.[122] The principle that clogs on the equity of redemption are void applies to all types of mortgages and also to charges, including floating charges.[123]

Charges

Every equitable mortgage is also an equitable charge but the converse is not true:[124] a mortgage, like a charge, appropriates property for the payment of a debt or the discharge of an obligation but a mortgage goes further than a charge and also operates to transfer ownership in equity to the creditor, subject to the chargor's equity of redemption.[125] A charge gives its holder rights in relation to the property which is the subject-matter of the security but does not effect a transfer of the legal or beneficial ownership of that property.[126] Except in relation to land where, by statute, a mortgage by way of legal charge can be created,[127] a charge is a form of equitable security. A charge would normally be created by an agreement between the parties supported by consideration or in the form of a deed but, as Slade J noted in *Re Bond Worth Ltd*,[128] an equitable charge can also be created by the chargor declaring himself a trustee of the relevant assets for the purposes of the security. Where the charge extends to future property, consideration is always required and a deed alone will not suffice.

The importance of the distinction between mortgages and charges is said to lie in the range of remedies available to the creditor in the event of default as a matter of general law. Broadly speaking, a chargee has available to it under the general law a more limited range of remedies than is available to a mortgagee.[129] However, well-drafted charges invariably expand the chargee's remedies with the result that, in practice, there is usually little difference between the remedies enjoyed by a mortgagee and by a chargee. In *Re Bond Worth Ltd* Slade LJ acknowledged that the words 'mortgage' and 'charge' are often used interchangeably.[130]

---

[122] eg *Noakes & Co Ltd v Rice* [1902] AC 24, HL, 28 *per* Earl of Halsbury LC and 30 *per* Lord Macnaghten.

[123] *Kreglinger v New Patagonia Meat and Cold Storage Co Ltd* [1914] AC 25, HL dispelling doubts raised by *De Beers Consolidated Mines v British South Africa Co* [1912] AC 52, HL.

[124] *Shea v Moore* [1894] IR 158, Ir CA.

[125] *Re Bond Worth Ltd* [1980] Ch 228, 250.

[126] *National Provincial and Union Bank of England v Charnley* 1924] 1 KB 431, CA, 449–50 *per* Atkin LJ; *Re Bond Worth Ltd* [1980] Ch 228, 250 *per* Slade J; *Swiss Bank Corpn v Lloyds Bank Ltd* [1982] AC 584, CA and HL, 594–5 *per* Buckley LJ; *Re Charge Card Services Ltd* [1987] Ch 150, 176 *per* Millett J; *Re BCCI (No 8)* [1998] AC 214, HL, 226 *per* Lord Hoffmann; *Re Cosslett (Contractors)* [1998] Ch 495 CA, 508 *per* Millett LJ.

[127] Law of Property Act 1925, s 87.

[128] [1980] Ch 228, 250.

[129] H Beale, M Bridge, L Gullifer, and E Lomnicka, *The Law of Personal Property Security* (OUP, 2007) 92–3.

[130] [1980] Ch 228, 250.

In *Buchler v Talbot*,[131] a case concerning the question of whether by virtue of section 175(2)(b) of the Insolvency Act 1986 the liquidator's costs and expenses were payable out of the proceeds of the realization of assets subject to a charge, all three members of the House of Lords who delivered reasoned speeches described a charge in terms that are more usually associated with a mortgage: 'the charged assets belong to the debenture holder to the extent of the amounts secured';[132] 'the proceeds of the assets comprised in a floating charge which belong to the charge holder to the extent of the security';[133] 'the company has only an equity of redemption; the right to retransfer of the assets when the debt secured by the floating charge has been paid off'.[134] The use of such language has attracted critical comment[135] but it is impossible to think that their Lordships simply ignored the basic and very familiar differences between mortgages and charges and the speeches are best read as supporting those who argue that it is a mistake to over-theorize in abstract terms about the nature of charges because their operation depends on the statutory context to which questions relate (in the *Buchler* case, the insolvency legislation and the distribution of assets by a liquidator) and on the particular rights and obligations that the parties have granted each other in the charging documentation.[136]

Fixed and floating charges—a comparison of their key features

Fixed charges

For companies, the category of charges has to be sub-divided into fixed charges and floating charges. A fixed charge is similar to a mortgage in that the holder immediately obtains rights in relation to the secured property and can restrict the chargor company from disposing of it or destroying it. The chargee may obtain an injunction to restrain unauthorized disposals[137] and, if property which is subject to an enforceable fixed charge is wrongfully disposed of by the chargor, the person acquiring the property will take it subject to the charge unless he can claim to be a bona fide purchaser of the legal title to the property who is without notice of the existence of the fixed charge. A fixed charge is said to fasten on the assets which are the subject-matter of the security; thus in the leading case of *Illingworth v Houldsworth*[138] Lord Macnaghten described a fixed charge as 'one that without

---

[131] [2004] 2 AC 298, HL.
[132] At para 16 *per* Lord Nicholls.
[133] At para 62 *per* Lord Millett.
[134] At para 29 *per* Lord Hoffmann.
[135] RJ Mokal, 'Liquidation Expenses and Floating Charges—the Separate Funds Fallacy' [2004] LMCLQ 387.
[136] J Armour and A Walters, 'Funding Liquidation: a Functional View' (2006) 122 LQR 295; Beale, Bridge, Gullifer, and Lomnicka (n 129 above) 102.
[137] *Holroyd v Marshall* (1862) 10 HL Cas 191, HL, 211–12 *per* Lord Westbury.
[138] [1904] AC 355, HL, 358.

more fastens on ascertained and definite property or property capable of being ascertained or defined'. In a much more recent case Lord Walker echoed these views: 'Under a fixed charge the assets charged as security are permanently appropriated to the payment of the sum charged, in such a way as to give the chargee a proprietary interest in the assets. So long as the charge remains unredeemed, the assets can be released from the charge only with the active concurrence of the chargee.'[139] The subject-matter of a fixed charge security may extend to future property in accordance with the principles in *Holroyd v Marshall*.[140]

Floating charges

In his speech in *Illingworth v Houldsworth* Lord Macnaghten described the floating charge in these terms:[141] 'a floating charge, on the other hand, is ambulatory and shifting in its nature, hovering over and so to speak floating with the property which it is intended to affect until some event occurs or some act is done which causes it to settle and fasten on the subject of the charge within its reach and grasp'.

The essence of the floating charge, and the key factor which distinguishes it from the fixed charge, is that the chargor can continue to deal with the assets which are the subject of the security and can transfer them to third parties unencumbered by the security.[142] However, as is discussed later in this chapter, some degree of restriction on dealings by the chargor with the secured assets is not incompatible with a floating charge. Whether a charge can be categorized as a fixed charge where it allows the chargor a degree of freedom to deal with the secured assets and to withdraw them from the security is much more questionable.

Floating charges can, and commonly do, extend to future property as well as to property presently owned by the chargor company. The effect of a floating charge on present and future property, such as stock in trade, is that as the stock turns over in the ordinary course of trade, items sold pass out of the security but new items come within the scope of the charge as soon as they are acquired by the company. It is not clear that a floating charge on chattels extends to the proceeds when those assets are sold by the company for its own benefit as permitted by the terms of the charge[143] but well-drafted security documentation will include express provision for the security to cover receivables and their proceeds.

Much of the wealth of a business may be in tied up in raw materials, goods in process of being manufactured, or stock in trade. The floating charge is ideally suited to unlock the potential of items such as these as a valuable source of security.

---

[139] *Re Spectrum Plus Ltd* [2005] 2 AC 680, HL, para 138.
[140] (1862) 10 HLC 191, 11 ER 999, [1861–73] All ER Rep 414, HL.
[141] [1904] AC 355, HL, 358.
[142] *Re Spectrum Plus Ltd* [2005] 2 AC 680, HL, para 111 *per* Lord Scott.
[143] See discussion in Law Commission, *Company Security Interests* (Law Com Rep No 296, 2005) paras 3.51–3.52.

Since the items comprising raw materials, goods being manufactured, or stock are circulating assets which necessarily fluctuate in the ordinary course of trade, fixed security under which the lender has power to restrain disposals tends not to be an attractive option. The floating charge was developed in the nineteenth century by practitioners and the Chancery courts[144] at a time when industrial and commercial expansion meant that the demand for corporate finance was very strong and smaller companies, which were either unable or unwilling to raise it by issuing equity securities, were largely dependent on loans.[145]

There is an obvious risk to a lender who takes floating as opposed to fixed security in that the company may dispose of the subject-matter of the security unprofitably, thereby undermining the value of the security and potentially putting its solvency at risk. Floating charges lack one of the important features associated with security, which is that the collateral remains with the chargor or is readily recoverable from transferees, a feature which Westbrook has labelled 'asset constraint'.[146] Furthermore, if the company does become insolvent, the lender with a floating charge may find that other lenders have taken fixed charges ranking in priority to the floating charge with the consequence that the company has insufficient assets to satisfy the debt secured by the floating charge.

There are certain devices available to strengthen the floating charge without destroying its flexibility. First, it is established that there are certain restrictions on dealings which are not incompatible with the floating nature of a floating charge and the lender can seek to include these in the charge in order to protect its interests.[147] Secondly, the lender with a floating charge can also try to protect its interest through provisions in the terms of the charge relating to crystallization. A floating charge need not continue to float forever but can convert into a fixed charge, a process normally described as crystallization. Once a floating charge crystallizes it operates from that point onwards as a fixed charge and, as such, it attaches to the company's existing assets which fall within the description of the subject-matter of the security and, if the security extends to future property,

---

[144] *Re Panama, New Zealand and Australia Royal Mail Co* (1870) 5 Ch App 318; *Re Florence Land and Public Works Co, ex p Moor* (1878) 10 Ch D 530, CA; *Moor v Anglo-Italian Bank* (1878) 10 Ch D 681; *Re Hamilton's Windsor Ironworks Co, ex p Pitman and Edwards* (1879) 12 Ch D 707; *Re Colonial Trusts Corp, ex p Bradshaw* (1879) 15 Ch D 465. The development of the floating charge in response to the industrial and commercial expansion of 19th-century Britain and the increasing need by companies for more capital is explored in *Re Spectrum Plus Ltd* [2005] 2 AC 680, HL, paras 95–96 *per* Lord Scott and in *Agnew v The Commissioner of Inland Revenue* [2001] 2 AC 710, PC, paras 5–7 *per* Lord Millett.

[145] RR Pennington, 'The Genesis of the Floating Charge' (1960) 23 MLR 630. WJ Gough, 'The Floating Charge: Traditional Themes and New Directions' in PD Finn (ed), *Equity and Commercial Relationships* (Law Book Company, 1987) 239 describes the floating charge as being 'one of the great legal success stories of Victorian times'.

[146] JL Westbrook, 'The Control of Wealth in Bankruptcy' (2004) 82 *Texas Law Review* 795, 808.

[147] In particular the negative pledge whereby the company covenants not to create any new security ranking in priority to or equally with the floating charge. The priority effect of the negative pledge is discussed later in this chapter.

to property matching that description which is subsequently acquired by the company. In other words, crystallization brings about asset constraint. Certain crystallizing events are implied by law into a floating charge unless they are expressly excluded by the parties. It is possible to extend the range of crystallizing events by express provision to that effect in the terms of the charge.[148] However, devices such as these, though of some effect in priority disputes between private parties, do not override public law provisions in the insolvency legislation that have redistributive effects. Those provisions apply primarily to charges created as floating charges and can have the effect of redistributing part of the floating charge collateral to unsecured creditors.

Since the floating charge does not provide asset constraint until crystallization and it has only limited effect as a mechanism for establishing a priority claim, its importance as a type of security can be called into question.[149] Recent changes in insolvency law[150] that have to a large extent removed the right for holders of floating charges to appoint administrative receivers and require them to look instead to the collective procedure of administration[151] deepen the doubts about its usefulness. Notwithstanding that floating charge holders enjoy certain special rights in administration, including the right to choose the administrator, the administration procedure is fundamentally different from administrative receivership because it has features of independence and altruism that did not apply to administrative receivership.[152] As the changes in the law are not retrospective, and there are various exceptional cases in which administrative receivers can still be appointed under post-15 September 2003 floating charges, it will take some time before their practical impact can be properly evaluated. However, it seems reasonable to predict some diminution in the perceived advantages associated with the floating charge by the lending community, which could affect the pricing of debt secured by a floating charge. The case for the abolition of the floating charge is becoming stronger.[153]

The nature of the floating charge

The nature of the floating charge is intriguing. It is undoubtedly an immediate security interest and not merely an agreement to create a security in the future

---

[148] See further below.

[149] R Mokal, 'The Floating Charge—An Elegy' in S Worthington (ed), *Commercial Law and Commercial Practice* (Hart, 2003) ch 17.

[150] By the Enterprise Act 2002, taking effect by way of amendment to the Insolvency Act 1986, with effect from September 2003.

[151] Insolvency Act 1986, Sch B1, para 14.

[152] M Simmons, 'Some Reflections on Administrations, Crown Preference and Ring-fenced Sums in the Enterprise Act' [2004] JBL 423, 425.

[153] RM Goode, 'The Case for the Abolition of the Floating Charge' in J Getzler and J Payne (eds), *Company Charges: Spectrum and Beyond* (OUP, 2006), ch 2.

at the time of crystallization.[154] As conventionally understood, the holder of a security interest has a proprietary interest in the debtor's property and can control dealings in that property, yet where the charge is floating the debtor remains, broadly, free to deal with the assets as if they were unsecured.[155] How can this be explained? The cases do not provide a clear answer but they have provided plenty of ideas to feed a lively academic debate.

One theory on the nature of the proprietary interest created by the floating charge is that is in essence the same as that it created by a fixed charge but coupled with a licence from the creditor to the debtor to continue to deal with the assets. It is now generally accepted that the floating charge is a distinct type of security and is not merely a fixed charge with a special feature.[156] However, that the nature of the interest created by a floating charge is the same as that in a fixed charge has some strong support. In particular, Worthington argues that a floating charge is best understood as giving rise to a proprietary interest that is of precisely the same type as that held by the owner of a fixed charge but which is defeasible when the charged assets are dealt with in accordance with the permitted licence to deal.[157] Nolan also suggests that the standard default entitlements associated with a floating charge are that it behaves as an ordinary equitable fixed charge but he differs from Worthington by suggesting that it is better to describe the floating charge not as defeasible but as an interest which is inherently limited because it can be overreached. He also emphasizes that the parties can adjust the standard terms with the consequence that the precise nature of the interest created may vary from case to case.[158]

Another view is that the floating charge, as a security interest entirely distinct from the fixed charge, gives the creditor an immediate proprietary interest of some sort in the property owned by the company from time to time but one that does not attach specifically to any of the assets until crystallization.[159] The theory enjoys considerable academic support[160] but a difficulty with it is that it

[154] Buckley LJ in *Evans v Rival Granite Quarries Ltd* [1910] 2 KB 979, CA, 999: 'A floating charge is not a future security; it is a present security which presently affects all of the assets of the company expressed to be included in it.'

[155] This apparent paradox led the US courts to deny the effectiveness of floating security: *Benedict v Ratner* 268 US 353, 45 S Ct 566, 69 L Ed 991 (1925).

[156] In particular Buckley LJ in *Evans v Rival Granite Quarries Ltd* [1910] 2 KB 979, CA, 999: 'A floating charge is not a specific mortgage of the assets, plus a licence to the mortgagor to dispose of them in the course of his business.'

[157] S Worthington, *Proprietary Interests in Commercial Transactions* (Clarendon Press, 1996) 81; S Worthington, *Personal Property Law: Text, Cases and Materials* (Hart, 2000) 129.

[158] R Nolan, 'Property in a Fund' (2004) 120 LQR 108.

[159] RR Pennington, 'The Genesis of the Floating Charge' (1960) 23 MLR 630, 646 and RR Pennington, *Company Law* (Butterworths, 8th edn, 2001) 539–41.

[160] Although there are differences of emphasis and on points of detail, the following writers agree that the holder of a uncrystallized floating charge has some form of proprietary interest: RM Goode, *Legal Problems of Credit and Security* (Sweet & Maxwell, 3rd edn, 2003) ch 4; JH Farrar, 'World Economic Stagnation puts the Floating Charge on Trial' (1980) 1 *Company Law* 83; EV Ferran, 'Floating Charges—The Nature of the Security' [1988] CLJ 213.

does not give a clear indication of the nature and quality of the proprietary interest created by the floating charge.[161] Goode has attempted to capture the special nature of the proprietary interest created by the floating charge by suggesting that the floating charge gives the holder a present interest in a *fund* of assets which the debtor is free to manage in the ordinary course of its business.[162] The fund concept has some explanatory power in relation to landmark cases on the floating charge that emphasize that the holder of such a security does not have an interest attaching specifically to the debtor's property and it has attracted significant judicial support in modern leading cases. In *Re Spectrum Plus Ltd (in liquidation)*[163] Lord Walker said that: 'the chargee has a proprietary interest but its interest is in a fund of circulating capital, and unless and until the chargee intervenes (on crystallization of the charge) it is for the trader, and not the bank, to decide how to run its business'.[164]

This comment from Lord Walker implicitly rejects yet another theory on the nature of the floating charge. This is the view, of which the major proponent is Gough, that although the floating charge is a present equitable security, it does not give the holder any equitable proprietary interest until crystallization.[165] The floating charge, in his view, gives rise to a deferred equitable interest and, prior to crystallization, the holder of a floating charge has a personal or 'mere' equity against the chargor arising under the charge contract.

The conceptual uncertainty about the nature of the floating charge that has intrigued many commentators has not stood in the way of the floating charge becoming a commercially important element of corporate financing. Furthermore, even though they have often had to resort to using rather vague metaphors to describe the floating charge,[166] through an incremental process the courts have been able to work out answers to many questions about the floating charge to the point where many clear and well understood principles governing its operation are now established.[167] For example, the priority of the floating

---

[161] *Re Margart Pty Ltd; Hamilton v Westpac Banking Corpn* (1984) 9 ACLR 269, NSW SC-EqD, 272 *per* Helsham CJ, 'while the charge is a floating charge that interest may or may not be an interest of the same dimension as that which he would obtain if the charge became a fixed charge'.

[162] Goode (n 160 above) 113–118.

[163] [2005] 2 AC 680, HL, para 139. See also S Atherton and RJ Mokal, 'Charges Over Chattels: Issues in the Fixed/Floating Jurisprudence' (2005) 26 *Company Lawyer* 10.

[164] See also *Agnew v The Commissioner of Inland Revenue* [2001] 2 AC 710, PC, para 11 *per* Lord Millett.

[165] WJ Gough, *Company Charges* (Butterworths, 2nd edn, 1996) 97–101 and ch 13.

[166] *Re New Bullas Trading Ltd* [1993] BCC 251, 260.

[167] *Evans v Rival Granite Quarries Ltd* [1910] 2 KB 979, CA stands out as a case where the English Court of Appeal attempted to grapple with the theoretical nature of the interest created by the floating charge before proceeding to consider its effect in a particular context (competition with a judgment creditor). The Australian courts have demonstrated a willingness to embark upon a discussion of the theoretical nature of the floating charge or, at least, to acknowledge the different theories that have been put forward. The authorities in support of both arguments are reviewed in *Lyford v CBA* (1995) 17 ACSR 211, Fed Ct of Aust-GenD where the Gough view is adopted and

charge and the extent to which a prohibition in the terms of the charge on the subsequent creation of prior ranking security on any part of the charged property is effective to postpone such security to the floating charge, are well-known and undisputed.[168] This makes it pertinent to ask whether pinpointing in an exact manner the abstract nature of the proprietary interest created by a floating charge actually matters that much: need we be concerned if, on the whole, the law seems to function perfectly well without it? The deficiency in the law, to the extent that there is one and this is not simply a consequence of the fact that the rights that the floating charge holder has before crystallization cannot be universally defined because they depend to some extent on the terms of the charge and the context in which questions have arisen,[169] does not appear to cause major practical problems and its significance should not be exaggerated. However, where a particular aspect of the operation of a floating charge is not clearly determined by existing authority, the lack of an authoritative general understanding of its proprietary effect makes it hard to predict how a case would be decided. For example, the proprietary consequences of a sale of assets that breaches a restriction in a floating charge has yet to be fully explained in the British cases,[170] and it is an issue on which commentators have suggested different views.[171]

Australian cases supporting the alternative view (*Landall Holdings Ltd v Caratti* [1979] WAR 97, WA SC; *Hamilton v Hunter* (1982) 7 ACLR 295, NSW SC Eq D; *Re Margart Pty Ltd (in liquidation), Hamilton v Westpac Banking Corp* (1984) 9 ACLR 269, NSW SC Eq D) are not followed. *Lyford* was followed in *Wily v St George Partnership Banking Ltd* (1997–98) 26 ACSR 1, Fed Ct of Aust.

[168] Priority rules are considered further below. Other situations in which arise questions about the proprietary effects of a floating charge include: whether the court can appoint a receiver and manager on the application of the holder of a floating charge (*Re Victoria Steamboats Ltd, Smith v Wilkinson* [1897] 1 Ch 158 ('yes')); competing claims of floating charge holders and judgment creditors (*Evans v Rival Granite Quarries Ltd* [1910] 2 KB 979, CA); the application of particular statutory provisions (eg *Re Margart Pty Ltd; Hamilton v Westpac Banking Corp* (1984) 9 ACLR 269, NSW SC-EqD where it was held that a payment to a creditor who held an uncrystallized floating charge did not contravene the New South Wales equivalent of the Insolvency Act 1986, s 127 because that section did not apply to the process whereby a person with a beneficial interest in property obtained the property or the proceeds of its realization from the company—the floating charge conferred a beneficial interest for this purpose).

[169] R Nolan, 'Property in a Fund' (2004) 120 LQR 108; PG Turner, Floating Charges—A "No Theory" Theory' [2004] LMCLQ 319.

[170] As was noted in *National Westminster Bank Plc v Spectrum plus Ltd* [2004] Ch 337, CA, paras 25–30 *per* Lord Phillips MR. In *Ashborder BV v Green Gas Power Ltd* [2005] 1 BCLC 623 disposals were held to be in breach of restrictions in floating charges limiting the chargor's dealings to the ordinary course of its business but the proprietary consequences of that finding were not fully explored.

[171] However, the clearest view and most persuasive view (not following EV Ferran, 'Floating Charges—The Nature of the Security' [1988] CLJ 213, 231) is that even before crystallization, the equitable interest created by the floating charge is capable of binding a third party who has acquired property with notice of the charge and of the circumstances of the transfer: R Nolan, 'Property in a Fund' (2004) 120 LQR 108, 127. See also Law Commission, *Company Security Interests* (Law Com Rep No 296, 2005) para 3.219, which assumes that buyers will not take free of a charge if they know that the disposition is not permitted because of some explicit restriction in the charge.

Establishing whether a charge is fixed or floating

An issue of considerable practical significance is that of distinguishing between fixed and floating charges. Whether a charge is fixed or floating is relevant to questions about its priority against competing securities. It is also relevant for the purposes of many of the provisions of the Insolvency Act 1986 that have redistributive effect because these mostly affect floating, but not fixed, charges.[172] Many of the modern landmark cases on the categorization of charges arose from disputes between preferential creditors and holders of security over the order of payment.[173] With the abolition of the Crown's preferential status with regard to tax claims, effected by section 251 of the Enterprise Act 2002, the classes of debt entitled to this statutory priority have been significantly reduced.[174] A consequence may be that in future there will be less controversy about this aspect of the insolvency regime and its interaction with consensual security interests.

However, other provisions of the Insolvency Act 1986 may take the place of the preferential debts regime as a key factor that drives disputes about the correct categorization of a charge. First, under section 176A of the Insolvency Act 1986, introduced by the Enterprise Act 2002, in insolvency proceedings a certain portion of a company's net property must be ring-fenced and not distributed to the holder of a floating charge except to the extent that it exceeds the amount required to satisfy unsecured debts. Secondly, the general expenses of administration (one type of insolvency proceeding) can be recouped out of assets that are subject to a floating charge but not from assets that are subject to a fixed charge.[175] This was also thought to be the position in liquidation until the decision of the House of Lords in *Buchler v Talbot*,[176] where it was held that assets secured by a floating charge were not available to meet general liquidation expenses. The more favourable position in liquidation for holders of floating charges was, however, short-lived because it was reversed by section 176ZA of the Insolvency Act 1986, inserted by the Companies Act 2006. Thirdly, floating (but not fixed) charges may be invalid if they are created within a certain period before the onset of insolvency proceedings and other specified conditions are satisfied.[177]

---

[172] J Armour, 'Should We Redistribute in Insolvency?' in J Getzler and J Payne (eds), *Company Charges: Spectrum and Beyond* (OUP, 2006) ch 9.

[173] Such as *Agnew v The Commissioner of Inland Revenue* [2001] 2 AC 710, PC and *Re Spectrum Plus Ltd* [2005] 2 AC 680, HL.

[174] Insolvency Act 1986, Sch 6 lists the remaining categories of preferential debts (contributions to occupational pension schemes and state pension schemes; remuneration and related payments owing to employees; and levies on coal and steel production).

[175] Insolvency Act 1986, Sch B1, para 99(3). J Armour, 'Floating Charges: All Adrift' [2004] CLJ 560, 564. However, *Buchler v Talbot*, considered next, complicated the position: R Henry, 'The New World of Priority for Floating Charge Holders' (2004) 20 *Insolvency Law and Practice* 194.

[176] [2004] 1 BCLC 281, HL.

[177] Insolvency Act 1986, s 245.

It is also possible that a dispute about the correct categorization of a charge could have its roots in the provisions for registration of charges contained in the Companies Act 2006 because failure to register a registrable charge can result in statutory invalidation.[178] The list of registrable charges is not comprehensive: although it includes all floating charges, fixed charges on certain asset classes are outside its scope.[179]

Fixed and floating charges are both consensual securities created by agreement between the parties. Freedom of contract prevails to the extent that the parties can choose what rights and obligations to grant each other. However, whether the particular package of rights and obligations that they have chosen amounts to a fixed or floating charge is a question of law. Any label that the parties may attach to the security documentation is not determinative of the nature of a charge: if the rights and obligations that the parties have granted each other in respect of the charged assets are inconsistent with the label attached to the charge by the parties, that description will be disregarded and, as a matter of law, the security will be categorized in accordance with the substantive rights and obligations that it creates.[180] The two-stage process—(1) ascertainment of the rights and obligations that the parties have given each other; and (2) attribution of the correct legal label to that package of rights and obligations—will be followed in any case where the nature of a charge is in doubt.

What, then, is the package of rights and obligations that the law will recognize as giving rise to a floating charge or, as the case may be, a fixed charge? Their consensual nature and the very flexible character of English law on security interests imply that neither type of charge should be expected to have a rigidly fixed set of terms that cannot be departed from in any respect. So, in considering this question, it needs to be borne in mind that what we are seeking to identify are the standard, or default, terms from which parties may have some freedom to depart without necessarily creating a different security from that which was their original intention. As Hoffmann J said, when he noted that the floating charge could not be exhaustively defined:[181]

All that can be done is to enumerate its standard characteristics. It does not follow that the absence of one or more of those features or the presence of others will prevent the

---

[178] As in *Smith (Administrator of Cosslett (Contractors) Ltd) v Bridgend County Borough Council* [2002] 1 AC 336, HL, where a clause conferring a power of sale on a provider of finance was held to be a floating charge which was void against the company in administration because it had not been registered.

[179] See eg *Arthur D Little Ltd (in administration) v Ableco Finance LLC* [2003] Ch 217, where a charge on shares was held to be a fixed charge not requiring registration.

[180] *Agnew v The Commissioner of Inland Revenue* [2001] 2 AC 710, PC, para 32. Much of the debate on proper characterization has focused on whether charges carrying the label 'fixed charge' are really floating charges but the characterization issues can also run the other way: *The Russell Cooke Trust Co Ltd v Elliot* [2007] EWHC 1443 (Ch) (charge labelled as 'floating' held to be a fixed charge).

[181] *Re Brightlife Ltd* [1987] Ch 200, 214–15.

charge from being categorised as 'floating'. There are bound to be penumbral cases in which it may be difficult to say whether the degree of deviation from the standard case is enough to make it inappropriate to use such a term. But the rights and duties which the law may or may not categorise as a floating charge are wholly derived from the agreement of the parties, supplemented by the terms implied by law. It seems to me fallacious to argue that once the parties have agreed on some terms which are thought sufficient to identify the transaction as a floating charge, they are then precluded from agreeing to any other terms which are not present in the standard case.

When seeking to establish the characteristics of the floating charge, it is usual to cite the following passage from the judgment of Romer LJ in *Re Yorkshire Woolcombers Ltd*:[182]

... I certainly think that if a charge has the three characteristics that I am about to mention, it is a floating charge.

(1) If it is a charge on a class of assets of a company present and future;
(2) if that class is one which, in the ordinary course of the business of the company, would be changing from time to time; and
(3) if you find that by the charge it is contemplated that, until some future step is taken by or on behalf of those interested in the charge, the company may carry on its business in the ordinary way as far as concerns the particular class of assets I am dealing with.

These three characteristics are indicative of a floating charge but, as Romer LJ emphasized,[183] they do not amount to a precise definition of a floating charge. A charge can still be a floating charge even though it does not meet all of the criteria. This is evident from *Re Croftbell Ltd*[184] where a charge was held to be a floating charge notwithstanding that the secured property (shares in subsidiaries) was not expected to be the subject of regular turnover in the ordinary course of business.[185] In a similar vein, in *Re ASRS Establishment Ltd*[186] it was said to be 'irrelevant' to the determination that a charge on an escrow account was floating that the escrow moneys were not a regular source of working capital and would not thus be subject to fluctuation. In *Smith (Administrator of Cosslett (Contractors) Ltd) v Bridgend County Borough Council*[187] a clause which gave the provider of finance a right of sale in respect of constructional plant, temporary works goods, and materials (whose nature came to be tested with respect to heavy-duty

---

[182] [1903] 2 Ch 284 CA; affirmed *sub nom Illingworth v Houldsworth* [1904] AC 355, HL.
[183] At 295. See also 298 *per* Cozens Hardy LJ.
[184] [1990] BCLC 844.
[185] See also *Welch v Bowmaker (Ireland) Ltd* [1980] IR 251, Ir SC, where the majority of the Irish Supreme Court held that a charge secured on land could be a floating charge notwithstanding that the debtor company was not in the business of property trading and the land was not a class of asset changing from time to time in the course of the company's business.
[186] [2000] 2 BCLC 631.
[187] [2002] 1 AC 336, HL.

coal-washing plants which were used to separate usable coal from residue) was held to be a floating charge.

Although it would be very unusual for a floating charge not to extend to future, as well as presently owned, assets of the debtor company, it has been held that a charge on present property only can be a floating charge.[188] Likewise, a charge on future property only can also be a floating charge and it is not essential to bring existing assets within the scope of the charge for it to be so classified.[189]

The most important of the three criteria is thus the third one: the extent to which the charge contemplates that the company will continue to be free to deal with the assets which are the subject-matter of the security without having to refer back to the creditor for authorization. In *Agnew v Commissioners of Inland Revenue* Lord Millett said of the three criteria that 'the first two characteristics are typical of a floating charge but they are not distinctive of it'.[190] His Lordship continued: 'It is the third characteristic which is the hallmark of a floating charge and serves to distinguish it from a fixed charge.'[191] In *Re Spectrum Plus Ltd*[192] Lord Scott went even further: 'Indeed if a security has Romer LJ's third characteristic I am inclined to think that it qualifies as a floating charge, and cannot be a fixed charge, whatever may be its other characteristics.' In the factual circumstances of the *Spectrum* litigation, which concerned the legal nature of a charge on book debts, which are fluctuating assets, Lord Scott's comment is noteworthy but not especially startling. However, if it is read as indicating a more general principle—that any freedom to deal with the assets that are the subject-matter of security means that a security must be categorized as a floating charge regardless of its other characteristics, such as the nature of the assets secured, it takes on a more controversial character.[193] This is because a line of case law stretching back to some of the classic cases on fixed and floating charges appears to establish that some degree of licence to deal with assets is not necessarily incompatible with a fixed charge and that the extent to which the licence to deal is compatible with a fixed charge depends on all the circumstances of the case.[194] It has been suggested that cases that sanction a limited power to deal as being compatible with a fixed charge are now very doubtful because of *Smith (Administrator of Cosslett (Contractors) Ltd) v Bridgend County Borough Council*[195] where a charge on assets,

---

[188] *Re Bond Worth Ltd* [1980] 1 Ch 228, 267; *Re Cimex Tissues Ltd* [1994] BCC 626, 635.
[189] *Re Croftbell Ltd* [1990] BCLC 844, 848.
[190] [2001] 2 AC 710, PC, para 13.
[191] ibid.
[192] [2005] 2 AC 680, HL, para 107.
[193] N Frome, '*Spectrum*—An End to the Conflict or The Signal for a New Campaign?' (2005) 20 *Butterworths Journal of International Banking and Financial Law* 433, 434; N Frome and K Gibbons, '*Spectrum*—An End to the Conflict or the Signal for a New Campaign' in J Getzler and J Payne (eds), *Company Charges: Spectrum and Beyond* (OUP, 2006) ch 5.
[194] The cases are reviewed in *Re Cimex Tissues Ltd* [1994] BCC 626, 634–640.
[195] [2002] 1 AC 336, HL.

including heavy duty machinery, was held to be a floating charge.[196] However, the case was decided on the basis that the property subject to the charge was a fluctuating body of assets which could be consumed or (subject to the approval of the engineer) removed from the site in the ordinary course of the contractor's business.[197] It may therefore still be open to argue that the case is not determinative of the position in different circumstances, such as where a charge is confined to non-fluctuating assets and the licence to withdraw assets from the security is limited.

The two-stage process for ascertaining whether a charge is fixed or floating, which the *Agnew* and *Spectrum* cases firmly establish as the method for determining the legal nature of a charge, emphasizes the rights and obligations that the parties have granted to each other and the legal categorization associated with that package of rights and obligations. The nature of the asset class to which the security relates is relevant in this process as part of the factual background against which the standard process of documentary interpretation takes place.[198] It may have particular significance in certain circumstances[199]—for instance, in the absence of an express provision permitting disposals in the ordinary course of business, a charge on assets that would ordinarily fluctuate in the ordinary course of business is likely to be categorized as a floating charge, as to classify it as a fixed charge would be likely to paralyse the chargor's business and the courts will favour a commercially sensible construction if the words used can bear it.[200] However, for the purposes of characterization, asset-class character is, at best, of second-order[201] importance only and, on one view, is actually irrelevant in determining whether a charge is fixed or floating.[202]

The essence of the floating charge, on the other hand, is that the assets that are the subject-matter of the security remain under the management and control of the chargor.[203] A charge does not cease to be a floating charge merely because it includes certain restrictions on dealing with the secured assets by the chargor;[204] the question remains whether overall control lies with the chargor, in which case the charge is floating, or with the chargee, in which case it may be fixed. The most familiar example of a restriction that is not incompatible with a floating charge is the covenant whereby the chargor promises not to create any subsequent security

---

[196] P Walton, 'Fixed Charges Over Assets Other Than Book Debts—Is Possession Nine-tenths of the Law?' (2005) 21 *Insolvency Law and Practice* 117.

[197] At para 41.

[198] *Ashborder BV v Green Gas Power Ltd* [2005] 1 BCLC 623, para 183.

[199] ibid.

[200] *Mannai Investment Co Ltd v Eagle Star Life Assurance Co Ltd* [1997] AC 749 HL, 771 *per* Lord Steyn.

[201] *Re Cosslett (Contractors)* [1998] Ch 495 CA, 510 *per* Millett LJ, affirmed *Smith (Administrator of Cosslett (Contractors) Ltd) v Bridgend County Borough Council* [2002] 1 AC 336, HL.

[202] S Worthington, 'Floating Charges: Use and Abuse of Doctrinal Analysis', in J Getzler and J Payne (eds), *Company Charges: Spectrum and Beyond* (OUP, 2006) 25, 29.

[203] *Re Cosslett (Contractors)* [1998] Ch 495 CA, 510 *per* Millett LJ

[204] ibid.

on the charged assets which would rank before or equally with the floating charge. Negative pledge covenants of this type are very common and their compatibility with a floating charge is now unquestionable.[205] Another example is provided by *Re Brightlife Ltd*[206] where a prohibition on the company selling debts which were the subject-matter of the security was held to be consistent with the charge being a floating charge. This case was part of a long and complex saga on the legal categorization of charges on book debts, to which we now turn.

Classification of a charge as fixed or floating and the nature of the secured property—charges on book debts

In *Siebe Gorman & Co Ltd v Barclays Bank Ltd*[207] the agreement between the company and its creditor Barclays Bank, charged the company's present and future book debts and other debts by way of first fixed charge. Under the terms of the charge, the company was required not to charge or assign any part of the charged property without the consent of Barclays. The company was permitted to continue to collect the proceeds of its book debts itself but was required to pay those proceeds into an account with Barclays. Slade J held that the restrictions on dealing with the debts (albeit that only certain forms of dealing were prohibited) together with the requirement to pay the proceeds into an account with Barclays from which, as the debenture was construed, Barclays could prevent withdrawals (although this right to block withdrawals was not expressly stated in the terms of the charge) were sufficient to constitute a fixed charge.

Siebe Gorman[208] was a breakthrough decision. It appeared to resolve a problem that practitioners had been grappling with since the early days in the nineteenth century when the forms of security with which we are now familiar were starting to emerge, namely, that creditors need control over the secured assets if their security is to be regarded as fixed but companies need to have ready access to the proceeds of their book debts, which are an important element of their cash flow. In the *Yorkshire Woolcombers* litigation, the fact that a fixed charge on book debts could have prevented the continued operation of the company's business by depriving it of an important source of cash was regarded as significant and as pointing towards the conclusion that the parties intended to create a floating

---

[205] ibid.

[206] [1987] Ch 200.

[207] [1979] 2 Lloyd's Rep 142.

[208] Generally, on the development of the concept of fixed charges on book debts, see: RA Pearce, 'Fixed Charges over Book Debts' [1987] JBL 18; RR Pennington, 'Fixed Charges Over Future Assets of a Company' (1985) 6 Company Law 9; G McCormack, 'Fixed Charges on Future Book Debts' (1987) 8 *Company Law* 3.

charge.[209] *Siebe Gorman* confirmed that dual control—on the debts and on the proceeds of the debts—was essential to the creation of a fixed charge on book debts and that, in relation to the proceeds of the debts, the creditor had to be able to prevent withdrawals from the account into which they were paid. The court's intepretation of the charge was the dual control requirement was satisfied. The cash-flow implications of that conclusion were not explored.

After the *Siebe Gorman* case, corporate finance practice quickly embraced the fixed charge on book debts as a standard part of the package of security sought by lenders but a steady stream of cases, in England and elsewhere in common law countries, gave some indication of difficulties with the decision that were eventually to culminate in the decision of the House of Lords in *Spectrum Plus*[210] in which it was overruled. There were two core problems: the construction of the charging document used by Barclays Bank which was litigated in the *Siebe Gorman* case—did it actually give the chargee sufficient control over the proceeds of the book debts for the charge to be regarded as fixed?; and a deeper problem as to whether control over proceeds, as well as the debts themselves, was necessary for the existence of a fixed charge on book debts.

On the first issue, in *Supercool v Hoverd Industries Ltd*[211] the New Zealand High Court declined to follow *Siebe Gorman* in a case involving charging documentation that was substantially the same as that litigated in the English case and did not draw the implication found in the *Siebe Gorman* case that the company was not free to make withdrawals from the account into which the proceeds were paid without the creditor's consent. Therefore, since the company's access to the proceeds was not restricted, the charge was only a floating charge. Doubts about whether the court in *Siebe Gorman* has correctly construed the charging documentation used by Barclays Bank were further reinforced by decisions elsewhere in the common law world.[212] The *Spectrum Plus* case finally provided an opportunity for the House of Lords to consider this issue of construction because there were no material differences between the charge used by the National Westminister Bank in that case and the Barclays Bank debenture in issue in *Siebe Gorman*.[213] The seven-person House concluded, unanimously, that the charge, properly construed in the context of the matrix of facts in which it was created, placed no restrictions on the use that the company could make of the balance on the account into which the proceeds of the book debts were paid and that therefore the charge, though labelled as fixed, was in law only a floating charge. *Siebe Gorman* was overruled and the Court refused to take the exceptional step of limiting the overruling so as to have prospective effect only; the argument that the

---

[209] [1903] 2 Ch 284, 288 *per* Farwell J, 296 *per* Romer LJ, and 297 *per* Cozens-Hardy LJ. See also A Berg, 'Charges Over Book Debts: A Reply' [1995] JBL 433, 436–40.
[210] *Re Spectrum Plus Ltd* [2005] 2 AC 680.
[211] [1994] 3 NZLR 300, NZ HC.
[212] *Re Holidair* [1994] 1 IR 416, Ir Sc.
[213] At para 86 *per* Lord Scott.

Siebe Gorman debenture had become a widely-used precedent for a fixed charge and that lenders should be shielded from the consequence of full, retrospective overruling found no favour.

The House of Lords in the *Spectrum* case also overruled the decision of the Court of Appeal in *Re New Bullas Trading Ltd*.[214] That case had involved a form of charge on book debts which differed from the standard *Siebe Gorman*-style precedent in a significant respect. Whereas the conventional form of charge treated book debts and their proceeds as indivisible, the charge in issue in the *New Bullas* case had treated the debt and its proceeds as divisible. The charge included the usual restrictions on dealings with the book debts themselves and required the chargor company to pay the proceeds of those debts into a designated bank account with a specified bank. However, the charge further stipulated that, once the proceeds had been paid in, they would be released from the fixed charge on the book debts and would be subject only to the creditor's general floating charge on the company's assets in the absence of any written directions from the creditor concerning the use of the money. The Court of Appeal had held that it was legally possible to separate a debt from its proceeds and that the debts could be the subject of a fixed charge, whilst the proceeds were subject only to a floating charge. That decision, though consistent with the English judiciary's tendency to look favourably on practitioner ingenuity in moulding the law to suit commercial needs, was widely criticized because it allowed a charge to be categorized as fixed even though assets that were the subject-matter of the security would be extinguished through collection of the proceeds, an event over which the holder of the charge did not have control.[215] Shortly before the decision of the House of Lords in *Spectrum*, the *New Bullas* case was said to have been wrongly decided by the Privy Council in *Agnew v Commissioner of Inland Revenue*.[216] The Privy Council, speaking through Lord Millett, reasoned:

While a debt and its proceeds are two separate assets, however, the latter are merely the traceable proceeds of the former and represent its entire value. A debt is a receivable; it is merely a right to receive payment from the debtor. Such a right cannot be enjoyed in specie; its value can be exploited only by exercising the right or by assigning it for value to a third party. An assignment or charge of a receivable which does not carry with it the right to the receipt has no value. It is worthless as a security. Any attempt in the present context to separate the ownership of the debts from the ownership of their proceeds (even if conceptually possible) makes no commercial sense.

. . .

The company was left in control of the process by which the charged assets were extinguished and replaced by different assets which were not the subject of a fixed charge and

214 [1994] BCLC 485.
215 RM Goode, 'Charges Over Book Debts: a Missed Opportunity' (1994) 110 LQR 592; and S Worthington, 'Fixed Charges over Book Debts and other Receivables' (1997) 113 LQR 562. Cf A Berg, 'Charges Over Book Debts: A Reply' [1995] JBL 433.
216 *Agnew v The Commissioner of Inland Revenue* [2001] 2 AC 710, PC.

were at the free disposal of the company. That is inconsistent with the nature of a fixed charge.[217]

In the *Spectrum* case the House of Lords agreed that the essential value of a book debt as a security lay in the money that could be obtained from the debtor in payment and that a security that did not allow its holder to control the proceeds of the debt should be categorized as a floating security.[218] This is not to say that a debt and its proceeds can never in law be regarded as separate assets—for example, it would be possible to take a fixed charge on proceeds without also controlling the debts themselves;[219] rather, it is simply that a chargee must control the proceeds of debts for its charge on those debts to be a fixed charge.

Post-*Agnew* and *Spectrum* it remains conceptually possible to create a fixed security over book debts[220] but, although the heresy that it is possible in this context to separate debts and proceeds as envisaged in the *New Bullas* case has been erased, problems remain in working out exactly what minimum degree of control a chargee must have over debts and their proceeds for its security on book debts to be fixed. Concern about technical legal uncertainty overlaps with a deeper policy concern: that the control legally required to create a fixed charge over book debts may exceed what is commercially acceptable because vesting that degree of control in the providers of debt finance could paralyse businesses by depriving companies of essential access to working capital.

It is clear that if the chargee collects the proceeds of book debts for its own benefit or allows the chargor to collect them on its behalf and requires them to be paid into an account from which no withdrawals can be made without its specific consent, the charge will be fixed. However, such arrangements would be administratively burdensome and likely to be commercially unworkable.[221] On the other hand, if the chargor has complete freedom to collect and use the proceeds in the course of its business, the charge will undoubtedly be floating, which may not satisfy the chargee's desire for strong priority. Commercial considerations suggest that the parties should aim for some type of middle ground, such as a standing authorization in the terms of the charge for the chargor to draw on the account when the credit balance exceeds a specified security cover. However, it is by no means certain that such an arrangement would be effective to create a fixed charge: in the *Spectrum* case Lord Walker suggested that assets could only be released from a fixed charge with the *active* concurrence of the chargee[222] and

---

[217] At para 49.

[218] *Re Spectrum Plus Ltd* [2005] 2 AC 680, HL, para 110 *per* Lord Scott.

[219] Re *SSSL Realisations (2002) Ltd* [2005] 1 BCLC 1, para 54, appeal dismissed [2006] Ch 610, CA.

[220] *Spectrum*, para 54 *per* Lord Hope; para 136 *per* Lord Walker. See also S Worthington, 'An "Unsatisfactory Area of the Law"—Fixed and Floating Charges Yet Again' (2004) 1 *International Corporate Rescue* 175.

[221] G Yeowart, 'Spectrum Plus: The Wider Implications' (2005) 20 *Butterworths Journal of International Banking and Financial Law* 301, 302.

[222] *Re Spectrum Plus Ltd* [2005] 2 AC 680, HL, para 138.

passages in speeches of other members of the House of Lords can also be read as casting doubt on whether any pre-agreed drawing rights on a supposedly blocked account in favour of the chargor can be accommodated within the terms of a fixed charge on book debts.[223] In the Court of Appeal in the *Spectrum* case Lord Phillips MR had said that it would seem to be 'beyond dispute' that a requirement to pay book debts into a blocked account would be sufficient restriction to render a charge over book debts a fixed charge, even if the chargor was permitted to overdraw on another account, into which from time to time transfers were made from the blocked account.[224] However, even this seemingly firm guidance must be treated with caution because the Court of Appeal was reversed by the House of Lords and Lord Walker, in the Lords, noted that the structure mentioned by the Master of the Rolls, although no doubt appropriate and efficacious in some commercial contexts, might not provide a simple solution in every case.[225]

Must the chargor actually block withdrawals from the account into which the proceeds of book debts are paid or are the legal requirements for a fixed charge on book debts satisfied so long as the proceeds are to be paid into an account that, on the face of the documents, is adequately blocked? Lord Millett's answer to this question in the *Agnew* case was unequivocal: 'But their Lordships would wish to make it clear that it is not enough to provide in the debenture that the account is a blocked account if it is not operated as one in fact.'[226] In *Spectrum* Lord Walker twice referred to Lord Millett's statement with evident acceptance of its correctness,[227] though with an acknowledgement that it could raise difficult questions with regard to the construction of commercial contracts. The difficulty is that conventional principles of contractual interpretation suggest that whether the account is actually operated as a blocked account is irrelevant to the question of construction because evidence of the parties' conduct after the conclusion of a contract is not generally admissible as an aid to interpretation of the terms of a contract.[228] In several cases that are part of the saga from *Siebe Gorman* to *Spectrum*, the inadmissibility of evidence relating to post-contractual conduct played a part in the courts reaching a conclusion that charges were fixed rather than floating.[229] Shams are an exception to the principle that post-contractual

---

[223] A Berg, 'The Cuckoo in the Nest of Corporate Insolvency: Some Aspects of the Spectrum Case' [2006] JBL 22; F Oditah, 'Fixed Charges and the Recycling of Proceeds of Receivables' (2004) 120 LQR 533.

[224] *National Westminster Bank plc v Spectrum Plus Ltd* [2004] Ch 337, CA, para 99.

[225] [2005] 2 AC 680, HL, para 160.

[226] [2001] 2 AC 710, PC.

[227] At paras 140 and 160. See also Lord Scott, para 119.

[228] *James Miller & Partners v Whitworth Street Estates (Manchester) Ltd* [1970] AC 583, HL; *Wickman Ltd v Schuler AG* [1974] AC 325, HL; *Re Armagh Shoes* [1984] BCLC 405; *Re Wogan's (Drogheda) Ltd* [1993] 1 IR 157, Ir SC.

Post-contractual conduct is, of course, relevant to questions about variation of existing contracts, contractual waivers, and estoppels.

[229] In particular *Re Wogan's (Drogheda) Ltd* [1993] IR 157, Ir SC. See also *Re Keenan Bros Ltd* [1985] BCLC 302, Ir HC, [1986] BCLC 242 Ir SC, where a special blocked account was

conduct is inadmissible but the courts are usually rather reluctant to invoke the doctrine of shams. It is not clear whether Lord Millett's warning is best interpreted merely as a reminder of the existence of the sham doctrine as conventionally understood, as signalling a departure from the traditional approach to construction, or as indicating one of the consequences of the two-stage process for the categorization of charges, with general principles of contractual interpretation[230] governing the first stage of the process (what rights and obligations have the parties granted each other?) but not the second stage (what is the legal categorization of their rights and obligations?). The third alternative—that post-charge conduct is relevant to the second stage legal categorization of the rights and obligations because it indicates that one of the legal features of a fixed charge, namely permanent appropriation of the secured assets to the payment of the sum charged,[231] is not present—has been strongly argued.[232] Whatever its precise meaning, it is not credible to suppose that a judge with such experience and distinction in this field as Lord Millett[233] would have included such a warning or that the equally eminent Lord Walker would have mentioned it specifically in the later case if they did not intend it to be taken seriously.[234] There would thus appear to be significant legal risk in corporate finance practice now proceeding on the basis that there is room for much divergence between the terms of a charge on book debts that provide for a blocked account and how that account is actually operated in practice.

Implications of *Agnew* and *Spectrum* for other asset classes

Queens Moat Houses plc v Capita IRG Trustees Ltd[235] is a recent case that supports the proposition that a limited power for the chargor to release property from the security is not incompatible with a fixed charge provided the chargee remains in overall control. A portfolio of hotels was charged as security for debenture stock. The charging deed gave the chargor power unilaterally to withdraw property

---

not opened for some 5 months after the charge documentation was concluded and during that period the company was apparently free to deal with the proceeds of its book debts. The trial judge rejected the admissibility of the evidence concerning the conduct of the parties during that 5 months and the Irish Supreme Court did not question that approach.

[230] On which, see *Mannai Ltd v Eagle Star Assurance Co Ltd* [1997] AC 749, HL; *Investors Compensation Scheme Ltd v West Bromwich Building Society* [1998] 1 WLR 896.

[231] *Re Spectrum Plus Ltd* [2005] 2 AC 680, HL, para 138 *per* Lord Walker.

[232] A Berg, 'The Cuckoo in the Nest of Corporate Insolvency: Some Aspects of the Spectrum Case' [2006] JBL 22.

[233] On Lord Millett's contribution to the law see G McCormack, 'Lords Hoffmann and Millett and the Shaping of Credit and Insolvency Law' [2005] LMCLQ 491.

[234] A Berg, 'The Cuckoo in the Nest of Corporate Insolvency: Some Aspects of the Spectrum Case' [2006] JBL 22, 36.

[235] [2005] 2 BCLC 199.

from the charge in certain circumstances. It was held that the existence of this unilateral right in favour of the chargor did not change what was otherwise a fixed charge into a floating charge. Lightman J reasoned that there was a critical difference between a corporate chargor's right to deal with and dispose of property free from a charge without reference to the chargee and a chargor's right to require the chargee to release property from the charge, in that the former right was consistent only with the existence of a floating charge and was inconsistent with the existence of a fixed charge, whereas there was no inconsistency between the existence of a fixed charge and a contractual right on the part of the chargor to require the chargee to release property from the charge. However, *permanent* appropriation of the secured assets for payment of the debt and *active* concurrence of the chargee in the release of any assets from the security are emphasized in the *Spectrum* decision as being crucial to the fixed charge.[236] Whether the *Queens Moat Houses* case, which was decided before *Spectrum*, is compatible with the decision of the House of Lords is thus open to question. The different nature of the assets in the two cases offers a possible line of distinction but many of the key passages in the *Spectrum* speeches are worded in general terms and do not obviously appear to be confined to charges on book debts. Furthermore, as noted earlier in this chapter, there is a strong trend in the modern cases to downgrade the significance of asset class in determining whether a charge is fixed or floating. Notwithstanding that English law on security interests has traditionally been characterized by its flexibility within the bounds of legal possibility and the cases have established the standard terms of different types of security without defining them exhaustively, the recent authorities suggest that total control of the assets secured, whatever their nature, may be necessary for a fixed charge.

Whether it is possible to distinguish *Spectrum* in the context of security relating to asset classes other than book debts is relevant in relation to project financing and structured financing transactions. In a securitization, for example, income producing assets, such as mortgages, equipment leases, consumer loans, credit card receivables, commercial loans, property rents, car finance loans, or trade receivables (for example commodities), are transferred by an originator to a special purpose vehicle (SPV) and the payment of principal and interest on the bonds issued by the SPV to fund the acquisition is met from the income stream produced by those assets. The SPV grants 'fixed' security over all of its assets and undertaking in favour of the trustee for the bonds, including its bank accounts but the security documentation will set out the order of payments from the bank accounts (a payment waterfall), which, typically, will include the possibility of a payment to the originator after the payment of fees and expenses and of amounts due to the bondholders. Payment waterfalls, which are also common in project

---

[236] In particular by Lord Walker, para 139.

financing,[237] are essentially pre-agreed arrangements for withdrawals from bank accounts and the effect is that the chargee does not give consent on a drawing-by-drawing basis. There is thus a risk that the security over the bank accounts could be characterized as a floating charge. A further risk is that, applying *Agnew* and *Spectrum* reasoning, the security on the assets that have produced the income stream paid into the bank accounts could also be held to be floating. In some cases before *Spectrum* it was held that charges on income producing assets, such as leases and shares, could be fixed even though the chargor had free use of the income but the correctness of those decisions is now in doubt.[238]

The risk of the security arrangements being recharacterized as floating rather than fixed could affect the credit rating of a structured financing. The rating agency Fitch, has given specific advice on this matter.[239] It says that given the legal uncertainty surrounding the application of *Spectrum* to asset classes other than book debts and the factual issues surrounding the level of control exercised by the chargee in practice, in respect of each charge in the transaction structure (including those granted by bankruptcy-remote SPV issuers), Fitch will expect the transaction legal counsel to:

(1) give a clean opinion that the relevant charge constitutes a fixed (rather than a floating) charge;

(2) give a reasoned (rather than 'clean') opinion as to whether the relevant charge constitutes a fixed (rather than floating) charge. In these circumstances, Fitch and its legal counsel will review the reasonableness of the views and analysis provided. If the conclusion expressed in the opinion is that the charge is or is likely to be held to be floating, the legal consequences of this need to be clearly stated (for example any impact on enforcement rights or recoveries in an administration, or risk of avoidance) so that these consequences can be factored into Fitch's rating analysis; or

(3) in circumstances where the transaction lawyers cannot express any legal conclusion on the recharacterization risk (in which case Fitch will assume in its analysis that the charge is floating), specify clearly what the legal consequences are if the fixed charge is recharacterized as a floating charge (for example any impact on enforcement rights or recoveries in an administration, or risk of avoidance), so that these consequences can be factored into Fitch's rating.

---

[237] G Yeowart, 'Spectrum Plus: The Wider Implications' (2005) 20 *Butterworths Journal of International Banking and Financial Law* 301, 302.

[238] *Re Atlantic Computer Systems plc* [1992] Ch 505, CA; *Re Atlantic Medical Ltd* [1992] BCC 653; *Arthur D Little Ltd (in administration) v Ableco Finance LLC* [2003] Ch 217. Cf *Royal Trust Bank v National Westminster Bank plc* [1996] BCC 613, CA, 618 *per* Millett LJ.

[239] Fitch Ratings, 'Spectrum Plus—Implications for Structured Finance Transactions?', Special Report (December 2005) available at <http://www.fitchratings.com/corporate/reports/report_frame.cfm?rpt_id=259190&sector_flag=1&marketsector=2&detail=> (accessed December 2007).

Assessment of the post-*Spectrum* position

While there are different views on the extent to which the post-*Spectrum* position is uncertain, particularly with regard to asset classes other than book debts, commentators tend to agree that costly efforts will continue to be made both by transactional lawyers and, in cases of dispute, by the judiciary to establish which side of the fixed/floating boundary a particular security structure falls.[240] If the control requirements set by the judiciary for fixed charges on circulating or other assets prove to be commercially unworkable, a possible policy response would be a statutory reformulation of security interests to provide a type of security that gives lenders the benefits associated with the fixed charge and, at the same time, allows companies free use of income streams.[241] However, to date, the legislature has not shown any willingness to intervene in this way. A more likely prospect for the short and medium term is that corporate finance practitioners will seek to find constructive solutions that avoid difficulties and uncertainties in the general law.[242] One possible solution is for companies to make greater use of alternative products and systems that allow borrowers to realize the value of their book debts through outright sales (invoice discounters and factors) rather than by granting security.[243] Another is for more debt finance to be raised through SPVs that are structured so as to be bankruptcy-remote (insolvency being when the status of a charge matters most).

Crystallization of a floating charge

Until a floating charge crystallizes, a company can continue to deal with the assets that are the subject-matter of the security in the ordinary course of its

---

[240] This point is made in many of the essays in J Getzler and J Payne (eds), *Company Charges: Spectrum and Beyond* (OUP, 2006).

[241] The idea of a third category of charge because the conceptual apparatus of fixed security and floating security may be inadequate to accommodate new forms of security has been mooted: A Berg, 'Charges Over Book Debts: The Spectrum Case in the Court of Appeal' [2004] JBL 581, 608; A Berg, 'Brumark Investments Ltd and the "Innominate Charge"' [2001] JBL 532.

[242] N Frome, 'Spectrum—An End to the Conflict or the Signal for a New Campaign' (2005) 11 *Butterworths Journal of International Banking and Financial Law* 433: 'Ultimately the lending community will always find a way of achieving their control objectives even if the law requires them to use more complex methodologies (such as off balance sheet structures) to do so. Unfortunately, in that event, the additional cost will have to be borne by the borrower community.' Also noting the potentially economically damaging consequences of additional costs: G Moss, 'Fictions and Floating Charges: some Reflections on the House of Lords' Decision in Spectrum' in J Getzler and J Payne (eds), *Company Charges: Spectrum and Beyond* (OUP, 2006) 1.

[243] P Flood, 'Spectrum Plus: Legal and Practical Implications' (2006) 17(2) *International Company and Commercial Law Review* 78. Under a factoring arrangement, the body providing finance purchases and collects trade debts (with or without recourse to the company if debtors fail to pay). Invoice discounting involves the financier purchasing the debts, but the company collects them and the debtors are not notified.

business.[244] The expression 'ordinary course of its ... business' has to be given the meaning which ordinary business people in the position of the parties to the security would be expected to give them against the factual and commercial background in which those documents were made.[245] A transaction can be in the ordinary course of business even if it is exceptional or unprecedented or even if it might be a fraudulent or wrongful preference in the context of a winding up.[246] The existence of an uncrystallized floating charge does not prevent the company's debtors from claiming rights of set-off against it,[247] nor does it preclude any of the company's other creditors from enforcing judgment against its assets.[248]

When a floating charge crystallizes into a fixed charge, it attaches to the existing assets of the company within the ambit of the charge and, unless the charge excludes this, all such assets as are subsequently acquired.[249] A crystallized floating charge ranks as a fixed charge for the purposes of determining its priority against other interests in the company's property which are created or acquired after crystallization.[250] Although there is one case that suggests otherwise,[251] the better view is that crystallization does not affect the priority of a floating charge against other interests in the same property which pre date crystallization. Crystallization has the effect of postponing execution creditors to the chargee's interest,[252] and once debtors of the company have notice of crystallization they are largely precluded from claiming rights of set-off.[253]

As charges are essentially consensual securities, it is for the parties to determine crystallizing events but, in the absence of any other provision, three crystallizing

---

[244] *Re Panama, New Zealand & Australia Royal Mail Co* (1870) 5 Ch App 318; *Re Florence Land & Public Works Co, ex p Moor* (1878) LR 10 Ch D 530, CA; *Wallace v Evershed* [1899] 1 Ch 189; *Re Yorkshire Woolcombers Ltd* [1903] 2 Ch 284, CA; affirmed *sub nom Illingworth v Houldsworth* [1904] AC 355, HL.

[245] *Ashborder BV v Green Gas Power Ltd* [2005] 1 BCLC 623, applying *Countrywide Banking Corp Ltd v Dean* [1998] 1 BCLC 306.

[246] ibid.

[247] *Biggerstaff v Rowatt's Wharf Ltd* [1896] 2 Ch 93, CA.

[248] *Evans v Rival Granite Quarries Ltd* [1910] 2 KB 979, CA, not following *Davey & Co v Williamson & Sons* [1898] 2 QB 194, CA.

[249] *NW Robbie & Co Ltd v Witney Warehouse Co Ltd* [1963] 3 All ER 613, CA. But Cf *Re Dex Developments Pty Ltd* (1994) 13 ACSR 485, CT SC, criticized by CH Tan, 'Automatic Crystallisation, De-Crystallisation and Convertibility of Charges' [1998] CFILR 41, 44.

[250] This is subject to the special considerations that may apply where there is no public indication of the fact of crystallization.

[251] *Griffiths v Yorkshire Bank plc* [1994] 1 WLR 1427.

[252] *Re Standard Manufacturing Co* [1891] 1 Ch 627, CA; *Re Opera Ltd* [1891] 3 Ch 260, CA; *Taunton v Sheriff of Warwickshire* [1895] 1 Ch 734; *Norton v Yates* [1906] 1 KB 112; *Cairney v Back* [1906] 2 KB 746. This is a complex area. The difficulties lie mainly in determining whether, for the mode of execution in question, the execution process has been completed by the time of crystallization. See further, WJ Gough, *Company Charges* (Butterworths, 2nd edn, 1996) 319–28.

[253] *NW Robbie & Co Ltd v Witney Warehouse Co Ltd* [1963] 3 All ER 613, CA. This is another difficult area which is considered further in PR Wood, *English and International Set-Off* (Sweet & Maxwell, 1989) 925–9; Gough (n 252 above) 281–302; EV Ferran, 'Floating Charges—The Nature of the Security' [1988] CLJ 213, 217–27.

events will be implied.[254] These are intervention by the holder of the charge to take control of the security, such as by appointing a receiver under the terms of the charge,[255] the commencement of the winding-up of the company,[256] and the cessation of its business.[257] It is also possible for the parties to agree additional crystallizing events in the terms of the charge. For example, a floating charge may contain a provision which entitles its holder to trigger crystallization by serving a notice to that effect on the company.[258] Until the 1980s, it was uncertain whether under English law it was possible to provide for automatic crystallization upon the happening of an event that did not require intervention from the holder of the charge and which, unlike liquidation or cessation of business, did not signal the end of the company's business. Dicta in some old cases suggested that, outside situations of cessation of business, the holder of the charge had to intervene positively in order to bring about crystallization.[259] In England, the powerful dicta of Hoffmann J in *Re Brightlife Ltd*[260] and his decision in *Re Permanent Houses (Holdings) Ltd*[261] heralded the acceptance of the legal effectiveness of automatic crystallization clauses that did not require the charge holder actively to intervene. Elsewhere in the Commonwealth, it has also been held that automatic crystallization in this form is possible.[262] This acceptance of non-interventionist automatic crystallization clauses, despite certain policy objections,[263] represents a triumph

---

[254] *Edward Nelson & Co Ltd v Faber & Co* [1903] 2 KB 367.

[255] *Evans v Rival Granite Quarries Ltd* [1910] 2 KB 979, CA; *NW Robbie & Co Ltd v Witney Warehouse Co Ltd* [1963] 3 All ER 613, CA. The appointment of a receiver by the court at the instance of a debenture holder would also trigger crystallization but appointment of a receiver via this route would be very unusual.

[256] *Re Panama, New Zealand and Australian Royal Mail Co* (1870) 5 Ch App 318; *Re Colonial Trusts Corp, ex p Bradshaw* (1879) 15 Ch D 465, CA, 472 *per* Jessel MR.

[257] *Re Woodroffes (Musical Instruments) Ltd* [1986] Ch 366; *William Gaskell Group Ltd v Highley* [1993] BCC 200; *Re The Real Meat Co Ltd* [1996] BCC 254.

[258] *Re Brightlife Ltd* [1987] Ch 200. The effectiveness of crystallization notices was conceded in *Re Woodroffes (Musical Instruments) Ltd* [1986] Ch 366.

[259] In particular *Evans v Rival Granite Quarries Ltd* [1910] 2 KB 979, CA, 986–7 *per* Vaughan Williams LJ and 992–3 *per* Fletcher Moulton LJ; *Reg in right of British Columbia v Consolidated Churchill Copper Corp Ltd* [1978] 5 WWR 652, BC SC.

[260] [1987] Ch 200. This case was actually about crystallization by service of a notice but there is no important difference in the legal analysis between that type of clause and 'pure' non-interventionist automatic crystallization provisions. See further, Gough (n 252 above) 233.

[261] (1989) 5 BCC 151. Counsel conceded the point but Hoffmann J reiterated the view that he had expressed in the earlier case that there was no conceptual reason why parties should not agree that any specified event should cause the charge to crystallize (at 154–5).

[262] *Stein v Saywell* [1969] ALR 481, H Ct of Aust (although the point was not argued); *Fire Nymph Products Ltd v The Heating Centre Pty Ltd* (1991–92) 7 ACSR 365, NSW CA; *Re Manurewa Transport Ltd* [1971] NZLR 909, NZ SC; *DFC Financial Services Ltd v Coffey* [1991] 2 NZLR 513, PC, 518 *per* Lord Goff; *Dovey Enterprises Ltd v Guardian Assurance Public Ltd* [1993] 1 NZLR 540, NZ CA.

[263] Historically, the effect of automatic crystallization clauses on the ranking of preferential debts was one of the issues that concerned writers on this topic. Before the Insolvency Act 1986, the position was that the floating charge had to continue to float up to the date of the liquidation for preferential debts to rank for payment ahead of the debt secured by the floating charge: *Re Griffin Hotel Co Ltd* [1941] Ch 129. The Insolvency Act 1986 reversed the position so that preferential debts now

for freedom of contract: a floating charge is a consensual security and it is for the parties to determine its features, including the circumstances in which it will crystallize.

Drafting of automatic crystallization clauses

There are now two main recognized forms of automatic crystallization clause: the first is where crystallization is to happen upon the occurrence of specified events without positive intervention from the holder of the charge; and the second is where crystallization is to happen if and when the holder of the charge serves a notice to that effect. The first type of clause places the occurrence of crystallization outside the control of the holder of the charge and, unless the clause is narrowly and carefully drafted, may result in situations where the charge crystallizes even though the charge holder is content for it to continue to exist in uncrystallized form. In anticipation of this, an automatic crystallization clause may be coupled with an express clause entitling its holder to de-crystallize it again.[264] In the absence of such a clause, it should be possible to achieve de-crystallization with the express or implied consent of the holder of the charge.[265] However, there is a risk that if the automatic crystallization clause is so widely drafted that the holder of the charge has frequently to agree to de-crystallization, this pattern of events may lead a court to conclude that the original agreement was later varied by the parties so as to exclude the automatic crystallization provision. The second form of automatic crystallization clause avoids the issue of unwanted crystallization by keeping the trigger for crystallization within the control of the holder of the charge by stipulating for crystallization on service of a notice. On the other hand, automatic crystallization clauses in this form have an in-built delay factor, which could operate to the detriment of the holder of the charge in its claim to priority over other interests in the same property.[266]

The commencement of administration proceedings in respect of a company in accordance with the Insolvency Act 1986 does not constitute an implied crystallizing event. This is an example of the type of event that could be covered by an express automatic crystallization clause in either of the forms outlined in the previous paragraph.

---

rank ahead of a debt secured by a charge which, as created, was a floating charge. Generally, on policy objections to automatic crystallization see: AJ Boyle, 'The Validity of Automatic Crystallisation Clauses' [1979] JBL 231; Cork Committee Report (n 5 above) paras 1570–1580. Academic opinion in favour of automatic crystallization clauses pre-dating the 1980s cases on the point included JH Farrar, 'The Crystallisation of a Floating Charge' (1976) 40 *Conv* 397.

[264] As in *Covacich v Riordan* [1994] 2 NZLR 502, NZ HC.

[265] But note R Grantham, 'Refloating a Floating Charge' [1997] CFILR 53; CH Tan, 'Automatic Crystallisation, De-Crystallisation and Convertibility of Charges' [1998] CFILR 41.

[266] However, the extent to which third parties will be affected by crystallization if they do not know, and have no means of knowing, that it has occurred is limited. See below.

Automatic crystallization and third parties

An argument against automatic crystallization provisions is that they are unfair because they can cause a charge to crystallize without that fact becoming apparent to others who deal with the company and advance credit to it. It has been suggested that any unfairness to third parties that results from recognizing that automatic crystallization clauses are effective may be mitigated by estoppel[267] or agency[268] principles: this is to say that until the fact of crystallization has been drawn to the attention of outsiders dealing with the company, the holder of the charge may be estopped from denying that the charge remains floating or, alternatively, that outsiders can continue to rely on the company's ostensible authority to deal with its assets as if they were subject only to an uncrystallized floating charge. In circumstances where a subsequent chargee is unaware of the crystallization of the earlier charge, application of either set of principles would mean that a debt secured by a floating charge that has crystallized into a fixed charge by operation of an automatic crystallization notice could lose priority to a debt secured by a subsequent fixed charge on the same property even though, in accordance with the normal priority rules that are discussed in the next section of this chapter, it would rank ahead of it.

The operation of estoppel or agency principles in relation to automatic crystallization clauses has not been litigated. In its recent work on company charges, the Law Commission for England and Wales adopted the agency reasoning suggested by Goode and concluded that it was extremely unlikely that such a device would be effective against a subsequent chargee without actual knowledge of the automatic crystallization clause because the company would still have apparent authority to dispose of its assets in the ordinary course of business.[269] Likewise, purchasers without notice would not be affected.[270] Judgment creditors would, on Goode's reasoning be in a different position because they are unsecured creditors with no interest in its assets.[271] The Law Commission has accepted that judgment creditors are at risk of automatic crystallization clauses.[272]

A system for registration of crystallization has been advocated from time to time[273] and the Companies Act 1989 contained a provision to that effect. That

---

[267] WJ Gough, *Company Charges* (Butterworths, 2nd edn, 1996) 252–6 discusses the operation of estoppel in this context and its limits. See also WJ Gough, 'The Floating Charge: Traditional Themes and New Directions' in PD Finn (ed), *Equity and Commercial Relationships* (Law Book Company, 1987), 239, 251–2.

[268] RM Goode, *Legal Problems of Credit and Security* (Sweet & Maxwell, 3rd edn, 2003) 146–8 and 181–2.

[269] Law Commission, *Registration of Security Interests: Company Charges and Property other than Land* (Law Com CP No 164, 2002) para 2.44.

[270] ibid para 4.143.

[271] RM Goode (n 268 above) 181–2.

[272] Law Commission, *Company Security Interests* (Law Com Rep No 296, 2005) para 3.201.

[273] AJ Boyle, 'The Validity of Automatic Crystallisation Clauses' [1979] JBL 231, 240.

provision would have authorized the Secretary of State to make regulations stipulating requirements for registration of notice of crystallizing events and providing for the consequences of failure to give notice. It was specifically stated that
those consequences could have included the ineffectiveness of the crystallization
against such persons as might be prescribed. This provision was part of a series of measures that were intended to revise and update the requirements of the
Companies Act 1985 on the registration of charges. Various difficulties in the
drafting of the new provisions emerged after the passing of the legislation and
they were never brought into force.

Priority rules for competing interests in the same property

A company may use its assets as security for more than one debt. When this happens and the value of the security proves to be insufficient to pay off all of the
debts that were secured on it, it becomes necessary to work out the respective
priorities of the various charges. Priority disputes can also arise where a company
charges property in favour of one person and then agrees to sell that property to
someone else: here the issue is whether the purchaser takes the property subject
to, or free from, the charge. The English courts worked out a series of rules for
resolving priority disputes and these rules continue to apply to company charges
even though certain aspects of them are affected by the statutory requirements for
the registration of charges. English law on security interests in personal property
differs from many other modern legal systems by not providing for a statutory
system of priority based primarily on the timing of the registration of charges on
a public register.[274] Reform bodies have periodically considered English law to be
deficient in this respect and have called for a complete overhaul of the law relating
to credit and security, including the establishment of a priority system based on
filing but, to date, legislation has not been forthcoming.[275]

There follows an outline of the various rules. At the outset of this discussion,
it is pertinent to note that these priority rules are default rules that apply where
the parties have not made alternative provision. It is open to secured creditors
to vary the priority afforded to their charges under the general law by a priority
agreement. Also to be noted at the outset is that land, ship mortgages, and other
asset classes where priority is affected by the requirements of specialist legislation
are excluded from this discussion. The special rules that apply where there are

---

[274] See, in particular the Uniform Commercial Code, art 9 (US); the Uniform Personal Property
Security Act 1982 (Canada), and the various Personal Property Security Acts, based on the model
of art 9, adopted in the various provinces of Canada. Article 9 has also served as a basis for a new
statutory system in New Zealand: Personal Property Securities Act 1999, which is described in
D McLauchlan, 'Fundamentals of the PPSA: An Introduction' (2000) 6 *New Zealand Business Law
Quarterly* 166.
[275] See below.

competing interests in debts or other forms of intangible personal property are considered separately after the general rules have been outlined.

Competing interests in tangible personal property

There are two main rules.[276] The first rule is that where the equities are equal the first in time prevails.[277] This is the priority rule that governs, for example, priority disputes between two fixed equitable charges on the same property. The charge that was created first has priority unless the equities are not equal. A situation where the equities would not be equal is where the first chargee's conduct has led the second to believe that the property is unencumbered. The second rule is that a person who bona fide purchases for value a legal interest in property takes free of existing equitable interests in that property provided he does not have notice of their existence and there is no fraud, estoppel, or gross negligence on his part.[278] By application of this rule a bona fide purchaser for value without notice takes property that is subject to a fixed charge free of the charge. The creditor is obliged to pursue his remedies against the company that has disposed of the security in breach of the terms of the charge.

A key feature of the floating charge is that it allows the company to continue to deal with its assets in the ordinary course of business as if they were unsecured. This power to continue trading includes power to grant subsequent mortgages and charges and accordingly, although the security is first in time, the holder of a floating charge is estopped from denying the priority of later legal or fixed equitable interests.[279] A subsequent fixed chargee or purchaser takes free of an earlier floating charge even where he is aware of the existence of that charge.[280] This modification of the normal first-in-time rule does not apply as between two floating charges on the same property. Here, in accordance with the general principle, the first in time takes priority[281] unless the first charge expressly permits the creation of subsequent floating security ranking in priority to, or equally with, the first floating charge.[282]

---

[276] For detailed treatment: J McGhee (gen ed), *Snell's Equity* (Sweet & Maxwell, 31st edn, 2005) ch 4.

[277] *Cave v Cave* (1880) 15 Ch D 639; *Rice v Rice* (1853) 2 Drew 73, 61 ER 646.

[278] *Pilcher v Rawlins* (1872) 7 Ch App 259.

[279] *Re Castell & Brown Ltd* [1898] 1 Ch 315; *Re Valletort Sanitary Steam Laundry Co Ltd* [1903] 2 Ch 654.

[280] *Moor v Anglo-Italian Bank* (1878) 10 Ch D 681; *Re Hamilton's Windsor Ironworks Co, ex p Pitman and Edwards* (1879) 12 Ch D 707; *Wheatley v Silkstone & Haigh Moor Coal Co* (1885) 29 Ch D 715; *English and Scottish Mercantile Investment Co v Brunton* [1892] 2 QB 700, CA; *Re Standard Rotary Machine Co Ltd* (1906) 95 LT 829.

[281] *Re Benjamin Cope & Sons Ltd* [1914] 1 Ch 800. *Griffiths v Yorkshire Bank plc* [1994] 1 WLR 1427, which is to the effect that a second floating charge can take priority by being the first to crystallize, is inconsistent with earlier authorities.

[282] *Re Automatic Bottle Makers Ltd* [1926] Ch 412, CA where a second floating charge on part of the property that was the subject-matter of the security in an earlier floating charge took priority

It is commonplace for floating charges to contain a promise from the chargor company not to use the assets that are the subject-matter of the security as security for any subsequent borrowing that would rank ahead of, or equally with, the floating charge, without the consent of the holder of that charge. This 'negative pledge' has a twofold purpose. Its internal purpose is to ensure that if the promise is broken, the holder of the charge can sue the company for breach of contract. In a well-drafted agreement, this breach will be an event of default that entitles the chargee to call in the loan. Its external purpose is to reverse the ordinary priority rule applicable to floating charges by ensuring that the floating charge ranks ahead of the security created in breach of the covenant. Contractual promises do not normally affect third parties who are not party to the agreement but it is established that a person who obtains security, legal or equitable, on property that is already subject to a floating charge containing a negative pledge takes subject to that charge if he has notice of the existence of the negative pledge.[283] It is insufficient that the subsequent creditor has notice simply of the existence of the floating charge; he must have notice of the fact that it contains a negative pledge.[284] An explanation for the priority effect of a negative pledge in a floating charge is that it is an equity attached to an equitable interest which, on general principles, is binding on persons who have notice of it.[285]

Priority rules for competing interests in intangible property

The priority rules for competing interests in intangible property are relevant where, for example, a company grants a series of charges, fixed or floating, on its book debts, or sells book debts that were subject to a charge. Priority here is governed by the rule in *Dearle v Hall*,[286] which is that priority is governed by the order in which notice is given to the debtors. Notice does not have to be in a particular form and it can be given orally.[287] Accordingly, the purchaser of the legal title to debts[288] takes them subject to an earlier fixed charge where the chargee is the first to give notice of his interest to the debtors, even though the purchaser may be unaware of the existence of the fixed charge when he acquires

---

to the earlier charge. This decision turned on the terms of the first floating charge, which reserved to the company the right to create certain specific charges ranking in priority. The Court of Appeal concluded that a charge in floating form could be within the scope of the reserved power.

[283] *Cox v Dublin City Distillery Co* [1915] 1 IR 345, Ir CA.

[284] *Re Valletort Sanitary Steam Laundry Co Ltd* [1903] 2 Ch 654; *Siebe Gorman & Co Ltd v Barclays Bank Ltd* [1979] 2 Lloyd's Rep 142.

[285] *Rother Iron Works Ltd v Canterbury Precision Engineers Ltd* [1974] QB 1, CA.

[286] (1823) 3 Russ 1, 38 ER 475, 492.

[287] *Lloyd v Banks* (1868) 3 Ch App 488.

[288] An assignment of the legal title to debts must comply with the formal requirements of the Law of Property Act 1925, s 136(1). These formalities include a requirement to give written notice of the assignment to the debtors. This written notice suffices for the purposes of the rule in *Dearle v Hall* but it does not override notices, in whatever form, of prior interests that were given earlier.

the debts.[289] It is axiomatic that a company that has charged its debts by way of a floating charge can continue to deal with the debts and to collect their proceeds; no notice of the existence of the floating charge will be given to the company's debtors, with the consequence that the charge will rank behind notified interests.

The rule in *Dearle v Hall* is subject to the qualification that where, at the time that a person acquires an interest, he is aware of the existence of other interests, apart from floating charges, in the same property, he takes subject to those interests irrespective of the order in which notice is given to the debtors.[290]

Priority of purchase money security interests

This is a special case of a priority conflict. The situation arises where a company which has created a charge covering future property acquires property fitting the description of the subject-matter of the security but that acquisition has been funded by borrowing from a third-party lender and that lender requires an interest in the acquired property in order to secure its advance. Assuming that the bona fide purchaser rule is inapplicable, which security interest has priority: the charge that was first in time or the later purchase money security? In *Abbey National Building Society v Cann*[291] the House of Lords held that the provider of the purchase money finance took priority. Lord Jauncey stated the basis for the decision in these terms: 'a purchaser who can only complete a transaction by borrowing money ... cannot in reality ever be said to have acquired even for a *scintilla temporis* the unencumbered freehold or leasehold interest in the land whereby he could grant interests having priority over the mortgage'.[292] For the the after-acquired property to feed the existing charge in priority to the new charge would constitute an unwarranted windfall in favour of the holder of the existing charge.[293]

---

[289] The displacement of the rule that a bona fide purchaser for value of a legal interest who is without notice of a prior equitable interest takes free of it is supported by recent case law (*E Pfeiffer Weinkellerei-Weinenkauf GmbH & Co v Arbuthnot Factors Ltd* [1988] 1 WLR 150; *Compaq Computers Ltd v Abercorn Group Ltd* [1991] BCC 484). The contrary view in favour of the application of the bona fide purchaser rule to this situation, developed by F Oditah, (1989) OJLS 513 and restated in F Oditah, *Legal Aspects of Receivables Financing* (Sweet & Maxwell, 1991) 154–63 has not been accepted.

[290] *Re Holmes* (1885) 29 Ch D 786, CA; *Spencer v Clarke* (1878) 9 Ch D 137.

[291] [1991] 1 AC 56, HL. G McCormack, 'Charges and Priorities—The Death of the Scintilla Temporis' (1991) 12 *Company Law* 10; RJ Smith, 'Mortgagees and Trust Beneficiaries' (1990) 106 LQR 545; R Gregory, 'Rompala Clauses as Unregistered Charges—A Fundamental Shift?' (1990) 106 LQR 550; J de Lacy, 'The Purchase Money Security Interest: A Company Charge Conundrum' [1991] LMCLQ 531.

[292] For some doubt about the extent of the decision see RM Goode, *Legal Problems of Credit and Security* (Sweet & Maxwell, 3rd edn, 2003) 190–193.

[293] Diamond Report (n 45 above) para 17.7.

Registration of charges—outline of requirements

A statutory system for the registration of company charges dates back to 1900. The Law Commission for England and Wales has summarized its intended purposes in the following terms:[294]

(1) it provides information on the state of the encumbrances on a company's property to those who may be interested (for example creditors and those considering or advising on dealing with the company, including credit reference agencies, financial analysts, and potential investors);
(2) it assists companies in enabling them to give some form of assurance to potential lenders that their property is unencumbered;
(3) it provides a degree of protection to a chargee, in relation to the validity and priority of its registered charge; and
(4) it assists receivers and liquidators in deciding whether or not to acknowledge the validity of a mortgage or charge.

However, the current legislation, which is contained in Part 25 of the Companies Act 2006,[295] does not fully achieve these goals. Improving the system for the registration of charges has been much debated by reform bodies, practitioners, and academics over the years and there was even legislative intervention in the form of Part IV of the Companies Act 1989, which contained a proposed new Part XII to the 1985 Act, which would have corrected some of the deficiencies of the present law. However, potential problems with the new regime that emerged after its enactment, including its inter-relationship with other applicable registration requirements, such as those relating to registered land, meant that it could not be brought into force. The Companies Act 1989, Part IV scheme was intended to be an improvement rather than a radical change.[296] Put 25 of the Companies Act 2006 is a consolidated version of the Companies Act 1985 Part XII. The substantive content of the law was not changed on consolidation (save for an extension of the legislation generally to Northern Ireland).

In outline, the structure of Part 25 of Companies Act 2006 is that prescribed particulars of most, but not all, charges created by companies must be

---

[294] Law Commission, *Registration of Security Interests: Company Charges and Property other than Land* (Law Com CP No 164, 2002) para 2.21.

[295] This Part applies to charges created by companies registered in England and Wales and in Northern Ireland (Pt 25, ch 1) and also to charges created by companies registered in Scotland (Pt 25, ch 2). Only the former are considered here. Charges created by oversea companies which may require registration at the English companies registry are also outside the scope of the discussion in this chapter: see *NV Slavenburg's Bank v Intercontinental Natural Resources Ltd* [1980] 1 All ER 955.

[296] Companies Act 1989, Part IV was to some extent based on recommendations in the Diamond Report (n 45 above) Pt III. These recommendations were made as proposed interim measures pending the complete overhaul of the general law relating to security interests in personal property that formed the main recommendation in the report.

delivered to the companies registry within twenty-one days of creation. The facts that not all charges are registrable and that there is a twenty-one-day registration period are key defects of the registration system. A person who searches the register can never be sure from that search alone[297] that he has discovered all of the charges affecting a company's property or even, because of the permitted twenty-one-day registration period, that he has discovered all of the existing registrable charges. When this point is considered in conjunction with the priority rule of first in time, its significance can be readily appreciated. The registrar of companies is required to maintain a register of charges and this is available for public inspection. The registrar has to check whether the requirements for registration have been complied with and, if he is satisfied that they have been, his certificate of registration in respect of the charge is conclusive. Whether the registrar of companies should carry the administrative burden of filtering out defective applications is debatable but the certainty provided by the system is valued in practice.[298] Failure to file as required by the legislation results in the charge becoming void against specified persons, including subsequent secured creditors. In this respect, the registration requirements can affect priority by withdrawing from a registrable, but unregistered, charge the priority over subsequent interests that it would have enjoyed under the first-in-time rule. However, where there is proper compliance with the filing requirements, the order of priority is not affected by order of filing. This is a complexity that many argue the system could do without: a system of priority based on date of filing would be far more straightforward than a series of rules that depend on order of creation of competing securities, equality of equities, and notice. Where the obligation to file particulars of registrable charges is overlooked, the court may authorize late filing. There is no mechanism for late filing without a court order.

Registration requirements—detailed aspects

Charges requiring registration

Certain charges created by a company are registrable. The term 'charge' in this context includes 'mortgage'.[299] Charges arising by operation of law, as opposed

---

[297] Inquiries of the company may elicit further information. Also, a company has to keep its own register of *all* charges at its registered office and this register can be searched to obtain a more complete picture (Companies Act 2006, ss 875–876); but a charge is not rendered void if it is not entered on this register, which means that there is less incentive to ensure its accuracy.

[298] The proposal in the Companies Act 1989 to relieve the registrar of this obligation and, as a consequence, to remove the conclusive certificate of registration was one of the most controversial aspects of the proposed new regime. For a more detailed examination of the 1989 Act see G McCormack, 'Registration of Company Charges: The New Law' [1990] LMCLQ 520; EV Ferran and C Mayo, 'Registration of Company Charges—The New Regime' [1991] JBL 152.

[299] Companies Act 2006, s 861(5).

to act of creation by the company, are not registrable.[300] The list of registrable charges is in Companies Act 2006, section 860(7). It is as follows:

(a) a charge on land or any interest in land, other than a charge for any rent or other periodical sum issued out of land;
(b) a charge created or evidenced by an instrument which, if executed by an individual, would require registration as a bill of sale;
(c) a charge for the purpose of securing any issue of debentures;
(d) a charge on uncalled share capital of the company;
(e) a charge on calls made but not paid;
(f) a charge on book debts of the company;
(g) a floating charge on the company's property or undertaking;
(h) a charge on a ship or aircraft, or any share in a ship;
(i) a charge on goodwill, or on any intellectual property.

Detailed commentaries on each of these categories of registrable charge can be found in the main company law texts. Here, just a few comments are made on some of the categories of registrable charge.

Charges on goods

Section 860(7)(b) of the Companies Act 2006 is the provision under which fixed charges on goods may be registrable. To determine whether a charge on goods is in fact registrable it is necessary to refer back to the Bills of Sale Acts 1878–82, which refer to mortgages or charges on personal chattels, personal chattels being defined as goods and other articles capable of complete transfer by delivery. Among the categories of security excluded from the registration requirements under the bills of sale legislation are pledges. There is an obvious case for this provision to be redrafted so as to make its purpose plain and to remove the obscure reference to the bills of sale legislation. Reform would provide an opportunity to close the gap whereby, under the present law, oral fixed charges on goods are not registrable.

Charges on book debts

'Debts arising in a business in which it is the proper and usual course to keep books and which ought to be entered in the books'[301] is one definition of the term 'book debts'. It has been held that where accountancy practice is not to treat certain debts as book debts, those debts should not be regarded as book debts for the purposes of the registration requirements of the companies

---

[300] *London and Cheshire Insurance Co Ltd v Laplagrene Property Co Ltd* [1971] Ch 499.
[301] *Official Receiver v Tailby* (1886) 18 QBD 25, CA, 29 *per* Lord Esher MR (affirmed *sub nom Tailby v Official Receiver* (1888) 13 App Cas 523, HL). See also *Shipley v Marshall* (1863) 14 CBNS 566, 570–1 *per* Erle CJ; *Independent Automatic Sales Ltd v Knowles and Fowler* [1962] 3 All ER 27.

legislation.[302] Accountancy practice is not normally to treat the credit balances on a company's bank accounts as book debts and, although there is no ruling precisely on the point, it would seem therefore that a charge on a bank account should not normally be registrable under section 860(7)(f) of the Companies Act 2006.[303] In practice, however, the companies registry will accept for registration particulars of fixed charges on bank accounts.[304]

Floating charges

All floating charges are registrable.[305] This is in contrast to fixed charges, which are only registrable if they fall under one of the specific headings. Where a charge has not been registered, one of the reasons for arguing that it is a fixed charge rather than a floating charge may be to establish that the charge was outside the category of registrable charge.[306]

Non-registrable charges

Fixed charges on insurance policies and on shares are among the categories of fixed charge that fall outside the registration requirements.[307] Those advocating reform of the system for the registration of charges have from time to time recommended that these types of fixed charge should become registrable.[308]

---

[302] *Paul & Frank Ltd v Discount Bank (Overseas) Ltd* [1967] Ch 348.

[303] In *Re Brightlife Ltd* [1987] Ch 200 and *Re Permanent Houses (Holdings) Ltd* (1988) 5 BCC 151 Hoffmann J held that for the purposes of particular charging documents, credit balances were not within the scope of the charge on 'book debts'. In the latter case, however, Hoffmann J stated specifically that he was not expressing any opinion on whether credit balances were book debts for the purposes of the registration requirements of the companies legislation. As Lord Hoffmann in *Re Bank of Credit and Commerce International SA (No 8)* [1998] AC 214, HL 227, he again declined to express a view on whether charges on bank accounts were registrable as charges on book debts, since the point did not arise for decision, but he referred to *Northern Bank Ltd v Ross* [1991] BCLC 504, NI CA, with the comment that the judgment in that case 'suggests that, in the case of deposits with banks, an obligation to register is unlikely to arise'. See also *Re Greenport Ltd (in liquidation); Obaray v Gateway (London) Ltd* [2004] 1 BCLC 555.

[304] Letter from the Companies Registration Office, dated 6 August 1985.

[305] Companies Act 2006, s 860(7)(g).

[306] As in *Smith (Administrator of Cosslett (Contractors) Ltd) v Bridgend County Borough Council* [2002] 1 AC 336, HL, where a clause conferring a power of sale on a provider of finance was held to be a floating charge, which was void against the company in administration.

[307] See *Arthur D Little Ltd (in administration) v Ableco Finance LLC* [2003] Ch 217, where a charge on shares was held to be a fixed charge not requiring registration.

[308] See Diamond Report (n 45 above) para 23.5 and para 23.8 considering the arguments for and against registration in these cases and the views put forward by earlier committees including the Jenkins Committee (*Report of the Company Law Committee* (Cmnd 1749, para 962)). Under the Law Commission's 2005 proposals for improvements to the system for the registration of charges, all charges would be registrable unless specifically exempted: Law Commission, *Company Security Interests* (Law Com Rep No 296, 2005).

The registration requirement

The prescribed particulars of a registrable charge created by a company must be delivered to the registrar of companies for registration within twenty-one days after its date of creation.[309] If there is an instrument creating or evidencing the charge, that instrument must accompany the application.[310] It is the duty of a company that creates a registrable charge to file particulars in respect of it but this task may, instead, be carried out by any person who is interested in the charge.[311] In practice, the person in whose favour the charge is created normally undertakes the task of filing the required particulars. It is in that person's interest to do so because his security will become void if the required filing is not made.[312]

The prescribed particulars of a charge created by a company, other than certain charges relating to debentures and certain Northern Irish charges, are: (a) the date of creation; (b) a description of the instrument (if any) creating or evidencing the charge; (c) the amount secured; (d) the name and address of the person entitled to the charge; and (e) short particulars of the property charged.[313] There are special requirements for the prescribed particulars of a charge relating to a series of debentures[314] and certain Northern Irish charges.[315] The existence (or not) of a negative pledge in a floating charge is not a prescribed particular but it is common practice for details of such clauses to be included in the form used to apply for registration of a floating charge. Where this common practice is followed, the existence of a negative pledge in a floating charge will be included in the registered details of the charge and, so, will become known to anyone who actually searches the register. The status of the negative pledge, as an item that is filed voluntarily rather than being a prescribed particular, is relevant to the question of the inter-relationship between the registration requirements and the priority rules and it is discussed further in that context.[316]

---

[309] Companies Act 2006, ss 860 and 870. There is also a registration requirement in relation to any charge on property that is acquired by the company subject to the charge where that charge would have been registrable had it been created by the company itself (Companies Act 2006, s 862). Non-compliance with this registration requirement does not make the charge void but the company and its responsible officers are liable to a fine. This registration requirement is not considered further in this chapter.

[310] Companies Act 2006, s 860(1).

[311] ibid s 860(2) permits someone other than the company to register a charge created by the company.

[312] ibid s 874. Under the Law Commission's 2005 proposals for improvements to the system for the registration of charges, the time limit for registration would be removed, as would the placing of the filing obligation on the company itself: Law Commission, *Company Security Interests* (Law Com Rep No 296, 2005). Pre-transaction filing would be allowed (ibid).

[313] The Companies (Prescribed Particulars of Company Charges) Regulations 2007, SI 2007/ (draft), reg 2. Companies Act 2006, s 1167 expressly defines 'prescribed' as meaning 'prescribed by statutory instrument made by the Secretary of State'. See also Companies Act 2006, s 869(4): *Grove v Advantage Healthcare (T10) Ltd* [2000] 1 BCLC 661.

[314] Companies Act 2006, ss 863–864, 869(2)

[315] ibid ss 868, 869(3).

[316] See below.

The role of the registrar and the issue of the certificate of registration

The role of the registrar is to check that the application is in order.[317] If it is not and the application is rejected, the defective filing cannot be relied upon in satisfaction of the Companies Act 2006 registration requirement and, to avoid the charge becoming void, a second, correct, application must be made within the original twenty-one-day filing period.[318] Once correct particulars relating to a registrable charge are filed with the registrar of companies, the statutory filing obligation is fulfilled and the charge cannot thereafter be held to be void for non-registration even if it does not actually appear on the register until some time after the twenty-one-day period for filing. Upon registration of a charge, the registrar issues a certificate of registration stating the amount secured by the charge.[319] This certificate is conclusive evidence that the requirements for registration in Part 25 of the Companies Act 2006 have been complied with.[320] The conclusive nature of the certificate means that, with possible exceptions for manifest error on the face of the certificate or evidence that it was obtained by fraud, it cannot be challenged by any person other than the Crown.[321] Thus, for example, where the registrar issues a certificate even though the application was in fact out of time, it is not open to any person (apart from the Crown) to argue that the charge is void for non-registration.[322]

Where the registrar fails to notice a mistake in filed particulars that misstates the chargee's rights in some respect, this does not estop the chargee from asserting his rights under the terms of the charge. This is illustrated by a case where the filed particulars understated the amount secured. It was held that the chargee was nevertheless entitled to enforce the charge to the full secured amount as stated in the charge.[323] This is an unfortunate outcome that further undermines the status of the register of charges as a source of useful information. Where the filed particulars understate a creditor's rights, he should not be entitled to assert rights which have not been publicly disclosed against other persons who have acquired an interest in the company's property. Another illustration of the deficiencies of the registration system is provided by *Grove v Advantage Healthcare (T10) Ltd*[324] where, in the particulars delivered for registration, the registered number of the

---

[317] Under the Law Commission's 2005 proposals for improvements to the system for the registration of charges, the Registrar would be relieved of this obligation and conclusive certificates would not be issued: Law Commission, *Company Security Interests* (Law Com Rep No 296, 2005).

[318] *R v Registrar, ex p Central Bank of India* [1986] QB 1114, CA.

[319] Companies Act 2006, s 869(5)–(6).

[320] ibid.

[321] *R v Registrar, ex p Central Bank of India* [1986] QB 1114, CA.

[322] *Re CL Nye* [1971] Ch 442, CA; *Re Eric Holmes Ltd* [1965] Ch 1052.

[323] *Re Mechanisations (Eaglescliffe) Ltd* [1966] Ch 20. See also *National Provincial and Union Bank of England v Charnley* [1924] 1 KB 431, CA.

[324] [2000] 1 BCLC 661, noted A Walters, 'Registration of Charges: Wrong Company Number in Particulars Submitted to the Registrar' (2000) 21 *Company Lawyer* 219.

chargor company was incorrectly stated as being that of another company in its group and the error was not noticed, with the result that the charge was registered against the wrong company. It was held that the failure to provide the correct registered number did not constitute a failure to comply with the registration obligation because the number was not a prescribed particular. Accordingly, the charge was registered and valid even though its existence would not have been discovered by a search against the correct registered number. The Court noted that this outcome could have led to the prejudice of third parties who dealt with the company and suggested that a remedy might in those circumstances have been available to the third party in the form of a claim to recover any loss occasioned from the registrar or the party who misinformed the registrar as to the registered number of the company.

Registration and notice

Registration of a registrable charge serves to give constructive notice of the existence of that charge to such persons as can be reasonably expected to search the register.[325] The category of persons who can reasonably be expected to search the register includes subsequent chargees but it is doubtful whether it covers purchasers of the company's property.[326] It does not constitute notice to debtors for the purposes of the rule in *Dearle v Hall*. Constructive notice of a charge covers the prescribed particulars of a charge but it is widely accepted, and has been specifically so held in Ireland,[327] that it does not extend to information that chargees voluntarily include in the application for filing of a charge but which are not required to be there as a matter of law. It is at this point that the inclusion of the existence (or not) of a negative pledge in a floating charge in the list of prescribed particulars comes into sharp focus. The fact that the existence of a negative pledge clause is not a prescribed particular, so as to come within the scope of constructive notice, undermines the protection to the floating charge holder of including such a provision.

Non-registration

'Non-registration' in this context means failure to file correct particulars of a registrable charge within twenty-one days of creation of the charge. Provided filing within the twenty-one-day period has taken place, it does not matter that the charge may not actually appear on the register until some time after the

---

[325] *Re Standard Rotary Machine Co Ltd* (1906) 95 LT 829; *Wilson v Kelland* [1910] 2 Ch 306.

[326] Law Commission, *Registration of Security Interests: Company Charges and Property other than Land* (Law Com CP No 164, 2002) paras 2.60–2.61. Under the Law Commission's 2005 proposals for improvements to the system for the registration of charges, registration would affect purchasers: Law Commission, *Company Security Interests* (Law Com Rep No 296, 2005).

[327] *Welch v Bowmaker (Ireland) Ltd* [1980] IR 251, Ir SC.

twenty-one-day registration period. Where there is non-registration in the relevant sense, the charge becomes void against the company's liquidator or administrator and also against the company's other secured creditors.[328] The reference to the charge becoming void against the liquidator or adminstrator means that it is void against the company in liquidation or administration or (another way of saying the same thing) against the company when acting by its liquidator or administrator.[329] Failure to register a registrable charge does not render it void against purchasers of the company's property although they may take free of it under the bona fide purchaser for value without notice rule.[330] Also, so long as it is not in liquidation or administration, the security remains valid against the company itself.[331] When a charge becomes void for want of registration, the money secured by the charge becomes immediately repayable.[332]

Late registration

Section 873 of the Companies Act 2006 provides for the late registration of charges. On the application of the company, or any person interested, the court may order the extension of the time for registration. Before making such an order the court must be satisfied that the failure to register in time was accidental, or due to inadvertence or some other sufficient cause, or is not of a nature to prejudice the position of creditors or shareholders of the company, or that on other grounds it is just and equitable to grant relief. The court may impose such terms and conditions as seem to it to be just and expedient. The usual form for such orders is to extend the registration period, subject to the proviso that this 'is to be without prejudice to the rights of parties acquired during the period between the date of creation of the said charge and the date of its actual registration'.[333] Errors in, or omissions from, the registered particulars or in a memorandum of satisfaction may also be corrected by a court order.[334] However, since charges are

---

[328] Companies Act 2006, s 874. This section refers to 'creditors' but it is clear from case law (*Re Cardiff's Workmen's Cottage Co Ltd* [1906] 2 Ch 627) that unsecured creditors have no standing to challenge the validity of a security that has not been duly registered.

[329] *Smith (Administrator of Cosslett (Contractors) Ltd) v Bridgend County Borough Council* [2002] 1 AC 336, HL.

[330] Law Commission, *Registration of Security Interests: Company Charges and Property other than Land* (Law Com CP No 164, 2002) para 2.58.

[331] *Re Monolithic Building Co Ltd* [1915] 1 Ch 643 CA, 667 *per* Phillimore LJ.

[332] Companies Act 2006, s 874(3). Under the Law Commission's 2005 proposals for improvements to the system for the registration of charges, there would be no time limit for registration but lenders would have strong incentives to register because priority would be determined by filing: Law Commission, *Company Security Interests* (Law Com Rep No 296, 2005).

[333] This proviso is derived from the decision in *Watson v Duff Morgan & Vermont (Holdings) Ltd* [1974] 1 WLR 450. On applications under this section generally, see G McCormack, 'Extension of Time for Registration of Company Charges' [1986] JBL 282.

[334] Companies Act 2006, s 873.

still fully enforceable notwithstanding errors in the registered particulars,[335] this reduces the incentive for creditors to apply to correct inaccurate particulars.

Clearing the register—memoranda of satisfaction

When a debt secured by a registered charge is wholly or partly repaid, or property has been released from a registered charge or is no longer part of the company's property, that fact may be publicly advertised by filing with the registrar of companies a memorandum of satisfaction in the prescribed form.[336]

Modification of registration requirements for financial collateral

The Companies Act 2006 registration obligations do not apply (if they would otherwise do so) in relation to a security financial collateral arrangement or any charge created or otherwise arising under a security financial collateral arrangement.[337] This modification derives from the Financial Collateral Directive,[338] which aims to safeguard financial stability and also to promote cross-border efficiency by simplifying the processes for using financial collateral. It insulates financial collateral (ie collateral in the form of cash or investment securities) from aspects of company, property, and insolvency laws that could otherwise apply.[339]

Reform[340]

In 2002, the Department of Trade and Industry asked the Law Commission for England and Wales to consider the case for reforming the law on company charges.[341] This followed a recommendation in the Final Report of the Company Law Review Steering Group.[342] The Steering Group reported that it had received substantial criticism of the current system for registering charges and for deciding priority between them. However, because of lack of time for

---

[335] *Re Mechanisations (Eaglescliffe) Ltd* [1966] Ch 20; *National Provincial and Union Bank of England v Charnley* [1924] 1 KB 431, CA.

[336] Companies Act 2006, s 872.

[337] The Financial Collateral Arrangements (No 2) Regulations 2003, SI 2003/3226, reg 4(4).

[338] Directive (EC) 2002/47 of the European Parliament and of the Council of 6 June 2002 on financial collateral arrangements [2002] OJ L168/43.

[339] See further ch 15 below.

[340] H Beale, M Bridge, L Gullifer, and E Lomnicka, *The Law of Personal Property Security* (OUP, 2007) ch 21.

[341] The Scottish Law Commission was also asked to conduct an inquiry. The two Law Commissions conducted broadly parallel but separate consultative exercises. The law of security in Scotland is different from that in England and Wales. An overview of the Scottish exercise can be found in Law Commission, *Company Security Interests* (Law Com Rep No 296, 2005) paras 1.42–1.43.

[342] 'Final Report', URN 01/942, paras 12.8–12.10.

consultation, it was able itself to present only provisional conclusions in favour of reform. The Law Commission published a consultation paper in 2002,[343] and a more detailed consultative report in 2004.[344] These papers floated some radical ideas for an entirely new scheme for security interests created by companies. The Law Commission's provisional proposals included the suggestion that the floating charge should disappear and be replaced by a new form of security that would allow the debtor to dispose of collateral without specific transaction-by-transaction consent from the holder of the charge. The Commission raised the possibility of extending the new scheme to title-retention devices such as finance leases, hire purchase, and conditional sale agreements. It thought that a system of effectiveness and priority against third parties based on filing should replace the existing complicated common law rules. These proposals proved to be controversial[345] and in its report, published in August 2005, the Law Commission set out revised proposals, which were intended to remove some of the more controversial features of the provisional scheme.[346] The 2005 proposals involved preservation of the distinction between fixed and floating charges, principally because of its importance in insolvency, and the exclusion of title-retention devices from the scheme, in response to the criticism that it would be illogical to have one set of rules applying to title-retention devices entered into by companies, and another for those involving unincorporated businesses and individuals. Sales of receivables of the kind which factoring and discounting agreements cover would be brought within the scheme and would need to be registered to preserve validity on insolvency. The Law Commission continued to advocate reforms to the filing system for company charges, including electronic filing, the abolition of the conclusive certificate of registration, removal of the twenty-one-day time limit for registration, extension of the list of registrable charges, and clearer priority rules based on filing. However, in July 2005 the government launched its own consultation seeking views on the economic impact of the recommendations of the Law Commission in respect of company charges. This was followed by a Ministerial announcement in November 2005 that it was clear from the consultation that there was not a consensus of support for the Law Commissions'[347] proposals and that therefore the new companies legislation would not include a specific power to implement charges measures but that the Bill would include a new power to

---

[343] Law Commission, *Registration of Security Interests: Company Charges and Property other than Land* (Law Com CP No 164, 2002).

[344] Law Commission, *Company Security Interests, A Consultative Report* (Law Com CP No 176, 2004).

[345] One prominent group with concerns was the Financial Law Committee of the City of London Law Society, a group comprising partners of City of London international law firms: R Calnan, 'The Reform of Company Security Interests' (2005) 20(1) *Butterworths Journal of International Banking and Financial Law* 25; R Calnan, 'The Reform of the Law of Security' (2004) 19(3) *Butterworths Journal of International Banking and Financial Law* 88.

[346] Law Commission, *Company Security Interests* (Law Com Rep No 296, 2005).

[347] This rejection extended to the proposals of the Scottish Law Commission as well as those made by the Law Commission for England and Wales.

make company law reform orders and this would provide a mechanism for implementing certain changes in respect of company charges, on matters of company law (as against property law), if wished.[348] The government said it would continue to consider and to discuss with interested parties exactly what changes should be implemented.[349] The proposed general power to make company law reform orders was dropped from the Bill during its passage through Parliament but there has been enacted a new power for the Secretary of State to amend part 25 by regulations.[350]

The resistance to change of English law relating to corporate security interests is remarkable given the severe criticism stretching back over many years that it has attracted, the attention it has received from law reform bodies, and also the examples provided by the generally well-received adoption of more modern systems in other countries that have a common legal heritage with Britain.[351] Yet there are some serious voices who question the value of notice filing systems[352] or who suggest that there may be good reason to draw back from convergence toward a US-inspired model that may not fit well with established local circumstances or with future EU or international initiatives in this field.[353] The fate of the company charges provisions of the Companies Act 1989, which were never implemented, demonstrates the difficult challenges involved in successfully legislating in such a technically difficult area. All in all, the most prudent course of action may be to eschew radical change in favour of incremental modest improvements to the existing regime, including making it more consonant with the electronic era,[354] but even this may not be an urgent policy priority.[355]

---

[348] Written Ministerial Statement, Alun Michael, Minister for Industry and the Regions, 3rd November 2005, 'Company Law Reform Government Statement Following the White Paper and Related Consultations', reported *Hansard*, HL, vol 675, col WS 27 (3 Nov 2005).

[349] ibid.

[350] See Companies Act 2006, Pt 25, ch 3.

[351] Most Canadian provinces and also New Zealand have introduced schemes of notice filing and priority rules that were modelled on the American Uniform Commercial Code, art 9: Law Commission, *Company Security Interests* (Law Com Rep No 296, 2005) para 1.8.

[352] U Drobnig, 'Present and Future of Real and Personal Security' [2003] *European Review of Private Law* 623, 660; R Calnan, 'The Reform of the Law of Security' (2004) 19(3) *Butterworths Journal of Banking and Financial Law* 88.

[353] R Calnan, 'The Reform of Company Security Interests' (2005) 20(1) *Butterworths Journal of International Banking and Financial Law* 25: 'we believe that the Model Security Law produced by the European Bank for Reconstruction and Development is a much more suitable starting point than art 9 of the UCC'; G McCormack, 'The Law Commission Consultative Report on Company Security Interests: An Irreverent Riposte' (2005) 68 MLR 286, 307–9. However, see S Worthington, 'Floating Charges: Use and Abuse of Doctrinal Analysis', in J Getzler and J Payne (eds), *Company Charges: Spectrum and Beyond* (OUP, 2006) 25, 49 who argues that the UK might have been well advised to update its law in order to participate effectively in the making of European and international law.

[354] McCormack, (n 353 above) 309.

[355] Calnan (n 353 above) 30.

PART IV

CAPITAL MARKETS FINANCE

13

Public Offers of Equity Securities

Scope of this part

This part of the book looks at the raising of corporate finance by issuing securities directly to investors. It focuses first on issues of equity securities and then on corporate bonds.

In this chapter the focus is on the process whereby for the first time a company raises finance by offering its equity securities to investors in the market. Although not strictly necessary, the initial public offer (IPO) process is usually coupled with the admission of the securities to trading on an organized trading platform so as to ensure easy access to trading and settlement facilities and coverage from investment analysts, and generally to enhance the liquidity of the securities. In considering IPOs, this chapter will generally assume that the securities are to be admitted to trading on a formal trading platform contemporaneously with the offer. It will also assume a domestic offering—ie an IPO by a UK incorporated company where the securities are to be offered to investors in the UK and admitted to trading on a UK market. Chapter 14 below is about international equity offerings. Corporate bonds are considered in chapter 15 below.

Reasons for going public

There are various reasons why the controllers of a business may consider that the time is ripe to embark on an IPO or a flotation, as this process is commonly described.[1] First, and most obviously, an IPO allows a company to raise new equity finance. Accessing the capital markets by an IPO expands the range of sources of corporate finance and reduces a company's dependence on internally generated capital, its controllers' personal resources, bank finance, trade finance (such as debt factoring), and venture capital. Cash raised from the flotation will reduce gearing and, once quoted, the issuer has then the option of going back to the market for secondary issues of securities in order to raise further cash.

---

[1] T Jenkinson and A Ljungqvist, *Going Public: The Theory and Evidence on How Companies Raise Equity Finance* (OUP, 2nd edn, 2001).

Being quoted may also improve the rate at which a company can borrow from banks.[2] As an illustration of the impact of a flotation on capital structure we can consider the Yell Group, which floated in July 2003 and raised £433.6 million (gross proceeds) in its IPO. It used the proceeds to settle £109.5 million payable on loan notes; to pay share issue costs of £23.7 million; to pay £79.6 million of exceptional costs; to repay £48.3 million of debt under senior credit facilities; and to redeem 35 per cent (£172.5 million) of senior notes pursuant to the optional redemption features in the terms of issue. It also replaced remaining senior credit facilities with new senior credit facilities of £664 million and US$596 million and a revolving credit facility of £200 million. Overall, it achieved a decrease in net debt from £2.4 billion to £1.3 billion.

Exit is a second reason for the controllers of a business to consider a flotation. A flotation provides existing controllers with an immediate opportunity to offer their existing shares to the market alongside the offer of new shares made by the company to raise new equity finance. Using a flotation as an exit mechanism can be especially important for venture capital firms, which provide specialized finance to small and medium-sized companies with high growth potential[3] and for private equity firms that sponsor leveraged buyout transactions.[4] One study of British IPOs found that, on average, almost as many shares in the offerings came from pre-IPO holders as from issuers themselves.[5] Furthermore, a flotation establishes a public market in the company's shares, thereby providing the opportunity of exit at a later date for those controllers who choose to retain the bulk of their shares at flotation. In some instances, flotation may be a step that is taken in order to draw attention to the company as a potential takeover target and with a view to facilitating an acquisition of the company's business at a higher price than would be attracted in a private sale.[6] A flotation may also enhance a company's position as a bidder in the takeover market by enabling it to use its shares, which post-flotation are liquid investments, as consideration for acquisitions.

In Anglo-American conventional market practice, the IPO is regarded as a watershed in the process whereby managerial control and share ownership

---

[2] M Pagano and A Röell, 'The Choice of Stock Ownership Structure: Agency Cost, Monitoring, and the Decision to Go Public' (1998) 113 *Quarterly Journal of Economics* 187.

[3] DJ Cumming and JG MacIntosh, 'The Extent of Venture Capital Exits: Evidence from Canada and the United States' in J McCahery and L Renneboog (eds), *Venture Capital Contracting and the Valuation of High Technology Firms* (OUP, 2004) ch 15.
Venture capital can be seen as a subset of private equity investment, with its distinguishing feature being that funds are advanced to early-stage businesses.

[4] PS Sudarsanam, 'Exit Strategy for UK Leveraged Buyouts: Empirical Evidence on Determinants' (February 2005) available at SSRN <http://ssrn.com/abstract=676849>.
However, private equity exits are more commonly achieved through trade sales than through IPOs: Centre for Management Buyout Research, *Exit* (Issue 8, 2006) (published by Barclays Private Equity).

[5] MJ Brennan and J Franks, 'Underpricing, Ownership and Control in Initial Public Offerings of Equity Securities in the UK' (1997) 45 *Journal of Financial Economics* 391, 406.

[6] L Zingales, 'Insider Ownership and the Decision to Go Public' (1995) 62 *Review of Economic Studies* 425.

become separated. A key feature of market practice that leads to this result is the prevalence of straightforward, one-share one-vote, equity capital structures. Institutional investors in the UK markets, which are the dominant investor class, expect issuers involved in IPOs to have capital structures comprising a single class of ordinary shares adhering to the 'one share-one vote' principle.[7] This contrasts with Continental European market conditions, where institutional investors play a more limited role. In some countries, mechanisms such as dual-class structures, which allow the existing owners to preserve control by weighting voting rights in their favour, remain common. According to one major study of the capital structure of European companies, which was published in 2005, only 65 per cent of the companies in the study applied the 'one share-one vote' principle to equity securities.[8] The study found that the highest proportion of companies adopting this principle was in Belgium (100 per cent), followed by Germany (97 per cent), and the UK (88 per cent). 'One share-one vote' was only applied by a minority of companies in the Netherlands (14 per cent), Sweden (25 per cent), and France (31 per cent).[9] Yet dual-class structures are only part of the story because complex pyramid share ownership structures, cross shareholdings, and other mechanisms can also achieve the effect of concentrating power disproportionately to the level of investment.[10] Pyramid ownership structures were historically common in German corporations[11] but they are no longer such a typical feature of its

---

[7] Brennan and Franks (n 5 above) (None of a large sample of UK IPOs for the years 1986–89 included the issuance of dual-class shares, nor did any prospectus provide super priority rights to a particular group of shareholders, or other constraints on the control rights of a particular class of shareholders'; JR Franks, C Mayer, and S Rossi, 'Ownership: Evolution and Regulation', ECGI—Finance Working Paper No 09/2003 (14 November 2006); EFA 2004 Maastricht Meetings Paper No 3205; AFA 2003 Washington, DC Meetings available at SSRN: <http://ssrn.com/abstract=354381>.

[8] Deminor Rating, 'Application of the One Share-One Vote Principle in Europe', available at <http://www.abi.org.uk/BookShop/ResearchReports/DEMINOR_REPORT.pdf> (accessed December 2007). Non-voting preference shares were not regarded in this Report as breaching the 'one share-one vote' principle because the absence of voting rights was compensated by a preferential dividend.
A later study comes up with different figures but is consistent with the Deminor Study in identifying France, the Netherlands, and Sweden as the countries in which companies make most use of multiple voting right structures: Institutional Shareholder Services, Shearman & Sterling and European Corporate Governance Institute, 'Report on The Proportionality Principle in the European Union' (May 2007) (study commissioned by the European Commission) available at <http://www.ecgi.org/osov/documents/final_report_en.pdf> (accessed December 2007) figure 4–10 (herein after 'Report on the Proportionality Principle in the EU').

[9] On the Swedish position see also: P Högtfeldt and M Holmen, 'A Law and Finance Analysis of Initial Public Offerings' (2004) 13 *Journal of Financial Intermediation* 324. On Germany: M Goergen and L Renneboog, 'Why are the Levels of Control (so) Different in German and UK Companies? Evidence from Initial Public Offerings' (2003) *Journal of Law, Economics and Organization* 141.

[10] A pyramid is a chain of holding companies with ultimate control based on a small total investment: High Level Group of Company Law Experts, 'A Modern Regulatory Framework for Company Law in Europe' (Brussels, November 2001) 17.

[11] JR Franks, C Mayer, and HF Wagner, 'Ownership and Control of German Corporations' (2006) 10 *Review of Finance* 537.

corporate landscape.[12] A recent study indicates that pyramid structures are widely used throughout Europe (except in Ireland, Denmark, Finland, and the United Kingdom) with the frequency of their occurrence being highest in Belgium and Sweden.[13] That same study identified thirteen different control enhancing mechanisms available for use in the national regulatory frameworks that were examined and reported that, overall, such mechanisms were most commonly actually utilized in companies in (in descending order): France, Sweden, Spain, Hungary, and Belgium.[14]

Dual-class, pyramid, and other functionally equivalent structures can impede the process for the separation of ownership and control because they enable pre-flotation controllers to go public whilst still maintaining control through a disproportionate say in the company's affairs. Developments in the market, including the growing influence of institutional investors across Continental Europe, and regulatory policy initiatives to promote more competitive pan-European securities market activity have turned the spotlight onto structures that deviate from the proportionate allocation of ownership and control and sparked a lively debate on whether deviations from the 'proportionality principle' should be curtailed and, if so, whether this should be effected by a pan-European rule or left to evolve within the constraints of market forces and the different approaches under the national laws of Member States.[15] The European Commission commissioned a factual and descriptive study to examine these issues, the results of which were published in May 2007 and which are referred to in this part of the chapter.[16] This study examined the position in the national framework of nineteen jurisdictions and also drew upon a line of theoretical and empirical literature that places discussion of the proportionality principle within a broader debate about the relationship between law and finance. One strand of literature suggests that there are links between the differences in patterns of corporate ownership around the world, including in particular the persistence of deviations from the proportionality principle, and the protections that national legal systems provide to minority shareholders: weak legal protection can be taken to imply concentrated ownership.[17] However, this explanation of ownership patterns does not go uncontested, as it is possible to point to countries such as Sweden, where

---

[12] 'Report on The Proportionality Principle in the European Union' (n 8 above) para 4.3.4.
[13] ibid.
[14] ibid 9.
[15] GA Ferrarini, 'One Share-One Vote: A European Rule?' (2006) 4 *European Company and Financial Law Review* 147.
[16] 'Report on The Proportionality Principle in the European Union' (n 8 above). Two working papers were also published to accompany this report: MC Burkart and S Lee, 'The One Share-One Vote Debate: ECGI—Finance Working Paper No 176/2007 (May 2007) available at SSRN: <http://ssrn.com/abstract=987486>; RB Adams and D Ferreira, 'One Share, One Vote: The Empirical Evidence', ECGI—Finance Working Paper No 177/2007 (May 2007) available at SSRN <http://ssrn.com/abstract=987488>.
[17] R La Porta, F López de Silanes and A Shleifer, 'Corporate Ownership Around the World' (1999) 54 *Journal of Finance* 471.

concentrated ownership persists despite good law,[18] and, indeed, to the UK, where share ownership has become dispersed in spite of weaknesses in the legal protections afforded to minority shareholders.[19] A significant alternative suggestion emphasizes national politics as a powerful driver of concentrated ownership in many countries,[20] though this explanation has also been questioned.[21] Moreover, it has been pointed out that a distinction between 'concentrated' and 'dispersed' share ownership is too simplistic and that a more sophisticated taxonomy is required to reflect the different controlling shareholder models that can be found around the world.[22]

The review of the theoretical literature in the Report to the European Commission concluded that control-enhancing mechanisms had advantages and drawbacks.[23] The review of the empirical literature provided insights into the causes and consequences of disproportional ownership but did not give a robust answer to the question of whether disproportional ownership creates social costs by destroying firm value.[24] The Commission said in response to the Report that it would review the issues 'with an open mind' and later the Internal Market Commissioner said in a speech to the European Parliament that there would be no further action in this area.[25] That appeared to represent a change of stance on the part of the Commission, as earlier statements had created the impression that it was minded to intervene to regulate control-enhancing mechanisms. To the extent that the Commission adopted a more cautious stance as it became better informed about the issues, this reflects well on its processes. It could be a serious mistake to base policy on shaky assumptions about the intrinsic superiority of one corporate ownership model over another[26] or about the role of law reform as a catalyst for the growth of vibrant equity markets dominated by widely-held companies.[27] Increased transparency in relation to deviations from the

[18] RJ Gilson, 'Controlling Shareholders and Corporate Governance: Complicating the Comparative Taxonomy' (2006) 119 *Harvard Law Review* 1641.

[19] BR Cheffins, 'Does Law Matter? The Separation of Ownership and Control in the United Kingdom' (2001) 30 *Journal of Legal Studies* 459.

[20] MR Roe, *Political Determinants of Corporate Governance: Political Context, Corporate Impact* (OUP, 2003).

[21] BR Cheffins, 'Putting Britain on the Roe Map: The Emergence of the Berle-Means Corporation in the United Kingdom' in JA McCahery, P Moerland, T Raaijmakers, and L Renneboog (eds), *Corporate Governance Regimes: Convergence and Diversity* (OUP, 2002) 147.

[22] Gilson (n 18 above).

[23] 'Report on The Proportionality Principle in the European Union' (n 8 above), 6.

[24] ibid.

[25] C McCreevy, Speech to European Parliament Legal Affairs Committee, 3 October 2007.

[26] Gilson (n 18 above) 1649: 'Recognizing the various types of controlling shareholders and their potential for impacting minority shareholders differently gives rise to a second, and as yet more tentative, theme in the new generation of controlling shareholder scholarship: what, after all, is wrong with controlling shareholder systems? Here the concern is normative. If controlling shareholder regimes do not necessarily lead to the extraction of large private benefits of control at the expense of minority shareholders, is there really a problem?'

[27] BR Cheffins, 'Does Law Matter? The Separation of Ownership and Control in the United Kingdom' (2001) 30 *Journal of Legal Studies* 459.

proportionality principle—as in the 2007 Shareholder Rights Directive, which requires quoted companies to make public shareholder voting results, including the number of shares cast for a resolution and the proportion of the share capital represented by those votes[28]—may be the most appropriate form of regulatory intervention. In his speech to the European Parliament, the Internal Market Commissioner acknowledged that there was sufficient EC legislation on transparency.[29]

Thirdly, macro-economic conditions also influence decisions to go public. Thus, for example, the so-called 'dot-com' bubble of 1999–2001 prompted a surge in IPOs in Europe, whilst in the couple of years thereafter the different economic conditions meant less need for the corporate sector to seek external financing and, to the extent that it was required, more reliance on debt and private equity than on publicly issued securities.[30] The 'market timing' theory of capital structure is that firms' capital structures can be understood as the cumulative result of efforts to time the equity market—ie to issue shares when market prices are high and to repurchase them when market values are low.[31] Market conditions, together with the stage of the firm in its life cycle, are regularly cited as an important factor in the decision to go public.[32] IPOs can be timed to take advantage of 'hot' markets, in which prices are affected by excessive investor enthusiasm.[33] Country-by-country variations in the size, age, industry, and riskiness of companies that are regarded by the market as being ready to go public have been identified.[34] It has been noted that, on the whole, smaller and younger firms do not go public in Europe as much as they do in the US.[35]

Politics can also influence levels of IPO activity, as is most obvious in relation to the privatization and flotation of previously state-owned enterprises. Distinctive features of privatization IPOs can include incentives for employees and for retail investors to take up the offer.

Finally, there is a myriad array of other factors that may be relevant to the going public decision, although these tend to be subsidiary to the new financing

---

[28] Directive (EC) 2007/36 of the European Parliament and of the Council of 11 July 2007 on the exercise of certain rights of shareholders in listed companies [2007] OJ L184/17, art 14.

[29] C McCreevy, Speech to European Parliament Legal Affairs Committee, 3 October 2007.

[30] L Bê Duc, G de Bondt, A Calza, D Marqués Ibáñez, A van Rixtel, and S Scopel, 'Financing Conditions in the Euro Area', ECB Occasional Paper Series No 37 (2005) 27–9.

[31] M Baker, and J Wurgler, 'Market Timing and Capital Structure' (2002) 57 *Journal of Finance* 1.

[32] JR Ritter and I Welch, 'A Review of IPO Activity, Pricing and Allocations' (2002) 57 *Journal of Finance* 1795.

[33] A Ljungqvist, VK Nanda, and R Singh, 'Hot Markets, Investor Sentiment, and IPO Pricing' (2006) 79 *Journal of Business* 1667.

[34] M Goergen and L Renneboog, 'Why are the Levels of Control (so) Different in German and UK Companies? Evidence from Initial Public Offerings' (2003) *Journal of Law, Economics and Organization* 141.

[35] F Degeorge and EG Maug, 'Corporate Finance in Europe: A Survey', ECGI—Finance Working Paper No 121/2006 (23 March 2006) Available at SSRN <http://ssrn.com/abstract=896518>.

and exit considerations and associated benefits. They include enhanced prestige, which may enable the company to attract a higher quality of professional managers and a higher public profile, which may help to attract customers in product markets. In a survey conducted on behalf of the London Stock Exchange, one in ten of all respondents stated that the extra credibility and profile afforded by being traded on a stock market was the major motivator in going public.[36] The liquidity associated with publicly quoted securities provides greater scope for companies to offer remuneration packages that include shares and options.

There are drawbacks associated with going public that also need to be considered. The process of flotation is complex and costly. Underwriting and other direct IPO costs, such as lawyers' fees, are lower in Europe than in the US but in total can still amount to at least 6 per cent of the proceeds of the issue.[37] Research conducted for the London Stock Exchange found that flotation costs were typically about 10 per cent of capital raised.[38] The process is likely to entail a significant corporate reorganization involving the status of the company, its constitutional framework, and its managerial structure. The status of the company may have to change because of the rules that private companies may not make public offers of their securities[39] or have their securities admitted to official listing.[40] Its constitutional framework, as set out in its articles, will need to be reviewed so as to remove provisions, such as restrictions on the transfer of shares, which will cease to be appropriate once its shares are publicly traded. Independent non-executive directors will have to be appointed in order to meet the expectations of the market with regard to good corporate governance and the terms of employment of existing executive directors may need to be made more transparent, particularly with regard to remuneration entitlements and notice periods.[41] There are also significant ongoing obligations associated with going public. Once a company has become a public company with outside investors, it will be subject to more stringent legal requirements and to the discipline imposed by market forces and by increased visibility.

Going public is not an irreversible step. Companies that are experiencing some difficulties may 'go private' in order to effect a turnaround away from the harsh gaze of the public markets. Reverting to the private arena may also appeal to companies which have failed to attract significant investor interest and have thus

---

[36] Eversheds, 'Going Public 2: A Survey of Recently Floated Companies' (2003).

[37] L Bell, L Correia da Silva, and A Preimanis, *The Cost of Capital: An International Comparison* (City of London, 2006) present research showing underwriting fees of 3–4% on average in European transactions and underwriting fees of 6.5–7% on US transactions. Legal, accounting, and advisory fees, as well as the marketing and PR costs, can add another 3–6%.

[38] Eversheds (n 36 above).

[39] Companies Act 2006, s 755.

[40] Financial Services and Markets Act 2000 (Official Listing of Securities) Regulations 2001, SI 2001/2956, reg 3.

[41] On the corporate governance implications of going public, see generally I Filatotchev and K Bishop, 'Board Composition, Share Ownership and "Underpricing" of UK IPO Firms' (2002) 23 *Strategic Management Journal* 941.

not gained sufficient benefits from being public to outweigh the disadvantages of a heavier regulatory burden and harsh public scrutiny.[42] In particular, entrepreneurial characters who have built up companies from scratch may chafe against the constraints of the public arena. An economically significant public-to-private market has developed in the UK since the late 1990s.[43]

Choice of trading platform

The standard option for a company coming to market for the first time is to have its securities admitted to trading on an exchange in its home country. This primary listing may be supplemented, either initially or at some later date, by a secondary listing, or cross listing on a foreign exchange. An important study of the geography of equity listings found that during the 1990s European companies that cross-listed in the US were mainly high-tech companies motivated by the need for infusions of new equity. The authors suggested as factors contributing to the US's competitive advantage in this respect: the presence of skilled analysts and institutional investors specializing in evaluating these companies; the liquidity of American exchanges; the quality of US accounting standards and shareholder rights' protection; and the huge US product market which provided a natural springboard for foreign companies with a strong export orientation.[44] Another powerful line of analysis from the same period emphasized 'bonding'— voluntarily subjecting themselves to the US's higher disclosure standards and greater threat of enforcement—as the reason why issuers from around the world came to the US stock markets.[45] The number of European issuers listing in the US has been in decline since 2002.[46] In 2003, 31 per cent of the New York Stock Exchange's IPO volume on the New York Stock Exchange (NYSE) came from foreign issuers (including Europe) but by 2005, foreign issuers accounted for only 8 per cent of this volume.[47] Only 5 per cent of the value of global initial public

---

[42] European Commission, 'Report of Alternative Investment Group: Developing Private Equity' (July 2006) 13.

[43] L Renneboog, T Simons, and M Wright, M, 'Why Do Firms Go Private in the UK?' (2007) 13 *Journal of Corporate Finance* 591.

[44] M Pagano, AA Röell and J Zechner, 'The Geography of Equity Listing; Why Do Companies List Abroad?' (2002) 57 *Journal of Finance* 2651.

[45] JC Coffee, 'Racing Towards the Top?: The Impact of Cross-Listings and Stock Market Competition on International Corporate Governance' (2002) 102 *Columbia Law Review* 1757; C Doidge, GA Karolyi, and RM Stulz, 'Why Are Foreign Firms That List in the U.S. Worth More?' (2004) 71 *Journal of Financial Economics* 205; R Stulz, 'Globalization, Corporate Finance, and the Cost of Capital' (1999) 12 *Journal of Applied Corporate Finance* 8.

[46] L Bell, L Correia da Silva and A Preimanis, *The Cost of Capital: An International Comparison* (City of London, 2006) 32–4.

[47] McKinsey & Co, 'Sustaining New York's and the US' Global Financial Services Leadership', report commissioned by MR Bloomberg and CE Schumer (January 2007) 46, available at <http://www.nyc.gov/html/om/pdf/ny_report_final.pdf> (accessed December 2007).

offerings (ie IPOS done outside the issuer's home country) was raised in the US in 2005 compared to 50 per cent in 2000.[48]

There are many factors that could explain this trend but one that has attracted particular attention is the tougher US regulatory environment, in particular the Sarbanes-Oxley Act of 2002, that emerged in response to certain high-profile corporate collapses and scandals of that period, and the propensity for litigation.[49] Clearly it does not make sense to remain bonded to a national regime unless the extra that investors are willing to pay for the shares of a company which is adhering to those standards outweighs the compliance costs.[50] Some analysis in relation to foreign companies trading in the US in the period leading up to and immediately after the adoption of the Sarbanes-Oxley Act found that the premium associated with being subject to US regulation declined during the period, an outcome that led the author to conclude that investors perceived Sarbanes-Oxley to have greater costs than benefits for cross-listed firms on average, especially for smaller firms and already well-governed firms.[51] On the other hand, a different study of the determinants and consequences of cross-listings on the New York and London stock exchanges from 1990 to 2005 found no deficit in cross-listing counts on US exchanges related to Sarbanes-Oxley.[52] The authors of this study concluded that their evidence supported the theory that an exchange listing in New York has unique governance benefits for foreign firms that have not been seriously eroded by Sarbanes-Oxley and cannot be replicated through a London listing.

[48] 'Interim Report of the Committee on Capital Markets Regulation' (November 2006) 2. This report (commonly referred to as the 'Paulson Committee Report') is available at <http://www.cap mktsreg.org/pdfs/11.30Committee_Interim_ReportREV2.pdf> (accessed December 2007).

[49] Some consider the Sarbanes-Oxley Act to be a serious policy blunder, which was enacted too quickly amidst a media frenzy over corporate scandal: see eg R Romano, 'The Sarbanes-Oxley Act and the Making of Quack Corporate Governance' (2005) 114 *Yale Law Journal* 1521.

In 2006–07 various initiatives were launched to examine concerns about the competitiveness of the US capital markets, including how this was being affected by the tough regulatory framework. These initiatives included the establishment of the Committee on Capital Markets Regulation (the 'Paulson Committee'), an independent, bipartisan committee composed of 22 corporate and financial leaders from the investor community, business, finance, law, accounting, and academia. See <http://www.capmktsreg.org/index.html>.

The McKinsey Report commissioned by Schumer and Bloomberg on the potential for New York to lose its status as the financial capital of the world was also a product of this period: McKinsey & Co, *Sustaining New York's and the US' Global Financial Services Leadership* (2007).

See also Commission on the Regulation of US Capital Markets in the 21st Century, 'Report and Recommendations' (March 2007) (bipartisan commission established by the US Chamber of Commerce), report available at <http://www.uschamber.com/publications/ reports/0703capmarketscomm.htm> (accessed December 2007).

[50] Bell, Correia da Silva, and Preimanis (n 46 above) 33–4.

[51] K Litvak, 'Sarbanes-Oxley and the Cross-Listing Premium' (2007) 105 *Michigan Law Review* 1857. See also K Litvak, 'The Effect of the Sarbanes-Oxley Act on Foreign Companies Cross-Listed in the U.S.' (2007) 13 *Journal of Corporate Finance* 195.

[52] CA Doidge, GA Karolyi, and RM Stulz, 'Has New York Become Less Competitive in Global Markets? Evaluating Foreign Listing Choices over Time', Charles A Dice Center Working Paper No 2007–9; Fisher College of Business Working Paper No 2007–03–012 (July 2007) available at SSRN: <http://ssrn.com/abstract=982193>.

Empirical evidence suggests that competition did not, historically, have a strong impact on the market for primary listings of European issuers: very few European issuers chose to list outside their home country because it was in their home market that issuers could generally expect to find the warmest reception for their securities.[53] However, there are indications that within the Euro-area country-by-country home bias in the construction of investment portfolios is diminishing in favour of more pan-European portfolio allocation strategies.[54] Consolidation of stock exchanges leading to international trading platforms,[55] cross-border takeovers of commercial companies that lead to foreign owner-ship (perhaps by a private equity firm intent on unlocking value by relisting on another market at a higher valuation) and firms' increasingly ambitious inter-national business strategies are among the factors that may erode further home biases and generate more competition for primary listing business. Indeed, in some market segments there is already a significant element of foreign primary listing activity. The London Stock Exchange's junior-tier market, the Alternative Investment Market (AIM), has achieved particular success in attracting for-eign issuers with a sole or primary listing in London.[56] In September 2005 there was a notable landmark event when SQS Software Systems AG became the first German company to have its primary quotation on AIM.[57] Overall, AIM accounted for 52 per cent of total European IPOs in 2005, which was a year when European exchanges in 2005 raised more new money from IPOs and attracted more international IPOs than the US exchanges.[58] Overall, for the first ten months of 2006, the value of IPO transactions was 270 per cent higher in Europe than in the US.[59]

AIM's regulatory status calls for comment. AIM is not a 'regulated market' for the purposes of the application of pan-European securities laws on prospectus and periodic disclosures. Ahead of the deadlines for implementing new European laws on the initial and periodic disclosures required of issuers with securities admitted to trading on regulated markets, the London Stock Exchange took the decision to relinquish AIM's status as an EEA regulated market and to operate it as an exchange-regulated market under the oversight of the Financial Services

---

[53] HE Jackson and EJ Pan, 'Regulatory Competition in International Securities Markets: Evidence From Europe in 1999—Part I' (2001) 56 *Business Lawyer* 653.

[54] L Baele, A Ferrando, P Hördhal, E Krylova, and C Monnet, 'Measuring Financial Integration in the Euro Area', ECB Occasional Paper Series No 14 (April 2008) ch 8.

[55] H Schmiedel and A Schönenberger, 'Integration of Securities Market Infrastructures in the Euro Area', ECB Occasional Paper Series No 33 (2005).

[56] Grant Thornton, *Global Growth Markets Guide 2007* reported that AIM attracted 462 new listings in 2006, of which more than one-quarter came from abroad.

[57] London Stock Exchange, 'London Stock Exchange aims for Europe: AIM is the Solution to Europe's SME Capital Funding Gap', LSE Press Release, 4 October 2005.

[58] L Bell, L Correia da Silva, and A Preimanis, *The Cost of Capital: An International Comparison* (City of London, 2006) 3.

[59] McKinsey & Co, 'Sustaining New York's and the US' Global Financial Services Leadership', (January 2007) 46.

Authority (FSA), which is the UK's financial regulator.[60] The decision was driven by concerns that the regulatory burden associated with being admitted to trading on a regulated market could undermine AIM's competitive position as a market for smaller and younger companies. It is worthwhile to note that AIM is playing a leading role in promoting transnational IPO activity[61] but it is doing so outside the regulatory framework that EU policy and lawmakers have recently put in place with a view to achieving that goal. However, AIM's approach, broadly speaking, is to use the framework of EC law as a starting point but to adapt it so as to make it more suitable for a market that is designed for smaller companies, so the divergence between the regimes should not be overstated.

Forms of public offer of shares

There are a number of ways in which an IPO can be structured, of which some of the most important are as follows.[62]

Offer for subscription

In an offer for subscription the public are invited to subscribe directly for new securities of the issuer that are not yet in issue. An offer for subscription of new shares may be combined with an offer for sale of existing shares by vendor shareholders.

Offer for sale

In an offer for sale the public are invited to purchase securities of the issuer that are already in issue or allotted. Where this marketing method is used in an IPO, the company allots the new issue of securities to an investment bank which then invites the general public to apply for the securities. The investment bank may acquire securities from existing holders and offer them to the public at the same time.

Placings and intermediaries offers

A placing is a marketing of securities by the investment bank which is sponsoring the issue to its clients or to clients of any securities house assisting in the placing.

---

[60] London Stock Exchange, 'London Stock Exchange Confirms Change to AIM's Regulatory Status', LSE Press Release, 18 May 2004.
[61] Price WaterhouseCoopers, 'IPO Watch Europe: Review of the Year 2005'.
[62] The definitions in this section are taken from the FSA, *Listing Rules*, Appendix 1.1. The *Listing Rules* form a part of the FSA *Handbook*.

An intermediaries offer is a marketing of securities by means of an offer by, or on behalf of, the issuer to intermediaries for them to allocate to their own clients. As selective methods of marketing, placings and intermediaries offers present potential transaction cost savings, which will be a key consideration where the costs of an offer for subscription or offer for sale would be disproportionate relative to the issuer's needs for new capital. In an international IPO a full retail offering in one country, typically the issuer's home State, may be combined with placings to institutional investors in other countries.

Determining the issue price—underwriting and bookbuilding

Historically, UK market practice was that the price at which shares were to be offered was determined by the underwriter to the issue in consultation with the company before the commencement of the official offer period. Although the underwriter would have had an idea as to the price at which sub-underwriters would be willing to take the issue, the actual sub-underwriting and formal marketing to other institutions and the public did not take place until the offer price had been set and the primary underwriter was contractually bound to take up shares not subscribed or purchased in the offer. The underwriter and sub-underwriters would then be on risk for the offer period, typically ten days to two weeks, at the end of which allocations would be determined and shares admitted to listing. The standard fee for underwriting was 2 per cent of the proceeds of the issue.

Since the 1990s it has become more common for the issue price of securities to be determined through a process known as bookbuilding. The principal difference between bookbuilding and traditional UK-style underwriting relates to the timing of the determination of the offer price relative to the underwriting and marketing of the issue. Where bookbuilding is used, the marketing of the securities effectively precedes the determination of the offer price. After some initial investigatory pre-marketing work by the bookrunner, the bookbuilding period commences with the publication by the company of an approved price range prospectus which indicates a range of price and the conditions for the final determination of the price. The bookrunner, acting through a network of managers, assesses the level of interest in the shares to be offered. During this period, sophisticated communications systems and computer programmes enable the bookrunner to monitor and analyse the level of demand. At the end of the bookbuilding period, the price is determined by reference to the level of demand.

Various advantages have been claimed for bookbuilding over the traditional UK method of price-setting. It is said to match price with demand more accurately and reduce the risk of the underwriters being left with a large 'stick' (ie securities not taken up by investors); to create price tension between prospective investors; and to encourage investor transparency. However, the advantages of bookbuilding as a more accurate pricing mechanism come at a cost because fees tend to be higher than for the more traditional method.[63] Bookbuilding also presents potential regulatory problems because of the wide discretion (and hence scope for abuse) with regard to allocations that it gives to the investment bank that is running the book[64] and the potential for conflicts between the obligations that it owes to the issuer and those that it may owe to its investment clients,[65] or its own proprietary interests.[66]

Notwithstanding developments in price-setting mechanisms, it is well established in the empirical literature that IPOs are routinely 'underpriced'—meaning that the share price jumps significantly on the first day of trading.[67] The level of underpricing fluctuates over time but can be particularly high in 'hot' markets, such as the technology stocks boom at the end of the 1990s. Underpricing is a major curiosity because it implies a significant transfer of value from the existing owners to the new investors. The literature offers various explanations for underpricing, of which the most established are models based on information asymmetries, such as: that the investment bank running the transaction knows more about demand conditions than the issuer; that the issuer knows more than other key players about the true value of the firm; or that some investors are better informed than others. However, information-based models do not fully explain IPO underpricing and there is considerable ongoing debate about other causes, including behavioral theories that look at the influence of 'irrational' investors in the marketplace or biases that affect the decisions made by those in control of companies that are launching IPOs.

The current UK regulatory framework in outline

Admissions to trading on regulated markets and public offers of securities are principally regulated by Part 6 of the Financial Services and Markets Act 2000 and the FSA *Handbook*, in particular the *Prospectus Rules* (or '*PR*'), the *Disclosure Rules and Transparency Rules* (or '*DTR* ') and the *Listing Rules* (or '*LR*'). Part 6 was extensively amended by the Financial Services and Markets Act

---

[63] F Degeorge and EG Maug, 'Corporate Finance in Europe: A Survey', ECGI—Finance Working Paper No 121/2006 (23 March 2006) available at SSRN <http://ssrn.com/abstract=896518>.

[64] Systematic evidence on how investment banks use their discretion over allocations is limited: TJ Jenkinson and H Jones, 'Bids and Allocations in European IPO Bookbuilding' (2004) 59 *Journal of Finance* 2309, 2336. However, the level of fees charged in London is still below that in New York: McKinsey & Co, *Sustaining New York's and the US' Global Financial Services Leadership* (January 2007) 43.

[65] FSA, 'Conflicts of Interest: Investment Research and Issues of Securities. Feedback on CP171', CP 205, (October 2003) ch 5.

[66] The FSA has taken enforcement action for failure to observe proper standards of market conduct in a book-built transaction: FSA Final Notice, 10 April 2006 against Deutsche Bank.

[67] A Ljungqvist, 'IPO Underpricing: A Survey' in BE Eckbo (ed), *Handbook of Corporate Finance: Empirical Corporate Finance* (Elsevier/North-Holland Handbook of Finance Series, 2007), vol 1, ch 7.

2000 (Market Abuse) Regulations 2005[68] and by the Prospectus Regulations 2005.[69] Some further changes were made via the Companies Act 2006.[70] These changes to the principal Act were driven by the need to implement new EC Directives: Directive (EC) 2003/6 of the European Parliament and of the Council of 28 January 2003 on insider dealing and market manipulation (market abuse) (the 'Market Abuse Directive');[71] Directive (EC) 2003/71 of the European Parliament and of the Council of 4th November 2003 on the prospectus to be published when securities are offered to the public or admitted to trading on a regulated market (the 'Prospectus Directive');[72] and Directive (EC) 2004/109 of the European Parliament and of the Council of 15 December 2004 on the harmonization of transparency requirements in relation to information about issuers whose securities are admitted to trading on a regulated market and amending Directive (EC) 2001/34 (the 'Transparency Obligations Directive').[73] Changes to the FSA *Handbook* were also prompted by the need to give effect to the Directives.

A 'regulated market' means a trading system which is authorized and functions regularly in accordance with the Markets in Financial Instruments Directive (MiFID).[74]

Admission to trading on a UK market that is not a regulated market, such as AIM, is not subject to EC-derived mandatory prospectus disclosure requirements (unless there is a public offer of the securities) or periodic disclosure requirements. Issuers admitted to trading on these markets are exchange-regulated under the oversight of the FSA.

The financial promotion and market abuse regimes established under section 21 and Part 8 of the Financial Services and Markets Act 2000 (as amended by the Financial Services and Markets Act 2000 (Market Abuse) Regulations 2005) respectively also impinge on this topic, as does the general law on deceit, misrepresentation, and negligent misstatement. Where securities issuance activity is conducted fraudulently, aspects of the criminal law will also be relevant.

European background

To appreciate the context within which the current UK regulatory regime operates it is necessary briefly to trace its recent historical development, which, since

---

[68] SI 2005/381, effective in part from 17 March 2005 and in full from 1 July 2005.
[69] SI 2005/1433, effective from 1 July 2005.
[70] Companies Act 2006, Pt 43.
[71] [2003] OJ L339/70.
[72] [2003] OJ L435/64.
[73] [2004] OJ L390/38.
[74] Directive (EC) 2004/39 of the European Parliament and of the Council of 21 April 2004 on markets in financial instruments [2004] OJ L145/1.

the late 1970s, has been increasingly shaped by legislative intervention at EU level intended to promote the establishment of an integrated pan-European securities market. Early EC laws, in the late 1970s and early 1980s, applied to the 'officially listed' segment of the securities market. Issuers that sought to raise finance by offering their securities to the public via a market for officially listed securities (usually the main stock exchange in each Member State) or which sought to facilitate the secondary market trading of their securities by their admission to such a market were required to make initial mandatory disclosures in the form of a set of listing particulars.[75] They were also subject to certain mandatory qualitative admission criteria.[76] Once officially listed, issuers were subject to certain continuing periodic disclosure and other requirements.[77] Member States were free to vest responsibility for the implementation and supervision of the regime for officially listed securities in their stock exchanges. This freedom was exploited in the UK, where the London Stock Exchange was the competent authority for matters relating to official listing. The regime for officially listed securities was followed towards the end of the 1980s by further EC law whereby prospectuses became mandatory for public offers of both officially listed and other securities.[78]

Market changes during the 1990s, such as the emergence of new trading platforms, made the regulatory emphasis on the officially listed segment of securities markets seem increasingly anomalous. The reliance on exchanges—which were converting from not-for-profit entities to commercial companies in order to operate more effectively in a new, more competitive, environment—to perform regulatory and supervisory functions came under increasing scrutiny. Other aspects of the EC regulatory regime for official listing and public offers of securities also proved to be ill-suited to the changing market conditions.

In 1999, the European Commission adopted the Financial Services Action Plan (FSAP).[79] The FSAP was an attempt by the European Commission to equip the Community better to meet the challenges of monetary union and to capitalize on the potential benefits of a single market in financial services. It set out an

---

[75] Council Directive (EEC) 80/390 co-ordinating the requirements for the drawing-up, scrutiny and distribution of the listing particulars to be published for the admission of securities to official stock exchange listing, [1980] OJ L100/1 (the 'Listing Particulars Directive').

[76] Council Directive (EEC) 79/279 co-ordinating the conditions for the admission of securities to official stock exchange listing [1979] OJ L66/21 (the 'Admission Directive').

[77] Council Directive (EEC) 82/121 on information to be published on a regular basis by companies shares of which have been admitted to official stock-exchange listing [1982] OJ L48/26 (the 'Interim Reports Directive').

[78] Council Directive (EEC) 89/298 co-ordinating the requirements for the drawing-up, scrutiny and distribution of the prospectus to be published when transferable securities are offered to the public [1989] OJ L124/8 (the 'Public Offers Directive').

[79] European Commission, 'Financial Services: Implementing the Framework for Financial Markets: Action Plan' (COM (1999) 232). See also A Alcock, 'The Rise and Fall of UK Quoted Company Regulation?' [2007] JBL 733.

ambitious plan for new legislation, including a revamped regime for public offers of securities and the admission of securities to trading platforms. FSAP ideas eventually crystallized into a considerable corpus of new EC securities law, of which the Prospectus, Transparency Obligations, and Market Abuse Directives represent a significant part.

Under the Prospectus Directive, Member States are obliged to enact laws requiring a prospectus to be published in respect of all non-exempt offers of securities to the public. The Prospectus Directive also requires Member States to pass laws imposing the requirement for a prospectus to be published on the admission of securities to trading on a 'regulated market'. Regulated markets can include second-tier markets as well as markets for officially listed securities but, as the repositioning of AIM by the London Stock Exchange demonstrates, steps can be taken to avoid the status where a more flexible regulatory regime is desired. The use of 'regulated markets' as a significant regulatory category continues into other Directives. Under the Market Abuse Directive, Member States are obliged to require issuers that have their securities admitted to trading on a regulated market also to comply with an obligation of continuous disclosure in respect of inside information.[80] The regulatory obligations associated with being admitted to trading on a regulated market are further reinforced by the Transparency Obligations Directive. This Directive makes it obligatory for Member States to require issuers that have their securities admitted to trading on a regulated market to comply with periodic disclosure requirements. It also requires shareholders to disclose major holdings. The issuer disclosure obligations that are imposed by the Market Abuse and Transparency Obligations Directives are considered further at the end of this chapter.

Another EC law of particular significance is Regulation (EC) 1606/2002 of the European Parliament and of the Council of 19 July 2002 on the application of international accounting standards (the 'IAS Regulation'), which, with effect from January 2005, imposes a requirement for the consolidated accounts of EEA issuers with securities admitted to trading a regulated market to be drawn up in accordance with the standards now known as International Financial Reporting Standards (IFRS) that have been adopted by the EU.[81]

Official listing—its continuing significance in the UK

The regulatory significance at the EU level of the officially listed segment of the market is now reduced to a shadow of its former self. The initial and ongoing

---

[80] Market Abuse Directive, Art 6.
[81] [2002] OJ L243/1.

disclosure regime in the Prospectus, Transparency Obligations, and Market Abuse Directives applies across all regulated markets and the officially listed segment of regulated markets is subject only to relatively minor additional requirements in relation to qualitative admissions criteria. These criteria are set out in Directive (EC) 2001/34 of the European Parliament and of the Council of 28 May 2001 on the admission of securities to official stock exchange listing and on information to be published on those securities ('CARD'), which is a consolidated version of the Directives passed in the late 1970s and 1980s that have been largely (but not completely) overtaken by the more recent EC laws.[82]

Although policy at EU level is moving firmly away from targeting regulation at the officially listed segment of the market, within UK domestic law there remains quite a significant, distinct body of regulation relating to official listing. The UK has made a policy decision to continue to single out the officially listed segment of the securities market and to subject it to public regulation that extends beyond the minimum that is necessary to give effect to Directives. It does so via provisions in the Financial Services and Markets Act 2000 (FSMA 2000) and associated regulations,[83] and the *Listing Rules*, which are part of the FSA *Handbook*.[84] The FSA has explained why:

However, we have applied higher standards to issuers admitted to the Official List, and our consultation has shown that market participants value many of these tougher, or super-equivalent, standards as providing additional investor protection and contributing to deep and liquid markets. We will continue to apply certain super-equivalent standards to issuers of equity securities that are admitted to the Official List.[85]

The FSA is now the competent authority for matters relating to official listing. It assumed that function in May 2000 as one of the consequences of the re-organisation of the London Stock Exchange into a publicly quoted commercial company. Part 6 of the Financial Services and Markets Act 2000 provides the FSA with statutory authority to act as the competent authority for listing and sets out its general duties and responsibilities in that capacity, as well as an outline framework governing the listing process and the mechanisms for its enforcement.

Super-equivalent provisions of the *Listing Rules* include a set of listing principles. The purpose of the listing principles is to ensure that listed companies

---

[82] [2001] OJ L184/1.

[83] Financial Services and Markets Act 2000 (Official Listing of Securities) Regulations 2001, SI 2001/2956.

[84] The complete *Handbook* is available online at <http://www.fsa.gov.uk/Pages/handbook>.

[85] FSA, 'The Listing Review and Implementation of the Prospectus Directive—Draft rules and feedback on CP203' (CP04/16) para 1.8.

pay due regard to their fundamental role in maintaining market confidence and ensuring fair and orderly markets.[86] The listing principles are as follows:[87]

Principle 1	A listed company must take reasonable steps to enable its directors to understand their responsibilities and obligations as directors.
Principle 2	A listed company must take reasonable steps to establish and maintain adequate procedures, systems and controls to enable it to comply with its obligations.
Principle 3	A listed company must act with integrity towards holders and potential holders of its listed equity securities.
Principle 4	A listed company must communicate information to holders and potential holders of its listed equity securities in such a way as to avoid the creation or continuation of a false market in such listed equity securities.
Principle 5	A listed company must ensure that it treats all holders of the same class of its listed equity securities that are in the same position equally in respect of the rights attaching to such listed equity securities.
Principle 6	A listed company must deal with the FSA in an open and cooperative manner.

Another significant super-equivalent domestic requirement in the *Listing Rules* is for companies to appoint a sponsor when they are applying for a primary listing of equity securities and on specified occasions thereafter.[88]

The most stringent official listing admission criteria apply in respect of the admission of equity securities to primary listing.[89] A primary listing means a listing by the FSA by virtue of which the issuer becomes subject to the full requirements of the *Listing Rules*. This contrasts with a secondary listing, available to overseas companies, which is a listing by the FSA other than a primary listing. The admission criteria for a primary listing include the following (some are derived from CARD):

(1) The company being floated must (unless an exception applies) have filed properly prepared and audited consolidated accounts for the last three years.
(2) At least 75 per cent of the applicant's business must be supported by a historic revenue earning record covering the period of the required accounts; the applicant must control the majority of its assets and must have done so for at least the period of the required accounts; and the applicant must carry on an independent business as its main activity.
(3) A sufficient number of the class of shares to be listed (normally at least 25 per cent) must be held by the public in one or more states in the EEA when the shares are admitted.

---

[86] *LR* 7.1.2.
[87] *LR* 7.2.1.
[88] *LR* 8.2.1.
[89] *LR* chs 2 and 6.

(4) The applicant company's group must have available sufficient working capital for its requirements for at least the next twelve months.

(5) The securities must be freely transferable and admitted to trading on a market for listed securities (such as the London Stock Exchange's main market).

(6) The expected market capitalization of the listed securities must be at least £700,000 for shares (in practice the market capitalization of applicants will tend to be much higher because the costs associated with listing make it unfeasible to proceed in this way unless significantly larger amounts are involved).

Officially listed companies are subject to certain continuing obligations under the *Listing Rules*. These requirements (which in certain detailed respects depend for their application on whether the listing is a primary or secondary listing and on whether the issuer is a UK incorporated company) are in addition to the periodic and other disclosure requirements that are imposed on all companies with securities admitted to trading on a regulated market and which are contained in the *Disclosure Rules and Transparency Rules* (discussed later in this chapter). The continuing obligations in the *Listing Rules* are a manifestation of the FSA's policy choice to provide a 'gold-plated', robust regulatory regime for the officially listed segment. Significant continuing obligations in the *Listing Rules* include:[90]

(a) stating how the listed company has applied the principles set out in the Combined Code on corporate governance, to confirm compliance with the Combined Code or to indicate and explain areas of non-compliance;[91]

(b) reporting on directors' remuneration policies and packages;[92]

(c) complying with the Model Code restricting dealings in securities;[93] and

(d) notifying shareholders of certain transactions and providing them with the opportunity to vote on larger proposed transactions.[94]

If the FSA considers that an issuer of officially listed securities or an applicant for listing has contravened any provision of the *Listing Rules*, it can impose a financial penalty.[95] Directors of issuers or applicants are also personally at risk of having a fine imposed on them if the FSA considers that they were 'knowingly concerned' in the contravention.[96] If the FSA is entitled to impose a penalty on a person for breach of the *Listing Rules*, it may alternatively publicly censure that person.[97] Sponsors of listed companies are also at risk of public censure if they fail to comply with the duties imposed on them by the *Listing Rules*.[98] This is in addition to the disciplinary sanctions that the FSA can impose on them if they

---

[90] The examples assume a UK incorporated issuer with a primary listing.
[91] *LR* 9.8.6.
[92] *LR* 9.8.8.
[93] *LR* 9.2.7R–9.2.8.
[94] *LR* ch 10.
[95] FSMA 2000, s 91(1).
[96] ibid s 91(2).
[97] ibid s 91(3).
[98] ibid s 89.

fail to comply with the general regulatory requirements applicable to them as authorized persons. In certain circumstances breach of the *Listing Rules* could also amount to market abuse contrary to Part 8 of FSMA 2000. The FSA has the power to impose an unlimited fine on any person who engages in market abuse[99] and to require restitution.[100] The FSA also has power to seek restitution orders against persons who have been knowingly concerned in a contravention of the *Listing Rules*.[101] The FSA has made only limited use of these powers thus far (which is consistent with its general supervisory policy of relying on a range of strategies to ensure compliance).[102] Its most prominent scalp to date has been Shell Royal Dutch plc which, in 2004, was fined £17 million by the FSA for market abuse and breach of the *Listing Rules* in misstating over a number of years its proved reserves of oil and gas.

Regulatory implications of admission to trading on AIM

Admission to trading on AIM falls outside the scope of mandatory disclosure requirements derived from European law, unless there is also a public offer of securities. Nor must prospective AIM issuers meet mandatory minimum qualitative criteria. The AIM *Rules for Companies* impose no requirements on the minimum percentage of shares to be in public hands post-admission, minimum prior trading records before admission, or minimum market capitalization. There is no pre-vetting of admission documents by a regulatory agency, as there is in the mandatory regime. Instead, the AIM *Rules* require companies applying to join AIM to appoint a nominated adviser ('Nomad') and to retain a Nomad at all times after admission.[103] It is the responsibility of the Nomad to warrant that the applicant is appropriate for AIM and it must be available at all times to advise and guide the directors of the company about their obligations to ensure compliance on an ongoing basis with the AIM *Rules*.[104] The AIM *Rules* require applicants to produce an admission document, the prescribed contents of which are less onerous than, but to a significant extent equivalent to, those that would be required in a mandatory prospectus.[105] Likewise, the ongoing disclosure requirements

---

[99] Ibid s 123.

[100] ibid s 384.

[101] ibid s 382.

[102] According to the FSA *Annual Report 2005/6* only one new *Listing Rules* case was opened during that year (see Appendix 9). However the FSA *Annual Report 2004/5* indicates that 11 new cases were brought that year, and that there were 8 new cases the previous year. For a general statement of the FSA's approach to using its disciplinary powers in respect of FSMA 2000, Pt 6, see FSA *Handbook*, DEPP 6.2, in particular DEPP 6.2.10G–6.2.14G.

[103] AIM *Rules for Companies* (herein after 'AIM *Rules*') r 1.

[104] AIM *Rules*, r 39 and AIM *Rules for Nominated Advisers*.

[105] AIM *Rules*, r 3 and sch 2.

to which AIM-quoted companies are subject under the AIM *Rules* are, broadly speaking, a lighter version of those under the general law for issuers admitted to trading on regulated markets.[106] There are a number of other continuing obligations following admission to AIM, including a requirement for shareholder consent before making a reverse takeover[107] or a major disposal resulting in a fundamental change of business.[108] AIM companies are not subject to disclosure requirements in respect of their compliance with the Combined Code on Corporate Governance.

The principle of mandatory prospectus disclosure

That securities markets are efficient in the sense that prices adjust quickly to new information is the cornerstone of modern securities regulation.[109] Even though there is considerable debate in the literature about the desirability of mandatory disclosure and its value in improving both the fundamental accuracy of share prices as best possible estimates of future risks and returns[110] and the efficient allocation of scarce resources to the most deserving projects,[111] policy and lawmakers have inclined to accept that there are connections between publicly available information, the accuracy of securities prices, and the allocation of resources and, furthermore, that there are imperfections in market mechanisms for voluntary disclosure that could lead to sub-optimal levels of disclosure in the absence of regulatory intervention, with adverse ramifications for allocative efficiency and investor protection.[112] In having a set of mandatory prospectus disclosure requirements that must be satisfied by an issuer which is offering its securities to investors, the UK (giving effect to EC Directives) thus conforms to the international norm.

---

[106] AIM *Rules*, rr 11 (prompt disclosure of price sensitive information), 17 (disclosure of miscellaneous information) 18 (half year reports), and 19 (annual financial statements).

[107] AIM *Rules*, r 14.

[108] AIM *Rules*, r 15.

[109] RJ Gilson and RH Kraakman, 'The Mechanisms of Market Efficiency' (1984) 70 *Virginia Law Review* 549.

[110] LA Stout, 'The Mechanisms of Market Inefficiency: An Introduction to the New Finance' (2003) 28 *Journal of Corporation Law* 635, 640.

[111] MB Fox, R Morck, B Yeung, and A Durnev, 'Law, Share Price Accuracy, and Economic Performance: The New Evidence' (2003) 102 Michigan Law Review 331, pt I, reviews important contributions to the literature. See also the Summer 2003 issue of the Journal of Corporation Law, which contains a series of papers from a symposium that revisited the seminal Gilson and Kraakman paper cited above.

[112] JC Coffee, 'Market Failure and the Economic Case for a Mandatory Disclosure System' (1984) 70 *Virginia Law Review* 717 remains the classic statement of the case for mandatory disclosure. A recent review of the literature on mandatory disclosure is provided by RA Prentice and FB Cross, *Law and Corporate Finance* (Edward Elgar, 2007) 28–69.

The operation of the mandatory prospectus disclosure regime

When is a prospectus required?

It is unlawful to offer prescribed transferable securities to the public in the UK or to request that they be admitted to trading on a regulated market situated or operating in the UK unless an approved prospectus has been made available to the public before the offer or, as the case may be, request is made.[113] Contravention is a criminal offence[114] and is actionable as a breach of statutory duty by any person who suffers loss as a result of the contravention.[115] Shares are prescribed transferable securities for this purpose.[116] All IPOs will thus prima facie fall within the scope of the mandatory prospectus requirement for public offers, including those which are to be admitted to AIM rather than the Main Market of the London Stock Exchange. However, the mere admission of securities to AIM is not an admission to trading on a regulated market and therefore will not trigger the mandatory prospectus requirement in the absence of a public offer but disclosure requirements under the AIM *Rules for Companies* will apply instead.

An offer of transferable securities to the public in the UK is broadly defined. There is an offer of transferable securities to the public if there is a communication in any form or by any means to any person which presents sufficient information on the securities and the terms on which they are offered to enable an investor to make an investment decision in respect of them.[117] This definition embraces secondary offers by shareholders as well as offers of new shares by issuers. A placing of securities through a financial intermediary is included[118] but communications in connection with trading on certain markets or facilities are not.[119] To the extent that an offer is made to a person in the UK, it is an offer to the public in the UK.[120]

There are certain exclusions and exemptions from the mandatory prospectus requirements that apply by reference to the amount of capital being sought, the number of investors to whom the offer is made, the nature of the investors to whom the offer is made (broadly, exemptions for offers to non-retail investors), or the minimum purchase price of the securities. There is no need for a public offer prospectus where transferable securities are part of an offer for which the total consideration is less than €2.5 million or an equivalent amount.[121] In response to the question

---

[113] FSMA 2000, s 85(1) and (2).
[114] ibid s 85(3).
[115] ibid s 85(4).
[116] ibid s 102A
[117] ibid s 102B(1) and (3).
[118] ibid s 102B(4).
[119] ibid s 102B(5).
[120] ibid s 102B(2).
[121] ibid s 85(5) and (6), and Sch 11A, para 9.

of whether, in applying this limit, the total consideration of the offer should be calculated on an EEA-wide basis or a country-by-country basis, the European Commission has opted for an EEA basis.[122] It is not clear whether elements of an offer that are made into non-EEA countries should be counted as well but it is arguable that they should be. This exclusion was introduced to enable small and medium-sized enterprises raise finance more easily. So far as EC prospectus law is concerned, offers of less than €2.5 million fall entirely outside its scope (save for a qualification that flows from the interpretation of the exemption that is discussed immediately below), with one consequence of this being that Member States are free to impose their own domestic prospectus law on offers below this size (subject to other exemptions) should they wish to do so. The UK position is that prospectus-style documents are not required for offers of less than €2.5 million.[123]

An overlapping exemption provides that an offer to the public of securities is exempt from the public offer prospectus requirement where the total consideration cannot exceed €100,000 or an equivalent amount.[124] Where the €100,000 exemption applies, Member States are not permitted to impose prospectus requirements under their domestic law.[125] Here it is less clear whether the limit is to be calculated on an individual Member State, EEA, or even global basis, though a case can be made for saying that it is territorially (ie Member State) based.[126] The costs involved in producing a prospectus would be disproportionate where such small amounts of capital are sought.

Offers made or directed at fewer than 100 people per Member State are also exempt from the public offer prospectus requirement,[127] as are offers made or directed to qualified investors only.[128] There is a further exemption from the public offers prospectus requirement for offers where an investor must pay at least €50,000 (or equivalent) to acquire the securities.[129] These exemptions facilitate non-retail offers, including IPOs made only to institutions. They are especially useful in international IPOs where, conventionally, an issuer makes a full retail offer in its home country (for which a prospectus is required) and makes selective placings of its securities to institutional investors in other countries, and in the marketing of international bond issues. These exemptions are considered further

---

[122] CESR, 'Frequently asked questions regarding Prospectuses: Common positions agreed by CESR Members' (CESR/07–651) 15 (Q 23(a)).

[123] UKLA, *List!* Issue 11, (September 2005).

[124] FSMA, s 86(1)(e).

[125] UKLA, *List!* Issue 11, (September 2005). This interpretation of how of the €2.5m exclusion and €100,000 exemption fit together is not straightforward. The two provisions were inserted into the draft Directive at different times and the relationship between them may not have been fully thought through.

[126] FSMA 2000, s 86(1) provides safe harbours from contravention of s 85, which is territorially based. See also Prospectus Directive, Art 3.1 (territorially-based) and Art 3.2 (which qualifies Art 3.1). On the other hand, s 86(1)(e) makes reference to the 'total' consideration.

[127] FSMA 2000, s 86(1)(b).

[128] ibid s 86(1)(a). S 86(7) defines 'qualified investor'.

[129] ibid s 86(1)(c) and (d).

in chapter 14 below, on international equity offerings, and in chapter 15, on corporate bonds.

In the case of all the exemptions just considered, it is only the public offers prospectus requirement that is avoided. If the securities are to be admitted to trading on a regulated market, an admission prospectus will be required unless another exemption is available. Exemptions from the admission prospectus requirement, and also further exemptions from the public offer prospectus requirement, are provided by the *Prospectus Rules*, made by the FSA as the competent authority for prospectuses.[130] These exemptions under the *Prospectus Rules* have little significance so far as IPOs are concerned.

Prospectus form and contents

A mandatory prospectus may be drawn up as a single or a tripartite document, the latter comprising a registration document (containing information relating to the issuer), a securities note (containing details of the securities to be offered or admitted), and a summary note.[131] Issuers contemplating an issue of securities may file a registration document with the FSA which will then be valid for twelve months. When the issuer is ready to issue securities to the public or to apply for their admission to trading on a regulated market, it will need to submit only the securities note (which will also provide information on any significant change since the registration document was approved, if this could affect the investors' assessment of the securities since the latest updated registration document was published) and the summary.[132] Having a tripartite prospectus will therefore enable an issuer to be in a position to issue securities more quickly once the registration document is published. The first major UK securities offering to adopt the new tripartite format was the flotation of Standard Life plc in July 2006.[133]

The detailed contents of a mandatory prospectus are prescribed by the Prospectus Directive Regulation, which, under EC law, is directly applicable in the UK.[134] The Prospectus Directive Regulation is an example of 'Level 2' legislation made under the Lamfalussy Process for EC securities law-making.[135] The approach adopted in the Prospectus Directive Regulation is to require a prospectus to be drawn up using a combination of schedules and building blocks, as

---

[130] *PR* 1.2.2 and *PR* 1.2.3. The statutory authority for the FSA to limit the scope of the mandatory prospectus requirement in this way is provided by FSMA 2000, s 85(5) and (6).

[131] *PR* 2.2.

[132] *PR* 2.2.5.

[133] E Ferran, 'Cross-border Offers of Securities in the EU: The *Standard Life* Flotation' (2007) 4 *European Company and Financial Law Review* 462.

[134] Commission Regulation (EC) 809/2004 of 29 April 2004 implementing Directive (EC) 2003/71 of the European Parliament and of the Council as regards information contained in prospectuses as well as the format, incorporation by reference and publication of such prospectuses and dissemination of advertisements [2004] OJ L149/1 ('Prospectus Directive Regulation').

[135] On the Lamfalussy Process generally, E Ferran, *Building an EU Securities Market* (CUP, 2004) 58–126.

appropriate to the type of issuer and relevant securities involved.[136] There are, *inter alia*, separate schedules and building blocks relating to shares, debt securities with a denomination of less than €50,000, debt securities with a denomination of at least €50,000, asset-backed securities, and derivative securities. Annex XVIII to the Prospectus Directive Regulation provides a table of combinations that is designed to enable issuers to determine the specific content requirements for a particular prospectus. As an aid to readers, the FSA *Prospectus Rules* include lengthy extracts from the Prospectus Directive Regulation but it is the Regulation itself that is the definitive source.[137]

The disclosure regime set by the Prospectus Directive and the Prospectus Directive Regulation is one of maximum harmonization. This means that the FSA cannot adopt general rules requiring a prospectus to contain items of information which are not included in relevant schedules and building blocks of the Prospectus Directive Regulation.[138] However, on a case-by-case basis as a condition of approving a prospectus, the FSA can require the inclusion in a prospectus of supplementary information that it considers necessary for investor protection.[139] There is also scope for the FSA, on a specific basis, to authorize the omission of information that would otherwise be required where disclosure would be contrary to the public interest or seriously detrimental to the issuer (provided that, in this case, the omission would be unlikely to mislead the public) or where the information is only of minor importance.[140]

The Committee of European Securities Regulators (CESR), which is a network organization of the EEA countries' national securities regulatory agencies, has issued recommendations for the consistent implementation of prospectus requirements.[141] Under the *Prospectus Rules* those responsible for drawing up a prospectus must consider the CESR recommendations as part of the determination of prospectus contents, as this will be taken into account by the FSA in the prospectus approval process.[142]

In addition to the detailed requirements derived from the Prospectus Directive Regulation, a prospectus must contain the 'necessary information', which is defined by section 87A(2) of the Financial Services and Markets Act 2000 as information necessary to enable investors to make an informed assessment of:

(1) the assets and liabilities, financial position, profits and losses, and prospects of the issuer of the transferable securities and of any guarantor; and
(2) the rights attaching to the transferable securities.

---

[136] Prospectus Directive Regulation, Art 21.
[137] *PR* 1.1.7.
[138] Prospectus Directive, rec 15.
[139] FSMA 2000, s 87J.
[140] ibid s 87B.
[141] CESR, 'Recommendations for the Consistent Implementation of the European Commission's Regulation on Prospectuses', No 809/2004, CESR/05-054b (2005).
[142] *PR* 1.1.6 and 1.1.8.

The necessary information must be presented in a form which is comprehensible and easy to analyse.[143] It must be prepared having regard to the particular nature of the transferable securities and their issuer.[144]

This general duty of disclosure in prospectuses is similar to the one that applied before the new regime came into effect from 1 July 2005. However, there are certain differences that could prove to have some significance in practice. The new disclosure obligation relates to information that is 'necessary' for investors to make informed assessments, whereas the old obligation related to information that investors and their professional advisers would reasonably require and reasonably expect to find there for the purposes of making informed assessments. Arguably a requirement for disclosure based on necessity is narrower than one based on reasonableness. On the other hand, the old limitation of the general disclosure obligation to information that was known to persons responsible for the prospectus or which it would be reasonable for them to have obtained by making inquiries is not continued. Nor is it expressly provided, as it used to be, that regard may be had to the fact that certain information may reasonably be expected to be within the knowledge of those professional advisers whom likely purchasers may reasonably be expected to consult and to the fact that certain information may be otherwise available as a result of requirements imposed on the issuer by a recognized investment exchange, by listing rules, or by or under any other enactment. Whilst the current regime does allow for regard to the nature of the securities and their issuer, it does not, unlike its predecessor, also expressly permit regard to likely purchasers. Under the Prospectus Directive itself, the viewpoint of investors is relevant only to the determination of the contents of prospectuses relating to non-equity transferable securities that have a denomination of at least €50,000.[145]

In the past, UK prospectus requirements did not permit incorporation of information by reference. This restriction has been relaxed. References are now allowed in a prospectus to information which is contained in one or more previously or simultaneously published documents that have been approved by or filed with the FSA or which have been provided to the FSA in accordance with regulatory requirements.[146] Information that may be incorporated by reference includes annual accounts and reports, and half-yearly reports.[147]

All IPO prospectuses, whether in single or tripartite form, must contain a summary.[148] The summary should generally not be longer than 2,500 words in its original language[149] and should, in clear and non-technical language, convey

---

[143] FSMA 2000, s 87A(3).
[144] ibid s 87A(4).
[145] Prospectus Directive, Art 7.2(b).
[146] *PR* 2.4.1.
[147] *PR* 2.4.2.
[148] FSMA 2000, s 87A(5).
[149] Prospectus Directive, rec 21.

the essential characteristics of, and risks associated with, the issuer, any guarantor, and the transferable securities to which the issue relates.[150] The summary must also contain risk warnings informing readers that it is only an introduction, that investment decisions should be based on the prospectus, and that certain pitfalls may be encountered in litigation arising from civil claims relating to prospectus information.[151] Incorporation by reference is not permitted in summaries.[152] There is room for a divergence of views between national regulators on how restrictively to interpret the requirement that the summary should not generally exceed the 2,500-word limit. So far as the UK is concerned, the FSA has indicated that it will adopt a 'reasonably strict' approach but it has acknowledged that there will be circumstances when, due to the particular complex nature of the securities, the 2,500-word limit would make it very difficult, if not impossible, to reasonably explain the 'essential characteristics of and risks associated with, the issuer, any guarantor and the transferable securities'. In these circumstances, the FSA would be prepared to allow the summary to be longer than 2,500 words, but not excessively so.[153]

If a prospectus for which approval is sought does not include the final offer price or the amount of transferable securities, as would be the case in a price range prospectus, the missing details must be filed with the FSA as soon as practicable,[154] whereupon limited withdrawal rights may be triggered.[155] Withdrawal rights are considered further later in this chapter.

Financial information in prospectuses

Historical financial information in prospectuses of EEA issuers must generally be drawn up in accordance with EU-adopted International Financial Reporting Standards (IFRS).[156] For third country issuers, the position, as originally envisaged, was that from 2007 such financial information would have to be prepared according to IFRS or a third country's national accounting standards, provided those standards were equivalent to IFRS.[157] However, the requirement for foreign issuers to present financial information according to IFRS or an 'equivalent' accounting system quickly became one of the most controversial features of the regime established by the Prospectus Directive. There were serious concerns that

---

[150] FSMA 2000, s 87A(6).
[151] *PR* 2.1.7.
[152] *PR* 2.4.4.
[153] *List!* (Issue 10, June 2005). *List!* is a UKLA newsletter that seeks to give broad coverage of topical issues of both a technical and non-technical nature. It does not give formal guidance but it provides valuable insights to the FSA's thinking on issues. *List!* is accessible via <http://www.fsa.gov.uk/Pages/Library/Communication/NewsLetters/newsletters/index.shtml>.
[154] FSMA 2000, s 87A(7).
[155] ibid s 87Q.
[156] Prospectus Directive Regulation, Annexes.
[157] ibid Art 35.

rigid requirements for restated accounts could make the European capital market prohibitively expensive for foreign issuers.[158] Attention focused on the equivalence determination process, in which the European Commission was to play the leading role, advised by the CESR.[159] Some work was done towards a decision by 2007, most significantly the publication of advice from the CESR to the effect that there was no need for reconciliation between Canadian GAAP, Japanese GAAP, or US GAAP and IFRS but that there was a need for a combination of qualitative and quantitative disclosures to address the significant differences that had been identified between the respective third countries' GAAP and IFRS, so as to ensure better and more comparable information for European investors.[160] However, it then became clear that the EU's original timescale did not fit comfortably with developments internationally and it had to be revised.[161] The following paragraphs provide an overview of recent developments but the issues are discussed in more depth in the context of international equity offerings.[162]

From 2005 onwards, efforts by major economies (including Japan, Canada, and the US) to reduce differences between IFRS and national GAAP intensified. In response to these efforts, and to enable work on the determination of 'equivalence' of different sets of accounting standards to continue,[163] the European Commission first extended the transitional period for foreign issuers to 2009 and then added a further extension to 2011, on certain conditions.[164] In making this further extension, the Commission noted that 'to encourage the use of IFRS throughout the global financial markets, and to minimise disruption to markets in the Community' it was appropriate to take account of convergence programmes.[165]

A significant step forward in the process occurred in November 2007, when the SEC adopted rules to permit foreign issuers to file accounts without reconciliation to US GAAP provided that they were prepared in accordance with

---

[158] E Ferran, *Building an EU Securities Market* (CUP, 2004) 160–4.

[159] Prospectus Directive, Art 20.

[160] CESR, 'Technical Advice on Equivalence of Certain Third Country GAAP and International Financial Reporting Standards', (CESR/05–230b, 2005).

[161] The way in which events unfolded is summarized in Commission Regulation (EC) 1787/2006 of 4 December 2006 amending Commission Regulation (EC) 809/2004 implementing Directive (EC) 2003/71 of the European Parliament and of the Council as regards information contained in prospectuses as well as the format, incorporation by reference and publication of such prospectuses and dissemination of advertisements, [2006] OJ L337/17. The next paragraph of the text draws on this source.

[162] See ch 14 below.

[163] European Commission, 'First Report to the European Securities Committee and to the European Parliament on Convergence Between International Financial Reporting Standards (IFRS) and Third Country National Generally Accepted Accounting Principles (GAAPs)' (COM (2007) 405) 3.

[164] Commission Regulation (EC) 1569/2007 of 21 December 2007 establishing a mechanism for the determination of equivalence of accounting standards applied by third country issuers of securities pursuant to Directives (EC) 2003/71 and (EC) 2004/109 of the European Parliament and of the Council [2007] OJ L340/66, Art 4.

[165] ibid rec 5.

IFRS.[166] This is subject to the qualification that only IFRS as issued by the International Accounting Standards Board will do. Subject to a limited transitional arrangement, accounts that are drawn up in accordance with a version of IFRS that has been modified in some respect (as can occur within the EU's system for the adoption of IFRS) are not within the scope of the permission.[167] The ball is now in Europe's court.

The European Commission and the other players in the accounting standards convergence or equivalence deliberations are involved in a complex, politically charged process of negotiation. Burdensome regulatory requirements that damage the attractiveness of a market to foreign issuers are problematic but waiving those requirements is not an easy step to take domestically because of the implicit double standards: why, it may be asked, do the market stability or investor protection considerations that are used to justify the imposition of those requirements on domestic issuers not also apply to foreign issuers? Standardization of information is generally favoured by regulators on the basis that it enables investors to make well-informed comparative assessments,[168] and allowing foreign issuers to make different disclosures erodes that principle. A strong element of bargaining also comes into the picture—one side may view it as worthwhile to soften its requirements for the other side's issuers in return for an equivalent softening the other way, but neither side will want to concede ground too soon.

Language in which non-financial prospectus contents are written

Where, as is usual in an IPO, an issuer is making an offer to the public and/or applying for its securities to be admitted to trading in its home state, it must write its prospectus in a language accepted by its home state regulator.[169] Where the issuance activity is to extend cross-border into other states as well as the home state, the prospectus must also be made available in languages that are acceptable to the competent authorities in each of the host states or, at the issuer's choice, in a language that is customary in the sphere of international finance.[170] Where, as would be unusual in an IPO, the issuer is not directing its efforts into its home state, the language requirement is for the issuer to satisfy each of the relevant host states or else to write its prospectus in a language that is customary in the

---

[166] SEC Press Release, 'SEC Takes Action to Improve Consistency of Disclosure to U.S. Investors in Foreign Companies', (15 November 2007). available at <http://www.sec.gov/news/press/2007/2007-235.htm> (accessed November 2007).

[167] The 'Community filter' on the adoption of IFRS in Europe is considered further in ch 14 below.

[168] JD Cox, 'Regulatory Duopoly in U.S. Securities Markets' (1999) 99 *Columbia Law Review* 1200; JC Coffee, 'Racing Towards the Top?: The Impact of Cross-listings and Stock Market Competition on International Corporate Governance' (2002) 102 *Columbia Law Review* 1757.

[169] Prospectus Directive, Art 19.1. For the UK implementation of the language rules, see *PR* 4.1.

[170] Prospectus Directive, Art 19.2.

sphere of international finance.[171] Where a prospectus that has been drawn up in accordance with these language rules is used for cross-border issuance activity within the EEA, host Member States can require only the summary to be translated into their official language.[172]

Historically, the EU's multi-lingual character was a significant barrier to the use of prospectuses for cross-border offers of securities because Member States could insist upon the translation of the entire prospectus into their local language. Compliance with such requests would have necessitated time-consuming, intensive cross-checking and verification exercises to counter the risk of inaccuracies creeping into disclosures via the translation process, hence adding to the overall transaction costs. In practice, cross-border use of prospectuses was a rare event. The new regime put in place by the Prospectus Directive is intended to address the problems that were encountered previously. The costs involved in translating short summaries should be trivial compared to the costs of full prospectus translation.

Supplementary prospectuses

There is a Directive-derived requirement for a supplementary prospectus where, following the publication of a prospectus and prior to the close of the offer or admission to trading, there arises a significant new factor or a material mistake or inaccuracy is noted.[173] A factor is significant if it would be significant for the purposes of making an informed assessment of the kind mentioned in the general duty of disclosure.[174] There is, however, no express statutory test for judging materiality in this context. A supplementary prospectus must provide sufficient information to correct any mistake or inaccuracy which gave rise to the need for it.[175] The FSA has taken the view that where the relevant transaction involves both an offer and admission to trading on a regulated market, the relevant period during which a supplementary prospectus may be required ends at the later of the closure of the offer or when trading of the securities on a regulated market begins.[176]

Withdrawal rights

An entirely new feature of the regime introduced by the Prospectus Directive is that statutory withdrawal rights arise in certain circumstances, namely:

---

[171] ibid Art 19.3.
[172] ibid Arts 19.2 and 19.3.
[173] FSMA 2000, s 87G.
[174] ibid s 87G(4).
[175] ibid s 87G(6).
[176] *List!* (Issue 11, September 2005).

(1) where a person has agreed to buy or subscribe for transferable securities where the final offer price or the amount of transferable securities on offer was not included in the prospectus, unless the prospectus disclosed the criteria and/or the conditions in accordance with these elements will be determined;[177] or

(2) where a supplementary prospectus has been published.[178]

In view of the potentially destabilizing effect of the exercise of withdrawal rights, it is reasonable to suppose that market practice will evolve in the direction of ensuring prospectuses generally do contain sufficient information to avoid such rights arising in the first set of circumstances. Price-range prospectuses stating the indicative offer price range should not give rise to withdrawal right complications so long as the criteria/conditions for the determination of the offer price are disclosed and the final price is within the range.

However, the risk of withdrawal rights arising from the publication of a supplementary prospectus cannot be avoided altogether. The right to withdraw is for two working days from the date of publication of the supplementary prospectus.[179] There are various uncertainties about the practical operation of withdrawal rights. For example, where an agreement to take shares has been completed, does the completion terminate withdrawal rights? There would appear to be a plausible argument to that effect as withdrawal rights arise only in favour of persons who have agreed to buy or subscribe and cease to operate once the contract has been completed. Although this point is not beyond doubt, the FSA has said that in its view withdrawal rights conferred by the Financial Services and Markets Act 2000 do not apply in relation to any investor whose agreement to buy or subscribe for securities has been effectively performed by the payment of consideration for the issue.[180] The statutory right to withdraw would appear to be non-excludable but it is unclear whether an undertaking not to exercise withdrawal rights, which in form at least leaves such rights in place, would be struck down as an attempt in substance to opt out of a mandatory regime.

Prospectus approval

A prospectus must be approved by the competent authority of the issuer's home state and made available to the public before an offer of securities to the public or a request for admission of securities to trading on a regulated market.[181] The scheme for establishing an issuer's home state is established by the Prospectus Directive.[182] For a Community issuer its home state for approval of share

---

177 FSMA 2000, s 87Q(1)–(2).
178 ibid s 87Q(4).
179 FSMA 2000, s 87Q(4).
180 *List!* (Issue 11, September 2005).
181 FSMA 2000, s 85.
182 Prospectus Directive, Art 2(1)(m).

prospectuses is the state in which it has its registered office. Thus a UK issuer has to apply to the FSA for prospectus approval. A foreign (non-EEA) issuer has a one-off opportunity to choose its EU home state.[183]

The rigidity of the approval regime has generated some controversy. Before the Prospectus Directive, issuers were tied to their home state only where an element of their securities issuance or listing activity was taking place there.[184] If the home state was not involved, an issuer could seek regulatory approvals from any one of the states in which that activity was occurring. The reduction of issuer mobility in this respect is based on the assumption that states are assumed to be in the best position to regulate and supervise those issuers that have their registered office within their jurisdiction. However, tying issuers in this way means that, in effect, national regulators are shielded from competition by their monopoly with regard to their home issuers. This removes some incentives for national regulators to improve their efficiency and effectiveness.

An approved prospectus has Community scope, which means that it is valid for public offers or the admission of the securities to trading on a regulated market in any number of the states within the EEA.[185] The only permissible additional formalities are that the home state must notify host states that the prospectus has been approved in accordance with the Prospectus Directive and send a copy of the prospectus, and host states may require translation of the summary into their official language. Host states cannot impose their own approval requirements.[186]

Prospectus publication

An approved prospectus must be filed with the competent authority and made available to the public.[187] The requirement for 'publication' does not mean that a prospectus must be sent directly to prospective investors. Instead, under the *Prospectus Rules*, and giving effect to the Prospectus Directive,[188] a prospectus is deemed to be made available to the public when it has been published in any one of the following ways:

(1) inserted in one or more newspapers, circulated in the states in which the securities are to be offered or admitted to trading;[189]

(2) in printed form, free of charge to the public at the offices of the regulated market on which the securities are being admitted to trading, or at the registered

---

[183] ibid Art 2(1)(m)(iii).
[184] CARD, Art 37 and Public Offers Directive, Art 20.
[185] Prospectus Directive, Art 17.
[186] ibid Art 18.
[187] ibid Art 14. For UK implementation, see *PR* 3.2.
[188] Prospectus Directive, Art 14.
[189] *PR* 3.2.4(1). Note Prospectus Directive Regulation, rec 32 provides that where a newspaper is used for the publication of a prospectus it should have a wide area of distribution and circulation. For further requirements on publication in newspapers, see Prospectus Directive Regulation, Art 30.

office of the issuer and at the offices of the financial intermediaries placing or selling the securities, including paying agents;[190]

(3) in electronic form on the issuer's website and, if applicable, on the website of the financial intermediaries placing or selling the securities, including paying agents;[191] or

(4) in electronic form on the website of the regulated market where admission to trading is sought.[192]

Where a prospectus is published by one of the electronic methods, a paper copy must be delivered free of charge to those investors who request it.[193]

There is provision in the Prospectus Directive for the publication requirement to be satisfied by publication in electronic form on the website of the home State competent authority if the said authority has decided to offer this service.[194] The FSA does not offer this service at present. The FSA is therefore required by the Prospectus Directive to publish on its website a list of all the prospectuses it has approved.[195] The FSA has implemented this by providing a list of approved prospectuses with a hyperlink, where applicable, to the websites of the specific issuers.[196]

Except in the case of an IPO of securities that are to be admitted to trading, a prospectus must be filed with the FSA and made available to the public as soon as practicable, and in any case at a reasonable time in advance of, and at the latest at the beginning of, the offer.[197] Where there is an IPO of securities that are to be admitted to trading on a regulated market for the first time, the prospectus must generally be made available to the public at least six working days before the end of the offer.[198] The FSA has taken the view that this six-day rule does not apply where there is an exemption from the public offers prospectus requirement and a prospectus is required only for the admission of the securities to trading on a regulated market.

Once published, a prospectus is valid for twelve months provided it is updated by supplementary prospectuses as required.[199] Once the registration document for a tripartite prospectus has been approved, it will remain valid for twelve

---

[190] *PR* 3.2.4(2).
[191] *PR* 3.2.4(3). For further requirements on publication in electronic form, see Prospectus Directive Regulation, Art 29.
[192] *PR* 3.2.4(4).
[193] *PR* 3.2.6.
[194] Prospectus Directive, Art 14.2(e).
[195] ibid Art 14.4.
[196] *PR* 3.2.7. See <http://www.fsa.gov.uk/ukla/officialPublicationOfProspectuses.do?view=true&listType=publicationOfProspectuses> and <http://www.fsa.gov.uk/ukla/officialProspectusesPassported.do?view=true&listType=prospectusesPassported>.
[197] *PR* 3.2.2, implementing Prospectus Directive, Art 14.1.
[198] *PR* 3.2.3, implementing Prospectus Directive, Art 14.1
[199] *PR* 5.1.1 and Prospectus Directive, Art 9.

months and can be combined with a new or updated securities note and summary note for future issues of securities during that period.[200]

Advertisements, pathfinder prospectuses, and mini prospectuses

The *Prospectus Rules* impose specific constraints relating to advertisements.[201] An advertisement relating to an offer or to an admission to trading on a regulated market must not be issued unless:

(1) it states that a prospectus has been or will be published and indicates where investors are, or will be, able to obtain it;
(2) it is clearly recognizable as an advertisement;
(3) information in the advertisement is not inaccurate, or misleading; and
(4) information in the advertisement is consistent with the information contained in the prospectus, if already published, or with the information required to be in the prospectus, if the prospectus is published afterwards.[202]

To comply with this requirement, a written advertisement should also contain a bold and prominent statement to the effect that it is not a prospectus but an advertisement and that investors should not subscribe for any transferable securities referred to in the advertisement except on the basis of information in the prospectus.[203] All information concerning an offer or an admission to trading disclosed in an oral or written form (even if not for advertising purposes), must be consistent with that contained in the prospectus.[204]

An advertisement for this purpose means an announcement:

(1) relating to a specific offer to the public of securities or to an admission to trading on a regulated market; and
(2) aiming to specifically promote the potential subscription or acquisition of securities.[205]

Article 34 of the Prospectus Directive Regulation sets out a non-exhaustive list of the types of document or event that could amount to an advertisement as so defined. The list is very wide and includes standard letters, newspaper advertising (with or without an order form), seminars and presentations, posters, brochures, and faxes. Arguably, it is sufficiently wide to cover brokers' research reports, invitation telexes, and other communications that are involved in an offer to the public or an admission to trading. There is some uncertainty about the impact of the control on advertisements on pre-IPO research and marketing reports, which

---

[200] *PR* 5.1.4 and Prospectus Directive, Art 9.4.
[201] Implementing Prospectus Directive, Art 15.
[202] *PR* 3.3.2.
[203] *PR* 3.3.3.
[204] *PR* 3.3.4.
[205] Prospectus Directive Regulation, Art 2(9).

are typically produced well in advance of the finalization of the contents of the prospectus. Much is likely to turn on how 'aiming to specifically promote' is interpreted; the FSA has not published a view on this matter.

Pathfinder prospectuses, which are draft prospectuses not yet formally approved by the FSA, can be issued as advertisements in accordance with the *Prospectus Rules*.[206] Pathfinders are only likely to be used where an offer is exempt from the public offers prospectus requirement, as in an institutional offering. In IPOs that have a retail as well as an institutional element, issuers are likely to prefer FSA-approved price range prospectuses so as to start the six-day publication period required under the *Prospectus Rules* as soon as possible.[207]

The Financial Services and Markets Act 2000 contains a general prohibition on the communication of invitations or inducements to engage in investment activity in the course of business otherwise than by authorized persons or with their approval of the contents.[208] This is known as the 'financial promotion' regime. The restriction on financial promotions does not apply to FSA-approved prospectuses and certain related documents.[209] However, advertisements produced under the *Prospectus Rules* are not covered by these exemptions and will therefore require approval under the financial promotion regime unless some other exemption applies.

It used to be a common practice to issue mini prospectuses to prospective retail investors. Under the regime that is now in force, an old-style mini prospectus would be an advertisement and, as such, would be subject to the *Prospectus Rules* and, unless an exemption can be found, the financial promotions regime. The FSA has suggested that as an alternative, an issuer could circulate the summary of a tripartite prospectus.[210] An advantage of this route is that, under the requirements relating to summaries, it will contain a statement that any investment decision should be based on the prospectus as a whole[211] and civil liability will only arise if the summary is misleading, inaccurate, or inconsistent when read together with the other parts of the prospectus.[212] A drawback is that summaries are normally limited to 2,500 words.[213] Were an old-style mini prospectus to be published as an advertisement, it would not be subject to a specific word limit but there could be a higher risk of liability arising because there is no equivalent requirement for liability to depend on a reading of the document together with the whole prospectus.

---

[206] *List!* (Issue 10, June 2005).

[207] *List!* (Issue 11, September 2005) indicates that it is the FSA's view that the 6-day requirement does not apply if there is no public offer for which a prospectus is required.

[208] FSMA 2000, s 21.

[209] Financial Services and Markets Act 2000 (Financial Promotion) Order 2005, SI 2005/1529, regs 70–71.

[210] *List!* (Issue 11, September 2005).

[211] *PR* 2.1.7.

[212] FSMA 2000, s 90(12).

[213] Prospectus Directive, Art 21.

Enforcement of securities laws regulating public issues and admission to trading—overview

UK law employs a mix of public and private enforcement strategies to underpin the regulatory framework governing public issues of securities and the admission of securities to trading on organized markets. On the private side, investors have available to them the rights under the general law of tort and contract to sue where they have acquired information on the basis of false information. Additionally, the securities legislation not only mandates a broader range of disclosures than would be required of issuers under the general law but also gives investors a special right to sue, which is more favourable in certain respects than claims based on tort or contract. The strategy of combining regulatory intervention to establish the rules for securities issuance with private enforcement of those rules by investors has been commended by commentators, who point out that it may be easier, and therefore cheaper, for investors to establish in a trial that the issuer has failed to reveal specific information, disclosure of which was mandated by law, than to prove the issuer's negligence in the absence of a statute, and that subversion of judges becomes more difficult when a statute describes precisely what facts need to be established for a claim to succeed.[214] In one line of study the development of stock markets has been found to be strongly associated with measures of private enforcement, such as extensive disclosure requirements and a relatively low burden of proof on investors seeking to recover damages resulting from inaccurate or incomplete prospectuses.[215] However, private enforcement mechanisms also have at least the potential to damage a securities market, where the checks and balances to curb manipulation of the system simply in order to extract settlements rather than to obtain redress for genuine grievances are inadequate. During the mid-2000s the propensity for civil litigation in the US featured significantly in important reports as a threat to the international competitiveness of its capital markets.[216]

As yet there is no meaningful degree of EU-wide harmonization of the mechanisms of private enforcement of securities laws. This is a specific aspect of a much broader point, namely, that the EU still remains far away from being a genuine European area of justice in civil and commercial matters in which people

[214] S Djankov, EL Glaeser, R La Porta, F López de Silanes, and A Shleifer, 'The New Comparative Economics' (2003) 31 *Journal of Comparative Economics* 595.
[215] R La Porta, F López de Silanes, and A Shleifer, 'What Works in Securities Laws?' (2006) 61 *Journal of Finance* 1. Further on the relationship between (private and public) enforcement of securities laws and market development: U Bhattacharya, 'Enforcement and its Impact on Cost of Equity and Liquidity of the Market', Study Commissioned by the Task Force to Modernize Securities Legislation in Canada (May 2006) available at SSRN: <http://ssrn.com/abstract=952698>.
[216] McKinsey & Co, *Sustaining New York's and the US' Global Financial Services Leadership* (January 2007), 73–5; 'Interim Report of the Committee on Capital Markets Regulation' (November 2006) 71–91.

can approach courts and authorities in any other Member State as easily as in their own.[217] Mutual recognition of judgments and judicial cooperation, rather than harmonization, serve as the focus for the as yet tentative policy initiatives in the field of EU civil justice.[218] Although securities law Directives are not completely silent on civil liability in that they do contain provisions requiring Member States to apply their national laws on civil liability, they do not prescribe the contents of those laws or regulate the process by which they are to be applied.[219] This means that those engaging in share issuance activity on a cross-border basis within Europe must still take account of multiple, potentially quite divergent, liability regimes.

On the public side of enforcement, the FSA is equipped with a wide array of tools. It can impose administrative sanctions, including fines and public censure, and can seek restitution of profits. It can suspend or prohibit issuance or listing activity and can instigate criminal proceedings. Pan-European coordination of public enforcement is more advanced than with regard to private mechanisms of enforcement. The securities law Directives tend to concentrate supervisory and enforcement competencies in home state regulatory authorities.[220] The Directives contain provisions requiring Member States to impose 'effective, proportionate and dissuasive' administrative measures or sanctions.[221] They also stipulate a minimum range of investigative tools that national securities regulators must have at their disposal[222] and provide for information-sharing and cooperation.[223]

Civil liability in the UK for defective prospectuses—rescission of contracts

An investor who is induced[224] to acquire securities on the basis of factual information provided by or on behalf of the other party which later turns out to have

---

[217] The task of the civil justice unit within the Justice, Freedom and Security Directorate of the European Commission is to promote the creation of a European justice area. See further <http://ec.europa.eu/dgs/justice_home/judicialcivil/dg_judicialcivil_en.htm> (accessed December 2007).

[218] M Andenas, 'National Paradigms of Civil Enforcement: Mutual Recognition or Harmonization in Europe?' (2006) 17 *European Business Law Review* 529.

[219] Prospectus Directive, Art 6.2; Transparency Obligations Directive, rec 10 and Art 7.

[220] Prospectus Directive, Art 23; Transparency Obligations Directive, Art 22. However, the Market Abuse Directive is more territorially based (rec 35).

[221] Prospectus Directive, Art 25; Transparency Obligations Directive, Art 24; Market Abuse Directive, Art 14.

[222] Prospectus Directive, Art 21; Transparency Obligations Directive, Art 20; Market Abuse Directive, Art 12.

[223] Prospectus Directive, Art 22; Transparency Obligations Directive, Art 21; Market Abuse Directive, Art 16.

[224] The false statement need not be the sole inducement: *Re Royal British Bank, Nicol's Case* (1859) 3 De G&J 387. If a statement would have influenced a reasonable person in deciding to

been false or misleading can seek rescission of the contract by which he acquired the securities. It is clear from case law that a company is unlikely to be able to distance itself from statements in a prospectus issued by or on its behalf, even where those statements are the work of specialists who have contributed to the compilation of the prospectus.[225] The statement complained of must have been a statement of fact not of law, intention, or opinion, but a prospectus that states that it is the company's intention to do something which it has, in fact, no intention of doing contains a false statement of fact.[226] Silence is not actionable as a general rule, but a claim may lie if the effect of an omission is to render what is said false or misleading.[227] In cases on the prospectus requirements of older companies legislation, it was held that a mere failure to comply with the mandatory disclosure requirements relating to prospectuses did not entitle an investor to rescind a contract to take shares.[228] These cases still appear to represent the law. An ambiguous statement may be actionable but it is for the claimant to prove that he interpreted the words in their false sense and was thereby induced to take the securities.[229] A person who was unaware of the false statement or who did not rely on it cannot claim that he was induced to acquire the shares by reason of it.[230]

The person claiming rescission must be within the class of persons to whom the false statement was addressed.[231] Where shares are offered to the public generally, this requirement should be easily satisfied since everyone is within the category of addressee. Identifying the class of person to whom the statement was addressed is more problematic where the offer is directed to particular investors as, for example, in a rights issue where the offer is to the company's existing shareholders. In a typically structured rights issue, the company's offer of new securities to its existing shareholders is in a form whereby it can be renounced by those shareholders in favour of other investors. A sensible interpretation of this structure is that the offer, and the documentation supporting it, is addressed to existing shareholders and to persons in whose favour they renounce their entitlements, although there is no clear modern authority in support of this view.[232]

---

acquire the securities, the court will readily infer that the claimant was induced: *Smith v Chadwick* (1883) 9 App Cas 187, HL, 196 *per* Lord Blackburn.

[225] *Lynde v Anglo-Italian Hemp Co* [1896] 1 Ch 178; *Mair v Rio Grande Rubber Estates* [1913] AC 853, HL.

[226] *Edgington v Fitzmaurice* (1885) 29 Ch D 459, CA.

[227] *Derry v Peek* (1889) 14 App Cas 337, HL. See also *R v Kylsant* [1932] 1 KB 442, CCA.

[228] *Re Wimbledon Olympia Ltd* [1910] 1 Ch 630; *Re South of England Natural Gas and Petroleum Co Ltd* [1911] 1 Ch 573. In *Re Wimbledon Olympia Ltd* at 632 Neville J said: 'I cannot attribute to the Legislature the intention that the mere fact of the omission of any of the facts required by this section to be stated should give the shareholders the right to get rid of their shares.'

[229] *Smith v Chadwick* (1883) 9 App Cas 187, HL.

[230] ibid.

[231] *Peek v Gurney* (1873) LR 6 HL 377; *Al Nakib Investments (Jersey) Ltd v Longcroft* [1990] 1 WLR 1390.

[232] The situation described in the text is different from that considered in the cases such as the *Al Nakib* decision, where an investor who acquired shares in the secondary market could not base

Rescission involves unwinding the contract and putting the parties back into their pre-contractual position. Its great advantage from an investor's perspective is that it enables the investor simply to hand back the shares and recover all of the money that was paid for them.[233] The investor does not need to become embroiled in the complications that can arise in relation to the assessment of compensation for deceit, misrepresentation, or negligence. The operation of rescission in relation to modern securities markets has not produced much case law, but whether this is because the remedy is little used or rarely leads to argument when it is invoked is hard to tell.[234] Older cases suggest that the remedy of rescission may have limited practical significance in this context. As a general rule, a party seeking rescission must act promptly after the discovery of the fraud or misrepresentation, and the need for swift action is particularly emphasized in nineteenth-century cases concerning contracts to take shares:

Where a person has contracted to take shares in a company and his name has been placed on the register, it has always been held that he must exercise his right of repudiation with extreme promptness after the discovery of the fraud or misrepresentation.[235]

If a man claims to rescind his contract to take shares in a company on the ground that he has been induced to enter into it by misrepresentation he must rescind it as soon as he learns the facts, or else he forfeits all claims to relief.[236]

The delay of a fortnight in repudiating shares makes it to my mind doubtful whether the repudiation in the case of a going concern would have been in time. No doubt where investigation is necessary some time must be allowed . . . But where, as in the present case, the shareholder is at once fully informed of the circumstances he ought to lose no time in repudiating.[237]

If, after learning of an entitlement to reject, the investor does something which amounts to accepting ownership of the shares, this will bar the right to rescind. The following acts have been held to have this effect: trying to sell the shares;[238] attending company meetings;[239] and signing proxies, paying calls, or accepting dividends.[240] There are conflicting authorities on whether it is possible to rescind if some of the shares originally acquired have since been sold.[241] Since shares are

---

a claim on false statements contained in a prospectus issued in connection with an offer of new shares.

[233] *Re Scottish Petroleum Co* (1883) 23 Ch D 413, CA. The investor may also recover interest: *Karberg's Case* [1892] 3 Ch 1, CA.

[234] *Smith New Court Securities Ltd v Scrimgeour Vickers (Asset Management) Ltd* [1997] AC 254, HL, 262 *per* Lord Browne-Wilkinson.

[235] *Aaron's Reefs v Twiss* [1896] AC 273, HL, 294 *per* Lord Davey.

[236] *Sharpley v Louth and East Coast Rly* (1876) 2 Ch D 663, CA, 685 *per* James LJ.

[237] *Re Scottish Petroleum Co* (1883) 23 Ch D 413, CA, 434 *per* Baggallay LJ.

[238] *Ex parte Briggs* (1866) LR 1 Eq 483.

[239] *Sharpley v Louth and East Coast Rly* (1876) 2 Ch D 663.

[240] *Scholey v Central Rly of Venezuela* (1869) LR 9 Eq 266n.

[241] *Re Metropolitan Coal Consumers' Association Ltd* (1890) 6 TLR 416 (no rescission if part sold); *Re Mount Morgan (West) Gold Mines Ltd* (1887) 3 TLR 556 (rescission still possible despite sale of part).

fungible securities, it is doubtful in principle whether disposal of part of the original holding should bar rescission: the investor can always go into the market to buy substitute shares and in that way put himself into a position to give back the full portion of what he acquired in return for his money back.[242] If the acquirer of the shares has used them as security for its own borrowings, or third parties have otherwise acquired an interest in them, this may bar rescission unless those rights can be unwound or arguments based on fungibility are accepted. Rescission cannot be sought against a company that has gone into liquidation because, at that point, the rights of the creditors of the company intervene.[243] This bar applies even though the company which is in liquidation may be solvent.[244]

The mechanics of rescission of a contract to subscribe shares are that the investor must notify the company that the shares are repudiated and take steps to have his name removed from the register[245] or some other equivalent action.[246]

In some offering structures, an investor may acquire shares otherwise than from the company directly. Indeed the company may have no direct involvement in the offer or the prospectus documentation relating to it, such as where it is an offer for sale by a major shareholder. In such a case the investor's claim for rescission for false information in the prospectus would lie against the vendor of the shares rather than the company. The investor must first establish that there is an actionable misrepresentation of fact for which the vendor is responsible and must then give notice to the vendor of the intention to repudiate the shares.[247] If the vendor does not accept the claim, the investor may seek an order for rescission from the court. The investor may have been registered by the company as the owner of shares but this does not preclude rescission[248] and the investor can

---

[242] *Smith New Court Securities Ltd v Scrimgeour Vickers (Asset Management) Ltd* [1997] AC 254, HL, 262 *per* Lord Browne-Wilkinson.

[243] *Tennent v City of Glasgow Bank* (1879) 4 App Cas 615, HL; *Oakes v Turquand* LR 2 HL 325, HL. The investor must have repudiated the shares and taken active steps to be relieved of them (or reached some agreement with the company whereby that particular investor is dispensed from having to take active steps (eg where another investor has taken action and the result of that case will determine whether other claims stand or fall)) before the commencement of the winding up: *Re Scottish Petroleum Co* (1883) 23 Ch D 413, CA, 433–4 *per* Baggallay LJ.

[244] *Re Hull and County Bank, Burgess's Case* (1880) 15 Ch D 507.

[245] *Re Scottish Petroleum Co* (1883) 23 Ch D 413 CA. The company may agree to rectify the register (as in *Re London and Mediterranean Bank* (1871–72) 7 LR Ch App 55) but if the company disputes the claim, the investor may apply to court for rectification. It has been said that a court order should normally be obtained: *Re Derham and Allen Ltd* [1946] 1 Ch 31, 36 *per* Cohen J.

[246] *Re General Rly Syndicate* [1900] 1 Ch 365, CA (the investor, when sued for unpaid calls, filed a counter-claim for rescission; this was held to be sufficient). Contrast *First National Reinsurance Co v Greenfield* [1921] 2 KB 260 where the defendant claimed, as a defence to an action for unpaid calls, that he was entitled to rescission but he did not, because it fell outside the jurisdiction of the court, claim rescission or rectification; his action was held to be insufficient and he was therefore liable for the calls.

[247] Giving notice of the intention to rescind to the other contracting party is a general requirement although it may be waived in unusual circumstances: *Car and Universal Finance Co Ltd v Caldwell* [1965] 1 QB 525, CA.

[248] See eg *Cory v Cory* [1923] 1 Ch 90 where the possibility of the register being rectified where a transfer which has been registered has been shown to have been induced by fraud or misrepresentation

seek to have the register rectified. Section 125 of the Companies Act 2006 provides a summary mode of rectifying the register in any circumstance where the name of a person is, without sufficient cause, entered in the company's register of members. This power, which is discretionary,[249] is a general one and it can be exercised in circumstances where shares have been improperly transferred as well as in cases of improper allotments.[250] However, the summary procedure should not be used in complicated cases, such as where an investor's right to seek rectification is disputed.[251] The bars to rescission of a contract to purchase shares from a vendor shareholder should, on general principles, be the same as those that apply to a contract to subscribe for shares and would thus include failing promptly to take steps to rescind once the false statement has been discovered or, in those circumstances, acting in a way which amounts to affirmation of the contract.

Civil liability for defective prospectuses—compensation claims

An investor who has acquired shares on the basis of a false prospectus may seek financial compensation in addition to, or instead of rescission. There are various different claims that are potentially available to the aggrieved investor. Anyone who is induced to enter into a contract by false statements that were addressed to him can sue those who are responsible for those statements in tort for deceit. If there is a contractual relationship between the maker of the statements and the person seeking compensation, the innocent party may be able to seek compensation under the Misrepresentation Act 1967 and may also have a claim for breach of contract. Another possible claim is for the investor to allege that the maker of the statements is in breach of a duty of care and is liable to pay damages under the tort of negligence. These remedies are generally available and they are not unique to securities transactions. Under the Financial Services and Markets Act 2000, there is, in addition, a statutory claim for compensation that is exclusive to prospectuses and listing particulars (which is a type of securities disclosure document that now has limited significance).[252]

was considered, although the judgment related only to procedural questions concerning discovery against the company.

[249] *Re Piccadilly Radio plc* [1989] BCLC 683.

[250] *Re London, Hamburgh and Continental Exchange Bank, Ward and Henry's Case* (1867) 2 Ch App 431; *Ex parte Shaw, Re Diamond Rock Boring Co* (1877) 2 QBD 463, CA; *Re Tahiti Cotton Co, ex p Sargent* (1874) 17 Eq 273.

[251] *Reese River Co v Smith* (1869) LR 4 HL 64, HL, 80 *per* Lord Cairns; *Re Greater Britain Products Development Corp Ltd* (1924) 40 TLR 488; *Re Hoicrest Ltd* [1998] 2 BCLC 175.

[252] FSMA 2000, s 90. For the application of this provision to prospectuses see in particular s 90(11). Listing particulars are required for admission to official listing where no mandatory prospectus is required: (*LR* 4.1). The Professional Securities Market run by the London Stock Exchange is a market for officially listed securities but it is not a regulated market. So long as the securities are not being offered to the public, an admission of securities to this market would not trigger a mandatory prospectus requirement.

The following text concentrates on the statutory claim under the Financial Services and Markets Act 2000 because, when it is compared to the general financial remedies for deceit, misrepresentation, or breach of duty of care, it is the remedy that is likely usually to produce the most favourable result for the investor. In outline, there are various reasons why this is so. The statutory claim under the Financial Services and Markets Act 2000 can be made in relation to the omission of information and, unlike other claims, is not limited to positive misstatements. It is also available to a potentially wider range of aggrieved investors than other claims. The persons against whom a claim under the Financial Services and Markets Act 2000 can be brought are clearly set out. The elements that an investor must establish in order to succeed are softer than with other claims; in particular, there is no need to show that the inaccuracies were included knowingly or negligently (though lack of knowledge and proper care can be a defence) or that the investor positively relied on the inaccurate information (though, again, the fact that an investor did not rely on the prospectus can operate as a defence). The statutory claim is, however, only available in respect of false or incomplete information in a prospectus. Where the allegedly false information is contained in another document, such as a broker's circular, this is a situation where the investor will need to look outside the Financial Services and Markets Act 2000 for a remedy.

Potential claimants

Any person who has acquired, or agreed to acquire securities to which a prospectus applies or any interest in them and who has suffered loss in respect of them as a result of untrue or misleading statements in the prospectus or the omission of any matter required to be included can bring the statutory claim.[253] Likewise, a person who has suffered loss in respect of such securities because of a failure to publish a required supplementary prospectus can sue.[254] The claim is open not only to original subscribers but also to subsequent purchasers in the market so long as they can show that the securities they acquired were ones to which the prospectus applied.[255] The requirement for a causal link between the inaccurate prospectus and the loss will, however, serve to exclude purchasers whose acquisition occurs after the distorting effect of the wrong information has been exhausted.

---

[253] FSMA 2000, s 90(1).
[254] FSMA 2000, s 90(4).
[255] Note *Possfund Custodian Trustee Ltd v Diamond* [1996] 2 All ER 774 where it is suggested that a reference to the 'person who has acquired the securities to which the prospectus relates', refers only to the placee in respect of the shares originally allotted to him, thereby excluding secondary purchasers. The interpretation which was not decisive to the decision in question appears to be unduly narrow. See also J Cartwright, *Misrepresentation, Mistake and Non-Disclosure* (Sweet & Maxwell, 2007) para 7.52; P Davies, 'Review of Issuer Liability: Final Report' (HM Treasury, June 2007), para 2, n 4.

In allowing claims by persons other than initial subscribers or purchasers, the statutory remedy under the Financial Services and Markets Act 2000 compares favourably to the civil remedies available under the general law. In an action based on deceit, the claimant must show that the false statement was made with the intention that it should be acted on by the claimant or by a class of persons of whom the claimant is a member. A deceit claim brought by a market purchaser of shares in respect of which a false prospectus had been issued failed on this ground because the House of Lords held that the purpose of the prospectus had been exhausted when the initial allotment was complete.[256] It is for the investor to establish that the purpose for which a prospectus was issued was to induce purchasers in the market to acquire the shares as well as initial subscribers.[257] A claim for compensation under the Misrepresentation Act 1967 depends on there being a contractual nexus between the parties and is thus limited to those who acquire the shares initially.[258] In a claim based on breach of duty of care the claimant must establish that the defendant owed him a duty of care and was in breach of that duty. In the leading case of *Caparo Industries Ltd v Dickman*[259] the House of Lords held that for such a duty to arise, the following must be established: (a) foreseeability of damage to the claimant; (b) a relationship of proximity between the claimant and the defendant; and (c) that the situation is one in which it is fair, just, and reasonable to impose a duty of care. The concept of 'proximity' is not one that is precisely defined: in the words of Lord Oliver of Aylmerton in the *Caparo* decision,[260] 'it is no more than a label which embraces not a definable concept but merely a description of circumstances from which, pragmatically, the courts conclude that a duty of care exists'. As such, it can overlap with, and shade into, the third criterion, which explicitly acknowledges that the existence or otherwise of a duty of care is not a matter of scientific deduction and can be affected by policy considerations as perceived by the courts. In a later case, *Henderson v Merrett Syndicates Ltd*,[261] Lord Goff thought that tortious liability for misstatements could be explained on the basis of an 'assumption of responsibility' by the person making the statement. The assumption of responsibility criterion has been found helpful in some subsequent cases.[262]

The English courts are generally reluctant to impose a duty of care on the makers of statements to persons who rely on those statements and suffer economic

[256] *Peek v Gurney* (1873) LR 6 HL 377, HL.

[257] *Andrews v Mockford* [1896] 1 QB 372, CA; *Peek v Gurney* (1873) LR 6 HL 377, HL, 412–13 *per* Lord Cairns.

[258] Under the Misrepresentation Act 1967, s 2(1) a claim lies 'where a person has entered into a contract after a misrepresentation has been made to him by another party thereto and as a result thereof he has suffered loss...'; the claim is against the other party. Under the Misrepresentation Act 1967, s 2(2) the court may in its discretion order damages in lieu of rescission of the contract between the parties.

[259] [1990] 2 AC 605, HL.

[260] ibid 633.

[261] [1995] 2 AC 145, HL.

[262] See in particular *Williams v Natural Life Health Foods Ltd* [1998] BCC 428.

loss. One consideration that the court regards as important in limiting the duty of care in these circumstances is the 'floodgates' argument: it is said that if the maker of a statement put into general circulation were to be held to owe a duty of care to everyone who relied on it, this would open up 'liability in an indeterminate amount for an indeterminate time to an indeterminate class'.[263] Another argument against the imposition of a duty of care is that persons who are concerned about the accuracy of statements on which they seek to rely should protect themselves by obtaining contractual warranties from the maker or by taking out insurance, and that it is beyond the proper ambit of the law of negligence to provide a claim in such circumstances.

A claim involving an allegedly false rights issue prospectus based on duty of care largely failed in *Al-Nakib Investments (Jersey) Ltd v Longcroft*.[264] The claim was brought by an existing shareholder in the company but it was struck out in so far as it related to the acquisition of shares in the market over and above its rights issue entitlement. The court held that the purpose of the prospectus was to do no more than to encourage shareholders to take up their rights and there was not sufficient proximity between the directors and those who bought shares in the secondary market. This is not to say that investors in the market who rely, for example, on statements in a prospectus relating to an offer for sale could never succeed in a claim based on a duty of care—indeed, in a case decided after the *Al Nakib* decision the court held that there was an arguable case for the existence of such a duty of care owed by a company, its directors, auditors, and financial advisers to purchasers in the market and that the issues merited full consideration at trial.[265] However, the onus is on the investor who is seeking compensation to establish that there exists the necessary proximity for such a duty to arise.

Persons who can be sued

The range of potential defendants also puts the claim under the Financial Services and Markets Act 2000 into a favourable light because of its clarity compared to other civil law remedies.

The *Prospectus Rules* set out a list of persons who are responsible for a prospectus and, as such, potentially liable to compensate investors.[266] The persons responsible for a prospectus relating to equity shares, warrants, or options to subscribe for equity shares that are issued by the issuer of the equity shares or other transferable securities with similar characteristics are:

(a) the issuer;
(b) if the issuer is a body corporate:

---

[263] *Ultramares Corp v Touche* (1931) 174 NE 441, 444 *per* Cardozo CJ.
[264] [1990] 1 WLR 1390.
[265] *Possfund Custodian Trustee Ltd v Diamond* [1996] 2 All ER 774.
[266] *PR* 5.5.

    (i)   each person who is a director of that body corporate when the prospectus is published; and

    (ii) each person who has authorized himself to be named, and is named, in the prospectus as a director or as having agreed to become a director of that body corporate either immediately or at a future time;

(c)   each person who accepts, and is stated in the prospectus as accepting, responsibility for the prospectus;

(d)   in relation to an offer:

    (i)   the offeror, if this is not the issuer; and

    (ii) if the offeror is a body corporate and is not the issuer, each person who is a director of the body corporate when the prospectus is published;

(e)   in relation to a request for the admission to trading of transferable securities:

    (i)   the person requesting admission, if this is not the issuer; and

    (ii) if the person requesting admission is a body corporate and is not the issuer, each person who is a director of the body corporate when the prospectus is published; and

(f)   each person not falling within any of the previous paragraphs who has authorized the contents of the prospectus.[267]

An issuer and its directors are not responsible persons for this purpose if the issuer has not made or authorized the offer or the request for admission to trading in relation to which the prospectus was published.[268] A director is not responsible for a prospectus if it is published without his knowledge or consent and on becoming aware of its publication he, as soon as practicable, gives reasonable public notice that it was published without his knowledge or consent.[269] An offeror is not responsible for a prospectus where the issuer is responsible for it, the prospectus was drawn up primarily by or on behalf of the issuer, and the offeror is making the offer in association with the issuer.[270] Where, for example, employees seek to realize their holding in their company by offering their shares for purchase in conjunction with a public offer of new securities by the company itself, this rule protects the employees from personal statutory liability relating to the prospectus information. This is a reasonable outcome since those employees are unlikely to have played a significant role in the preparation and production of the prospectus.

A person who accepts responsibility for a prospectus or who authorizes the contents of a prospectus may state that they do so only in relation to specified parts of the prospectus, or only in specified respects, and in that case the person is responsible only to the extent specified and only if the material in question is included in (or substantially in) the form and context to which the person has agreed.[271] The inclusion of persons who have accepted responsibility for the prospectus in

---

[267] *PR* 5.5.3.
[268] *PR* 5.5.5.
[269] *PR* 5.5.6.
[270] *PR* 5.5.7.
[271] *PR* 5.5.8.

the list of responsible persons has to be read together with the requirements of the Prospectus Directive Regulation on prospectus contents, which mandate a declaration from the persons responsible for the information in the prospectus (whether legal persons or natural persons, whose names are to be listed in the prospectus) that to the best of their knowledge information contained therein (or information contained in the parts for which they are responsible) is in accordance with the facts and contains no omission likely to affect its import.[272] In the UK, the reporting accountants are required to take responsibility for the historical financial information in a prospectus. Not surprisingly, their standard practice is to limit their responsibility to that part only.

A person is not responsible for any prospectus by reason only of giving advice about its contents in a professional capacity.[273] The FSA does not expect the investment banks that act as sponsors to flotations and the lawyers who advise on them to give prospectus responsibility statements.

The existence of this detailed code of responsibility relieves investors from having to show that statements are attributable to particular persons and that they are legally responsible for them. Whilst investors cannot recover compensation in respect of the same loss from more than one responsible person, the fact that various persons are clearly identified as being liable, subject to defences, may increase the chances of finding a sufficiently deep financial pocket to cover the amount of the claim. In a deceit claim or a claim based on breach of duty of care, investors have a heavier burden because they must establish that the defendants were legally responsible for the making of the offending statement in accordance with common law rules. So far as deceit claims are concerned, directors have been held personally liable for common law deceit, alongside their company, for knowingly or recklessly issuing a false prospectus[274] and more recent authority has confirmed that the courts will not look kindly on directors who attempt to use the company's separate legal personality as a shield against liability for fraudulent behaviour.[275] In principle, directors, reporting accountants, financial advisers, and other professional intermediaries could be liable for negligent misstatements contained in a prospectus but the rules on duty of care liability mean that it would be necessary to establish that such persons have assumed personal responsibility for that information, which may not be easy.[276] The position under the Misrepresentation Act 1967 is that there must be a contractual nexus between the claimant and the defendant.

---

[272] Prospectus Directive Regulation, Annex I, item 1 and Annex III, item 1.
[273] PR 5.5.9.
[274] *Edgington v Fitzmaurice* (1885) 29 Ch D 459.
[275] *Standard Chartered Bank v Pakistan National Shipping Corp and ors (Nos 2 and 4)* [2003] 1 AC 959, HL.
[276] *Al Nakib Investments (Jersey) Ltd v Longcroft* [1990] 1 WLR 1390.

Defences to liability

A responsible person may escape liability under section 90 of the Financial Services and Markets Act 2000 by establishing that one of the exemptions from liability specified in Schedule 10 to the Act is applicable. The exemptions are:

1. that the responsible person reasonably believed, having made reasonable enquiries, in the accuracy of the prospectus or, in the case of the omission of information, that the omission was proper, at the time when the prospectus was submitted to the FSA and any one of the following applies—
   a. that he continued to hold that belief until the time when the securities were acquired; or
   b. that the securities were acquired before it was reasonably practicable to bring a correction to the attention of likely purchasers; or
   c. that he had already taken all steps that were reasonably practicable to bring a correction to the attention of likely purchasers; or
   d. that he continued in the belief until after the securities were admitted to trading on a regulated market and dealings in them had commenced and further, that the securities were acquired after such a lapse of time that he ought to be reasonably excused; this exemption will limit the potential liability of responsible persons to a chain of market purchasers but it should be noted that it is a discretionary exemption, not available as of right;[277]

2. if the loss in question is incurred as a result of an incorrect statement by an expert,[278] other responsible persons may claim an exemption on the grounds that they reasonably believed that the expert was competent and had consented to the inclusion of the statement in its particular form and context at the time when the prospectus was submitted to the FSA and that any one of the conditions equivalent to those specified in (a) to (d) above is satisfied;[279]

3. irrespective of the responsible person's original belief, he is exempt if he satisfies the court that he had published a correction in a manner calculated to bring it to the attention of likely purchasers before the acquisition or had taken all reasonable steps to secure such publication and reasonably believed that it had in fact taken place;[280]

4. liability is not incurred in respect of an incorrect statement made by an official person or stated in an official public document provided it is accurately and fairly reproduced in the prospectus;[281]

5. no liability arises in relation to any person who acquired the securities in the knowledge that the prospectus was inaccurate;[282] and

---

[277] FSMA 2000, Sch 10, para 1.
[278] Defined in ibid Sch 10, para 8.
[279] ibid Sch 10, para 2.
[280] ibid Sch 10, paras 3–4.
[281] ibid Sch 10, para 5.
[282] ibid Sch 10, para 6.

6. a responsible person is exempt from liability for failure to comply with the obligation to produce a supplementary prospectus if he satisfies the court that he reasonably believed that a supplementary prospectus was not required.[283]

It should also be noted that statutory liability for summaries is regulated. Statutory liability will attach to those persons who are responsible for the summary but only if the summary is misleading, inaccurate, or inconsistent when read together with the other parts of the prospectus.[284]

Elements of the claim

Causation

Section 90 of the Financial Services and Markets Act 2000 allows an investor to claim compensation for the distortion of the operation of the market through the provision of false information. The investor must establish a causal link between the inaccurate prospectus and the loss suffered; this means that an investor must establish that the price at which he acquired the shares was a price that was distorted by the wrong information. However, there is no further requirement that the investor should have been specifically aware of the false information and have relied upon it in making an investment decision. In this respect the securities law claim contrasts favourably with a deceit claim or a claim under the Misrepresentation Act 1967 where the investor must show that he was induced to act by the false statement[285] and if the evidence shows that the investor was unaware of the statement or took no notice of it, the claim will not succeed.[286] Evidence that the price at which securities were sold was affected materially by the false statement or omission could establish causation.

Investor's knowledge of falsehood

A claim brought by an investor who knows that the information contained in a prospectus is false is likely to fail irrespective of the particular remedy pursued. An investor who knows that information is false cannot claim to have been induced to act on it and a deceit or misrepresentation claim will fail for that reason.[287] Equally, in a case based on breach of the duty of care, an investor could not credibly claim that the mistaken advice caused the loss when he or she was actually aware of the mistake and proceeded anyway. Under the Financial Services and Markets Act 2000, a person who would otherwise be a responsible

---

[283] ibid Sch 10, para 7.

[284] ibid s 90(12).

[285] *Edgington v Fitzmaurice* (1885) 29 Ch D 459, CA; *Standard Chartered Bank v Pakistan National Shipping Corp and ors* [2003] 1 AC 959, HL.

[286] *Smith v Chadwick* (1881) 9 App Cas 187, HL.

[287] But the investor is not required to make inquiries to verify the accuracy of information: *Aaron's Reefs Ltd v Twiss* [1896] AC 273, HL, 279 *per* Lord Halsbury LC.

person can defend the claim by showing that the investor acquired the shares with knowledge of the inaccuracy.[288]

Knowledge of falsehood by the persons responsible for the statement

An investor bringing a claim under the securities legislation is not required to show that the responsible persons knew that the offending statements were wrong. Lack of such knowledge on the part of responsible persons is relevant only to the extent that this may provide the basis for a defence where they can establish that they believed on reasonable grounds that the information was true. There are some similarities in this respect with the claim for compensation under the Misrepresentation Act 1967. There the claimant is not required to prove negligence but the defendant can escape liability by establishing that he or she reasonably believed that the statements were true.[289] The mental element is important in an action for deceit where the claimant must establish that the maker of a statement knew that it was false, did not have an honest belief in its truth, or was reckless as to its veracity.[290] In a claim based on breach of duty of care, it is for the claimant to show that the maker of the statement failed to act with sufficient care.

Liability for silence

The general law regarding liability for silence or failure to warn is restrictive. Keeping quiet does not, as a general rule, amount to deceit and the law of tort does not readily impose a duty of care to warn others of potential dangers.[291] Equally, unless silence has the effect of making what is said untrue, there is no claim for misrepresentation under the Misrepresentation Act 1967. Under the Financial Services and Markets Act 2000, however, inadequate information can give rise to liability even if it does not render what is said inaccurate. The omission of information required in order to satisfy the prospectus disclosure requirements is actionable, as is the failure to produce a supplementary prospectus when required.[292]

Amount of compensation

The rules relating to the amount of damages that may be awarded to a successful claimant are more generous in deceit claims than those based on breach of duty

---

[288] FSMA 2000, Sch 10, para 6.
[289] Misrepresentation Act 1967, s 2(1). *Howard Marine & Dredging Co Ltd v A Ogden & Sons (Excavations) Ltd* [1978] QB 574, CA.
[290] *Derry v Peek* (1889) 14 App Cas 337, HL.
[291] *Smith v Littlewoods Organization Ltd* [1987] 2 AC 241, HL.
[292] FSMA 2000, s 90(1)(b)(ii) and (11).

of care because the latter are subject to remoteness rules limiting liability only to foreseeable losses, whereas a person who can establish that he was deceived can claim all losses flowing directly from the wrong whether or not those losses were foreseeable.[293] The deceit rules have also been held to apply to claims under the Misrepresentation Act 1967.[294] The Financial Services and Markets Act 2000 provides no explicit guidance on the basis upon which statutory compensation is to be assessed. Cases on old companies legislation provisions that provided for compensation for untrue prospectuses applied the deceit rules.[295] Whilst the different statutory context means that such cases need to be treated with some caution, there is sufficient similarity between the modern statutory regime and its predecessors in this respect to suggest that the courts may continue to apply the deceit rules.[296]

In *Smith New Court Securities Ltd v Scrimgeour Vickers (Asset Management) Ltd*[297] the House of Lords reviewed the rules governing the assessment of damages in tort for deceit. This case involved a sale and purchase of shares that had been induced by deliberate misstatement. The House of Lords rejected a simple but inflexible rule to the effect that the claimant's basic measure of damages was the difference between the price paid for the shares and the market price that the shares would have had on the date of purchase if the market had not been distorted by the false information as being both wrong in principle and liable to produce manifest injustice. The overriding principle was that the victim of the tort was entitled to be compensated for all actual loss flowing directly from the transaction induced by the wrongdoer. In some circumstances, the difference between the price paid for property and the market price that it would have had on the date of the transaction but for the tort might be the appropriate measure of this loss, but in others a different measure, such as the difference between the price paid for the property and the price at which it was later disposed of, might

---

[293] *Doyle v Olby (Ironmongers) Ltd* [1969] 2 QB 158, CA.

[294] *Royscot Trust Ltd v Rogerson* [1991] 2 QB 297, CA. This extension of the deceit rules to circumstances where the defendant has not deliberately misled the claimant has been criticized: RJA Hooley, 'Damages and the Misrepresentation Act 1967' (1991) 107 LQR 547. In *Smith New Court Securities Ltd v Scrimgeour Vickers (Asset Management) Ltd* [1997] AC 254, HL, 282–3 Lord Steyn noted that there was a question whether the loose wording of the Misrepresentation Act 1967 compelled the Court so to extend the deceit rules, but he expressly refrained from giving a concluded view on the correctness of the *Royscot* decision. Lord Browne-Wilkinson was equally restrained (at 267).

[295] *Clark v Urquhart* [1930] AC 28, HL. Viscount Sumner (at 56) explained that the statutory action was intended to give the remedy which in *Derry v Peek* the House of Lords had limited to those who could prove deceit. See also Lord Tomlin (at 76): 'the effect of the section is to create a statutory tort having within the ambit prescribed by the section the same characteristics and consequence as the corresponding common law tort based on misrepresentation except that the complainant is relieved of the necessity of alleging and proving fraud'.

[296] P Davies, 'Liability for Misstatements to the Market: A Discussion Paper' (HM Treasury, March 2007) para 107 takes the view that 'It seems likely that the courts would apply the same approach as is followed in the case of common law claims for deceit, since the section is closely modelled on the common law tort.'

[297] [1997] AC 254, HL.

be required in order to give the claimant full compensation in accordance with the general principle.

An issue that is likely to concern an investor is whether he can recover for the decline in the value of the shares that reflect post-acquisition movements in the market generally, as well as for the loss resulting from the distortion to the share price because of the misstatements. An inflexible date of transaction rule would preclude recovery for losses resulting from post-acquisition market movements, but under the more flexible approach adopted in the *Smith New Court* case they are potentially recoverable. However, to succeed in this claim, the investor must still show that the defendant's misstatements caused the loss. Establishing legal causation is a complex issue of which it has been said that: 'no satisfactory theory capable of solving the infinite variety of practical problems has been found'.[298] Practical causation problems in the context of securities transactions are that an investor might not have paid the price that he did but for the misleading statement, but he might still have bought the shares for a lower price or he might have invested his money in other shares that would also have been affected by general movements in market prices. Pragmatic or common-sense solutions to practical problems such as these need to ensure that an investor does not recover for losses that he would have incurred in any event as a result of investment decisions that were entirely unaffected by the false or misleading information.[299]

Under section 74(2)(f) of the Insolvency Act 1986 a sum due to any member of a company in his character of a member by way of dividends, profits, or otherwise is not deemed to be a debt of the company payable to that member in a case of competition between himself and any other creditor not a member of a company. This statutory subordination in liquidation does not apply to claims for damages for misrepresentation by a purchaser of shares but the position of a subscriber for shares is more uncertain.[300]

Civil liability for false prospectuses—assessment

Standards of accuracy in relation to prospectuses are perceived to be high in the UK and this has been linked in part to civil liability standards.[301] Yet one of the most noticeable features of the UK position is the paucity of modern cases in which investors have pursued civil claims, statutory or otherwise, relating to

---

[298] *Smith New Court Securities Ltd v Scrimgeour Vickers (Asset Management) Ltd* [1997] AC 254, HL, 284–5 *per* Lord Steyn.

[299] On how causation principles can affect the assessment of damages, see also *South Australian Asset Management Corp v York Montague Ltd* [1997] AC 191, HL, 214 *per* Lord Hoffmann.

[300] *Soden v British & Commonwealth Holdings plc* [1998] AC 298, HL.

[301] P Davies, 'Liability for Misstatements to the Market: A Discussion Paper' (HM Treasury, March 2007) para 71 reporting the views of respondents consulted by Professor Davies in the first stage of his review.

allegedly false prospectuses. There is no reported case of an investor succeeding in bringing a claim for compensation under the special statutory regime in the Financial Services and Markets Act 2000 or its predecessor, the Financial Services Act 1986. Nor is there much evidence in the reported decisions of investors even commencing such claims—the LexisNexis database from 1986 onwards reveals just one case where the statutory claim was directly in point: aggrieved investors in a rights issue tainted by an inaccurate set of listing particulars sought orders for discovery to obtain documentary evidence and information with a view to establishing whether it would be worthwhile to sue the issuer's accountants under the Financial Services Act 1986 or for common law negligence. The application was rejected on grounds relating to civil procedure rules on discovery.[302] (The investors' case against the accountants and the company's banks was eventually settled out of court; the company's managing director was convicted of fraud and given an eight-year prison sentence.)[303] In one other case, claims for compensation under the Financial Services Act 1986 were relevant but the litigation was primarily about a compromise of claims in insolvency.[304] It is relatively uncommon even to find newspaper stories to the effect that investors are considering suing for having been sold securities on the basis of a false prospectus.[305]

Resorting to civil litigation is not a prominent feature of established securities market practice in the UK. However, it is unlikely that the lack of a rampant litigation culture provides a full explanation for the dearth of cases.[306] An additional contributing factor could be the effectiveness of civil sanctions as a deterrent: the background threat of civil sanctions may be enough to remove incentives for corporate managers to fabricate prospectus information and/or for financial and professional intermediaries to take risks in checking its accuracy and completeness. If, or to the extent that, this is so, it is interesting that the low level of actual enforcement activity has not compromised the deterrent force of civil sanctions.

Administrative sanctions for defective prospectuses

The FSA has power to exert specific administrative sanctions against issuers, offerors, and other persons who breach regulatory obligations relating to prospectuses

---

[302] *Axa Equity and Law Life Assurance Society plc and others v National Westminster Bank plc* Chancery Division, 2 February 1998, Court of Appeal, 7 May 1998.

[303] J, Willcock, 'Resort Hotels Chief Jailed for Eight Years', *The Independent* (London), 2 April 1997, Business Section, 21.

[304] *Re Barings plc* [2001] 2 BCLC 159.

[305] A LexisNexis search for 2004–5 turns up only one reported example of a threatened UK action, which concerned a rights issue prospectus published by Mayflower plc, a company which later collapsed.

[306] On whether there are grounds for thinking that things are changing in the UK in the direction of an increasing propensity for civil litigation see P Davies, 'Review of Issuer Liability: Final Report' (HM Treasury, June 2007) paras 12–18.

in respect of transferable securities. These include: ordering the suspension or prohibition of an offer to the public or admission to trading on a regulated market of transferable securities[307] issuing public censure notices;[308] and imposing fines.[309] Restitution can also be sought in respect of profits made or losses or other adverse effects resulting from requirements imposed by or under the Act, which would include the *Prospectus Rules*.[310] If the contravention also amounts to market abuse, the FSA may itself order restitution without the need for court proceedings.[311] Where there is market abuse, the FSA may also impose penalties including the possibility of unlimited fines.[312]

When the FSA was first established, there was considerable concern about how it would use its large armoury of enforcement powers.[313] Certain aspects of its enforcement practices and procedures have since proved to be controversial and it has found it necessary to engage in a significant internal reorganization to provide a more transparent system of operation in enforcement matters.[314] As yet, however, the FSA has not exercised its enforcement powers in relation to information contained in a published prospectus. Of course, the FSA has an opportunity to exert control over the contents of prospectuses at the pre-publication stage in its role as the competent authority for the approval of prospectuses.

Criminal liability for defective prospectuses

Issuing a prospectus that contains false information, promises, or forecasts, or which conceals material facts could be an offence under section 397 of the Financial Services and Markets Act 2000. It must be shown that the maker of a statement, promise, or forecast acted knowingly or recklessly with regard to its misleading, false, or deceptive nature. Dishonesty is required for the concealment offence. In all cases it is necessary also to show that the action was taken for the purpose of inducing, or recklessly as to whether it may induce, another person to enter into a relevant agreement, a category which includes agreements to acquire securities. A person who is found guilty under this section is liable to a maximum penalty of seven-years' imprisonment plus a fine.[315] The application of this sanction in relation to public offers of securities is illustrated by *R v Feld*[316] where the

---

[307] FSMA 2000, ss 87K and 87L.
[308] ibid ss 87M and 91(3).
[309] ibid s 91(1A).
[310] ibid ss 382–386.
[311] ibid s 384.
[312] ibid Pt 8.
[313] E Ferran, 'Examining the United Kingdom's Experience in Adopting the Single Financial Regulator Model' (2003) 28 *Brooklyn Journal of International Law* 257.
[314] FSA, *Annual Report 2005/6*, Chairman's Statement.
[315] FSMA 2000, s 397(8).
[316] 6 April 1998, CCA.

Court of Appeal upheld a six-year sentence against a director for offences relating to a rights issue prospectus under the statutory predecessor to section 397. The prospectus had contained serious misinformation that overstated profits and understated liabilities. The figures had been supported by forged documents supplied to the company's auditors by its managing director, Feld. The company had raised over £20 million by the rights issue but went into insolvent liquidation the following year. In upholding the length of the conviction, the court emphasized the vital importance of maintaining the confidence of the City and financial institutions in the veracity of information contained in prospectuses and similar documents.

The issuance of a false prospectus may be part of a broader scheme that falls within the scope of a number of criminal offences. For example, in 2003, two directors, Nicolaides and Atkins, were convicted under section 12 of the Criminal Justice Act 1987 of defrauding shareholders of two companies. The companies were supposedly established to provide internet access to subscribers and low-cost telephone calls and were promoted, in various prospectuses, as attractive investment opportunities in a new and apparently lucrative technology market. In fact the companies were used as vehicles by which the defendants fraudulently enriched themselves using a variety of intermediate companies and businesses which were controlled by the defendants.[317] However, Atkins and another director were found not guilty of an offence under the statutory predecessor to section 397 of the Financial Services and Markets Act 2000.[318]

The Fraud Act 2006, in force from 15 January 2007, provides for a new general statutory criminal offence of fraud that can be committed by false representation, by failure to disclose information, or by abuse of position. In each case the act must be done dishonestly and with the intention of making a gain or causing a loss or risk of loss to another, but the gain or loss does not actually have to take place. On conviction a defendant may be sentenced to up to ten years in prison and/or a fine. This new fraud offence has been enacted with a view to removing the complications that can be encountered in prosecuting fraudulent activity. It may be used alongside or in preference to other existing offences.

Public offers of securities by private companies

The Companies Act 2006 provides that private limited companies that have a share capital must not offer their securities to the public or allot or agree to allot their securities with a view to their being offered to the public.[319] The inclusion of

---

[317] This description of the facts and the decision is taken from a press release by the Serious Fraud Office, 'Two Guilty of Defrauding Company Shareholders'(4 April 2003) at <http://www. sfo.gov.uk/news/prout/pr_199.asp?seltxt=> (accessed July 2006).

[318] FSA/PN/091/2005 (18 August 2005) and FSA/PN/106/2005 (7 October 2005).

[319] Companies Act 1986, s 755. There is a presumption that an allotment or an agreement to allot is made with a view to a public offer if that offer is made within 6 months of the allotment or

a prohibition on private companies offering their securities to the public long pre-dates the very detailed regulation of public offers now contained in the Financial Services and Markets Act 2000. The approach to defining an offer of securities to the public in the companies legislation is not the same as that in section 102B of the Financial Services and Markets Act 2000. Although it would be superficially appealing to align the definitions, in the debates in Parliament on the Bill that became the Companies Act 2006 the government maintained the view that the two statutes were directed at different things and that this precluded making the definitions exactly the same.[320]

The Companies Act 2006 does not contain a comprehensive definition of an 'offer to the public' but the essence of the approach in that legislation is that it is an offer that does not have a private character because there is no close connection between the company and the persons to whom the offer is made.[321] Thus an offer to the public includes an offer to any section of the public, however selected.[322] However, an offer is not regarded as an offer to the public if it can properly be regarded, in all the circumstances, as not being calculated to result, directly or indirectly, in securities of the company becoming available to persons other than those receiving the offer, or otherwise being a private concern of the person receiv-ing it and the person making it.[323] An offer is to be regarded (unless the contrary is proved) as being a private concern of the person receiving it and the person making it if:

(a) it is made to a person already connected with the company and, where it is made on terms allowing that person to renounce his rights, the rights may only be renounced in favour of another person already connected with the company; or

(b) it is an offer to subscribe for securities to be held under an employees' share scheme and, where it is made on terms allowing that person to renounce his rights, the rights may only be renounced in favour of another person entitled to hold securities under the scheme, or a person already connected with the company.[324]

Persons already connected with the company for this purpose are existing members or employees of the company, members of the family of members or

agreement or before the company receives the whole of the consideration due to it in respect of the securities (s 755(2)).

[320] The evolution of the debate on this issue is traced briefly by Lord McKenzie, speaking on behalf of the government in the Lords: *Hansard*, vol 679, GC 455–6 (14 March 2006), *Hansard*, vol 679, GC 471–3 (15 March 2006). The debate on the point in the House of Commons is at *Hansard*, Standing Committee D, cols 819–825 (18 July 2006).

[321] As indicated by Lord McKenzie on behalf of the government in Parliamentary debate dur-ing the passage of the Companies Bill 2006: *Hansard*, vol 679, GC col 472 (15 March 2006).

[322] Companies Act 2006, s 756(2).

[323] ibid s 756(3).

[324] ibid s 756(4).

employees, widows, widowers, or surviving civil partners of members or employees, existing debenture holders, and trustees of trusts of which the principal beneficiaries are persons in the preceding categories.[325]

The meaning of 'securities' for the prohibition on public offers by private companies is limited to shares or debentures.[326] It is possible that an offer of other securities, such as options or warrants, could be caught as amounting to an indirect offer of shares or debentures.[327]

The prohibition on public offers of securities by private companies could impinge upon preparatory steps taken by a private company that is intending to convert to a public company in order to make an IPO. However, the Companies Act 2006 provides a carve-out that should be helpful in this situation: a company is not in breach if either it acts in good faith in pursuance of arrangements under which it is to re-register as a public company before the securities are allotted, or as part of the terms of the offer it undertakes to re-register as a public company within a specified period of not more than six months, and that undertaking is complied with.[328]

Under the predecessor legislation to the Companies Act 2006, it was an offence for a private company to infringe the prohibition on offers to the public. Criminal sanctions are no longer used in this context. On the application by any member or creditor of the company or the Secretary of State, the court can restrain a proposed contravention.[329] If the contravention has already occurred, the court must require the company to re-register as a public company unless it does not meet the requirements for re-registration or it would be impractical or undesirable to require it to do so.[330] In those circumstances, the court may make a remedial order (which may require a person knowingly concerned in the contravention to purchase the securities) and/or order the compulsory winding up of the company.[331] The persons who have standing to apply for a post-contravention order are those who were members or creditors at the time of the offer, those who became members as a result of the offer, and the Secretary of State.[332] Contravention does not affect the validity of an allotment of securities.[333]

---

[325] ibid s 756(5)–(6).

[326] ibid s 755(5).

[327] This was suggested by Lord McKenzie, the government spokesperson, in Parliamentary debate during the passage of the Companies Bill 2006: *Hansard*, vol 679, GC col 453 (14 March 2006).

[328] Companies Act 2006, s 755(3)–(4).

[329] ibid s 757.

[330] ibid s 758.

[331] ibid ss 758(3)–(4) and 759.

[332] ibid s 758(4).

[333] ibid s 760.

Continuing obligations

Although this chapter is primarily concerned with the regulation of public offers of securities it would be incomplete without some reference to the disclosure and other continuing obligations that are imposed on companies that have taken the key step of opening up to outside investors by having their securities admitted to trading on an organized trading platform. Continuing obligations that the UK of its own volition has chosen to impose on officially listed issuers via the FSA *Listing Rules* have been considered already. This section deals with obligations derived from the Transparency Obligations Directive and the Market Abuse Directive.

Obligations derived from the Transparency Obligations Directive

Periodic financial reporting obligations

The Transparency Obligations Directive sets out requirements on the content and timing of annual and half-yearly financial reports and introduces the concept of interim management statements (IMS) for issuers of shares that do not produce quarterly reports.[334] The requirements must be applied (with certain exceptions) to issuers that have securities admitted to trading on a regulated market situated or operating within a Member State. For an issuer of shares, the home state for the purposes of this Directive is the state in which it has its registered office.[335] In the UK, implementation of the Transparency Obligations Directive was effected by means of changes to the Financial Services and Markets Act 2000 that were inserted by the Companies Act 2006 and by FSA rules made under the new statutory powers.[336]

Under the FSA's *Disclosure Rules and Transparency Rules* issuers whose transferable securities are admitted to trading and whose home state is the UK are required to make public their annual financial reports at the latest four months after the end of each financial year and to ensure that they remain publicly available for

---

[334] Transparency Obligations Directive, Arts 4–6.
[335] Art 2(1)(i).
[336] FSMA 2000, ss 89A–89N (inserted by Companies Act 2006, ss 1266–1268), and FSMA 2000, ss 90A and 90B (inserted by Companies Act 2006, s 1270), FSMA 2000, s 100 (inserted by Companies Act 2006, s 1271) and FSMA 2000, s 103(1) (amended by Companies Act 2006, s 1265). The Companies Act 2006 also made certain minor and consequential amendments: (Companies Act 2006, s 1272 and Sch 15). The new FSA rules are in the FSA *Handbook, Disclosure Rules and Transparency Rules* (*DTR*).
The Companies Act 2006, ss 1269 and 1273 also inserts a new provision into FSMA 2000 relating to corporate governance rules: (FSMA 2000, s 89O).

at least five years.[337] The annual financial report must include the audited financial statements, a management report, and responsibility statements.[338] For EEA-incorporated issuers, consolidated financial statements will normally be prepared in accordance with IFRS.[339] The signed audit report must be disclosed in full to the public together with the annual financial report.[340] The management report must contain a fair review of the issuer's business and a description of the principal risks and uncertainties facing the issuer.[341] Responsibility statements must be made by the persons responsible within the issuer and in respect of each such person must set out to the best of his or her knowledge that: the financial statements give a true and fair view of the assets, liabilities, financial position and profit or loss of the issuer and the undertakings included in the consolidation taken as a whole; and the management report includes a fair review of the development and performance of the business and the position of the issuer and the undertakings included in the consolidation taken as a whole, together with a description of the principal risks and uncertainties that they face.[342] Half-yearly financial reports must be made public as soon as possible, but no later than two months after the end of the period to which the report relates and they must remain available to the public for at least five years.[343] Half-yearly financial reports must include a condensed set of financial statements, an interim management report, and responsibility statements.[344] For an issuer of shares, the half-yearly report must also include a fair review of major related party transactions.[345] Interim management statements must be made public during the first six-month period of the financial year and during the second six-month period of the financial year.[346] The interim management statement must contain information that covers the period between the beginning of the relevant six-month period and the date of publication of the statement.[347] The interim management statement must provide: an explanation of material events and transactions that have taken place during the relevant period and their impact on the financial position of the issuer and its controlled undertakings, and a general description of the financial position and performance of the issuer and its controlled undertakings during the relevant period.[348] For issuers that publish quarterly financial reports, voluntarily or otherwise, that publication is taken to satisfy the requirement to make public interim management statements.[349]

---

[337] *DTR* 4.1.1R–4.1.4.
[338] *DTR* 4.1.5.
[339] *DTR* 4.1.6.
[340] *DTR* 4.1.7(3).
[341] *DTR* 4.1.8.
[342] *DTR* 4.1.12.
[343] *DTR* 4.2.2.
[344] *DTR* 4.2.3.
[345] *DTR* 4.2.8.
[346] *DTR* 4.3.2–4.3.3.
[347] *DTR* 4.3.4.
[348] *DTR* 4.3.5.
[349] *DTR* 4.3.6.

There is provision for non-EEA issuers that are incorporated in countries whose relevant laws are considered 'equivalent' by the FSA to be exempted from the rules on annual financial reports, half-yearly financial reports and interim management statements. The issue of equivalence of accounting standards is as controversial in this context as it is in relation to prospectuses. To enable work on convergence to continue, in December 2006 the transitional exemption in the Transparency Obligations Directive for foreign issuers was extended by a further two years so that in respect of a financial year starting before 1 January 2009 such issuers could continue to use financial statements prepared in accordance with the generally accepted accounting principles of Canada, Japan or the US or of other third countries provided that, in the latter case, certain additional conditions were satisfied.[350] In December 2007, the Commission provided a further extension to 2011 for the use of financial statements prepared in accordance with a third country's accounting standards provided certain conditions relating to that country's adoption of IFRS or convergence of national standards with IFRS are satisfied.[351] This corresponds to an extension that has also been made for prospectuses, as discussed earlier in this chapter.

Civil liability for periodic financial disclosures

Section 90A of the Financial Services and Markets Act 2000 (inserted by section 1270 of the Companies Act 2006) imposes civil liability on issuers in relation to reports and statements published in response to requirements under provisions implementing Articles 4, 5, and 6 respectively of the Transparency Obligations Directive and preliminary statements made in advance of such reports or statements to the extent that they contain information that is intended to appear in the report or statement and that information will be presented in the report or statement in substantially the same form in which it appeared in the preliminary statement. This statutory liability regime applies to issuers of securities traded on a regulated market situated or operating in the UK and to issuers with securities traded on regulated markets elsewhere that have the UK as their home state.[352] The enactment of a dedicated statutory issuer liability regime was driven by Article 7 of the Transparency Obligations Directive, which requires Member States to ensure that their laws, regulations, and administrative provisions on liability apply at least to issuers. The common law position regarding the liabilities of issuers in respect of false accounts was not free from doubt. Although no

---

[350] Commission Decision of 4 December 2006 on the use by third country issuers of securities of information prepared under internationally accepted accounting standards [2006] OJ L343/96.

[351] Commission Regulation (EC) 1569/2007 of 21 December 2007 establishing a mechanism for the determination of equivalence of accounting standards applied by third country issuers of securities pursuant to Directives (EC) 2003/71 and (EC) 2004/109 of the European Parliament and of the Council [2007] OJ L340/66, Art 4.

[352] FSMA 2000, s 90A(2).

issuer had been found liable in damages under English law in respect of financial statements, it was recognized that the law relating to financial markets and to the obligations of issuers to investors on those markets was dynamic and that the Transparency Obligations Directive could increase the level of uncertainty as to whether any actionable duty was owed by an issuer to investors. The British government took the view that this uncertainty needed to be to be clarified by establishing a clear statutory liability.[353] The statutory regime is exhaustive: except to the extent provided by section 90A, there is no additional liability in respect of the disclosures to which it relates.

There are some stringent conditions attaching to issuer liability under section 90A that are designed to prevent company resources being inappropriately diverted from shareholders, employees, and creditors to the benefit of a much wider group of investors. Liability is owed to persons who *acquire* securities[354] but it does not extend to persons who sell securities. The acquirer must have suffered loss in respect of the securities *as a result* of any untrue or misleading statement in a publication to which the section applies or the omission from any such publication of any matter required to be included in it.[355] There is also a reliance requirement that further limits the scope of the liability: a loss is not regarded as suffered as a result of the statement or omission in the publication unless the person suffering it acquired the securities in reliance on the information in the publication, and at a time when, and in circumstances in which, it was reasonable for him to rely on that information.[356] This means that existing shareholders who retain their holdings do not have a claim. Liability is further qualified in so far as it only arises where a person discharging managerial responsibilities within an issuer knew, in the case of a statement, that it was untrue or misleading or was reckless or knew, in the case of omission, that this was a dishonest concealment of a material fact.[357] Directors (including *de facto* directors) and senior executives who have responsibilities in relation to the publication are persons discharging managerial responsibilities.[358]

Issuers are not subject to any liability other than that provided for by the section in respect of loss suffered as a result of reliance by any person on an untrue or misleading statement in a publication to which the section applies, or the omission from any such publication of any matter required to be included in it.[359] However, this safe harbour does not affect any liability of the issuer in respect of any loss or damage arising otherwise than as a result of reliance by any person on an untrue or misleading statement in, or omission from, a publication

---

[353] See further P Davies, 'Liability for Misstatements to the Market: A Discussion Paper' (HM Treasury, March 2007) paras 46–47.
[354] FSMA 2000, s 90A(3).
[355] ibid s 90A(3).
[356] ibid s 90A(5).
[357] ibid s 90A(4).
[358] ibid s 90A(9).
[359] ibid s 90A(6)(a).

to which section 90A applies. Nor does the safe harbour extend to liability for a civil penalty, for a criminal offence, or the powers of the court and the FSA with respect to restitution.[360]

A director of an issuer that is within the scope of the statutory liability regime is not subject to any liability, other than to the issuer, in respect of any loss suffered as a result of reliance by any person on an untrue or misleading statement in a publication to which s 90A applies, or the omission from any such publication of any matter required to be included in it.[361]

Certain aspects of the section 90A liability regime have generated controversy, in particular that: it is limited to investors who acquire securities; it applies only to reports and statements published in response to requirements implementing the Transparency Obligations Directive and not to other disclosures, such as those required to comply with obligations under the Market Abuse Directive; and there is no equivalent regime for issuers of securities traded on markets other than regulated markets, such as AIM issuers.[362] There are also some uncertainties about its scope, in particular whether it applies to quarterly reports. The mandatory obligation in Article 6 of the Transparency Obligations Directive to publish interim management statements does not apply to issuers that, under either national legislation or the rules of the regulated market or of their own initiative, publish quarterly financial reports. However, the approach adopted under the FSA's *Disclosure Rules and Transparency Rules* is that publication of a quarterly financial report will be taken as satisfying the requirement to make public the interim management statements required by the rules.[363] This approach makes it possible to argue that publication of a quarterly report is 'in response to a requirement imposed by a provision implementing' the Transparency Obligations Directive and, therefore, within the scope of section 90A, but the matter is not entirely free from doubt.

The provision inserting section 90A into the Financial Services and Markets 2000 was added to the Companies Act 2006 at a relatively late stage during its passage through Parliament. Although the government conducted a brief consultation on the regime, there was not time to address all of the issues fully and to arrive at properly thought-through conclusions. The regime enacted as section 90A of the Financial Services and Markets Act 2000 represents what the government thought it needed to do to implement the Transparency Obligations Directive, with an extension to cover preliminary statements which the government accepted were a special case because of the unusually high degree of overlap between the content of disclosures required under the Transparency Obligations Directive and the content of preliminary announcements. In the consultation

---

[360] ibid s 90A(8).
[361] ibid s 90A(6)(b).
[362] In August 2006, HM Treasury issued a consultation paper addressing these issues: 'Extending the Scope of the Statutory Damages Regime for Disclosures Required under the Transparency Directive' (9 August 2006).
[363] *DTR* 4.3.6.

exercise, the government noted that not extending the regime to cover preliminary statements could have perverse effects, encouraging opportunistic legal action by investors and encouraging issuers to reduce the content of preliminary announcements, or to abandon them altogether (if voluntary).[364]

To deepen its understanding of the wider issues on issuer liability, in October 2006 the government appointed Professor Paul Davies to conduct a formal review of the liability of issuers in respect of damage or loss suffered as a consequence of inaccurate, false, or misleading information disclosed by issuers or their managements to financial markets (including to their own shareholders or bondholders) or of failure to disclose relevant information promptly or at all.[365] Professor Davies issued a discussion paper in March 2007 and a final report in June 2007.[366] In the Final Report he recommended a number of changes, namely: to extend the statutory regime to cover ad hoc disclosures; to apply the statutory regime to all announcements made through a Regulatory Information Service (RIS); to extend the statutory regime to apply to disclosures by issuers with securities traded on exchange-regulated markets, including AIM and the PLUS-quoted Market, and to all 'multilateral trading facilities' and other trading platforms for securities; to extend the statutory regime to encompass liability for dishonest delay in making RIS announcements; and to extend the statutory regime to confer rights on both buyers and sellers of securities.[367]

At the time of writing it is not yet clear whether the government intends to amend the statutory regime so as to give effect to the recommendations made by Professor Davies. Should it decide to do so, there is scope for the changes to be made by means of regulations. Section 90B of the Financial Services and Markets Act 2000 (inserted by section 1270 of the Companies Act 2006) empowers HM Treasury to make provision for the liability of issuers of securities traded on a regulated market and other persons in respect of information published to holders of securities, to the market, or to the public generally.

Administrative and criminal sanctions

The FSA has power to take disciplinary action against issuers that fail to comply with transparency obligations. These powers include public censure of the issuer[368] and suspension or prohibition of trading in its securities.[369] The FSA may impose a civil penalty of such amount as it considers appropriate on any person

---

[364] It used be a mandatory continuing obligation under the *Listing Rules* to publish preliminary results but as a result of changes linked to the implementation of the Transparency Obligations Directive, this became a permissive regime with effect from 20 January 2007. See *LR* 9.7A.

[365] *Hansard*, HC vol 450, col 93 WS (26 October 2006).

[366] P Davies, 'Liability for Misstatements to the Market: A Discussion Paper' (HM Treasury, March 2007); P Davies, 'Review of Issuer Liability: Final Report' (HM Treasury, June 2007).

[367] 'Final Report' (n 365 above) executive summary.

[368] FSMA 2000, s 89K.

[369] ibid s 89L.

who contravenes transparency obligations.[370] Restitution orders may also be sought.[371] If the contravention amounts to market abuse, the FSA may impose penalties including the possibility of unlimited fines[372] and may itself require restitution.[373] Criminal sanctions under section 397 of the Financial Services and Markets Act 2000 (misleading statements and practices) and under the Fraud Act 2006 may apply.

Other continuing obligations derived from the Transparency Obligations Directive

The Transparency Obligations Directive contains provisions relating to the notification obligations in respect of the acquisition or disposal of major holdings in shares and certain other financial instruments. These requirements are implemented in the UK by chapter 5 of the FSA *Disclosure Rules and Transparency Rules*.[374] Chapter 5 imposes obligations on holders to notify the issuer and, in the case of a notification relating to shares admitted to trading on a regulated market, the FSA. The issuer must then make public all of the information contained in the notification through an RIS. An issuer must also, at the end of each calendar month during which an increase or decrease has occurred, disclose to the public the total number of voting rights and capital in respect of each class of share in issue and the total number of voting rights attaching to shares of the issuer which are held by it in treasury. There are also disclosure obligations in respect of the acquisition or disposal by an issuer of its own shares.

Chapter 6 of the FSA *Disclosure Rules and Transparency Rules* implements other continuing obligations under the Transparency Obligations Directive.[375] These include an obligation, which in the UK was previously found in the *Listing Rules*, to ensure equal treatment for all holders of shares who are in the same position.[376] Other continuing obligations in this chapter are concerned with ensuring that holders of securities can exercise their rights, including using proxies, and with ensuring that they are informed of changes in the rights attaching to securities and about arrangements for meetings, issues of new shares, and the payment of dividends.

The continuing obligations in Chapters 5 and 6 of the *Disclosure Rules and Transparency Rules* are underpinned by the range of administrative and criminal sanctions outlined in the previous section.

---

[370] ibid s 91(1B), as inserted by Companies Act 2006, Sch 15, para 6(3).
[371] FSMA 2000, s 382.
[372] ibid Pt 8.
[373] ibid s 384.
[374] Under statutory authority provided by FSMA 2000, ss 89A and 89B–89D (inserted by the Companies Act 2006).
[375] Under statutory authority provided by FSMA 2000, ss 89A and 89E (inserted by the Companies Act 2006).
[376] *DTR* 6.1.3.

AIM issuers[377]

AIM issuers are required by the AIM *Rules for Companies* to produce annual and half-yearly reports. EEA incorporated issuers must prepare and present their accounts in accordance with IFRS but other issuers are not required to reconcile accounts that have been drawn up under US GAAP, Canadian GAAP, Australian IFRS, or Japanese GAAP.[378] The statutory issuer liability regime in section 90A of the Financial Services and Markets Act 2000 does not apply to AIM issuers (although an extension in their direction is under consideration as a consequence of the Davies review). Hence, the directors of AIM issuers do not benefit from the safe harbour against liability that is afforded by that section to directors of issuers with securities admitted to trading on a regulated market.

The rules relating to the acquisition or disposal of major shareholdings contained in chapter 5 of the FSA *Disclosure Rules and Transparency Rules* have been applied to AIM issuers incorporated under the Companies Act 2006 (or predecessor legislation) and any other bodies that are incorporated and have their principal place of business in Great Britain. This represents an intensification of the regulatory regime under which AIM issuers operate but it is not wholly alien territory for them because prior to the implementation of the Transparency Obligations Directive, they were subject to obligations with regard to disclosures of interests that were imposed by Part VI of the Companies Act 1985. The FSA *Disclosure Rules and Transparency Rules* replace, and in some respects extend, Part VI of the Companies Act 1985.

Obligations derived from the Market Abuse Directive

Article 6 of the Market Abuse Directive completes the regulatory framework for disclosure by issuers by obliging Member States to require an issuer of financial instruments to inform the public as soon as possible of inside information which directly concerns the said issuer, save where this would prejudice its legitimate interests. The Directive applies to issuers with securities admitted to trading on a regulated market. The Directive provides that each Member State must apply the requirements provided for in the Directive to (a) actions carried out on its territory or abroad concerning financial instruments that are admitted to trading on a regulated market situated or operating within its territory or for which a request for admission to trading on such a market has been made; and (b) actions carried out on its territory concerning financial instruments that are admitted to trading

---

[377] Companies admitted to the PLUS-quoted Market are in the same position as regards the general law.
[378] *AIM Rules*, r 19.

on a regulated market in a Member State or for which a request for admission to trading on such market has been made.[379] So far as issuer disclosure required by Article 6 is concerned, implementation is effected by chapter 1 of the FSA *Disclosure Rules and Transparency Rules*. The usual range of administrative and criminal sanctions would apply in the case of a failure by an issuer to comply with the obligations of timely disclosure imposed by this chapter.

AIM issuers are subject to a duty of general disclosure of price-sensitive information under the AIM *Rules*.[380]

---

[379] Market Abuse Directive, Art 10.
[380] AIM *Rules*, r 11.

14

International Equity Offerings

Introduction

An issuer makes an international (or global) offering when it offers its securities directly to investors outside its home market. The international offer may be made alongside an offering to investors in the home market or, less commonly, instead of it. The modern market for international equity offerings emerged in the 1980s, driven by political and economic changes that included the emergence of market economies in the formerly communist countries of Eastern Europe, the privatization of large utility companies that had been state-owned and which typically had capital needs that were too large to be absorbed easily by their domestic market, reforms in developing countries that led to the abolition of exchange controls and the creation of emerging markets attractive to international investment funds, and a deepening investor appetite for foreign securities as part of portfolio diversification strategies.[1] This segment of the market is now of considerable economic significance. For example, of the 603 initial public offers (IPOs) on European exchanges in 2005, 126 were international IPOs by issuers from outside the EEA.[2] These international IPOs raised €.9.6 billion, slightly short of 20 per cent of the total offering value of €50.7 billion.[3] Indian, Australian, and Israeli companies dominated with 32, 16, and 14 IPOs respectively.[4] Most of the international IPOs in Europe (90 of the 126) took place in London.[5] The US markets, which until the 2000s were the undisputed top destination for issuers in search of international capital,[6] did not fare so well: in 2005 only 23 overseas companies chose US exchanges for their IPOs, raising €3.0 billion.[7] Far from

---

[1] The importance of wide portfolio diversification is a central element of modern finance theory: M Rubinstein, 'Markowitz's "Portfolio Selection": A Fifty-Year Retrospective' (2002) 57 *Journal of Finance* 1041.

[2] Price Waterhouse Coopers, 'IPO Watch Europe Review of the Year 2005', 6.

[3] ibid.

[4] ibid.

[5] ibid.

[6] McKinsey & Co, 'Sustaining New York's and the US' Global Financial Services Leadership', report commissioned by MR Bloomberg and CE Schumer, (January 2007) 45 notes that a listing on a US exchange was until relatively recently considered de rigueur for a non-US company that wanted to capitalize on the deepest and most liquid market in the world.

[7] ibid 16.

being a 'blip', the 2005 figures appeared to be indicative of a broader trend for foreign companies to shun the US markets. The US regulatory system, in particular the enhanced corporate governance obligations that were imposed by the Sarbanes-Oxley Act of 2002,[8] and its propensity for private litigation, shouldered much of the blame for the declining international appeal of the US markets,[9] although other factors, including the emergence of markets that could credibly compete with the US markets on technology, investor confidence, and liquidity measurements, the development of significant pools of capital elsewhere in the world, and improvements in the mechanisms whereby investors could trade in securities outside their home markets (in other words, investors going to issuers rather than issuers coming to them), were also acknowledged to have played a part.[10]

Each issuer will have its own reasons for making an equity offering outside its home jurisdiction, but the following are commonly mentioned: to establish access to well-developed foreign capital markets for immediate and future financing needs; to overcome limited investor appetite in the home market and/or to tap into foreign investor interest; to achieve a desired investor base in a particular foreign country for strategic/business reasons; to gain attention from analysts; to bond voluntarily with the regulatory regimes in which the offer is made with a view to boosting investor confidence (this reason is of particular relevance to issuers whose home regimes are regarded as being relatively weak by international

---

[8] Work by Professor Litvak in relation to foreign companies trading in the United States in the period leading up to and immediately after the adoption of the Sarbanes-Oxley Act found that the premium associated with being subject to US regulation declined. The biggest losers were companies that were more profitable, riskier, and smaller, companies with a higher level of pre-SOX disclosure, and companies from well-governed countries. She concluded that these results were consistent with the view that investors expected SOX to have greater costs than benefits for cross-listed firms on average, especially for smaller firms and already well-governed firms: K Litvak, 'Sarbanes-Oxley and the Cross-Listing Premium' (2007) 105 *Michigan Law Review* 1857. See also K Litvak, 'The Effect of the Sarbanes-Oxley Act on Foreign Companies Cross-Listed in the U.S.' (2007) 13 *Journal of Corporate Finance* 195.

[9] The 'Interim Report of the Committee on Capital Markets Regulation' (November 2006) concluded that that the solution to the competitive problem of US capital markets lay, on the one hand, in reducing the burden of litigation and regulation and, on the other hand, in increasing shareholder rights. The report of the committee (widely referred to as the 'Paulson Committee') is available at <http://www.capmktsreg.org/pdfs/11.30Committee_Interim_ReportREV2.pdf> (accessed December 2007).

See also Commission on the Regulation of US Capital Markets in the 21st Century, 'Report and Recommendations' (bipartisan commission established by the US Chamber of Commerce), (March 2007) report available at <http://www.uschamber.com/publications/reports/0703capmarketscomm.htm> (accessed December 2007).

EJ Pan, 'Why the World No Longer Puts its Stock in Us', (13 December 2006). Cardozo Legal Studies Research Paper No 176 available at SSRN <http://ssrn.com/abstract=951705>. The cross-border regulatory conflicts that result from Sarbanes Oxley and which create problems for foreign issuers listed in the US are discussed in E Tafara, and RJ Peterson, 'A Blueprint for Cross-Border Access to U.S. Investors: A New International Framework' (2007) 48 *Harvard International Law Journal* 31.

[10] 'Interim Report of the Committee on Capital Markets Regulation' (November 2006) x.

standards);[11] and to gain publicity or to enhance international prestige. These reasons overlap and for any particular issuer a combination of factors is likely to influence a decision to make an international offering. Prominent among the factors militating against an international offering will be the extra costs involved in making a multi-jurisdictional offer, which will embrace both the costs of the offering itself and on-going costs associated with having a presence in several different securities markets and being subject to local regulation in each of those markets.

Strategies for developing a regulatory framework for international offerings

International offerings of securities, in common with other types of cross-border capital market activity, present profound challenges for regulators and policymakers. On the one hand, there is an obvious attraction in removing local regulatory barriers that deter foreign issuers from entering a market and thereby undermine its international competitiveness. On the other hand, waiving requirements for foreign issuers touches upon sensitive issues relating to national sovereignty, the mission of national regulatory authorities to protect their own markets from fraud or other destabilizing activities and to ensure investor protection, and the equal treatment of all market participants whether they be domestic or foreign. Two strategies have emerged in practice as the leading mechanisms for steering a course between these competing considerations: convergence or equivalence and mutual recognition. These terms are not precisely defined and it is not always clear that contributors to debates on the development of the international framework are using these terms consistently. The following paragraph provides interpretations for the purposes of this chapter.

Convergence/equivalence

Convergence means reducing or eliminating differences between sets of national or regional requirements.[12] 'Harmonization' is another term that is sometimes used interchangeably with convergence but 'convergence' has come to be preferred because it is thought to capture the idea of an exercise that is designed to arrive at the 'best' standard, whereas harmonization suggests a compromise where differences exist.[13] Full convergence implies a single, generally applicable, set of

---

[11] JC Coffee, 'Racing Towards the Top?: The Impact of Cross-listings and Stock Market Competition on International Corporate Governance' (2000) 102 *Columbia Law Review* 1757.

[12] G Whittington, 'The Adoption of International Accounting Standards in the European Union' (2005) 14(1) *European Accounting Review* 127, 133.

[13] E Tafara and RJ Peterson, 'A Blueprint for Cross-Border Access to U.S. Investors: A New International Framework' (2007) 48 *Harvard International Law Journal* 31, n 72; DT Nicolaisen,

standards. The EU has achieved this for prospectus disclosures and consolidated financial reporting of a significant segment of EU issuers but that achievement has to be set in the context of the overall EU market integration project. This demanding interpretation of the concept is not often realistically achievable at the global level for political reasons, nor is it necessarily optimal anyway. Whilst a single set of standards would have certain advantages in terms of facilitating issuer access and comparability by investors, these advantages cannot be viewed in isolation and need to be set against possible disadvantages, including unwieldiness and lack of receptiveness to important regional variations in market conditions and legal environments. At the global level it usually makes more sense to think about 'practical' convergence, which is about achieving a robust degree of similarity between different sets of standards but not necessarily making them identical.[14] The term 'equivalence' is increasingly used to denote this degree of convergence, particularly in the accounting field. In an exercise to determine the equivalence of various sets of accounting standards, the Committee of European Securities Regulators (CESR) interpreted its task as being to look at whether differences in the standards under consideration would affect investors' decisions. The CESR said:

CESR's outcome-based approach to the GAAP equivalence, as a form of direct comparison of standards, has been predicated on the basis that investor's decision should be unaffected by the use of different accounting standards when assessing their buy, hold, sell investment decision. By analysing and evaluating financial information based on third country GAAP, investors should be able to make similar decisions irrespective of whether they are provided with financial statements based on IFRS or not. This outcome based definition of equivalence combined with how the market reacts to accounting differences are considered particularly relevant in the assessment of significance.[15]

The European Commission adopted a definition of equivalence for the purposes of Directives relating to the prospectus and periodic disclosures that draws upon the advice from CESR but does not follow it exactly. Other accounting systems may be deemed equivalent to IFRS where financial statements prepared in accordance with them:

… enable investors to make a similar assessment of the assets and liabilities, financial position, profit and losses and prospects of the issuer as financial statements drawn up in accordance with IFRS, with the result that investors are likely to make the same decisions about the acquisition, retention or disposal of securities of an issuer.[16]

'A Securities Regulator Looks at Convergence' (2005) 25 *Northwestern Journal of International Law and Business* 661, 672.

[14] Nicolaisen (n 13 above) 672–3.

[15] CESR, 'Equivalence of Certain Third Country GAAP and on Description of Certain Third Countries Mechanisms of Enforcement of Financial Information' (CESR/05-230 b) para 9. Later advice from CESR to the Commission reiterated the point: CESR, 'Advice to the European Commission' (CESR/07-138).

[16] Commission Regulation (EC) 1569/2007 of 21 December 2007 establishing a mechanism for the determination of equivalence of accounting standards applied by third country issuers of

Mutual recognition

Mutual recognition involves at least two countries agreeing on an essentially reciprocal basis to allow participants from the other into their markets on condition of adherence to foreign regulatory requirements and with a waiver of some local requirements.[17] Convergence or equivalence and mutual recognition strategies are not mutually exclusive. Countries are unlikely to enter into mutual recognition agreements unless they are satisfied that the foreign systems in question are sufficiently similar to their own to avoid problems of regulatory arbitrage.[18] Trust and confidence in foreign systems are the essential underpinnings of mutual recognition and these can be fostered by convergence around similar standards.

Also relevant in this context are similarities (or differences) in oversight and enforcement. Since making concessions for foreign issuers could mean placing considerable reliance in respect of these matters on the foreign regulator and the foreign laws, a country is unlikely to be willing to proceed in that direction unless it is confident that the quality of the foreign oversight and enforcement is at least comparable to its own.[19] Furthermore, if confidence in the quality of foreign oversight and enforcement erodes, that is likely to undermine support for the continuance or extension of such arrangements.[20] Mutual recognition requires continuing confidence by participating national regulators that their regulatory counterparts in other countries are fairly and adequately applying and enforcing standards.

Regulatory competition

Before turning to examine some major recent practical initiatives to develop an acceptable framework for international issuance activity that have employed convergence and mutual recognition strategies, this section closes with a brief examination of a third strategy that has received considerable academic attention.

securities pursuant to Directives (EC) 2003/71 and (EC) 2004/109 of the European Parliament and of the Council [2007] OJ L340/66, Art 2.

[17] SJ Choi and AT Guzman, 'Portable Reciprocity: Rethinking the International Reach of Securities Regulation' (1998) 71 *South California Law Review* 903, 907 use the term 'normal reciprocity' to describe such arrangements.

[18] Tafara and Peterson (n 13 above) 31, n 79.

[19] Various authors have made the point that the mutual recognition agreement between the US and Canada, noted later in the text, was only possible because of the similarity of their standards: Choi and Guzman (n 17 above) 920; DS Ruder, 'Reconciling U.S. Disclosure Practices with International Accounting and Disclosure Standards' (1996) 17 *Northwestern Journal of International Law and Business* 1, 11.

[20] W Hicks, 'Harmonisation of Disclosure Standards for Cross-Border Share Offerings: Approaching an "International Passport" to Capital Markets?' (2002) 9 *Indiana Journal of Global Legal Studies* 361, 377 outlines problems with the Canadian/US mutual recognition agreement for issuer disclosure which, it is said, nearly collapsed because of eroding US confidence in the quality of Canadian oversight.

Some authors have written strongly in favour of opening up capital market activity to 'regulatory competition', whereby, in essence, market participants would be free to operate internationally on the basis of adherence to a single national regime of their choice. Regulatory competition can be seen to come from the same base as mutual recognition in so far as it implies that countries will allow securities market activity to take place in their territory on the basis of compliance with the laws of another country but it is considerably broader than mutual recognition, particularly with regard to the extent to which it would allow market participants to choose the law governing their activity. Some supporters of regulatory competition argue that if issuers, for example, are free to choose the regulatory regime governing their issuance activity, this will promote a 'race to the top' because issuers have incentives to select disclosure regimes that offer good investor protection laws because such choices lower the cost of capital.[21] In turn, governmental responsiveness to regulatory competition should mean that countries around the world will adapt their standards so as to bring them into line with issuer and investor preferences.[22] In other words, regulatory competition could lead to convergence, but convergence that is market-driven and therefore arguably more in tune with market preferences and needs.[23]

From other quarters, however, come doubts about issuers' incentives to select regimes with good investor protection laws[24] and about investors' ability to collect and process all of the information that would be needed to make meaningful assessments of differences in quality between different investor protection regimes and to reflect these accurately in the cost of capital.[25] Whether there are sufficient

---

[21] Fierce debate has raged among leading scholars on the merits of regulatory competition in securities market regulation. Key articles include: R Romano, 'Empowering Investors: A Market Approach to Securities Regulation' (1998) 107 *Yale Law Journal* 2359; R Romano, 'The Need for Competition in International Securities Regulation' (2001) 2 Theoretical Inquiries in Law 387; SJ Choi and AT Guzman, 'Portable Reciprocity: Rethinking the International Reach of Securities Regulation' (1998) 71 *South California Law Review* 903; MB Fox, 'Securities Disclosure in a Globalizing Market: Who Should Regulate Whom' (1997) 95 *Michigan Law Review* 2498; MB Fox, 'Retaining Mandatory Securities Disclosure: Why Issuer Choice is Not Investor Empowerment' (1999) 85 *Virginia Law Review* 1335; MB Fox, 'The Issuer Choice Debate' (2001) 2 *Theoretical Inquiries in Law* 563. HE Jackson, 'Centralization, Competition, and Privatization in Financial Regulation' (2001) 2 *Theoretical Inquiries in Law* 649, 659–62 provides a valuable overview of the debate.

[22] HE Jackson and E Pan, 'Regulatory Competition in International Securities Markets: Evidence from Europe in 1999—Part I' (2001) 56 *Business Lawyer* 653 note that an implicit assumption in the debate over regulatory competition is that at least some governments will make meaningful changes in their legal regimes in order to preserve or expand the number of entities under their regulatory oversight.

[23] One of the most commonly cited benefits of regulatory competition is that it provides a market-driven mechanism for discovering what people want: JM Sun and J Pelkmans, 'Regulatory Competition in the Single Market' (1995) 33 *Journal of Common Market Studies* 67.

[24] JC Coffee, 'Law and Regulatory Competition: Can They Co-exist?' (2002) 80 *Texas Law Review* 1729.

[25] JD Cox, 'Regulatory Duopoly in U.S. Securities Markets' (1999) 99 *Columbia Law Review* 1200, 1234: 'Before we embrace multiple standards in the belief that a disclosure hierarchy will develop among the securities of a particular market, we need better evidence that securities

regulatory jurisdictions to engage in meaningful competition is questioned.[26] Some commentators have identified enforcement as a likely weak spot in that issuer freedom of choice as regards investor protection could imply highly contentious extraterritorial enforcement by the securities regulatory agency of the chosen national regime or unskilled and inexperienced enforcement of that regime by the agencies of other countries.[27] Fraud concerns, in particular, lead regulators to question whether regulatory competition is capable of promoting a race to the top.[28]

Practical initiatives to develop a regulatory framework for international issuance activity

IOSCO international disclosure standards for non-financial information

The International Organization of Securities Commissions (IOSCO) was formed in 1983, from the transformation of an inter-American regional association (created in 1974), to facilitate cooperation between securities regulators. It now has over 150 members and affiliated members representing regulatory authorities and self-regulatory organizations from around the world. Cooperation between members to promote high standards of regulation in order to maintain just, efficient, and sound markets is one of its functions. IOSCO also seeks to promote the exchange of information between regulators, to unite efforts on effective surveillance, and to provide mutual assistance in the application and enforcement of standards.

In September 1998, IOSCO published International Disclosure Standards (IDS) for cross-border offerings and initial listings of equity securities by foreign issuers.[29] The underlying aim of the IDS is to enhance comparability of information while ensuring a high level of investor protection.[30] The IDS are designed to

---

markets are capable of making discrete judgments among issuers using different disclosure standards.' Being fully informed is one of the conditions which, according to the classic theory of regulatory competition (the 'Tiebout model' from C Tiebout, 'A Pure Theory of Local Expenditures' (1956) 64 *Journal of Political Economy* 416), needs to be satisfied for it to operate effectively: JP Trachtman, 'Regulatory Competition and Regulatory Jurisdiction in International Securities Regulation' in DC Esty and D Geradin (eds), *Regulatory Competition and Economic Integration* (OUP, 2001) 289–310. However, this exacting condition can never be fully met (ibid); HS Scott, 'Internationalization of Primary Public Securities Markets' (2000) 63 *Law and Contemporary Problems* 71.

   [26] JD Cox, 'Regulatory Duopoly in U.S. Securities Markets' (1999) 99 *Columbia Law Review* 1200, 1232–3.
   [27] ibid 1239–44; JC Coffee, 'Law and Regulatory Competition: Can They Co-exist?' (2002) 80 *Texas Law Review* 1729.
   [28] E Tafara and RJ Peterson, 'A Blueprint for Cross-Border Access to U.S. Investors: A New International Framework' (2007) 48 *Harvard International Law Journal* 31.
   [29] 'International Disclosure Standards for Cross-border Offerings and Initial Listings by Foreign Issuers' (IOSCO, 1998) (hereinafter 'IOSCO, IDS'). These standards are available via the IOSCO online library at <http://www.iosco.org>.
   [30] ibid 3.

apply to international listings and public offers and sales of equity securities for cash.[31] They set out disclosure requirements for prospectuses, offering and initial listing documents, and registration statements relating to such listings and offerings.[32] The IDS are not automatically binding on states as a matter of law but some countries have taken steps to implement them into their national requirements, either just for foreign issuers or for both foreign and domestic issuers. In 1999, the US adopted revised disclosure requirements for foreign issuers that were based on the IOSCO model.[33] Within the EU, the IDS were the starting point for the disclosure requirements in the Prospectus Directive.[34]

However, the IDS are not comprehensive: in particular, in relation to financial information, whilst the IDS identify the types of financial statements that are required to be included, specify the periods that they should cover, and impose independent audit requirements, they do not prescribe the contents of financial statements.[35] It is left open to individual countries to choose whether or not to require profit forecasts or other forward looking statements.[36] Another noticeable gap in the coverage of the IDS relates to 'materiality'. As well as specific disclosure requirements, most countries rely on an overriding principle of disclosure of material information in prospectuses or other offering documents. Thus, for example, section 87A of the UK Financial Services and Markets Act 2000 provides that a prospectus must contain the 'necessary information', which means 'the information necessary to enable investors to make an informed assessment of (a) the assets and liabilities, financial position, profits and losses, and prospects of the issuer of the transferable securities and of any guarantor, and (b) the rights attaching to the transferable securities'. Different countries interpret the concept of materiality in different ways. The IDS note this divergence of approach but they do not seek to challenge it directly.[37] This means that there is still room for considerable divergence in the disclosure expectations of countries that have adopted the IDS for international offerings, a feature that undermines their role as a single set of common disclosure requirements for international offerings. Another tricky issue that can act as an obstacle to cross-border issuance and listing activity that is side-stepped in the IDS is the language of non-financial information: it is simply assumed that all information contained in a document will be provided in a language acceptable to the host country,[38] which means that issuers may have to contend with onerous translation burdens. More generally,

---

[31] Companies Act.
[32] ibid.
[33] HS Scott, *International Finance: Law and Regulation* (Sweet & Maxwell, 2004) 41.
[34] Directive (EC) 2003/71 of the European Parliament and of the Council of 4th November 2003 on the prospectus to be published when securities are offered to the public or admitted to trading on a regulated market [2003] OJ L435/64 (the 'Prospectus Directive'), rec 22.
[35] IOSCO, IDS, 20–23, Standard VIII (Financial Information).
[36] IOSCO, IDS, 14.
[37] IOSCO, IDS, 5 and Pt II.
[38] IOSCO, IDS, 6.

the IDS envisage host states having considerable room to tailor international disclosure requirements to their home market, which, again, lessens their impact as a standardizing force.[39] The IDS may be best regarded as containing the 'seeds of true harmonisation'[40] but clearly they are not a fully grown plant. In a more recent project to develop common standard for debt issuance activity, IOSCO's Technical Committee itself is relatively modest about the achievements of the IDS.[41] It refers to the IDS as being *broadly* accepted as a disclosure *benchmark*, and it notes that the equity disclosure regimes of many IOSCO members are *based* on them (emphasis added).[42]

IASB international financial reporting standards

The International Accounting Standards Committee was created in 1973 to set international accounting standards and issue discussion documents on international accounting issues.[43] Its objectives were to harmonize existing diverse standards, to formulate and publish in the public interest accounting standards to be observed in the presentation of financial statements, and to promote a common international approach. In 1997, the board of the Committee commenced a review of its objectives and structure. The outcome of the review was a new organizational structure in which the International Accounting Standards Board (IASB), an independent, privately-funded[44] body based in London, assumed the standard-setting role. The new structure took effect in April 2001. According to the revised constitutional arrangement, the IASB's role is to:

(1) develop in the public interest a single set of high quality, understandable, and enforceable global accounting standards that require high quality, transparent, and comparable information in financial statements, and other financial

---

[39] W Hicks, 'Harmonisation of Disclosure Standards for Cross-Border Share Offerings: Approaching an 'International Passport' to Capital Markets?' (2002) 9 *Indiana Journal of Global Legal Studies* 361, 372.

[40] TG Siew, 'Regulatory Challenges in the Development of a Global Securities Market—Harmonisation of Mandatory Disclosure Rules'[2004] *Singapore Journal of Legal Studies* 173, 186.

[41] IOSCO, 'International Disclosure Principles for Cross-border Offerings and Listings of Debt Securities by Foreign Issuers' (Consultation Report, 2005).

[42] ibid 1.

[43] This paragraph draws on information available for the IASB website: <http://www.iasb. co.uk/>. For a more detailed explanation of the structure and how it operates in practice see G Whittington, 'The Adoption of International Accounting Standards in the European Union' (2005) 14(1) *European Accounting Review* 127.

[44] IASB funding historically has come largely from voluntary contributions from a relatively small number of private companies, accounting firms, international organizations, and central banks. As the demands on and expectations for the organization have grown, this funding arrangement is becoming unsustainable and moves are afoot to shift to an internationally-applied mandatory levy system: International Accounting Standards Committee Foundation, *Annual Report* 2006, 6.

reporting to help participants in the world's capital markets and other users make economic decisions;

(2) promote the use and rigorous application of those standards;

(3) in fulfilling objectives (1) and (2), take account of, as appropriate, the needs of small and medium-sized entities and of emerging economies;

(4) bring about convergence of national accounting standards and International Accounting Standards to high quality solutions.

The International Accounting Standards Committee had, over the years, published a series of International Accounting Standards (IAS). Since April 2001, any new standards made by the IASB are known as International Financial Reporting Standards (IFRS) but existing IAS that remain extant have not been renamed. This chapter uses the more modern terminology except where the particular context calls for a reference to IAS.

The IASB is not itself a regulatory body. It does not have power to enforce international standards or to require compliance. Its standards only achieve legal force where, either by a process of transposition of IFRS or by convergence of the contents of national standards towards IFRS, they become part of national law or where market participants adopt them in particular transactional contexts.[45] The IASB is committed to working with other standard setters in the achievement of its goals, especially standard setters in jurisdictions that have adopted or converged with IFRS, or which are in the process of doing so.[46]

Adoption of IFRS, especially in Europe

International financial reporting standards have acquired considerable practical significance.[47] As of the beginning of 2007, nearly 100 countries around the world required or permitted the use of, or had a policy of convergence with, IFRS.[48] One of strongest endorsements of the IFRS as a set of enforceable disclosure standards came from Europe in June 2000, when the European Commission announced a new proposed law that by January 2005 would require all companies listed on regulated markets within the EU to prepare consolidated accounts using IASB accounting standards.[49] This goal was realized with the adoption of Regulation (EC) 1606/2002 of the European Parliament and of the Council of

---

[45] Whittington (n 43 above) notes that the initial success of international standards was market based and that arguably it was because of their established importance in practice that governments were forced to take a position in relation to them.

[46] 'Statement of Best Practice: Working Relationships between the IASB and Other Accounting Standard-Setters' (February 2006) available at <http://www.iasb.co.uk>.

[47] Whittington (n 43 above) 127–8 provides background on the adoption of international standards around the world.

[48] <http://www.iasb.co.uk> (accessed January 2007).

[49] European Commission Communication, 'EU Financial Reporting Strategy' (COM (2000) 359). This step was described by a former SEC Chief Accountant as the primary driver of significantly expanded use of IFRS: DT Nicolaisen, 'A Securities Regulator Looks at Convergence'

19 July 2002 on the application of international accounting standards.[50] The IAS Regulation stipulates that for each financial year starting on or after 1 January 2005, companies governed by the law of a Member State must prepare their consolidated accounts in conformity with Community-adopted IFRS if, at their balance sheet date, their securities are admitted to trading on a regulated market of any Member State.[51] This Regulation applies to EEA countries not in the EU as well as EU Member States. Issuers that are subject to the IAS Regulation must present historical financial information in any prospectus they issue in conformity with IFRS[52] and, for such issuers, periodic financial disclosures required by the Transparency Obligations Directive must also conform to Community-adopted IFRS.[53] The Prospectus and Transparency Obligations Directives also in principle extend the mandatory use of IFRS to issuers from third countries but make provision for non-EU issuers to use financial statements prepared otherwise than in accordance with these IFRS provided the accounting standards under which they have been drawn up have been deemed 'equivalent' in accordance with EC mechanisms.[54]

It is important to note that the effect of the IAS Regulation is to impose a Community filter on the mandatory application of IFRS. The Regulation provides a procedure for Community adoption of IFRS and obliges listed companies to draw up their consolidated accounts in accordance with only those IFRS that have been so adopted. The adoption mechanism thus provides for EU oversight and control over the application of IFRS. Although the European Commission has said that the role of the mechanism is not to reformulate or replace IFRS, but to oversee the adoption of new standards and interpretations, intervening only when these contain material deficiencies or have failed to cater for features specific to the EU environment,[55] there are some concerns that the adoption mechanism provides scope for the EU to tamper with IFRS in ways that could impede

---

(2005) 25 *Northwestern Journal of International Law and Business* 661. European Commission, 'EU Financial Reporting Strategy: The Way Forward' (COM (2000) 359)).

[50] [2002] OJ L243/1 (the 'IAS Regulation').

[51] IAS Regulation, Art 4.

[52] Commission Regulation (EC) 809/2004 of 29 April 2004 implementing Directive 2003/71 (EC) of the European Parliament and of the Council as regards information contained in prospectuses as well as the format, incorporation by reference and publication of such prospectuses and dissemination of advertisements [2004] OJ L149/1 ('Prospectus Directive Regulation') Annex 1, para 20.

[53] Directive (EC) 2004/109 of the European Parliament and of the Council of 15 December 2004 on the harmonisation of transparency requirements in relation to information about issuers whose securities are admitted to trading on a regulated market and amending Directive (EC) 2001/34 [2004] OJ L390/38 ('Transparency Obligations Directive') Arts 4–5.

[54] Prospectus Directive Regulation, Annex 1, para 20.1 and Transparency Obligations Directive, Art 23. The debate on equivalence is considered in more detail later in this chapter.

[55] European Commission, 'EU Financial Reporting Strategy' (COM (2000) 359) 7.

broader international efforts to establish common accounting standards.[56] Such concerns acquired a practical focus in 2003–04 in a controversy over the accounting treatment of derivatives and other complex financial instruments because the European Commission's efforts to secure changes to the relevant standard (IAS 39) before it adopted it was seen by US regulators as potentially jeopardizing efforts to achieve convergence between IAS/IFRS and US generally accepted accounting principles (US GAAP).[57] In the end, the EU voted to adopt a version of IAS 39 that had two carve-outs from IAS 39 as published by the IASB.[58] The Commission sought to justify this departure from the IASB's standard by describing it as 'an exceptional situation caused by particular prudential and technical complexities which … [had] not been resolved'.[59] The IASB later revised its IAS 39 in respect of one of the matters that had been carved out and thereafter the Commission adopted the revised IASB standard in respect of that matter.[60]

IOSCO has also endorsed IFRS but some major economies that are IOSCO members, in particular the US, have been slow historically to adopt fully IFRS for domestic or foreign issuers. However, in late 2007 the US Securities and Exchange Commission (SEC) made what could prove to be a historic decision to sanction the use of IFRS in its markets. The following paragraphs outline the background leading up to that decision.

US position—from reconciliation to US GAAP to acceptance of IFRS

In the 1980s, the US adopted a position with regard to foreign issuers that were subject to US reporting requirements that allowed them to prepare their financial

---

[56] N Moloney, *EC Securities Regulation* (OUP, 2002) 240. The historic decision by the US SEC in November 2007 to allow foreign issuers to file financial statements prepared in accordance with IFRS relates only to accounts that are prepared using IFRS as issued by the International Accounting Standards Board, not regional variants thereof: SEC Press Release, 'SEC Takes Action to Improve Consistency of Disclosure to U.S. Investors in Foreign Companies' (15 November 2007) available at <http://www.sec.gov/news/press/2007/2007-235.htm> (accessed November 2007). However, there is a 2-year transitional arrangement during which time foreign issuers using the EU IAS 39 carve-out may reconcile their financial statements to IFRS as issued by the IASB in lieu of reconciling their financial statements to US GAAP. If after the 2-year transition period those issuers are still applying the carve-out version, they will have to revert to performing a reconciliation of their financial statements to US GAAP. The SEC's decision is considered further later in this chapter.

[57] A Michaels and A Parker, 'US Warns Europe on Accounting Rules' *Financial Times*, 2 February 2004, 1.

[58] Declaration by the Commission on the adoption of IAS 39 at the meeting of the accounting regulatory committee of 1 October 2004, available at <http://ec.europa.eu/internal_market/accounting/docs/ias/declaration-ias39_en.pdf> (accessed August 2007).

The formal adoption was effected by Commission Regulation (EC) 2086/2004 of 19 November 2004 amending Regulation (EC) 1725/2003 on the adoption of certain international accounting standards in accordance with Regulation (EC) 1606/2002 of the European Parliament and of the Council as regards the insertion of IAS 39 [2004] OJ L363/1.

[59] Declaration (n 58 above).

[60] Commission Regulation (EC) 2106/2005 of 21 December 2005 amending Regulation (EC) 1725/2003 adopting certain international accounting standards in accordance with Regulation (EC) 1606/2002 of the European Parliament and of the Council, as regards International Accounting Standard (IAS) 39 [2005] OJ L337/16.

statements using a body of generally accepted accounting principles other than US GAAP but, if they did so, they had also to include a reconciliation of significant variations from US GAAP.[61] When it was introduced, reconciliation was intended to be a concession in favour of foreign issuers but it came to be regarded as an expensive and time-consuming process that served as a barrier against foreign issuers entering the US markets.[62] Some relatively modest relaxations of the reconciliation requirements for accounts drawn up in accordance with IAS/IFRS were made in 1994 but deepening demand from market participants for a single set of high-quality international accounting standards that facilitates both the comparability of issuers by investors and issuer access to pools of capital kept the spotlight on this issue.

One way of eliminating the need for reconciliation is through convergence. Since October 2002, the IASB and the US Financial Accounting Standards Board (FASB) have been engaged in a long-term project on the convergence of IFRS and US GAAP. This project, known as the 'Norwalk Agreement', commits both sides to use their best efforts to make their existing financial reporting standards fully compatible as soon as is practicable and to coordinate their future work programmes to ensure that once achieved, compatibility is maintained.[63] The Norwalk Agreement embraces both relatively straightforward short-term projects to remove technical detailed differences between different standards and thereby reduce the need for reconciliation and also longer-term, more ambitious, projects to find common solutions on issues of principle. According to an IASB-FASB memorandum of understanding published in February 2006, the goal is to reach a conclusion on some short-term convergence issues by 2008.[64]

Also important is this context is the agreement in January 2005 between the Accounting Standards Board of Japan (ASBJ) and the IASB to launch a joint project to reduce differences between IFRS and Japanese GAAP and to work towards the convergence of Japanese GAAP with IFRS. In January 2006, the Accounting Standards Board of Canada publicly stated its objective to move to a single set of globally accepted high-quality standards for public companies and concluded that this objective was best accomplished by converging Canadian accounting standards with IFRS within five years.[65]

---

[61] The history is reviewed by the SEC in a paper published in July 2007 announcing its proposal to drop reconciliation requirements for issuers filing IFRS financial statements: SEC, 'Acceptance From Foreign Private Issuers of Financial Statements Prepared in Accordance With International Financial Reporting Standards Without Reconciliation to U.S. GAAP', Release Nos 33–8818; 34–55998; International Series Release No 1302; File No S7–13–07 (July 2007) ('hereinafter SEC, Proposed Rules on Reconciliation').

[62] HS Scott, *International Finance: Law and Regulation* (Sweet & Maxwell, 2004) 41.

[63] IASB and FASB, 'Memorandum of Understanding' (October 2002) available at <http://www.fasb.org/news/memorandum.pdf> (accessed January 2007).

[64] <http://www.fasb.org/intl/mou_02-27-06.pdf>.

[65] These developments are noted in the recitals to Commission Regulation (EC) 1787/2006 of 4 December 2006 amending Commission Regulation (EC) 809/2004 implementing Directive (EC) 2003/71 of the European Parliament and of the Council as regards information contained in prospectuses as well as the format, incorporation by reference and publication of such prospectuses

Another way of avoiding costly reconciliation requirements for issuers involved in international securities issuance or listing activity is for the regulatory authorities in each of the countries in which they have a presence to agree that their systems for drawing up financial statements are 'equivalent' to each other in spite of differences. When the Prospectus and Transparency Obligations Directives were adopted, they envisaged that the position in Europe as from 2007 would be that foreign issuers that were subject to disclosure requirements under those Directives would be required to use IFRS or an equivalent system of accounting disclosure.[66] Some steps were taken towards the making of equivalence determinations within that time frame. In particular, in June 2005 CESR advised the Commission that the GAAP of Canada, Japan, and the US, each taken as a whole, were equivalent to IFRS adopted in the EU, subject to certain additional disclosures and supplementary financial statements.[67] However, the deadline for implementation of the disclosure regimes for foreign issuers contemplated by the Directives was later postponed to 2009, and then, subject to certain conditions, to 2001.[68] Making more time available for the operation of programmes to converge foreign national accounting systems with IFRS and to enable determinations of equivalence to be made was a significant factor underlying these postponement decisions.[69] A key event in the development of an international framework based on equivalence was the announcement in 2005 that the European Commission and the Securites and Exchange Commission (SEC) had agreed on a 'roadmap' towards equivalence between IRFS and US GAAP.[70] The roadmap outlined an iterative series of reviews to enable the SEC to decide whether it could recommend the abolition of reconciliation requirements. These steps included examination by SEC staff of the quality of foreign issuer IFRS financial statements.[71] The target date for

and dissemination of advertisements [2006] OJ L337/17 and Commission Decision of 4 December 2006 on the use by third country issuers of securities of information prepared under internationally accepted accounting standards [2006] OJ L343/96.

[66] Prospectus Directive Regulation, Annex 1, para 20; Transparency Obligations Directive, Art 23.

[67] CESR, 'Equivalence of Certain Third Country GAAP and on Description of Certain Third Countries Mechanisms of Enforcement of Financial Information' (CESR/05-230 b).

[68] Commission Regulation (EC) 1787/2006 of 4 December 2006 amending Commission Regulation (EC) 809/2004 implementing Directive (EC) 2003/71 of the European Parliament and of the Council as regards information contained in prospectuses as well as the format, incorporation by reference and publication of such prospectuses and dissemination of advertisements [2006] OJ L337/17 and Commission Decision of 4 December 2006 on the use by third country issuers of securities of information prepared under internationally accepted accounting standards [2006] OJ L343/96; Commission Regulation (EC) 1569/2007 of 21 December 2007 establishing a mechanism for the determination of equivalence of accounting standards applied by third country issuers of securities pursuant to Directives (EC) 2003/71 and (EC) 2004/109/EC of the European Parliament and of the Council [2007] OJ L340/66, Art 4.

[69] Ibid, recs 4–5.

[70] SEC, *Proposed Rules on Reconciliation*, sec D. See further DT Nicolaisen, 'A Securities Regulator Looks at Convergence' (2005) 25 *Northwestern Journal of International Law and Business* 661.

[71] In 2006, the SEC staff reviewed the annual reports of more than 100 foreign private issuers containing financial statements prepared for the first time on the basis of IFRS: SEC, *Proposed Rules on Reconciliation*.

the decision under the roadmap, as originally announced, was 2009. However, things moved more quickly: in November 2007 the SEC voted to adopt rules to allow foreign private issuers to file financial statements prepared in accordance with IFRS without reconciliation.[72]

The SEC's decision with regard to dropping its reconciliation requirements is bound to have a significant impact on the equivalence decisions on the European side. In welcoming the SEC's decision to drop its reconciliation requirement, the European Commissioner for the Internal Market said: 'Now it will be Europe's turn to accept accounts in US GAAP. This decision will have to be taken next year [2008]. And it is certainly my intention to propose that no reconciliation to IFRS will be needed for companies filing their accounts under US GAAP. This is the only sensible way forward.'[73] Pending that decision, the EU position is that third country issuers may be permitted to use financial statements drawn up in accordance with the accounting standards of a third country, provided the standard-setting authority in that country has made a public and credible commitment either to adopt IFRS before December 2011 or to converge its national standards with IFRS before that deadline.[74] CESR will play an important role in monitoring, and advising the Commission on, the progress of convergence or, as the case may be, adoption programmes.[75]

Some mutual recognition agreements

There is an agreement in place between the US and Canada whereby Canadian companies can issue securities into the US on the basis of Canadian disclosure rules rules and US companies can issue securities into Canada on the basis of US rules.[76] This agreement is known as the Multi-jurisdictional Disclosure System (MJDS). The MDJS regime is limited in a variety of ways and it is subject to important qualifications, in particular the requirement for financial statements to be reconciled to US GAAP. Relatively little use has been made of the MJDS and its future is in doubt.[77]

---

[72] SEC Press Release, 'SEC Takes Action to Improve Consistency of Disclosure to U.S. Investors in Foreign Companies' (15 November 2007). available at <http://www.sec.gov/news/press/2007/2007-235.htm> (accessed November 2007). This permission relates only to accounts they are prepared using IFRS as issued by the International Accounting Standards Board, not regional variants thereof.

[73] C McCreevy, Speech, 27 November 2007, text available at <http://www.europa.eu/rapid/pressReleasesAction.do?reference=SPEECH/07/757&format=HTML&aged=0&language=EN&guiLanguage=en> (accessed November 2007).

[74] Commission Regulation (EC) 1569/2007 of 21 December 2007 establishing a mechanism for the determination of equivalence of accounting standards applied by third country issuers of securities pursuant to Directives (EC) 2003/71 and (EC) 2004/109 of the European Parliament and of the Council [2007] OJ L340/66, Art 4.

[75] ibid Art 4(5).

[76] Securities Act Release No 6902 (21 June 1991).

[77] HS Scott, *International Finance: Law and Regulation* (Sweet & Maxwell, 2004) 53.

Historical European experience is also of mutual recognition arrangements being put in place but then little use being made of them in practice. Under the regulatory framework that preceded the current disclosure regime, there was provision for mutual recognition by other Member States of any prospectus that had been approved by the securities regulator in one state.[78] However, very few issuers took advantage of these arrangements.[79] They came to be seen as being flawed because host Member States could require prospectuses to include additional information for their local market and could insist on full translation of the documents. The additional costly complexity involved in tailoring documentation so as to satisfy various different sets of national regulatory requirements undermined the appeal of the mutual recognition procedures. Under the new Prospectus Directive of 2003,[80] these design flaws have been addressed. The basic idea that once a prospectus has been approved in one state it can then be used for issuance activity in other EEA states without the need for any further approvals is retained but the ability of host states to require additional local information and to insist on full translation is removed. It is early days for the operation of this revised arrangement but there are indications that issuers are willing to make active use of it. Its operation is considered in more detail later in this chapter.

The European and North American experiences can both be seen to support the view that lack of common standards in significant areas is an impediment to effective mutual recognition: one explanation for low use of the MJDS is the need for GAAP reconciliation; and one explanation for the low use of the old European mutual recognition procedures was the need to add local information relating to each of the Member States in which the prospectus was used. They can also be interpreted as saying something about the importance of maintaining mutual trust and confidence in the quality of oversight and enforcement: the rumoured demise of the MJDS has been associated with US lack of confidence in Canadian enforcement.[81]

However, it is also important to note that, to a large extent, the low use of these arrangements may be attributable to causes other than flaws in details of their internal design. This could simply be a case where regulatory policy design is out of step with the major needs of the market. Globalization is a force that has affected all aspects of capital market activity and not just issuers. Investors, especially institutional investors and financial intermediaries, have also become international in outlook and often in their organizational structures. So too have stock exchanges and other securities trading platforms. Institutional investors can now trade relatively easily in securities that are listed on foreign exchanges—and

---

[78] N Moloney, *EC Securities Regulation* (OUP, 2002) 198–205.
[79] ibid 209–13.
[80] Directive (EC) 2003/71 [2003] OJ L435/64.
[81] W Hicks, 'Harmonisation of Disclosure Standards for Cross-Border Share Offerings: Approaching an 'International Passport' to Capital Markets?' (2002) 9 *Indiana Journal of Global Legal Studies* 361, 377.

even retail investors, for whom the traditional strong home bias in investment strategies may be starting to erode, have been able to find ways of investing in securities listed abroad.[82] As secondary market trading in foreign securities becomes easier and more commonplace, some of the considerations that historically might have led a company to consider making a direct offer of its securities into the primary market of another country and/or to have its securities listed there begin to lose their force. Even for those companies whose needs for new equity capital are too large to be absorbed by their domestic primary markets, a multi-jurisdictional public offer made in accordance with laws relating to prospectuses is not the only option, as it may be possible to satisfy those needs with a full retail offering at home that is combined with a wholesale offer to professional investors abroad, with the wholesale offer being structured so as to fall within professional and other exemptions from the requirements for mandatory prospectuses.[83]

Even though there are quite persuasive arguments to the effect that the emphasis in international policy-making should shift from the primary to the secondary market, new international arrangements for the mutual recognition of prospectuses continue to be developed. For example, in 2006 Australia and New Zealand reached agreement on a regime for mutual recognition of securities offerings between the two countries. Given their geographical proximity and the close historic, political, and economic relationship between them, that these two countries were able to feel sufficiently comfortable with each other's regime to enter into such an arrangement is not surprising.[84]

Cross-border issuance in the European Economic Area using a prospectus passport

Obtaining a passport

An issuer that is proposing to offer its securities to the public and/or apply for admission of its securities to trading on a regulated market within the EEA must draw up a prospectus that, in form and content, complies with the requirements of the Prospectus Directive itself and with those of the Prospectus Directive Regulation, which is a secondary measure adopted by the European Commission to prescribe the details of the information to be disclosed in a prospectus.[85] The

---

[82] HE Jackson, 'A System of Selective Substitute Compliance' (2007) 48 *Harvard Journal of International Law* 105.

[83] E Ferran, *Building an EU Securities Market* (CUP, 2004) 200–1.

[84] Full Text of the Agreement between the Government of Australia and the Government of New Zealand in Relation to Mutual Recognition of Securities Offerings (22 February 2006), available at <http://www.med.govt.nz/templates/MultipageDocumentTOC____22301.aspx (accessed August 2007).

[85] [2004] OJ L149/1.

disclosure regime set by the Prospectus Directive and the Prospectus Directive Regulation is one of maximum harmonization. This means that national regulatory authorities cannot adopt general rules requiring a prospectus to contain items of information which are not included in relevant schedules and building blocks of the Prospectus Directive Regulation.[86] Chapter 13 above, considers in detail the implementation and operation of that regime in the UK domestic context. Here, there follows an overview of the general scheme of the EC legal regime.

An issuer must apply to the competent authority of its home state for regulatory approval of the prospectus before it is published.[87] For European issuers, the home state is the state in which their registered office is located.[88] Once a prospectus is approved it has Community scope, which means that it is valid for public offers or the admission of securities to trading on a regulated market in any number of states within the EU.[89] The home state authority must, if so requested by the issuer, notify host state authorities that the prospectus has been approved in accordance with the Prospectus Directive and send a copy of the prospectus.[90] Host states cannot impose their own approval requirements.[91] Host states may require translation of the summary of the prospectus (which should not normally exceed 2,500 words in the original language) into their official language but not of the entire document, provided that the prospectus has been drawn up in either a language accepted by the competent authorities of those Member States or in a language customary in the sphere of international finance.[92] Approved prospectuses must be made available to the public in any one of a number of prescribed ways, including insertions in newspapers circulating in the Member States where the offer is made or admission is sought and on the issuer's website, but need not be sent directly to investors unless they so request.[93] Advertisements relating to offers to the public or admission of securities to trading on a regulated market are regulated.[94] Supplementary prospectuses are required in certain circumstances and these must be published in accordance with at least the same arrangements as were applied when the original prospectus was published.[95]

The design of this regime reflects lessons learnt from past experience: the disclosure requirements are standardized, host states cannot require the inclusion of additional local information for the home market and translation burdens have been significantly lightened. The regime has also to be seen in the context of the institutional framework for its implementation and supervision. Oversight

---

[86] Prospectus Directive, rec 15.
[87] ibid Art 13.
[88] ibid Art 2.1(m)(i).
[89] ibid Art 17.
[90] ibid Art 18.
[91] ibid Art 18.
[92] ibid Art 19.2.
[93] ibid Art 14.
[94] ibid Art 15.
[95] ibid Art 16.

of prospectuses takes place at national level and is primarily the responsibility of the issuer's home state securities regulator. Where a host state finds irregularities, it must refer these findings to the competent authority of the home Member State and it is only where irregularities persist, despite the measures taken by the competent authority of the home Member State or because such measures prove inadequate, that the host state can itself take all the appropriate measures in order to protect investors.[96] This fragmentation of responsibility carries the risk that standardization objectives will not be met because they are undermined by differences in the way that national regulators interpret and apply the rules. One strategy for addressing this risk is to draft the rules in such a way as to leave little room for differing interpretations. The very detailed nature of the prospectus disclosure requirements applies this strategy to some extent. It is reflected also in the choice of legal instrument in which the requirements are contained: the Prospectus Directive *Regulation* applies directly in Member States without the need for transposition via a domestic instrument, as would be required for a Directive and which could provide opportunities for differences to creep in via the transposition process. However, excessive detail carries its own dangers and thus this strategy for drafting the content of rules cannot be taken too far. Nor can too much reliance be placed on the choice of legal instruments because regulations may often be inappropriate, perhaps because there are legitimate local specificities of which account needs to be taken or because of the need to adhere to the EU subsidiarity principle whereby decisions should be taken at the closest possible level to the citizen.[97] Another way in principle of addressing the problem of different national authorities taking different views is to remove from them the responsibility for oversight, giving it instead to a supra-national pan-European agency formed especially for that purpose. However, whatever merits a Euro-SEC, or a Euro-FSA with responsibility across all financial market segments, may have, and these are debatable,[98] there is little prospect of such an agency being established in the short to medium term. Instead, a different approach is favoured, whereby national agencies are allowed to retain oversight responsibilities but an institutional framework has been put in place to foster convergence in the way that they perform these tasks.

Lamfalussy and the establishment of the Committee of European Securities Regulators

In July 2000, the European Council (in its Economic and Finance Ministers formation ('ECOFIN')) appointed a Committee of 'Wise Men', under the

---

[96] ibid Art 23.

[97] Inter-institutional Monitoring Group, 'Second Interim Report Monitoring the Lamfalussy Process' (January 2007), para 34.

[98] The extensive debate on this topic is reviewed in E Ferran, *Building an EU Securities Market* (CUP, 2004) 119–122.

chairmanship of Baron Alexandre Lamfalussy, to conduct a broad examination of the mechanisms for regulating and supervising EU securities markets. The Lamfalussy Committee published an initial report in November 2000 and a final report in February 2001.[99] The work of the Lamfalussy Committee was very influential. It led to the adoption of a new structure for rule-making and supervision of securities market activity (generally known as the 'Lamfalussy Process') involving four levels:

- Level 1 (in essence primary legislation decided upon by the Council and Parliament in accordance with established law-making procedures—of which the Prospectus Directive is an example);
- Level 2 (implementing measures, or more detailed rules, decided upon by the Commission acting in accordance with EU comitology procedures—of which the Prospectus Directive Regulation is an example);
- Level 3 (a drive towards consistent implementation and transposition of legislation at Member State level); and
- Level 4 (greater emphasis on monitoring and enforcement).

The Committee of European Securities Regulators (CESR), which was formally established by the Commission in June 2001 (although it can trace its origins back to the Forum of European Securities Commissions which was established on an informal basis in 1997), performs the Level 3 role of promoting the drive towards consistency, as well as providing technical advice to the Commission on legislative proposals.[100] There are now also similar coordinating committees for banking and for insurance.[101] CESR comprises representatives from national regulators (in practice usually the heads of the national securities regulator) of Member States plus Norway and Iceland, which are members of the EEA but not the EU. As part of its Level 3 role, CESR performs a standard-setting function, ie it can issue standards, rules, and guidance that are not binding EC rules but which, in a manner akin to the 'enforceability' of other forms of international 'soft law', are underpinned by loose commitments from CESR members to give effect to them in their national regulatory systems.[102] The Committee also plays a

---

[99] The 'Regulation of European Securities Markets: Final Report' (Brussels, 15 February 2001), in which 'The Regulation of European Securities Markets: Initial Report' (Brussels, 9 November 2000) appears as Annex 5, with the ECOFIN Council's terms of reference included as Annex 1 to the 'Initial Report'.

[100] See Commission Decision (EC) 2004/7 of 5 November 2003 amending Decision (EC) 2001/527 establishing the Committee of European Securities Regulators [2004] OJ L3/32. On CESR's Level 3 role see N Moloney, 'Innovation and Risk in EC Financial Market Regulation: New Instruments of Financial Market Intervention and the Committee of European Securities Regulators' [2007] *European Law Review* 627.

[101] See Commission Decision (EC) 2004/5 of 5 November 2003 establishing the Committee of European Banking Supervisors [2004] OJ L3/28 and 2004/6/EC Commission Decision of 5 November 2003 establishing the Committee of European Insurance and Occupational Pensions Supervisors [2004] OJ L3/30.

[102] CESR Charter, art 4.

peer review role, monitoring regulatory practices within the single market.[103] It is envisaged that over time CESR's role in relation to peer review and peer pressure could bring about significant convergence in securities regulatory practices across Europe.[104] CESR is also charged with keeping an eye on global developments in securities regulation and considering their impact on the regulation of the single market for financial services.[105]

An example of CESR's 'soft' standard-setting role is provided by its recommendations for the consistent implementation of prospectuses requirements.[106] The recommendations provide clarification in relation to issues such as working capital disclosure, profit forecasts, capitalization and indebtedness, and also on the detailed disclosure items under the Prospectus Directive Regulation. These recommendations are not binding as a matter of European law but CESR members are introducing them into their national requirements on a voluntary basis. This voluntary incorporation has taken place in the UK: the FSA requires issuers to have regard to the CESR recommendations and will take account of them in the prospectus approval process.[107] Also relevant in this context is a 'Q and A' publication relating to prospectuses, published by CESR, that outlines common positions agreed by CESR members and also some points where views diverge.[108] This document, which was produced at the behest of market participants, is intended to provide the market with responses in a quick and efficient manner to everyday questions which are commonly posed to the CESR Secretariat or CESR members. It is sensible for CESR to focus on improving mechanisms for the pooling and publication of regulatory know-how that have been hammered out on the anvil of real transactional experience. The benefits for market participants and regulators of being able easily to tap into the results of such experience are readily apparent.[109]

Prospectus liability—a gap in the standardization agenda?

It is common for national legal systems to provide a special civil remedy to investors who have acquired securities on the basis of a false prospectus. This dedicated

---

[103] ibid.

[104] C Scott, 'The Governance of the European Union: The Potential for Multi-Level Control' (2002) 8 *European Law Journal* 59, 68 sees the emergence of CESR as the body responsible for implementation and application of EU securities law as 'displacing' the Commission from this role.

[105] CESR Charter, art 4.5.

[106] CESR, 'Recommendations for the Consistent Implementation of the European Commission's Regulation on Prospectuses No 809/2004' (CESR/05-054b).

[107] FSA *Handbook, Prospectus Rules*, 1.1.6G and 1.1.8G.

[108] CESR, 'Frequently Asked Questions Regarding Prospectuses: Common Positions Agreed by CESR Members' (CESR/07-651).

[109] Practical guidance is also being published at national level: see FSA, *Passporting Fact Sheet* (UKLA Publications, Factsheet No 4, October 2006).

remedy is often more favourable to investors than claims that are available under the general law, for example because there is less that the investor needs to prove in order to win the claim or because the range of defendants against whom the claim can be brought is wider. Section 90 of the UK Financial Services and Markets Act 2000, considered in chapter 13 above, provides an example of such a claim.

The Prospectus Directive does not attempt to harmonize the contents of civil remedies available to investors. All it does is to say that such liability should exist under national laws and that it must apply to the persons who are responsible for the information in the prospectus.[110] Exactly who is to be regarded as a responsible person is not exhaustively prescribed but there is provision for responsibility to attach to the issuer or its management.[111] This relatively light touch form of intervention means that there is considerable room for variations between the liability regimes of different Member States. This has potentially adverse implications for those engaged in cross-border securities issuance activity when it is combined with applicable conflict of laws rules. Civil jurisdiction within the EU is regulated by EC Regulation 44/2001 (the 'Brussels Regulation')[112] which, as a general rule, allocates jurisdiction on the basis of domicile of the defendant[113] but which, in tort claims (ie claims where a defendant's non-contractual civil liability is in question), provides also for jurisdiction in the courts of the location of the harmful event.[114] The place where the damage occurs is the general rule for the choice of law governing a tort claim under the EC Rome II Regulation governing non-contractual obligations.[115] Applying these rules, there is a risk that participants in cross-border issuance activity on the basis of a prospectus passport could

---

[110] Prospectus Directive, Art 6.

[111] ibid Art 6.

[112] Council Regulation (EC) No 44/2001 of 22 December 2000 on jurisdiction and the recognition and enforcement of judgments in civil and commercial matters [2001] OJ12/1.

[113] The domicile of legal persons is determined by Art 60, which provides three possible solutions: the statutory seat, or the place of the central administration or the principal place of business of the company.

[114] Brussels Regulation, Art 5(3). This place can be either where the harm was directly suffered or where the acts giving rise to the harm were done (Case C-21/76 *Bier v Mines de Potasse* [1976] ECR 1735). The claimant has a free choice between these two (or more) courts as an alternative to the courts of the defendant's domicile. Locating financial loss can be challenging (see eg Case C-364/93 *Marinari v Lloyds Bank* [1995] ECR I-2719 and Case C-220/88 *Dumez France v Hessische Landesbank* [1990] ECR I-49). These add to the uncertainties which an issuer may face in determining where a suit might be brought. However, there is a movement towards limiting the jurisdiction of the court under Art 5(3) to the damage suffered within that jurisdiction (Case C-68/93 *Shevill v Presse Alliance* [1995] ECR I-415). That may prevent parallel litigation on the same damage, but will permit a claimant to split up the claim to pursue an issuer in several jurisdictions.

[115] Regulation (EC) 864/2007 of the European Parliament and of the Council of 11 July 2007 on the law applicable to non-contractual obligations (Rome II) [2007] OJ L199/40, Art 4(1) applies the law of that country 'irrespective of the country in which the event giving rise to the damage occurred and irrespective of the country or countries in which the indirect consequences of that event occur'. There are exceptions to the general rule, including one where there is a 'manifestly closer connection' with another country, which could be based in a pre-existing relationship or a contract between the parties to the litigation. The limits and applicability of the exception will require elucidation from the ECJ, if the experience follows that of the similar wording in the equivalent EC measure relating to contractual obligations.

face the possibility of multiple prospectus liability suits in the various countries in which the prospectus is used; if so, liability could fall to be determined under different national laws and in accordance with different civil procedure rules. Some groups could find themselves within one country's list of responsible persons to whom liability can attach but outwith another country's list. Overall, the lack of standardization with regard to the civil liability position could quite significantly undermine the appeal of the prospectus passport.

Civil liability position under the Transparency Obligations Directive

It is worthwhile also to consider here the civil liability position under the Transparency Obligations Directive.[116] This Directive broadly follows the Prospectus Directive in requiring Member States to ensure that civil liability attaches to responsible persons for the periodic financial disclosures required of issuers with securities admitted to trading on a regulated market, with at least the issuer being so responsible; but it does not prescribe in detail the contours of that liability regime.[117] Some Member States may determine that the remedies available under the general civil law already satisfy this requirement. Others may conclude that a new specially dedicated remedy is needed. As discussed in chapter 13 above, the UK took the latter view and, in order to meet the requirements of the Transparency Obligations Directive, enacted section 90A of the Financial Services and Markets Act 2000.

Where the Transparency Obligations Directive differs from the Prospectus Directive in a way that could have significant implications for liability concerns, is with regard to publication venues. Under the Prospectus Directive, an issuer can pick and choose: it is not required to make an offer on the basis of a passported prospectus into all Member States. However, under the Transparency Obligations Directive, issuers with securities admitted to trading on a regulated market are required to disseminate regulated information effectively to the public throughout the Community.[118] An implementing measure made under the Transparency Obligations Directive fleshes out what this means:

Directive 2004/109/EC sets high-level requirements in the area of dissemination of regulated information. The mere availability of information, which means that investors must actively seek it out, is therefore not sufficient for the purposes of that Directive. Accordingly, dissemination should involve the active distribution of information from the issuers to the media, with a view to reaching investors.

Minimum quality standards for the dissemination of regulated information are necessary to ensure that investors, even if situated in a Member State other than that of the issuer, have equal access to regulated information ...

---

[116] [2004] OJ L390/38.
[117] Transparency Obligations Directive, Art 7.
[118] ibid Art 21.

Additionally, by way of minimum standards, regulated information should be disseminated in a way that ensures the widest possible public access, and where possible reaching the public simultaneously inside and outside the issuer's home Member State . . .[119]

Once admitted to a regulated market, issuers must therefore contend with the possibility of multi-jurisdictional litigation in respect of their periodic disclosures, as liability could arise in each of the jurisdictions in which the information is received and acted upon.[120] Of course, in a sense there is nothing new here because, even before the Transparency Obligations Directive, issuers with publicly quoted shares faced the risk that investors in various countries might acquire their securities and later sue in their local courts. However, the Transparency Obligations Directive has led to fears in some quarters of an increased risk of multiple civil liability suits under different national laws, for example because, even though national laws may remain the same, investors may find it easier to establish the factors (such as receipt of information within the jurisdiction) on which liability depends or because the Directive may have a dynamic effect on Member States' liability laws and result in the enactment of new remedies that are more favourable to investors.

Position of issuers from third countries

Issuers from third countries are entitled to use the passport in respect of any prospectus that has been approved by the issuer's home state. For a third country issuer of equity securities, the home state is the Member State where the securities are intended to be offered to the public for the first time after the date of entry into force of the Prospectus Directive or where the first application for admission to trading on a regulated market is made, at the choice of the issuer.[121]

The contents of the prospectus drawn up by a third country issuer are determined by reference to the Prospectus Directive, subject to concessions on grounds of equivalence of third country laws. As discussed earlier in this chapter, the major sticking point here is in relation to accounting standards for financial disclosures, where an interim arrangement is in place up to 2011.

Third country issuers that have their securities admitted to trading on an EEA regulated market are subject to obligations that give effect to the Transparency

---

[119] Commission Directive (EC) 2007/14 of 8 March 2007 laying down detailed rules for the implementation of certain provisions of Directive (EC) 2004/109 on the harmonisation of transparency requirements in relation to information about issuers whose securities are admitted to trading on a regulated market [2007] L69/27, recs 15–17.

[120] This issue has been considered in some detail by the UK Financial Markets Law Committee (FMLC), which identifies issues of legal uncertainty in the framework of the wholesale financial markets and considers how such issues should be addressed. See 'Issue 76—Transparency Obligations Directive' (January 2004); 'Issue 76—Transparency Obligations Directive' (October 2004), and 'Issue 76—Transparency Obligations Directive' (September 2006). These memoranda, together with an exchange of correspondence between Lord Woolf (FMLC) and Alexander Schaub (European Commission), are available via the FMLC website at <http://www.fmlc.org>.

[121] Prospectus Directive, Art 2(1)(m)(iii).

Obligations Directive, again subject to concessions based on equivalence. Outside the area of accounting standards, where the interim arrangements up to 2011 apply, the Commission has made some progress towards the determination of equivalence for aspects of the Transparency Obligations Directive. For this purpose the Commission has taken the view that equivalence should be able to be declared when general disclosure rules of third countries provide users with understandable and broadly equivalent assessments of issuers' positions that enable them to make similar decisions as if they were provided with the information according to requirements under the Transparency Obligations Directive, even if the requirements are not identical.[122] On certain matters, national regulatory agencies have made their own determinations of equivalence. For example, the UK FSA has determined that the laws of the US, Japan, Israel, and Switzerland on major shareholdings are equivalent to the notifications required under its rules implementing the Transparency Obligations Directive and that issuers with securities admitted to trading on a regulated market in the UK that are incorporated in any of these countries are exempt from the FSA's requirements.[123] Swiss issuers also enjoy further 'equivalence' exemptions.[124]

Cross-border share issuance activity in the EEA without a passport—making use of exemptions

As an alternative to a full public offer in a number of countries made on the basis of a prospectus passport, the Prospectus Directive provides a number of exemptions that enable an issuer to conduct cross-border share issuance activity without a prospectus. This may be an attractive option where the issuer's need for capital or likely international investor interest in its offering is limited or where considerations such as the risk of facing multiple prospectus liability suits under a number of different legal systems are seen to outweigh the benefits of making an offering to a widely-drawn group of investors. A study of capital raising practices in the EU in 1999 found that prospectus passports were rarely used by European issuers to make offerings in European capital markets and that the much more common structure was for the home element of the offering to be made on a basis of a prospectus but for the cross-border element to be structured so as to come within exemptions.[125] That study obviously pre-dated the new Prospectus Directive and the significant improvements to the design of the passport regime that it has made. However, some considerations, such as prospectus liability concerns,

---

[122] Commission Directive (EC) 2007/14 [2007] OJ L69/27, rec 18 and Arts 13–23.
[123] The list is published at <http://www.fsa.gov.uk/Pages/Doing/UKLA/company/non_eea/index.shtml> (accessed December 2007).
[124] ibid.
[125] HE Jackson and E Pan, 'Regulatory Competition in International Securities Markets: Evidence from Europe in 1999—Part I' (2001) 56 *Business Lawyer* 653.

that militate against using the passport remain. The option of a full retail offer to investors in the home market which is accompanied by a prospectus, combined with an exempt wholesale offer to professional investors in other countries, may thus continue to hold considerable attraction.

Private placements have to be structured so as to comply with local requirements relating to investment advertisements and resale restrictions under local law that are designed to prevent seepage into the retail market of securities sold on a prospectus-exempt basis to professionals only. The exact scope of the relevant exemptions under the local law in each of the countries where they are to be relied upon also needs to be checked. As the exemptions are derived from the Prospectus Directive, which is a maximum harmonization measure, in theory they should be identical across the EEA but, as noted earlier in this chapter, differences in interpretation can creep in as part of the process whereby Directives are incorporated into national laws. One of the weaknesses of the old European regime that the Prospectus Directive of 2003 sought to address was that the drafting of the prospectus exemptions was imprecise and led to considerable variation in how they were interpreted. The wording of the Prospectus Directive is much tighter and therefore the problem should recede, though cautious issuers engaging in cross-border activity will probably still seek reassurance from local lawyers on the interpretation of the scope of the exemptions in their jurisdiction.

Relevant exemptions

The general rule is that Member States must not allow any offer of securities to be made to the public within their territories without prior publication of a prospectus.[126] Likewise Member States must ensure that any admission of securities to trading on a regulated market situated or operating within their territories is subject to the publication of a prospectus.[127] However, the obligation to publish a prospectus is qualified in certain cases. The exemptions in respect of public offer prospectuses that are of most relevance for cross-border equity issuance activity are those relating to offers of securities addressed solely to qualified investors; and offers of securities addressed to fewer than 100 natural or legal persons per Member State, other than qualified investors.[128] So long as the issuer is not seeking to list its securities on regulated markets in any of the territories in which the offer is made (in which case a prospectus obligation under that heading would arise unless a relevant exemption is available), it can rely on these exemptions to make its offering. The category of qualified investors includes firms operating in the financial markets, national and regional governments, central banks,

---

[126] Prospectus Directive, Art 3(1).
[127] ibid Art 3(3).
[128] ibid Art 3(2).

international and supranational institutions, other legal entities that are not small and medium-sized enterprises (SMEs), SMEs that expressly ask to be considered as qualified investors, and natural persons who expressly ask to be considered as qualified investors provided they meet at least two of the specified criteria relating to experience of securities market transacting, portfolio size, and professional employment in the financial sector.[129] Any subsequent resale of securities to which an exemption applied is regarded as a separate offer and may require a prospectus unless an exemption applies.[130]

One area where different regulators might take different views on the interpretation of these exemptions is where offers are made to a trust or to a partnership: for the purposes of the 100 persons exemption, is this to be regarded as an offer to each of the trustees or partners, or to the trust or partnership as a single person?[131] Another area of possible divergence is where an offer is made to brokers who have the ability to decide to buy on behalf of clients without reference to these underlying clients: is this to be regarded as an offer to the brokers, who should be qualified investors, or to the underlying clients, who may not be?[132]

US securities law and relevant exemptions

Section 5 of the US Securities Act of 1933 generally prohibits an issuer from making any public offer or sale of any security in the US unless a registration statement with respect to that security filed with the SEC has become effective and delivery of a prospectus forming a part of such registration statement accompanies (or precedes) confirmation of the sale. The prohibition may in certain circumstances extend to the sale of securities outside the US to US persons. However, there are several exemptions from the section 5 registration requirements. The exemptions that are of most significance in relation to international equity offerings are: sales of securities outside the US (Regulation S); private placements (Section 4(2) and Regulation D); and resales to qualified institutional buyers (Rule 144A).

Regulation S: sales and resales outside the US[133]

The SEC adopted Regulation S in 1990 in order to clarify the circumstances under which the Securities Act 1933, section 5 registration requirements would not be applied extraterritorially. Regulation S replaced a complicated set of selling restrictions with a more territorial approach to the application of US law.[134]

---

129   ibid Art 2(1)(e)–(g) and Art 2(2).
130   ibid Art 3(2).
131   FSMA 2000, s 86(3) treats each of these as being an offer to a single person.
132   ibid s 86(2) treats this situation as being covered by the qualified investor exemption.
133   <http://www.sec.gov/about/forms/reg_s.pdf>.
134   HS Scott, *International Finance: Law and Regulation* (Sweet & Maxwell, 2004) 59.

Where the requirements of Regulation S are met, US registration requirements will not apply. Regulation S does not affect the extraterritorial application of the anti-fraud provisions of the US federal securities laws.

The effect of Regulation S is that for the purposes of the registration requirements of the Securities Act of 1933, the terms 'offer' and 'sale' are deemed to exclude offers and sales that occur 'outside the United States'. By way of non-exclusive safe harbours, an offer or sale is deemed to take place outside the US when two general conditions are satisfied: (a) it is an 'off-shore' transaction, and (b) there are no directed selling efforts in the US. In addition, there is a further condition on the Regulation S safe harbour for primary offerings, which operates by reference to whether there is substantial US market interest (SUSMI) in the issuer's securities.

Offshore transaction

An offshore transaction is one where the offer is made outside the US and the buyer is, or is reasonably believed by the seller to be, outside the US at the time of origination of the buy order. Alternatively, it is a transaction where the offer is made outside the US and the transaction is executed through a securities exchange located outside the US (for a primary offer) or the facilities of a designated offshore securities market (in the case of a resale). Offshore transactions are not restricted to sales to non-US residents.

No directed selling efforts in the US

Directed selling efforts are any activities that could reasonably be expected to have the effect of conditioning the market in the US for any of the securities being offered. Directed selling efforts could include advertisements with television or radio stations reaching the US (though there are certain specific exemptions for particular types of advertisement). Marketing efforts in the US for an offering that is otherwise exempt from the registration requirements of the Securities Act will not generally be treated as directed selling efforts of a simultaneous offering outside the US under Regulation S.

Substantial US market interest

The primary offer safe harbour in Regulation S distinguishes between three categories of offerings. The thinking that underlies this three-tier structure is that there is a risk that securities that have been sold initially on an exempt basis could flow back into the US markets by unregulated routes and the more the issuer is connected with the US the greater the risk of flow back.

Category I offerings include offerings of equity securities of foreign issuers for which there is no substantial US market interest. Whether there is a substantial US market interest is determined by reference to whether the US represents the largest single market for such securities of the issuer or to a comparison of the percentage of dealings in that class of securities that takes place via US market facilities and of dealings via the facilities of the securities market of a single foreign country. As a matter of practice, the view generally taken is that there will be a substantial US market interest for very few foreign issuers, including even those foreign issuers that have obtained a listing on a securities exchange in the US. Category I offerings need only comply with the general conditions discussed above.

Category II offerings include equity offerings by foreign issuers that are subject to periodic reporting requirements under US securities law that do not fit within Category I because there is substantial US market interest. For Category II offerings, in addition to satisfying the offshore transaction and directed selling efforts requirements, the issuer must also comply with certain selling restrictions. Offers and sales of the securities in the US or to US persons (defined by reference to residency rather than nationality) are prohibited during a restricted period lasting forty days. There are also certain procedural requirements relating to legends that must appear on all offering material and agreements that must be obtained from distributors on their efforts to conform to the safe harbour.

Category III offerings include equity offerings of foreign issuers not subject to the periodic reporting requirements under US securities law that do not fit into Category I because there is a substantial US market interest for the class of securities being offered. Very few offerings of foreign issuers will fall into this category. Equity offerings by US issuers also fall into this category. The most rigorous restrictions apply in this case: in addition to the general conditions, selling restrictions apply for a period of one year for offerings of equity securities, and there are additional procedural requirements.

Resales

Securities may also be re-sold under Regulation S so long as the transaction is offshore and there are no directed selling efforts in the US. The resale provisions are not limited to securities originally sold under the Regulation. Securities privately placed in the US or acquired in another exempt sale can be re-sold offshore in reliance on Regulation S. Equally, securities offered outside the US using the Regulation S exemption can then be immediately re-sold in the US using the Rule 144A exemption, considered later.

Private placements and Regulation D[135]

Section 4(2) of the Securities Act of 1933 exempts from registration requirements transactions by an issuer not involving any 'public offering'. In Regulation D the SEC addressed uncertainties in determining whether a 'public offering' has occurred by providing a non-exclusive safe harbour for offerings made under section 4(2). The background to the adoption of Regulation D was Congressional demands for a relaxation of the registration burden on smaller issuers.[136] Regulation D provides a number of safe harbours for small offerings but, for the

---

[135] <http://www.sec.gov/divisions/corpfin/ecfrlinks.shtml>.
[136] JD Cox, RW Hillman, and DC Langevoort, *Securities Regulation Cases and Materials* (Aspen Law & Business, 3rd edn, 2003) 400–401.

purposes of this account, it is the safe harbour it provides for private offerings that is most important. Regulation D allows sales to an unlimited number of accredited investors. The category of 'accredited investor' includes banks, insurance companies, registered and small business investment companies, certain business development companies, certain employer benefit plans, organizations with total assets in excess of US$5 million and certain wealthy individuals (individuals with a net worth or joint net worth with his or her spouse exceeding US$1 million, or with individual income in excess of US$200,000 (US$300,000 joint with spouse) in each of the two most recent years and if the individual has a reasonable expectation of reaching the same income level in the current year).[137] Regulation D also allows sales to no more than 35 non-accredited investors who meet certain sophistication standards.[138] A significant drawback of selling to non-accredited investors is that the offering becomes subject to considerably more onerous disclosure requirements, as discussed next.

Disclosure requirements

Regulation D does not mandate specific disclosures if sales are made only to accredited investors. However, if a sale is made to even one non-accredited investor, the issuer will be required to deliver to all investors within a reasonable time prior to any sale a disclosure document, often called a private placement memorandum, containing much of the information that would be required in a registration statement filed with the SEC. Also, investors should be given the opportunity to ask management questions that are material to making an informed investment decision.

Resales

Securities offered under section 4(2) and Regulation D are 'restricted securities' and may not be re-sold unless they are registered or qualify for an exemption from registration.

Rule 144A: resales of restricted securities to qualified institutional buyers[139]

Rule 144A is a non-exclusive safe harbour that exempts from registration requirements resales to qualified institutional buyers (QIBs) of securities issued in a non-public offering that are not of the same class or fungible with securities listed or

---

[137] In August 2007, the SEC proposed certain modifications of the Regulation D safe harbour, including the creation of a new safe harbour for offerings to 'large accredited investors', a modest expansion of the categories of investors who would qualify as 'accredited investors', and the addition of inflation adjustments to increase over time the minimum standards for accredited investors and large accredited investors.

[138] Cox, Hillman, and Langevoort (n 136 above) 409–10.

[139] HS Scott, *International Finance: Law and Regulation* (Sweet & Maxwell, 2004) 46–9.

quoted on a US exchange or market. As such, the rule addresses the circumstances in which a person who has purchased securities from an issuer in a transaction which was itself exempt from registration under the Securities Act of 1933, such as an offshore transaction made in accordance with Regulation S, or a private placement made in reliance on Regulation D, may resell those securities without destroying the original exemption or otherwise being subject to the Securities Act registration requirements. The rationale behind the Rule 144A exemption is that the benefit of disclosure-based investor protection is outweighed by the benefit of more rapid access to capital markets when securities are exclusively placed with experienced, sophisticated investors.

Criteria for safe harbour

Under Rule 144A, a person may resell securities to any QIB provided that: (a) the securities are not of the same class when issued as securities of the issuer quoted in NASDAQ or listed on a US stock exchange (the fungibility prohibition); (b) the buyer is advised that the seller is relying on Rule 144A (the notice requirement); and (c) certain information is made available (although this last requirement does not always apply).

Who is a qualified institutional buyer?

Resales under Rule 144A must be made exclusively to QIBs. A QIB is (a) an institution that owns and invests on a discretionary basis at least US$100 million in qualifying securities (US$10 million if the person is a US broker-dealer), or (b) an entity owned by a QIB, or (c) a US broker-dealer buying as agent for, or in a riskless principal transaction for resale to, a QIB. If the person is a bank or lending institution, it must also have a net worth of at least US$25 million to qualify.

Eligible securities—the fungibility prohibition

Both debt and equity securities are eligible for resale under Rule 144A, provided they are not, at the time of issuance, of the same class as securities which are listed on a national exchange or quoted through the NASDAQ system. This means, for example, that common stock of US listed companies cannot be sold under Rule 144A. The goal of this requirement is to prevent trading of essentially the same securities simultaneously in public and private markets.

Notice to purchaser

The seller of the securities must take 'reasonable steps' to ensure that the purchaser is aware of the seller's reliance on Rule 144A. Obtaining representations from the purchaser and/or including legends in the offering memorandum may satisfy this condition. In the secondary market, a special confirmation notice is used which specifies the seller's potential reliance on the Rule.

Available information

The information that must be made available must be reasonably current and should include (a) a very brief statement of the nature of the business of the issuer and the products and services it offers, and (b) the issuer's most recent balance sheet and profit and loss and retained earnings statements, and similar financial statements for such part of the two preceding fiscal years as the issuer has been in operation (the financial statements should be audited to the extent reasonably available). To be 'reasonably current', with regard to a foreign issuer, the required information must meet the timing requirements of the issuer's home country or principal trading markets. If the issuer is subject to periodic reporting requirements under US securities law it need not make such information available.

Liability position

Rule 144A sales are not subject to the stringent liability provisions that apply to registered public offers. However, Rule 10b-5 liability under the Exchange Act of 1934 is applicable. This is the basic anti-fraud provision of the federal securities law. It prohibits fraudulent devices, schemes, and practices, and also misstatements/omissions of material facts (but negligence is not enough). It gives rise to a private remedy in the hands of injured investors.

Making a public offer and obtaining a listing in the United States—a brief outline of the law relating to foreign issuers

This chapter concludes with a very brief overview of the US legal framework governing (non-exempt) public offers and listing of securities by foreign issuers.[140] A public offer will trigger registration under the Securities Act of 1933 and a listing will trigger registration under section 12 of the Securities Exchange Act of 1934. The disclosure requirements for making a public offering and for listing are substantially identical. A listed issuer also becomes subject to the periodic reporting and other requirements under sections 13 and 15 of the Exchange Act of 1934.

Foreign private issuers use SEC Form 20-F for their original registration and for subsequent periodic filings. A foreign company is a 'foreign private issuer' for this purpose unless more than 50 per cent of its outstanding voting securities are owned directly or indirectly by US residents, and any of the following conditions is satisfied: (a) the majority of executive officers/directors are US citizens or residents; (b) more than 50 per cent of the assets of the issuer are located in the US; or (c) the business is administered principally in the US.

In 1999, the SEC adopted a complete revision of Form 20-F that replaced most of the other requirements with IOSCO international disclosure standards. As discussed earlier in this chapter, foreign issuers' financial reports have historically

---

[140] For detailed treatment see Cox, Hillman, and Langevoort (n 13 above) 205.

generally been required to be drawn up in accordance with US GAAP or reconciled to it, but the SEC has voted to drop this requirement. Certain other
requirements of the US securities regulatory regime are also modified for foreign
issuers.[141] These accommodations reflect efforts by the SEC to balance investor
protection considerations and an interest in maintaining the international competitiveness of the US securities markets.

The Sarbanes-Oxley Act of 2002, which is concerned with corporate governance matters including senior officer certification of financial statements, independent audit committees, audit partner rotation, and auditor oversight, applies
to foreign issuers that are listed in the US as well as to domestic issuers. The Act,
as originally enacted, treated domestic and foreign companies in the same way
but, in implementing it, the SEC has made some accommodations for foreign
companies in order to avoid conflicts with corporate governance requirements
and practices under issuers' domestic laws.[142] One of the most controversial
aspects of the Sarbanes-Oxley Act is section 404, which requires annual reports
to include a report by management on the company's internal control over financial reporting and also requires the company's auditor to attest to, and report on,
management's assessment of the effectiveness of the company's internal control
over financial reporting. Producing section 404 reports is a time-consuming and
expensive exercise.[143] In principle, foreign issuers are required to comply with
section 404, but some deadlines were extended as indicated by the following table
provided by the SEC.[144]

The extension of the deadlines was linked to initiatives aimed at making it
easier for foreign issuers to terminate their obligations under US securities law.
The enactment of the Sarbanes-Oxley Act made this a more pressing concern
because the additional compliance costs that it imposed (especially with regard
to section 404 reports) affected cost-benefit calculations. It is relatively easy for
an issuer to delist its securities in the US but this does not terminate registration
and obligations that are associated with registration.[145] Until 2007 an issuer was
not entitled to terminate registration of a class of securities not listed on a US
exchange unless the class was held by fewer than 300 persons worldwide or fewer
than 300 US residents. The '300 US resident holders' test had not kept pace with

---

[141] R de la Mater, 'Recent Trends in SEC Regulation of Foreign Issuers: How the U.S. Regulatory
Regime is Affecting the United States' Historic Position as the World's Principal Capital Market'
(2006) 39 *Cornell International Law Journal* 109 provides an overview.

[142] JC Coffee, 'Racing Towards the Top?: The Impact of Cross-listings and Stock Market
Competition on International Corporate Governance' (2000) 102 *Columbia Law Review* 1757,
1757, 1824–6.

[143] One survey of 70 UK-based companies estimated that the aggregate cost of Sarbanes-Oxley
compliance for these companies could be as high as US $860m: cited in EJ Pan, 'Why the World
No Longer Puts its Stock in Us', Cardozo Legal Studies Research Paper No 176 (13 December 13,
2006) available at SSRN <http://ssrn.com/abstract=951705>.

[144] <http://www.sec.gov/news/press/2006/2006-210.htm> (accessed February 2007).

[145] R Pozen, 'Can European Companies Escape U.S. Listings?', Harvard Law and Economics
Discussion Paper No 464 (March 2004) available at SSRN <http://ssrn.com/abstract=511942>.

	Accelerated Filer Status	Revised Compliance Dates and Final Rules Regarding the Internal Control Over Financial Reporting Requirements	
		Management's Report	Auditor's Attestation
U.S. Issuer	Large Accelerated Filer OR Accelerated Filer ($75MM or more)	Already complying (Annual reports for fiscal years ending on or after November 15, 2004)	Already complying (Annual reports for fiscal years ending on or after November 15, 2004)
	Non-accelerated Filer (less than $75MM)	Annual reports for fiscal years ending on or after December 15, 2007	Annual reports for fiscal years ending on or after December 15, 2008
Foreign Issuer	Large Accelerated Filer ($700MM or more)	Annual reports for fiscal years ending on or after July 15, 2006	Annual reports for fiscal years ending on or after July 15, 2006
	Accelerated Filer ($75MM or more and less than $700MM)	Annual reports for fiscal years ending on or after July 15, 2006	Annual reports for fiscal years ending on or after July 15, 2007
	Non-accelerated Filer (less than $75MM)	Annual reports for fiscal years ending on or after December 15, 2007	Annual reports for fiscal years ending on or after December 15, 2008
U.S. or Foreign Issuer	Newly Public Company	Second Annual Report	Second Annual Report

Source: Securities and Exchange Commission, 'Further Relief from the Section 404 Requirements for Smaller Companies and Newly Public Companies', Press Release of 15 December 2006.

the internationalization of investment portfolios, which has meant that many foreign issuers have well in excess of that number of US investors. In 2007, the SEC accepted that the test was inadequate and amended its rules so as to permit foreign private issuers to deregister on the basis of specified criteria designed to measure US market interest for any class of securities by reference principally to the US trading volume of that class as compared to the trading volume in the primary trading market for that class.[146] Under the amended rules, a foreign private issuer is eligible to terminate its Exchange Act registration and reporting obligations regarding a class of equity securities if the US average daily trading volume of the class of securities has been no greater than 5 per cent of the average daily trading volume of that same class of securities on a worldwide basis during a recent 12-month period and certain other conditions are met.[147]

[146] SEC Release No 34-55005, File No S7-12-05 (22 December 2006).
[147] <http://www.sec.gov/news/press/2007/2007-55.htm> (accessed December 2007).

15

Corporate Bonds

Introduction

Bond markets are a source of debt financing for companies. The economic benefits that can flow from well-functioning corporate bond markets include:[1]

(1) diversification of sources of funds for the corporate sector, thereby making it less vulnerable to collapses in bank lending;
(2) increased choice and flexibility, which enhance the ability of firms to raise finance that is a good match for the timing and currency of their cash flows;
(3) strengthening of the balance sheets of pension funds and life insurance companies by providing institutional investors with instruments that satisfy demand for fixed-income assets with long maturities, higher returns than government bonds, and less risk than equity.

The UK Financial Services Authority (FSA) has described the bond markets as 'a core sector of the capital markets in the UK...a major financing tool for the private sector'.[2] According to Bank for International Settlements (BIS) statistics, at the end of 2005 the amount outstanding of international debt securities issued by the UK corporate sector (excluding banks and other financial institutions) stood at US$203.9 billion and the outstanding amount of UK corporate domestic debt securities was US$24.2 billion.[3] Broadly speaking, international debt securities are securities that are issued into the international marketplace and which are usually denominated in a currency other than the issuer's home currency,[4] but the BIS uses a more complex test, based on the location of the transaction, the currency of issuance, and the residence of the issuer, in compiling its data.[5] The heavy

[1] IMF, 'Global Financial Stability Report' (September 2005) ch IV (Development of Corporate Bond Markets in Emerging Countries).
[2] FSA, 'Trading Transparency in the UK Secondary Bond Markets' (Discussion Paper 05/5) para 2.3.
[3] BIS, 'Securities Statistics' (December 2005).
[4] FSA, 'Trading Transparency in the UK Secondary Bond Markets' (Discussion Paper 05/5) para 2.6.
[5] Bank for International Settlements Monetary and Economic Department, 'Guide to the International Financial Statistics', BIS Papers No 14 (February 2003) 13–14. International issues comprise all foreign currency issues by residents and non-residents in a given country and all domestic currency issues launched in the domestic market by non-residents. In addition, domestic

reliance of the UK corporate sector on the international market contrasts with the US position, where the equivalent 2005 amounts were US$27.4 (international debt securities) and US$2,695.7 (domestic debt securities);[6] this difference is readily explicable by reference to the breadth and depth of US domestic capital markets and the dollar's predominance as the currency of international finance.

Historically, the bond markets did not play a significant role in the financing of the Continental European, especially German, corporate sector[7] but political and economic developments during the 1990s, including the introduction of the euro, led to significant change.[8] Although bank lending still remains the main source of external finance in the EU,[9] euro-area issuers have increasingly sought to expand their range of funding sources by issuing bonds.[10] According to one study, the overall euro-area bond market achieved a growth rate of 283 per cent between 1994 and 2004, outstripping its US equivalent, where the market grew by 35 per cent over the same period.[11] Private-sector debt issuance in the euro-area rose from US$124 billion to US$273 billion between 1994 and 1998 and, after the introduction of the euro, increased to US$657 in 1999.[12] By 2004, private-sector bond issuance in the euro-area was about US$550 billion.[13] Going to the debt capital markets for finance allowed European corporate issuers to access new investors and diversify their liabilities. Bond issues played a significant part in the financing of the wave of mergers and acquisitions that swept across Europe in the 2000s.[14] Issuers found a rapidly growing community of investors pursuing internationally-diversified investment strategies for bonds, especially within the euro-area. In the bond markets, the traditional home bias in investment has eroded,[15] although some have suggested that it may have been replaced

currency issues launched in the domestic market by residents are also considered as international issues if they are specifically targeted at non-resident investors. The empirical classification of bond issues denominated in euros is controversial: M Pagano and EL von Thadden, 'The European Bond Markets under EMU' (2004) 20 *Oxford Review of Economic Policy* 531.

    [6] BIS, ' Securities Statistics' (December 2005).
    [7] ECB, 'The Euro Bond Market Study' (December 2004) 45, available at <http://www.ecb. int/pub/pdf/other/eurobondmarketstudy2004en.pdf> (accessed December 2007), concedes that France has had a long history of corporate bond financing (eg in September 2003 the outstanding amount of corporate bonds as a percentage of GDP in France amounted to 23%) but maintains that overall in the euro-area bank-based financing is still the dominant source of corporate finance.
    [8] Pagano and von Thadden (n 5 above); G de Bondt and JD Lichtenberger, 'The Euro Area Corporate Bond Market: Where Do We Stand Since the Introduction of the Euro?' (2003) 4 *European Business Organization Law Review* 517.
    [9] European Commission, 'Financial Integration Monitor 2004' (SEC (2004) 559) 3.
    [10] ECB, 'The Euro Bond Market Study' (December 2004) 21–2. The euro-area embraces the major Continental European economies, such as France, Germany, Italy, and Spain.
    [11] JP Casey and K Lannoo, 'Europe's Hidden Capital Markets', Centre for European Policy Studies (Brussels, 2005) 8.
    [12] Pagano and von Thadden (n 5 above).
    [13] ibid.
    [14] ECB, 'The Euro Bond Market Study' (December 2004) 22.
    [15] European Commission, 'Financial Integration Monitor 2004' (SEC (2004) 559) 9.

with a euro-area home bias.[16] The financial services industry responded quickly to new business opportunities and helped to push forward changes in the market through more aggressive competition for underwriting and other intermediary services and the provision of more standardized electronic trading services.[17] One illustration of the changes in the market for the provision of intermediary services is that in the six-year period from 1995 to 2001, US investment banks increased their market share of euro-denominated bond underwriting business from 2 per cent to 32 per cent,[18] and underwriting fees became much lower.[19] Continuous product development, including innovative asset-backed securitization structures and credit derivative products, also played a role in broadening and deepening the European corporate debt market.[20]

The emergence of the euro-denominated bond market is a major indication of the changing European environment for corporate finance. The origins of this market were in the redenomination of bonds from former national currencies into euros at the beginning of monetary union but the market has since become much larger and more liquid.[21] Public and private-sector bodies, from both within and outside the euro-area, can issue euro-denominated bonds. Banks and other financial institutions are the dominant group of private-sector issuers of euro-denominated bonds.[22] Financial institutions issue numerous different types of bonds, from straightforward unsecured bonds through to complex asset-backed securities that enable them to remove risk from their balance sheets.[23] At present, private-sector bonds by issuers outside the financial sector constitute only a small percentage of the total volume of euro-denominated debt,[24] but the rate of growth is significant: in the period from the end of 1998 to the end of 2003, the outstanding volume of euro-denominated corporate bonds grew by 95 per cent compared to a growth rate of only 37 per cent in the case of financial sector bonds (excluding covered bonds).[25] There is a significant presence of non-euro-area issuers

[16] L Baele, A Ferrando, P Hördhal, E Krylova, and C Monnet, 'Measuring Financial Integration in the Euro Area', ECB Occasional Paper Series (No 14) (April 2004) 54; ECB, 'The Euro Bond Market Study' (December 2004), 5.

[17] Pagano and von Thadden (n 5 above).

[18] European Commission, 'Financial Integration Monitor 2004' (SEC (2004) 559) 14.

[19] ibid 16.

[20] ECB, 'The Euro Bond Market Study' (December 2004) 6.

[21] ibid 8.

[22] Based on the European Commission's Directorate-General for Economic and Financial Affairs regular statistics and other information on developments in the euro-denominated bond markets. The data includes the volumes of debt issued, the maturity structures, and the conditions in the market. This data is available at <http://ec.europa.eu/economy_finance/publications/publ_list 2007.htm> (accessed December 2007).

[23] ECB, 'The Euro Bond Market Study' (December 2004) 24–5.

[24] 7% in 2005 according to the European Commission's Directorate-General for Economic and Financial Affairs data, noted above (n 22).

[25] ECB, 'The Euro Bond Market Study' (December 2004) 25. Covered bonds are bonds used by banks to refinance loans secured by mortgages or loans to the public sector. They differ from securitization structures because, broadly speaking, they do not shift risk from the balance sheet. They are most commonly issued by German banks but there is also significant issuance by banks

(mainly from the UK and the US) in the euro-denominated corporate bond market, reflecting the euro's increasing importance as an international currency.[26] The European Central Bank (ECB) has suggested two reasons why the role of the debt capital markets in the financing of the corporate sector may become increasingly significant: first, the new supervisory rules of Basel II may make bank loans more expensive and thus intensify disintermediation tendencies in the financial sector; and, secondly, the pool of investors will be enlarged as the problems of ageing societies become more immediate and the pension systems in many European countries move towards funded pension plans.[27]

Institutional investors are the major investors in bonds and they are especially dominant in the UK market.[28] Direct retail investment in bonds is rare historically in the UK but more common elsewhere in Europe, with, for example, direct investment in bonds estimated to account for 42 per cent of total Italian retail savings and investments during 2003.[29] In the UK, retail investor interest in the bond markets is growing.[30] In recent years, hedge funds have played an increasingly significant role in the burgeoning European debt capital market.[31]

Law and the development of corporate bond markets in Europe

The creation of a fully integrated internal financial market is a major policy objective for the EU. So far it is in bond markets that there has been the most significant progress towards the achievement of that goal.[32] The introduction of the euro provided a catalyst for bond market integration, first in relation to sovereign

in other Continental European countries. 2003 saw the start of covered bond issuance by Irish and UK banks (ibid 38–9).

[26] ibid 29. However, others are rather sceptical about the importance of the euro-denominated market for non-European corporates: J Gregson, 'Adapting to the Euro' (2005–2006) *International Capital Market* 89.

[27] ECB, 'The Euro Bond Market Study' (December 2004) 23.

[28] FSA, 'Trading Transparency in the UK Secondary Bond Markets', Discussion Paper 05/5, paras 2.12–2.13. See also IOSCO, 'Transparency of Bond Markets', Report of the Technical Committee of the International Organization of Securities Commissions (May 2004) section B.2, available at <http://www.iosco.org/library/pubdocs/pdf/IOSCOPD168.pdf> (accessed December 2007).

[29] FSA, 'Trading Transparency in the UK Secondary Bond Markets', Discussion Paper 05/5, para 2.14.

[30] H McKenzie, 'The Lure of Steady Returns' (2005–2006) *International Capital Market* 85.

[31] Bond Market Association, 'Primary Market Survey' (2006) reported that hedge funds were contributing an average of nearly 14% of total investment across the asset classes but were most heavily invested in high yield bonds. This report is accessible at <http://archives1-sifma.org/story.asp?id=2653> (accessed December 2007).

[32] 'With regard to the euro-denominated bond market, a relatively high degree of integration can be observed': ECB, 'The Euro Bond Market Study' (December 2004) 7. See also, M Pagano, and EL von Thadden, 'The European Bond Markets under EMU' (2004) 20 *Oxford Review of Economic Policy* 531; JP Casey and K Lannoo, 'Europe's Hidden Capital Markets', Centre for European Policy Studies (Brussels, 2005).

debt but thereafter spreading into the private sector.[33] The significance of the part played in stimulating bond market development by the major EU legislative programme for the regulation of financial markets—which began in 1979, intensified significantly around the turn of the century, and now extends far beyond merely removing barriers to cross-border economic activity—is more debatable.[34] Ragan and Zingales, for example, suggest that the shift in the European financial system towards a more market-based approach is attributable to a fortunate coincidence of favourable international conditions (an increase in international trade and capital movements), economic conditions (improvements in processing and transmission of information that have made arm's-length markets more efficient), and local political conditions (the transition from separate national governments to a more unified European government).[35] As discussed later in this chapter, changes in EC law have led to some market innovations but not always in the way that the designers of the laws may have intended.

Terms of bonds[36]

Bonds generally have three basic features—the par value (which will normally also be the redemption value), the interest rate, (or coupon), and the length of time to maturity—but these can be freely added to or varied, so as most effectively to meet particular investor preferences and market conditions at the time of issue. Accounting and regulatory considerations can have a significant impact on the terms included in bond issues, as in the case of some hybrid securities, which are debt instruments that replicate some features of equity so as to be treated as equity for accounting purposes or to be classified as equity for the purposes of capital adequacy requirements applying to financial institutions.[37] Another relevant factor can be the views of rating agencies, which perform a valuable information gathering, evaluation, and dissemination function by assigning ratings to many bonds when they are issued. Documentation provisions can affect the rating assigned to a particular issue of bonds and may result in a difference between the rating applied to the issue and the general credit rating applied to the issuer.[38]

---

[33] Pagano and von Thadden (n 32 above).

[34] Casey and Lannoo (n 32 above) ch 3.

[35] R Rajan and L Zingales, 'Banks and Markets: The Changing Character of European Finance', in V Gaspar, P Hartmann, P and O Sleijpen (eds), *The Transformation of the European Financial System* (Frankfurt: ECB,2003) 124.

[36] This section draws on FSA, 'Trading Transparency in the UK Secondary Bond Markets', Discussion Paper 05/5, para 2.4.

[37] Herbert Smith, 'Hybrid Capital for Corporates' (March 2006) available at <http://www.herbert-smith.com/NR/rdonlyres/8571D1F7-8E21-4CA5-A9BC-FA8FF568F0B0/1880/DCM_hybrid_capital_for_corporates_Mar06.html>(accessed December 2007); J Leavy and F Nizard, 'How Hybrid Capital Rules Help French Issuers' (2005) 24(11) *International Financial Law Review* 47.

[38] Fitch Ratings, 'Jumping The Queue: Ineffective European Bond Documentation's Negative Pledge and Structural Subordination-Related Provisions: Ratings Cliffs Waiting to Happen', European Corporates Special Report (2003).

An illustration of the importance of the role played by rating agencies in driving the structure of bond issue documentation is provided by the development of the European market for corporate hybrid bonds, which began around 2003 but took off significantly in 2005 after the rating agencies clarified their methodologies for rating these instruments.[39]

Interest

Fixed rates of interest are common: for instance, in 2003 more than 80 per cent of the newly issued euro-denominated corporate bonds were fixed-rate coupon bonds, which was consistent with the pattern in recent previous years.[40] Floating rate bonds, where the coupon is set at a predetermined margin above a specified money market rate, are also possible, as are deep discount bonds, which typically offer a zero coupon but allow the investor to make a return by acquiring the securities at a significant discount to their redemption price. Another possibility is the step-up bond, which gives investors a higher coupon after an initial period. The step-up may be coupled with an issuer call option to enable the issuer to redeem the bond before it matures; the increase in the interest charge will act as an incentive for the issuer to exercise that option. Ordinarily, interest on bonds is payable whether or not the issuer is profitable but in some types of hybrid bonds, which seek to replicate equity instruments, interest payments may be deferred until maturity in certain circumstances, such as where certain preset financial ratios are not met.[41]

Maturity

Most bonds have an original maturity of at least a year, but this can range up to thirty years, and beyond for some issues. Hybrid bonds may have a very long maturity or be perpetual, so as to replicate the permanence which is a feature of equity capital.[42] Issuer call options are likely to be included in long-dated bonds so as to bolster their appeal to investors. Bonds increasingly include bondholder put options, which allow bondholders to force redemption in certain circumstances, such as a change of ownership or a restructuring event within the issuer that triggers a ratings downgrade.[43]

---

[39] D Andrews, 'Corporate Hybrids Edge Towards Mainstream' (2006) 25(3) *International Financial Law Review* 7; B Maiden, 'Moody's Defends Hybrid Securities' (2006) 25(4) *International Financial Law Review* 68.

[40] ECB, 'The Euro Bond Market Study' (December 2004) 29.

[41] Herbert Smith, 'Hybrid Capital for Corporates' (March 2006) (n 37 above).

[42] ibid.

[43] Fitch Ratings, 'Jumping The Queue: Ineffective European Bond Documentation's Negative Pledge and Structural Subordination-Related Provisions: Ratings Cliffs Waiting to Happen', *European Corporates Special Report* (2003) 3.

Ranking

Corporate bonds are normally unsecured. A major exception is the securitization, including the collateralized debt obligations(CDOs), segment of the market: bonds issued by special purpose vehicles that are secured on a pool of income-producing assets, such as mortgages, leases, credit card debts, bonds, or loans.[44] Collateralized bond issues tend to involve several tranches of debt with 'senior secured' securities on top, followed by 'second lien' securities, and then more 'junior' securities.[45] Unsecured bonds may also be subordinated so as to rank behind other unsecured debts in the event of the issuer's insolvency. Subordination is a feature of hybrid bonds that seek to mimic equity instruments whilst retaining the favourable tax deductibility status of debt. Historically, there was some doubt about the legal effectiveness under English law of contractual subordination of unsecured debt and rather complex structures were developed to safeguard against that legal risk.[46] However, concerns have receded because straightforward subordination clauses have been upheld in recent cases.[47] In particular circumstances, more complex subordination structures may still be employed, such as where multiple layers of unsecured subordination are sought.[48]

Covenants

The covenants that are included in bond issues tend to be less extensive than in term loans.[49] This aspect of bond market practice is related to the obvious practical problems that would be involved in seeking the consent of a large, dispersed group of investors for changes to covenants that prove to be unduly restrictive.[50] Some have gone as far as to suggest that covenants written into public debt instruments are virtually impossible to renegotiate with the consequence that all but the

---

[44] ECB, 'The Euro Bond Market Study' (December 2004) 41–2.

[45] S Whitehead, 'Managing Demand for Debt Puts Documentation Issues in the Spotlight' (2006) 25(1) *International Financial Law Review Private Equity Supplement* 17; G Fuller and F Ranero, 'Collateralised Debt Obligations' (2005) 20(9) *Butterworths Journal of International Banking and Financial Law* 343.

[46] E Ferran, *Company Law and Corporate Finance* (OUP, 1999) ch 16.

[47] *Manning v AIG Europe UK Ltd* [2006] Ch 610, CA; *Re Maxwell Communications Corporation plc* [1993] 1 WLR 1402.

[48] eg a trust may be used in a turnover subordination where the junior creditor is permitted to prove in the liquidation of the debtor but is required to account to specified senior creditors for liquidation dividends. By requiring the junior creditor to hold the liquidation dividends on trust, the arrangement is shielded from the effects of the junior creditor's own insolvency.

[49] WW Bratton, 'Bond Covenants and Creditor Protection: Economics and Law, Theory and Practice, Substance and Process' (2006) 9 European Business Organization Law Review 39. However, note the increasing use of 'covenant lite' loan agreements in private equity deals in 2007, where some loan deals contained the lighter covenants more usually associated with bond issues: (Q2 2007) *Bank of England Quarterly Bulletin* .

[50] PR Wood, *International Loans, Bonds, Guarantees, Legal Opinions* (Sweet & Maxwell, 2nd edn, 2007) ch 5.

standard boilerplate covenants are useless in the public debt market.[51] Structures have evolved to mitigate the problem of having to negotiate with a large number of bondholders. In UK market practice, this typically involves the appointment of a trustee which is empowered to make certain, usually largely immaterial, changes to the bond issue terms and which is responsible for convening meetings of bondholders to consider matters affecting their interests, including changes to the terms, and for taking enforcement action in response to the occurrence of an event of default.[52] The appointment of a trustee for a bond issue is not, however, mandatory under English law.[53]

Common types of protective covenants in bonds in US public markets are restrictions on additional debt, payout constraints, asset sale restrictions, investment restrictions, restrictions on mergers, negative pledges, and restrictions on transactions with affiliates.[54]

Historically, sterling and euro-denominated bonds have tended to include comparatively less covenant protection.[55] The presence of mandatory legal capital rules in Europe that constrain payouts may go some way towards explaining this.[56] Where negative pledge covenants are used they often have limitations, such as carve-outs permitting the creation of security at subsidiary level or allowing

---

[51] MH Bradley and MR Roberts, 'The Structure and Pricing of Corporate Debt Covenants' (13 May 2004) available at SSRN <http://ssrn.com/abstract=466240>.

[52] On the position of the trustee with regard to enforcement, see *Concord Trust v Law Debenture Trust Corp plc* [2005] 2 Lloyd's Rep 221, HL. Financial Markets Law Committee, 'Trustee Exemption Clauses' Issue No 62 (May 2004), ch 2 gives an outline of the variety of transactions in which trusts are used in the financial markets and a brief description of the role of the trustee in each case. Ch 3 looks specifically at the role of the trustee in international bond issues. Ch 4 provides some sample clauses. This paper is available at <http://www.fmlc.org/papers/trustee_exemption_clauses_issue62.pdf> (accessed December 2007).
See also P Rawlings, 'The Changing Role of the Trustee in International Bond Issues' [2007] JBL 43.

[53] cf the mandatory requirements under the US Trust Indenture Act 1939.

[54] N Reisel, 'On the Value of Restrictive Covenants: An Empirical Investigation of Public Bond Issues' (January 2007). available at SSRN <http://ssrn.com/abstract=644522>; WW Bratton, 'Bond Covenants and Creditor Protection: Economics and Law, Theory and Practice, Substance and Process' (2006) 9 *European Business Organization Law Review* 39; M Kahan and B Tuckman, 'Private Versus Public Lending: Evidence from Covenants' in JD Finnerty and MS Fridson (eds), *The Yearbook of Fixed Income Investing 1995* (Irwin Professional Publishing, 1996) 253 comparing covenants in private and public debt; K Lehn and A Poulsen, 'Contractual Resolution of Bondholder-Stockholder Conflicts in Leveraged Buyouts' (1991) 34 *Journal of Law and Economics* 645; CW Smith, Jr and JB Warner, 'On Financial Contracting: An Analysis of Bond Covenants' (1979) 7 *Journal of Financial Economics* 117.

[55] A study of 439 international bonds launched by 146 non-financial UK based companies during 1986 to 1999 found that protective provisions were included in the bonds of only 3% of higher credit quality firms included but that the figure rose to 31% in lower quality firms: M do Rosario Correia, SC Linn, and A Marshall, 'An Empirical Investigation of Debt Contract Design: The Determinants of the Choice of Debt Terms in Eurobond Issues', FEP Working Paper No 148, Faculdade de Economia do Porto (June 2004) available at <http://www.fep.up.pt/investigacao/workingpapers/WP148Rosario.pdf> (accessed December 2007).

[56] See ch 7 above.

security for specified types of new indebtedness or within certain parameters, that undermine their usefulness.[57] In 2003 the rating agency, Fitch Ratings, published a research paper exposing what it saw as deficiencies in European bond market practice with regard to the drafting of conventional negative pledge covenants.[58] The Fitch paper was also critical of market practice on covenants restricting new debt at subsidiary level. For subsidiaries of an issuer of bonds to be free to incur new debt is potentially harmful to the bondholders because the parent's claims, as shareholder, to the subsidiary's assets rank behind (or, putting it another way, are structurally subordinated to) those of the subsidiaries' creditors. Fitch's overall assessment was that Continental European bond issuers often offered a much weaker covenant package than their counterparts elsewhere.[59]

Around the same time as the Fitch paper, a major group of investors[60] launched its own initiative to bring what it saw as comparatively poor disclosure and documentation standards in both the sterling and euro markets more into line with those in the US.[61] That group identified three structural features that it would like to see as standard practice in investment grade bond issues: a bondholder put option linked to change of control and rating downgrade; a strong negative pledge provision with many fewer restrictions and carve-outs; and an effective covenant against disposal of assets. However, later dialogue between representatives of institutional investors, intermediaries, and issuers moved the debate away from seeking harmonized standards and towards greater education about the scope of typical covenants and promoting ways of flagging the key features in covenants so that the market would be better able to judge their implications and value.[62] This shift may to some extent have been influenced by the economic conditions of the period, which included a strong flow of funds into the European debt capital markets and a growing divergence in the calibre of European issuers, a segment which had, historically, been dominated by investment-grade issuers. In overall terms, the proportion of 'junk' bonds in issue—ie high yield bonds with low credit ratings—is lower in Europe than it is in the US,[63] but, with a boom in leveraged buyout activity and with more investors searching for higher

---

[57] Fitch Ratings, 'Jumping The Queue: Ineffective European Bond Documentation's Negative Pledge and Structural Subordination-Related Provisions: Ratings Cliffs Waiting to Happen', *European Corporates Special Report* (2003), 3–4.

[58] ibid.

[59] ibid.

[60] Estimated to represent about one-quarter of the US$980bn Eurobond market: R Mannix, 'Investors Push for Rewrite of Eurobond Covenants' (2003) 22(11) *International Financial Law Review* 33.

[61] 'Improving Market Standards in the Sterling and Euro Fixed Income Credit Markets' (October 2003), available at <http://www.treasurers.org/technical/papers/resources/credit-code2003.pdf> (accessed December 2007).

[62] ABI/BVI, 'Bond Dialogue Conclusions' (April 2006) available at <http://www.treasurers.org/purchase/customcf/download.cfm?resid=1858> (accessed December 2007).

[63] 10% of the corporate bond market, compared with around 40% in the US: ECB, 'The Euro Bond Market Study' (December 2004) 25.

yields than on investment-grade securities, the market was growing at a significant rate in the mid-2000s. Some professional investors may have been happy to
trade weak covenant protection for higher yields but, arguably, the unprecedented
flow of funds into the markets and the increasing competition among investment
banks for underwriting mandates, led to undue relaxation of market discipline
and resulted in the unwarranted persistence of inferior documentation.[64]

However, one area where documentation tightened up during that period was
in relation to change of control bondholder put options, which became more
common in bonds issued by large investment-grade issuers during the 2000s.[65]
These can be seen as provisions that protect existing bondholders from prejudicial consequences of a buyout, which will usually be that the issuer is saddled
with repayment obligations in respect of the acquisition financing and its existing
bonds are downgraded. It is, of course, also possible to view them as anti-takeover
shielding mechanisms that favour the existing management but it would be contrary to company law for an issuer's management to structure a bond issue to
achieve this goal rather than to promote the success of the company.

Conversion rights

Restrictive covenants limit the future actions of the issuer and thereby protect
bondholders from opportunistic conduct by management and controlling shareholders. An alternative mechanism for protecting bondholders from conduct that
is favourable to shareholders but potentially disadvantageous for them is provisions for conversion.[66] Conversion terms entitle bondholders to force conversion
of their debt instruments into equity securities of the issuer or of another company in its group.[67] Empirical data provides some evidence of conversion mechanisms and restrictive covenants acting as substitutes for each other.[68]

Convertible bonds work by giving the holder the option to convert the bonds
into a fixed number of shares at a conversion price which is determined at the

---

[64] E Russell-Walling, 'Bigger LBOs and Decline of House Banking Drive European Market'
(2005–2006) *International Capital Market* 65 quoting C Dammers, head of regulatory policy at
the International Capital Market Association as saying that: 'Deals are getting bigger and more
investors want to buy—but looser documentation is part of the price they are paying. In the mature
US market, high-yield investors protect themselves. Here it may take some serious losses before
investors focus on this issue.'

[65] M Hartley, 'Beyond Change of Control' 21(11) *Butterworths Journal of International
Banking and Financial Law* 475.

[66] M Jensen and W Meckling, 'Theory of the Firm: Managerial Behavior, Agency Costs and
Ownership Structure' (1976) 3 *Journal of Financial Economics* 305; CW Smith, Jr and JB Warner,
'On Financial Contracting: An Analysis of Bond Covenants' (1979) 7 *Journal of Financial
Economics* 117.

[67] Similar to convertible bonds are exchangeable bonds, which are exchangeable into shares
of another company, which need not be part of the bond issuer's corporate group: M Asmar and
J Cowan, 'Convertible and Exchangeable Bonds' (2001) 12(5) *Practical Law for Companies* 21.

[68] M Kahan and D Yermack, 'Investment Opportunities and the Design of Debt Securities'
(1998) 14 *Journal of Law, Economics and Organization* 136.

time of issue of the bonds. The conversion price is typically at a significant premium (around 25 to 30 per cent) to the market price of the shares at the time of issue. The coupon on convertible bonds tends to be lower than on plain bonds of the same issuer because investors can trade interest expectations against the benefit of equity linkage. Should the market price of the conversion shares fail to rise to a level that makes the conversion price commercially attractive, bondholders can retain the bond and are not obliged to exercise the option to convert. Exercise of the conversion option has the effect of releasing the debt and converting it into equity capital. A variant on the convertible bond structure is the bond with warrant, which gives investors a debt instrument and also an entitlement to subscribe for shares. The warrant is usually detachable from the bond and can be traded separately; exercise of the warrant results in an injection of new equity capital and the bonds remain in issue.

Publicly issued convertible bonds usually contain special covenants that are intended to protect bondholders against actions by the issuer that would dilute the economic value of the conversion option.[69] Dilution could result from actions that result in value leaving the company, such as distributions to existing shareholders or disposals of assets at an undervalue. An issue of new shares could also cause economic dilution where the offer price of the shares is at a significant discount to the market price because the aggregate assets of the issuer would not increase sufficiently to compensate for the additional number of shares in issue. Capital reorganizations, such as share splits, could also be prejudicial to convertible bondholders, as where, for example, a company sub-divides its shares, but the conversion price remains unchanged—in effect the bondholder would have to pay the 'full' price for only part of the original assets. In overall terms, anti-dilution provisions will address voluntary action by the issuer of the bonds that could decrease the value of the equity into which the bonds are to be converted.[70] Catering for some possible future events, such as share splits, is a relatively straightforward matter of making mechanical adjustments but other possible future events can present more complex drafting challenges as well as questions of principle about how restrictive the covenants should be.[71] In publicly issued convertible bonds, anti-dilution provisions are usually limited to voluntary corporate actions in which there are clear agency problems flowing from divergence of interests between shareholders, and bondholders: thus, typically, rights issues, bonus issues, disposals of assets to shareholders and so forth, are addressed but not transactions with outsiders in the ordinary

---

[69] MA Woronoff and JA Rosen, 'Understanding Anti-dilution Provisions in Convertible Securities' (2005) 74 *Fordham Law Review* 129, 133; M Kahan, 'Anti-dilution Provisions in Convertible Securities' (1995) 2 *Stanford Journal of Law, Business and Finance* 147; PR Wood, 'International Convertible Bond Issues' [1986] *Journal of International Banking Law* 69.

For an overview of formulae used in anti-dilution covenants, see Asmar and Cowan (n 67 above) 27.

[70] Woronoff and Rosen (n 69 above) 133.

[71] SI Glover, 'Solving Dilution Problems' (1996) 51 *Business Lawyer* 1241.

course of business.[72] Furthermore, convertible bonds do not usually provide for adjustment on the payment of ordinary cash dividends or straightforward share buy-backs, as such restrictions would hamper routine corporate activity.[73]

Takeovers leading to the end of an active market in the shares into which bonds are convertible represent a significant potential threat to the interests of convertible bondholders. There are various ways in which the terms of the bonds can safeguard against this risk, such as by permitting bondholders to convert their bonds at an adjusted conversion price on a change of control of the issuer or to exercise a put option, or by imposing an obligation on the issuer to procure that the bidder extends its offer to the bondholders. Under the UK City Code on Takeovers and Mergers, contractual provisions in bond terms are bolstered by a specific requirement whereby a bidder is obliged to make an appropriate offer or proposal to the bondholders to ensure that their interests are safeguarded and that they receive equal treatment.[74]

Structure of bond issues

Various parties are usually involved in a bond issue, including, as well as the issuer, a lead manager to coordinate arrangements among the managers of the issue for the subscription and distribution of the bonds, a trustee to act as the intermediary between the issuer and the bondholders, a listing agent to assist with the listing process (for bonds that are to be admitted to listing), and fiscal, or paying, agents through which are channelled interest and other payments to bondholders and which, in the case of convertible bonds, will have responsibility for conversion mechanics.[75] The documents will include a subscription agreement, which is the agreement in which the managers agree to purchase the bonds and the issuer agrees to issue them, a trust deed, and a paying agency agreement.[76] There will also be an offering circular, the contents and arrangements for approval of which will depend on whether the mandatory requirements for prospectuses relating to public offers or admission of securities to trading on a regulated market are applicable.

In committing their company to a bond issue, the responsible officers of the issuer must, of course, ensure that they are acting within their authority and in accordance with their duties. Particular restrictions that need to be checked are borrowing limits in articles, which limit the debt that the directors can add to

---

[72] If the terms of the bonds include an investor put option this may be triggered by an extraordinary transaction, such as the sale or cessation of the principal part of the issuer's business followed by a credit rating downgrade.

[73] Asmar and Cowan (n 67 above) 27 note the extension of protective provisions to special (ie exception one-off) cash dividends and share repurchases at a significant premium.

[74] Rule 15.

[75] Asmar and Cowan (n 67 above); A Carmichael and T Wells, 'Eurobonds' (1996) 7(7) *Practical Law for Companies* 41.

[76] ibid.

the capital structure without reverting to the shareholders for approval, and covenants in existing loans whereby lenders limit the amount of additional debt that can be taken on. Issues of equity-linked debt, such as convertible bonds, also attract company law requirements that are protective of existing shareholders. These are, first, that directors must be specifically authorized, either by the company's articles or an ordinary resolution of the shareholders, to allot shares or securities with equity subscription or conversion rights.[77] An allotment authority must state the maximum number of shares that may be allotted, which, in the case of equity-linked securities, means the maximum number of shares that may be allotted pursuant to the subscription or conversion rights.[78] The authority must also specify an expiry date, which must be not more than five years from the date when it is given.[79] The allotment of shares on the exercise of subscription or conversion rights does not, however, need to be separately authorized and may take place after the authority for the issue of the equity-linked securities has expired.[80] Secondly, equity-linked securities are 'equity securities' for the purposes of statutory pre-emption rights, which means that prima facie equity-linked securities must be offered first to existing shareholders.[81] Pre-emption rights may, however, be disapplied, usually by special resolution.[82] Ordinary resolutions authorizing directors within limits to allot shares and equity-linked securities and special resolutions disapplying within limits pre-emption rights are routine, but would need to be carefully checked to ensure that a proposed bond issue does not exceed the limits. Another company law point that may be noted in relation to equity-linked securities is the rule that shares may not be allotted at less than their nominal value, which could be infringed, for instance, by the issue of a convertible bond at a discount to its nominal value of £1 which entitles the holder immediately to convert it into a £1 nominal value share.[83] However, this point is unlikely to have much practical significance because shares tend to trade at a price which is far in excess of their par value and the conversion price is set by reference to, and above, the market price of the shares. Company law rules on the valuation of non-cash consideration[84] do not apply where convertible bonds are converted into shares of the issuer of the bonds because, technically, the shares are issued for cash in this case;[85] but they would need to be considered where bonds are convertible into newly-issued shares of, say, the parent company of the issuer of the bonds.[86]

---

[77] Companies Act 2006, s 551 (replacing Companies Act 1985, s 80). The text assumes that the issuer is a public company.

[78] ibid s 551(3)(a) and (6).

[79] ibid s 551(3)(b).

[80] ibid s 551(7).

[81] ibid s 561. For the meaning of equity securities see Companies Act 2006, s 560.

[82] ibid ss 570–571.

[83] *Mosely v Koffyfontein Mines* [1904] 2 Ch 108, CA.

[84] Companies Act 2006, s 593.

[85] ibid s 583(3)(c) provides that shares are deemed paid up in cash where the consideration is a release of a liability of the company for a liquidated sum.

[86] In this case, the liability released belongs to the subsidiary rather than the parent which is issuing the shares and therefore s 583(3)(c) is not satisfied.

Issuance and trading of bonds

Bond issues may listed or unlisted. A factor that is relevant to the decision of whether or not to list is that listing may attract institutional investors that are subject to regulatory constraints that limit their holdings of unlisted securities. The London Stock Exchange and the Luxembourg Stock Exchange dominate the market for listing of international bond issuance activity in Europe.[87] Secondary market trading of bonds, including listed bonds, generally takes place outside exchanges.[88] Multilateral electronic trading systems have grown in importance in Europe, especially in relation to secondary market trading of government bonds.[89] Clearing and settlement services for the international bond markets in Europe are provided primarily by Euroclear Bank SA/NV,[90] and Clearstream, which is part of the Deutsche Börse Group.[91] Bonds may be issued in bearer or registered form. Bonds issued in bearer form will normally take the form of a single global bond which is held by a common depositary for both Euroclear and Clearstream. Bondholders hold their bonds through participants in Euroclear and Clearstream; participants are institutions that have their own accounts to trade and settle through these systems. Bonds may be issued in registered form to appeal to particular investors that are subject to regulatory requirements that restrict the sale to them of bearer bonds.[92] Where bonds are issued in registered form, arrangements can be made for them to be traded through Euroclear and Clearstream, which are paperless systems.[93]

Regulation of the issuance process

In 1963, the US government introduced a tax regime that discouraged foreign issuers from raising dollar-denominated finance directly from US investors. This

[87] JP Casey and K Lannoo, 'Europe's Hidden Capital Markets', Centre for European Policy Studies (Brussels, 2005) 33.
[88] ibid, 49–53.
[89] ECB, 'The Euro Bond Market Study' (December 2004) 30–36. The effects of electronization of secondary trading are less marked in relation to corporate bonds but are beginning to take effect especially for highly rated issues: Casey and Lannoo (n 87 above) 42 and 49.
[90] <http://www.euroclear.com>.
[91] <http://www.clearstream.com>.
On both Euroclear and Clearstream, see The Giovannini Group, 'Cross-Border Clearing and Settlement Arrangements in the European Union' (Brussels, November 2001) 30, available at (accessed December 2007)
[92] <http://ec.europa.eu/internal_market/financial-markets/docs/clearing/first_giovannini_report_en.pdf> eg under the US Tax Equity and Fiscal Responsibility Act 1982 debt securities in bearer form cannot be sold in the US as part of their initial issue without incurring significant tax penalties.
[93] M Asmar and J Cowan, 'Convertible and Exchangeable Bonds' (2001) 12(5) *Practical Law for Companies* 21.

step was a catalyst for the development in Europe of an offshore market for US dollar-denominated bonds, which was originally known as the 'eurobond' bond but which has since come to be known as the international securities market. The international securities market has become a very successful and economically significant part of the European economy. It now provides a facility for public and private-sector issuers around the world to raise capital in many different currencies by issuing a diverse range of financial instruments.[94] The origins of the international securities market, as an entrepreneurial response by sophisticated practitioners to an opportunity created by a restrictive regulatory step, and its inherently international character influenced the way in which the regulatory system responded to it. It has been suggested that the 'hidden' nature of the market—with trading taking place off-exchange—meant that in its early days it largely escaped the attention of national regulators within Europe, who were, understandably, more concerned with activities that could more directly affect retail investor protection in local, domestic markets.[95] Initiatives at national and at Community level to upgrade securities market regulation brought the international securities market onto the regulatory radar screen during the 1980s but, broadly speaking, it continued to enjoy light-touch regulation, a stance that could be justified in policy terms because issuers tended to be public authorities and highly-rated private sector entities, and investors tended to be sophisticated professionals who could be expected to look after themselves. The adoption of the Financial Services Action Plan (FSAP) by the European Commission marked the start of a more interventionist phase at EU level in relation to the regulation of financial markets generally and led to the adoption of a series of new EU-wide laws affecting the issuance and trading of securities.[96] The potentially adverse impact of rigid regulatory requirements on the international securities market received considerable attention during the passage of those laws through the Community's law-making processes and certain modifications were made so as not to disrupt its operation unduly. However, it is open to question whether the modifications fully achieve this goal.

The Prospectus Directive,[97] which was adopted in 2003 and was due for implementation into Member States' national laws by July 2005, now sets the pan-European framework for prospectus disclosure.[98] The general scheme is that a prospectus must be published when securities are offered to the public or admitted to trading on a regulated market. The contents of a prospectus are exhaustively prescribed by Community law and Member States do not have discretion

---

[94] P Krijgsman, 'A Brief History: IPMA's Role in Harmonising International Capital Markets 1984–1994', International Primary Market Association, London (2000).

[95] ibid.

[96] See generally, E Ferran, *Building an EU Securities Market* (CUP, 2004).

[97] Directive (EC) 2003/71 of the European Parliament and of the Council of 4 November 2003 on the prospectus to be published when securities are offered to the public or admitted to trading and amending Directive (EC) 2001/34, [2003] OJ L345/64.

[98] See generally, Ferran (n 96 above) ch 5; see also chs 13 and 14 of this book.

to set additional 'super-equivalent' prospectus disclosure requirements. Some incorporation of information by reference is permitted. Subject to certain transitional arrangements, financial information in a prospectus must be compiled in accordance with International Financial Reporting Standards (IFRS) or, for foreign (non-EU) issuers, in accordance with another accounting system, so long as it has been deemed 'equivalent' to IFRS by the EU.[99] A prospectus must be approved before publication by the issuer's home state securities regulator; for EU issuers, the home state is the state of their registered office and for non-EU issuers it is the state that they have chosen as their EU home state by offering securities or having them admitted to trading on a regulated market in that jurisdiction (but once that choice is made by a non-EU issuer it cannot subsequently be changed for new issues). An approved prospectus can be used throughout the EU without any need to obtain local approvals from host state regulators. A prospectus can be in the form of a single document or separate documents comprising a registration statement, a securities note, and (where relevant) a summary. Base prospectuses are allowed for non-equity securities, including warrants in any form, issued under an offering programme.[100] Where securities are offered cross-border, the whole prospectus need not be translated into local languages so long as it is written in a language customary in the sphere of international finance, such as English.

This scheme is modified for debt securities, and some equity and equity-linked securities, in the following ways. First, the requirement to publish a prospectus does not apply to certain offers of debt or equity securities (assuming the securities are not also being admitted to trading on a regulated market).[101] The category of excluded unlisted offers includes offers to 'qualified investors',[102] offers to fewer than 100 people per Member State (other than qualified investors),[103] offers of large denominated securities (minimum €50,000),[104] and offers with high minimum subscriptions (minimum €50,000 per investor).[105]

Reliance on a high monetary threshold (€50,000) as a *de facto* mechanism for excluding the general public from wholesale issues that are not supported by the full range of retail investor protection requirements is also the basis of

---

[99] Commission Regulation (EC) 809/2004 of 29 April 2004 implementing Directive (EC) 2003/71 of the European Parliament and of the Council as regards information contained in prospectuses as well as the format, incorporation by reference and publication of such prospectuses and dissemination of advertisements [2004] OJ L149/1, Annex 1, para 20.1.

[100] Prospectus Directive, Art 5(4).

[101] ibid Art 3(2).

[102] ibid Art 3(2)(a). Qualified investors include financial industry firms, governments and central banks, and large corporates; Member States have the option to treat certain sophisticated individuals and also certain SMEs as qualified investors if they so request (Prospectus Directive, Art 2(1)(e) and (f) and Art 2(2).

[103] ibid Art 3(2)(b).

[104] ibid Art 3(2)(c).

[105] ibid Art 3(2)(d).

the second modification.[106] Where a prospectus is required—such as where securities are to be admitted to trading on a regulated market (as they may well be in order to enhance their attractiveness to regulated institutional investors)— the prospectus content requirements are modified in certain respects. The most important difference[107] is that the requirement to give financial information drawn up under IFRS, or an equivalent set of accounting standards, is disapplied for non-EU issuers of large denominated securities (minimum €50,000) of non-equity securities.[108] Non-EU issuers can instead use accounts based on other accounting standards so long as the prospectus contains an appropriate warning and provides a narrative description of the differences between the standards in question and IFRS.[109] Debt securities that are convertible into new shares of the issuer of the debt instruments or of another company in its group would be equity securities for this purpose and thus would not benefit from this modification.[110]

Thirdly, the requirement tying issuers to their home states for regulatory approvals is relaxed for issues of non-equity securities denominated in units of least €1,000, and also certain derivatives. In these cases, the issuer (whether EU incorporated or non-EU) can choose to obtain its regulatory approvals from either its home state or the Member State where the securities are offered to the public or admitted to trading on a regulated market.[111] Debt securities that are convertible into equity of the company that issued the debt securities or equity of another company in its group do not benefit from this modification because they are classified as equity securities for this purpose. The official justification for the general rule requiring issuers to obtain regulatory approval from their home state is that states are assumed to be in the best position to regulate and supervise those issuers that have their registered offices within their jurisdiction.[112] During the passage of the Prospectus Directive into law, it was heavily argued that this rule should not apply to bond issues because of the concentration of relevant supervisory expertise in London and Luxembourg, which are the principal centres for bond issuance and listing activity in the EU. The European Commission had proposed to use the €50,000 threshold for the relaxation of the general rule but that

---

[106] European Commission, 'Amended proposal for a Directive of the European Parliament and of the Council on the prospectus to be published when securities are offered to the public or admitted to trading and amending Directive 2001/34/EC' (COM (2002) 460), explanatory memorandum, 4.

[107] There is also the more modest difference that the requirement for prospectus summaries does not apply (justifiable on the basis that people with such large amounts of money can be expected to read and evaluate full information) (Prospectus Directive, Art 5(2)). Also, the annual updating requirement does not apply (ibid Art 10).

[108] Prospectus Directive, Art 7(2)(b). On the definitions of equity and non-equity securities (ibid Art 2(1)(b) and (c)).

[109] Prospectus Directive Regulation, Annex IX, para 11.1.

[110] This is in contrast to the position with regard to exchangeable bonds.

[111] Prospectus Directive, Art 2(1)(m)(ii).

[112] ibid rec 14.

was resisted by participants in the bond markets.[113] No threshold at all would have been the preferred outcome for many;[114] its survival, but in a minor form at a €1,000 threshold,[115] may perhaps be best regarded as a face-saving compromise for those who had originally pressed for the threshold to be set at the much higher level.

As well as having to comply with the requirement to compile financial information for the prospectus in accordance with IFRS or an equivalent system, issuers of 'retail' bonds, ie bonds with a minimum denomination of less of €50,000, that are admitted to trading on a regulated market must also comply with periodic disclosure requirements under the Transparency Obligations Directive.[116] Subject to certain transitional arrangements, the basic position for non EU-issuers is that mandatory annual and half-yearly financial disclosures under the Transparency Obligations Directive must be drawn up in accordance with IFRS or an alternative system which has been deemed to be equivalent to IFRS by EU authorities.[117] The legislative choice of €50,000 as the wholesale/retail threshold does not reflect existing market practice within the EU, which instead is for wholesale issues to be in smaller denominations so as to facilitate portfolio diversification and management.[118] For instance, one study of the European bond market in the first half of 2002 found that over 77 per cent of issues had a denomination of less than €5,000.[119] The misalignment between the regulatory regime and market practice prompted concerns that foreign issuers might shun the European international securities market and look elsewhere for capital in order to avoid the costly burden of restating their accounts to IFRS. However, efforts to establish the 'equivalence' of different accounting regimes and, in the interim, the extension of transitional arrangements postponing the coming into effect of the new reporting requirements mitigate these concerns.[120]

---

[113] Various key stages in the battle garnered press attention: eg 'Uncommon Market: Senseless Decision on Bonds must be Reversed' *Financial Times*, 6 May 2003, Leader Column, 20.

[114] International Primary Market Association & European Banking Federation, 'Banking Sector Satisfied with Progress on Prospectus Directive', Joint Press Release, (5 November 2002) states: 'There is no logical connection between issuer choice and minimum denomination.'

[115] It is estimated that freedom of choice will be available in around 95% of bond issues despite the threshold: Brussels Bureau, 'Brussels Agenda: Bonds Foreign and Financial', *FT.com*, 1 July 2003.

[116] Directive (EC) 2004/109 of the European Parliament and of the Council of 15 December 2004 on the harmonisation of transparency requirements in relation to information about issuers whose securities are admitted to trading on a regulated market and amending Directive (EC) 2001/34 [2004] OJ L390/38.

[117] Transparency Obligations Directive, Art 23.

[118] Freshfields Bruckhaus Deringer, 'The Prospectus Directive', Client Publication (2003) available at <http://www.freshfields.com/publications/pdfs/practices/4968.pdf> (accessed December 2007). R Northedge, 'An Instant Hit' (2005–2006) *International Capital Market* 41.

[119] International Primary Market Association and European Banking Federation, 'Banking Sector Satisfied with Progress on Prospectus Directive', Joint Press Release, (5 November 2002).

[120] See ch 14 above for detailed discussion.

Exchange-regulated markets for bonds

Markets can move much more quickly than politicians, bureaucrats, and regulators and the initially uncertain prospects for quick and workable solutions to the problems generated by the design of the wholesale regime in the Prospectus and Transparency Obligations Directives provided an opportunity for a demonstration of market strengths in ingenious, rapid innovation. For actors outside the EU, particularly in Singapore and Switzerland, the prospect of more burdensome regulation within the EU triggered more intense efforts to attract bond listing business that would historically have gone to London or Luxembourg.[121] Within the EU, in July 2005, the London Stock Exchange opened a new trading platform called the Professional Securities Market (PSM). The PSM is a market for officially listed debt securities and depository receipts, with the consequence that securities trading on it can be freely acquired by institutional investors that are constrained from buying unlisted securities.[122] PSM securities also qualify for favourable tax treatment under English law.[123] However, the PSM is not a 'regulated market' for the purposes of the Prospectus and Transparency Obligations Directives. Accordingly, securities that are admitted to trading on the PSM fall outside the scope of the EU-wide mandatory requirements for IFRS (or equivalent) financial information (provided that they are not the subject of a public offer). The disclosure requirements for listing particulars (the term used in this context for the offering circular rather than 'prospectus' relating to securities that are to be admitted to the PSM are set and monitored by the FSA, as the UK listing authority.[124] The requirements for PSM listing particulars are substantially based on Prospectus Directive disclosure requirements for wholesale debt—in effect, 'cherry picking' those parts of the EU-wide regime that fit comfortably with the international securities market and, to that extent meeting investor preferences for information standardization, and dispensing with those that do not. As at December 2007, there were 772 securities listed on the PSM, of which the majority were medium-term notes. The desire of the British players to maintain a competitive position as an international market for listed securities is, unsurprisingly, also evident elsewhere within the EU. In July 2005, the Luxembourg Stock Exchange launched a similarly structured platform, the Euro MTF market, which by early February 2006 already had over 1,000 listings.[125]

[121] FH Kung, 'The Regulation of Corporate Bond Offerings: a Comparative Analysis' (2005) 26 *University of Pennsylvania Journal of International Economic Law* 409, 427.

[122] London Stock Exchange, 'Implementing the Professional Securities Market: an exchange regulated market for debt and depository receipts' (May 2005) available at <http://www.londonstockexchange.com/NR/rdonlyres/A05EB887-2BE3-4903-B68E-10AFAF73DDA1/0/Marketstructureservicedescription.doc> (accessed December 2007).

[123] HM Revenue and Customs, '*Quoted Eurobonds: launch of new markets in London and Luxembourg*' at <http://www.hmrc.gov.uk/euro/quoted-eurobonds.htm> (accessed December 2007).

[124] *Listing Rules*, ch 4.

[125] 'One Thousand Securities Listed on the Euro MTF Market of the Luxembourg Stock Exchange', Luxembourg Stock Exchange Press Release (March 2006); J Weydert,

Securities admitted to trading on the PSM or the Euro MTF market do not benefit from the European passport for prospectuses. However, this is not a major problem because the principal purpose of having international bonds admitted to trading on a formal market is not to open up direct investor access but rather to ensure their acceptability to investors that must invest in 'listed securities' and to obtain favourable tax treatment. Secondary market trading of bonds listed on the PSM, Euro MTF, or any similarly organized platform can take place on a cross-border basis through intermediaries which themselves hold passports to operate across the EU. Secondary market trading will not trigger a requirement to produce a prospectus so long as it remains within the public offer exemptions provided by the Prospectus Directive.

Stabilization

It is common for the bond issuance process to include some stabilization activity to maintain and support the price of the bonds in the immediate post-issuance period. In policy terms, a degree of stabilization is permissible because it alleviates sales pressure generated by short-term investors and maintains an orderly market in the relevant securities.[126] Stabilization can thus contribute to greater confidence of investors and issuers in the financial markets.[127] However, stabilization needs be carefully controlled to avoid infringing laws prohibiting market abuse. This, too, is an area that is now regulated at the EU level, by the Market Abuse Directive. The Market Abuse Directive, which addresses insider dealing and other forms of abusive conduct as well as imposing on issuers an obligation of prompt disclosure of inside information, is limited in scope to financial instruments admitted to trading on a regulated market in at least one Member State, or for which a request for admission to trading on such a market has been made, and to financial instruments not admitted to trading on a regulated market in a Member State, but whose value depends on a financial instrument so admitted or for which admission has been sought.[128] However, it is open to Member States to extend the scope of their national laws on market abuse and to set more stringent rules. The British market abuse regime does have a broader scope: conduct occurring in relation to securities listed on the PSM would be caught because all markets established under the rules of UK recognized investment exchanges

---

'Luxembourg's Prospectus Rules in Line with EU' (2006) 25(2) *International Financial Law Review* 72.

[126] Commission Regulation (EC) 2273/2003 of 22 December 2003 implementing Directive (EC) 2003/6 of the European Parliament and of the Council as regards exemptions for buy-back programmes and stabilisation of financial instruments [2003] OJ L336/33, rec 11.

[127] ibid.

[128] Directive (EC) 2003/6 of the European Parliament and of the Council of 28 January 2003 on insider dealing and market manipulation (market abuse) [2003] OJ L96/16, Art 9.

(of which the London Stock Exchange is one) are prescribed for this purpose.[129] There is a safe harbour, under European and domestic law, for stabilization activity provided it conforms to prescribed requirements.[130]

In the bond issuance process it is also necessary to pay attention to controls on advertisements and other promotional materials. In the UK, the principal control is section 21 of the Financial Services and Markets Act 2000, which requires 'financial promotions' in the course of business to be made only by authorized persons or with the contents having been approved by an authorized person. This requirement does not apply to exempt communications, which include certain communications to overseas recipients, investment professionals, high net worth individuals, companies and firms, and sophisticated investors.[131] Prospectuses and listing particulars are also within the scope of an exemption under the financial promotions regime.[132] The Prospectus Directive, implemented in the UK in the FSA *Handbook*, also regulates advertisements relating to public offers of securities or the admission of securities to trading on a regulated market by requiring advertisements to be accurate, complete, and consistent with the prospectus and to alert people to the fact that there is a prospectus containing the information that investors should use as the basis for their investment decisions.[133] As bonds tend to be targeted at an international community of investors, foreign (in particular US), selling restrictions must also be considered.

Bond market transparency—a growing concern

The transparency of the secondary bond markets has come to the foreground of policy attention in recent years. It has been suggested that the collapse of certain prominent issuers of corporate bonds focused regulators' attention on the significance of the bond markets as a source of capital for the corporate sector and on the potential within them for fraud and abuse that could undermine investor protection and the maintenance of orderly markets.[134] The growing complexity of the bond markets is another factor that has made regulators more aware

---

[129] Financial Services and Markets Act 2000, s 118 and Financial Services and Markets Act 2000 (Prescribed Markets and Qualifying Investments) Order 2001, SI 2001/996 (as amended).

[130] Commission Regulation (EC) 2273/2003 of 22 December 2003 implementing Directive (EC) 2003/6 of the European Parliament and of the Council as regards exemptions for buy-back programmes and stabilisation of financial instruments [2003] OJ L336/33; Financial Services and Markets Act 2000, s 118A(5) and FSA *Handbook*, MAR 2 (Stabilisation).

[131] The exemptions are provided by the Financial Services and Markets Act 2000 (Financial Promotion) Order 2005, SI 2005/1529.

[132] ibid reg 70.

[133] Prospectus Directive, Art 15 and FSA *Handbook*, PR 3.3.

[134] FH Kung, 'The Regulation of Corporate Bond Offerings: a Comparative Analysis' (2005) 26 *University of Pennsylvania Journal of International Economic Law* 409, 410–11.

of the need to pay them close attention.[135] Enhanced regulatory scrutiny of the bond markets has also been linked to increased retail participation. Recent data suggests that direct retail investment in bonds is more significant than had been generally perceived[136] and it could increase further as demographic and other economic and social changes lead more retail investors to the bond markets in search of long-term investments with predictable cash flows to fund their retirement.[137] Easier access to the market due to new technology, including electronic systems and internet access, may also increase retail participation.[138]

The structure of the secondary market for bonds, in which most trading takes place off-exchange in bilateral transactions between clients and bond dealers, means that there is not the flow of readily available pricing information in relation to bond trades that there is in respect of equity securities.[139] In a major international study, the International Organization of Securities Commissions (IOSCO) found considerable international variation regarding pre- and post-trade transparency requirements in respect of listed and unlisted bonds.[140] Overall, bond price transparency was regarded as being weaker in Europe than in the US, where the TRACE system for reporting and dissemination of last sale information on corporate bonds has been in operation since 2002 and requires dealers to report trades on all eligible US corporate bonds within 45 minutes.[141] According to IOSCO:

The introduction of TRACE in the United States has been a significant development in enhancing regulatory reporting and market transparency for corporate bond trades in the United States. Information provided by TRACE enables regulatory authorities to assess the status of, and monitor trading in, the corporate bond markets. It also provides the public—both retail and institutional investors—with information that enables them to assess whether they are obtaining fair and reasonable prices for their trades.[142]

Within Europe there has recently been vigorous debate, at EU and Member State levels, about whether greater transparency should be imposed on the secondary bond markets by regulatory intervention. There is the possibility to do so

---

[135] IOSCO, 'Transparency of Corporate Bond Markets', Report of the Technical Committee of the International Organization of Securities Commissions (May 2004) 25, available at <http://www.iosco.org/library/pubdocs/pdf/IOSCOPD168.pdf> (accessed December 2007).

[136] ibid 4, reporting data from TRACE, the trade reporting and dissemination system introduced by the National Association of Securities Dealers (NASD) in the US: although representing less than 2% of total value, 65% of the trades in reportable corporate debt transactions were valued at less than US $100,000, the NASD benchmark value for retail trades. H McKenzie, 'The Lure of Steady Returns' (2005–2006) *International Capital Market* 85, reporting that in the UK corporate bonds were the most popular retail investment sector in July 2005.

[137] IOSCO, 'Transparency of Corporate Bond Markets' (n 135 above) 4.

[138] ibid.

[139] ibid, 7.

[140] ibid 11–22.

[141] ibid 24; also Kung (n 134 above) 421.

[142] IOSCO, 'Transparency of Corporate Bond Markets (n 135 above) 34.

under the Markets in Financial Instruments Directive 2004 (MiFID).[143] MiFID contains a range of transparency-orientated provisions that, initially, were limited to equities. The possibility of extending them to bond trades was envisaged by Article 65(1) of MiFID, which required the European Commission to submit a review to the European Parliament on the possible extension of the scope of the transparency provisions to markets other than equities. The merits of such an extension were hotly contested and numerous public and private sector bodies compiled papers and reports to feed into the Commission's review.[144] A debate on transparency versus liquidity lay at the heart of the controversy because of the risk that increased mandatory transparency requirements could lead dealers, on whom the market is heavily reliant for liquidity, to withdraw their capital from the market. The Committee of European Securities Regulators (CESR) played a key role in advising the Commission on this matter.[145] CESR did not identify any evident market failure in respect of market transparency on bond markets. It found that wholesale participants generally seemed content with the way in which the cash bond markets currently operate and their level of access to transparency information. Access to transparency information for smaller participants, including retail investors, was not as great, and this led CESR to believe that there would be value to such users in receiving access to greater trading transparency. Greater transparency might also encourage higher levels of retail participation in the markets. On the other hand, CESR noted that various other factors, including the structure of the bond markets, retail investors' understanding of them, and the distribution channels used also played an important role in determining the level of retail involvement. Given this, CESR advised that any increase in transparency would need to be carefully tailored to ensure that liquidity provision and levels of competition were not damaged as a result of dealers reducing or withdrawing their commitment to the markets. The European Securities Market Expert Group (ESME), which was also mandated by the Commission to provide advice, reached a similar conclusion: that there did not appear to be convincing evidence of market failure with respect to market transparency in wholesale bond

[143] Directive (EC) 2004/39 of the European Parliament and of the Council of 21 April 2004 on markets in financial instruments amending Council Directives (EEC) 85/611 and (EEC) 93/6 and Directive (EEC) 2000/12 of the European Parliament and of the Council and repealing Council Directive (EEC) 93/22 [2004] OJ L145/1. Directive (EC) 2006/31 [2006] OJ L114/60 extended the transposition and implementation dates for MiFID. The deadline by which Member States had to transpose MiFID into their national laws was 31 January 2007 and the deadline for the relevant national laws coming into force was extended to 1 November 2007.

[144] eg FSA, 'Trading Transparency in the UK Secondary Bond Markets', FSA Discussion Paper, DP05/5 (2005); FSA, 'Trading Transparency in the UK Secondary Bond Markets', FSA Feedback Statement, FS06/4, 2006); JP Casey and K Lannoo, 'Europe's Hidden Capital Markets', Centre for European Policy Studies (Brussels, 2005) ch 4; P Dunne, M Moore, and R Portes, European Government Bond Markets: Transparency, Liquidity, Efficiency (City of London, 2006); B Biais, F Declerck, J Dow, R Portes, and EL von Thadden, European Corporate Bond Markets: Transparency, Liquidity, Efficiency (City of London, 2006).

[145] CESR, 'Response to the Commission on Non-equities Transparency', CESR/07-284b (June 2007).

markets but that, as regards retail bond markets, there appeared to be some evidence of sub-optimality and even market failure with respect to market transparency.[146] ESME was in favour of a market-led solution to correct these problems. The next stage is for the European Commission to publish a report taking stock of the discussion. In view of the broad consensus from CESR, ESME, and industry bodies that there is no market failure in wholesale markets, intervention in that area seems very unlikely but whether a regulatory or a market-led solution to the problem of improving access to price information by retail investors will be preferred remains unclear.

EU regulatory intervention to enhance certainty in market transactions involving financial collateral

Collateral is an immensely significant part of financial market activity generally. It has been noted that collateral is used throughout the EU in all types of transactions, including capital markets, bank treasury and funding, payment and clearing systems, and general bank lending, and that collateral is the main tool for reducing systemic risk in payment and securities settlement systems.[147] Although corporate bonds are themselves normally unsecured, corporate bonds are one of the asset classes that can be used as collateral for asset-backed securities.[148] Collateralized debt obligations, which use bonds and loans as collateral, were first issued in the late 1980s, and by the late 1990s they were the fastest growing segment of the asset-backed securities market.[149] There was particularly rapid growth in the European CDO market during the 1990s.[150]

Financial collateral is commonly in the form of cash or securities that are held in or through accounts with custodians and clearing systems.[151] Putting in place effective arrangements for collateral involving investment securities is technically complex and involves working through a wide range of matters including the form in which they were issued (registered or bearer, certificated or uncertificated) and any arrangements that have been made for the trading and settlement through a system such as Euroclear or Clearstream.[152] The cross-border nature of

[146] ESME, 'Non-equities Market Transparency', Report to the European Commission (June 2007).

[147] K Löber and E Klima, 'The Implementation of Directive 2002/47 on Financial Collateral Arrangements' [2006] *Journal of International Banking Law and Regulation* 203; K Löber, 'The Developing EU Legal Framework for Clearing and Settlement of Financial Instruments', ECB Legal Working Paper No 1 (February 2006) 19–25, available at SSRN <http://ssrn.com/abstract=886047>.

[148] Löber and Klima (n 147 above).

[149] 'The Barclays Capital Guide to Cash Flow Collateralized Debt Obligations' (2002) 2.

[150] ibid.

[151] Löber and Klima (n 147 above).

[152] R Goode, *Legal Problems of Credit and Security* (Sweet & Maxwell, 3rd edn, 2003) ch VI; R Cranston, *Principles of Banking Law* (OUP, 2nd edn, 2002) 407–9.

much of this activity adds to transactional complexity and potential legal uncertainty. The EU's initial steps to harmonize the law in this area were taken in the Settlement Finality Directive,[153] which provided a legal framework for payment and securities settlement systems, including provision for collateral security provided in connection with operations of the Central Banks of the Member States and the ECB in the performance of their central banking functions.[154] That was followed by the selection of a Directive on the cross-border use of collateral as a top priority in the FSAP.[155] The European Commission argued that a harmonizing measure was needed to relieve market participants of the burden of checking the different laws on perfection of security interests (ie procedures a collateral taker must follow to ensure that the rights to the collateral are good against third parties, including a liquidator in the event of bankruptcy) in each of the Member States, grappling with uncertainties as regards the law applicable to cross-border transfers of book entry securities, and considering the impact of all the different bankruptcy legislations which exist in Member States.[156]

The Financial Collateral Directive was adopted in 2002.[157] It aims to safeguard financial stability and also to promote cross-border efficiency by simplifying the processes for using financial collateral.[158] Where it applies, it requires Member States to remove formal requirements under their national laws for the creation validity, perfection, enforceability, or admissibility in evidence of a financial collateral arrangement, save for requirements for an arrangement to be evidenced in writing or in a legally equivalent manner. It provides certainty with regard to the law governing the legal nature and proprietary effects of book entry securities collateral and related matters by stipulating that this is to be the law of the country in which the relevant account is maintained.[159] Any laws that might cast doubt on the ability of a collateral taker to exercise rights conferred by a financial collateral arrangement to use the collateral must be disapplied.[160] So too must national laws that could lead to recharacterization of a financial collateral arrangement

---

[153] Directive (EC) 98/26 of the European Parliament and of the Council of 19th May 1998 on settlement finality in payment and securities settlement systems [1998] OJ L166/45.

[154] European Commission, 'Proposal for a Directive of the European Parliament and of the Council on financial collateral arrangements' (COM (2001) 168) 2.

[155] ibid.

[156] ibid 3.

[157] Directive (EC) 2002/47/EC of the European Parliament and of the Council of 6 June 2002 on financial collateral arrangements [2002] OJ L168/43.

[158] HM Treasury, 'Implementation of the Directive on Financial Collateral Arrangements', (July 2003) 4.

[159] Financial Collateral Directive, Art 9. The 2002 Hague Convention on the law applicable to certain rights in respect of securities held with an intermediary allows parties some choice with regard to governing law, which is incompatible with the wording of Art 9. The Directive will need to be modified if the Community decides to sign and ratify the Hague Convention.

[160] Of which an example under English law is the equitable rule prohibiting clogs on the equity of redemption: HM Treasury, 'Implementation of the Directive on Financial Collateral Arrangements' (July 2003) 16.

that, by its terms, involves a transfer of title.[161] The Financial Collateral Directive also provides for the enforcement of financial collateral arrangements through sale or appropriation (taking the collateral in settlement), subject to the terms of the collateral arrangement but free of formalities under the general law, such as public notice or the obtaining of court orders.[162] Financial collateral arrangements must also be given certain exemptions from national insolvency laws that could prevent them from taking effect or under which they could be invalidated or reversed.[163] Specified netting arrangements must also be insulated from the effects of insolvency law.[164]

'Financial collateral' for this purpose means cash or financial instruments.[165] Title transfer collateral arrangements, as well as security arrangements, are within the scope of the Directive.[166] Both types of arrangement have the same basic aim: to give the holder of the collateral a proprietary interest that will protect its interests should the collateral provider default.[167] The Directive is limited to transactions where both parties are non-natural persons, including unincorporated firms and partnerships as well as companies, and one of them is: (a) a public body; (b) a financial institution subject to prudential supervision; or (c) a regulated central counterparty, settlement agent, or clearing house.[168] However, Member States can extend the Directive's scope, and the UK is among those that have chosen to do so.[169] The British regime applies where the collateral-provider and the collateral-taker are both non-natural persons and it is not necessary for one of the parties to be within any of the groups specifically identified in the Directive.[170]

---

[161] Financial Collateral Directive, Art 6.

[162] ibid Art 4. HM Treasury (n 160 above) 17 notes that appropriation is permitted in the UK and therefore an opt-out in the Directive for Member States that do not permit appropriation under their local law does not apply.

[163] Financial Collateral Directive, Arts 4(5) and 8.

[164] ibid Art 7.

[165] ibid Art 1(4).

[166] ibid Art 2.

[167] The distinction between security (rights in another's property) and ownership that is usually emphasized in English credit and security law is overridden in this context.

[168] Financial Collateral Directive, Art 1; HM Treasury (n 160 above) 6.

[169] For a pan-European review of implementation see K Löber and E Klima, 'The Implementation of Directive 2002/47 on Financial Collateral Arrangements' [2006] *Journal of International Banking Law and Regulation* 203.

[170] Financial Collateral Arrangements (No 2) Regulations 2003, SI 2003/3226.

Index